Close Encounters

Close Encounters

Communicating in Relationships

Laura K. Guerrero

Arizona State University

Peter A. Andersen

San Diego State University

Walid A. Afifi

Penn State University

Boston   Burr Ridge, IL   Dubuque, IA   Madison, WI   New York
San Francisco   St. Louis   Bangkok   Bogotá   Caracas   Kuala Lumpur
Lisbon   London   Madrid   Mexico City   Milan   Montreal   New Delhi
Santiago   Seoul   Singapore   Sydney   Taipei   Toronto

McGraw-Hill Higher Education

A Division of The **McGraw-Hill** Companies

CLOSE ENCOUNTERS
COMMUNICATING IN RELATIONSHIPS

Published by McGraw-Hill, a business unit of The McGraw-Hill Companies, Inc. 1221 Avenue of the Americas, New York, NY, 10020. Copyright © 2001 by The McGraw-Hill Companies, Inc. All rights reserved. No part of this publication may be reproduced or distributed in any form or by any means, or stored in a datbase or retrieval system, without the prior written consent of The McGraw-Hill Companies, Inc., including, but not limited to, in any network or other electronic storage or transmission, or broadcast for distance learning.

Some ancillaries, including electronic and print components, may not be available to customers outside the United States.

This book is printed on acid-free paper.

3   4   5   6   7   8   9   0   BAH/BAH   0   9   8   7   6   5   4   3   2

ISBN 0-7674-1082-3

Sponsoring editor, Holly Allen; production editor, Holly Paulsen; manuscript editor, Tom Briggs; design manager, Jean Mailander; text designer, Ellen Pettengell; cover designer, Lisa Buckley, art editor, Rennie Evans; illustrator, Judith Ogus; photo researcher, Brian Pecko; permissions editor, Martha Granahan; manufacturing manager, Randy Hurst. The text was set in 10/12 Palatino by Thompson Type, Inc. and printed on acid-free 45# Chromatone Matte by Banta Book Group.

Cover art: Judy Dunworth, *Indeterminate Space #6*, 36" × 22".

Photo credits appear on page C-1 following the references, which constitutes an extension of the copyright page.

Library of Congress Cataloging-in-Publication Data
Guerrero, Laura K.
    Close encounters : communicating in relationships / Laura K. Guerrero, Peter A. Andersen, Walid A. Afifi.
        p.   cm.
    Includes bibliographical references and index.
    ISBN: 0-7674-1082-3
    1. Interpersonal communication.   I. Andersen, Peter A.   II. Afifi, Walid A.   III. Title.
BF637.C45.G83   2001
153.6—dc21

                                                                    00-053285

www.mhhe.com

Preface

In recent decades, scholarly research on close relationships has flourished. Instructors teaching courses on relationships and interpersonal communication can now draw upon an impressive body of knowledge based on sound research. At the same time, the popular press, including talk shows, self-help books, and popular magazines increasingly give people advice about how to have better relationships. Yet, as professors who study relationships know, this popular advice does not always correspond with research findings. Thus, one of our goals in writing *Close Encounters* was to present students with an informative, yet readable textbook that would help them understand their relationships better and be more critical consumers of information about relationships. For us, this is an important goal. Writing this textbook helps us reach beyond the pages of scholarly journals to share information with students who are eager to learn more about relationships.

Close Encounters provides more in-depth coverage of theory than is typical in most interpersonal communication textbooks. We hope this balance of theoretical coverage and an accessible writing style will be helpful to students and professors alike.

Approach

This book takes a relational approach to the study of interpersonal communication by focusing on issues that are central to describing and understanding close relationships, particularly between romantic partners and friends. We also touch upon family relationships throughout the book. One of the most exciting trends in the field of personal relationships is that scholars from different disciplines are all working toward the common goal of understanding relationships. Researchers from fields such as communication, family studies, psychology, and sociology have all made important contributions to scholarly knowledge about relationships. This book reflects the interdisciplinary nature of the field of personal relationships while focusing strongly on interpersonal communication.

Organization

In line with the relational approach, this book is organized loosely around relational trajectories. We use the term *trajectory* loosely because all relationships are different, with no two following exactly the same path. Nonetheless, from a communication perspective, it is helpful to think of relationships in terms of how they progress from initial meetings toward farewells. Of course, interesting and important communication occurs throughout a relationship's course. For example, conflict can be studied in terms of a couple's first big fight, the mundane disagreements that people have on a fairly regular basis, the conflicts that enhance relational functioning, or the argument that ultimately leads to the destruction of a relationship. Thus, even though this book is organized somewhat chronologically, we believe that relationships do not always unfold in a linear fashion and that many types of events, such as having conflicts, communicating love, and reducing uncertainty, can occur at various stages during the life course of a relationship.

Part I focuses on processes that are often associated with relational development, such as uncertainty reduction, impression management, and self-disclosure. In Part II, the focus shifts to messages and processes that help maintain relational satisfaction, intimacy, and fairness. Topics in this section include sex, love, social exchange, equity, relational maintenance, and intimacy. In Part III, we examine *potential* relational problems, such as issues of power, the need for privacy, relational transgressions, and conflict, as well as disengagement. When we teach our relational communication courses, we note that many of the topics covered in this last section have both a bright and a dark side. For instance, being able to influence a friend or sibling to engage in safe behavior is a positive way of using relational power, while coercing someone to stay in a dissatisfying or abusive relationship is a negative way of exerting power. Similarly, maintaining some level of privacy is usually highly beneficial for a relationship even though too much privacy can lead to alienation and loneliness. Even conflict, which many people think of only in negative terms, can help relational partners solve problems and become even closer. Relationship termination can also have a bright side—sometimes ending one relationship opens the door to new experiences.

Although we organized the book based on a loosely defined chronological order, the discussion of various topics departs from this structure when appropriate. For example, the chapter on uncertainty reduction includes information relevant to both new and developed relationships, while the chapter on relational maintenance discusses behaviors used to sustain closeness and those used to keep relationships from disengaging. We have found that students like discussing topics in a chronological order, but it is critical to remind them that many relational processes are important throughout the course of a relationship.

Features

In addition to the features we have already outlined, following are other key features we believe will appeal to students and instructors alike:

- **Current, interdisciplinary research:** The research in *Close Encounters* reflects the interdisciplinary nature of the study of personal relationships and draws from across the social science disciplines.

- **High-interest topics:** Intriguing subjects, such as long-distance relationships, cross-sex friendships, flirting, the "dark side" of relational communication, and sexual interaction, are explored in depth.

- **Pedagogical features:** *Close Encounters* also has a number of pedagogical features to enhance student interest:

  Put Yourself to the Test—These exercises, found throughout the text, assess various aspects of students' own relational interactions.

  Highlights—Found in each chapter, these boxes take a closer look at issues in relational research and challenge students to think critically about research and popular concepts.

  Discussion Questions—Found at the end of each chapter, these questions can help students prepare for class, or they can be used as springboards for classroom discussions.

  Research References—A comprehensive list will help students explore topics of interest in more depth.

Finally, the instructor's manual that accompanies *Close Encounters,* written by Stephen Yoshimura, Christina Granato, and Laura Guerrero, contains chapter outlines, test bank questions, and classroom activities. The test bank includes both multiple choice and essay questions. Activities involve generating class discussion and/or debate, using role plays, and using excerpts from popular movies to illustrate points.

Acknowledgments

Writing a textbook is an exciting challenge, as well as a time-consuming task. During the nearly three years we spent writing this book, our dens were cluttered with hundreds of articles on relationships, and our families had to listen to the click-click-click of our computer keyboards even more than they usually do. The support of our families and colleagues was critical in helping us complete this project, and we owe them our sincere gratitude. We are especially indebted to Vico, Jan, Kirsten, and Tanya, who provided not only social support but also examples and feedback. Vico provided many hours of babysitting as well.

We would also like to thank the many people who helped during the writing and editing process. Our editor, Holly Allen, provided outstanding leadership and guidance, as well as patience (especially when the first author went on maternity leave for a semester). Holly Paulsen and Melissa Williams were great production editors. Several other members of the Mayfield staff deserve thanks, including Jean Mailander, design manager; Brian Pecko, photo researcher; and

Rennie Evans, art editor. We also thank Tom Briggs for his careful copyediting. Additionally, we'd like to thank Stephen Yoshimura and Christina Granato for all their hard work on the instructor's manual.

The reviewers for this textbook provided superb feedback. We took their comments very seriously and incorporated many of their suggestions (although including all of them would have meant a 1,000-page book!). The book is definitely better because of their careful scrutiny and insightful commentary. Thus, we would like to extend a special thank you to Katherine Adams, California State University at Fresno; Daniel Canary, Arizona State University; Victoria DeFrancisco, University of Northern Iowa; Katherine Dindia, University of Wisconsin–Milwaukee; Renee Edwards, Louisiana State University; Michael Hecht, Pennsylvania State University; Larry Nadler, Miami University; Donna Pawlowski, Creighton University; Glen Stamp, Ball State University; Claire Sullivan, University of Maine; and Richard West, University of Southern Maine.

We are also grateful to our mentors and to the colleagues with whom we work on a day-to-day basis. Directly or indirectly, these scholars helped shape this book. In particular, we would like to acknowledge our colleagues at Arizona State University, Penn State University, and San Diego State University for their support, encouragement, and interesting conversation. Judee Burgoon also deserves special recognition, not only for serving as a mentor for the first and third authors but also for suggesting that we use "close encounters" as part of the title.

Finally, we would like to thank all the students we have had in our interpersonal courses over the years. Our students have provided us with valuable feedback about what they would like to see in a textbook on communication in relationships. Just as importantly, lively dialogue with students has helped sustain our enthusiasm for teaching courses on interpersonal communication and relationships. We hope this book contributes to spirited discussions about relationships in your classroom as well.

Brief Contents

Contents

2 Making a Good Impression: Identity Management in Relationships   28

3 Drawing People Together: Forces of Social Attraction   56

4 Making Sense of Our World: Coping with Uncertainty and Expectancy Violations   85

7 The Closest Encounter: Sexual Interaction 169

8 All Relationships Are Not Created Equal: Social Exchange, Equity, and Commitment 200

9 Staying Close: Maintaining Intimate Relationships   225

10 Communicating Closeness: Intimate Interaction   252

11 Power Plays: The Politics of Close Relationships 281

12 Getting Too Close for Comfort: Privacy in Relationships 312

Hurting the Ones We Love: Relational Transgressions

 When People Disagree: Interpersonal Conflict

15 In the End: Relationship Disengagement and Termination   402

The Building Blocks of Close Encounters

An Introduction to Communication in Relationships

What would life be like without close relationships? Imagine attending a joyous event such as a wedding or graduation without the presence of friends or family, or grieving without the comfort of loved ones. Close relationships provide much of the meaning in people's lives. Relationships are the source of people's deepest, most inspiring experiences, as well as their greatest hurts and sorrows. Gibran (1923/1970) captured the essence of close relationships:

> Your friend is your needs answered. He is the field you sow with love and reap with thanksgiving. You come to him with hunger and you seek him with peace. And let there be no purpose in friendship save the deepening of the spirit. And let your best be for your friend. If he must know the ebb of your tide, let him know its flood also. (pp. 64–65; original masculine voice retained)

In a less philosophical vein, McAdams (1988) suggested that, "through personal relationships, we may find our most profound experiences of security and anxiety, power and impotence, unity and separateness" (p. 7). Indeed, personal relationships are central to being human.

People are born into relationships and live their lives in webs of friendships, family networks, romances, marriages, and work relationships. In fact, research has shown that when people talk, the most common topics are relationship problems, sex, family, and romantic (or potentially romantic) partners (Haas & Sherman, 1982). The capacity to form relationships is innate and biological, a part of the genetic inheritance that has enabled the human race to survive over time. As social creatures humans have less potential for survival, creativity, and innovation as individuals than in relationships. Experts in personal relationships attempt to unlock the mysteries of these universal human experiences, to assist people with problematic relationships, and to help people achieve greater satisfaction in their close encounters.

In this introductory chapter we provide a brief history of the field of personal relationships. Then we define and discuss three important terms that are central to this book: relationships, interpersonal communication, and relational communication. We also discuss issues related to each of these concepts.

The Field of Personal Relationships: A Brief History

People have been curious about their relationships for thousands of years, but the formal study of personal relationships is a recent phenomenon. Today we take the study of personal relationships for granted. A few decades ago, however, the scholarly investigation of relationships was considered unscientific and a waste of resources. In 1975 two of the finest and earliest relationship researchers, Ellen Berscheid and Elaine Hatfield (formerly Elaine Walster), were publicly criticized by Senator William Proxmire of Wisconsin for their research on love. Proxmire gave the "Golden Fleece Award" for wasteful government spending to the National Science Foundation for supporting Berscheid and Walster's research on love with an $84,000 grant. The senator's objections to "squandering" money on love research were twofold: (1) Scientists could never find an answer to the mystery of love, and (2) even if they did, he didn't want to hear it and was confident that no one else did either (Hatfield, 1999). Of course, like many Americans Proxmire had problematic relationships of his own and had just been divorced at the time he gave his "award." Months of harassing phone calls and even death threats to Berscheid and Walster followed (Hatfield, 1999). Even Ellen Hatfield's mother's bishop, whose name is changed in the letter below, got into the act.

> Dear Faithful in Christ:
> This week, the *Chicago Tribune* announced that the National Science Foundation will unravel the most sacred mysteries of love and life. Soon they will be in a position to dictate to the whole world. If "Science" were not such a sacred cow, we would all laugh at such ponderous nonsense. Who has granted these "scientists" the ability to see into men's minds and hearts? Are their "findings" going to eliminate pride, selfishness, jealousy, suffering, and war? Sex research. Birth control. "Swinging." This is not the face of America. . . .
>   Rev. Richard S. Moody
>   Bishop, Diocese of Chicago (Hatfield & Rapson, 2000)

Within decades, however, most people, including priests and politicians, would come to realize that understanding the many facets of close relationships is as important as research on earthquakes or nutrition. Most people now find social scientific knowledge compatible with personal political and religious beliefs. In fact, some churches conduct premarital workshops and marriage encounters based on this research. Also, bookstores and newsstands are crammed with books and magazines that focus on every aspect of relationships, providing advice (of variable quality) on topics such as how to "Get a Guy by the 4th of July" (Miller, 1999), how to "Keep Your Marriage Strong" (Russo, 1999), how to decide "On What Date Do You Do It?" (Kornreich, 1999), and how "Women Size [Men] Up"

BOX 1.1 HIGHLIGHTS

The Importance of Being a Critical Consumer— Comparing John Gottman to John Gray

People are bombarded with advice about relationships from best-selling books, magazine articles, and talk shows. How accurate is this advice? The answer is, it depends. Sometimes the advice given in the media is consistent with social scientific research; other times it is not. In a *Psychology Today* article, Marano (1997) put John Gray to the test by comparing his credentials and conclusions to those of John Gottman.

John Gray is the author of the number-one bestseller in nonfiction, *Men Are from Mars, and Women Are from Venus*. John Gottman is one of the premier social psychologists in the study of personal relationships. So how did Gray stack up to Gottman? Here is what *Psychology Today* reported after researching and interviewing both men.

	John Gray	John Gottman
Education	Ph.D. through correspondence school	Ph.D. from the University of Illinois
Licensing	Driver's license	Licensed psychologist
Number of Journal Articles	None	109
Number of Couples Formally Studied	None	760
The Cardinal Rule of Relationships	Men and women are different.	What people think they do in relationships and what they actually do are very different.
Defining Statement	"Before 1950, men were men and women were women."	"It's the everyday mindless moments that are the basis of romance in marriage."
What Makes Marriage Work?	Heeding gender stereotypes	Making mental maps of each other's world
What Makes Marriage Fail?	Gender differences in communication style	Gender stereotypes; reactions to stress
What They Say About Each Other	"John who?"	"I envy his financial success."

Source: Adapted from Marano (1997).

(Williams, 1999), to name just a few. One important function of scientific research on relationships is to provide a check-and-balance system for the popular advice given in the media. Critical consumers can compare the scientific literature to the popular, but sometimes inaccurate, advice they receive in magazines, best-selling books, and television shows. Box 1.1 presents one such comparison.

Several major tributaries have contributed to the now steady stream of scholarly research on personal relationships. The early pioneers in the field could not have envisioned the vast amount of research on relationships that exists in several disciplines today. The young field of personal relationships has always been interdisciplinary, although it sometimes took years for scholars from different disciplines to discover one another's work. Duck (1988) commented that the field of personal relationships is unusual because it is truly interdisciplinary and has the power to impact people's everyday lives. Groups of scholars from the disciplines of communication, social psychology, child development, family studies, sociology, and anthropology are all in the business of studying human relationships. Next, we take a closer look at how research in interpersonal communication, social psychology, and other disciplines has contributed to the establishment and evolution of the field of personal relationships.

Contributions of Interpersonal Communication Research

Although the earliest research in this area dates back to the 1950s, the study of interpersonal communication began in earnest in the 1960s and 1970s (Andersen, 1982). Previously, communication scholars had been mainly preoccupied with public speeches, political rhetoric, and mass communication. In the 1960s scholars realized that most communication takes place in small groups and dyads consisting of close friends, family members, and romantic partners (Miller, 1976). The study of interpersonal communication thus began to focus on how people communicate in dyads and small groups. The first books on interpersonal communication emerged soon thereafter (see McCroskey, Larson, & Knapp, 1971).

Scholars also began to realize that interpersonal communication differs depending upon the type of relationship people share. Miller and Steinberg (1975) proposed that the defining characteristics of interpersonal relationships are that they are unique, in most respects irreplaceable, and require an understanding of the psychological makeup of the partner. By contrast, noninterpersonal or "role" relationships, such as those with store clerks or phone operators, possess few unique qualities, are entirely replaceable, and involve only stereotypic perceptions of roles.

These shifts in communication scholarship reflected broader social changes. In part, the youth movement of the 1960s represented a rebellion against a society perceived to be impersonal and manipulative. Sensitivity training, encounter groups, and other personal growth movements of the 1960s and 1970s turned people's attention inward to the dyad and to close relationships.

The evolution of interpersonal communication as one of the primary emphases in the communication discipline was a natural outcome of the realization that relationships are the primary locus for communication. In addition, scholars recognized that relationships are an inherently communicative phenomenon. Indeed, it is difficult to imagine how human relationships might exist in the absence of communication. This realization was well stated by Miller

(1976): "Understanding the interpersonal communication process demands an understanding of the symbiotic relationship between communication and relational development: communication influences relational development, and in turn (or simultaneously) relational development influences the nature of the communication between parties to the relationship" (p. 15). Communication has also been called "the lifeblood of relationships" (Knapp & Vangelisti, 1996, p. 3). Since the 1970s, the sophistication of interpersonal and relational communication research has increased, and the work has become more theoretically driven (Andersen, 1982).

Contributions of Social Psychology

Early research in social psychology also laid the groundwork for the scientific investigation of interpersonal relationships, with much of this work focused on social development and personality differences. From the late 1950s through the mid-1970s, however, social psychologists increasingly began studying interaction patterns related to group and dyadic processes (for some of the major early works, see Altman & Taylor, 1973; Berscheid & Walster, 1969; Heider, 1958; Thibaut & Kelley, 1959). This movement was not limited to social psychologists in the United States; in Great Britain, Argyle and his associates also spent several decades studying aspects of relationships (see Argyle & Dean, 1965; Argyle & Henderson, 1985).

During this time several highly influential books were published. For example, Thibaut and Kelley's (1959) *The Social Psychology of Groups* eventually led to an explosion of research on social exchange processes in groups and dyads, bringing issues such as rewards (the positive outcomes people get from relationships) and reciprocity (the way one person's behavior leads to similar behavior in another) to the forefront. Berscheid and Walster's (1969) *Interpersonal Attraction* also had a major impact on both interpersonal communication research and the study of dyadic behavior in social psychology. This book focused on emerging relationships between strangers, as much of the early research in social psychology did (see Altman & Taylor, 1973). A short time later, however, relational research began to focus on love, and the study of close relationships began to bloom (see Berscheid & Walster, 1974; Rubin, 1970, 1973). Finally, Altman and Taylor's (1973) *Social Penetration: The Development of Interpersonal Relationships*, which examined the role of self-disclosure in relationships, helped generate research in communication, relationship development, and relationship disengagement.

The prestigious *Journal of Personality and Social Psychology* also includes a section on "Interpersonal Processes"; indeed, this journal publishes some of the best research on relationships. However, until the mid-1980s there were no journals devoted entirely to the study of relationships. In fact, the first professional conference devoted entirely to interpersonal relationships was held in the 1980s, again indicating the youthfulness of the field of personal relationships (see Kelley, 1986). This conference, which was organized primarily by social psychologists, laid the roots for the creation of two organizations that focus exclusively on personal relationships: the International Network on Personal Relationships (INPR), which was established by Steve Duck, and the International Society for the Study of Personal Relationships (ISSPR), which was founded by Robin Gilmour and Steve Duck. In 1984, the INPR established the first journal dedicated solely to the study of personal relationships, the prestigious *Journal of Social and Personal Relationships*. A decade later the ISSPR launched a second journal, called *Personal Relationships*.

Roots in Other Disciplines

Although the most identifiable bodies of research on personal relationships come from scholars in communication and social psychology, disciplines such as family studies, sociology, developmental and child psychology, clinical psychology, humanistic psychology, and anthropology have made important contributions as well. A recent study reported that approximately 37% of the research on personal relationships comes from social psychologists and another 37% comes from communication experts. In addition, sociologists and family studies scholars contribute substantially to the field of personal relationships (Hoobler, 1999).

Relationship researchers in the areas of communication and social psychology also draw on work from disciplines such as developmental psychology and family studies. For example, a series of books by Bowlby (1969, 1973, 1980) on attachment processes in parent-child relationships examined how interactions between infants and their care-givers influence whether children develop secure or insecure personalities. Subsequently, researchers applied Bowlby's work on attachment to adult romantic relationships to distinguish between people who are secure and comfortable with relational closeness and people who are insecure and/or uncomfortable with relational closeness (see Hazan & Shaver, 1987).

This interdisciplinary element gives the field of personal relationships a richness and diversity of ideas that often is absent in other fields. It is precisely because scholars in the various disciplines—communication, social psychology, sociology, family studies, and so on—think in different ways and have different theoretical and methodological approaches that the field of personal relationships has been so vital and is evolving so quickly (Duck, 1988).

Although this book draws upon knowledge from various fields, the primary focus is on communication in close relationships. Next, we define and discuss three terms that are central to this book: relationships (role, interpersonal, and close), interpersonal communication, and relational communication. Box 1.2 gives definitions for each of these key terms.

Relationships

Think about all the different people with whom you interact in a given day. Do you have relationships with all of them or only some of them? With how many of these people do you have close or intimate relationships? Defining the term

BOX 1.2 HIGHLIGHTS

Definitions of Key Terms

Role relationship: Two people who share some degree of behavioral interdependence, although people in such relationships are usually interchangeable and are not psychologically or behaviorally unique. One person in a role relationship can easily replace another.

Interpersonal relationship: Two people who share repeated interactions over time, can influence one another, and have unique interaction patterns.

Close relationship: Two people in an interpersonal relationship that is characterized by enduring bonds,

emotional attachment, personal need fulfillment, and irreplaceability.

Interpersonal communication: The exchange of nonverbal and/or verbal messages between people, regardless of the relationship they share.

Relational communication: A subset of interpersonal communication that focuses on the expression and interpretation of messages within close relationships. Relational communication includes the gamut of interactions from vital relational messages to mundane everyday interactions.

relationship can be tricky. When do we cross the line from interacting with someone to having a relationship? And when do we move from having a casual or functional relationship to having a close or intimate relationship?

Features of Relationships

According to many relationship scholars, the basic requirement for having a relationship is that two individuals share some degree of behavioral interdependence (Berscheid & Peplau, 1983). This means that one person's behavior somehow affects the other person's behavior, and vice versa. Based on this definition, we have relationships with a variety of people, including the salesclerk who helps us make a purchase, the waiter who takes our orders and serves us dinner, and the boss whom we rarely see but on whom we depend for leadership and a paycheck. These basic "relationships," known as **role relationships,** are not true interpersonal relationships. Rather, role relationships are functional and/or casual, and often are temporary; also, people in such relationships are usually interchangeable and are not unique. A close or intimate relationship with someone requires more than simple behavioral interdependence.

In addition to basic behavioral independence, **interpersonal relationships** require that people's lives be intertwined in important ways, that the two individuals influence each other in meaningful ways, that they have unique interaction patterns, and that they have repeated interactions over time. Thus, behavioral interdependence is an enduring feature of **close relationships** (see Berscheid & Peplau, 1983) but is merely a fleeting feature of functional relationships, such as those with salesclerks and waiters.

Brehm (1992) discussed two other features that help distinguish close relationships from more casual ones: emotional attachment and need fulfillment.

When we have a close relationship with someone, we feel connected to that person emotionally; he or she can make us feel happy or sad, proud or disappointed. Similarly, our close relational partners fulfill interpersonal needs, such as the need to belong to a social group, to feel loved and appreciated, or to care for and nurture someone (Brehm, 1992). Together, these attributes suggest that close relationships can be defined by the bonds people share. When that bond is characterized by enduring behavioral interdependence, repeated interactions, emotional attachment, and need fulfillment, a close relationship has emerged. Our closest relationships are also characterized by **irreplaceability**. This means that the other person has a special place in our thoughts and emotions, as well as in our social network.

Types of Relationships

Another way to think about relationships is to categorize them based on type. In fact, we do this every day in our ordinary language. For example, we refer to some relationships as "friendships" and to others as "romances" or "marriages." We introduce someone as our "best friend," "brother-in-law," "wife," and so forth. These categorizations, although simple, help people understand the type of relationship we share with someone.

Relationships come in all shapes and sizes. When college students think about what constitutes a close relationship, they mainly think about dating or romantic relationships. However, as the different categories or types just listed suggest, we live in a web of relationships that includes family members, lovers, acquaintances, coworkers, employers, and so forth. We also have "blended" relationships, such as those with a teacher who also becomes a friend or with a coworker who becomes a lover.

Moreover, most of us are apt to think only of typical "mainstream" relationships. The media, as well as most research, traditionally have focused on young, white, middle-class heterosexuals (Wood & Duck, 1995). But relational researchers have begun to examine many other types of relationships as well, including gay, lesbian, and bisexual relationships (Huston & Schwartz, 1995; Kurdek, 1991); polygamy (Altman & Ginat, 1996); cohabitation between unmarried individuals (Cunningham & Antil, 1995); single-parent families, orphans, and interracial couples (Gaines, 1995; Williams & Andersen, 1998); cross-generational and Internet relationships (Lea & Spears, 1995); and long-distance relationships (Rohlfing, 1995). Unfortunately research in these areas still lags far behind the research on heterosexual romantic relationships. For example, Peplau and Spalding (2000) reported that, of the 312 articles published in the *Journal of Social and Personal Relationships* from 1980 to 1993, only 3 focused on some aspect of sexual orientation.

Because this book is based on the existing research, the majority of the discussion necessarily revolves primarily around romantic relationships between heterosexuals. We also discuss research related to friendships and family relationships, albeit less often. We make an effort, however, to include relevant work on understudied relationships whenever possible. Thus, as you read this book, keep in mind that the traditional models of relationships do not apply to all relationships. Nonetheless, many types of relationships have elements in common: connection and conflict, joy and grief, and so forth. Indeed, the more scholars study less common relationships, the more they conclude that all relationships are cut from part of the same patchwork quilt. Of course, there are important differences sprinkled in with the similarities. Relationships are as unique as the different combinations of patchwork that can come together to create a quilt, and individuals in certain types of relationships do encounter particular difficulties that can affect communication processes. For example, Huston and Schwartz (1995), in their research on gay men and lesbians, stated: "The relationships formed by lesbians and gay men are in many ways very similar to heterosexual ones; in other ways distinct factors influence relationship formation and survival" (p. 120). Gay and lesbian couples, as well as interracial couples, often have to deal with societal prejudices and pressures with which opposite-sex and same-culture couples do not have to cope.

Characteristics Distinguishing Different Relationship Types

All types of intimate relationships vary on a number of different characteristics or dimensions. First, relationships can be either **voluntary** or **involuntary.** That is, people make a conscious choice to be involved in some of their close relationships but they enter other close relationships without choosing to do so. For instance, children cannot choose their family; rather, they are born or adopted into relationships with parents, siblings, aunts and uncles, grandparents, and other relatives. By contrast, people typically choose their friends. In most Western cultures people also choose their romantic partners, whereas in many other cultures spouses are selected through arranged marriages, thus becoming less voluntary.

Second, relationships are characterized by their **romantic** versus **platonic** nature. Typically friendships and relationships with family members are platonic, which means they do not include sexual attraction or sexual involvement. Dating and marital relationships, by contrast, are often marked by romantic feelings and sexual activity. Of course, some relationships fall in the middle. Sometimes an individual has romantic or sexual feelings for someone who is only supposed to be a good friend, or someone feels little sexual attraction for a well-liked dating partner. In these cases, the line between romance and friendship is likely to be blurred. In addition, both platonic and romantic relationships can be characterized as **intimate.** In everyday use some people use the terms *intimate* and *sexual* synonymously. But intimate relationships are defined by the characteristics mentioned previously: behavioral independence, repeated interactions, emotional attachment, and need fulfillment. Thus, people can have intimate relationships with friends, family members, and romantic partners.

Third, relationships can be either **satisfying** or **dissatisfying.** Satisfying relationships make people feel good about themselves. The relational partners feel close and connected, and emotions usually are more positive than negative. Dissatisfying relationships, by contrast, often make people feel badly about themselves. Partners often feel disconnected from one another, and emotions generally are more negative than positive. All relationships go through rough stretches, and some dissatisfaction not only is inevitable but also can lead partners to work through and solve problems, which can improve the relationship. At any given time, and in general, a relationship can be characterized by some degree of satisfaction or dissatisfaction. Think of the different close relationships that you have. You are likely to feel more satisfied in some of these relationships than others. For example, you might share a close relationship with both of your siblings, but you tend to be happier when with your brother than your sister, perhaps because you have more in common with your brother and get into more conflicts with your sister.

Fourth, relationships can be either **long-term** or **short-term.** For many people their sibling relationships are the longest lasting relationships they will experience—from infancy through old age. Thus, the history that siblings share with one another is unique. Other relationships are short-term, sometimes by choice and other times due to circumstances. Think about old friends you have lost touch with but wish you could contact today. Commitment levels also factor into the long- versus short-term distinction. For example, if you are highly committed to your romantic partner, this makes a long-term relationship much more likely than if you want to "play the field" and see other people. Some romantic relationships fall in the middle. For instance, if you are in a romantic relationship that is on a "commitment roller coaster," you and your partner may frequently break up and then make up. In any case, both commitment levels and relational length help define the nature of a given relationship.

Other dimensions characterize certain types of relationships. For example, Fitzpatrick (1988) suggested that marriages can be viewed in terms of how **traditional** or **nontraditional** the relationship is. In traditional marriages husbands and wives often adhere to established gender roles, with the man expected to earn more money and the woman expected to take primary responsibility for the home. In less traditional marriages these gender roles are blurred, and partners need to negotiate how tasks will be handled. Fitzpatrick also suggested that marriages differ based on how **connected** versus **separate** partners are. Partners who value connection are highly interdependent and readily share their experiences with each other. These couples are also likely to engage in activities together with common friends. By contrast, partners who value separation are likely to be less self-disclosive and to engage in more activities without their spouses, such as spending time with friends. Finally, Fitzpatrick distinguished marriages based on whether spouses tend to avoid or engage in conflict. **Conflict avoiders** dislike conflict, often because they believe that disagreement is unpleasant and can harm the relationship; **conflict engagers** believe that it is important to air grievances and to discuss problems.

Finally, some scholars have labeled **sex** or **gender** as a component defining different types of relationships (Brehm, 1992; Wood, 1996). Sex refers to an individual's biological makeup as male or female, whereas gender refers to how masculine, feminine, or androgynous the person is, with androgynous individuals possessing some feminine and some masculine traits (Bem, 1974). Sex is biologically determined, whereas gender is socially and culturally constructed. Sex can help define family relationships into categories such as father-son or father-daughter, or romantic relationships into categories such as lesbian, gay, or heterosexual. Much of the research on friendship also makes these distinctions by comparing male friendships to female friendships, or same-sex friendships to cross-sex friendships. Other research focuses more on gender by looking at how masculine, feminine, or androgynous individuals are within a relationship. For example, a romantic couple consisting of a feminine person and a masculine person is likely to function much differently than a romantic couple consisting of two androgynous individuals. In this book we use the term *sex* to refer to biological sex (male versus female) and the term *gender* to refer to culturally constructed images of men and women as masculine versus feminine.

Need Fulfillment in Close Relationships

Researchers suggest that a plethora of human needs are satisfied in close personal relationships, with the three most central interpersonal needs being affection, inclusion, and control (Schutz, 1958). **Affection** is satisfied through our ability to love other people and through having other people love us (Schutz, 1958). Throughout life our need for love and affection is satisfied through close relationships. Neglected infants who are never touched suffer from "failure-to-thrive syndrome" and even risk death (Andersen, 1999; Montagu, 1971/1978). Adults also need love and affection to validate their self-worth (Morris, 1971). Affection, according to Schutz (1958), occurs only in dyads. Inclusion and control, by contrast, can occur either "between pairs of people or between one person and a group of persons" (p. 23). Affection forms the basis for our most powerful relationships.

   Social inclusion, or the need to feel part of a group, is another crucial need (Schutz, 1958). It is through primary group relationships that basic needs such as safety and survival are satisfied. As Ruesch (1951) observed: "In the fold of the family, clan or group or in the widest sense of the world, the herd, he [or she] feels secure. Reliance on other members of the group increases his [or her] chance for survival in a troubled world" (p. 36). Humans evolved as members of hunting and gathering bands of 100 to 200 people (Donald, 1991). This may explain why belonging to groups—from youth groups to corporations, from sports teams to service clubs, from street gangs to fraternities and sororities— is so important to most people. In any case, Schutz (1958) suggested that feeling included is a crucial part of social development that enables us to have successful interactions and associations with other people. A lack of social interaction and inclusion can contribute to loneliness and low self-esteem (Segrin, 1998).

   The third basic interpersonal need, **behavioral control,** refers to the need people have to feel in control of their lives (Schutz, 1958). People in successful interpersonal relationships share control over their lives (Scott & Powers, 1978), including important decisions involving work, money, sex, children, and household chores. Indeed, a whole body of research suggests that partners who share tasks and resources in a fair manner are more satisfied with their relationships

In today's busy society, many people fulfill their need for social inclusion by joining groups where they can interact with others.

(see Chapter 8). By contrast, partners who believe they lack control or who are denied free choice may deliberately sabotage their relationships, defy rules, and engage in other destructive behavior. For example, if you have a friend who always shows up late, you might retaliate by leaving before he or she arrives. Prohibition on a relationship by parents sometimes increases the attractiveness of the relationship. According to Cialdini (1988), this effect is based on the idea that objects or people observed to be scarce or hard to obtain are most attractive. This explains why advertisers offer "limited time offers" and sales "while the supply lasts" and why people who are "hard to get" are more attractive than people who are "easy to get"—except, of course, if they are only easy for you to get.

Although these needs undoubtedly are important to some degree in most of our close relationships, keep in mind that needs vary from relationship to relationship. As Scott and Powers (1978) put it, "In a romantic relationship the need for affection may dominate your feelings and characterize your relationship. At school, however, the psychological need to know and understand may dominate your feelings and characterize your relationships with classmates" (pp. 7–8). Similarly, at particular points in a given relationship, certain needs may dominate. For example, teenagers often feel a strong need to assert their independence and escape parental control, while also wanting to be part of a social group of peers (Guerrero & Afifi, 1995b).

Goals in Relationships

Of course, humans are driven by more than needs; they also have aspirations and goals. College students' goals might include graduating, making friends, acquiring skills, partying, meeting their future spouse, getting into graduate or professional school, living up to parental expectations, and preparing for a career. Spouses' goals might include maintaining a happy marriage, raising their children to be "good" people, buying their dream home, and saving for retirement. Within the context of interpersonal interaction, Canary and Cody (1994) suggested that people strive for three overriding sets of goals: self-presentational goals, relational goals, and instrumental goals.

Self-presentational goals have to do with the image we convey to others. Andersen (1999) claimed that "selling ourselves is the most common objective of persuasion" (p. 265). Other scholars have contended that people often resemble actors on a stage, trying to present themselves in the most favorable light possible (see Chapter 2). Indeed, a central set of communication principles suggests that we are as attractive, credible, competent, or honest as others think we are. Objective personal qualities sometimes have little to do with our image, especially when we first meet people. From an interpersonal standpoint we are what people think we are. As Andersen (1999) put it, "Impressions we form of others are not just part of the communication game, they are the whole game" (p. 265). Not surprisingly, people spend a lot of time trying to look and act just right for that big date or that important interview.

Relational goals have to do with how we communicate our feelings about others, including the type of relationships we desire. Canary and Cody (1994) maintained that "nothing brings us more joy than our personal relationships. We spend significant amounts of time, energy and emotion in the pursuit of quality relationships" (p. 6). At every stage in a relationship, we have goals and plans for the future of that relationship. For example, you might want to meet that attractive student in your class, impress your date, avoid the person who won't let you alone, or spend time with your sister whom you haven't seen all year. Canary and Cody (1994) described three primary groups of relational goals. The first is activity based and involves sharing an activity with someone, such as attending a party or going skiing. The second is relationship based and involves wanting to initiate, escalate, maintain, or deescalate a relationship. The third is advice based and involves giving advice to peers and parents.

Instrumental goals have to do with accomplishing specific tasks, including obtaining goods and services, that promote self-advancement. For example, making money, getting good grades, buying a car, getting a ride to school, and completing a homework assignment are all instrumental goals. Usually, although not always, instrumental goals involve other people. Often people facilitate attainment of instrumental goals by asking for advice or assistance from a friend, getting permission from a parent or boss, eliciting support from a friend, or influencing someone's attitudes or behaviors (Canary & Cody, 1994). Thus, whereas achieving relational goals involves *giving* advice to help others, achieving instrumental goals involves *seeking* advice and assistance to meet one's own task-related goals. It is through networks of relationships that many of our instrumental goals are facilitated. For example, suppose you want to get a pay raise at work. To do this you have to communicate your wishes to your boss, and you also have to make a convincing argument that your performance merits a raise. People in close relationships also commonly try to achieve instrumental goals. For instance, think about the times you have asked a friend for a favor, tried to convince others to see the movie that you want to see, or perhaps asked a family member to loan you some money. All of these situations involve instrumental goals.

Principles of Interpersonal Communication

Whether you are trying to fulfill self-presentational, relational, or instrumental goals, communication is the vehicle through which you attain these goals. This is not to say that all communication is strategic and goal oriented. Much of our communication is relatively mindless and routine (Burgoon & Langer, 1995; Langer, 1989). Nonetheless, communication is the mechanism by which relationships are developed, the glue that holds them together, and often the means by which they are dissolved.

The terms *interpersonal communication* and *relational communication* are used to describe the process whereby people exchange messages within the context of different types of relationships. The goal of message exchange is the cocreation of meaning, although as we shall see shortly not all message exchanges are effective and miscommunication occurs frequently. A broader concept than relational communication, **interpersonal communication** refers to the exchange of messages, verbal and nonverbal, between people, regardless of the relationship they share. These people could be strangers, acquaintances, coworkers, political candidate and voter, teacher and student, superior and subordinate, friends, or lovers, to name just a few types of relationships. Thus, interpersonal communication includes the exchange of messages in all sorts of relationships, ranging from functional to casual to intimate. **Relational communication,** by contrast, is narrower in that it typically focuses on messages exchanged in intimate, or potentially intimate, relationships. In this section we focus on specific principles related to interpersonal communication.

Principle 1: *Interpersonal communication consists of nonverbal and verbal messages.*

Although much of our communication consists of verbal messages, nonverbal communication is at least as important as verbal communication (Andersen, 1999). In fact, studies suggest that 60–65% of the meaning in most interactions is derived from nonverbal behavior. And when emotional messages are exchanged, even more of the meaning may be gleaned from nonverbal behaviors (see Burgoon, Buller, & Woodall, 1996). Words are not always to be trusted. For example, someone can say "I love you" and not really mean it. But the person who spends time with you, gazes into your eyes, touches you lovingly, tunes into your moods, interprets your body language, synchronizes with your behavior, and uses a loving tone of voice sends a much stronger message. Nonverbal actions often do speak louder than words. As Eliza Dolittle sings in *My Fair Lady,* "Don't talk to me, show me. / When we sit together in the middle of the night, don't talk at all just hold me tight. / Anyone who's ever been in love can tell you that this is not time for a chat."

Nonverbal communication encompasses a wide variety of behaviors, including **kinesics** (facial expressions, body and eye movements), **vocalics** (silence and the way we say words, including vocal pitch, loudness, tone, and speed), **proxemics** (the way we use space), **haptics** (the use of touch), **appearance** (physical attributes such as height, weight, and general attractiveness, as well as clothing), **environmental cues** (such as using candles and soft music to set a romantic mood), and **chronemic cues** (the use of time, such as showing up for a date early or late). Clearly these types of behaviors can send powerful messages. Of course, interpersonal communication also consists of many forms of verbal behavior, including self-disclosure and verbal content. Self-disclosure, through which people reveal information about themselves to others, is a particularly important form of interpersonal communication (see Chapter 5). The use of formal or informal language, nicknames, and present or future tense are other examples of verbal behavior that affect interpersonal interactions. For example, when dating partners first start talking about sharing a future, such communication is likely to reflect a shift toward a more committed relationship.

Principle 2: One cannot not communicate in interpersonal settings.

In one of the important early works on communication, Watzlawick, Beavin, and Jackson (1967) stated: "Activity or inactivity, words or silence, all have message value: they influence others and these others, in turn, cannot not respond to these communications and thus are themselves communicating" (p. 49). Thus, unless two people simply do not notice each other, some degree of communication is inevitable when they are in contact. Even if someone does not mean to send a message, something that person says or does is likely to be interpreted as meaningful by the other person. This does not mean, however, that everything people do is communication. For communication to occur, a person has to send a message intentionally, or a receiver has to perceive and assign meaning to a behavior. So, for example, if you are blinking in a normal fashion while interacting with a friend, your friend is unlikely to attach any meaning to such an ordinary, involuntary, and biologically based behavior. Similarly, not every body movement counts as communication since many of these movements go unnoticed. But some of the movements you make and most, if

or, not and?

not all, of the words you say will be received and interpreted by others, making it impossible not to communicate at some level (Andersen, 1991).

To illustrate, recall the last time you sat down next to a stranger—perhaps at the mall, in a movie theater, or on a bus. What did you notice about the person? Did you check to see if he or she looked friendly before sitting down? Did you notice his or her appearance? Did he or she look older or younger than you? If you can answer any of these questions, Andersen (1991) argued that communication took place because you perceived and interpreted the stranger's behavior. In our relationships much of what we do is interpreted as meaningful by our partners. For example, a smile might be perceived as heartfelt or condescending, while a neutral facial expression might be perceived as reflecting boredom. Even silence can communicate a message. For instance, if a close friend stops calling you and does not return your messages, you will likely suspect that something is wrong. Perhaps your friend is mad at you, or perhaps he or she is ill or depressed. In either case your interpretation of your friend's silence will probably lead you to communicate with her or him in particular ways that will, in turn, further influence the exchange of messages between you.

Principle 3: *Every message contains both content and relational information.*

Bateson (1951a) observed that messages, whether verbal or nonverbal, send more than literal information; they also tell people something about their relationship: "Every courtesy term between persons, every inflection of the voice denoting respect or contempt, condescension or dependency, is a statement about the relationship between two persons" (p. 213). Bateson (1951b) labeled these two functions of communication the report and command features of messages. The **report** function refers to the literal content of the message; the **command** function refers to the part of the message that signals status and other aspects of the interpersonal relationship.

Building on Bateson's work, Watzlawick et al. (1967) labeled these two functions the **content** and **relationship** levels of communication: "The report of a message conveys information and is therefore synonymous in human communication with the content of the message. . . . The command aspect, on the other hand, refers to what sort of message it is taken as, and ultimately to the relationship between the communicators" (p. 51). Thus, a statement as simple as "Hand me your book" contains both content (namely, the request to hand over the book) and information about the relationship. This relational information depends on whether the request is delivered in a harsh, polite, sarcastic, bored, or warm vocal tone. It also depends on the communicator's facial expressions, posture, gestures, use of touch, attire, eye contact, and a host of other nonverbal behaviors. Finally, the context or situation can affect how the relational information in a message is interpreted.

Another example may be helpful here. Suppose that late on Friday afternoon your romantic partner calls and asks, "So what are we doing tonight?" At the content level this seems to be a simple question. But at the relationship level this question could be interpreted a variety of ways. You might think, "It sure is nice to know that we always do something together on Friday nights, even if we don't plan it in advance." Alternatively, you might think that your partner takes you for granted and assumes that you have nothing better to do than wait around for her or him to call before you make plans. Or, if you had argued with your partner the day before, you might think that this is his or her way of making up. Yet another possibility is that you might think your partner always leaves it up to you to decide what to do. Based on which relational information you get from the message, you are likely to react in very different ways.

Principle 4: Interpersonal communication can be effective or ineffective.

When one person sends an intentional message, understanding occurs when the receiver attaches approximately the same meaning to the message as did the sender. Of course, such perfectly effective communication may never occur since people typically attach somewhat different meanings to the same messages. It is impossible to get inside people's heads and to think their thoughts and feel their emotions. Thus, it is difficult to truly and completely understand "where someone is coming from." Nonetheless, the most effective communication occurs when sender and receiver attach very similar meanings to a behavior. Less effective (or less accurate) communication occurs when sender and receiver attach different meanings to a behavior.

Some scholars claim that shared understanding must take place for an exchange of messages to qualify as true communication (see Motley, 1990, 1991). Andersen (1991), however, disputed that claim, arguing that if complete understanding "were a necessary ingredient, then communication would be impossible because receivers never have exactly the same meaning for a message as does the sender" (p. 319). Indeed, Watzlawick et al. (1967) stated that communication is not limited to only those instances when mutual understanding occurs.

Similarly, Hecht, DeVito, and Guerrero (1999) suggested that effective or "successful" communication is only one form of message exchange and that other forms of message exchange should also be viewed as interpersonal communication. Specifically, Hecht et al. discussed miscommunication, attempted communication, misinterpretation, and accidental communication as important forms of interpersonal communication that are less-than-perfect in terms of creating shared meaning between sender and receiver. **Miscommunication** occurs when someone sends an intentional message that is misinterpreted by the receiver. For example, you might teasingly say "I hate you" to someone who takes your message literally. **Attempted communication** occurs when someone sends an intentional message that the receiver fails to receive or interpret; in other words, he or she misses the message. For example, you might hint that you want to leave a party you think is boring, but your partner might not get the message and keep on socializing. **Misinterpretation** occurs when someone unintentionally sends a message that is misinterpreted by the receiver. For example, you might be scowling simply because you are in a bad mood after a long, trying day at work, but your roommate misinterprets your facial expression as reflecting anger toward her or him. Finally, **accidental communication** occurs when someone does not mean to send a message, but the receiver observes the behavior and interprets it correctly. For example, you might try to hide your joy at acing an exam from a classmate who studied harder than you and did poorly, but your classmate sees your nonverbal reaction and correctly assumes that you did well. As you can see, all of these forms of communication can impact the communication process and people's relationships. Certainly effectiveness is important to high-quality communication, but it is not an attribute of all interpersonal communication.

Principle 5: Interpersonal communication can be symmetrical or asymmetrical.

This principle of communication, which is taken from Watzlawick et al. (1967), emphasizes the dyadic nature of the communication processes. That is, communication unfolds through a series of messages and countermessages that all contribute to the meaning people attach to a given interaction. **Symmetrical communication** occurs when people exchange similar relational information, or messages that are similar in meaning. For instance, a dominant message may be met with another dominant message (she says, "Take out the trash!" and he responds, "Do it yourself!"), or an affectionate message may be met with another affectionate message (she says, "I love you," and he says, "I love you too"). Nonverbal messages can also be symmetrical, as when someone smiles at you and you smile back, or when your date gazes at you lovingly and you touch her or him gently on the arm.

   Asymmetrical communication occurs when people exchange different kinds of information. One type of asymmetry occurs when people exchange messages that are opposite in meaning. For example, a dominant message such as "Take out the trash!" might be met with a submissive message such as "Okay, whatever you say, honey." Or a declaration of love might be met with an embarrassing silence and shuffling of feet, after which the beloved person might say something like "Thanks, but I'm not ready for that right now." Another type of asymmetry occurs when one person uses more of a certain behavior than another. For instance, Michael might tell Ashley he loves her several times during a conversation while Ashley might say "I love you" only once. Or Darnell might touch Tasha 10 times while Tasha initiates touch only once. As these examples suggest, the verbal and nonverbal messages that two people send and receive work together to create a unique pattern of communication that reflects their relationship.

Principles of Relational Communication

As mentioned previously, relational communication can be thought of as a subset of interpersonal communication that focuses specifically on the messages exchanged within relationships. Most often, research on relational communication examines messages in relationships that are, were, or have the potential to become intimate. Thus, all of the principles of interpersonal communication discussed previously are applicable to communication in relationships. Relational communication includes the entire range of communication behaviors, from vital relational messages to mundane everyday interaction. Thus, relational communication reflects the nature of a given relationship at a particular time. Communication both constitutes and defines relationships. In other words, communication is the substance of close relationships. Wilmot (1995) provided several principles of relational communication that are consistent with these ideas. These principles are paraphrased below.

Principle 1: *Relationships emerge across ongoing interactions.*

Relationships form not out of thin air, but across repeated interactions. Cappella (1998) argued that "experience and common sense tell us that relationships are formed, maintained and dissolved in interactions with partners. At the same time interactions reflect the kind of relationship that exists between the partners" (p. 325). According to Wilmot (1995), "Relational definitions emerge from recurring episodic enactments" (p. 25). In part, relationships represent collections of all the communication episodes in which two partners have engaged over time, and each episode adds new information about the relationship. In new relationships each episode may add considerably to the definition of the relationship. Even in well-developed relationships critical turning points such as a declaration of love, a heated argument, or an anniversary can alter the course of the relationship.

Principle 2: *Relationships contextualize messages.*

In different relationships messages have various meanings. For example, a frown from your relational partner does not have the same meaning as a frown from a stranger; a touch from your mother does not have the same meaning as a touch from your date or spouse; and disclosure from an acquaintance at work does not have the same meaning as disclosure from a good friend. In Wilmot's (1995) words, "Relationship definitions 'frame' or contextualize communication behavior" (p. 27). Thus, the context is critical to understanding the message. According to Andersen (1989), "It has become axiomatic that no human action can be successfully interpreted outside of its context. The term 'out of context' has become synonymous with meaningless or misleading" (p. 27).

Principle 3: *Relational types overlap one another.*

While some relationships fit into neat categories such as boyfriend, coworker, wife, or student, many relationships fit more than one category. For example, a colleague might also be a basketball teammate, a close friend, and a fellow member of a service organization. As Wilmot (1995) put it, "Relational types are not necessarily mutually exclusive—their boundaries are often fuzzy" (p. 28).

Moreover, relationships often move from one category to another as when a coworker becomes a friend, a friend becomes a dating partner, or a fraternity brother becomes an employee. In these "fuzzy" relationships people can be uncertain about how to behave appropriately, especially when they are using different relational definitions.

Principle 4: Relational definitions and communication
episodes frame each other.

This paraphrase of Wilmot's (1995) fourth principle suggests that relational communication is a highly dynamic, interrelated process. As definitions of a relationship change, so does the communication within that relationship, and vice versa. For instance, if you start dating a coworker, your communication with that person will reflect this change in relationship status. You are likely to discuss more intimate topics and to engage in more frequent interaction. Of course, your conversations at work might remain somewhat formal if you both want to project a professional demeanor. Similarly, two rivals at work who are stuck together in a stalled elevator might pass the time by talking and joking. As a result they might reassess their relationship and see each other in friendlier, less competitive terms.

Relational Messages

People can send a variety of messages to one another about their relationships. After reviewing the literature from a range of disciplines, Burgoon and Hale (1984, 1987) outlined seven types of relational messages that people commonly communicate to one another: (1) dominance/submission, (2) level of intimacy, (3) degree of similarity, (4) task-social orientation, (5) formality/informality, (6) degree of social composure, and (7) level of emotional arousal and activation. These messages, which have been referred to as the *fundamental relational themes,* all reflect the nature of a relationship. Of these seven themes, dominance/ submission and intimacy are the two primary dimensions that characterize relationships (Burgoon et al., 1996).

These seven message themes are important within all types of interpersonal interaction, but especially in close relationships. In role relationships relational messages stay fairly constant, with people generally following prescribed rules and scripts. For instance, in manager-employee relationships a certain level of formality, friendliness, dominance, and task orientation usually prevails across most interactions. By contrast, in intimate relationships the range and impact of relational messages typically is much greater. For example, a romantic couple might be hostile during an argument and then intimate when making up; a parent might act with an unusual level of formality and dominance when having a serious talk with a child; or friends might have a hard time switching gears and moving from a conversation to a task. Such messages can have a powerful impact on how relational partners view each other and their relationship.

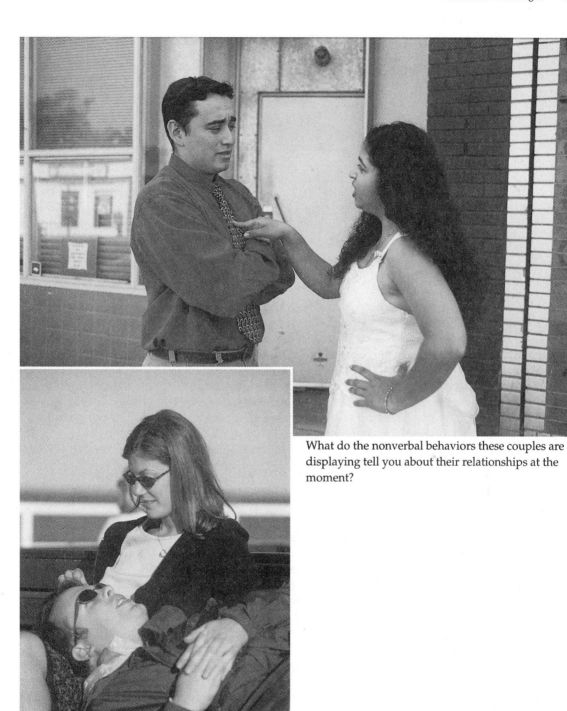

What do the nonverbal behaviors these couples are displaying tell you about their relationships at the moment?

Dominance/Submission

Dominance is often defined as the actual degree to which a person can influence others, and **submission** as the actual degree to which a person gives up influence and/or yields to the wishes of others. As such, dominance is a "social and relational phenomenon. That is, dominance is determined by the subservient or submissive responses of others. It is not dominance unless it works" (Burgoon et al., 1996, p. 306). Dominance is closely related to power and status, with **power** defined as a person's ability to control valuable resources, and **status** defined by a person's place in a social hierarchy (Patterson, 1983). For example, your boss is likely to have power because she controls your work schedule and has the power to promote you and give you a raise. She also has status because of her position within the company. And because she has power and status, she may be able to influence you more easily. Similarly your friends are likely to be able to influence you to some extent because you like them and want to maintain positive relationships with them.

Dominance is communicated in a variety of ways. Verbal statements that take the form of commands are a key form of dominant behavior, as are many verbal messages delivered using assertive or aggressive language. Nonverbal behaviors can also reflect dominance. For example, dominant individuals tend to look at people more when they are speaking and less when they are listening (Exline, Ellyson, & Long, 1975), which suggests that they believe what they are saying is more important. Dominant individuals also tend to take up more space and to speak in a moderately loud, fast, and authoritative tone of voice. Interestingly, dominant individuals also have the prerogative to violate norms by keeping others waiting, dressing casually when others are expected to dress formally, talking for longer periods of time than others, and initiating touch (Burgoon et al., 1996). (More information on dominance is provided in Chapter 11.)

Level of Intimacy

According to Burgoon and Hale (1984), intimacy is a multidimensional construct that has five subthemes: (1) affection/hostility, (2) inclusion/exclusion, (3) trust, (4) depth/superficiality, and (5) intensity of involvement. Intimate communication conveys affection, inclusion, and trust. It is also high in depth. In other words, intimate communication deals with personal rather than superficial topics. In addition, intimate communication typically is characterized by high levels of nonverbal involvement and positive affect, which means that the two people are actively engaged in conversation and attentive to each other.

Intimacy is conveyed in a variety of ways. Verbal statements of affection, such as "I love you," are highly valued within relationships (Marston, Hecht, & Robers, 1987). Personal nicknames, such as "honey bunny" for a romantic partner or "pumpkin" for a child, also convey intimacy. Self-disclosure is important in communicating intimacy as well. As you will learn in Chapter 5, self-disclosure occurs when individuals reveal personal information about themselves to others. The more in-depth this self-disclosure is, the more intimate the communication.

Nonverbal behaviors are extremely powerful in conveying intimacy. A special set of behaviors called **nonverbal immediacy cues** send messages of physical and psychological closeness, as well as interpersonal warmth (Andersen, 1985). Primary immediacy cues include touch, close proxemic distancing, direct body orientation, forward lean, and attention gaze. Andersen also included positive affect cues such as smiling and vocal warmth as part of nonverbal immediacy. (More information on intimacy is provided in Chapter 10.)

Degree of Similarity

Shows of similarity are an important way for people to identify with one another and to show inclusion. Similarity is achieved through a wide array of verbal cues, such as expressing similar opinions and values, agreeing with each other, reciprocating self-disclosure, and communicating empathy and understanding. Nonverbal cues conveying similarity are very common. For example, people may sit in similar positions or mirror one another's facial expressions. Indeed, research has shown that people's emotions are often "contagious," with one person's emotional state influencing the other's, leading to similar displays of affect (Hatfield, Cacioppo, & Rapson, 1994). Other research has shown that people often adapt their vocal intonations and speech to match that of their friends or other people they like (Street & Giles, 1982). For example, you might pick up some of the slang that a friend uses, and you might talk with a slightly different accent when at home with your family on the East Coast than when with friends from the Midwest. Street and Giles (1982) referred to this process as **communication accommodation,** whereby people's verbal and nonverbal behaviors become more similar to or different from those around them. Generally, when we like people and want to identify with them, our behavior becomes more similar to theirs. By contrast, when we dislike people and want to dissociate ourselves from them, our behavior becomes more dissimilar to theirs.

People also alter their physical appearance to show similarity and dissimilarity. For example, group members might get tattoos, as many players on college basketball teams do. In addition, body piercings can reveal that people belong to a particular group or generation. More temporary signs of similarity, such as getting similar haircuts or wearing similar clothing, are common as well. As Guerrero (1995) put it:

> Clothing often identifies people as members of a group or dyad. In particular, high school cliques, gangs, coworkers, and fraternity/sorority members often adopt similar forms of dress. Romantic dyads and best friends often engage in rituals such as wearing similar rings or exchanging jewelry that is marked with similar sayings such as "friends forever." (p. 75)

Thus, people communicate similarity and dissimilarity in a variety of verbal and nonverbal ways. Such messages help form a foundation for inclusion in or exclusion from groups and also can signal individuals' connection to one another.

Task-Social Orientations

As noted previously, some people are connected only through task-oriented or role relationships. Common examples of task-oriented relationships include teachers and students, superiors and subordinates, doctors and patients, and lawyers and clients. Unless a friendship develops, communication between these people generally focuses almost exclusively on the task at hand—for example, getting a good grade, doing a job properly, seeking medical treatment, or trying to win a settlement. By contrast, our close relationships, as well as many of our casual acquaintanceships, tend be characterized by more social orientations. Here communication involves conversing and having fun, rather than trying to accomplish a particular task. Importantly, our closest relationships often include both task and social orientations. For example, a married couple may have a task orientation when doing chores together or discussing important issues such as how to discipline a rebellious child. But this same couple may shift to a social orientation when they out having fun with some friends or spending a quiet, romantic evening together away from their rebellious child.

Burgoon and Hale (1987) found certain types of communication to reflect a task orientation. Specifically, when people seemed sincere, work oriented, reasonable, and more interested in the task at hand than the conversation, they were rated as being highly task oriented. This makes sense. Think about a time when you tried to have a serious conversation with a romantic partner. Perhaps you were concerned about a problem that had emerged in your relationship, and you were intent on working it out. How would you feel if your partner seemed uninterested in solving the problem? What if she or he wanted to watch TV instead of talking, or kept changing the subject to something less serious? These actions probably would be distressing to you. In this case your task orientation would be in direct contrast to your partner's more social orientation.

Formality/Informality

When an interaction is formal, people maintain their distance, and the overall tone of the interaction is serious. By contrast, informal interactions are characterized by less distance and a more casual approach. One of the key verbal behaviors associated with formality is forms of address. For example, calling your professor Dr. Brown is more formal than calling her Dr. B., which is more formal than calling her Lisa. Similarly, the way you address your romantic partner's parents sends a strong message regarding formality. Do you call your partner's father Mr. Garcia or José? If you marry your partner, will he still be Mr. Garcia or José, or will you call him Dad? These seemingly trivial differences in forms of address can affect the intimacy level of the relationship. In some cases too much formality sends a strong negative message. For instance, someone who considers you a close friend might be offended by your use of formal address. When parents are angry with a child, they sometimes use the child's full name ("Jonathan Martin Hall, stop that this minute!"), and romantic partners sometimes use formal names sarcastically during an argument ("Whatever you say, MISS Green!"). Of course, using too little formality can also send a strong negative message. For example, calling your date Christy when she prefers Christine would not be a wise move on a first date, nor would it be wise to call your spouse by a nickname such as "sweet-ums" when at a formal company party.

Nonverbal cues are also important in conveying formality. Burgoon and Newton (1991) found that interactions characterized by the use of anxiety cues (such as speaking too fast, using nonfluencies like "um," and twisting one's hands in one's lap), inexpressiveness (such as neutral facial expressions and a lack of gestures and vocal animation), and low levels of eye contact combined to convey formality. This is probably because people are less comfortable in formal than informal situations. Environmental cues are important in conveying formality as well. To illustrate, think about the different ways that lunch might be served at a birthday party. If there is assigned seating and someone serves you lunch, the atmosphere is probably much more formal than if everyone helps themselves to a buffet and finds a place to sit or stand while eating. Similarly, the way people use time differs based on the level of formality. If the birthday party is a formal affair, people are expected to be there on time, or at least before the meal is served. Time of arrival is more lax if the party is a casual affair.

Degree of Social Composure

Social composure is related to the level of anxiety and communication competence people show in a given interaction. When people are socially composed, they appear confident and sure of themselves, and other people are likely to regard them as competent communicators. Social composure is conveyed through verbal cues such as making strong, convincing arguments and saying the appropriate words at the right time. For example, if you are arguing with your roommate about the household chores, you will appear composed and competent if you present a logical argument about why you think the chores are not being distributed fairly. If you are asking someone out on a date, you will appear more composed if you make your request in a charming and appropriate fashion ("I feel so comfortable with you; I'd enjoy spending more time with you. Would you like to go to a party with me next Saturday night?") rather than stammering or becoming tongue-tied.

Nonverbal behavior also sends powerful messages about social composure. Canary and Cody (1993) listed several types of nonverbal messages that are related to competence and composure. These include (1) maintaining a high level of, but not continuous, eye contact, (2) speaking in a confident, moderately fast, and fairly loud voice, and including purposeful pauses, and (3) wearing clothing that is appropriate for the situation. By contrast, low levels of social composure and competence are conveyed by anxiety cues such as using nonfluent speech, moistening one's lips, and fidgeting. Other behaviors such as looking down before responding to a question, displaying smiles that look fake or insincere, and taking too long to resume one's speaking turn also are associated with a low level of social composure (Burgoon et al., 1996; Canary & Cody, 1994). So, if your heart starts pounding when you are arguing with your roommate or asking someone out, you might appear anxious and sound nervous, which could undermine perceptions of your composure.

Level of Emotional Arousal and Activation

Relational messages also influence the emotional tone of an interaction. Interactions can be characterized by two emotional dimensions: (1) **pleasantness,** which refers to how positive or negative the emotions experienced are, and (2) **activity,** which refers to how active or bored a person feels (see Burgoon et al., 1996). For example, if you are in an argument with your romantic partner, the interaction is likely to be characterized by low pleasantness and high activity. But if you are having a serious, loving conversation with your romantic partner about your future together, the interaction is likely to be high in both pleasantness and activity. Other times, interactions are characterized by low activity. For example, two strangers sitting next to each other at the department of motor vehicles might chat to pass the time, but they are unlikely to be very involved in the conversation. Instead, such interactions typically are socially polite (pleasant) but low in activity. In other situations, such as having to talk to someone you would rather avoid, the interaction is likely to be low in both pleasantness and activity.

Research has shown that people usually perceive moderate to moderately high levels of arousal as most appropriate when interacting with relational partners, particularly when arousal is positive (see Burgoon et al., 1996). Negative forms of arousal include experiencing distress or nervousness; positive forms of arousal include experiencing excitement, interest, and elation. We do not expect our friends and loved ones to be nervous around us, except maybe at the beginning of a relationship, but we do expect them to be interested and involved in the conversations we have with them. Perhaps surprisingly, research also suggests that individuals sometimes are less relaxed with people they like than with people they dislike (Burgoon et al., 1996). This is because people care more about making a good impression on those they like and because they are often more affected by what close relational partners say about them than by what strangers say.

In any given interaction these relational messages work together to create a pattern of themes that reflects the nature of a relationship at a particular point in time. Over time, different patterns of themes emerge to characterize the type of communication and the type of relationship that people share. Think about your closest relationships. How would they compare in terms of these message themes? Chances are that each relationship is characterized by a somewhat unique profile of relational messages.

Conclusion

This chapter introduced you to the field of personal relationships and provided information on some key concepts that will be discussed in this book. After reading this chapter, you should have a better appreciation for the complexity of your relationships and the communication that occurs within them. Communication does not occur in a vacuum. Rather, communication is shaped by contextual and relational factors, and communication both reflects and influences the nature of a given relationship.

A large assortment of verbal and nonverbal behaviors are relevant to relational communication. In this book several chapters focus on ways that verbal and nonverbal messages are used to communicate messages related to love, intimacy, power and influence, and privacy. We also look at how communication is used to communicate identity (Chapter 2) and reduce uncertainty (Chapter 4). Communication is instrumental throughout the lifespan of a relationship, so this book contains chapters that focus on communication during initial attraction (Chapter 3), relationship development (Chapter 5), relational maintenance (Chapter 9), and relationship termination (Chapter 15). Finally, some of the chapters in this book emphasize interactions that occur during important relational events, such as sexual interaction (Chapter 7), the exchange of resources (Chapter 8), relational transgressions, such as infidelity and deception (Chapter 13), and conflict (Chapter 14). We hope these chapters will give you fresh insight into how communication functions during the many different stages and events of your personal relationships.

Discussion Questions

1. What qualities distinguish your close relationships from your casual relationships?
2. In this chapter we defined interpersonal communication as the exchange of nonverbal and verbal messages between people, regardless of their relationship. Do you agree or disagree with this definition of interpersonal communication? What types of behavior should not count as communication?
3. As illustrated by the comparison of John Gottman and John Gray, there is a lot of popular press material on relationships that does not necessarily correspond with what researchers have found. Why do you think the public is so fascinated with popular books, talk shows, and magazine articles on relationships? What type of role, if any, do you think relationship researchers should play in this process?

Making a Good Impression

Identity Management in Relationships

"What do you think of my new haircut?" "Honey, do these pants make me look fat?" "Isn't my new velvet Elvis painting great?" Truthful answers to questions such as these can harm a relationship. Suppose you think the haircut looks awful, the pants make the person look unappealing, and the Elvis painting is tasteless. How are you to respond? Researchers have shown that the answers to these types of questions have important relational consequences because they are tied to people's identities. Research on identity management offers a glimpse into how people develop and maintain their perceptions of self. Identity management is particularly important at the beginning of relationships when people are trying to make a good initial impression, but even in developed relationships identity management takes place.

In this chapter we examine how people use communication to manage their identities during social interactions. First, we briefly discuss the development of personal identities and the role that relationships play in their development. Second, we discuss some general issues related to identity management, such as whether trying to make a good impression is deceptive and manipulative or is simply a natural, often unconscious process. Finally, we review literature related to two major theories of identity management—Goffman's (1959) dramaturgical perspective and Brown and Levinson's (1987) politeness theory—as well as research on facework.

The Development and Expansion of Identities

Sociologists, anthropologists, psychologists, family researchers, and communication scholars, among others, have studied how our identities influence us throughout life. Although several definitions have been offered, we define **identity** here as "a theory of self that is formed and maintained through actual or imagined interpersonal agreement about what self is like" (Schlenker, 1985, p. 67). The key theme underlying this definition is that "a person's identity is forged, expressed, maintained, and modified in the crucible of social life, as its contents undergo the continual process of actual or imagined observation, judgment, and reaction by audiences (oneself and others)" (Schlenker, 1985, p. 68). In other words, the way we see ourselves is shaped by our interactions with other people, including the way they respond to and judge us.

Identity, Perceptions, and Social Interaction

Our identities help us understand ourselves in relation to the world around us. Self-esteem and identity are part of a person's **theory of self. Self-esteem** refers to how positively or negatively we view ourselves. People with high self-esteem perceive themselves as possessing valuable personal characteristics; people with low self-esteem perceive themselves to lack such characteristics. Identity defines who we are and what we are like (see Schlenker, 1985) by specifying the characteristics that define us (African American, student, smart, attractive, introvert) and placing us on a comparative continuum with others (smarter than John, not as smart as Haley). Unlike self-esteem, however, our identity is not based on whether we consider these aspects of ourselves to be positive or negative qualities. Identity simply specifies what these qualities are. Self-esteem and identity, although sometimes related, are clearly distinct. For example, both Sally and Scott may smoke and have "smoker" as part of their identities. However, Sally may think that her smoking is part of what makes her cool, while Scott may be depressed because he sees smoking as an expensive, unhealthy habit that he cannot stop. Thus, smoking could contribute to high self-esteem for Sally and to low self-esteem for Scott. In this chapter we focus on identity and identity management rather than self-esteem, despite their influences on one another.

Many factors other than self-perception affect our identities. Hecht (1993) argued that identity construction can be viewed through four "frames of identity" or "lenses" (see also Hecht, Collier, & Ribeau, 1993). First, identity is viewed through a personal frame. In this sense, identity is an image we construct within ourselves: We perceive ourselves to possess certain characteristics and not others. Second, identity can be viewed through an enactment frame. In other words, identities develop through communication with others; the way we respond to others and the way they respond to us reflects and shapes our theories of self. Third, identity can be viewed through a relationship frame whereby we define ourselves in terms of relationships with other people. For example, your identity might be shaped by the kind of friend, romantic partner, and son or daughter you are. Moreover, you might portray yourself differently depending on whether you are with your best friend, a first date, your spouse, or your parents. Finally, identity can be viewed through a communal frame. As such our identities are integrally tied to the groups to which we belong, and the development of our identities often is constrained by our cultural or group identities. For example, in childhood we are taught rules of cultural appropriateness, such as norms of politeness. These rules become so ingrained that they necessarily affect our identities.

Hecht (1993) argued that these four frames work together to affect identity development. All couples routinely deal with these identity issues, but interracial or intercultural couples often face special challenges. They must each deal with who they are as individuals—for example, as a white man and an African American woman (personal frame). They must also deal with how they present themselves to others (enactment frame), what it means to be an interracial couple (relationship frame), and how to best blend their different cultural backgrounds (communal frame).

Hecht's theory, as well as other research, suggests that identity, perception, and social interaction are related to one another in various ways. Next, we discuss seven principles that show how identity affects how we perceive ourselves, how others perceive us, how we behave, and how we evaluate our behavior and our relationships with others.

Principle 1: Our identities provide us with a hierarchical structure of who we are.   Although we define ourselves in myriad ways, our identity helps organize these many characteristics into a hierarchical structure that fluctuates according to context (Schenkler, 1985). In other words, the importance of various aspects of ourselves changes depending on the situation in which we find ourselves. The content of our identity includes our roles (student, son, friend), goals (live in Europe, get a job helping others), personal qualities (friendly, honest), accomplishments (3.5 GPA, president of an organization), group/cultural membership (sorority member, Asian), and appearance (am moderately attractive, like Abercrombie clothes), among others. These contents vary in the degree to which they *centrally* define who we are. The more central they are to our definition of self, the more likely they are to be stable across our lifetime and to be prominent as we present ourselves to others during interactions.

Principle 2: The feedback we receive from others helps shape our identities.   Charles Horton Cooley (1922) first developed the notion of the **looking-glass self,** a metaphor that helped describe his belief that identity is shaped by feedback from others. He argued that social audiences provide us with the image of ourselves that we see when we look into a mirror. Therefore, the way people treat us is reflected in the way we see ourselves. For example, think of how you came to believe that you were smart enough to pursue a college degree. Your identity as an intelligent person was most likely cultivated through interactions with parents, teachers, and/or peers. Perhaps a specific teacher in high school said you were smart enough to go to college, or your parents or spouse gave you positive feedback and encouragement, or a friend kept complimenting you on your ability to learn quickly. Regardless of the source, one or more of these people likely helped develop that aspect of your identity. Other parts of our identities are similarly formed through our interactions with others.

Principle 3: Our identities help us interpret feedback from others.   Just as people's feedback affects our identities, so, too, can our identities affect how we perceive feedback from others (Schlenker, 1980). For example, people who see themselves as introverts will likely react very differently from those who define themselves as extroverts when someone says to them, "You're awfully quiet today." The emotions they experience and the perceptions of what the statement means about them, what it means about the sender of the message, and what the sender intends by the statement—all are influenced by their identity as an introvert or extrovert, to say nothing of other aspects of their theory of self.

Research also suggests that we are likely to interpret feedback from others as consistent with our identity (Swann, 1983; Swann & Read, 1981). For example, people who consider themselves attractive may interpret someone's negative comment about their appearance as an expression of envy rather than a true reflection of their attractiveness. Moreover, we are generally more likely to remember information that is consistent with our identity and to discount information that is inconsistent (Kahneman, Slovic, & Tversky, 1982). However, some research suggests that this tendency applies only to those aspects of our identity that are central to our definition of self and for which we have strongly held beliefs (Stangor & Ruble, 1989). For less central aspects of self, inconsistent information is more easily assimilated. For example, a 21-year-old who is just beginning to adopt an identity as someone who enjoys drinking on weekends may struggle mightily when a friend tells him that she thinks people who drink are irresponsible. This feedback may influence his identity development. However, if the negative feedback comes after drinking has become a more stable aspect of the person's identity, it will likely be ignored.

Principle 4: Identity incorporates expectations and guides behavior. The central characteristics that we see ourselves as possessing create social expectations for our behavior (Schenkler, 1985), as well as self-fulfilling prophecies (Merton, 1948). These expectations strongly influence how we act (Bandura, 1986). As such, our identity carries with it expectations for how people with that identity typically behave. To live up to that identity means to behave in a certain manner. For example, if a person's identity includes being a good student, he or she must behave in ways that reflect such a characteristic or the identity will not be maintained. Such individuals are likely to study harder and to attend classes more regularly than those who see themselves as average or poor students. In other words, the maintenance of our identity requires us to behave in an identity-consistent manner.

Self-fulfilling prophecies also are related to identity. A **self-fulfilling prophecy** occurs when an expectation exists that something will happen, and a person behaves in a way (often unconsciously) that actually makes it more likely that the anticipated event will occur. For example, if you think someone will refuse your request for a date, you might be hesitant and nervous when approaching the person, which could lead your intended date to turn you down. By contrast, if you think someone is likely to accept your request for a date, you will probably ask in a confident, competent manner, which could lead your intended date to accept your invitation.

Principle 5: Identity influences our evaluations. The expectations and behavioral guidelines connected to identity provide people with comparison points against which to judge their performance (Schenkler, 1985). As a result, our identity influences our evaluation of how well or poorly we performed. For example, good students are likely to get upset if they receive a C on an exam or a paper, whereas those who see themselves as poor students might be delighted to receive a C. Interestingly, self-esteem and identity may be most closely connected through this expectation-evaluation link. Unrealistically flattering self-definitions lead to expectations of self that are unlikely to be met, which leads to a string of perceived failures. As a result, self-esteem can suffer.

Principle 6: Identity influences the likelihood of goal achievement. Our identity helps determine what goals we are likely to achieve. The achievement of goals is facilitated by the presence of qualities that are consistent with that particular goal. Thus, people who see themselves as good students are likely to get better grades because they see studying and attending class as important behaviors that help them maintain their identities. The same type of process influences goal achievement in our relationships. For example, the likelihood that Bill will achieve his goal of dating David depends on the extent to which Bill believes he possesses characteristics desired by or appealing to David. If an important aspect of Bill's identity is his sensitivity and David prefers a dating partner who is relatively tough, Bill might feel he has little hope of attracting David. Self-fulfilling prophecies are also related to goal achievement. For instance, if Nikki believes that she can make it as a dancer on Broadway, she is likely to have confidence, be more motivated, and perhaps work harder, all of which will make it easier to achieve her goal.

Principle 7: Our identities influence what social relationships we choose to pursue and maintain. Robinson and Smith-Lovin (1992) found that people prefer interactions with individuals who provide identity-consistent feedback, even if such feedback produces emotional hurt. In other words, those who define themselves in negative terms, such as not intelligent, unconsciously seek partners who confirm that negative identity. Why would this be the case? Apparently people distrust feedback that is not consistent with what they believe, so they perceive those who offer such feedback as dishonest and less likable (Swann, Griffin, Predmore, & Gaines, 1987). The consequences of this tendency can be serious, especially for abused women, who often unconsciously find themselves attracted to individuals with the same characteristics as those who abused them in the past.

Identity-consistent behavior may be particularly important in established relationships. Swann, De La Ronde, and Hixon (1994) examined this issue by investigating whether our preference for "authentic" feedback (feedback consistent with our identity) or "positive" feedback (feedback that is more favorable than our view of self) changes according to the stages of our relationships. They asked partners in marriages and dating relationships about their self-identity, their partner's assessment of their identity, and the level of relationship intimacy. Their results showed that a shift occurs between dating relationships and marriages. Although intimacy was highest in dating relationships when a partner's view of the individual was more positive than the individual's view of his or her self, the most intimate marriages were those in which "authenticity" prevailed—that is, in which the partner's view of the individual matched the individual's view of his or her self. It seems that we want others to view us through rose-colored glasses while dating but that successful marriages are those in which the partners, at some point before or during marriage, view each other in a more authentic way.

Identity Management in Relationships

So far, we have shown that identity influences our interactions with others and our selection of relationship partners, but we have not yet addressed how identity is intertwined with relationship development. To do this, we review principles related to impression formation and self-expansion theory.

Impression Formation You may have heard the expression "you never get a second chance to make a first impression." When we first meet people, they quickly assess us, often based on outward cues such as physical appearance and facial expression. In fact, Zunin (1972) contended that most people make these assessments within the first 4 minutes of an initial interaction. This is because people feel a need to be able to predict and explain other people's behavior (see Berger, 1987, and Chapter 4). In addition, people like consistency. Therefore, in initial encounters people try to determine what the individual with whom they are interacting is like. To do this, they "latch" onto external characteristics, such as physical appearance, clothing, and facial expressions, to try to generate a consistent picture. For example, if a woman is wearing professional business attire, she may be judged to be educated, intelligent, and successful. If a man is smiling and laughing, he may be judged to be friendly and fun-loving. Of course, these snap judgments can be wrong because they are based on stereotypes rather than true aspects of a person's identity.

Work by Duck (1976) gives further insight into this process of evaluating people during initial encounters. Duck described four types of personal constructs that people use to judge others in initial encounters: (1) physical constructs, such as a person's height, weight, and attractiveness; (2) role constructs, such as whether a person is a manager or an entry-level employee, or a student or a teacher; (3) interaction constructs, such as whether a person appears friendly or hostile, or introverted or extroverted; and (4) psychological constructs, such as judgments about a person's intelligence, motivation level, and laziness. According to Duck, most initial impressions are based on the physical construct. From the physical construct people think they can determine a number of personality characteristics, such as age, physical fitness, strength or athletic ability, and even friendliness and trustworthiness. This goes back to the idea of looking for a "consistent package." If people latch onto the physical construct and perceive someone as attractive, then they are also likely to judge the person positively in terms of interactional and psychological constructs.

Although the physical construct typically has the most power during initial interactions, the other constructs can also have an impact. For example, a common question people ask when first meeting someone is "What do you do for a living?" Think of the different impressions you have of people based on whether they disclose that they are a lawyer, construction worker, secretary, flight attendant, IRS agent, or professional athlete. Similarly, you will likely have very different impressions of the same person depending on whether he or she is in a "bad" or "good" mood when you first meet. The person in a good mood will probably be viewed as friendly and nice; the person in a bad mood will probably be viewed as hostile, withdrawn, and/or mean. Fair or not, these types of first impressions set the stage for relationship development by determining how attracted people are to one another.

Research on nonverbal communication paints a similar picture. Burgoon, Buller, and Woodall (1996) reviewed research showing that first impressions are usually influenced more by nonverbal than verbal communication. They outlined three types of nonverbal cues that are particularly important in forming and managing impressions: (1) physical appearance cues, (2) positive affect cues, and (3) immediacy cues.

Consistent with Duck's research, Burgoon and her colleagues discussed physical appearance as the most important of these cues in many (although not all) situations. Considerable research has been conducted on the role that physical appearance plays in the attraction process (see Chapter 3). For example, beautiful people are often perceived to possess more positive qualities, including trustworthiness, friendliness, talent, and social skills, than more average-looking people. This tendency to overgeneralize someone's positive qualities based on an attractive physical appearance has been called the **what-is-beautiful-is-good hypothesis** or the **halo effect** (Dion, Berscheid, & Walster, 1972; Hatfield & Sprecher, 1986b). However, it is important to keep in mind that the halo effect is based on snap judgments and stereotypes. As Hatfield and Sprecher's research showed, beautiful people do not really differ in terms of talent or virtue, although they may possess a small advantage in terms of social skills because they have had more positive interactions with others, and thus more opportunities to develop these skills.

Aspects of people's physical appearance are linked with a number of other stereotypes (see Burgoon et al., 1996, for a review). For example, tall, muscular people typically are perceived as dominant and athletic; short, chubby individuals are stereotyped as cheerful but lazy, and tall, thin individuals are stereotyped as sensitive but tense and awkward. Think about how these physical appearance stereotypes are reinforced by folklore and the media. Santa Claus is big and jolly, while Olive Oyl from *Popeye* is skinny and high-strung. In the same vein it is usually easy to separate the heros from the villains in cartoons because the "good" characters are often more attractive than the "bad" ones.

Positive affect cues and immediacy cues are also important in impression formation and management. **Positive affect cues** convey warmth and pleasantness. Woodall, Burgoon, and Markel (1980) found that smiling and head nodding in particular make a person appear more attractive and likeable. Burgoon et al. (1996) defined **immediacy cues** as behaviors that signal availability for and interest in interaction (see also Chapter 10). Immediacy cues such as gaze,

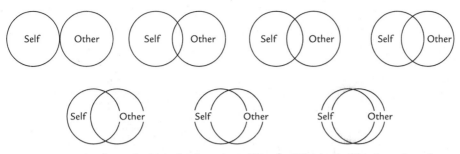

FIGURE 2.1 The Inclusion-of-Others-in-Self Scale Which drawing best describes your relationship? *Source:* Aron and Aron (1996).

close proximity, forward lean, open body positions, and direct body orientation (facing toward rather than away from someone) have been found to be especially important in promoting positive first impressions because they make a person appear approachable.

This basic research on impression management suggests that relationship development is enhanced when people are physically attractive and use positive affect and immediacy cues during initial interactions. Because these cues lead people to attribute positive characteristics to a person's identity, they increase the probability that attraction and future interaction will occur.

Self-Expansion Theory Research on impression formation investigates how people make identity judgments in initial encounters. Aron and Aron's (1986, 1996a) **self-expansion theory** goes a step further by explaining how identity influences the development of close relationships after first impressions are made. The theory is framed around three primary predictions. First, people seek to expand the self. Several studies have shown that one of our fundamental desires as human beings is to broaden our experiences and extend our identity (Aron & Aron, 1996b). We do not seem satisfied with a static sense of self. Instead, we seek to develop our sense of self as part of our physical, cognitive, and emotional development. For example, if you are good at oil painting, you might try other kinds of art, such as ceramics or watercolors.

Second, people enter into relationships because of the opportunities they provide to expand their identity. One of the best ways to expand the self is by becoming close to someone who can contribute to our identity development by exposing us to new experiences. In fact, Aron, Aron, and Smollan (1992) found that the more partners defined their relationship as a meshing of both identities, the closer they were likely to be. Figure 2.1 shows the inclusion-of-others-in-self scale that these authors have used in most of their studies. They have consistently found that close relationships are characterized by an expansion of self through inclusion of others. Rather than having two separate identities, people in close relationships combine identities, thereby allowing each partner's identity to expand through new experiences.

In a novel test of this prediction, Aron, Paris, and Aron (1995) asked 325 students to list as many self-descriptive words or phrases that came to mind in response to the question "Who are you today?" The students performed this task four times across a 10-week period (once every 2½ weeks), as well as answering questions about whether they had fallen in love since their previous completion of the task. Consistent with the theory's prediction, those who reported falling in love since the previous task showed a marked increase in the number of self-definitions they could list, an apparent indication that their identity had expanded. This does not mean, however, that strong relationships are those in which partners are completely intertwined. It is important to keep in mind that the theory emphasizes the importance of self in relationships. As such, losing one's sense of self or one's individual identity in favor of a relational identity is *not* what the theory would predict as a "healthy" relationship outcome. Instead, the theory predicts that close relationships are those in which both individuals have strong self-identities that can grow from the new experiences that each partner's identity brings.

Third, a relationship's success depends on the ability of the relationship to expand the partners' experiences and sense of self. A common phenomenon in many relationships is stagnation; that is, over time the relationship becomes bogged down by routine, which decreases satisfaction for both partners. Self-expansion theory offers an interesting explanation and remedy for this common problem. Specifically, Aron and Aron (1986, 1996a) argued that relationships stagnate when they stop serving their self-expansion function. In other words, when the partners' identities stop benefiting from the relationship, personal growth, and thus relational growth, stops.

To avoid such stagnation, relational partners should engage in new and challenging activities—for example, train for a marathon or learn how to kayak. The key is that this activity is done together. To test this theory, Reissman, Aron, and Bergen (1993) placed married couples into one of three groups. They instructed the first group to spend 1½ hours every week participating in a set of activities that both partners viewed as exciting, the second group to spend 1½ hours each week engaging in activities that both partners viewed as pleasant, and the third group not to deviate from their normal routine. After 10 weeks, the researchers investigated the groups for changes in satisfaction levels. As predicted by self-expansion theory, satisfaction increased more for couples who engaged in exciting activities than for couples who engaged in pleasant activities or stayed with their normal routine. The mere act of spending time together was not what increased satisfaction. Rather, for satisfaction to rise, the time spent together needed to involve exciting activities, which presumably led to self-expansion.

In sum, how we view ourselves plays a critical role in what interactions we select, what relationships we pursue, and how these interactions and relationship develop. Thus far, however, we have not addressed how we communicate our identity to others, how we manage to maintain our identity despite threats to its validity, and what social rules are in place to help us navigate the pitfalls of identity management. In the next section, we discuss how identity management influences our behavior across a variety of situations.

Shakespeare and Goffman both believed that all the world is a stage, with people merely players. How does this famous quote relate to impression management and identity?

Communicating Our Identities to Others

Antonio: *I hold the world but as the world, Gratiano;*
                A stage where every man must play a part,
                And mine a sad one.
Gratiano: *Let me play the fool . . .*
—WILLIAM SHAKESPEARE, *The Merchant of Venice,* **Act I, Scene I**

Shakespeare's writing popularized the notion that all the world's a stage upon which we are merely players. Social scientists, including Goffman (1959, 1967, 1971), have also embraced this idea when describing the process of identity management. As a sociologist Goffman was particularly interested in how individuals communicate their identities to others and how others help confirm these identities. He saw identity management as an intrinsic part of social interaction that depends on involvement from all group members to be successful. Goffman used the term *self-presentation* to describe people's tendency to manage their behavior to create particular images of themselves for others. Other scholars have used the terms *facework* (Cupach & Metts, 1994), *impression management* (Tedeschi, 1981), *identity management* (Schlenker, 1985), and *politeness* (Brown & Levinson, 1987) to describe this process of managing behavior. Although these terms differ slightly, with some terms encompassing a broader range of behaviors than others, they are used interchangeably in this chapter.

Besides *self-presentation, facework* is the most common term used to describe behaviors that help people make positive impressions on others (see Tracy, 1990, for a review of work in this area). In fact, you have probably heard the word *face* used this way in everyday conversation. Examples include describing someone as "saving face" (when trying to remedy an embarrassing situation), noting that it is "face time" (when there is an opportunity to present a positive image of oneself), talking about putting on a "happy face" (when we are actually feeling bad), and trying to "put the best face forward" (when in situations such as job interviews). In more technical terms, Brown and Levinson (1987) defined *face* as a person's publicly displayed image of self.

To better understand how people use communication to present themselves in a positive light, we will discuss research and theory related to three general perspectives: (1) Goffman's dramaturgical approach, (2) Brown and Levinson's politeness theory, and (3) preventive versus corrective facework. First, however, we should examine some general issues related to self-presentation and how it functions in everyday life.

General Issues in Self-Presentation

On any given day, chances are that you are trying to make a good impression on someone. Doing so often requires managing your behavior to hide or minimize potential faults while maximizing strengths. Impression management also involves adapting your behavior to particular audiences and situations. For example, the image Melanie presents to a group of her close friends when at a nightclub on Saturday night is likely to be very different from the image she displays to upper management when at work. Some people question whether these types of behavioral shifts are hypocritical, manipulative, and deceptive; reflect communication competence; or simply represent the way people unconsciously present themselves to others.

Issue 1: Is self-presentation hypocritical, manipulative, or deceptive?   When discussing self-presentation in class, we typically find that a majority of students think, at first, that self-presentation is the height of hypocrisy, is evidence of insecurity, is tantamount to being phony, or is downright deceptive. Moreover, many students are uncomfortable with the notion that we are all chameleon-like in our behavior, changing it according to the audience and situation. Are we not trying to deceive the audience into thinking we are something or someone we are not? The answer is no, not typically. Most instances of self-presentation are merely a matter of highlighting certain *aspects* of ourselves to different audiences. We may have elements of intelligence, sociability, respect, crassness, career orientation, and laziness in our identity, but we segregate these different elements when communicating to various audiences. This segregation is not deception because those characteristics are all true aspects of ourselves.

Of course, people do fabricate identities periodically. Indeed, the news is littered with cases of people leading double lives or individuals in an Internet chatroom posing as someone or something they are not. These instances, and others like them, are examples of deceptive self-presentations. Most of us, how-ever, have neither the ability nor the desire to completely fabricate our identity.

Other less extreme examples may relate to your life experiences more di-rectly. Have you ever hidden your anger or sorrow from others and "put on a happy face," feigned interest in a boring conversation, or acted as if you liked someone you actually disliked? We act these ways for a variety of reasons, but all involve a belief in the importance of self-presentation. We may not want people to know that we are angry or sad because that knowledge would reveal something about us, we may not want to show boredom because that would be disrespectful, and we may not want to express our dislike because that would hinder group dynamics.

Attempts to manage impressions in the hope of advancing a desirable im-age of ourselves sometimes backfire. One of the key elements of a successful performance is that it is perceived as sincere (Goffman, 1959) and as a true reflection of one's personality. Cases in which individuals are caught lying in their efforts to manage their identity will produce the opposite results from those sought. Research has shown that when deception is detected it produces detrimental personal and relational consequences (Buller & Burgoon, 1994; O'Hair & Cody, 1994; see also Chapter 13). Indeed, honesty may be one of the most important impressions that we want to foster in others because it goes to the core of our identity. Being perceived as untrustworthy or fake will likely put in doubt the sincerity of all other positive qualities that we have successfully portrayed and that accurately reflect who we are.

Exaggerating the truth or putting too much effort into self-presentation sometimes produces negative outcomes as well. For example, research on nar-cissism (self-focusing behavior) has shown that boastful individuals are gener-ally rated as less socially attractive and are liked less than those who enact less self-promotion (Vangelisti, Knapp, & Daly, 1990). These findings are interesting in that they show that behaviors meant to bolster one's image in the eyes of an audience can backfire if the person is perceived as selfish or insincere. Indeed, Schlenker (1980, 1984, 1985) has discussed a dilemma that people often face of having to choose between presenting the best possible image of self and pre-senting a plausible or realistic image. Jones and Wortman (1973) used an exam-ple of a first date to show how this dilemma may play out in our behavioral choices. When people on a first date describe all their positive qualities and accomplishments, they can come across as conceited and, as a result, be consid-ered unattractive. But, if they neglect to mention these qualities and accomplish-ments, they may be perceived as undesirable. Thus, the ideal self-presentation strikes a balance between positivity and plausibility.

Issue 2: How is self-presentation related to communication competence? According to researchers who study communication competence, people who are socially skilled have a knack for engaging in behavior that is both polite and situationally appropriate (Spitzberg & Cupach, 1988). People who possess these skills are also generally more successful at developing relationships. This makes sense when you think about all the ways in which you manage impressions based on the audience and the situation. For example, you would probably not have many friends if you acted as formally with them as you would during a job interview. In a similar vein you would probably not be hired if you acted too informally when meeting a prospective employer. Among friends we act relaxed, discuss social activities, and often trade stories about humorous events that have occurred in our lives. We want to promote ourselves as a good friend, a good person, and someone who can contribute to the group's fun. During the job interview we want to emphasize very different aspects of ourselves—as a reliable colleague, a smart person, and someone who can contribute to the company's development. If we switch gears this way, does this mean that we are phonies? No. It means we understand that we must fulfill different roles for different audiences, just as they do for us. Being flexible in terms of the roles that we play can help us be more effective communicators, as long as we are not manipulating others for nefarious purposes.

Several different studies confirm that people change their behavior based on the audience and/or the situation. As mentioned previously, to be socially competent people must strike a balance between showing their most positive characteristics and still appearing modest. Interestingly, this balance is affected by whether we are interacting with friends or strangers. Research suggests that we are more likely to present an overly favorable impression of ourselves to strangers than to friends. We can assume that strangers do not know much about us, so the importance and utility of disclosing favorable information about ourselves is relatively high. By contrast, our friends probably already know of our accomplishments, so pointing them out again would likely be perceived as conceited, thus backfiring. Moreover, our friends probably know us well enough to recognize realistic from unrealistic stories, while strangers may be unable to make such a distinction. Tice, Butler, Muraven, and Stillwell (1995) conducted five studies that compared the differences in people's self-presentations to friends and to strangers. They concluded that "people habitually use different self-presentation strategies with different audiences, relying on favorable self-enhancement with strangers but shifting toward modesty when among friends" (Tice et al., 1995, p. 1120).

Several studies also show that we vary the impression that we project of ourselves based on the audience or situation. For example, Daly, Hoggs, Sacks, Smith, and Zimring (1983) observed restroom behavior of men and women in restaurants and bars. They recorded the amount of time that people spent preening (adjusting their clothes, straightening their hair, looking at themselves in the mirror) and then asked them about their relationship with the person with whom they attended the establishment. Not surprisingly, they found that those who spent the most time managing their appearance were also in the newest relationships. In fact, research on affinity-seeking behavior (behavior done to attract others) discovered a variety of impression management activities that we do early in relationships to increase our partner's attraction to us (Daly & Kreiser, 1994). These include attending carefully to how we look, appearing interested in what the person has to say, emphasizing similarities, and portraying an image as a "fun" person. In sum, the way people present themselves to others is flexible and dynamic, with people managing their behavior differently depending on the situation and the audience so as to maximize positive impressions and social competence.

Issue 3: To what extent is self-presentation a deliberate, conscious activity?   Self-presentation is so commonplace that it often becomes routine, habitual behavior that is encoded unconsciously. DePaulo (1992) offered several examples of habitual impression management behavior, including the postural etiquette that girls learn as they are growing up and the ritualistic smiles given by the first runner-up at beauty pageants. Other examples include the ritualistic exchange of "thank you" and "you're welcome," table manners, classroom etiquette, and the myriad taken-for-granted politeness strategies (which we will address in more detail later in this chapter). All these behaviors were probably enacted deliberately and consciously at some time but have since become automatic aspects of interaction.

However, at times even behaviors that are typically habitual become more deliberate. Specifically, when we especially want to make a good impression or when we expect difficulty in achieving our desired impression, our self-presentational activity will likely be more deliberate and controlled (Leary & Kowalski, 1990; Schlenker, 1985). For example, when you first meet the parents of your girl- or boyfriend, you will probably be more aware than usual of your posture, politeness rituals, and other normally habitual impression management behaviors. Your deliberateness in enacting these behaviors may be further heightened if your partner's parents do not approve of the relationship and/or you expect resistance from them. In sum, in certain circumstances we are very deliberate and conscious in our use of impression management tactics—for example, on first dates, at the dean's office, or in an interview—but the majority of our self-presentational strategies are relatively habitual and performed unconsciously.

Interestingly, even people who claim not to care about what others think of them tend to manage their identities in ways that make them more socially competent, which provides further evidence that self-presentation is often an unconscious, habitual process. Schlenker and Weigold (1990) compared "autonomous" individuals, who claim to be very individualistic and not to care about audience opinions, with individuals who claim to place significant weight on others' attitudes. If self-presentational concerns are irrelevant to autonomous individuals, then we would expect their attitudes to be unaffected by audience attitudes. Instead, Schlenker and Weigold found that autonomous individuals changed their attitudes "if expressing their actual beliefs would have jeopardized their appearance of independence" while more socially driven individuals did so "in order to conform to the expectations of their partner" (p. 826). In other words, both autonomous and more socially driven people are motivated to maintain a certain image of themselves; it is the image itself that differs. Thus, even those who claim not to care about societal attitudes seem to be motivated by self-presentational concerns. Indeed, research shows that those who are not sensitive to audience characteristics and self-presentation needs are less successful relationally and professionally than those who are (Schlenker, 1980). This suggests that there is considerable social incentive for people to adapt their behavior based on the audience.

The Dramaturgical Perspective

The dramaturgical perspective helps explain how people adapt their behavior to various audiences. In his book *The Presentation of Self in Everyday Life*, Goffman (1959) advanced a revolutionary way of thinking about identity management. Based primarily on his observations of behavior in a Shetland Islands (Scotland) farming community, he presented a **dramaturgical perspective** on identity management behavior. Borrowing from Shakespeare, Goffman used the metaphor of theater to describe our everyday interactions. Specifically, he argued that we continually enact performances that are geared for particular audiences, with the purpose of advancing an image that is beneficial to us. In other words, we are always concerned about appearances and work to ensure that others view us the way we would like them to.

Goffman, like others, argued that we are highly motivated to present a positive image of ourselves to others. Indeed, the evidence for such a claim is strong. For example, several studies have shown that some sexually active individuals refrain from using condoms because they are afraid such an action may imply that they (or their partners) are "uncommitted" or "diseased" (Lear, 1997). Holtgraves (1988) argued that gambling enthusiasts pursue their wagering habits partly because they wish to portray themselves as spontaneous, adventurous, and unconcerned about losing money. Snow and Anderson's (1987) year-long observational study revealed how homeless people present themselves to their communities in ways that help restore their dignity. For instance, a 24-year-old male who had been homeless for 2 weeks told them: "I'm not like the other guys who hang out at the 'Sally' [Salvation Army]. If you want to know about street people, I can tell you about them; but you can't really learn about street people from studying me, because I'm different" (p. 1349). This individual clearly made an effort to distance himself verbally from what he considered to be an undesirable identity: being homeless. In fact, distancing was the most common form of self-presentation these authors found among the homeless.

Since Goffman's early work, scholars have outlined certain conditions under which impression management becomes especially important to us (Schlenker, Britt, & Pennington, 1996). Although researchers still consider impression management to be something that is always salient to us, the following three conditions seem to make it especially important.

Condition 1: The behavior reflects highly valued and central aspects of the self. In other words, we are more concerned about the success of our impression management when we try to portray an image that is at the core of our identity than when our efforts involve less central aspects of ourselves. For example, if Kathryn sees herself as highly career oriented but only somewhat outgoing, she is likely to portray herself as more professional than social. Situations that require a professional image, such as job interviews or business presentations, are likely to call forth a particularly strong need for Kathryn to manage her self-presentation.

Condition 2: Successful performance is tied to vital positive or negative consequences.   For example, if the success of a cherished relationship depends on your ability to convince your partner of your commitment, the importance of your impression management efforts is heightened. You might start sending your partner flowers, giving him or her gifts, and saying "I love you" more often as ways of showing that you are a devoted, committed partner. In a similar vein, if you are told that your raise at work is contingent on evidence that you are a team player, you may devote considerable attention to that aspect of your identity. Consistent with this notion, several studies have shown that we are especially motivated to be perceived in a positive light when interacting with attractive or highly valued others (see Jellison & Oliver, 1983; Schlenker, 1984). In one study participants were less likely to ask for help on a task from attractive opposite-sex strangers than from unattractive opposite-sex strangers, presumably because of their desire to come across as competent to attractive others (Alain, 1985).

Condition 3: The behavior reflects directly on highly valued rules of conduct.   We all consider certain rules of conduct to be especially important. For example, some people strongly believe that engaging in conflict in a public setting is inappropriate (Jones & Gallois, 1989). These people will be especially careful not to engage in public conflict because violating that norm would be especially threatening to the public identity they wish to portray. Similarly, some people believe that public displays of affection are inappropriate. If someone shows too much public affection to these people, they might become embarrassed and then back away to try to maintain a comfort level. When important relational rules such as these are violated frequently, it not only is very face threatening but often leads to relationship deterioration (Argyle & Henderson, 1984; Metts, 1994).

It is worth noting that these three factors are often quite prominent in close relationships, especially in the early stages, when partners are busy trying to make positive first impressions (Swann et al., 1994). In these early stages people typically display central aspects of themselves to their partners (condition 1); success in these displays can make the difference between attracting or repelling a potential friend or romantic partner (condition 2); and ground rules are often set as to what rules of conduct will be most highly valued (condition 3). For these reasons (and others discussed throughout the chapter), studying identity and identity management is critical to understanding the success and failure of relationships.

To the extent that the three conditions outlined here are salient, people will engage in impression management. Consistent with his dramaturgical perspective, Goffman (1959) referred to social behavior designed to manage impressions and influence others as a **performance.** An **actor** gives a performance in front of a set of observers, or an **audience,** and in a particular location, which Goffman referred to as the **stage.**

Front Versus Back Stage   As in any theatrical venue there are two general types of stages: front and back. The **front stage** is where our performances are enacted and our behaviors are observed by an audience. This is where impression management is particularly important. Conversely, the **back stage** is where we can let our guard down and do not have to think about staying in character. According to Goffman (1959) the back stage is "where the performer can reliably expect that no member of the audience will intrude" (p. 113). In the backstage and surrounding area, which Goffman referred to as **wings,** we can often find materials and individuals who assist us in giving a successful performance. For example, cologne/perfume, a hairbrush, and a mirror are all backstage materials that we use to improve our appearance, thereby increasing the potential success of our self-presentational performance on a first date. We might also ask friends to assist us in our appearance or to give us information about the person whom we are about to date. In fact, one of the primary ways that we gain information about someone is by consulting other people (see Berger, 1987). We then use this information to improve our impression management strategies. Answers to questions like "Is he dating anyone right now?" and "Does she like sports?" can help reduce uncertainty and give people an idea of how to manage their impressions. For example, if you learn that someone you want to date is interested in sports, you might portray yourself as a sports enthusiast and invite that person to a college sporting event. If you learn that the person dislikes sports, you will probably take a different approach.

Tedeschi (1986) made a distinction similar to front and back stages by comparing public versus private behavior, with public behavior being subject to observation and private behavior being free from such scrutiny. Indeed, several studies have shown that we often behave differently in public than in private (for a review, see Baumeister, 1986). Can you think of something that you typically do only in the back stage? Singing is a common example of a backstage behavior. Many people are too embarrassed to sing in front of others (in the front stage) but, when pressed, admit to singing in the shower or in their cars (which are both backstage regions). In a similar vein, hygienic activity, despite its universality, is reserved for backstage regions. These may seem to be obvious examples of backstage behavior, but you might have noticed the complexity of these "stages." For example, unless you have a good singing voice, you would probably not sing in front of strangers, but you might not hesitate to sing in front of your best friend or a romantic partner. When people are with their closest friends and intimate partners, behaviors that typically are reserved for the back stage are often moved to the front stage. In other words, what is considered back stage behavior is very much dependent on the audience; our closest friends and family members are back stage, so they get a more authentic and unrehearsed version of us.

Role, Audience, and Context Whether behaviors occur in the front or back stage is dependent on the role enacted, the audience being targeted, and the context in which the activities are performed. For example, you might feel free to sing in front of strangers at a karaoke bar. Similarly, some teenagers manage their use of swearing differently depending on the audience. When with their parents or other adults, they might want to advance an identity of being proper and respectful, which would preclude them from swearing. With their friends, by contrast, they might want to convey a carefree, rebellious, and "cool" identity that is bolstered by the use of swearing. The only viable criterion on which performance success is judged is whether it successfully advances the image that the performer desires to advance for a particular audience (Baumeister, 1982; Leary, 1995; Schlenker, 1980). When a performance threatens the image that one wants to convey to a certain audience, it is reserved for the back stage. Thus, in the swearing example, the teenagers would consider swearing a back-stage activity when they are interacting with their parents but a front-stage activity when they are interacting with peers.

This discussion of stage-appropriate behavior also highlights the relative difficulty of defining what constitutes a "back" stage. "Public" and "private" may capture part of what is meant by such a distinction, in that "front" stage is that area to which the particular audience in question has access, and the "back" stage is that area to which the audience presumably has little access. Thus, parents may be unaware that their teenage son or daughter swears when in the company of peers because they have little or no access to that part of their child's communication performance.

Finally, it is important to mention the audience's role in the impression management process. When self-presentation is successful, the audience and "actor" interact to help each other validate and maintain their identities. After all, we can work hard to establish a certain identity, but it rests on the audience to either accept or reject our self-presentation. In fact, Goffman (1967) argued that the validation of another person's identity is a "condition of interaction" (p. 12). In other words, we expect other people to accept the identities we show them and to help us save face when we accidentally put forth an undesired image. We have all been in situations in which we inadvertently said or did something embarrassing, and the last thing we wanted was for someone to emphasize the error or laugh at our mistake. In fact, Goffman (1967) called people who can watch another's "face" being damaged without feeling sorrow, hurt, or vicarious embarrassment "heartless" human beings. Moreover, research shows that people who fail to help others save face are often disliked and shunned (see Cupach & Metts, 1994; Schlenker, 1980). Most people know how it feels to be made fun of after an embarrassing event, so instead of laughing they try to relieve the distress that the embarrassed person is feeling. This leads to the next theory of impression management we discuss in this chapter— politeness theory.

Politeness Theory

As an extension of Goffman's work, Brown and Levinson (1987) developed **politeness theory,** which focuses on the specific ways that people manage face using communication. A large portion of their theorizing revolved around a distinction they made between positive and negative face.

Positive Versus Negative Face　Brown and Levinson (1987) defined **positive face** as the favorable image that people portray to others and hope to have validated by others. In other words, positive face is the identity that we have been discussing as part of self-presentation, impression management, and identity management. It describes a person's need to have an identity that is desirable to at least some other people. By contrast, they defined **negative face** as the perception that a person can do what he or she wants without having to worry about others' reactions.

According to social politeness theory, people face a constant struggle between wanting to do whatever they want (which satisfies their negative face needs) and wanting to do what makes them look good to others (which satisfies their positive face needs). Of course, on some occasions the same action can satisfy both aspects of face. For example, suppose your best friend asks you to help prepare food for a party he or she is giving. You might agree to help your friend, which supports your positive face needs because it makes you look good. But if you happen to love to cook, your negative face needs also would be satisfied because you are doing exactly what you wanted to do. However, it is much more likely that a behavior will fall somewhere between the two face needs or that supporting one face need will threaten the other. For example, you may agree to help a friend move despite your desire to relax at home. In this case, in attending to your negative face needs by staying home, you would come across as a poor friend and threaten your positive face needs.

During interaction with others, people's positive and negative faces can be validated or threatened. Identity is validated when a person's behavior and the audience's response to that behavior support the image the individual is trying to advance. For example, you may validate your identity as a caring partner by taking your significant other for an unexpected dinner date after he or she had a long week at work. In return your partner may validate your identity as a caring partner by telling you or others how appreciative he or she is when you do nice things like arranging special dinners out.

A study by Albas and Albas (1988) examined how students validated their positive faces following receipt of a good exam grade. The researchers identified several strategies that "acers" (as they labeled them) used to reveal their grade to others as a way to bolster their positive faces without directly bragging. These strategies included "repressed bubbling" (nonverbal signals of elation), "accidental revelation" (leaving the test facing upward, with the grade in full display), and "question-answer chain" (asking other students how they did, which sets the stage for them reciprocating with a similar question). In this way students who performed well on the test could "publish" that fact to others, thereby supporting their identity as an intelligent person and good student. However, as mentioned previously, if the person appears to be bragging or fishing for a compliment, these strategies could backfire. That is, in addition to validating one's identity as an intelligent person, such strategies could threaten one's identity as a nice and modest person.

Face-Threatening Acts   When a person's behavior is at variance with the identity he or she wants to convey, a face-threatening situation occurs. Face-threatening acts (FTAs) are behaviors that detract from an individual's identity and often make the person look foolish (Brown & Levinson, 1987). For example, forgetting a dinner date with your significant other is a self-inflicted threat to your identity as a caring partner. Your partner may further contribute to this face threat by publicly chiding you for stranding her or him at the restaurant. Of course, not all behaviors are equally face threatening. Certain behaviors cause people to lose more face and lead to more negative personal and relational consequences than others.

Research suggests that at least six factors affect the degree to which an FTA is perceived to be severe. The first three factors, identified by Schlenker and his colleagues (Schlenker, Britt, Pennington, Murphy, & Doherty, 1994; Schlenker & Weigold, 1992), focus on behavior that threaten a person's own face. The remaining three factors, from Brown and Levinson's (1987) politeness theory, focus on behaviors that threaten either an individual's or his or her partner's face.

1. **The more important the rule that is violated, the more severe the FTA.** For example, forgetting your relational partner's birthday usually will be more of a rule violation than forgetting to call your partner to tell her or him that you will be late coming home from work.

2. **The more harm the behavior produces, the more severe the FTA.** For example, if you trip and lose your balance, you are likely to feel some loss of face. However, if you trip, fall to the ground, and scatter your paperwork, the loss of face is likely to be much greater. Similarly, if you get caught telling a lie about something that has serious implications for your relationship, the loss of face will be greater than if you get caught telling a "little white lie."

3. **The more the actor is directly responsible for the behavior, the more severe the FTA.** For example, if a store clerk refuses to accept your credit card because the expiration date is past, it is much less face threatening than if the clerk phones in your card number and is asked to confiscate your card and cut it up because you are late on your payments.

4. **The more of an imposition the behavior is, the more severe the FTA.** For example, you will probably be more concerned about your face when asking for help moving furniture to a new house (which is quite an imposition on the person's time and energy) than when asking for help solving a simple riddle (which is hardly an imposition).

5. **The more power the receiver has over the sender, the more severe the FTA.** For example, if you make a silly comment that your boss could misconstrue as an insult, you will probably be more worried than if you make the same silly comment in front of a friend. With the boss you are more likely to worry about appearing incompetent and incurring negative consequences.

6. **The larger the social distance between sender and receiver, the more severe the FTA.** For example, you will probably worry less about threatening the face of your best friend than that of an acquaintance, presumably because the foundation of the friendship is more solid and less susceptible to harm from face threats.

Although research has generally supported the validity of these factors, some research has shown that factor 6, which relates to the social distance between receiver and sender, may not always hold true. Work by Holtgraves and Yang (1990, 1992) suggests that in many cases, instead of being *less* concerned about threatening the identity of those close to us, we are actually *more* concerned about doing so. The context and purpose of the self-presentation strategy may make a difference here. Sometimes we are particularly concerned about making a good impression and getting along well with a new acquaintance; other times we are more concerned with protecting our close relationships from harm. The main point here is that identity management concerns become more salient as the consequences of impression management failure increase.

Facework Strategies   Given the importance of facework in people's everyday lives, it should come as no surprise that people use a variety of intricate strategies to manage these face needs during interaction. In fact, most, if not all, interactions inherently include examples of facework that help people maintain or repair, or that strategically threaten their own faces or those of others. Even simple requests ("Since we live so far apart, would you mind meeting at a restaurant that is somewhere halfway between us?") are phrased in a way that respects the positive and negative face needs of the other person. This fact becomes clear if you think of other ways that these requests may be phrased ("I don't want to drive that far. You have to meet me halfway").

Given the many ways that concerns for facework influence our interactions, Brown and Levinson (1987) offered five options that individuals have when considering an FTA. The strategies differ in the degree of balance achieved between the goals of accomplishing a face-threatening task and managing face concerns.

1. **The "bald on-record" strategy.** This strategy is characterized by primary attention to task and little or no attention to helping the partner save face. It is the most efficient strategy but also the most face threatening. Brown and Levinson (1987) offered the examples of a mother telling her child to

"Come home right now!" or someone in need of assistance telling a by-stander to "Lend me a hand here!" Bald on-record strategies are typically used when maximum task efficiency is important or where there are large differences in power or status between actors.

2. **The "positive politeness" strategy.** This strategy is intended to address the receiver's positive face while still accomplishing the task. It includes explicit recognition of the receiver's value and his or her contributions to the process, and couches the FTA (often a request) as something that does not threaten the identity of the receiver. For example, complimenting someone on her or his attire, haircut, or performance is an example of positive politeness that might precede a request. Similarly, if you want a friend to help you write a resume and cover letter, you might say, "You are such a good writer. Would you help me edit this?"

3. **The "negative politeness" strategy.** This strategy is intended to address the receiver's negative face while still accomplishing the task. The key is that receivers not feel coerced into doing something, but instead feel that they are performing the act of their own volition. Often, negative polite-ness also involves deference on the part of the sender to ensure that he or she does not come across as coercive. For example, you might say to a friend, "I suppose there wouldn't be any chance of your being able to lend me your car for a few minutes, would there?" Brown and Levinson (1987) noted that requests phrased this way clearly emphasize the freedom of the receiver to decline.

4. **The "going off record" strategy.** This strategy is characterized by primary attention to face and little attention to task. As such it is a relatively ineffi-cient strategy for accomplishing tasks. However, given the importance of face, it may serve the participants well and so is often used. Examples include hinting, using an indirect nonverbal expression, or masking the request as a joke. For instance, if you want your partner to take you on a vacation, you might make comments such as "I've always wanted to go on a Caribbean cruise" or "It would be great to get away and go somewhere tropical." If you want your roommate to pick her or his socks off the floor, you might use indirect nonverbal communication such as frowning while looking at the socks for an extended period of time.

5. **The decision not to engage in the FTA.** Brown and Levinson (1987) noted that individuals often choose to forgo the face-threatening task completely in favor of preserving face. For example, even if you are upset because your roommate's partner always spends the night at your apartment, you might decide not to say anything for fear of embarrassing or angering your roommate (particularly if you do not want him or her to move out).

According to Brown and Levinson (1987), people perform a form of cost-benefit analysis when deciding what type of strategy to use. Bald on-record strategies are the most efficient but also the most damaging to face, and as such may be most damaging to the relationship. However, by going off record people run a much greater risk that the receiver will not recognize the request or will simply ignore it.

Metts (1992) applied this logic to the predicament of breaking up with a romantic partner. The act of breaking up with someone is face threatening in a variety of ways. For example, suppose Maria tells Carlos that she wants to end their relationship but Carlos does not want to break up. This act threatens Carlos's negative face because he is being forced to do something he does not want to do. Carlos's positive face may also be threatened because Maria's request suggests that he is no longer a desirable relational partner. Finally, Maria's positive face could be threatened because she might worry that Carlos (and perhaps other people) will see her as selfish, egotistical, or uncaring. According to Metts (1992) Maria is likely to use different strategies depending how face threatening she thinks the breakup will be for both herself and Carlos. If she thinks the breakup will be highly distressing, she is more likely to use an on-record-with-politeness strategy. Conversely, if Maria thinks the breakup will cause little distress, she is more likely to use an off-the-record strategy (such as avoiding the person) or a bald on-record strategy (such as blunt statements about wanting to break up).

Preventive and Corrective Facework

Certainly people sometimes are task driven, perform FTAs, and pay little attention to the consequences of threatening their own or another person's face. But people are more likely to try to avoid face threats and/or attempt to repair a damaged face. Research on preventive and corrective facework highlights other ways that concerns for face affect our interactions (Cupach & Metts, 1994).

Preventive facework is characterized by efforts to avoid or minimize potential face threat. Preventive strategies are like preemptive strikes in that they seek to prevent any future damage by framing the message in friendlier, softer terms. Studies have identified many types of preventive facework in our daily interactions. Perhaps the most common form of preventive facework is the use of disclaimers. Hewitt and Stokes (1975) outlined five general disclaimers that individuals often use before saying or doing something that may be face threatening: (1) hedging ("I may be way off here, but . . ."), (2) credentialing ("I'm your father, so I'm going to be straight with you"), (3) sin license ("Well, since we're all disclosing embarrassing situations"), (4) cognitive disclaimer ("I know you're going to think I've lost it, but . . ."), and (5) appeal for suspended judgment ("Hear me out before jumping to conclusions").

Other researchers have included the notion of verbal self-handicapping as a method of preventive facework (Higgins & Berglas, 1990). That is, people will sometimes offer an excuse that serves to minimize the face threat of a potential poor performance. For example, prior to an important game, Candace may inform her soccer team of a knee injury she has suffered. This strategic pregame disclosure serves two functions. If Candace plays well in the game, then she bolsters her identity as a "tough" team player who can play with pain. But if she plays poorly, she already has a built-in excuse for her subpar performance.

Unfortunately, research shows that these self-handicapping tactics often become self-fulfilling prophecies because they offer the individual a reason *not* to do as well as possible. In sum, the various disclaimers all serve to soften the potential face threat that might result from impending action and essentially ask the audience to consider the act within the perspective of the context.

Corrective facework is characterized by efforts to *repair* an identity already damaged by something that was said or done. Like preventive facework, corrective facework may be performed by the person whose face was threatened or by others who are assisting in the protection and/or repair of the person's face. Embarrassing moments are good examples of situations that often lead to corrective facework because they undermine a person's positive self-image. As Cupach and Metts (1994) argued, people become embarrassed when they are perceived to have acted incompetently—that is, when behavior is judged to be "inappropriate, ineffective, or foolish" (p. 18). Box 2.1 contains a brief test to assess how easily you are embarrassed.

In a comprehensive review of embarrassment research, Miller (1996) outlined 10 types of embarrassing behaviors that typically threaten one's face. The two most common causes of embarrassment were "physical pratfalls or inept performance" and "cognitive errors." The former category includes instances in which people appear unnecessarily awkward or incompetent—for example, missing a pole on which you intended to lean, tipping a chair over after leaning back too far, and catching your hair on fire as you light the grill. The latter category includes mistakes in judgment (trying every key before realizing you are at the wrong door), forgetfulness (forgetting your phone number or people's names), lack of attention or "temporary stupidity" (saying something that gives away a secret you are trying to keep for others), or clumsy answers. One of the best sources for examples of clumsy answers is Petra and Petra's 1993 book *The 775 Stupidest Things Ever Said.* One example of clumsy answers in this book is a response that then-vice-president of the United States George Bush gave at a campaign rally: "For 7½ years I've worked alongside President Reagan. We've had triumphs. Made some mistakes. We've had sex . . . uh . . . setbacks."

People typically use corrective facework in response to embarrassing situations such as these, as well as to other situations involving FTAs. There are six general types of corrective strategies for repairing a damaged face (Cupach & Metts, 1994; Schlenker & Weigold, 1992):

1. **Avoidance.** The common thread underlying avoidance behaviors is the goal of distancing oneself or one's partner from the act. Often, distancing occurs when individuals pretend that the act never happened or otherwise ignore its occurrence. For example, continuing to walk down the aisle after knocking over a display in a grocery store and glossing over an obvious Freudian slip are instances of avoidance. The hope is that the audience may pay less attention to the act if the actor avoids reference to it.

2. **Humor.** When the consequences of the FTA are relatively small, people often resort to humor as a way to deal with the threat. By using humor after an FTA, people show poise and come across as competent communicators,

BOX 2.1 PUT YOURSELF TO THE TEST

How Easily Are You Embarrassed?

Imagine that each of the events listed below happened to you. Rate how embarrassed you would feel using the scale below.

1 = Not at all embarrassed, uncomfortable, or awkward

2 = Slightly embarrassed, uncomfortable, or awkward

3 = Moderately embarrassed, uncomfortable, or awkward

4 = Quite embarrassed, uncomfortable, or awkward

5 = Strongly embarrassed, uncomfortable, or awkward

_____ 1. You were just beginning a talk in front of a class.

_____ 2. You slipped and fell on a patch of ice in a public place, dropping a bag of groceries.

_____ 3. You were a dinner guest, and the guest seated next to you spilled his plate on his lap while trying to cut his meat.

_____ 4. A group of friends was singing "Happy Birthday" to you.

_____ 5. You discovered you were the only person at a social gathering dressed in casual rather than formal attire.

_____ 6. You were calling up a person you had only met briefly to ask for a date.

_____ 7. You walked into a bathroom at someone else's house and discovered it was occupied by a member of the opposite sex.

_____ 8. You were being lavishly complimented on your pleasant personality by your companion on a first date.

_____ 9. You were in class and noticed that the teacher had neglected to zip his fly.

_____ 10. You were alone in an elevator with a professor who had just given you a bad grade.

_____ 11. You walked into a room full of strangers and were introduced to everyone.

_____ 12. You tripped and fell while boarding a bus full of people.

_____ 13. You entered an apparently empty classroom, turned on the lights, and surprised a couple who were kissing passionately.

_____ 14. Your mother started telling people all sorts of silly things you did as a child.

_____ 15. You said you disliked engineers and then found out that one of the people in your group was studying to be an engineer.

Add up your score. A score of 35 represents the highest level of "embarrassability"; a score of 15 represents the lowest level.

Source: Most items are adapted from Modigliani (1968).

thereby repairing their damaged faces. Sometimes it is best to laugh at yourself so others will laugh with you, not at you.

3. **Apologies.** Apologies are "admissions of responsibility and regret for undesirable events" (Schlenker & Weigold, 1992, p. 162). In that sense, they may help repair some of the damage to face by emphasizing the actor's nature as a moral individual who intends to take responsibility for his or her action. Unlike avoidance, in which actors deny responsibility, apologies tie the incident directly to the actor and, as such, may further threaten face—especially if the apology is deemed insincere.

4. **Accounts.** Accounts, or attempts to explain the FTA, come in the form of excuses or justifications. Excuses are explanations that minimize the personal responsibility of the actor for her or his actions. For example, if you engage in a silly fraternity or sorority prank that causes you to lose face, you might excuse your behavior by saying that your friends pressured you into action or that you had consumed too much alcohol. With justifications actors do not try to distance themselves from the act, but instead "reframe an event by downplaying its negative implications" (Cupach & Metts, 1994, p. 10). Arguing that your behavior at the fraternity or sorority party was "not that big of a deal" or that the prank did not really hurt anyone are examples of justifications for FTAs.

5. **Physical remediation.** This strategy involves attempts to repair physical damage. For example, you might quickly clean up a coffee spill on the table, or you might zip up your pants once you recognize that your fly is open. The audience, especially if sympathetic, often engages in physical remediation as well. For example, if you see a food smudge on your partner's chin, you might wipe it off before other people see it.

6. **Aggression.** In some cases individuals feel the need to repair their damaged face by using physical force. For example, people sometimes start a physical altercation in response to a put-down or personal attack. In fact, research shows that dating violence often follows a perception of face threats (for a review of violence research, see Gelles & Cornell, 1990). People may also become aggressive when they are embarrassed. In an attempt to shift the blame, they might yell at someone else. For example, if you accidentally bump into someone while walking through a crowded shopping mall, you might angrily tell your shopping companion to give you more space and stop walking so close.

Of course, several of these strategies may be combined in efforts to repair a damaged face. For example, after spilling coffee on the boss's desk, you might say you are sorry (apology), explain that you were distracted by the boss's stimulating presentation (account), and then clean up the mess (physical remediation). Indeed, the more face threatening the act, the more energy will be put toward multiple repair attempts.

In other situations people may be more likely to ignore face threats or to respond with humor. This is especially likely when FTAs are expected. For instance, embarrassing and face-threatening actions are more or less expected and accepted at wedding and baby showers. Common activities at baby showers include having people guess how big the mom-to-be's stomach is or how much she weighs, and at wedding showers the bride-to-be often receives revealing lingerie. Braithwaite (1995) observed behavior at coed wedding and baby showers to investigate what tactics people used to embarrass others and what tactics people used to respond to face threats. She found that wedding and baby showers are contexts in which some degree of embarrassment is expected, so the potentially embarrassing action is not as face threatening as it would be in other contexts. Yet the dance between embarrassment-producing face threats and face-repairing responses was still evident. Other situations, such as "roasting" someone at a retirement party, may require this same delicate dance.

Conclusion

Our desire to present particular images of ourselves shapes our social interactions and influences our relationships. In this chapter we outlined the factors that influence identity and the ways in which we communicate this identity to others during initial encounters and in established relationships. We also emphasized the ways in which other people help us maintain our public identities.

It is important to note, however, that this chapter covered only a small portion of the literature on identity and impression management. Research looking at psychological processes such as self-esteem and self-concept are also related to identity and impression management. In this chapter, our focus was on identity management within social and personal relationships. Other researchers have studied self-presentation within different contexts, such as first impressions during employment interviews or self-presentation strategies used by teachers in classrooms.

Interpersonal communication researchers have also studied identity and impression formation within the attraction process. People are attracted to those who convey a positive self-identity while appearing to be modest and approachable. Physical appearance, which plays a key role in impression management, is also one of several bases for attraction in close relationships (see Chapter 3).

As this chapter suggests, a person's identity is based on a complex theory of self that incorporates expectations, self-fulfilling prophecies, and feedback from others. People project a certain identity to the world, and that identity is either accepted or rejected by the audience, causing the identity to be either reinforced or modified. Relationships provide a venue for expanding one's identity and growing as a person. Facework is also important to project one's own desired image and to protect the positive and negative faces of a relational partner. Indeed, an awareness of the importance of face can go a long way toward helping people understand the development and deterioration of relationships.

Discussion Questions

1. What personal characteristics are most central to your theory of self?
2. In this chapter we discussed some ethical issues related to identity management. Under what circumstances do you think that techniques used to manage one's positive identity are unethical?
3. Think about one of your most embarrassing moments. Did you do any facework? If so, what identity management techniques did you employ? Did people around you help you save face? If so, how?

Drawing People Together

Forces of Social Attraction

Julie will never forget the moment she first saw Eric. They were at a social gathering when she spotted him across the room. There was something about him. Maybe it was his dark hair and piercing blue eyes, or maybe it was the confident way he stood or the way he threw back his head and laughed. Whatever it was, Julie felt an immediate surge of attraction. Her heart raced when their eyes met and he strode over to talk to her.

Andrew and Paula had been friends for nearly 3 years before they started dating. They had always been attracted to each other. They shared the same hobbies, family values, and religious beliefs, but when they first met they were involved with other people. When they eventually got together, it felt natural and comfortable—as if they had always been meant to be together.

◆ ◆ ◆ ◆

Attraction is a force that draws people together. Attraction can occur as quickly as a flash of lightning, or it can develop slowly over time. Sometimes attraction is accompanied by a surge of arousal, with heart pounding rapidly and palms sweating. Other times attraction is accompanied by a warm, cozy, comfortable feeling. Of course, attraction is not always mutual; people are often attracted to individuals who are not attracted to them.

The reasons people are attracted to some individuals and not others are complex and dynamic, and sometimes attraction is hard to explain or understand. For example, you may wonder why your friends are attracted to certain people you find unappealing, why partners in certain celebrity couples who seem so dissimilar are together, or even why you are attracted to a particular type of person. After breaking up with someone, a friend may ask you, "Whatever did you see in her [or him]?" and you may struggle to come up with an answer. Alternatively, you may know exactly what qualities first attracted you to your former partner, but you now realize that he or she does not really possess those qualities or that those qualities alone were not enough to sustain your relationship. After such an experience people sometimes tell themselves that they will never again be attracted to a certain type of person, only to later find themselves dating the same type of person.

Although attraction is complex, and the characteristics that attract people to others vary widely, there are some fundamental reasons attraction develops. Social scientists have devoted considerable energy to determining the causes of social attraction. In this chapter we review some of the research in this area. Specifically, we focus on how the personal attributes of two individuals work separately and together to affect attraction. We also look at the role that context and the environment play in the attraction process. This chapter will give you insight into the many factors that influence whom you are attracted to and why people are or are not attracted to you.

Defining Attraction

There are many types of attraction. We might be attracted to someone physically, socially, sexually, or relationally. We also might be attracted to someone because they can help us accomplish goals. Sometimes we are even attracted to people who are "bad" for us, which is a tendency called "fatal attraction." In this section we examine the differences among these forms of attraction.

The Big Three: Task, Physical, and Social Attraction

Usually people are attracted to someone based on their ability to complete tasks, their physical appearance, or their sociability (McCroskey & McCain, 1974). **Task attraction** refers to our desire to work with someone to fulfill instrumental goals, such as completing a project or making a presentation. Think of people with whom you would like to work on a group project; they are probably smart, hard-working, fair, and friendly. **Physical attraction** results when we like how people look, whether it be their body shape, their eyes, their attire, or other aspects of their appearance. Finally, **social attraction** reflects the feeling that we would like to "hang out" and be friends with someone. When people are socially attractive, we also usually think that they would fit in well with our circle of friends and our family. Box 3.1 lists some of the test items used to measure these three types of attraction.

Obviously these types of attraction are related. In fact, both task and physical attraction can contribute to more general perceptions of social attraction. For example, if you meet someone who is physically attractive, you might decide that she or he is also charming and intelligent, and therefore socially attractive. This tendency to perceive physically attractive people as more sociable is part of the halo effect, which we will discuss later in this chapter. You also might be socially attracted to certain people, such as roommates and coworkers, precisely because you find them task attractive. This is especially likely if you are the type of person who attends carefully to tasks and takes your work seriously.

BOX 3.1 PUT YOURSELF TO THE TEST

What Types of People Attract You Most?

To see what types of people attract you, try rating your closest friends and current and/or recent romantic partners using this scale. Think about the qualities that attracted you to them when you first met, and rate them accordingly by circling the appropriate number. Perhaps you are more attracted to people based on their ability to help with tasks, their sociability, or their physical appearance, or perhaps all of these types of attraction are important to you. You might also notice that different forms of attraction were present when you first met your close friends versus your romantic partners. Use the following scale to make your ratings:

1 = Strongly disagree . . . 7 = Strongly agree

Task Attraction

	Disagree					Agree	
1. If I wanted to get things done, I thought I could probably depend on her/him.	1	2	3	4	5	6	7
2. I had confidence in her/his ability to get the job done.	1	2	3	4	5	6	7
3. I thought I would enjoy working with her/him on a task.	1	2	3	4	5	6	7
4. I thought this person would be an asset in any task situation.	1	2	3	4	5	6	7
5. I thought this person would take her/his work seriously.	1	2	3	4	5	6	7

Social Attraction

1. I thought she/he could be a friend of mine.	1	2	3	4	5	6	7
2. I wanted to have a friendly chat with her/him.	1	2	3	4	5	6	7
3. I thought she/he would be easy to get along with.	1	2	3	4	5	6	7
4. I thought she/he would be pleasant to be with.	1	2	3	4	5	6	7
5. I thought I could become close friends with her/him.	1	2	3	4	5	6	7

Physical Attraction

1. This person struck me as handsome or pretty.	1	2	3	4	5	6	7
2. I found her/him attractive physically.	1	2	3	4	5	6	7
3. This person looked appealing.	1	2	3	4	5	6	7
4. I thought she/he was good looking.	1	2	3	4	5	6	7
5. I thought she/he had an attractive face.	1	2	3	4	5	6	7

Source: This table contains sample items adapted from McCroskey and Richmond's revised version of the Interpersonal Attraction Scale, as published in Tardy (1988).

Despite the similarities, these types of attraction are distinguishable. For example, the person you would like to be part of your group project may not always be the first person you would ask to a party. Engineers and accountants often get a "bad rap" for fitting that stereotypic mold of people who are respected for their knowledge but can be dull socially. In a similar vein, if you had a choice of partners for an important project, you would rarely use someone's physical appearance as the main criterion for selection. So, despite some overlap between these types of attraction, there are also definite differences.

Sexual Attraction

In many cases physical attraction leads to sexual attraction. (In Chapter 7 we review literature related to sexual attitudes and behaviors, part of which includes the notion of sexual attraction.) **Sexual attraction** reflects the desire to engage in sexual activity with someone and typically is accompanied by feelings of sexual arousal in the presence of the person. Although people can be sexually attracted to those they find socially attractive, social attraction is not necessarily accompanied by sexual thoughts. For example, your attraction to others as friends (part of what defines social attraction) is often a platonic feeling that does not include a sexual component. Even if we think of attraction to a potential dating partner, the qualities that attract us sexually may not be the same qualities that attract us socially. For example, Reyes et al. (1999) found that physical attractiveness is more closely related to sexual attraction than is social attractiveness. As this study suggests, physical and sexual attraction often occur together in romantic relationships. In other relationships, however, physical and sexual attraction may be unrelated. For instance, you might initially be physically attracted to someone because he or she dresses in the same style as you do and is about the same age. But this does not necessarily mean that you want to have sex with this person.

Relational Attraction

Another type of attraction, **relational attraction,** refers to the desire to have an intimate relationship with a person. Some scholars maintain that there are differences between initial feelings of social attraction and well-thought-out feelings of relational attraction, although relational attraction can be thought of as a subset of social attraction. Initially, you might feel social attraction to someone and say that you would really like to get to know her or him better. However, for other reasons you may not think that he or she would make a good long-term relational partner. For example, Anne might be socially attracted to Paul because he is attractive and fun to be around, but she might also think that Paul would be too flirtatious and fickle to be a serious boyfriend.

A study by Johnson, Afifi, and Duck (1994) found support for this difference between initial social attraction and long-term relational attraction. Specifically, in their study on attraction to partners after a first date (with the dates set up through a dating service), Johnson et al. distinguished between instant or "flashbulb attraction" and "expected relational course." Flashbulb attraction occurred when people felt a surge of immediate interest. Expected relational course was measured by asking participants to assess the potential for a future relationship with their date. Johnson et al. (1994) found that people who experienced flashbulb attraction did not always want to have a long-term relationship with someone.

Fatal Attraction

Regardless of whether we are initially attracted to individuals because of their winning personality, their ability to help us accomplish goals, or their good looks, we could eventually discover that the very qualities we once found attractive are not as desirable as first thought. Felmlee (1995, 1998) studied this phenomenon by conducting a number of studies on **fatal attraction,** which she defined as occurring when the very qualities that draw us to someone eventually contribute to relational breakup. That is, certain qualities may seem attractive initially but often spell danger ahead. For her studies she asked people to think of the last romantic relationship they were in that ended and then to describe both what initially attracted them to the person and what ultimately led to the breakup.

Felmlee's analysis of the answers led her to some interesting conclusions. First, differences were consistently the most common type of fatal attraction. In other words, being attracted to someone because he or she is one's "opposite" might be exciting in the short term, but this novelty is likely to wear thin over time. Second, initially attractive qualities such as being fun, exciting, or easygoing can also contribute to breakups, especially if someone has these qualities to an extreme. For example, if you are attracted to someone primarily because of her or his sense of humor, that attraction could turn to dislike if you realize that your partner can never be serious. Similarly, a partner's easygoing nature may become distressing when you notice that he or she is unambitious, lazy, and irresponsible. Thus, it is important to look for someone who is well balanced rather than to concentrate on one or two personality traits.

A Framework for Understanding Attraction

Unfortunately, few scholars have looked into the subtle differences between forms of attraction to see which types are most strongly associated with our relational decisions. Instead, many scholars define social attraction broadly as "a motivational state in which an individual is predisposed to think, feel, and usually behave in a positive manner toward another person" (Simpson & Harris, 1994, p. 47). Obviously, this definition embraces many motivations for thinking, feeling, and behaving positively toward someone. For instance, such motivation could stem from wanting to work with someone, wanting to be someone's friend, wanting to be someone's lover, or thinking that someone is physically attractive. However, when most relationship researchers measure attraction, they focus on social and/or physical attraction. Thus, the research reported in this chapter is most relevant to these two forms of attraction.

In the remainder of this chapter, we attempt to answer the question, What attracts us to others? As you will see, the answer to this question is quite complex. Indeed, researchers have found that many different factors influence attraction. To help organize these factors, we will use a framework first presented by Kelley and colleagues in 1983. Our application of this framework to the attraction process is depicted in Figure 3.1. Kelley argued that four general factors influence how we behave during interactions:

1. Personal qualities that we bring to the interaction, including our intepersonal needs, expectations, personality, mood, physical appearance, and level of communication skill, among other qualities

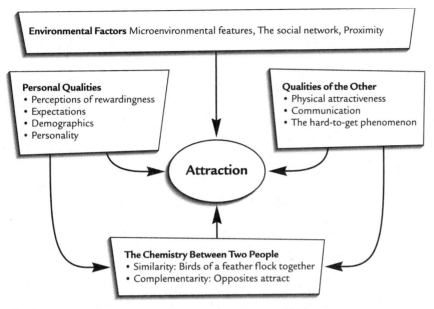

Environmental Factors Microenvironmental features, The social network, Proximity

Personal Qualities
• Perceptions of rewardingness
• Expectations
• Demographics
• Personality

Qualities of the Other
• Physical attractiveness
• Communication
• The hard-to-get phenomenon

Attraction

The Chemistry Between Two People
• Similarity: Birds of a feather flock together
• Complementarity: Opposites attract

FIGURE 3.1 **Factors Influencing Interaction and Attraction**

2. Qualities that the other person brings to the interaction

3. Qualities that reflect the chemistry or synergy between two people, including similarities and differences between relational partners across a range of characteristics, and that emerge only when the two of them are together

4. Features of the physical environment or context in which the interaction takes place, called environmental variables, including details of the location in which the interaction is taking place (size, temperature, furniture, public versus private setting, and so on) and feedback from friends and family

All of these factors have been shown to be related to how interactions develop (for a review see Kelley et al., 1983) and to whom people become attracted. Therefore, we review research relevant to each of these factors next.

Personal Variables Related to Attraction

What personal characteristics and perceptions do we possess that might influence our feelings of attraction to others? A considerable amount of research has focused on this question. This research suggests that our evaluations of a person's reward value, our expectations about a person's behavior, and a number of demographic and personality variables all impact how attractive we find people.

Perceptions of Reward Value

When people enter relationships, they hope to receive a number of benefits or rewards, such as companionship, affection, and sometimes even financial resources. Therefore, one of the most powerful influences on our attraction to others is our own perception of their reward value, which is related to our interpersonal needs and preferences. In fact, ideas from social exchange theory (see Chapter 8) serve as a foundation for research on attraction. According to this theory, we are attracted to others when we think they offer more rewards than costs. Thus, if someone seems to have a host of positive, rewarding qualities (such as a good sense of humor, a positive outlook, and a willingness to sacrifice for others) and only a few negative, costly qualities (such as being late all the time or being too possessive), attraction should be high. Furthermore, individuals will be perceived as especially attractive if they have more rewards to offer than other people.

Although many of these rewards can also be considered qualities possessed by the other person (such as the other person's physical attractiveness) or are associated with the chemistry between two people (such as similarity in beliefs and attitudes), it is people's own *perception* of these rewards that we are currently addressing. In that sense anything that impacts our perception of the rewards that others can offer will play a primary role in determining to whom we are attracted. Because these perceptions are our own and may have no basis in objective reality, they are personal variables. Additionally, what qualifies as "rewarding" varies from one individual to another. For example, one person might value intelligence as the most rewarding attribute in a relational partner; another might rate a good sense of humor as more rewarding than intelligence. Potential partners are only rewarding to the extent that they are perceived to be able to fulfill an individual's interpersonal needs by contributing valuable resources to a relationship.

Expectations

People's perceptions of reward value are influenced by behavioral expectations. Indeed, numerous studies have shown that people's expectations of others play a strong role in the attraction process (see Afifi & Burgoon, 2000, for a review). This process seems to operate in two ways. First, people's expectations determine what they notice as being unusual or usual, which influences their attraction to others. When people act in unusual ways, others take notice (Burgoon & Hale, 1988). In general, if the unexpected behavior is perceived as rewarding, attraction is likely to increase. By contrast, if the unexpected behavior is perceived as unrewarding, attraction is likely to decrease (Afifi & Burgoon, 2000). For instance, if Cheryl expects Jake to lend her his class notes and he refuses, her attraction for him is likely to decrease. In the same vein, people are likely to be attracted to those who positively violate their expectations. Thus, if Jake not only offers to lend Cheryl his notes but also tells her she can call him at home with questions, her expectations (for notes only) may be exceeded, and her attraction for him is likely to increase.

Second, people's expectations have a way of becoming reality, regardless of the other person's actual behavior, and in so doing influence to whom people are attracted. This suggests that our expectations of other people lead us to treat them in ways that make it more likely that they will confirm our expectations. For example, if Leon thinks Philip is a friendly, considerate person, he is likely to treat him with respect, which, in turn will make Philip more likely to treat Leon in a friendly, considerate manner. This also suggests that we tend to perceive people as acting in ways that fulfill our expectations, regardless of their actual behaviors. The extensive research on self-fulfilling prophecies supports these ideas. For example, in one study new teachers were told that certain students were "smart" and that other students were less smart (see Rosenthal & Jacobson, 1968). Although the two groups of students actually were no different from each other, by the end of the semester the teachers' expectations about the students' intelligence translated into different grades for the two groups. The students whom the teachers expected to be smart received better grades than the students saddled with lower teacher expectations despite the initial similarity in ability and intelligence between the two groups.

This important study was followed by a series of studies that investigated why the teachers' expectations resulted in different grades. At least two explanations have been given. First, teachers treated student comments and essays differently. Specifically, when supposedly poor students gave good answers, teachers focused on superficial aspects of their answers and attributed the smart-sounding parts of the responses to luck. By contrast, when supposedly smart students gave poor answers, teachers tended to look for something positive in their responses. For example, if a student labeled as smart commented that a political candidate won a debate because he or she "was nicer," the teacher might interpret the student's answer to mean that viewers put too much weight on style compared to substance.

Second, the teachers' expectations led them to treat the two groups differently, which eventually influenced the actual quality of the students' work. For example, the teachers gave mostly positive feedback to the supposedly bright students and mostly negative feedback to the supposedly poor students. Eventually, the students in the "poor group" simply stopped trying, while those in the "bright group" were encouraged to try harder (Rubovits & Mahen, 1973).

After these studies on teacher-student interaction were published, numerous other studies showed a similar pattern across a range of contexts, including courtrooms, job interviews, and athletic fields. Expectancy effects have also been found in research on attraction. For example, Snyder, Tanke, and Berscheid (1977) tested the impact of men's perceptions of women's physical attractiveness on the women's behavior. The researchers found that, when interacting with men who saw them as physically attractive, women behaved in a more sociable, likable, and friendly manner than when interacting with men who saw them as unattractive. Thus, subtle interpersonal cues of men's expectations had the power to actually influence the women's behavior.

Research on beliefs about future interactions provides another example of how expectations influence attraction. When people expect to see someone again, they are more likely to find that person attractive, regardless of his or her behavior, than if they do not have such expectations of future interaction (Kellermann & Reynolds, 1990). The expectation of future interaction motivates people to look for positive qualities in someone so that they will look forward to future interactions rather than dreading them. This motivation, in turn, increases the chances that people will find the individual attractive. Conversely, when people interact with someone whom they do not foresee meeting again, they have little reason to search for positive qualities. In fact, doing so may be depressing, given that they may not have the opportunity to get to know the person better in future interactions. Indeed, people are sometimes motivated to find negative qualities in individuals whom they do not expect to see again, thereby minimizing any attraction.

Demographic Characteristics

As we have seen, perceptions and expectations have a direct effect on whom people find attractive. Sex, age, and other demographic variables also affect attraction, although the effects of such variables appear to be somewhat weaker than those connected to expectations. The demographic characteristic that has received the most attention in the attraction literature is sex.

One of the most frequently asked questions is whether men and women differ in what qualities they find attractive. The popular belief is that men are primarily attracted by looks whereas women are more often attracted by personality, but is this belief supported by research findings? In fact, the majority of studies show that men are attracted to others based on physical appearance more than are women. For example, Feingold (1991) reviewed results from seven studies conducted in the 1970s and 1980s and concluded that "men valued physical attractiveness more than did women, and that women valued similarity more than did men" (p. 357). More recently, Sprecher (1998a) found that men rated physical attractiveness as a more important reason for attraction than did women, while women rated personality as a more important reason for attraction than did men.

One explanation for these sex differences, and others like them (see Hamida, Mineka, & Bailey, 1998), stems from social evolutionary theory (see Chapter 8). Social evolutionary theorists argue that sex differences in attraction are perfectly consistent with our evolution as a species. A central idea in social evolutionary theory is that humans, like all mammalian species, are driven by a desire to advance the species. Because only the strong survive, people are attracted to those whom they consider to be the "strongest" (see Buss, 1994). Because men and women fulfill different roles in the evolutionary chain, they look for different qualities in their mating partners. Specifically, theorists argue that women "are looking for men who are willing to commit and who can provide security for them and their offspring" (Pines, 1998, p. 148), whereas men are simply looking for the most attractive (and most potentially fertile) women available.

Social evolutionary theories suggest that these specialized sex roles evolved over thousand of years and are responsible for many of the sex differences observed today. According to this view, women are attracted to older men with more resources, whereas men typically are drawn to younger women in their re-productive prime (Buss, 1994). Also, men are more easily influenced by physical appearance, while women attend more closely to personality and compatibility.

However, sex differences in attraction may not be as clear cut as these stud-ies suggest. In fact, sex differences between men and women may be exagger-ated in studies in which the researchers rely on data from questionnaires. In these studies respondents rate the extent to which physical appearance is an important part of their attraction to others. The problem is that women appear to be more hesitant than men to report that physical attraction actually is an important part of their selection process. Indeed, when researchers use a differ-ent measure to test whether both men and women are more attracted to physi-cally appealing others, they find that men and women are both influenced by physical attraction. For example, Sprecher (1989) conducted a study in which men and women were given a wide range of information about someone of the opposite sex. Of all the information provided, that which was related to the person's physical attractiveness was found to be the most important determi-nant of attraction for both men and women. However, when Sprecher later asked them how much the person's physical attractiveness influenced their at-traction, men were more willing than women to acknowledge its effect. In sum, as is typical in much of the research that we will discuss in this book, sex differences in social attraction may be overstated. Men and women seem more similar than different in terms of what they find attractive in others.

Rather than studying sex differences, several scholars argue that we need to think of everyone as varying on a continuum of masculine-feminine qualities labeled as "gender orientation" or "sex-role orientation" (Archer, 1989; Bem, 1974). For instance, you may know men whose beliefs and behaviors are rela-tively feminine and women whose beliefs and behaviors are relatively mascu-line. Many men and women display a mix of feminine and masculine behaviors and beliefs, and are thereby classified as **androgynous** (Bem, 1974). Clearly, much behavior is affected by socialization. Thus, men who grow up in an envi-ronment that encourages emotional expression and that values personal quali-ties are not expected to behave similarly to or be attracted to the same types of partners as men who grow up in an environment in which emotional expres-sion is discouraged or masculinity is defined by inattention to relationships. The same can be said for women. Mayback and Gold (1994) found that women who agree with "traditional" female roles are more attracted to aggressive, "macho" men than are women whose attitudes toward female roles are more unconventional. Indeed, thinking about differences between people based on their location on a masculine-feminine continuum, rather than based simply on their biological sex, may be the better way to understand differences and simi-larities between people.

Two other important demographic characteristics that have received little attention from scholars are sexual orientation and age. The few studies that have examined the impact of these variables suggest that they do not have much effect on the qualities that people seek in their mates. For example, Boy-den, Carroll, and Maier (1984) asked 110 gay men to describe themselves and their ideal partner. These men desired partners who were similar to themselves in age and attitude—two qualities that are also important in heterosexuals' romantic attraction to others. In a similar vein, scholars studying the aging process have found that people show remarkable consistency in whom they find attractive, regardless of age. In fact, people seem to find essentially the same qualities attractive whether they are in their preteen or teen years or in their 70s or 80s (Aboud & Mendelson, 1998; Webb, Delaney, & Young, 1989). In sum, although these studies did not find differences in attraction due to sexual orientation or age, given the small number of studies conducted, it seems premature to dismiss the possibility that some differences may exist.

Personality

Many aspects of personality are important in relationships; one of the most important is attachment style (see Chapter 6). Considerable evidence suggests that people perceive relationships differently based on their past experiences with relational partners, starting with the parent-child relationship. These differing views of relationships are represented by four "attachment styles" (Bartholomew, 1990): (1) Secure individuals are comfortable both alone and in relationships, (2) dismissive individuals prefer to be alone and are unmotivated to develop and maintain relationships, (3) fearful avoidant individuals fear intimacy and lack self-confidence, and (4) preoccupied individuals want intimacy and fear being alone.

Studies have shown that people's attachment style influences their behavior in relationships. Therefore, it should come as no surprise that it also influences to whom we are attracted. For example, Bartholomew (1990) argued that one way people maintain their attachment styles is through the unconscious process of selectively choosing interaction partners who confirm their sense of self and others. This might explain why people who are treated badly as children are attracted to romantic partners who also treat them badly. In a related vein Sperling and Borgaro (1995) found that preoccupied individuals are more attracted to people who provide a hint of positive feedback than are securely attached persons. Apparently, because preoccupied individuals strongly desire to be in relationships, they grab onto the potential opportunity suggested by someone giving them a compliment. Secure individuals, by contrast, are not so quick to jump at the potential opportunity; they prefer to gather more information about others before developing a relationship.

Self-esteem and mood also are related to whom we are attracted. Have you noticed that about yourself? When you are feeling down, are you attracted to the same type of people as when you are feeling good about yourself? If your answer is no, you are not alone. In fact, several studies have shown that how people feel about themselves strongly influences whom they find attractive. For example, Joshi and Rai (1987) found that a person's self-esteem is directly related to his or her level of attraction to others. That is, those who have high self-esteem consistently find others more attractive than those whose self-esteem is low.

Self-esteem can operate in even more subtle ways. In two studies, Hoyle, Insko, and Moniz (1992) assessed students' self-esteem, asked students to complete a bogus test of intelligence, and then provided them with either positive or negative feedback about their performance. After this feedback the students talked briefly with another person and completed a survey about their attraction to the interaction partner. The students with low self-esteem were more attracted to the person if they talked to her or him after being told good news about their performance on the "intelligence test," as opposed to being told bad news about their performance. In other words, good news made them more attracted to others, perhaps because they associated the person with a rewarding situation, or perhaps because they were simply in better moods and more receptive to their interaction partner's positive qualities.

These findings may also be explained in relation to how we view others in comparison to ourselves. If we already have a poor image of ourselves and then are told that we lack intelligence, we are unlikely to consider others attractive. This is because finding them attractive but not feeling that we have a chance with them is just too threatening or discouraging. Instead, we convince ourselves that they are unattractive as a way to shield ourselves from what we perceive to be their eventual rejection of us.

People with high self-esteem showed the exact opposite pattern in Hoyle et al.'s (1992) study. That is, they were more attracted to others after hearing bad news about their performance on the intelligence test than they were after hearing good news. Why would that be? One explanation is that people with high self-esteem recognize the need to boost their self-image after receiving bad news, and one way to do so is to view others as attractive and to interact with them. By contrast, receiving good news only bolsters their already high self-esteem, which may lead them to view most others as unworthy partners and thereby lower their attraction to them. Thus, for example, if a person you are attracted to has high self-esteem and performs poorly on an exam, it might actually be a good time to ask her or him out. In a sense you would be the consolation prize.

Many other personality-related variables have been studied in connection to attraction. Two of the most important are the degree to which we are aware of our surroundings (self-monitoring) and our level of narcissism. You have probably known people who are oblivious to their surroundings and others who are hypersensitive to what is happening around them. The former wear the same type of clothes regardless of context and never brush their hair before leaving the house; the latter are always concerned about whether their clothes match the formality of the occasion and are always perfectly groomed before leaving the house. These two people differ on a personality trait called **self-monitoring,** which reflects the extent to which people regulate their behavior to fit the social context. High self-monitors attend to the rules of their surroundings and adjust accordingly, while low self-monitors rarely tailor their behavior according to context (Snyder & Gangestad, 1986; Snyder & Simpson, 1987). Given their greater concern for how they appear to others, it is not surprising that high and low self-monitors differ in what they find attractive in others.

In fact, research in this area shows that high self-monitors typically are first attracted to others based on their physical appearance, while low self-monitors are usually drawn by personality traits (Snyder, Berscheid, & Glick, 1985). High self-monitors also do not like being the "third wheel" in a social setting. At least partly for that reason, they are likely to enter into relationships more quickly than are people who care less about showing up alone at social functions (Glick, 1985).

Another personality trait that has been shown to influence our attraction to others is the degree to which we are narcissistic. Have you known people who always want to be the center of attention and/or are always bragging about their accomplishments? Do these people often dominate conversations and interrupt others to get their point across? If so, you know at least one person who would likely be categorized as a narcissist. *Narcissism* is characterized by an extreme focus on oneself during interaction, to the exclusion of others (Vangelisti, Knapp, & Daly, 1990). Campbell (1999) conducted five studies to determine how individuals' degree of narcissism affects their attraction to others. He found big differences between the qualities that are attractive to narcissists and to nonnarcissists. Most noticeably, narcissists are attracted to others who admire them, while nonnarcissists are drawn to others who exhibit caring qualities. Not surprisingly, Campbell (1999) also found that narcissists are partly drawn to these admiring others because of their own need to improve their self-esteem. In other words, as you may have suspected, narcissists are often those who, despite their outward appearance, have relatively low self-esteem and who seek self-esteem boosts.

Other People's Qualities

The personal qualities discussed previously should give you an idea of what kinds of predispositions you have when evaluating the attractiveness of others. Of course, other people possess certain qualities that increase your likelihood of being attracted to them. As noted earlier in the chapter, attraction ultimately boils down to a feeling that someone can offer us more rewards than costs relative to other potential relational partners. Thus, the key question becomes, What qualities do people find especially rewarding? Among other qualities, people seem to prefer those who are physically attractive and communicatively competent. People who are perceived to be in high demand and "hard to get" are also highly valued. In this section we discuss these variables, starting with the quality that has received the most attention—physical attractiveness.

Physical Attractiveness

Studies have consistently shown that physical attractiveness is one of the top two predictors of social attraction (Dion, 1986; Huston & Levinger, 1978). For example, Sprecher (1989) found that physical attractiveness is the most important predictor of attraction; in her study the more physically attractive the other person was, the more attracted participants were to him or her. Similarly, Johnson et al.'s (1994) research on first dates among dating club members showed that, more than any other quality, people's physical attractiveness determined whether their date found them socially attractive. These findings may not be surprising, but the more interesting question may be, What specific "looks" do we find attractive?

The answer to that question is too complex to be fully addressed here and in some ways is culturally determined, but several studies have yielded some insights. For instance, one feature that has been shown to have a very strong influence on attraction is height. In fact, studies have found that women tend to find very short men unattractive as potential mates even when the researcher assigns them a whole host of other rewarding qualities, such as a positive personality, intelligence, and high earning potential (Jackson & Ervin, 1992; Pierce, 1996). Tall women also seem to be at an advantage, but perhaps less than their male counterparts (Hensley, 1994). Across many different cultures, when men are being evaluated, a strong jawline, broad shoulders, and a hip-to-waist ratio of slightly less than one (in other words, hips that are slightly smaller than waist) contribute to judgments of physical attractiveness. For women a soft jawline and an hourglass figure (with the waist significantly smaller than the chest and hips) is preferred (Buss, 1989, 1994; Singh, 1995). Both men and women also value physical fitness and an athletic build in their dating partners. Overweight people, particularly in the United States, are not considered attractive.

You might think that this is quite unfair and that people should be judged by their inner character rather than their outward appearance. This may be true, but the research suggests that, fair or not, people use outward appearances to make judgments about people's inner character. Specifically, research has shown that people often associate good looks with a wide range of other positive qualities. This tendency, often called the halo effect or the what-is-beautiful-is-good stereotype, leads people to believe that physically attractive individuals are more likely to succeed, and are more sociable, popular, and competent than their less attractive counterparts (Dion, 1986; Dion, Berscheid, & Walster, 1972). With this halo effect people are drawn to attractive individuals because most people are looking for someone who offers the "complete package." Maybe because of that, researchers have found that physically attractive people receive more positive attention from others throughout life (Dion, 1972), often develop more positive self-esteem (Nell & Ashton, 1996), and may actually develop some of the skills people assume they have (Chaiken, 1979).

The halo effect helps explain why good looks are often an important part of the attraction process. Social evolutionary theorists offer a complementary explanation for why physical attractiveness matters. Specifically, they argue that people's attraction to particular physical traits is due to the genetic drive to mate with the fittest person possible (Buss, 1994). To that end physically attractive individuals should be socially attractive to the greatest number of people because they are essentially the most highly evolved physical specimens in our species and so are highly prized. Physical fitness, especially in terms of body shape and size, is also an outward sign of health and fertility. Thus, although cultural standards for beauty are somewhat different, social evolutionary theorists predict that some preferences cut across cultures. For example, dark hair is prized in some cultures, while light hair is prized in others. Yet physical attributes related to health and fertility, such as having a clear complexion and a physically fit body, have been found to be valued by most cultures around the globe (Buss, 1994).

Finally, people may be drawn to physically attractive individuals because they hope to gain rewards through association. Think about when you are with your most attractive friends; perhaps you have more opportunities to meet people and feel more attractive yourself. Research suggests that, whether intentional or not, people do benefit by interacting with more attractive others. Sigall and Landy (1973), for example, found that people were rated as more attractive when they were with comparatively more attractive individuals than when they were not. The idea here is that some of the attention that physically attractive people get spills overs to their friends through what is called the **assimilation effect.**

In sum, most people are attracted to good-looking persons, but what other qualities do we find attractive in potential partners or friends? Is physical appearance all that matters? The answer is a resounding no. People notice those who are physically attractive, but that does not guarantee that highly attractive people will continue to be valued after the initial attraction fades. In fact, they can be at a disadvantage in trying to live up to the high expectations imposed by the halo effect. For example, Hatfield (1984) wrote about a beautiful woman who was insecure because she worried that men would be disappointed if they saw her for what she really was, rather than what they dreamed a beautiful woman should be. Physical appearance only goes so far. Next we examine other qualities that make people attractive.

Interpersonal Communication Skills

Are we so drawn to physically attractive people that their interpersonal communication skills do not matter initially? For a long time scholars ignored the role of interpersonal communication in favor of studying the impact of other variables on our attraction. Recently, however, this pattern has changed. Sunnafrank (1991, 1992) was among the first scholars to study how communication influences attraction. In the mid-1980s he began a series of studies that added what was, until then, a novel element to studies of attraction—he actually had participants interact with the person they were rating on attraction! Most previous studies had only shown participants a picture or given them information about some fictitious character. Sunnafrank argued that, unless people were allowed to communicate, experiments would not be representative of the real qualities that people consider when evaluating the attractiveness of others. In fact, he suggested that many of the factors that scholars had found to predict attraction (such as physical attractiveness) might not matter as much once people started talking to one another. Instead, he claimed, people would attend to one another's communication style to determine how attracted they were to each other.

Many studies have supported Sunnafrank's contention. For example, Reyes et al. (1999) had students watch an interaction in which an opposite-sex actor was either very nice or acted like a jerk. Before watching the interaction, the students saw a still picture of the actor and were asked to answer several survey questions, including questions about their attraction to the actor. They then watched the interaction and answered the questions again. The power of communication was evident. Although physical attractiveness was one of the main qualities that drew people to the actor prior to watching the interaction, the actor's behavior during the interaction, whether positive or negative, was the primary determinant of their attraction to the actor afterwards; physical attractiveness hardly mattered. Thus, communication style plays a key role in determining to whom we are attracted. But what specific communication styles do we find appealing? Although the research on this issue is relatively sparse, enough studies exist to help us sketch an initial picture.

One communication quality that seems to emerge relatively consistently in studies of attraction is that of warmth. Warmth typically is communicated verbally by a generally positive attitude and a show of concern for others (Folkes & Sears, 1977) and nonverbally by such behaviors as smiling, making eye contact, and showing interest in the other person (Andersen & Guerrero, 1998a; Friedman, Riggio, & Casella, 1988). In fact, Sprecher (1998a) recently conducted three studies, all of which revealed that warmth and kindness were rated as the two qualities of the interaction partner that were most responsible for the participants' attraction to him or her.

Sociability and competence are two other communication qualities that have been shown to be related to attraction (Krueger & Caspi, 1993). Here, sociability refers to one's ability to communicate easily among a group of people. People who are extroverted and expressive are often perceived as highly sociable. Competence is determined by one's level of composure and knowledge. People are often evaluated as competent when they communicate without showing signs of nervousness and seem knowledgeable—although when people go out of their way to seem knowledgeable they are often rated as unattractive (Vangelisti et al., 1990).

In contrast to these "softer" qualities of warmth, sociability, and competence, some people are drawn to potentially "darker" qualities. For example, several studies have shown that women in particular are attracted to men who show a certain degree of assertiveness or power. This is consistent with social evolutionary theory in that women should be attracted to behavioral expressions of dominance in men because it reflects a reproductive advantage. In other words, women should be attracted to the strongest and fittest men. To test this idea, Sadalla, Kenrick, and Vershure (1987) created perceptions of dominance by having male actors take seats close to the subjects. The "nondominant" actors sat up straight and chatted quietly among themselves; the "dominant" actors sat in a very relaxed posture and showed a lack of interest in the women while talking loudly, quickly, and clearly. They found that the women were most attracted to the men who showed these signs of dominance.

More recently, however, Jensen-Campbell, Graziano, and West (1995), in an attempt to retest this hypothesis, asked whether "nice guys really finish last." Jensen-Campbell et al. argued that from an evolutionary perspective women should also value altruism in men because they would want partners who make sacrifices and invest considerable resources in the relationship. This is exactly what they found. First, women were attracted to altruistic men (men who were willing to do something boring so that the woman did not have to) much more than to nonaltruistic men (men who jumped at the opportunity to do something fun and left the boring task to the woman). In that sense the study was consistent with the research showing that people are attracted to individuals who are warm and caring. However, men who were altruistic but seemed otherwise unassertive and weak were not very attractive. In the same vein, though, and contrary to the Sadalla et al. study, men who were assertive/dominant and nonaltruistic were not attractive to the women either. Instead, women found the combination of assertiveness/dominance and altruism most appealing. Thus, strong but altruistic men may be perceived as most attractive.

Interestingly, the same results did not emerge with regard to men's attraction to women. That is, men's levels of attraction were unaffected by a woman's level of dominance but were highly dependent on whether the woman was altruistic. Altruistic women were attractive to men while nonaltruistic women were not. So, again, the importance of communicating care in interactions shines through; nice men (and women) do not necessarily have to finish last.

Finally, the timing of positive versus negative behavior seems to influence attraction. Several studies have identified what has been called the **loss-gain effect** (Afifi & Burgoon, 2000; Aronson & Linder, 1965; Sharma & Kaur, 1996). This effect reflects what happens to attraction when a person's behavior moves from positive to negative or from negative to positive. For example, if someone seems very nice to you early in the interaction, but then begins to act like a jerk, would you be more attracted to that person than if he or she was a jerk from the start? Studies suggest that you would not. In fact, people are more attracted to individuals who are consistently negative than to people who initially behave positively and then switch to negative behavior. People who start out being nice get our hopes up, so the letdown we experience when we discover that they are not as nice as we thought makes it worse than if they had acted badly from the start. Thus, as odd as it may seem, people are more attracted to individuals who are consistently unpleasant than to individuals who start out pleasant and then become unpleasant. Of course, people are most attracted to those who are pleasant throughout an interaction.

The "Hard-to-Get" Phenomenon

In some situations the person who acts somewhat hard to get is perceived as attractive. For example, Roberson and Wright (1994) put males in a situation in which they had to try to convince a female stranger (who was actually working for the experimenters) to be their coworker on a project. The men were told that the woman either would be easy to convince, might be difficult to convince, or would be impossible to convince. Results showed that the men rated the woman whom they were told would be moderately difficult to convince as the most attractive. The authors concluded that playing hard to get has its benefits but that it can backfire if the person is seen as unattainable.

These findings were consistent with prior research by Wright and colleagues. Wright, Toi, and Brehm (1984) were interested in whether the amount of energy that people put into pursuing someone is related to how much people like the individual they are pursuing. In this study Wright et al. told male participants that they could work with a female actor on a project if they could memorize a certain number of sentence combinations in 2 minutes. Participants were assigned to memorize either two (the easy condition), five (the moderately difficult condition), or eight (the very difficult condition) combinations. Right before the researchers had the men start trying to memorize these combinations, they asked them to rate the actor. Amazingly, given that the upcoming task was all that differed, the men who were about to try memorizing five combinations rated the actor as more attractive than the men in either the easy or the very difficult condition.

Similarly, Wright and Contrada (1986) found that people rated members of the opposite sex as most attractive when they were portrayed as moderately selective rather than as very selective or nonselective. Why is that? Again, apparently, we are initially more attracted to individuals who present a bit of a challenge than to those whom we perceive to be easily attainable or unattainable. One reason for this may be that, in our effort to shoot for the best possible "catch," we think that we are not shooting high enough if we are attracted to those who are not at least somewhat of a challenge. Consistent with this reasoning, research has shown that we are most likely to be attracted to hard-to-get people if they are easy for us to attract but difficult for others to attract (Walster, Walster, Pilivin, & Schmidt, 1973). This is probably because, when a person is hard for others to get but easy for you to get, people view you in a more positive light. In other words, people will likely perceive that you must have outstanding personal qualities if you were able to obtain such a high-quality partner.

Research also shows that people are attracted to members of high-status groups (Hogg & Hains, 1996). People who are in high-status groups or who hold positions of high status may be perceived as attractive for at least three reasons. First, high-status individuals typically are valued by many people. Therefore, they can be choosier when selecting relational partners, which makes them hard to get. Second, high-status individuals provide their partners with rewards by association. Thus, someone who has a high-status partner is likely to be viewed by others in a more positive light and to have access to the partner's resources. Finally, high-status individuals sometimes benefit from a halo effect similar to that experienced by physically attractive people. Social status helps explain why many college students are attracted to fraternities and sororities—they desire to belong to a high-status group.

In sum, in addition to individuals' own personal qualities, many qualities of other people increase or decrease feelings of attraction. However, unique qualities emerge when two people interact with each other. These factors, which we call the "chemistry" or "synergy" between people, also affect attraction.

The Interpersonal Chemistry Between Two People

When the personal qualities of two people are mixed together, they interact to create a certain chemistry or synergy that reflects the fit between them. One of the strongest and most important aspects of interpersonal chemistry is the degree to which people are similar to one another. This conclusion is far from new. As early as 1870, Sir Francis Galton, the cousin of Charles Darwin and a scientist best known for his research on intelligence and heredity, concluded that spouses usually are similar on several characteristics. Over the next century, many studies showed that friends and spouses tend to be similar on everything from attitudes and beliefs to height and visual acuity (Byrne, 1992). These studies all reached the same conclusion: the more similar others are to us, the more we will be attracted to them.

Similarity: "Birds of a Feather Flock Together"

Do birds of a feather really flock together? Think about your friends and dating partners. Do most of them have a lot in common with you? Maybe you like to do the same things, think the same way, and/or have similar personalities. Or perhaps you come from similar backgrounds. This preference for similarity has been shown to hold true across a whole host of personal qualities, although it has been studied most extensively in the context of similarity among attitudes.

Attitudinal Similarity   When people are similar in their attitudes, beliefs, and values, they are said to share attitudinal similarity. People can have perceived similarity (thinking that they are similar to the other person) and/or actual similarity (actually being similar to the other person). Two people may think they share attitudes and beliefs but later find out that they have very different likes and dislikes. The importance of this distinction quickly became evident to researchers. In one of the first extensive studies of attitudinal similarity, Newcomb (1961) found important differences between actual and perceived similarity. Newcomb gave a group of male undergraduates room and board in exchange for their participation in a study on friendships. The participants were randomly assigned roommates and were given surveys throughout the school year. The results showed that roommates liked one another more when they were similar. Interestingly, at the beginning of the year, perceived similarity and actual similarity did not match. New roommates were often oblivious to the actual level of similarity they shared, so they relied heavily on their perceptions of similarity to determine liking. As the year went on, however, the actual degree of similarity between roommates gradually became evident. By the end of the year those who were actually dissimilar did not like one another, even though their initial perceptions of similarity had led them to like one another at first.

At about the same time that Newcomb's now famous experiment was taking place, Byrne (1961, 1971) began to research the impact of attitudinal similarity on attraction. Byrne's work has contributed immensely to our understanding of the relation between similarity and attraction. One of his main methods for testing the effect of similarity on attraction was what he labeled the "bogus stranger" method. Byrne would first ask participants a series of questions assessing their likes and dislikes. He would then take the questionnaire to a different room and create answers on another, similar questionnaire that ranged from being almost identical to the participants' answers to very different from the participants' answers. The next step was to take that "bogus" survey back to the participants, tell them that the survey belonged to a participant who had already taken part in the study, and ask them to read it over and then rate the extent to which they would be attracted to this "bogus stranger." Byrne and his colleagues repeatedly found that participants were more attracted to bogus strangers who were similar to them (for a review, see Byrne, 1997).

As you might suspect, the real-life applicability of this method has been challenged, with some scholars arguing that this similarity effect disappears when two people communicate with each other (Sunnafrank, 1991). Nonetheless, the remarkable consistency of the finding that people are attracted to attitudinally similar individuals is hard to dispute. Thus, the question becomes, What is it that makes attitudinal similarity so important?

According to Byrne's (1971) **reinforcement model,** we are attracted to similar others because they reinforce our view of the world as the correct perspective. People do not like it when others challenge the correctness of their own attitudes and values. The best way to avoid such a challenge is to interact with individuals who think the same way as they do. Imagine disagreeing about everything with your friends or dating partner; that would get tiresome rather quickly, so you probably avoid people with whom you think that may happen. By contrast, when two people are similar, they usually have more in common to talk about and like to do the same things, which makes interaction enjoyable. All of these similarities make people's lives much easier, as well as making people feel that their way is the "right" way since their views are shared by others. The disadvantage, of course, is that people fail to grow very much if all their friends are just like them.

Demographic Similarity   Of course, attitudinal similarity is not the only way in which similarity draws people together. Studies show that people are attracted to others who are similar in demographic characteristics, communication style, and physical appearance. The number of demographic similarities that are associated with attraction is astounding. For starters, ask yourself these questions: How many people with a racial identity different from your own do you consider to be good friends? How many people do you know who were born and raised in a different country, and how many of them would you consider close friends? How many of your friends are 5 years older or younger than you? How many of your friends are not pursuing, have not pursued, or do not intend to pursue a college education? How many of your friends come from families that have half or less than half of your family's income? How many of your friends have a sexual orientation different from your own? The questions could go on and on. In all likelihood your answer to most of these questions was "very few" or "none." According to the research, our friendship choices are very homogeneous.

People tend to be attracted to individuals who are similar in age, race, cultural background, educational level, socioeconomic status, and religion, among other demographic characteristics (Hill, Rubin, & Peplau, 1976; Kandel, 1978). People are also attracted to individuals who behave and communicate in ways similar to themselves. In terms of behavior, several studies show that people are drawn to others who like to do the same things they do—from sports, to hiking, to reading, and even to more deviant activities. For example, Kandel, Single, and Kessler (1976), among others, have reported that drug users are strongly attracted to other drug users, which often results in the worsening of their addictions.

Similarity in Communication Skill   People also have a preference for similarity in communication style. Burleson (1998) tried to explain why people are attracted to others who have similar levels of communication skill and are happier with similarly skilled individuals than with those who are not similarly skilled. What intrigued Burleson was not that very good communicators are attracted to other good communicators, but that poor communicators are also drawn to other poor communicators. Why might people with limited communication skill be attracted to others who are similarly limited? Burleson (1998) advanced four possible explanations:

1. **The differential importance explanation.** Communication may not be a very frequent or important activity for those with low communication skill. As a result, low-skill people may not care if their partner is unskilled. In other words, since low-skill people do not engage in communication very often, they may not be looking for a high-skill partner. Other factors affecting attraction may be more important to them.

2. **The "ignorance is bliss" explanation.** Low-skill individuals are not aware that some people communicate better than they do. Because they have relationships with similar others, most of their interactions have been with people with relatively low social skills. As a result, they are happy with the way their low-skill partner communicates.

3. **The "sour grapes" explanation.** People who have poor communication skills are painfully aware of their shortcomings in the social arena. Although they might like to have partners who have better skills than they do, they perceive highly skilled communicators to be hopelessly out of their reach. As a result, they settle for partners with lower social skills, figuring that these partners are as good as they can get.

4. **The skill-as-culture explanation.** What some people consider to be poor communication might actually be seen as effective communication by

others. Thus, individuals who are defined as being low-skill communicators by researchers may be enacting communication behaviors that they and their partners consider to be quite competent. For example, low levels of expressiveness might be perceived as indicative of incompetence by some people, but an inexpressive dyad might feel most comfortable keeping their emotions hidden.

Unfortunately, researchers have not yet tested these explanations to discover which best explains the attraction between two people who lack communication skill.

Similarity in Physical Attractiveness   A final form of similarity that has been studied extensively for its impact on attraction is similarity in physical attractiveness. Have you ever noticed how people who are dating tend to be similar in terms of physical attractiveness? In fact, people take notice when one member of a romantic couple is much better looking than the other. Fair or not, the automatic assumption is that the less attractive partner must have other exceptional qualities (such as a great personality, wealth, or high social standing) that led the more attractive partner to choose her or him over better looking alternatives.

Our tendency to be attracted to people who are similar to ourselves in terms of physical attractiveness has been called the **matching hypothesis** (Berscheid, Dion, Walster, & Walster, 1971). This does not mean that people search for partners who look similar to themselves in terms of physical features—for example, brown-eyed people looking for brown-eyed partners, or people with high cheek bones and fair skin looking for partners who have similar bone structure and skin color. Instead, the matching hypothesis predicts that people look for partners who have roughly the same level of overall physical attractiveness as themselves. Thus, if you consider yourself to be fairly good-looking but not stunningly beautiful or devastatingly handsome, the matching hypothesis predicts that you will look for a partner who is somewhat above average but not extraordinarily attractive. By contrast, if you think you are gorgeous, you will look for a partner who is just as good-looking as you. Interestingly, the matching hypothesis has been shown to hold true across a wide variety of relationship types, from friendships to marriages, and cultures (Feingold, 1988).

However, this matching hypothesis seems to be in stark contrast to the research on physical attractiveness. Those studies found that people are most attracted to individuals who are very physically attractive. By contrast, research on the matching hypothesis suggests that people are most attracted to individuals who are similar to them in physical attractiveness. In other words, less attractive people should be attracted to other similarly less attractive people rather than to the best looking ones. These seemingly inconsistent findings lead to two questions: (1) Which of these hypotheses is right? and (2) Why would less attractive people be attracted to other less attractive individuals as opposed to more attractive ones?

The answers to both of these questions likely depend on people's sense of the ideal and the realistic. Ideally people want to date others who are more

Are these couples similar in terms of physical appearance? What other similarities do they share?

attractive than they are, but realistically they recognize that physically attractive individuals are likely to have many options and to be somewhat selective about whom they date. Recall the research on the hard-to-get phenomenon. These studies showed that people are attracted to individuals who are somewhat hard to get but tend to shy away from individuals who are too selective because they do not want to waste their effort and/or they see the selective people as too choosy or conceited. Thus, people may label someone who is much better looking than themselves as conceited and instead select a dating partner who is similar to themselves in terms of physical attractiveness. In short, the matching hypothesis is based on the idea that people want to maximize the attractiveness of their partner by choosing someone who is as attractive as themselves while minimizing their chances for rejection by choosing someone who is attainable. Based on this reasoning, both the beautiful-is-good and matching hypotheses appear to have some basis in truth.

With the matching hypothesis in mind, researchers have studied people's tendency to compare themselves to others (Wheeler & Miyake, 1992; Wood & Taylor, 1991). These researchers have shown that people often find fault with those whom they consider to be better than themselves (in whatever quality or characteristic is being considered) as a way to protect their self-esteem from damage. For example, Juan might believe that the really good-looking girl in his math class must be stuck up even though he has no evidence to back up this belief. Likewise, Monica might assume that a student who always does better than she does in school has no social life even though the A student may actually have a much more interesting social life than Monica. By making such favorable self-to-other comparisons, people can bolster their self-esteem. Downgrading highly attractive individuals is also related to the similarity hypothesis in that people typically pursue those who are initially perceived as similar to as opposed to better than themselves.

Complementarity: Sometimes Opposites Attract

Although the research discussed thus far shows that there is a strong similarity effect when it comes to attraction and liking, this does not mean that people are always similar on every valued characteristic. Sometimes relational partners or good friends also complement one another in some areas. For example, two best friends, Rick and Kevin, might both be intelligent, have good marriages and careers, and enjoy hiking and skiing. However, Rick might be the better skier while Kevin might be especially smart when it comes to making financial investments. Instead of envying each other's skills, they may be proud of each other's special talents. And they also might be completely different in some ways. For instance, Rick might be quiet and reserved, carefully thinking before talking, while Kevin is extroverted and impulsive. These qualities could complement one another; that is, Rick might appreciate having Kevin around to help him make new friends, while Kevin might appreciate it when Rick tells him to think before acting on certain impulses.

As this example suggests, the old saying that "opposites attract" has some basis in truth. However, **complementarity** seems to be a much better predictor of attraction and liking when it is linked to behavior or resources, and not attitudes and values (Strong et al., 1988). When it comes to people's core attitudes and beliefs, similarity seems to be much more important than complementarity. Additionally, as noted previously, sometimes people are initially attracted to someone who is completely unlike them, only to discover that those "opposite" characteristics eventually drive them crazy. As Felmlee (1998) suggested in her work on fatal attraction, "Be careful what you wish for," because sometimes you might get it and then regret it (p. 235)!

In sum, several studies have shown that similarities in attitudes, likes and dislikes, demographic characteristics, and physical attractiveness are all related to attraction and liking. Some complementary features may also be related to attraction, especially when there is complementarity in behavior (such as a shy person paired with an outgoing person) or resources (such as a wealthy person paired with a beautiful person). The final influence on people's attraction to others is environmental features. Although there is little research addressing environmental influences on attraction, these influences are nonetheless important to study.

Environmental Features Related to Attraction

How does the environment or context influence people's attraction to others? As you read through this section, you might be surprised by all the ways the environment can affect attraction and liking. Environmental features, social networks, and proximity are all contextual elements that are associated with attraction.

Microenvironmental Features

Research suggests that the environment has subtle effects on attraction and liking (see Andersen, 1999). For example, research on room features and their effects has shown that room temperature (Griffit, 1970), the presence of music (May & Hamilton, 1980), and even such seemingly irrelevant characteristics as the size of the room, the presence of high ceilings, the linear perspective of the room, the type of couch material, the color of the walls and ceilings, and the lighting may influence whether people are attracted to one another (Andersen, 1999; Burgoon et al., 1996). For example, environments that encourage interaction by providing a cozy atmosphere can promote attraction. Similarly, low lighting and soft colors may make certain people look particularly attractive, while brighter lighting and bolder colors may make other people look appealing. Environments that put people face-to-face in close proximity also enhance attraction (Andersen, 1999).

Environmental effects on attraction have also been explained by Byrne and Clore (1970; see also Clore & Byrne, 1974) using the **reinforcement affect model,** according to which certain types of environments are more likely to make people feel good. For example, an intimate setting with comfortable chairs and couches, soft wall colors, low lighting, and soft music relaxes people. These environmentally induced positive emotions then get transferred to whoever is present. In other words, people unconsciously associate the feelings they experience in a particular environment with the individuals who are part of that environment.

Other studies have shown that under some circumstances the emotions people experience due to the environment can also be related to attraction. Dutton and Aron (1974) conducted an unusual experiment to test the impact of environmental cues on attraction. They had male participants cross either a stable or a relatively unstable bridge. To make matters worse, the stable bridge was low-lying while the unstable bridge spanned a steep ravine. After crossing the bridges, the participants were met by either a male or female research assistant and told to write a brief story, which was later coded for sexual imagery. The participants also were given the phone number of the assistant and invited to call her or him at home if they wanted more information. Amazingly, the researchers found that the men who crossed the unstable bridge and met the female assistant included more sexual images in their stories and were more likely to call the assistant at home. Apparently their fear and arousal increased their attraction to the female assistant.

It may seem odd that a negative emotion such as fear can lead to attraction. Why does this happen? Zillman (1978), an emotions theorist, identified the presence of a process called **excitation transfer.** What sometimes happens, Zillman argued, is that people mistake the cause of their emotional arousal. This is especially likely to happen when people experience arousal in response to two different sources in close proximity to each other. In those cases, people mix the two states of arousal together and attribute excitement to the second stimulus. In the Dutton and Aron study, participants experienced high arousal/anxiety after walking over an unstable bridge and then immediately experienced emotional arousal when they met the female research assistant. In doing so, they may have unconsciously and mistakenly attributed their rapid heartbeats and other signs of intense emotional arousal to the presence of the female assistant, leading them to believe that they were much more attracted to her than they objectively might have been. Although this may sound a little far-fetched (and scholars have challenged the validity of excitation transfer; see Riordan & Tedeschi, 1983), other studies have confirmed this finding (White, Fishbein, & Rutstein, 1981). Apparently, in some cases, people who share scary experiences are more likely to be attracted to each other due to excitation transfer.

Social Networks

Another factor that impacts attraction is one's social network, including family and friends. Have you noticed that what you find attractive in others is often similar to what your friends find attractive? If so, you are not alone. In fact, hundreds of studies have shown that people's attitudes and intentions are strongly influenced by the attitudes of their friends and family (Sheppard, Hartwick, & Warshaw, 1988). Many scholars argue that the attitudes of members of our social circle (otherwise known as subjective norms) are the strongest predictor of our own attitudes and intentions. Given that attraction represents an attitude toward other people, the feedback we receive from friends and family certainly plays an important role in whom we find attractive.

In most cases the approval of one's social network promotes attraction and liking. For example, if you meet someone you would like to date, and your friends all tell you how wonderful she or he is, you are likely to feel even more positively toward this potential dating partner. However, the reverse can also occur. Perhaps you find someone attractive, but your friends question what you see in him or her and discourage you from pursuing a relationship, and your attraction decreases. There is one notable exception to this phenomenon, however. Some research has supported the **"Romeo and Juliet" effect,** which predicts that parental interference can strengthen attraction between two people. Specifically, Discoll, Davis, and Lipetz (1972) found that partners in dating couples reported more love for each other when their parents disapproved of their relationship. Discoll et al. retested their hypothesis 10 months later using the same couples and found the same results, with parental interference still positively related to the amount of love couples reported.

There are at least three viable explanations for the "Romeo and Juliet" effect. First, rebellious young couples may exert their power by defying their parents and becoming romantically involved with whomever they want. These feelings of power and excitement may be attributed to their relationship, much as the excitation transfer process suggests. Second, as discussed earlier, people may be attracted to individuals who are somewhat challenging or hard to get yet attainable. Third, if their love is especially strong, the partners can endure disapproval from the social network. Two people who are less in love might be quick to break up when parents and friends disapprove, making it unlikely that they would be together long enough to be in a research study.

Keep in mind that the "Romeo and Juliet" effect does not always hold true. In Chapter 15 we report research suggesting that some couples break up due to disapproval from parents and friends. Similarly, in Chapter 9, we report that involvement in each other's social network helps keep relational partners close. Sometimes interference from others draws people closer together, but other times such interference tears them apart.

Proximity

Of all the environmental features that impact attraction, proximity has received the most research attention. This is not surprising. Proximity gives people the opportunity to meet and be attracted to one another. Have you ever thought that the perfect friend or romantic partner was somewhere out there but that you would never find her or him? If so, you were worried that lack of proximity would prevent you from meeting someone to whom you would be attracted.

Several studies have confirmed that proximity is extremely important in attraction and relationship development. The earliest set of studies was conducted by Festinger, who found that the location of college students' apartments affected who became friends (see Festinger, Schachter, & Back, 1950). Students who lived close to one another were much more likely to become friends than were students who lived in the same building but farther apart. Similarly, Newcomb's (1961) famous dormitory roommates study demonstrated a strong proximity effect during the second year, even though proximity did not affect attraction during the first year. Newcomb's findings were especially intriguing because they suggested that proximity can outweigh similarity as a basis for attraction. Specifically, Newcomb paired half of the male undergraduates with similar others and the other half with dissimilar others (unbeknownst to the participants). Regardless of whether they were similar or dissimilar, the students were more likely to be friends with their roommates than with other dormitory residents.

The tendency for people to develop romantic relationships and friendships with individuals they meet in the workplace has also been attributed primarily to proximity. Indeed, 75% of the organizational members Dillard and Wittman (1985) surveyed could identify at least one workplace romance involving themselves or someone they knew. This statistic is not surprising given the amount of time most people spend in the workplace. As Westhoff (1985) put it, "Corporate romance is as inevitable as earthquakes in California" (p. 21). Similarly, a *New York Post* article began with the declaration that the workplace is "the best dating service" around ("The Best," 1988, p. 14). Other times, work associates become close friends (Bridge & Baxter, 1992). Proximity is a major contributor to the development of these friendships, as is similarity and shared tasks (Sias & Cahill, 1998; Sias, Smith, & Avdeyeva, 1999).

In sum, the effects of proximity are all around you. You are more likely to be friends with your neighbor than with someone who lives a few miles away, and you are more likely to marry someone you meet at work or school than someone you meet in a bar. This is because you have more opportunities to interact with and become attracted to people you see on a frequent basis.

Conclusion

Many factors help determine to whom you are attracted. Although knowledge of these factors does not guarantee that you will be attracted to the "right people," it should help you better understand why you are attracted to certain people and not others. You should also be aware of the ways you might stereotype people based on factors such as physical appearance, so that you will consider a more complete package of attributes when deciding whether to pursue a relationship with someone.

As the research on fatal attraction suggests, it is important to understand what is attractive to you over the long haul, rather than being lured by "flashbulb attraction." If you are attracted to someone only because he or she is opposite to you in some characteristics, research suggests that the attraction may not be lasting. Being similar on a number of key characteristics that are important to you, such as family values or life philosophies, is a better recipe for relational success. Indeed, social attraction is only a starting point. After two people who are attracted to each other meet, they usually have a long way to go before they develop a truly intimate relationship. In other chapters we discuss issues related to developing and intensifying relationships, maintaining close relationships, and communicating love and intimacy. Together, these chapters paint a picture of what happens in relationships that develop beyond initial attraction. Unfortunately, there is no magical way to determine if someone to whom you are attracted will be a true friend or a long-term romantic partner. But the research presented in this chapter should help you better understand why you are more attracted to some people than others.

Discussion Questions

1. Think about five people in your social network. What initially attracted you to these people? Do all of the qualities you thought of fit into the framework discussed in this chapter, or are there factors you would add to the model?
2. In this chapter we discussed an abundance of research on similarity as a force affecting attraction. Less research has been conducted on complementarity. Based on your own experiences, which old adage do you think is truer: Do "birds of a feather flock together," or do "opposites attract"?
3. This chapter also discussed the importance of proximity in the attraction process. In long-distance relationships proximity is missing, which has led people to debate whether "absence makes the heart grow fonder" or "out of sight means out of mind." Based on your experiences, which of these sayings is truer?

Making Sense of Our World

Coping with Uncertainty and Expectancy Violations

How often have you spent time observing others interact? As you walk around your college or university campus, you are likely to hear many conversations between people who are just getting to know one another. Recently, one of us overheard the following conversation while sitting outside the communication building on campus:

RYAN: Hi, I know this sounds corny, but you look really familiar. Are you a communication major?

CINDY: Yeah, actually, I am.

RYAN: Are you in COMM 330?

CINDY: Yeah. Are you in that class?

RYAN: Yeah, but I haven't been going much lately. By the way, my name is Ryan.

CINDY: Hi, I'm Cindy. How did you do on the test yesterday?

Their conversation continued for a little longer, with Cindy looking a bit bored with it. The conversation ended this way:

CINDY: Well, I'd better get going. I'm on my way to a meeting with a professor.

RYAN: Oh, all right . . . well, nice meeting you. I'll see you in class.

CINDY: Yeah, see ya.

This kind of conversation occurred time after time as people approached others in front of the communication building. But this should hardly be surprising to you. You probably have had many conversations similar to the one between Cindy and Ryan. In fact, research shows that people follow a typical pattern when they first meet and get to know one another. Kellerman (1995) has done several studies that reveal how similarly people converse during initial interactions. In one of her studies, she observed 212 pairs of strangers interacting and found that most of the conversations included the exact same topics, in almost the exact same order (Kellermann, 1991). Since then, she has confirmed that our initial interactions with strangers follow a very common path of topics: We start with some sort of initial greeting ("Hi"), then try to establish some commonalities ("Are you a communication major?"), and/or discuss generic topics like the weather or sports. If we are successful in establishing these commonalities, we may be able to extend the small talk. Finally, we give a reason for having to leave ("I'm on my way to a meeting with a professor") and end with some sort of goodbye ("See ya").

The question becomes, Why do we ask these questions and seek commonalities? The research on uncertainty reduction offers an answer. In this chapter we review three of the major principles of Berger and Calabrese's (1975) uncertainty reduction theory, which examines uncertainty within the context of initial encounters between people. We also discuss how uncertainty functions within established relationships and what factors affect how motivated people are to reduce uncertainty. Finally, we look at what happens when people's behavior deviates from expectations and thus creates uncertainty. As you will see, uncertainty-increasing events can have either positive or negative effects on relationships.

Uncertainty Reduction in Initial Encounters

Within Berger and Calabrese's uncertainty reduction theory, "uncertainty" refers to the inability to predict the attitudes and/or behaviors of an interactional partner. In other words, it is the extent to which someone believes that he or she does *not* know and understand someone else. For example, "high uncertainty" means that you do not feel confident in your ability to predict or explain someone's attitudes and behaviors, whereas "low uncertainty" means that you know someone well enough to be able to predict and explain her or his actions. We can have high or low uncertainty about a wide range of attitudes and behaviors. For example, Kurt might know his friend Jamal's attitudes about education and about academia very well but not have a clue about his political leanings. Janet might know how Carrie will act when the two of them are alone, but if she hasn't gone out with Carrie socially, she might not be confident in predicting how Carrie will act in more public settings, like parties or dance clubs.

According to **uncertainty reduction theory,** high uncertainty prevails in initial encounters because people do not yet know one another well. The theory suggests that the driving force in initial encounters is obtaining information about the other person in order to get to know her or him better and ultimately to reduce uncertainty. Berger and Calabrese very clearly laid out the framework of their theory, and Berger, among others, has done several studies to further clarify or modify the original theory (Berger, 1979, 1988, 1993; Berger & Douglas, 1981; Berger & Kellermann, 1983). Although the original theory offered 7 general predictions (called axioms) and 21 more specific predictions (called theorems), in this chapter we will focus on three general principles that seem to provide a foundation for the theory.

Principle 1: *People seek information to reduce uncertainty during initial encounters with others.*

Berger and Calabrese argued that our reason for behaving the way we do during initial interactions with strangers is simple: We want to get to know them better. Not only do we *want* to get to know them, we *have* to get to know them better if we hope to reduce uncertainty and create order in our world. In fact, Berger and Calabrese believed that we *need* to be able to predict and explain both our own behavior and that of others in any given situation. They called this our need to reduce uncertainty. In other words, they claimed that we dislike situations in which we are not sure about the outcome and that our primary motivation in initial interactions is to decrease uncertainty about what might happen and/or what someone might be like. In a sense we act as "naive scientists" who gather information and sort through alternative explanations to better understand the people around us.

Think about situations in which you have been uncertain about what might happen. A first date, your first prom, your first college class, your first roommate, your first job, a request for a raise—all might be good examples. But even in these cases we usually have some idea about what might happen and how to act because other people have talked about them with us. In fact, sometimes we have too much information, and we need to sort through it all to predict and explain someone's behavior. For example, you may have heard conflicting stories about blind dates and you are unsure which scenario, if any, will best apply to your blind date. Or you may lack information about appropriate behavior on blind dates. Either way, you will feel anxious and wonder, What will this person be like? What am I supposed to do? What am I supposed to say? According to Berger and Calabrese's theory, this state of uncertainty is the driving force behind our behavior during initial interactions.

When we experience uncertainty, we seek information in an attempt to understand the situation. We ask one another basic questions and try to establish commonalities because this type of information helps us get to know the person better and reduce uncertainty. As others tell us about themselves, we feel more confident in our ability to predict how they think and act. As a result, we feel more comfortable in the interaction. Initially, however, we ask "superficial" questions and engage in small talk. This type of communication helps give us a general sense of how the other person acts and thinks. In addition, by sticking to superficial topics, we can keep some things about ourselves private until we know the other person better and feel more comfortable disclosing.

Take the case of Ryan and Cindy from the beginning of this chapter. Ryan was able to confirm that Cindy was a communication student, which made him feel as if he knew her a little better. He knew what sort of courses she has to take, he could guess that she is outgoing and likes to interact with people, and he could estimate her age. So, Cindy's answer to that one question probably helped reduce Ryan's uncertainty about her tremendously. And if Cindy and Ryan had interacted longer, their uncertainty probably would have been reduced even more. According to uncertainty reduction theory, the more bits of information we have about someone, the more we "know" her or him, and the better we should be able to predict that person's attitudes and behaviors. Thus, as communication increases, uncertainty about the person with whom we are interacting should decrease. We should be more certain about someone after spending 20 minutes with that person than after spending 5, because we will have had four times as much time to seek information about him or her.

Several studies have confirmed that uncertainty is related to the number of questions people ask and the amount of time they spend interacting. Douglas (1990a) placed 78 college students in same-sex pairs of strangers and asked them to interact for either 2 minutes, 4 minutes, or 6 minutes. After the interactions the participants completed a measure of confidence in their ability to predict the other person's behavior and attitudes. The uncertainty levels of those who interacted for 6 minutes were much lower than the levels of those who interacted for only 2 minutes. Douglas also found that the students who asked more questions were more confident, thus suggesting that the amount of communication (in terms of responses to questions) was related to decreases in uncertainty. Other researchers extended the interaction time to a maximum of 16 minutes and obtained relatively similar results for the first 6 minutes but did not find that uncertainty decreased significantly from the 8th to the 16th minute of interaction (Redmond & Virchota, 1994). Apparently, people gather information rather quickly during initial interactions and then stick with their initial impressions.

In another study, Douglas (1990b) had students interact with a same-sex stranger for 4 minutes, after which they completed a survey measuring their uncertainty. He later analyzed their conversations for the amount of self-disclosure. His analysis showed that the participants' uncertainty was directly related to the amount of information disclosed by their interaction partner. As the amount of the first person's disclosure increased, the second person's uncertainty decreased. This study provides rather strong evidence supporting uncertainty reduction theory's prediction that communication helps decrease uncertainty.

Principle 2: People can reduce uncertainty using passive, active, or interactive strategies.

Sometimes people reduce uncertainty using strategies other than face-to-face or direct communication. Thus, our second principle of uncertainty reduction theory involves different strategies for reducing uncertainty.

Passive Strategies People who rely on nonintrusive observation of individuals are using passive strategies (Berger, 1979, 1987). This type of strategy involves behaviors such as looking at someone sitting alone to see if a friend or date comes along, observing how a person interacts with others, or paying attention to the kinds of clothes a person wears. These methods are passive in that they are indirect ways of gathering information and reducing uncertainty without having to interact with someone. For example, on the basis of observation, you might make assumptions about someone's age and level of expressiveness, and judgments about the appropriateness of his or her behavior.

Passive observations are most likely to be effective and informative when they are conducted in an informal setting, like a party, rather than in a formal setting, like a classroom or business office (Berger & Douglas, 1981). Moreover, people usually make more accurate judgments when watching someone interact with others than sitting alone. You might be wondering why this is so. The research suggests that informal situations involving interactions with others offer important information about how a person really acts and thinks. Most people behave in similar ways when they are in formal settings because the rules for behavior in these situations are fairly strict. For example, it is unusual to see people behave inappropriately in a fancy restaurant. By contrast, people act in various ways at an informal party because the "rules" are less rigid. When people are relaxed and interacting in an informal setting, their natural selves typically emerge. Therefore, it is much more informative, and consequently much more uncertainty reducing, to observe someone in an informal, as opposed to a formal, setting. Regardless of setting, though, we can detect only a limited amount of information by passive strategies alone.

Active Strategies   Often we resort to active strategies of uncertainty reduction. One type of active strategy involves purposefully manipulating the social environment in a certain way and then observing how someone reacts to this manipulation. The information seeker is not part of the manipulated situation although he or she sets the situation up. These tactics are like miniexperiments conducted with the intent of seeking information about the target person. For example, in the movie *Singles,* one of the lead actresses would sneeze to see if the person would say "Gesundheit," which to her indicated that the person was nice and well-mannered.

Manipulative tactics also occur in developed relationships. For example, one student of ours used an active strategy on her boyfriend. She typed a letter phrased as if it had come from a female admirer of her boyfriend. The letter included a request that they meet at a certain place and time, and was signed "your secret admirer." She then placed this letter on the windshield of her boyfriend's car. She had two goals in mind when she did this: (1) she wanted to see if her boyfriend would tell her that he received such a letter, and (2) she wanted to check whether he would show up at the location in search of this fictitious person. (In case you are wondering, he did not tell her about the letter, but he also never showed up to meet the fictitious person.) Several other students in our classes have admitted to using similar active uncertainty reduction strategies with their dating partners. This type of information-seeking strategy is useful because it can help reduce uncertainty without the need to rely on more direct methods. Of course, such manipulative attempts could backfire in

---

BOX 4.1 HIGHLIGHTS

"Hired Help"—Today's Relationship Information Seekers

More and more we hear stories of people hiring "relationship detectives" to check out their current or potential mates. Open the Yellow Pages or search the Web, and you will find long lists of agencies or people willing, for a fee, to investigate your significant other for anything from infidelity to use of a false identity. In essence these agencies are offering you the opportunity to reduce your uncertainty without having to personally work at it. Their list of services is long. For additional fees they can do a variety of "spy" activities, including videotaping the target (maybe catching him or her leaving a third party's residence or flirting with someone at a bar) and hiring a member of the opposite sex to approach him or her in a bar or restaurant and proposition him or her for a date and/or sex.

By hiring an agency to spy on your significant other, you are reducing uncertainty the easy way. The difficulties of interactive uncertainty reduction are replaced by passive (in the case of videotapes) or active (in the case in which they simply relay to you what they saw or have another individual flirt with him or her) strategies. More importantly, you don't have to do guesswork on the truthfulness of the information you are receiving from the third party, as typically is the case with the use of active uncertainty reduction methods. Also you don't have to decide whether the behavior you are observing is a reflection of the person's true character, because they videotape the person without his or her knowledge and do so in informal settings. Of course, the ethics of such practices and the implications of such distrust for the relationship's future are important issues for people choosing this tactic. But the fact remains that our need to reduce uncertainty in relationships has spawned a burgeoning industry of information seekers for hire.

---

the long run, making the person look paranoid and/or communicating distrust to her or his partner.

The second type of active uncertainty reduction strategy involves asking third parties (friends, family members) about the person in question. We often ask friends if they have heard anything about a particular person of interest or ask for help interpreting something that person did. Think back to the times you were attracted to someone in high school. Chances are, you asked others for information. For example, you might have asked her or his friends questions such as, Is she seeing anyone? Has he ever mentioned me? If so, what did he say? Do you think she'd go out with me? What types of things does he like to do? Indeed, studies have shown that we gather various information about people from their friends, ranging from their age and marital status to their hobbies and personality traits (Killworth, Bernard, & McCarty, 1984). In fact, one study found that 30% of the information we have about someone comes from asking others (Hewes, Graham, Doelger, & Pavitt, 1985). Box 4.1 details one increasingly popular method of obtaining information about people.

Interactive Strategies The third general type of uncertainty reduction is interactive (Berger, 1979, 1987). Interactive strategies involve direct contact between the information seeker and the target. Common interactive strategies include asking questions, encouraging disclosure, and relaxing the target. In the conversation between Ryan and Cindy at the beginning of this chapter, the questions that Ryan asked represent an example of interactive uncertainty reduction. We are especially likely to ask such questions the first time we meet someone. In studies of behavior during initial interactions, researchers have found that the frequency of question asking drops over time, coinciding with decreases in our level of uncertainty (Douglas, 1990a; Kellermann, 1995).

It is important to note, though, that the questions being asked in initial interactions are usually very general. Other research suggests that we hesitate to ask questions about intimate issues until we have a close relationship with the person and even then may avoid asking direct questions (Bell & Buerkel-Rothfuss, 1990). Studies have also shown that people sometimes disclose information about themselves with the specific hope that their disclosure will encourage the other person to do the same (Berger, 1979). Note, however, that we use disclosure as an uncertainty reduction strategy only after we reach a certain level of comfort in being able to predict the other person's attitudes and behaviors. This comfort level typically is reached through the general question asking that is so common during initial interactions. Finally, people sometimes try to relax the target so that she or he feels comfortable revealing information. People sometimes offer drugs or alcohol to achieve this effect; examples of more common and less manipulative strategies include creating a comfortable environment that is conducive to talking, smiling a lot, and acting interested to get the other person talking (Berger, 1979).

As these examples suggest, interactive strategies are not limited to verbal communication. We often reduce our uncertainty about someone through nonverbal cues (Kellerman & Berger, 1984). For instance, if you smile at and make eye contact with someone across a room, and the person motions you to come over, a very clear message has been sent. That one motioning gesture gives you quite a bit of information and reduces your uncertainty considerably. In fact, nonverbal behaviors can be the primary method of communicating our thoughts and feelings about other people and our relationships with them (Andersen, 1999; Burgoon, Buller & Woodall, 1996). For example, research on sexual behavior (see Chapter 7) has shown that the primary way we go about discovering whether a partner is interested in escalating the level of sexual activity—that is, reducing our uncertainty about the person's sexual desires—is through nonverbal cues. So, although much of the research on interactive uncertainty reduction methods has focused on verbal strategies, we often engage in nonverbal interactions that are potentially uncertainty reducing.

Of course, people can use multiple uncertainty reduction strategies in a single interaction. For example, suppose that Derek spots Michelle in a bar. She appears to be a fellow college student, seems very outgoing, and does not have other males around her (passive strategy), so he sends over a drink in hopes of receiving positive feedback to his gesture (active strategy using manipulation of the environment). The waiter brings her the drink and points over to Derek. Michelle takes the drink, glances at Derek, and appears to smile slightly. When the waiter walks back past Derek's table, Derek asks him if she said anything (active strategy using a third party). The waiter says that she didn't but that she looked pleased. Now that Derek has reduced his initial uncertainty somewhat, he feels confident enough to take the next step, so he approaches Michelle and starts engaging in conversation with her (interactive strategy).

Principle 3: As uncertainty decreases, attraction usually increases.

According to uncertainty reduction theory, the more we know about someone, the more we reduce uncertainty. This reduction in uncertainty then leads us to like the other person more. Remember that Berger and Calabrese argued that we are uncomfortable with uncertainty and will therefore be highly motivated to gain information so as to better predict and explain our partner's behavior. Therefore, it also makes sense that we would be less attracted to people whose behavior we can't predict and with whom we have high uncertainty.

Research generally supports this prediction. In most cases we are more attracted to people when we can predict their behavior (for a review see Douglas, 1990a or Kellermann & Reynolds, 1990). This association between attraction and uncertainty also appears to hold for members of different cultures. In fact, Gudykunst and his colleagues have argued that elevated uncertainty is one reason that many people feel less attracted to members of other cultures (see, for example, Gudykunst & Nishida, 1984). According to this perspective, you might feel more uncertain and anxious around people from other cultures simply because you are unsure of their cultural norms and customs. This uncertainty could prevent you from developing an attraction for these people.

However, when uncertainty is reduced, people from different cultures often like one another more. Gudykunst (1988, 1989), in his theory of **intergroup uncertainty reduction,** described several conditions that make it more likely that uncertainty will be reduced in intercultural interactions. First, he argued that people who identify strongly with their own group identity feel more confident about interaction with someone from a different social or cultural group. Second, when people perceive members of another culture or social group favorably, they are likely to look forward to interacting with them. These two factors combine to create a communication climate that makes information exchange and uncertainty reduction easier. For example, imagine visiting Brazil for the first time. If you are confident about your own cultural identity and are looking forward to communicating with Brazilians, you are likely to be comfortable and open during interactions, which will likely lead to uncertainty reduction and increased liking. By contrast, if you are unsure about your role as a person in a foreign country and you dread interacting with people who speak a different language, you are likely to avoid interaction and to remain uncertain and anxious.

Although getting to know people better often does lead to attraction and liking, as both uncertainty reduction and Gudykunst's theory of intergroup uncertainty reduction predict, there are times when uncertainty reduction leads to less attraction and liking. Think about your own experiences in initial encounters. You can probably recall times when, as you found out more about someone, you decided that you disliked that person rather than liking her or him more. For example, you might learn that someone you just met is a liar and a cheat. This discovery reduces your uncertainty about your new acquaintance, but it probably doesn't increase your attraction. Similarly, if someone makes a tasteless, offensive remark, it is likely to reduce your uncertainty about the kind of person he or she is, but it is also likely to decrease your attraction.

Even in relationships that have started to develop, uncertainty reduction can lead people to change their minds and feel less attracted to someone. A good example of this can be found in the movie *Casual Sex?* In this movie Stacy (played by Lea Thompson) falls in love with a musician she meets at a health spa. The man is tall and attractive and seems to be warm and sensitive. When Stacy returns to Los Angeles, he accompanies her and then moves into her apartment. Stacy quickly becomes familiar with all his irritating habits: He wants to sit around all day playing music while she works, he doesn't believe in checking accounts or credit cards, and he suddenly seems much more immature and unintelligent than she had previously thought. As a result, Stacy decides she wants to end the relationship. In this case uncertainty reduction certainly did not increase relational satisfaction! As this example illustrates, there are clearly situations in which uncertainty reduction leads to dislike rather than attraction. This is typically true when the information we receive about someone is negative.

Predicted Outcome Value Theory

An alternative to uncertainty reduction theory, called **predicted outcome value theory** (Sunnafrank, 1986, 1990), takes the positive versus negative aspects of information into account. According to Sunnafrank, people are not driven by a need to reduce uncertainty in all cases. Instead, whether we seek more information depends on whether outcome values are positive or negative. In this theory, outcome values relate to our predictions about future interactions with others. For example, if you like someone and think you would have positive interactions with her or him in the future, that person has a positive outcome value for you. Similarly, if you think your boss can provide you with rewards in the future, your boss has a positive outcome value. Other people have negative outcome values. For example, you might dislike someone and think that interaction with her or him would be difficult, embarrassing, and awkward.

According to Sunnafrank's theory, we initially reduce uncertainty as a way of finding out how we feel about a person or an interaction. After that, the positive or negative outcome value becomes the driving force behind whether we try to seek further information. Thus, when someone reveals negative information to us during an initial encounter, we are likely to predict negative outcome values and to cut off communication with that person. Put another way, when outcome values are positive, we will be motivated to seek information; when outcome values are negative, we will decrease communication and stop seeking information.

A practical example should make the importance of predicted outcome values even clearer. Imagine meeting someone named Fred for the first time. After a few minutes of conversation, you will probably come to some conclusions about Fred. If you decide that Fred is a really nice person who might be fun to have as a friend, you are likely to stay and chat with him longer. Perhaps you will ask Fred more questions about his interests and goals, and end up exchanging phone numbers and calling him later in the week. But if a few minutes of conversation convinces you that Fred is an oddball who makes you feel uncomfortable, you are likely to terminate the conversation and to avoid Fred if you see him in the future. Therefore, according to predicted outcome theory, the relationship between uncertainty reduction and attraction might be better stated as follows: When uncertainty is reduced as a result of learning positive information about someone, attraction increases; when uncertainty is reduced as a result of learning negative information about someone, attraction decreases.

Uncertainty in Established Relationships

Although uncertainty reduction is usually a much more prominent goal in initial encounters than in established relationships, uncertainty can pervade even the closest of our relationships. Indeed, Berger (1988, 1993) has argued that people feel a need to reduce uncertainty at various stages of a relationship's development and decline. Planalp and Honeycutt (1985) conducted a study to determine when people in established relationships experienced uncertainty. Specifically, they asked students whether they could recall a time when they learned something surprising about a friend, spouse, or dating partner that made them question the relationship. Ninety percent of the respondents in this study were able to recall such an instance, thus strongly supporting the claim that certain behaviors do increase, rather than decrease, uncertainty, even in developed relationships.

The researchers then categorized the responses into six uncertainty-increasing behaviors:

1. **Competing relationships** included the discovery that a friend or dating partner wanted to spend time with someone else.
2. **Unexplained loss of contact or closeness** occurred when communication and/or intimacy decreased for no particular reason.
3. **Sexual behavior** included discovering that a friend or dating partner engaged in sexual behavior that was not characteristic of her or his actions.
4. **Deception** involved discovering that friends or dating partners had lied or been misleading.
5. **Change in personality/value** occurred when people realized that their friends or dating partners were different from what they used to be.

6. **Betraying confidence** included instances in which people's friends or dating partners disclosed private information to others about them without their consent.

For all six types of behavior, the participants felt less able to predict their friend or dating partner's attitudes and behaviors following these events than they had before these events took place. In other words, they felt as if they "knew them less" following the behavior than they did prior to it. Studies confirm the high incidence of such uncertainty-increasing behaviors in close relationships. For example, one study found that 80% of marriages included uncertainty-increasing events (Turner, 1990).

The method that Planalp and Honeycutt (1985) used is also worth noting. They asked the participants to think about something "surprising." In fact, earlier, Berger had argued that unexpected (or surprising) behaviors increase uncertainty, and this study seems to support his claim. That is, when people do something unexpected, we should be less able to predict their attitudes and behaviors in the future. For example, if Rob thinks that Leah is shy and reserved, he is likely to be surprised to see her flirting with a large group of men at a party. Before the party, Rob would likely have predicted that Leah would not engage in such behavior, but now he would be uncertain about what to predict for her behavior at future parties. Thus, his uncertainty has increased, and his ability to predict has decreased. Rob's ability to explain Leah's behavior would also decline because he would be unsure about how shy she really is.

Rob and Leah's situation illustrates the type of reasoning that led Berger, as late as 1994, to claim that unexpected behaviors always lead to increases in uncertainty. But let's examine that claim. Think about behaviors that fit in any of the six uncertainty-increasing categories. It is easy to see how they might increase uncertainty, but might they not also *reduce* uncertainty in some cases? Couldn't these behaviors sometimes make us feel as if we now know how the person *really* is? To illustrate, suppose a friend lied to you about his past. The fact that he lied about such an important issue may tell you a lot about the kind of person he is. Discovering that lie may not increase your uncertainty, but instead reduce it. Similarly, Rob might think that he now knows the *real* Leah after he sees her flirting with a group of men. These counterexamples leave us with the question of whether all surprising events increase uncertainty or whether some actually reduce uncertainty.

Clearly, uncertainty is a complex and sometimes paradoxical concept. Sometimes behaviors that initially increase our uncertainty might reduce uncertainty in the long run, and sometimes these unexpected behaviors may even cause us to like someone more. This is precisely what happened in the movie *Casual Sex?* After Stacy ends her relationship with the musician, she gets to know another man, Vinny. She originally thought Vinny was obnoxious, so she is surprised when he shows himself to be quite sensitive. Stacy's expectations were violated, uncertainty was eventually reduced, and she became very attracted to (and eventually married!) Vinny. Box 4.2 contains a scale you can use to see how much certainty you perceive to exist in one of your relationships.

BOX **4.2** **PUT YOURSELF TO THE TEST**

The Attributional Confidence Scale

Respond to the following questions by circling the appropriate number. When responding, think of a specific person, such as a good friend or romantic partner.

1. How confident are you of your general ability to predict how he/she will behave?

   Very confident 7 6 5 4 3 2 1 **Not confident at all**

2. How certain are you that he/she likes you?

   Very certain 7 6 5 4 3 2 1 **Not certain at all**

3. How accurate are you at predicting the values he/she holds?

   Very accurate 7 6 5 4 3 2 1 **Not accurate at all**

4. How accurate are you at predicting his/her attitudes?

   Very accurate 7 6 5 4 3 2 1 **Not accurate at all**

5. How well can you predict his/her feelings and emotions?

   Very well 7 6 5 4 3 2 1 **Not well at all**

6. How much can you empathize with (share) the way he/she feels about himself/herself?

   Very much 7 6 5 4 3 2 1 **Not much at all**

7. How well do you know him/her?

   Very well 7 6 5 4 3 2 1 **Not well at all**

Add up your scores for the seven items. The maximum score is 49, and the minimum score is 7. The closer your score is to 49, the more uncertain you are. The closer your score is to 7, the more confident and certain you are about your prediction.

Source: This scale is adapted from Clatterbuck (1979).

You might want to reanswer these questions later in the semester to see if your certainty level changes.

Secret Tests

Regardless of whether uncertainty-reducing events lead to more positive or negative evaluations of a relational partner, such events often provoke a desire to seek more information. For instance, it is natural to wonder *why* your partner is suddenly showering you with unexpected gifts or is constantly staying out late and forgetting to call you. In these situations people in established relationships often use passive, active, and interactive strategies that are similar to those mentioned earlier in this chapter. But relational partners also have a number of other more specific strategies at their disposal. In a particularly insightful look at uncertainty reduction in ongoing relationships, Baxter and Wilmot (1985) described seven sets of "secret tests" that people use to reduce their uncertainty about their partner's commitment to the relationship:

1. **Asking-third-party tests.** This strategy relies on feedback from social network members. This test is identical to one of the active strategies described earlier. For example, Natalie might ask her boyfriend's best friend if he is still mad at her about something.

2. **Directness tests.** This strategy involves direct interaction with the partner. This test is identical to the interactive strategies described earlier. Here Natalie would go directly to her boyfriend and ask him if he is angry with her.

3. **Triangle tests.** This strategy is intended to test the partner's commitment to the relationship by creating three-person triangles. Fidelity checks (such as seeing if the partner responds to a fictitious "secret admirer" note) and jealousy tests (such as flirting with someone else to see how the partner responds) are two examples of triangle tests.

4. **Separation tests.** This strategy relies on creating physical distance between relational partners. The two primary methods here are having a long period of physical separation (such as seeing if your relationship can survive a summer of not seeing each other) and ceasing contact for an extended period of time to see how long it takes for your partner to call.

5. **Endurance tests.** This strategy increases the costs or reduces the rewards for the other person in the relationship. One such test, known as "testing limits," involves seeing how much the partner will endure. For instance, someone might dress down, become argumentative, start arriving late for dates, or fail to call at a designated time to see if the partner stays committed despite these irritations. Another test, known as "self putdowns," involves putting yourself down to see if the partner responds by offering positive feedback. For example, Chan may say that he feels overweight in the hope that Tamika will try to convince him that he looks great, thus indicating a high level of commitment to him.

6. **Public presentation tests.** This strategy involves watching for the other person's reaction to the use of certain relational labels. It is most commonly used in the early stages of a relationship. It is typified by the first public presentation of a partner as your "boyfriend" or "girlfriend" (whereas before, the partner may have been introduced only as a "friend"), followed by observation of the partner's reaction. Public presentation tests that might occur later in the relationship include asking someone to wear a ring or a sports or letter jacket, or asking someone to spend the holidays with your family.

7. **Indirect suggestion tests.** This strategy involves using hinting or joking to bring up a topic without taking direct responsibility. The partner's response then gives you insight into his or her feelings about the issue. For example, Patricia might joke about moving in with Peter to check his reaction to the

issue. Although Patricia may have been truly thinking about moving in, the fact that she said it as a joke gives her an "out" that allows her to save face if Peter rejects the idea. At the same time this strategy allows Patricia to seek information about Peter's attitudes toward cohabiting with her.

These categories of secret tests were derived from interviews with college students who were asked to discuss information acquisition strategies that they used in one of three relationship types: (1) a platonic opposite-sex friendship, (2) an opposite-sex friendship with romantic potential, or (3) a romantic relationship. Beyond identifying these secret tests, Baxter and Wilmot's (1985) study revealed an important point about our behavior in relationships—namely, the vast majority of uncertainty reduction strategies in relationships are indirect. The image of relationships as being completely open and of partners being totally direct was shattered in this study. In fact, only 22% of the students who reported on a romantic relationship listed direct strategies as a tactic they used to reduce their uncertainty. By contrast, 34% said they used triangle tests and 33% reported using endurance tests in their romantic relationships. Especially interesting is the extent to which indirectness was used in friendships with romantic potential. Consistent with research showing these relationships to be ambiguous and uncertain (O'Meara, 1989), the students who were reporting on a relationship with romantic potential were more likely than those reporting on the other relationship types to mention separation tests and indirect suggestion tests as information-seeking strategies. Perhaps this is because relationships with romantic potential are often still developing and so are more prone to uncertainty than are stable friendships or romantic relationships.

Other researchers have shown that people are also more likely to use indirect secret tests in the early stages of dating relationships, when using direct information-seeking strategies may be riskier than they are later in the relationship (Bell & Buerkel-Rothfuss, 1990). For example, Emmers and Canary (1996) found that, when romantic couples wanted to repair their relationship after encountering an uncertainty-increasing event such as deception or infidelity, they used direct strategies more often than passive or active strategies.

In sum, the type and stage of the relationship influence the use of various uncertainty reduction strategies. Relationships with ambiguous definitions, as well as early dating relationships, are characterized by reliance on indirect strategies. More developed relationships feature the use of both indirect and direct strategies.

Uncertainty Reduction and Relational Satisfaction

As discussed earlier, in initial interactions uncertainty reduction generally increases attraction as long as the information obtained is positive. Therefore, it is reasonable to suspect that uncertainty reduction might also be associated with satisfaction in established relationships. However, research suggests that high levels of either uncertainty or certainty can decrease relational satisfaction.

One study in particular (Parks & Adelman, 1983) showed that too much uncertainty may have a negative impact on relationships. In this study, Parks and Adelman recruited 172 students who were currently in romantic relationships and had them complete a questionnaire about their attraction to and uncertainty about their partner, among other variables. On average these students had been in their relationships for a little less than 1½ years. They then contacted these students 3 months later and asked them similar questions. Their results revealed several very interesting patterns related to uncertainty. The one most relevant here is that they confirmed the predicted link between uncertainty and attraction or satisfaction in relationships. In fact, the respondents who reported being relatively uncertain about their partner on the first questionnaire were more likely to have ended their relationship 3 months later than were the respondents who had initially felt relatively low uncertainty.

Other research suggests that too much certainty can also have a negative impact on relationships. According to this line of reasoning, knowing someone too well can become boring. Relationships that are stagnant are usually characterized by a lack of uncertainty, as well as a lack of growth. Being able to predict everything that someone is going to do or say is not necessarily a good thing, and some uncertainty may help keep the relationship exciting (Livingstone, 1980). One of the reasons that many heterosexual individuals enjoy cross-sex friendships is that there is often a sense of uncertainty or mystery about where the relationship is going. But that sense of mystery and excitement may eventually fade if the friendship turns romantic. Similarly, some people thrive on roller coaster–type relationships that are hot one day and cold the next. For these individuals uncertainty keeps the relationship challenging and exciting. Even in more stable relationships it is important to keep things from becoming too predictable.

The importance of both stability and excitement is also captured in **dialectics theory** (Baxter, 1990; Baxter & Montgomery, 1996; see also Chapter 9). According to this theory, people have opposing interpersonal needs. For example, people want to be close and connected to others, but they also want to be independent. People want to tell others about themselves, but they also want to keep some information private. Similarly, scholars adopting the dialectical perspective believe that we want both certainty (predictability) and uncertainty (novelty) in our relationships. Too much certainty or uncertainty can erode a relationship over time. Indeed, there is considerable evidence to support this claim. We don't like to be in situations in which we know everything about our partner, because that produces boredom. But we also don't like situations in which we can't predict what our partner is going to do from day to day, because that produces a lot of stress. Instead, we want a bit of both ends of this dialectic. As a result, people often swing back and forth between wanting more excitement/novelty and wanting more stability/predictability in their relationships.

Factors Affecting Motivation to Seek Information

All of the research discussed so far in this chapter is rooted in the assumption that people have a strong need to reduce uncertainty by seeking information, particularly during initial encounters and the early stages of relationships. In fact, the basic idea underlying uncertainty reduction theory is that we have a need to predict people's behaviors and that this need drives our constant search for information. But is that a valid assumption? Are we always motivated to find out more information? Or, as dialectics theory suggests, are we sometimes happier with some uncertainty? Research suggests that at least four conditions affect how motivated people are to reduce uncertainty. The first three of these conditions were discussed by Berger (1979). The fourth condition is from later research on uncertainty in illness theory and taboo topics in relationships.

Condition 1: High Incentive Value

Berger's (1979) first condition is that there must be high incentive value. In other words, people are particularly interested in reducing uncertainty about individuals who can provide them with important rewards and/or satisfy important needs. Thus, people are likely to have a lot of incentive to reduce uncertainty about a potential romantic partner, a boss, or someone who appears to have a great personality and would make a good friend; but they are likely to have little incentive to reduce uncertainty with strangers or other people who are likely to have little impact on their lives. This logic is similar to Sunnafrank's (1986) reasoning in predicted outcome value theory: People are most motivated to seek information when they see the partner as a rewarding and likable person.

Of course, sometimes we are motivated to seek information about people we dislike, especially if they can affect our lives in some way. Think about your enemies. Have you ever wanted to dig up some "dirt" about someone you really disliked? Have you ever wanted to get to know your enemies a little bit better—even if only to understand how they could be such jerks? We do seem to have an inherent interest in discovering information about people, even if we do not consider them to be pleasant or rewarding, but that interest seems stronger when we are interacting with people we actually like. Of course, there might also be a difference between our true enemies and those we just don't like very much. Enemies are typically people with whom we have repeated, and sometimes unavoidable, interactions. If these people affect our lives, we will have to think about them and seek information about them from time to time. In fact, it may be in our best interest to know what they are thinking and planning about us. By contrast, if someone is simply an acquaintance whom we do not like very much, we might feel indifferent and so abandon the search for information. In the latter case the incentive to reduce uncertainty would be low.

Condition 2: Deviations from Expected Behavior

Berger (1979) also predicted that deviations from expected behavior increase attentiveness to information seeking. If someone behaves in an unexpected or unpredictable way, Berger argued, our curiosity and need for predictability will increase. As a result, we are especially motivated to seek information that will help us predict future behavior, and we become very attentive. For example, if a friend of yours starts behaving strangely around you, perhaps acting defensive or being untalkative, you are likely to feel uncertainty and to seek information. Perhaps your friend is upset with you, or perhaps she or he simply had a bad day at school or work. In any case you are likely to use one or more of the strategies discussed earlier in this chapter to help you figure out what is wrong.

Later in this chapter we discuss other research related to expectancy violations. As you will see, when people's actual behavior deviates from what is expected, it can lead to a number of positive or negative consequences depending on whether the unexpected behavior is seen in a favorable or unfavorable light. Sometimes unexpected behavior leads to positive outcomes even if these behaviors initially create uncertainty.

Condition 3: Anticipation of Future Interaction

When people anticipate interacting with someone in the future, Berger (1979) predicted that the motivation to seek information is particularly strong. That is, our interest in reducing uncertainty about people is heightened when we expect to see them again. If we do not believe that we will ever see the person again, we will not have the same interest in getting to know her or him. Several studies confirm that anticipation of future interaction is an important influence on our motivation to reduce uncertainty and to seek information (Douglas, 1985, 1990a; Kellermann & Reynolds, 1990). Research has shown that we consider information seeking to be more important when we think we will need to predict and explain someone's future behavior.

Condition 4: The Anticipated Positive Versus Negative Content of the Information

Other research suggests that the type of information we expect to receive can influence how motivated we are to reduce uncertainty. Specifically, when people expect to uncover negative information, they may decide they would rather live with the uncertainty than confirm their fears. **Uncertainty in illness theory** (Mishel, 1981, 1988, 1990) supports this claim. Mischel claimed that sometimes we would rather not know something and so we will actively avoid opportunities to obtain information. According to uncertainty in illness theory, when we lack knowledge about something that might help us, we want to reduce the uncertainty by seeking the helpful information. However, in the context of diseases, when eliminating uncertainty might mean eliminating hope for recovery (by discovering that the disease is fatal), uncertainty is cherished because it keeps hope alive. In other words, we will avoid seeking information and will instead prefer to live with uncertainty if we fear that we might discover information about our health that makes us lose hope for the future.

There is considerable evidence supporting the logic of uncertainty in illness theory. Take people's sexual behavior, for example. Despite the fact that hundreds of thousands of college students are at high risk of contracting a sexually transmitted disease (STD), only a very small percentage ever get tested for such diseases. This pattern is even stronger if you consider fatal STDs, like AIDS. One of the reasons people give for not getting tested is that they would rather not know if they have an STD. For these people the uncertainty is preferable to the potential knowledge that they have a stigmatized disease that may change their life or even lead to their death. This attitude is especially worrisome given that many STDs are quite treatable, especially if diagnosed early. Research shows a similar pattern in tests for breast cancer and colon cancer. Only a very small percentage of the population most at risk for these types of cancer actually get regular checkups, again despite the fact that with early detection the consequences are relatively benign.

Similarly, research suggests that we sometimes prefer to keep a level of uncertainty in our relationships, especially if reducing uncertainty could reveal negative information or lead to negative relational consequences. For example, studies on "taboo topics" that people avoid discussing in relationships show that the future of the relationship is one of the most avoided topics among romantic partners. Studies have shown that even couples who have been together for a long time sometimes avoid seeking information and reducing uncertainty. For example, one study included long-term dating couples in which one of the partners would be graduating from college in a few months (Afifi & Burgoon, 1998). Many of these couples avoided having the "dreaded discussion" about their future. Why is that? Perhaps they were worried about their future together and feared that the relationship might change after graduation. In this case, uncertainty might be perceived as a better alternative than finding out that the relationship could be at risk.

Studies on cross-sex friendships also suggest that uncertainty is sometimes accepted in ongoing relationships. Some cross-sex friendships are full of uncertainty and ambiguity regarding issues such as whether romantic potential exists (O'Meara, 1989). In these cross-sex friendships "sensitive" topics—especially about the relationship—are typically avoided at all costs (Afifi & Burgoon, 1998; Baxter & Wilmot, 1985). In fact, the current and future status of the relationship is often the most commonly avoided topic in cross-sex friendships. Chavez and Guerrero (1999) found that individuals were especially likely to avoid discussing the status of the relationship when they were romantically attracted to their cross-sex friend but feared that he or she did not reciprocate their feelings. Thus, people sometimes prefer uncertainty when they fear that information seeking might confirm their worst fears—such as that the relationship does not have a future. As we discussed earlier, in other cases people might prefer some uncertainty to keep their relationships unpredictable and exciting.

Berger's (1979) article, as well as subsequent research on uncertainty in illness theory and taboo topics in close relationships, suggest an important change in the thinking behind uncertainty reduction theory. Berger's inclusion of the first three conditions discussed here made it clear that at certain times people are more motivated to reduce uncertainty. But Berger was not claiming that our need to reduce uncertainty disappears in the absence of these conditions. He still argued that we are *always* motivated to reduce uncertainty to some extent but that this desire is heightened when people can offer us rewards, when they behave in unusual ways that violate expectations, and when we expect to see them again. The research on uncertainty in illness theory and taboo topics in relationships also suggests that people are sometimes more motivated to reduce uncertainty when they expect to receive positive rather than negative information.

Personality Differences

In addition to these four conditions, personality factors may affect how motivated people are to reduce uncertainty. Several scholars have argued that some people have a greater need for uncertainty reduction than others. Social psychologists have suggested that, instead of always needing to seek information, as uncertainty reduction theory suggests, or having this need vary according to specific circumstances, as scholars such as Mishel have suggested, the need for information seeking varies from person to person. Depending on who you read, you will see a different label for this concept. Need for closure (Krugkanski, 1990), tolerance for uncertainty (Kellermann & Reynolds, 1990), uncertainty orientation (Sorrentino & Short, 1986), and coping style (Miller, 1987) are among the most popular labels. Regardless of the labeling, all of these scholars essentially propose the same thing: Some people have a high need to reduce uncertainty while others are much less concerned with predictability and certainty. You can probably think of people who are very uncomfortable in new situations or with people about whom they know little, as well as people who thrive in situations like that. Box 4.3 contains a scale to measure your own need for closure in relationships.

Uncertainty-oriented people are not afraid of uncertainty and, in fact, enjoy the opportunity to broaden their knowledge by seeking information regardless of whether it increases or decreases uncertainty. By contrast, certainty-oriented people are most comfortable in situations with little or no uncertainty, in which they can predict their behavior and that of others, and will find ways to ignore information that might increase uncertainty.

Studies have found that our uncertainty orientation influences us in a variety of ways. Not surprisingly, uncertainty-oriented individuals generally fare better than certainty-oriented ones in any situation of elevated uncertainty (Sorrentino, Short, & Raynor, 1984). The dating scene is full of uncertainty (What should I say? What does he mean? Does she like me? When should I call? Where should we go on the next date? When should I make my move?). As a result, if you are a certainty-oriented person, you probably are hesitant to initiate relationships with people and fare relatively poorly on first dates. But you also may be more satisfied in relationships than are uncertainty-oriented people. Certainty-oriented people have been shown to possess higher levels of trust for their partners (Sorrentino, Holmes, Hanna, & Sharp, 1995). Uncertainty-oriented people are adjusting their predictions about their partners with every new bit of information, which magnifies any inconsistency in the partner's behavior and hinders the achievement of complete trust in the partner. But certainty-oriented

BOX 4.3 PUT YOURSELF TO THE TEST

How Much Need for Closure Do You Have?

To determine your need for closure in relationships, mark the extent to which you agree or disagree with each of these statements using the following scale:
1 = Strongly disagree . . . 6 = Strongly agree

	Disagree				**Agree**	
1. I don't like situations that are uncertain. (A)	1	2	3	4	5	6
*2. I like to have friends who are unpredictable. (P)	1	2	3	4	5	6
3. When dining out, I like to go to places where I have been before so that I know what to expect. (P)	1	2	3	4	5	6
4. I feel uncomfortable when I don't understand why an event occurred in my life. (A)	1	2	3	4	5	6
5. I don't like to go into a situation without knowing what I can expect from it. (P)	1	2	3	4	5	6
6. When I am confused about an important issue, I feel very upset. (A)	1	2	3	4	5	6
*7. I think it is fun to change my plans at the last minute. (P)	1	2	3	4	5	6
*8. I enjoy the uncertainty of going into a new situation without knowing what might happen. (P)	1	2	3	4	5	6
9. In most social conflicts I can easily see which side is right and which is wrong. (A)	1	2	3	4	5	6
10. I don't like to be with people who are capable of unexpected actions. (P)	1	2	3	4	5	6
11. I prefer to socialize with familiar friends because I know what to expect from them. (P)	1	2	3	4	5	6
12. I like to know what people are thinking at all times. (A)	1	2	3	4	5	6
13. I dislike it when a person's statement could mean many different things. (A)	1	2	3	4	5	6
14. It's annoying to listen to someone who cannot seem to make up his or her mind. (A)	1	2	3	4	5	6
15. I feel uncomfortable when someone's meaning or intention is unclear to me. (A)	1	2	3	4	5	6
16. I'd rather know bad news than stay in a state of uncertainty. (A)	1	2	3	4	5	6
17. I dislike unpredictable situations. (P)	1	2	3	4	5	6

Add together the scores for the questions that are *not* asterisked. Then subtract the scores for the questions that are asterisked. The maximum score is 81, and the minimum score is −4. The closer you are to 81, the stronger your need for closure. The questions marked with a (P) measure your preference for predictability, whereas the items marked with an (A) measure your discomfort with ambiguity.

Source: The items in the scale are taken from Kruglanski, Webster, and Klem (1993).

people are not as concerned with every piece of information about the partner (they would rather ignore information that increases uncertainty, for example), so they find it easier to develop confidence in their partner.

So, who is better off in relationships—someone who can ignore inconsistent information, thus maintaining trust in his or her partner, or someone who is always trying to figure out his or her partner? Neither type of orientation seems to have a clear advantage. Because of their information vigilance, uncertainty-oriented people are more likely to detect changes in their partner's moods and to react accordingly. Their awareness of inconsistencies also means that they will likely discover more deceptions by their partner than will certainty-oriented people. But certainty-oriented people may have smoother, more stable relationships because of their relative disinterest in focusing on every piece of information about their partners.

In their research on monitoring by relational partners, Miller and her colleagues (Miller, 1987; Miller, Brody, & Summerton, 1988) have shown that some people tend to be information seekers (high monitors) and others information avoiders (low monitors). Most of their research has been conducted on health behavior. High monitors tend to be much more anxious in medical situations because they are always seeking information that might be threatening; low monitors tend to cope with stressful situations by distracting themselves and ignoring negative information. High monitors also tend to be more depressed and to visit physicians more often to seek information about illnesses. However, they tend to improve less rapidly because of the physiological effects of anxiety than do low monitors. In relationships we would expect monitors to exhibit greater anxiety and more distrust as well, just as uncertainty-oriented people do.

Expectancy Violations

As Berger (1979) suggested, behaviors that deviate from expectations are likely to increase a person's motivation to reduce uncertainty. This is because expectancy-violating behaviors make it more difficult for people to predict and explain someone's behavior. It is not surprising, then, that considerable research has been conducted on expectancy violations in both initial interactions and close relationships. In this section we discuss Burgoon's (1978; Burgoon & Hale, 1988) expectancy violations theory, as well as related research on expectancy violations in close relationships.

Expectancy Violations Theory

How do people react when they encounter unexpected behavior? Burgoon (1978; Burgoon & Hale, 1988; Burgoon, Stern, & Dillman, 1995) has attempted to answer this question by developing and testing **expectancy violations theory.** In its earliest form the theory focused on how people react to violations of personal space. Later, however, the theory was extended to encompass all types of behavioral violations, positive and negative. For example, a negative expectancy violation occurs when you expect your best friend to be smiling and happy for you when you win an award, but instead he or she frowns and looks envious. A negative expectancy violation also occurs when you expect someone to be honest and then you find out that she or he has lied to you. A positive expectancy violation occurs when you expect your significant other to be angry with you because you are late for a date, but instead he or she hugs you and expresses relief that you showed up. These examples show how commonplace expectancy violations are.

People build expectancies largely through interaction with others. In a sense, by observing and interacting with others, people reduce uncertainty about how these others behave under different circumstances. When uncertainty is reduced, an expectation is formed. These expectations can be either predictive or prescriptive. **Predictive expectancies** tell people what to expect in a given situation based on what normally occurs in that particular context and/or relationship (Burgoon et al., 1995). For example, if Sean always does the dishes at night after Larry cooks, Larry will be surprised to find a stack of dirty dishes sitting in the sink the morning after he cooked a special meal. Thus, predictive expectancies often are based on the norms or routines that typically occur within a given context and/or relationship. **Prescriptive expectancies,** by contrast, tell people what to expect based on general rules of appropriateness (Burgoon et al., 1995). For example, if you are driving during rush hour and let someone merge into your lane, you might expect the other driver to acknowledge your kind act by waving a friendly hand in your direction because that is what the rules of politeness demand. Similarly, you might expect your mom to hug you when she picks you up at the airport because that is how you think parents should greet their children.

According to expectancy violations theory, three factors affect expectancies: communicator characteristics, relational characteristics, and context. **Communicator characteristics** refer to individual differences, including age, sex, ethnic background, and personality traits. For instance, you might expect an elderly woman to be more polite than an adolescent boy, or you might expect your extroverted friend to be outgoing at a party and your introverted friend to be quiet and reserved. **Relational characteristics** refer to factors such as how close we are to someone, what type of relationship we share (platonic, romantic, business), and what types of experiences we have shared together. Hearing "I love you" from a romantic partner might be an expected behavior, but hearing the same words from a casual acquaintance might be highly unexpected. Similarly, certain types of intimate touch are usually expected in romantic relationships but not in platonic ones. Finally, **context** includes both the social situation and cultural influences. Clearly there are different behavioral expectations depending on the situation. For example, if you are in church attending a funeral, you expect people to act differently than if you were at the same church attending a wedding. Behavioral expectations may also shift depending on whether you are at work or out for a night on the town with friends. Similarly, expectations differ based on culture. For example, you might expect someone to greet you by kissing your face three times on alternating cheeks if you are in parts of Europe, but not if you are in the United States.

What happens when expectancies are violated? Maybe your platonic friend says "I love you" and touches you in an overly intimate fashion, or maybe you expect to be greeted affectionately by a European friend but the friend offers only a stiff handshake. According to expectancy violations theory, your response will be contingent on at least two factors: (1) the positive or negative interpretation of the behavior and (2) the rewardingness of the partner.

The Positive or Negative Interpretation of the Behavior   When unexpected events occur, people often feel heightened arousal and uncertainty, leading them to search for an explanation (Burgoon & Hale, 1988). To do this, people pay closer attention to their partner and the situation so that they can figure out what the unexpected behavior means. Eventually the unexpected behavior will be interpreted as positive or negative. As part of this process, the unexpected behavior is often compared to the expected behavior. When the unexpected behavior is perceived to be better than the expected behavior, a positive violation has occurred. By contrast, when the unexpected behavior is perceived to be worse than the expected behavior, a negative violation has occurred (Burgoon & Hale, 1988).

Floyd, Ramirez, and Burgoon (1998) gave a good example of how people's expectations affect whether they evaluate a behavior as positive or negative. They told the story of Louise, who dropped fairly obvious hints to her husband, Dan, that she wanted him to take her out to a fancy restaurant for her birthday. Because she had hinted so much, she felt certain that Dan would indeed take her someplace nice for her special day. In one scenario Dan gives Louise a birthday card, and they never go out to dinner. In this case a card falls short of Louise's expectations, leading to a negative violation. In the other scenario Dan tells Louise that he has booked them on a cruise to the Bahamas. In this case, even though Louise did not get what she expected, the cruise is likely to be perceived as an even better present than dinner out, leading to a positive violation.

As the example of Louise and Dan shows, expectancy violations can have positive or negative consequences for relationships. When positive violations occur, people are likely to be happier and more satisfied with their relationships. When negative violations occur, however, people might become angry and dissatisfied with their relationships (Burgoon et al., 1995; Levitt, 1991; Levitt, Coffman, Guacci-Franco, & Loveless, 1994).

The Rewardingness of the Partner   Sometimes people cannot determine the valence of a behavior simply by comparing the unexpected behavior to what they originally expected. This is because some behaviors are ambiguous; they can be positive in some circumstances and negative in others, depending on who enacts them. For example, imagine that you are working on a class project with several classmates. Because they are always together, you assume that two of the classmates, Terry and Alex, are a couple. However, Terry approaches you after the group meeting, smiles warmly, touches your arm, and asks you out on a date. You are surprised and ask, "Aren't you with Alex?" Terry replies, "Oh no, Alex and I are just really good friends."

How might you respond to Terry's unexpected behavior? The smile, touch, and request are not inherently positive or negative. Instead, the interpretation of these unexpected behaviors depends on how rewarding you perceive Terry to be. If you see Terry as attractive, charming, and intelligent, you likely will see the expectancy violation as positive and reciprocate by accepting the date. If, however, you see Terry as a deceitful person who is going behind Alex's back, you probably will see the expectancy violation as negative and refuse the date. In this case it is not the behavior per se that is positive or negative; instead, it is the combination of the behavior and the rewardingness of the partner.

Interestingly, research on expectancy violations theory has shown that nonrewarding communicators are evaluated the most highly if they stay within the norms and avoid violating expectations (Burgoon & Hale, 1988). For example, suppose you have to work on a project with a coworker whom you dislike. The two of you do not talk to each other much, but so far you have tried to keep your relationship civil. If the coworker suddenly starts asking you to go to lunch with her and telling you her life's story, you will probably evaluate her even more negatively because you will see her as pushy and overbearing. Similarly, if the coworker starts pointedly ignoring you and makes sarcastic remarks while you are speaking, you will likely evaluate her even more negatively as a mean, rude person. Notice that whether the expectancy violation involves behaviors that are more friendly or less friendly, you might still perceive the coworker negatively. This is because people tend to interpret unexpected behavior as consistent with their initial impressions of someone. To produce a more positive result, the coworker would probably be better off remaining civil and gradually becoming less distant. Such behavior would confirm your expectations and perhaps lay a foundation for a better relationship.

With rewarding communicators, however, expectancy violations theory suggests that positive expectancy violations actually produce better outcomes than expectancy-confirming behaviors (Burgoon & Hale, 1988; Burgoon et al., 1995). This can easily be seen in the Louise and Dan scenario presented earlier. If Dan had taken Louise out to dinner as she expected, she probably would have been happy and responded to him warmly and enthusiastically. But if Dan had booked a cruise instead, Louise likely would have been even happier. Thus, our behavior, as well as the emotions we feel, will be influenced by how positively or negatively we view an expectancy violation. When positive violations occur, people feel "bright emotions" such as joy, excitement, and relief. When expectancies are confirmed, people also feel bright emotions, but they are less intense. Finally, when negative violations occur, people feel "dark emotions," such as sadness, anger, and disappointment (see also Levitt, 1991). Positive violations are also met with reciprocity. In other words, the positive behavior that violated expectations will be met with positive behavior by the partner. So, when Dan shows Louise the tickets for the cruise, she is likely to show him affection by hugging and kissing him. That is, a positive behavior is met with a positive behavior.

Clearly, positive expectancy violations can be beneficial in close relationships even though they temporarily create uncertainty and reflect a lack of predictability. As Floyd et al. (1999) put it:

When unexpected events occur, . . . they force us to admit that our predictions were wrong and they can cause us to feel uncertain about the future. Expectancy violations theory concedes that expectancy violations often do produce more negative outcomes than expectancy confirmations. However, it parts ways with other theories by suggesting that, under certain circumstances, expectancy violations can produce outcomes that are actually more positive than those produced by expectancy confirmations. (p. 440)

Types of Expectancy Violations in Close Relationships

Given that expectancy violations can be beneficial or harmful to relationships, a sensible next question to ask is, Do certain behaviors tend to function as positive or negative expectancy violations in people's day-to-day relationships? In past research, such as that by Planalp and Honeycutt (1985), researchers focused primarily on negative events. Afifi and Metts (1998) extended this research by asking people in friendships and romantic relationships to think about the last time their friend or partner did or said something unexpected. They emphasized that the unexpected event could be either positive or negative. Participants reported on events that had occurred, on average, 5 days earlier. Some of the behaviors reported were relatively mundane, and others were quite serious. The outcome was a list of nine general categories of expectancy violations that commonly occur in relationships:

1. **Criticism or accusation:** actions that are critical of the person or that accuse her or him of some type of offense

2. **Relationship escalation:** actions that confirm or intensify the commitment of the person to the relationship, such as saying "I love you" or giving expensive gifts

3. **Relationship de-escalation:** actions that imply a desire to decrease the intimacy level in the relationship, such as reducing communication and spending more time apart

4. **Uncharacteristic relational behavior:** actions that are not consistent with the way the person defines the relationship, such as members of cross-sex friendships asking their supposedly platonic friend for a sexual relationship

5. **Uncharacteristic social behavior:** actions that do not have relational implications but that simply are not expected from that person in that context, such as a mild-mannered person raising his or her voice during an argument with a salesperson

6. **Transgressions:** actions that are violations of taken-for-granted rules of relationships, such as having an affair, being disloyal, sharing private information with other people, and being deceitful

7. **Acts of devotion:** actions that imply that the person really views the partner and/or the relationship as being special, such as going "above and beyond the call of duty" to help that individual through a difficult time

8. **Acts of disregard:** actions that imply that the person considers the partner and/or the relationship as unimportant, such as showing up late or being inconsiderate

9. **Gestures of inclusion:** actions that show an unexpected desire to include the partner in the person's activities or life, such as disclosing something very personal or extending an invitation to spend the holidays with his or her family

In addition to varying dramatically in terms of severity, these reported violations differed tremendously in the extent to which they were seen as positive or negative and, most importantly, the extent to which they increased or decreased uncertainty. Unlike earlier researchers, Afifi and Metts (1998) found that many expectancy violations *reduce* uncertainty by providing important information about the actor. In other words, apparently not all expectancy violations increase uncertainty, although certainly a good number do.

Conclusion

Uncertainty reduction plays an important role in the way people communicate with others. In initial interactions with strangers and acquaintances, people often feel a strong motivation to reduce uncertainty. Even in close, developed relationships, people sometimes feel strongly motivated to reduce uncertainty. People use a variety of strategies to try to reduce uncertainty. They might passively observe others, manipulate the social environment, question third parties, or interact directly with the person. In established relationships people also report using a variety of "secret tests" to help them determine how committed their partners are to the relationship.

Uncertainty reduction often leads to increased liking and attraction, especially when people discover positive information about others. However, in some cases uncertainty reduction can decrease attraction and liking. This most likely occurs when people uncover negative information about someone, such as finding out that a new friend has been deceptive or disloyal. In established relationships, too much uncertainty can lead to frustration and stress, whereas too little uncertainty can lead to boredom.

Expectancy violations also produce uncertainty. Interestingly, however, expectancy violations can be beneficial to relationships when they are interpreted positively. In other words, when unexpected behavior is perceived to be better than expected behavior, people experience positive outcomes despite the initial discomfort they might have felt at not being able to accurately predict their partner's behavior.

Collectively, the literature on uncertainty reduction suggests that people do indeed have a strong desire to reduce uncertainty and find out more about one another, especially in initial encounters. So, the next time you meet someone for the first time, think about the strategies you are both using to get to know each other. Chances are, like Cindy and Ryan at the beginning of this chapter, you will follow a fairly standard communication "script" that allows you to find out little bits of information about each other. Based on this information, you might decide that the person whom you have just met is someone you want to see in the future, or you might decide (as Cindy's boredom indicates she might) that a future relationship is not worth pursing. In either case, uncertainty reduction would play an important role in your decision.

Discussion Questions

1. According to uncertainty reduction theory, people are driven by the need to reduce uncertainty during initial encounters. Do you agree with this idea? Are there certain circumstances that make uncertainty reduction an especially salient goal?
2. Dialectics theory suggests that some level of uncertainty makes a relationship exciting. Do you agree or disagree?
3. Think about the last few times someone violated your expectations, either positively or negatively. Does expectancy violations theory help explain how you reacted to these expectancy violations? Why or why not?

Getting Closer

Initiating and Intensifying Relationships

Starting new relationships can be a wonderful, exciting, and almost magical enterprise. Whether it is being introduced to potential sorority sisters or fraternity brothers, starting a new job, or going on a first date, new relationships hold out the promise of relational opportunity, novelty, and connection. Of course, trying to start new relationships can also lead to an assortment of negative emotions, including anxiety, uncertainty, and embarrassment, especially if people worry about being rejected. It is no wonder, then, that relationship development has been of interest to communication researchers for decades. These researchers have tried to unlock the mysteries surrounding issues such as how people can best use communication to help them get closer to one another and why some people are better at developing close relationships than others.

In this chapter we discuss several different perspectives on relationship initiation and intensification. First, we address some of the barriers to initiating and/or intensifying relationships. Second, we examine the concept of self-disclosure. Many communication researchers believe that intimate self-disclosure, which involves sharing personal information with another person, is a basic requirement for relationship development. Third, we discuss two models of relationship development: Altman and Taylor's social penetration theory, and Knapp's coming-together stages. Finally, we discuss relational turning points, which are events associated with changes in the commitment level of a relationship.

Barriers to Initiating and/or Intensifying Relationships

Just as the beginning of a relationship can be wonderful, so, too, can it be awful. Some people have an easy time meeting others and developing satisfying relationships; other people have a hard time approaching people and developing intimate relations; and still others have no trouble initiating relationships but always seem to end up in "bad relationships."

Starting new relationships, or trying to make current relationships better, is no easy task. Considerable risk is involved. But the rewards of a new relational adventure can make these risks worth taking. There are some barriers, however, that make it more difficult for people to develop or intensify relationships. Therefore, it is important to study the forces that prevent relationships from developing, as well as those that propel relationships toward more intimacy. This is a relatively new area of research. As Baumeister, Wotman, and Stillwell (1993) argued, "Knowledge about relationships that fail to form and thrive has been relatively elusive" (p. 377). Thus far, at least three barriers to the initiation and intensification of relationships have been identified: (1) social anxiety, (2) rejection and unrequited love, and (3) interference or lack of opportunity.

Social Anxiety

Individual personalities have a major effect on how people approach new relationships. For example, extraverts and sensation seekers are more willing to take risks during initial encounters, probably because they focus on positive outcomes. For extraverts, new relationships mean excitement, happiness, passion, adventure, and the like. By contrast, shy and introverted individuals are likely to focus on the negative outcomes that might occur as a consequence of approaching others. For shy individuals the fear of rejection may dominate, with emotions such as anxiety, apprehension, embarrassment, and shame surfacing. Research also suggests that people labeled as "fearful-avoidant" hesitate to become involved in new relationships because they have been hurt or rejected in the past, leading to low self-esteem and a generally negative attitude toward relationships (Bartholomew, 1990).

When people are extremely shy and/or fearful-avoidant, they experience high levels of self-consciousness and tension when approaching new people and new social situations (Andersen, 1999; Andersen & Guerrero, 1989), leading to the **withdrawal response.** The withdrawal response causes shy and apprehensive people to avoid social situations such as attending parties or going out with a group of new acquaintances. For example, if Colin is shy and his friend Mark asks him to go camping with a bunch of people he doesn't know well, Colin is likely to decline Mark's invitation. He would prefer staying at home to spending an uncertain weekend with Colin's friends. Sometimes, however, apprehensive individuals cannot avoid social situations. In these cases the withdrawal response dictates that they minimize their presence by remaining apart from others, engaging in relatively low levels of eye contact, and failing to participate fully in interactions. So, if Mark was able to talk Colin into going camping, Colin would be unlikely to do much talking as they sat around the campfire roasting marshmallows and telling ghost stories.

Shy or apprehensive people also tend to focus on their own feelings of self-consciousness rather than trying to understand the people around them (Andersen, 1999). For example, rather than laughing spontaneously at the funny joke they just heard, they might be thinking about whether it would be appropriate to laugh. This type of intense, anxious self-focus results in a negative cycle: Anxiety leads to reduced social information, which leads to incompetent interpersonal behavior, which produces negative reactions from others, which then produces even more anxiety in the shy or apprehensive person (Segrin, 1998). Although most people feel at least some anxiety and self-consciousness in new interpersonal situations, these feelings overwhelm shy and apprehensive individuals, making it more difficult for them to develop new relationships.

Rejection and Unrequited Love

Sometimes shy and apprehensive people think that others will reject them even though this fear is unwarranted. Other times, however, this fear of rejection is highly warranted. Such is the case with unrequited love, whereby one person (the would-be lover) wants to initiate or intensify a romantic relationship, but the other person (the rejector) does not (Baumeister et al., 1993; Baumeister & Wotman, 1992; Bratslavsky, Baumeister, & Sommer, 1998). Unrequited love can characterize several types of situations. Sometimes the two people do not know one another well; other times they may be good friends but one person wants to intensify the relationship further and the other person does not; still other times unrequited love occurs in the initial stages of a relationship. For example, after going on a few dates, one of the dating partners may fall in love but the other might want to stop dating altogether.

When unrequited love is suspected, the would-be lover has two options: (1) to keep quiet about his or her feelings or (2) to try to win the partner's love (Baumeister et al., 1993). Either way, there are considerable risks for the would-be lover. On the one hand, approaching the loved one could lead to rejection, humiliation, or, in the case of an established friendship, the de-escalation or termination of the relationship. On the other hand, keeping quiet could cost the person any opportunity to win the other person over. The popular television series *Frasier* gave examples of both these options. Niles had been in love with Daphne for 6 years but had never disclosed his true feelings to her. When Daphne met another man (who ironically was introduced to her by Niles), they went through a whirlwind romance that led to a marriage proposal. When Daphne accepted the proposal, Niles was left wondering whether it would have been better to speak up about his feelings for Daphne. Eventually Niles told Daphne he loved her, and by doing so he won her over.

Of course, in real life a confession of love is sometimes met with rejection. When this happens, the situation can be difficult for both the rejector and the would-be lover. Although it is flattering to be the object of someone's affection, the rejector often feels guilty for being unable to return the would-be lover's sentiments. If the would-be lover is persistent in his or her pursuit, the rejector may feel frustrated and even victimized (Baumeister et al., 1993). In fact, Baumeister and his colleagues found that rejectors often report experiencing more negative emotions than do would-be lovers. According to their research, would-be lovers perceive the situation as having either extremely positive or negative outcomes, whereas most rejectors perceive only negative outcomes.

Unrequited love may also be a particularly challenging situation for the rejector because the communication script is unclear. In other words, it is difficult to find a way to reject the would-be lover's advances without hurting her or his feelings. Would-be lovers, by contrast, have a much clearer script for how to behave. As Baumeister et al. (1993) put it:

> The would-be lover's script is affirmed and reiterated from multiple sources; for example, one can probably hear a song about unrequited love in almost any American house within an hour, simply by turning on the radio. A seemingly endless stream of books and movies has portrayed aspiring lovers persisting doggedly to win the hearts of their beloveds. Many techniques are portrayed as eventually effective. If one is rejected in the end, the familiar script calls for heartbroken lovers to express their grief, perhaps assign blame, accept the failure, and then go on with their lives. (p. 379)

The rejector, however, does not have a clearly defined cultural prescription for how to deal with the would-be lover. Movies and novels often portray rejectors as "aloof, casual, teasing, or sadistic heartbreakers," but most rejectors are actually quite concerned with helping the would-be lover save face (Baumeister et al., 1993, p. 391). Thus, many rejectors initially resist making harsh declarations such as "I'm not attracted to you" and instead rely on more polite or indirect communication strategies, such as saying that they value the friendship too much to ruin it by pursuing a romantic relationship or that they are too busy to date anyone at this time. Folkes (1982) found that rejectors tend to keep the real reasons for their refusal to date hidden and instead try to let the other person down easily.

Of course, the problem with polite or indirect messages is that they can be misinterpreted (Cupach & Metts, 1991). Rejectors may feel that they have delivered the message, albeit nicely, while would-be lovers may cling to the hope that, since the rejector did not dismiss them directly, an intensified relationship is still possible. For example, would-be lovers who receive a message such as "I'm not interested in dating anyone right now, but I really value you as a friend" might hear this as "There might be a chance of a love relationship in the future since I like and value you." When the would-be lover continues to pursue a relationship, the rejector may wonder what she or he has to do or say to get the message of disinterest across. The rejector may resort to harsher and more direct messages, with strategies becoming increasingly direct if the would-be lover persists (Metts, Sprecher, & Regan, 1998). Indeed, Trost's (1997; Trost & Gabrielidis, 1994) research suggests that people use a variety of strategies to reject romance, with some strategies more direct than others; Box 5.1 lists these strategies. When clear sexual advances are made, women are likely to be verbally direct, and most men accept their refusals (Metts et al., 1998).

Unrequited love is a prime example of how it takes two people to develop a relationship. If one person is not interested, the relationship cannot flourish. Of course, this problem is not limited to romantic relationships. Sometimes the colleague we want to get to know better does not want to get to know us, or the person we would like to be friends with rejects us. In fact, most of us can probably remember times in middle or high school when we wanted to be friends with a certain group of people but were not readily accepted. These

BOX 5.1 HIGHLIGHTS

Common Strategies Used to Reject Romantic Advances

Strategy	Men	Women
Nonverbal Regulation	54.3%	68.5%
Ignoring the person		
Maintaining large distances		
Acting cold or casual		
Passively exhibiting wedding rings		
Acting nervous and uneasy		
Direct Notification	31.4	68.5
Telling the would-be lover that you are not interested		
Saying that you only want to be friends		
Talking about a current partner and/or relationship		
Conversation Regulation	42.9	35.2
Leaving the encounter		
Lying about involvement with someone else		
Keeping the conversation superficial		
Being blunt or rude		
Polite/Smoothing Strategies	25.7	25.9
Acting polite and grateful for compliments		
Saving face for the would-be lover		
Flirting with the person even if not interested		

Note: Percentages represent the number of men and women who reported using each type of strategy.

Source: Trost and Gabrielidis (1994).

types of situations illustrate the sad but true fact that, while it takes two people to develop a relationship, it only takes one to end it or to prevent it from developing in the first place.

Interference and Lack of Opportunity

As discussed in Chapter 3, proximity and the perceived elusiveness of a partner can be powerful bases of attraction. People generally are attracted to those with whom they are in close proximity and have repeated interaction. This helps explain why people who work for the same organization, live on the same street, have the same major, or belong to the same church or club often become friends or romantic partners. The proximity associated with these situations gives people an opportunity to get to know one another better (Brehm, 1992).

In addition, people who are in close proximity often have a lot in common, making it easier to initiate conversations. For example, students who have the same major might break the ice by talking about common classes, and members of the Sierra Club can approach one another and begin talking about their environmental concerns.

Sometimes, however, the opportunity to interact with a socially and/or physically appealing person is not there. For example, you might meet someone briefly, be very attracted to the person, and then never see her or him again. Long distances can also impede the intensification of relationships. You can probably recall instances in your own life when this happened. Perhaps you vowed to stay close to the new friend you met at summer camp, but gradually the letters and phone calls lessened and you lost contact. You might also remember friends from grade school or high school whom you meant to keep in touch with but no longer even know how to contact. Of course, the progress of romantic relationships also can be impeded by distance and lack of opportunity.

Interference from others is yet another impediment to the development of close relationships. As mentioned in Chapter 3, people are often attracted to those who are hard to get. Sometimes people are hard to get to know because other people interfere with the relationship. For example, the Romeo and Juliet effect is based on the idea that, when romantic partners face obstacles, such as parental disapproval of their relationship, they will be even more attracted to each other and work harder to maintain the relationship (Driscoll, Davis, & Lipetz, 1972). This can be hard to do, however. It is difficult to sustain close relationships without the support of one's social network. Think about times when your social network (perhaps your best friend or family members) disliked a potential or actual romantic partner. This probably put considerable strain on your relationships with the members of your social network, as well as with the romantic partner. Interference also occurs when a desired romantic partner is already in a relationship with someone else and when a potential friend or romantic partner is too involved in other aspects of his or her life (such as passing the bar exam, planning a wedding, or working overtime on an important project) to spend time developing a relationship.

Self-Disclosure

Once people overcome these barriers, they still must get to know one another better if the relationship is to progress and they are to become closer. Communication is the primary vehicle for achieving such closeness. In fact, much of the research on relationship development has examined how a specific type of communication—self-disclosure—helps people move from being strangers to being close friends or lovers. **Self-disclosure** occurs when people reveal something about themselves to others. Some self-disclosure, such as talking about where you grew up or what your major is, is fairly impersonal; other self-disclosure, such as talking about your future hopes and childhood insecurities, is much more intimate. As relationships develop, communication typically is characterized by increases in intimate self-disclosure. This is not to say that other forms of communication are unimportant. Affectionate displays of nonverbal communication, such as loving gazes and comforting touches, can also help people develop their relationships, as can other forms of verbal communication, such as specialized and/or intimate nicknames such as "honeybunch" or "sweetheart." Most research, however, has concentrated on self-disclosure. This is probably because people typically increase self-disclosure before they begin using intimate forms of nonverbal communication, such as touch, and other forms of intimate verbal communication, such as calling each other by pet names.

Dimensions of Self-Disclosure

One of the first theoretical explorations of self-disclosure was developed by Altman and Taylor (1973). According to **social penetration theory,** self-disclosure usually increases gradually as people develop their relationships. Altman and Taylor suggested that self-disclosure can be conceptualized in terms of three dimensions: depth, breadth, and frequency. Depth refers to how personal or deep the communication is, breadth to how many topics a person feels free to discuss, and frequency to how often self-disclosure occurs. Various types of encounters can be characterized differently based on these three dimensions. For example, when you have to work on a class project with someone you don't know well, you might talk a lot about school (a fairly superficial topic) but not about much else. However, you might need to get together with this person frequently in order to complete the class assignment. Your self-disclosure with this person could be described as low in depth and breadth but high in frequency. Of course, if you started to develop a close relationship with your classmate, the depth and breadth of your self-disclosure would probably increase, so that you'd be talking about more varied and more personal topics in addition to discussing the class assignment.

As relationships develop, they tend to increase in depth and breadth. In fact, according to social penetration theory, it is helpful to visualize the process of self-disclosure during relationship development as the slow unpeeling of an onion, as Figure 5.1 shows. An onion has a rather thin and flimsy outer layer, but as you peel through the various layers, they get harder, with the core of the onion very tightly bound. Similarly, Altman and Taylor (1973) suggested that there are three basic layers of self-disclosure: (1) a superficial layer that is easy to penetrate, (2) a social or personal layer that is easy for most friends, family members, and lovers to penetrate, and (3) a very intimate layer, or core, that is seldom revealed, and then only to people whom we trust completely.

At the superficial layer people reveal commonplace facts about themselves that are not threatening in any way. For example, telling someone your name, major, hometown, zodiac sign, and favorite color are benign self-disclosures. At the social/personal level people typically reveal more about their likes and dislikes, and hopes and fears, but they still keep their deepest hopes and fears a secret. For example, you might tell most of your friends that you'd like to

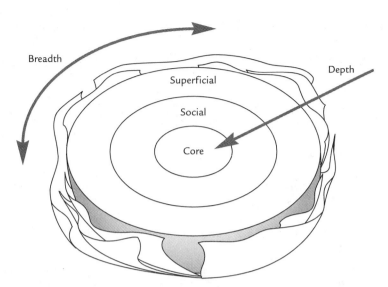

Breadth

Depth

Superficial

Social

Core

FIGURE 5.1 Depth and Breadth of Self-Disclosure Depth increases as people disclose about more intimate topics, while breadth increases as people talk about a wider range of topics. Different topics can be thought of as occupying different "wedges" of the onion.

marry a certain kind of person, that you had an unhappy childhood, or that you are worried about getting a good job when you graduate from college. But you might not tell them all the intimate details related to these topics. At the core people share all the personal details that make them who they are. Within the core are people's most secret, intimate feelings. For example, you might disclose negative childhood experiences that you would normally prefer not to think about, and you might confess all of your fears and insecurities about succeeding in your chosen profession. You might also reveal intimate, positive feelings about people by telling them how much they mean to you and how lost you would be without them.

In addition to depth, breadth, and frequency, research has uncovered two other dimensions relevant to self-disclosure: valence and duration (Gilbert, 1976; Tolstedt & Stokes, 1984). Although these two dimensions were not mentioned in the original social penetration theory, they appear to be critical for understanding the type of self-disclosure that characterizes a relationship.

Valence refers to the positive or negative "charge" of the self-disclosure. For example, if you disclose your dreams, your warm feelings for someone, or your happiest childhood memories, the self-disclosure has a positive valence. By contrast, if you disclose your fears, your hostile feelings for someone, or your unhappiest childhood memories, the self-disclosure has a negative valence. Valence is a crucial dimension of self-disclosure because it helps determine how people feel about one another. Think about friends who call you all the time to complain about their lives. Their self-disclosure might be full of breadth and depth, but instead of feeling closer to your friend, you might end up feeling depressed and want to avoid such conversations in the future. Similarly, some research has shown that couples show an increase in depth of self-disclosure when they are continually arguing or when their relationship is in decline (Tolstedt & Stokes, 1984). The types of comments they typically make, however, are negatively valenced ("I wish I'd never met you," "Why don't you ever listen to me?" "You make me feel unimportant"). Thus, high depth alone does not tell the whole story. Depth and valence work together to create the emotional climate of a self-disclosure. Of course, some negatively valenced self-disclosure can draw people closer. For example, when two individuals feel comfortable enough to reveal their deepest fears, worst failures, and most embarrassing moments, they probably have developed a particularly close relationship. The key is to limit the number of negatively valenced disclosures relative to the number of more positively valenced disclosures.

The other new dimension relevant to self-disclosure is duration, which reflects *how long* two people spend disclosing in a single conversation rather than *how often* they disclose (frequency). It is possible for people to have self-disclosures of limited frequency but long duration. A common example of this is the "stranger on the plane" (or train) phenomenon. When you sit down next to someone on a plane, you might chat with her or him for the entire duration of the flight. You might even disclose intimate details about your life to your seatmate, figuring that you probably won't see her or him again, so you are not really making yourself vulnerable. Thus, it is the limited frequency of the interaction that allows you to confidently engage in self-disclosure that is high in both depth and duration. In other cases you might have frequent self-disclosure with someone, but it usually is short in duration. For example, you might talk with a coworker every day, but only for limited amounts of time during a coffee break.

Risks Associated with Self-Disclosure

Disclosing personal and intimate information can be risky. When we tell other people our innermost thoughts and feelings, we become vulnerable and open ourselves up to criticism. Several scholars have used a dialectical perspective to explain the costs and benefits of self-disclosure (Baxter & Montgomery, 1996; Petronio, 2000; Rosenfeld, 2000). According to this perspective, people have opposing needs in their relationships. For example, Terrell might want to spend a lot of time with Monique, but he might also want to spend time alone and with his friends. Such opposing needs can cause tension (see Chapter 9). When self-disclosure is considered, scholars adopting a dialectical perspective have noted that people have strong needs for both openness and secrecy. As Rosenfeld (2000) put it:

> I want to be open because I want to share myself with others and get the benefits of such communication, such as receiving social support, the opportunity to think out loud, and the chance to get something off my chest. I do not want to be open because I might be ridiculed, rejected, or abandoned. Open or closed; let others in

or keep others out? Every interaction has the potential for raising the tension of holding both desires simultaneously. It is not that one desire "wins" and the other "loses." Rather, they exist simultaneously. Interpersonal life consists of the tension between these opposites. (p. 4)

Consistent with the dialectical perspective, scholars have delineated several risks associated with self-disclosure. One of the most comprehensive of these lists was compiled by Hatfield (1984), who argued that people avoid intimate self-disclosure for at least six different reasons: (1) fear of exposure, (2) fear of abandonment, (3) fear of angry attacks, (4) fear of loss of control, (5) fear of their own destructive impulses, and (6) fear of losing their individuality.

Fear of Exposure   Sometimes people worry that too much self-disclosure will expose their negative qualities and cause others to think badly of them or to like them less. For example, people might not want others to learn that they acted unethically or once had a problem with drugs. As the saying goes, "Some things are better left unsaid." As Hatfield (1984) put it, "One reason, then, that all of us are afraid of intimacy, is that those we care most about are bound to discover all that is wrong with us—to discover that we possess taboo feelings . . . have done things of which we are deeply ashamed" (p. 210).

Fear of Abandonment   The possibility of negative exposure can lead to the second fear—the fear of abandonment. Here people worry that, if others get to know them too well and start to like them less, they will reject or abandon them. Hatfield (1984) gave an excellent example of the fear of abandonment by telling the story of a graduate student with whom she had worked. This young European woman was beautiful, intelligent, and charming; in fact, many men were madly in love with her. Of course, she was not perfect—she had her insecurities and self-doubts, just as all of us do. But she put on a bright, charming facade in order to fit the perfect image that people had of her. The problem, however, was that, whenever she got close enough to a man to admit her insecurities, she fell off the pedestal that he had put her on. It was impossible to meet all of the high expectations of these men. When the perfect image was shattered, they lost interest and abandoned her.

Fear of Angry Attacks   People also worry that their partners might use what they disclose against them. For example, you might worry that your relational partner will retaliate if you confess to a one-night stand, admit telling a lie, or recount happy experiences you had with a former relational partner. Sometimes people even use the intimate information we share with them as ammunition against us. For example, if you ask a colleague to help you with something you do not understand, you might worry that, when it comes time for a promotion decision to be made, the coworker will tell others that you are incompetent. If you tell your best friend that you sometimes only pretend to pay attention to people, your friend might later accuse you of being selfish and of not really listening when he or she is disclosing personal problems.

Fear of Loss of Control   People also worry that if they engage in too much self-disclosure, they won't be able to control their thoughts and feelings or the thoughts and feelings of others. For example, Zachary may worry that, if he tells Brianna how much he cares for her, he will express his feelings too strongly, and perhaps scare her away. Similarly, Carl may worry that, if he tells his best friend how he feels about his recent relational breakup, he will lose control and start crying. Hatfield (1984) argued that these kinds of fear are more problematic for men than women: "Traditionally, men are supposed to be in control—of themselves, of other people, and of the situation" (p. 211). People may also fear losing control of information, especially if they think that the person to whom they disclose to might share the information with others (Phillips & Metzger, 1976). Additionally, people may worry that if they disclose personal weaknesses to their partner, they will lose their ability to influence the partner (Petronio, 1991).

Fear of Destructive Impulses   Sometimes people worry that self-disclosure might lead them to react in negative ways that could hurt themselves or others. For example, Pablo might decide to admire Gina from afar rather than confessing his feelings of love for her. Pablo might feel a sense of security in loving Gina from a distance rather than risking rejection. He might also fear that if he discloses his feelings and she rejects him, he will become so distraught that he will hurt himself or her. People also may avoid self-disclosure when they suspect that it will cause conflict or that in the heat of an argument they might say things that are destructive to the relationship.

Fear of Losing Individuality   Some people fear losing their personal identity and being engulfed by the relationship. According to Hatfield (1984), one of the "most primitive fears of intimacy" is that we could "literally disappear" if we become too engulfed in a relationship (p. 212). Consistent with the dialectical perspective, this fear represents the push and pull that many people feel between the competing forces of wanting to be closely connected to others and wanting to be independent and self-sufficient. The idea here is that, if we tell people too much about ourselves, they will know us so well that we risk losing our uniqueness and mysteriousness. Moreover, if we maintain high levels of self-disclosure, we may come to a point where there is nothing left to share. In this case, we may feel that we are part of a group or dyad, rather than a unique individual with some private, secret thoughts and feelings. We may even feel a need to "escape" from our relational partner in order to find privacy and assert our independence.

Self-Disclosure and Liking

Because self-disclosure comes with considerable risk yet also draws people together, the act of self-disclosure conveys both trust and closeness. Thus, according to social penetration theory, self-disclosure typically increases gradually as people get to know, like, and trust one another. If people do not develop trust or liking, self-disclosure will not progress very far, and the relationship will stagnate or terminate.

Many studies have examined the relationship between self-disclosure and liking. In a statistical review of 94 studies, Collins and Miller (1994) tested the **disclosure-liking hypothesis,** which predicts that, when a sender discloses to a receiver, the receiver will like the sender more. Collins and Miller's statistical review supported the disclosure-liking hypothesis, although this relationship appears to be stronger among acquaintances than strangers. Collins and Miller's statistical review also supported the **liking-disclosure hypothesis,** which predicts that people will disclose more to receivers they like. Thus, you are more likely to disclose to close relational partners and to people to whom you are attracted than to people you dislike.

In some cases, however, high levels of self-disclosure are not related to liking. Derlega, Metts, Petronio, and Margulis (1993) suggested that there are three reasons for this. First, when self-disclosure violates normative expectations, it will not lead to liking. Sometimes people disclose too much information too quickly, or they disclose negative information that leads others to dislike them (Bochner, 1982; Parks, 1982). As Derlega and colleagues observed, "Highly personal, negative disclosure given too soon inhibits liking unless some strong initial attraction already exists" (p. 31). Second, self-disclosure is a better predictor of liking when receivers think that the sender only discloses information to certain special people. If senders are perceived to disclose information indiscriminately, the self-disclosure may be seen as less valuable, and liking may not result. Third, "disclosure will not lead to liking if it is responded to in a negative manner" (Derlega et al., 1993, p. 32). If a sender discloses sensitive information and the receiver dismisses the information or responds in an unkind or critical manner, both sender and receiver are likely to feel negatively about the interaction and about each other. Usually, however, receivers match the intimacy level of a sender's self-disclosure. Box 5.2 gives examples of the relationship between self-disclosure and liking.

Reciprocity of Self-Disclosure

For relationships to flourish in the initial stages, self-disclosure must also be reciprocated. Considerable research has focused on the reciprocity or matching of self-disclosure, starting with Jourard's (1959, 1964) pioneering work on patterns of self-disclosure. Jourard believed that reciprocal self-disclosure, which he termed the **dyadic effect,** is the vehicle by which people build close relationships (see also Altman & Taylor, 1973; Gouldner, 1960). Reciprocal self-disclosure occurs when one person reveals information and his or her partner responds by offering information that is at a similar level of intimacy. For example, if Kayla tells Samantha about her secret career ambitions, Samantha might respond by sharing her future career goals and plans. Jourard's work suggests that self-disclosure usually begets more self-disclosure. In other words, people are likely to respond to high levels of self-disclosure by revealing similarly personal information. Of course, there are exceptions to this rule. For example, you might

---

BOX 5.2 HIGHLIGHTS

Examples of Relationships Between Liking and Disclosure

The Disclosure-Liking Hypothesis: Disclosure Leads to Liking

Wendy and Karen pair up to work on a school project. Although they have had a few classes together, they don't know each other well. However, one evening, after working on their project, they start talking about personal issues. Wendy tells Karen about her long-distance relationship with her boyfriend and confesses to really missing him. Karen tells Wendy about her 3-year-old son and confesses that it is difficult to concentrate on school when she is so busy as a single mom. The two women feel a new sense of connection to each other.

The Liking-Disclosure Hypothesis: Liking Leads to Disclosure

Patrick really likes his new neighbor, Spencer, who seems friendly, funny, and easygoing. Once in a while when they run into each other before work, Spencer tells Patrick a joke and makes him laugh. One day, Patrick wins a prestigious award at work. He doesn't talk about the award much at work because he does not want to appear boastful or conceited. But when he comes home after work, he sees Spencer out mowing his lawn. Spencer waves, and Patrick strides over to tell him the good news. Spencer shuts off the lawn mower, and the two men start to talk.

Too Much Disclosure Too Early Can Lead to Disliking

Tanya and Joel are on a first date. They go out to dinner at a fancy restaurant and engage in chit-chat. About halfway through dinner, Joel starts telling Tanya his life story. He starts by telling her about how he was an unpopular kid in elementary school. Then he talks about how his dog died when he was 10 years old. He is just starting to get into the adoles-

cent years when the waiter arrives to see if they want dessert. Tanya says she is full and asks the waiter to bring the check, hoping that she can get out of the restaurant before Joel starts talking about his first sexual experiences.

Indiscriminant Disclosure Is Less Likely to Lead to Liking

Travis and Angela meet at a company party. Angela tells Travis about her dreams and career aspirations. She tells him, "I wouldn't tell just anyone this, but my secret ambition is to be a rock star. I know it is silly and probably will never happen, but it would be so much fun to turn on the radio and hear myself singing." Later she says, "Don't tell anyone, but I might be leaving the firm to concentrate on a possible music career." Travis feels honored that Angela told him these things until he runs into a coworker who says, "Hey, I saw you talking to that woman who wants to be a rock star. She's been saying she's going to quit for the last year. I doubt she ever will." Suddenly, Travis doesn't feel special anymore.

Negative Responses to Disclosure Reduce Liking

Amy's sister has been dating Tyler for several months. Amy is very close to her sister and would like to get to know Tyler better. One day, at a family picnic, Amy approaches Tyler and says, "Hello." She asks him how he has been. He says, "Fine," and looks away from Amy and out at the lake. Undaunted, Amy continues the conversation: "My sister tells me that you just got a big promotion at work. What will you be doing?" "More of the same," he says, still looking at the lake. Amy tells him about her job, but he doesn't seem interested. Eventually, Amy gives up and walks away, wondering what her sister could possibly see in him.

not want to continue a conversation with someone because you don't want to "lead the person on," or you might decide that the other person's level of self-disclosure is inappropriate and makes you uncomfortable. In these cases you are less likely to reciprocate self-disclosure.

Nonetheless, research suggests that people typically feel a natural pull toward matching the level of intimacy and intensity present in their conversational partner's self-disclosure. In a statistical review of 67 studies involving 5,173 participants, Dindia and Allen (1995) concluded that the evidence overwhelmingly supports the tendency for people to reciprocate self-disclosure. Studies have shown that people typically match the intimacy level of their conversational partner's self-disclosure regardless of the context (face-to-face versus via telephone), the type of relationship (strangers versus intimates), or the amount of liking or disliking (Derlega, Harris, & Chaikin, 1973; Hosman & Tardy, 1980; Janofsky, 1971; Levinger & Senn, 1967). Research also suggests that individuals who violate the norm of reciprocity are perceived as cold, incompetent, unfriendly, and untrustworthy (Bradac, Hosman, & Tardy, 1978; Chaikin & Derlega, 1974).

There are two primary theoretical explanations for the dyadic effect (Davis & Skinner, 1974; Rubin, 1974). According to the **social exchange explanation,** when self-disclosure is reciprocated it is rewarding because it reflects mutual trust and liking. However, unreciprocated self-disclosure is costly because it unnecessarily makes a communicator vulnerable (Altman & Taylor, 1973; Hatfield, 1984). As Hendrick (1981) argued, "Self disclosure can be seen as something that has both costs and benefits" (p. 1150). To balance these costs and benefits, individuals can respond to intimate self-disclosure by engaging in a similarly rewarding level of intimate verbal communication that signals trust and liking. As Derlega et al. (1993) put it, reciprocity helps "equalize both the rewards and the risks of self-disclosure" (p. 33). Indeed, research has shown that moderate to moderately high levels of positive self-disclosure are perceived as the most rewarding (see Gilbert, 1976; Gilbert & Horenstein, 1975) and that moderately intimate self-disclosure is most likely to be reciprocated (VanLear, 1987). Therefore, the highest levels of reciprocity may occur when the disclosure is the most rewarding.

The **uncertainty reduction/modeling explanation** predicts that people will feel high levels of uncertainty during initial interactions (see Berger & Calabrese, 1975; see also Chapter 4). Because of this uncertainty, individuals pay attention to their partner's behavior to determine the most appropriate way to respond. If one partner initiates intimate self-disclosure, the other will likely follow suit in an effort to be socially appropriate. Thus, dyadic partners are likely to model each other's behavior. Recall that, according to uncertainty reduction theory (Berger & Calabrese, 1975), high levels of uncertainty also lead to information seeking and reciprocity as conversational partners strive to learn more about each other. Once uncertainty is reduced, the need to seek information decreases, as does reciprocity. Thus, the uncertainty reduction/modeling explanation may work best when applied to initial interactions. The social exchange explanation, by contrast, may explain the dyadic effect in both initial and developed relationships.

It is also important to note that reciprocity may be delayed in long-term, close relationships. For example, a husband might disclose his social anxieties to his wife, who simply listens patiently. Subsequently, the wife might reciprocate by sharing some of her deepest fears while the husband assumes the listening role. In initial encounters between people, future interaction is often uncertain so immediate reciprocity is more important.

Not surprisingly, research has also shown that partners who believe they reciprocate self-disclosure tend to be more satisfied with their relationships, particularly when the self-disclosure is positively valenced (Chelune, Rosenfeld, & Waring, 1985; Gouldner, 1960; Rosenfeld & Welsh, 1985; Webb, 1972). Studies have found that spouses are usually dissatisfied with their relationships when there is a large discrepancy between the amount of personal information they share with their partner and the amount of personal information they receive from their partner (Davidson, Balswick, & Halverson, 1983; Hansen & Schuldt, 1984). Similarly, Afifi, Guerrero, and Egland (1994) found that perceived reciprocity of self-disclosure was the main predictor of relational closeness for male friends. These studies showed that self-disclosure is important not only in building relationships but also in maintaining them.

Stage Theories of Relationship Development

As you might suspect, self-disclosure, along with other patterns of communication, changes as a relationship progresses. Indeed, much of the research on relationship development focuses on the stages of people's relationships. In this section we look at two popular stage theories of relational development. Both theories focus on how communication changes as people move from being strangers to being intimates.

Social Penetration Theory

To map out the progression of self-disclosure, Altman and Taylor (1973) described four stages that people can go through as they progress from being strangers to being intimates; Figure 5.2 shows the stages. As discussed earlier, social penetration theory originally focused specifically on how the dimensions of depth, breadth, and frequency change; more recent research suggests that valence and duration may also change as relationships move through the different stages.

Stage 1: Orientation   This stage occurs the first time people meet and sometimes lasts for two or three more encounters, particularly if each meeting is short in duration. The orientation stage involves low levels of depth and breadth. The two people do not know each other, so they stay at the superficial level of the self-disclosure "onion" (see Figure 5.1). This helps them avoid becoming vulnerable. Bits of information, such as one's name, occupation, or

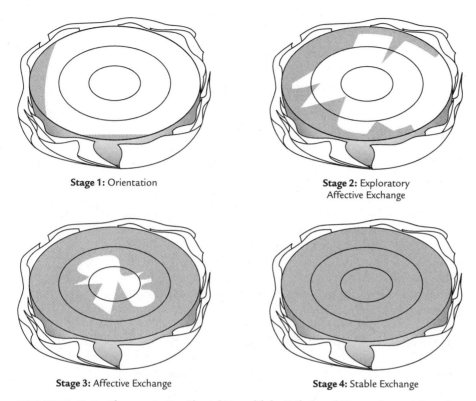

Stage 1: Orientation

Stage 2: Exploratory Affective Exchange

Stage 3: Affective Exchange

Stage 4: Stable Exchange

FIGURE 5.2 Changes in Depth and Breadth by Relational Stage *Source:* Adapted from Altman and Taylor (1973).

major, may be exchanged in an effort to reduce uncertainty. The valence of the disclosure is usually positive, with participants trying to make a good impression by following rules of social politeness.

Most initial encounters are characterized by disclosure that is low in depth and breadth, and positive in valence. There are exceptions, however. One is the stranger-on-the-plane (or train) phenomenon mentioned earlier. This type of situation is special because of the potential for high duration and low frequency. In other words, we do not expect to see the other person again. And if we do see the other person sometime in the future, we might feel uncomfortable about the depth and breadth of our self-disclosure. For example, there is a scene in an old movie in which two people meet on a train. The woman is heading to the West Coast to marry her long-time boyfriend, but she has started to doubt her feelings for her fiancé. She discloses her misgivings to the stranger on the train, confessing that she thinks she is only going along with the marriage because the relationship is old and comfortable, and that she no longer loves her fiancé. Later in the movie, the stranger on the train appears again—as her fiancé's best man! Needless to say, she is extremely embarrassed and uncomfortable. Another exception to the orientation stage's general pattern of low breadth and depth is a first session between counselor and client. Often the client will discuss his or her problems and concerns in great depth because the environment is considered safe and the counselor is a professional.

Stage 2: Exploratory Affective Exchange This stage is typical of acquaintances, casual friends, and casual daters. Sometimes people move beyond this stage and develop closer relationships; other times they stay at this stage and simply remain acquaintances or casual friends. The exploratory affective exchange stage is characterized by increasing breadth and frequency but relatively low depth of self-disclosure (Altman & Taylor, 1973). In other words, people in this stage will "explore" potential topics by increasing breadth. For instance, they might touch on a variety of subjects, ranging from sports, to politics, to adventures with family and friends. However, they will not delve too deeply into any of these topics. They might explain that they have a particularly good relationship with one parent but not the other, but they won't give a lot of emotional detail about their innermost feelings about either parent. The valence of the disclosure is still usually much more positive than negative because people are trying to maintain positive impressions as they get to know one another (Guerrero & Andersen, 2000).

Increasing the breadth of self-disclosure can help a relationship develop and intensify. People often discover what topics they can talk about comfortably, what they have in common, and what they like about one another. Thus, increasing breadth helps people explore one another's likes and dislikes, as well as other personality traits. Once individuals have explored enough that they begin to trust their partner, they will begin to disclose in more depth. At this point, duration often increases because they want to know each other even better. Long phone conversations and face-to-face interactions are commonplace at the end of this stage, as partners try to learn as much about each other as they can. In some cases, though, people in the exploratory affective exchange stage decide that they do not have much in common and that they should either remain casual friends or terminate the relationship.

Stage 3: Affective Exchange When relationships progress into the third stage, both breadth and depth of self-disclosure have increased significantly. This stage is usually reserved for people we consider to be good friends, as well as family members and romantic partners. Now we feel a sense of closeness and connection to the partner, and we feel less vulnerable. We believe that we can trust the partner and that the partner will accept us for who we are—flaws and all. At this point, however, we are still not completely open with our partner. There are certain types of information that we wish to keep hidden, certain parts of our inner selves that are still too private to share. For the most part, however, self-disclosure is high in breadth and depth.

The valence and duration of self-disclosure also may change in this stage. Rather than sticking mostly to positive self-disclosures, people in the affective exchange stage feel free to engage in negative self-disclosure. In some ways the "honeymoon period" has ended, and people no longer feel that they have to be on their best behavior. As a result, conflict may occur more frequently as people feel that they can express both positive and negative emotions more freely. The duration of the typical self-disclosure conversation may also lessen as people settle into this stage. The beginning of this stage, like the end of the exploratory affective exchange stage, often is marked by long, in-depth conversations as partners strive to get to know each other and then to show their affection and trust. However, as the relationship stabilizes, the need for long conversations diminishes because partners already know a considerable amount about each other.

Stage 4: Stable Exchange The final stage in social penetration theory involves complete self-disclosure. In terms of breadth, every topic is fair game. In terms of depth, partners feel free to disclose their innermost thoughts and feelings. This, of course, does not mean that partners always disclose everything to each other every time they talk. It does mean, however, that no topic is taboo. Achieving a true state of stable exchange is very difficult. Even in our closest relationships we tend to keep some secrets from our partner (Vangelisti, 1994). In fact, Baxter and Wilmot (1984) found that 91% of the partners in romantic couples they surveyed said that there was at least one topic that they never discussed with their relational partner. Common taboo topics included the state of the relationship, past relationships, and sexual experiences. Thus, although stable exchange may seem like a worthy goal, it is probably an unrealistic one. Partners in many couples exchange information on a regular basis, but very few actually share 100% of their thoughts and feelings.

In any case, complete self-disclosure is probably not the best prescription for a happy relationship. Elsewhere in this book we emphasize that many people have strong needs for privacy and autonomy (see Chapters 9 and 12). As Hatfield suggested, too much self-disclosure may rob us of our sense of privacy and make us feel overly dependent on others. In addition, it can be nice to keep some mystery in our relationships. This is not to say that people should purposely hide important information from their close relational partners. They should, however, feel that they have the right to keep certain innermost thoughts and feelings private. This helps explain why a stable rate of exchange is difficult to achieve in relationships. Although close relational partners may engage in many conversations that are completely open, sometimes they may keep information private. Complete self-disclosure also can require a lot of effort and energy. Thus, close relational partners often cycle back and forth between high and low levels of self-disclosure, even though the potential for high levels of self-disclosure is always there. Similarly, partners in stable relationships may go for a while without disclosing anything very intimate, but then "catch up" by engaging in a long, in-depth conversation.

Stages of "Coming Together"

A complementary stage model of relationship development was created by Knapp (Knapp & Vangelisti, 1996), who sought to describe the process of coming together by looking at a variety of communication behaviors beyond

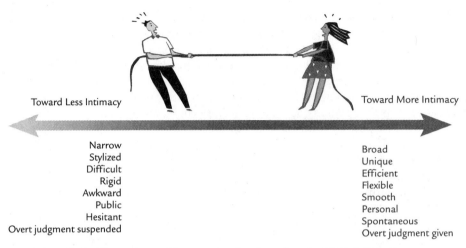

Toward Less Intimacy

Toward More Intimacy

Narrow	Broad
Stylized	Unique
Difficult	Efficient
Rigid	Flexible
Awkward	Smooth
Public	Personal
Hesitant	Spontaneous
Overt judgment suspended	Overt judgment given

FIGURE 5.3 **Dimensions of Communication Associated with Relationship Development and Decline** *Source:* Adapted from Knapp (1983).

self-disclosure. Knapp's model was based on the same general idea as social penetration theory. That is, as relationships develop, communication will become more personal, and people worry less about managing their impressions. Knapp visualized the stages of relational development as a staircase leading upward, with each step or stage representing an increase in intimacy (Knapp & Vangelisti, 1996). Knapp also visualized stages of relational disengagement as a descending staircase, with each stage characterized by more avoidance and separation. In this chapter we focus on Knapp's coming-together stages, or the ascending part of the staircase. In Chapter 15 on relational disengagement, we discuss Knapp's coming-apart stages.

Knapp's stages of coming together are based on dimensions similar to those originally identified by Altman and Taylor (1973). Knapp also proposed that relationships grow along eight dimensions, as depicted in Figure 5.3. According to this perspective, breadth (narrow to broad) and depth (public to personal) increase as relationships develop, and communication becomes less governed by social norms, more idiosyncratic (stylized to unique), and more accurate and rapid (difficult to efficient). People can also communicate the same message in multiple ways once a relationship has developed (rigid to flexible). For example, if you are uncomfortable at a party with a first date, you will probably have to tell your date that you'd like to leave. If you are at the same party with someone you know well, you may be able to use more subtle signals, such as looking pointedly at the door or raising an eyebrow, to indicate that you think it's time to go. As relationships develop, people can also predict each other's behaviors better, leading to synchronized interaction (awkward to smooth). They know one another's pause patterns and can take conversational turns without interrupting each other. People in close relationships also feel an openness about expressing themselves readily (hesitant to spontaneous) and voicing criticisms of their partner (overt judgment suspended to overt judgment given). Thus, people in close relationships often express themselves without first thinking about the impression that they are making.

As people move through these dimensions, Knapp suggested, they typically go through five stages that take them from an initial encounter to a fully committed relationship. Of course, most of our relationships do not progress that far. In fact, Knapp claimed, we usually stop at the second stage, deciding to remain casual friends or acquaintances but not to invest the time and effort needed to become close friends or romantic partners.

The Initiating Stage   The first stage in Knapp's model is similar to the orientation stage in social penetration theory. Here people are meeting each other for the first time. They are usually trying to make a positive impression, so they engage in polite, friendly, safe, and superficial communication. A greeting and reply are typical of the initiating stage. One person might say, "Hi. I'm Chantel. Is this your first day here?" The other might reply, "Yes, it is. My name is Paul." From there the conversation is likely to continue on a rather superficial level. Perhaps Chantel will tell Paul some innocuous facts about the company, and perhaps Paul will tell Chantel how pleased he is to be aboard. During this process, uncertainty is also likely to be reduced and a foundation set for future interactions, should they occur.

The Experimenting Stage   The second stage in Knapp's model is similar to the exploratory affective exchange stage in social penetration theory. Impression management is still a goal, but the more salient goal is to get to know the other person better to determine whether to pursue a relationship. Here people exchange fairly superficial information as they try to identify each other's likes and dislikes, values, attitudes, and personal opinions. For example, Paul might ask Chantel what she likes to do on the weekend, whether she has a family, and where her hometown is. Chantel might ask Paul about his previous job, his education, and the reasons he decided to take a job with the company. Each is likely to reciprocate as well. Thus, when Chantel says she likes to play tennis and watch sports on television during the weekend, Paul might say that he watches a lot of sports, too, and that he'd like to get out more to do things like play tennis. According to Knapp (Knapp & Vangelisti, 1996), this type of small talk is the key to understanding the experimenting stage. Both Chantel and Paul are "experimenting" in that they are trying to find out more about each other. Small talk allows them to fulfill a number of goals simultaneously, including discovering common interests, seeing if it would be worthwhile to pursue a closer relationship, reducing uncertainty in a safe manner that does not make them vulnerable, and allowing them to maintain a sense of connection with other people without putting themselves at much risk for hurt or rejection.

The Intensifying Stage   When experimenting leads people to decide to pursue a closer relationship, they usually move into the intensifying stage. Typically, movement into this stage is gradual. Breadth and depth of self-disclosure increase slowly but steadily, and displays of affection begin tentatively. For example, in a romantic relationship a peck on the lips is likely to precede a deeper kiss, which is likely to precede intimate touching. Other types of communication common in this stage include using nicknames or forms of endearment, making "we" instead of "I" statements ("We should go down to Mexico sometime"), and making statements that reflect positive regard and commitment, such as saying "I love you" or "You are my very best friend." Declarations such as these usually first occur in the intensifying stage and then continue into the next two stages as couples integrate and bond.

Work by Tolhuizen (1989) gives further insight into how people intensify their relationships. In his research, Tolhuizen found 15 different intensification strategies; Box 5.3 lists the strategies. The three most common strategies are increased contact, relationship negotiation (which involves talking about the relationship), and social support and assistance (which involves asking someone for advice and/or comfort). Nearly 40% of the people Tolhuizen surveyed described increased contact as an important intensification strategy, while 29% and 26% mentioned relationship negotiation and social support/assistance, respectively. Thus, these three strategies appear to be fairly common ways of intensifying various relationships. The other strategies listed in Box 5.3 appear to play more minor roles in the intensification process, but they still represent important means by which people escalate their relationships.

The Integrating Stage   By the time two people reach the integrating stage, they have already achieved a high level of intimacy. Now they are ready to show that intimacy to others by presenting themselves as a "couple." This type of presentation is not limited to romantic couples; friends often present themselves as a unified team as well. The key here is that "the two individual personalities almost seem to fuse or coalesce" (Knapp & Vangelisti, 1996, p. 38). Once this coupling has occurred, people outside the relationship begin to see the partners as two halves of a whole. It is easy to see when this has taken place. For example, you may be at a party without your best friend, and several people stop and ask you, "Hey, where is Chris?" They all expect to see the two of you together. Or you and your romantic partner may start to receive joint invitations to parties or joint Christmas gifts, which shows that other people see you as a committed couple.

Other types of changes occur within the dyad in this stage. Close friends or romantic partners may be able to complete each other's sentences, and their tastes, attitudes, and opinions may merge. For example, in the movie *When Harry Met Sally,* the last scene shows Harry and Sally talking about their wedding. Sally starts to describe their wedding cake, including the rich chocolate sauce that they had "on the side." Harry concludes the description by saying that it is important to have the sauce on the side, because not everyone likes the same amount of sauce on their cake. This is a good example of coupling since Sally, not Harry, was originally the person who insisted on ordering the sauce on the side. Other signs of coupling include wearing similar clothing, opening a joint bank account, designating a favorite tune as "our song," and merging social networks.

BOX 5.3 HIGHLIGHTS

Tolhuizen's Strategies for Intensifying Relationships

1. **Increased contact:** includes seeing or calling the person more often (39.2%)
2. **Relationship negotiation:** includes openly discussing the state of the relationship and the feelings the partners have for one another (29.1%)
3. **Social support and assistance:** involves asking people for support, advice, and comfort (26.1%)
4. **Increased rewards:** includes doing favors and making sacrifices for one another, such as helping someone move or helping with household tasks (17.6%)
5. **Direct definitional bid:** involves asking the partner to make a definite commitment, such as seeing each other exclusively, moving in together, or getting married (16.1%)
6. **Tokens of affection:** includes sending flowers, cards, and gifts, as well as exchanging rings (16.1%)
7. **Personalized communication:** includes using idiomatic communication, such as special nicknames and inside jokes, as well as listening empathically (15.1%)
8. **Verbal expressions of affection:** includes uttering declarations such as "I love you" and "I hope we are always this close" (14.1%)
9. **Suggestive actions:** includes flirting, trying to get someone jealous, and playing "hard to get" (13.1%)
10. **Nonverbal expressions of affection:** includes gazing at the partner lovingly, touching the partner, and smiling (12.1%)
11. **Social enmeshment:** involves getting to know and spending more time with the partner's family and friends, sometimes through activities such as spending a holiday together (11.6%)
12. **Acceptance of definitional bid:** involves redefining the relationship through actions such as saying "yes" when the partner asks for more commitment, or agreeing to date exclusively, move in together, or get married (9.5%)
13. **Personal appearance:** involves changing one's physical appearance to please the partner by engaging in behaviors such as trying to lose weight, changing one's hairstyle, or dressing particularly well (9.5%)
14. **Sexual intimacy:** involves engaging in increasingly intimate behavior, often including sexual relations (8%)
15. **Behavioral adaptation:** involves changing one's behavior to please the partner, perhaps by trying to secure a better job or to criticize the partner less and compliment the partner more (7.5%)

Note: The percentages in this table represent the percentage of people in Tolhuizen's study who described or reported using each strategy. Because people were allowed to describe as many strategies as they deemed relevant, the percentages add up to more than 100%.

The Bonding Stage   In the final stage of Knapp's model, partners find a way to publicly declare their commitment to each other, usually through the institutionalization of the relationship. Perhaps the most obvious way of institutionalizing a romantic relationship is through marriage. Getting married shows commitment, and also makes it harder to leave the relationship. Most people cannot simply walk away from a marriage. There are possessions to divide, perhaps children to provide for, and a socially shared history that is hard to leave behind. Marriage can also be thought of a social ritual, in that two people come together before family and friends to declare their love for each other.

Such a public declaration cements their bond even further. Importantly, in states that do not allow gay and lesbian couples to marry, these couples often still have public commitment ceremonies uniting them as life partners in front of friends and family. These ceremonies underscore how important public commitment is to most romantic couples.

Other types of relationships also reach the bonding stage, although the institutionalization of these relationships is more difficult. Friends and family members, however, can make public, enduring commitments to one another in many different ways. For instance, if you get married, the people you choose to stand up as your bridesmaids or groomsmen will be an important part of this critical life event, and they will hold that place in your memory forever. By choosing them, you are telling your social network that these people have a special place in your life. Similarly, if you have a child and choose godparents, these individuals will be part of a very important social ritual that publicly lets others know you value and trust them. Some friendship rituals, such as becoming blood brothers or getting matching tattoos, may also be ways to show a permanent bond.

The Ordering and Timing of Stages

When thinking about the two stage theories we have discussed, it is important to note that people do not always move through stages in an orderly manner. According to Altman and Taylor (1973), self-disclosure usually unfolds gradually, with people progressing through the various stages one at a time in the "proper" order. However, they acknowledge that this is not always the case, as the stranger-on-the-plane phenomenon suggests. Similarly, Knapp (Knapp & Vangelisti, 1996) believed that his five stages show the typical pattern of relational development for most couples but that variations frequently take place. Couples might go though the stages in a different order, or they might skip some stages entirely. For example, some romantic couples meet, fall in love at first sight, and quickly get married. Other couples move in together after only a few dates. The movie *About Last Night* shows a couple who appear to go through the stages too quickly. They have sex early in their relationship and decide to move in together without really getting to know each other. Eventually their relationship falls apart, and the woman moves out of their apartment. Later, they meet again, feel a mutual attraction, and decide to take things more slowly this time.

This may be typical; that is, when people skip stages or move too quickly through them, they might later go back and engage in communication appropriate for that stage. Take a couple who meets and soon gets married as an example. Their friends and family might be surprised at the news of their marriage, and the newlyweds may need to work on merging their social networks and gaining acceptance as a couple. In this case some of the processes that typically occur during the integrating stage would be occurring after the bonding stage.

Relational Turning Points

A turning point is "any event or occurrence that is associated with change in a relationship" (Baxter & Bullis, 1986, p. 469). Turning points can also be thought of as major relational events. Interestingly, most of the scenes in romantic movies and novels consist of significant relational events or turning points. This is probably because turning points help tell the story of relational change. Rather than focusing on the more mundane events that occur on a day-to-day basis, the turning point approach emphasizes those events that stand out in people's minds as having the strongest impact on their relationships. This is not to say that mundane events are unimportant. Indeed, mundane events help shape the way people see their relationships even if such events sometimes go unnoticed and unappreciated. These mundane events can be thought of as part of the regular road upon which a relationship travels. Turning points, by contrast, are the detours relationships sometimes take.

The turning point approach is very different from stage approaches to relationship development and disengagement even though turning points can mark entry into a new stage. Social penetration theory, for example, suggests that relationships develop fairly smoothly and gradually as people's communication becomes more personal. By contrast, the turning point approach suggests that relationships follow a choppier path, with both positive and negative events affecting their course. Research by Baxter and Bullis (1986; Bullis, Clark, & Sline, 1993) suggests that there are at least 12 major relational turning points.

Two turning points deal specifically with the time we spend with someone. The first of these, **get-to-know time,** includes initial interactions and focuses on the quantity rather than the quality of time spent together. First meetings, first dates, and activities such as playing basketball, typify this turning point. By contrast, the **quality time** turning point focuses on special occasions when two people had a high-quality interaction, such as having an especially long and intimate conversation, getting away for the weekend together, and meeting one partner's family for the first time.

Passion was also identified as a common turning point. **Passionate events** include the first kiss, the first time a couple exchanged the words "I love you," the first sexual encounter, and other passionate phenomena such as falling in love at first sight.

Another set of turning points deals with physical separation and reunion. **Physical separation** was reported when people were apart, often involuntarily, due to vacations, business trips, and school breaks. **Reunions** occurred when the period of physical separation was over and the couple was together again.

Couples also identified three turning points that revolve around the commitment level of the relationship: external competition, exclusivity, and serious commitment. **External competition** occurs when a person feels threatened by a third party or an activity that is taking up a lot of the partner's time. Sometimes an ex-spouse or former girlfriend or boyfriend re-emerges; other times a new rival starts to compete for the partner's affections; still other times responsibilities related to work, school, or childcare, or time spent with friends, interfere with the relationship. **Exclusivity** occurs when people decide to see each other exclusively and drop all other rivals. **Serious commitment** takes this a step further, usually by showing commitment through cohabiting and/or getting married.

Most relationships are also characterized by disengagement and conflict, as well as by making up. The category of **disengagement and conflict** includes a couple's first big fight, attempts to de-escalate or withdraw from the relationship, and actual relational breakups. **Making up** occurs when partners repair relational problems and/or feel close to each other again. Baxter and Bullis (1986) noted that there is not always a perfect correspondence between disengagement/conflict and making up. Sometimes the conflict is viewed as more significant than the making-up session or vice versa.

Sacrifice constitutes yet another relational turning point. Partners often make many sacrifices for each other, including doing favors and giving gifts. Perhaps more importantly, partners often are there to support and comfort each other in crisis situations, such as dealing with the death of a loved one or helping one regain confidence after an embarrassing failure. Seeing each other through such difficult times is a cornerstone of close relationships, as these times are often remembered as significant turning points.

Finally, couples sometimes report experiencing **positive or negative psychic change.** Unlike other turning points, psychic changes do not appear to have specific causes. People simply report that their attitudes toward the partner changed somehow, even though they cannot figure out exactly why. For example, a person might suddenly see her or his partner as more physically attractive and sexually appealing (a positive psychic change) without being able to pinpoint why. Or a person might suddenly see the relationship as boring and the partner as dull (a negative psychic change) even though nothing else has really changed.

These 12 turning points probably make sense to you. If you were asked to identify the events that had changed a relationship of yours in a significant way, you would likely list many of these events. In fact, you could create a map of your relationship, much like Baxter and Bullis (1986; Bullis et al., 1993) had the participants in their studies create. A sample of such a map, referred to as a **turning-point analysis,** is shown in Figure 5.4. As you can see, the turning-point approach does not depict a smooth, gradual increase in commitment. Instead, this approach reveals a rockier road that includes all of the important ups and downs that influence the growth, and in some cases the demise, of close relationships.

Conclusion

This chapter focused on some of the most influential theories of relationship development and intensification, as well as some barriers that prevent people from initiating and escalating relationships. Several points are important to keep in mind as you think about this body of literature. First, every relationship

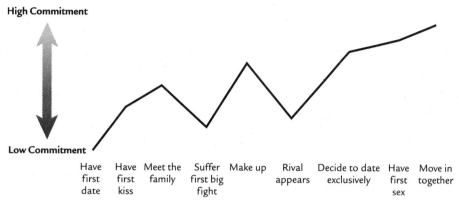

FIGURE 5.4 A Sample Turning-Point Analysis

follows a unique trajectory. Social penetration theory and Knapp's coming to-gether stages give us an idea of what to expect, but the specific paths our relationships travel will usually be filled with unexpected turns.

Second, many of the same strategies that people use to develop their relationships are used to help maintain satisfying relationships. However, some behaviors, such as self-disclosure, are most relevant in the initial stages of relationships when people are getting to know one another. Chapter 9 discusses a wide array of behaviors that people use to maintain relationships after the initial period of relational development. In addition, Chapter 9 discusses sex differences in communication behavior, including self-disclosure.

Third, while social penetration theory focuses on communication in developing relationships, the turning point approach emphasizes communication patterns that occur across the entire trajectory of a relationship. Similarly, Knapp's model of relational stages includes both coming-together and coming-apart stages, although this chapter examined only the former. In Chapter 15, Knapp's coming-apart stages are discussed.

Fourth, one person may want to intensify a relationship while the other person may not, so two people could actually want to be in different "stages." One person may be trying to reach the intensifying stage of Knapp's model, while the other is content to stay at the experimenting stage. Similarly, two people might map the turning points in their relationship differently. A good example of this is found in the movie *When Harry Met Sally.* After they have sex for the first time (a significant turning point), the camera zooms in to show their faces. Sally has a big smile on her face and looks very relaxed and happy. It might be assumed that her commitment level has increased. Harry, by contrast, looks scared to death, so his commitment level may well have decreased. They later have a big fight, after which Sally begins to disengage herself from Harry (showing decreased commitment), but Harry tries to make up (showing increased commitment). At this point Harry leaves all sorts of messages on Sally's answering machine, but she ignores him and does not answer the phone. Although fictional, these scenes ring true because most of us can recall times when a situation was interpreted differently, leading us to feel a different level of commitment from that of our partner.

In closing, the relational development models provide a nice blueprint of how close relationships typically unfold over time. Yet every relationship follows a different path, and rarely will relationships progress smoothly as people move from being strangers to being close friends or lovers. The joy of discovering a new friend or developing a new romantic relationship, however, makes the journey worthwhile.

Discussion Questions

1. Think about times when you felt uncomfortable because someone engaged in too much or too little self-disclosure. What circumstances caused you to feel uncomfortable? In other words, why is self-disclosure considered inappropriate in some contexts and appropriate in others?
2. Stage theories of relational development suggest that although there is some variation, most relationships follow a fairly predictable trajectory. Do you agree or disagree? Do your relationships typically follow the stages outlined by Altman and Taylor's social penetration theory or Knapp's coming-together stages, or do they take a different course?
3. Map out the major events that have occurred in one of your relationships over the past year. Do most of those events correspond with those mentioned by scholars studying turning points? What events might be missing, especially for non-college-age couples?

Making a Love Connection

Styles of Love and Attachment

In the 1960s the Beatles sang, "All you need is love." Later, in the 1990s, Elton John's ballad, entitled "Believe," told listeners that "everything crumbles sooner or later, but love." Alfred Lord Tennyson once wrote that it is "better to have loved and lost, than never to have loved at all." The prevalence of love in songs and poems illustrates just how important, and sometimes elusive, love is in people's everyday lives. Of course, love is not always a happy experience. Sometimes love is not returned, leading people to feel rejected and miserable. Reciprocated love, however, is one of the most wonderful of human experiences.

In this chapter we take a closer look at the concept of love, as well as a related concept known as attachment. First, we distinguish between liking and loving. Second, we cover three major perspectives on love: (1) Lee's love styles, (2) Sternberg's triangular theory of love, and (3) Marston and Hecht's love ways. These three perspectives show that people experience love in different ways. Sometimes love is passionate and driven by arousal and emotional highs and lows; other times love is more tranquil and secure, driven by friendship, respect, and liking. Finally, we review literature related to attachment theory, in which love is conceptualized as an attachment process whereby people become highly connected to each other (Hazan & Shaver, 1987). As we will see, attachment is an important part of many different loving relationships, including relationships between family members, romantic partners, and close friends.

Liking Versus Loving

Love is a complex concept that can refer to a set of feelings, a state of mind, or a type of relationship. Love is communicated in a variety of ways, such as by making sacrifices, disclosing one's innermost thoughts and feelings, showing nonverbal affection, and having sexual intercourse. Some researchers have tried to separate loving from liking. Rubin (1970, 1973, 1974) suggested that there are *qualitative* rather than *quantitative* differences between loving and liking.

In other words, just because you like someone a lot does not necessarily mean you love her or him. Love is more than merely an abundance of liking, and loving and liking can be thought of as related but distinctly different concepts. People can, in some cases, even love others without liking them very much. In general, however, individuals tend to like the people whom they love. For example, Rubin (1970, 1973) found that people reported liking their close friends and dating partners about equally but loving their dating partners more than their friends. Partners in romantic couples who were "in love" and planned to marry also reported loving each other more than dating partners who did not have concrete plans for the future. Thus, romance and commitment appear to be important in most love relationships.

Liking and loving can be distinguished from each other by certain feelings and relationship characteristics. Rubin (1973) suggested that liking is characterized by affection and respect. Affection is based on having enjoyable interactions with someone, which make one feel good when around that person. These types of interactions promote interpersonal warmth, or a feeling of cozy closeness, that helps cement the bond between two people (Andersen & Guerrero, 1998a). Respect is based on admiring a person's positive personal characteristics, such as a good sense of humor, a sense of integrity, or an inner strength and tenacity. Loving, by contrast, is characterized by attachment, caring, and intimacy (Rubin, 1973). When people feel attached to someone, they feel a strong need to win that person's approval. They are also drawn to that person when they need social support and comfort. The caring component, by contrast, refers to giving (rather than receiving) support and comfort, as well as to showing affection. Finally, intimacy involves the bond that is created when two people both give and receive care. Intimacy involves a sense of interdependence, whereby two people rely on each other to fulfill needs for attachment and caring.

A series of studies by Davis and his colleagues (Davis & Roberts, 1985; Davis & Todd, 1982) also supports the idea that loving is qualitatively different than liking and, again, that loving is special because it often includes more caring and passion than liking. As Rubin had suggested earlier, Davis found that friendship is defined by characteristics such as enjoyment, acceptance, trust, and respect, as well as doing things for one another, disclosing information, understanding each other, and feeling comfortable together (Davis & Todd, 1982, 1985). Love is defined by all of these friendship characteristics *plus* caring and passion. Caring includes making supreme sacrifices for the loved one and defending her or him to others; passion includes being fascinated by the loved one, feeling that the relationship is unique and exclusive, and experiencing strong sexual desire. Thus, for Davis and his colleagues, friendship, caring, and passion typically reflect love, whereas friendship reflects only liking.

Different Types of Love

Social scientists have also distinguished between love that is characterized primarily by friendship and love that is characterized primarily by passion. **Companionate love,** which is based on friendship, involves affection, trust, security, and caring. Walster and Walster (1978) defined companionate love as "the affection we feel for those with whom our lives are deeply intertwined" (p. 9). This kind of love is commonly experienced in family relationships and friendships, as well as romantic relationships. Hatfield (1988) labeled companionate love as the "warm" type of love because it tends to develop over time into a consistent, secure source of warmth. **Passionate love** is based on arousal and intense emotion. When the beloved person returns our passionate love, we feel ecstasy; when this person rejects our love, we feel agony. Thus, a passionate relationship often is characterized by emotional highs and lows, rather than a more consistent feeling of interpersonal warmth. Because of this, as well as the tendency for passionate love to develop rapidly but to decline over time, Hatfield (1988) labeled passion as the "hot" type of love that typically is sexual in nature. Many romantic couples experience passionate love at the beginning of their relationships, with companionate love emerging once the relationship has stabilized and become more committed (Kelley, 1983).

Companionate and passionate love appear to be the most common types of love. Moreover, these types of love tend to be experienced similarly across different cultures (Hatfield & Rapson, 1987; Jankowiak & Fischer, 1992). However, there are other types of love as well. For example, some people view love as highly practical while others see it as more spiritual. Love is also communicated in a variety of ways, including self-disclosure, emotional responses, and time spent together. In this section we examine three perspectives on different styles of loving. As you proceed, keep in mind that companionate and passionate love are represented in each of these perspectives.

Lee's Love Styles

Lee's (1973, 1977, 1988) work on love styles began with the notion that there are three primary styles of loving, much as there are three primary colors. When mixing paint, the primary colors are red, blue, and yellow. By mixing these three primary colors, you can create any color in the rainbow. Lee conceptualized styles of loving in a similar manner. He proposed that the primary love styles are **eros** (physical love), **storge** (companionate love), and **ludus** (game-playing love). And just as the primary colors can be mixed to create a multitude of different hues, Lee theorized that the three primary styles of love can combine to create a vast number of love styles. Specifically, different elements within each of the three primary styles of loving could be mixed in various ways, leading to many different combinations. Of these possible combinations, Lee suggested that three are the most common: **mania** (possessive love), **agape** (unselfish love), and **pragma** (practical love). Figure 6.1 depicts Lee's love styles as a color wheel.

As we shall see next, each style of love is defined by both positive and negative characteristics. The more strongly and exclusively a person identifies with a single style, the more likely he or she is to experience some of the negative characteristics. Most people, however, report identifying with a combination of styles, with one or two styles experienced most strongly. Box 6.1 gives a scale by which you can determine your own love style.

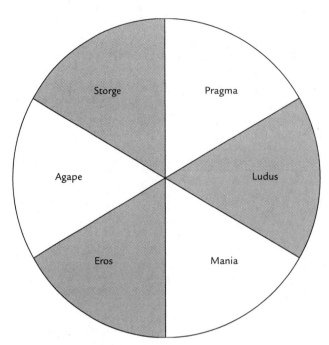

FIGURE 6.1 **Lee's Love Styles Represented as a Color Wheel** The primary styles are shaded; the secondary styles are composed of the aspects of the two primary styles adjacent to them.

Physical Love (Eros)   Erotic lovers are attracted to people who are physically attractive to them (Lee, 1988). They are eager to develop intense, passionate relationships, and they often experience fairly intense emotional highs and lows. They also feel high levels of arousal and desire physical contact. Thus, they often escalate sexual intimacy relatively quickly within their relationships. Because they feel such a strong attraction to each other, erotic lovers develop a sense of intimacy and connectedness relatively quickly. These individuals are also "intense communicators" (Taraban, Hendrick, & Hendrick, 1998, p. 346). Specifically, they show high levels of self-disclosure, are able to elicit similarly high levels of self-disclosure from their partners, and display high levels of touch and nonverbal affection. They want to be with each other, and they feel considerable distress when apart.

Eros is an important part of many love relationships. This type of love is common in the initial stages of romantic relationships and often leads into a more friendship-based and secure style of love (Hendrick, Hendrick, & Adler, 1988). Some level of eros also keeps relationships exciting and passionate. However, too much eros can have negative effects. For example, if you are only interested in someone because of the person's beauty, the attraction is likely to fade quickly. Also, some erotic lovers have trouble adjusting after the initially

BOX 6.1 PUT YOURSELF TO THE TEST

What Is Your Love Style?

To determine your dominant love style, rate yourself on each of these statements according to the following scale: **1 = Strongly disagree . . . 5 = Strongly agree**

	Disagree			Agree	

1. My partner and I were attracted to each other immediately when we first met. 1 2 3 4 5
2. My partner and I have the right physical chemistry. 1 2 3 4 5
3. The physical part of our relationship is intense and satisfying. 1 2 3 4 5
4. My partner and I were meant for each other. 1 2 3 4 5
5. My partner fits my ideal standards of physical attractiveness. 1 2 3 4 5
6. I try to keep my partner a little uncertain about my commitment to her/him. 1 2 3 4 5
7. I believe that what my partner doesn't know about me won't hurt her/him. 1 2 3 4 5
8. I could get over my relationship with my partner pretty easily. 1 2 3 4 5
9. When my partner gets too dependent on me, I back off. 1 2 3 4 5
10. I enjoy playing the field. 1 2 3 4 5
11. It is hard for me to say exactly when our friendship turned into love. 1 2 3 4 5
12. To be genuine, our love first required caring. 1 2 3 4 5
13. Our love is the best kind because it grew out of a close friendship. 1 2 3 4 5
14. Our love is really a deep friendship, not a mysterious or mystical emotion. 1 2 3 4 5
15. Our love relationship is satisfying because it developed from a good friendship. 1 2 3 4 5
16. I considered what my partner was going to become in life before committing myself to her/him. 1 2 3 4 5
17. I tried to plan my life carefully before choosing a partner. 1 2 3 4 5
18. In choosing my partner, I believed it was best to find someone with a similar background. 1 2 3 4 5
19. An important factor in choosing my partner was whether she/he would be a good parent. 1 2 3 4 5
20. Before getting very involved with my partner, I tried to figure out how compatible our goals were. 1 2 3 4 5
21. If my partner and I broke up, I don't know how I would cope. 1 2 3 4 5
22. It drives me crazy when my partner doesn't pay enough attention to me. 1 2 3 4 5
23. I'm so in love with my partner that I sometimes have trouble concentrating on anything else. 1 2 3 4 5
24. I cannot relax if I suspect that my partner is with someone else. 1 2 3 4 5
25. I wish I could spend every minute of every day with my partner. 1 2 3 4 5

(continued)

	Disagree				Agree

26. I would rather suffer myself than let my partner suffer.   1 2 3 4 5

27. I am usually willing to sacrifice my own wishes to let my partner achieve her/his goals.   1 2 3 4 5

28. Whatever I own is my partner's to use as she/he pleases.   1 2 3 4 5

29. When my partner behaves badly, I still love her/him fully and unconditionally.   1 2 3 4 5

30. I would endure all things for the sake of my partner.   1 2 3 4 5

Add up the following items to get your score on each love style.

Eros: items 1–5   _____

Ludus: items 6–10   _____

Storge: items 11–15   _____

Pragma: items 16–20   _____

Mania: items 21–25   _____

Agape: items 26–30   _____

Higher scores mean that you possess more of a particular love style. The highest possible score for a given love style is 25; the lowest possible score is 5.

Source: This is an abbreviated, modified version of Hendrick and Hendrick's (1990) Love Attitudes Scale.

"hot" attraction begins to cool or after they discover that the partner, who seemed perfect at first, cannot possibly live up to these unrealistically high expectations. Still, research suggests that maintaining some degree of eros is beneficial in a relationship. In fact, Hendrick et al. (1988) found that dating couples were more likely to stay together if the partners were high in eros and low in the ludic, game-playing style of love. This confirms the claim that passion and commitment are important in many love relationships.

Companionate Love (Storge) Storgic lovers have relationships based on friendship, shared values and goals, and compatibility (Lee, 1988). Physical attraction is not as important as security, companionship, task sharing, and joint activity. Although these relationships are not very exciting, they are dependable and stable. Love often is framed as a partnership or a lifelong journey. Thus, it is important that the two individuals want the same things—perhaps a home and family, or perhaps independence and the ability to travel together to exotic places. Storgic lovers feel extremely comfortable around each other, and emotions tend to be positive but muted. Unlike some of the other love styles, storgic lovers do not experience many intense emotional highs or lows.

Companionate love characterizes many long-term romantic relationships, as well as relationships between family members and between close friends. This type of love tends to be relatively enduring. Because storgic lovers trust each other and do not require very high levels of emotional stimulation and arousal, they are able to withstand long separations. For example, if Jeff is an officer in the Navy, he might have to go on ship duty for long stretches of time. If he and his partner, Sarah, are storgic lovers, they are likely to be sad when they are parted from each other, but their trust and relational security will keep them from being highly distressed. Other types of lovers (for example, erotic or manic lovers) would feel much higher levels of distress because their relationships are fueled by physical attraction and the physical presence of the loved one. Of course, it is important to keep in mind that, although trust and security can provide a safety net for a relationship, too much stability can lead to predictability and boredom. Thus, bringing excitement and emotion to the relationship is often the biggest challenge for storgic lovers.

Game-Playing Love (Ludus)   Ludic lovers see relationships as fun, playful, and casual; they view relationships as games to be played. They avoid commitment and prefer to play the field rather than settle down with one person (Lee, 1988). In fact, for the ludic lover the challenge of pursuit usually is much more rewarding than the actual relationship itself. Some ludic lovers are highly self-sufficient individuals who put their personal goals and activities ahead of their relationships. They share relatively little personal information with their partners and are slow to develop intimate relationships (Hendrick & Hendrick, 1987). Of course, sometimes only one person in the relationship is a game player. This can be very frustrating for the ludic lover's partner, who probably experiences considerable uncertainty about where he or she stands in the relationship. Many students and recent college graduates adopt the ludic style, especially if they feel they are not ready for a highly committed romantic relationship. Instead, they may feel that school or career takes precedence over relational involvements. When these individuals are ready or when they meet the right person, they are likely to move out of the ludic style and into a more committed style of loving.

In Margaret Mitchell's classic Civil War novel *Gone with the Wind*, the Scarlett O'Hara character provides a good example of an individual with a ludic love style. Scarlett is a notorious flirt. In an early scene she is at a party surrounded by dozens of admirers; she is careful not to commit to any one man. Later, Scarlett marries men she does not love to fulfill personal goals. For example, she marries her sister's boyfriend, Frank, to help pay the mortgage on the family plantation. Her ludic nature also shines through in her relationship with Rhett Butler. Scarlett and Rhett constantly compete with each other through glib and sarcastic remarks, and Scarlett often hides her warm feelings for Rhett. By the time she realizes she loves Rhett, it is too late. He has grown tired of her games and delivers the famous line, "Frankly, my dear, I don't give a damn."

Possessive Love (Mania)   Manic lovers are demanding, dependent, and possessive (Lee, 1988). They often feel a strong need to "be in control" and to know everything that the partner is doing. The song "Every Breath You Take," by the

Police, exemplifies the manic lover's desire to monitor "every breath you take, every move you make, every smile you fake." In extreme cases, manic lovers are obsessive individuals who are addicted to love, much as a drug addict is addicted to heroin or cocaine. The obsessed lover cannot get enough; he or she wants to spend every minute with the partner, and any perceived lack of interest or enthusiasm by the partner, or any physical separation, results in extreme emotional lows. By contrast, when the beloved person reciprocates affection, the manic lover experiences an emotional high. Manic lovers also become jealous easily and can be overly preoccupied with their relationships. Of course, many people experience a mild form of mania. For example, they get jealous when their partners flirt with an ex-boyfriend or -girlfriend, they find themselves constantly thinking about the partner, and their happiness seems to depend, at least in part, on having a relationship with the person they love. When these thoughts and feelings become extreme, a more negative form of possessive love emerges.

According to Lee (1973), the manic style is a combination of eros and ludus. Manic lovers feel high levels of physical attraction and passion for their partners, which is consistent with the erotic style (Hendrick et al., 1988). However, manic lovers also play games with their partners by manipulating and trying to control them. In addition, manic lovers sometimes worry about committing to a relationship because they fear that they will be hurt. To the manic lover, relationships represent a source of both extreme joy and extreme pain. Manic lovers can quickly become infatuated with someone even though they do not know the person very well. For example, manic lovers often are willing to break off an old relationship to pursue a new, seemingly more attractive alternative before they really get to know the new love interest. If you have ever been hotly pursued by someone who barely knew you, chances are that you were dealing with a manic lover.

Unselfish Love (Agape)   The type of love that agapic lovers experience is usually called "unselfish" or "altruistic" love. The agapic lover is more focused on giving than receiving (Lee, 1988). Moreover, these lovers are motivated by an intense concern for their partner's well-being. They are willing to make sacrifices for their partner, even at the expense of their own needs and desires. For example, an agapic lover might turn down a big promotion at work if it means relocating to a new city where her or his partner might be unhappy. Agapic love usually is unconditional, as well as spiritual and pure. In fact, the biblical description of love as patient, kind, and slow to anger and jealousy is very much in line with Lee's description of agape. Relationships between romantic partners, family members (especially parents toward children), and friends all can be characterized by agape.

The agapic style contains some elements of both eros and storge (Lee, 1973). An agapic lover has a deep, abiding, highly passionate love for his or her partner—although not usually in a physical sense. Passion instead revolves around loving the partner well and being motivated to help the partner be as happy as he or she can be. Thus, an agapic lover will show passion by giving gifts and making sacrifices for the partner, or sometimes by granting the partner sexual favors even if such activity is not personally arousing. Physical intimacy may also be an important part of agapic love, with sexual contact usually seen as something sacred that should only occur between two people who love each other deeply. The storge side of agapic love stresses the enduring and secure nature of the relationship, which helps explain why agapic individuals are able to love their partners unconditionally.

Given all this, it might seem as if having an agapic lover would be an ideal situation. There are, however, some drawbacks to this style. Agapic lovers sometimes seem to be "above" everyone else. Their partners often have trouble matching their high level of unconditional love, which can lead to feelings of discomfort and guilt. In addition, agapic lovers sometimes put their partners on too high of a pedestal. Their partners may worry that they cannot live up to such an idealized image.

Practical Love (Pragma)   Pragmatic lovers search for a person who fits a particular image in terms of vital statistics, such as age, height, religion, and occupation, as well as preferred characteristics, such as being a loyal partner or having the potential to be a good parent. Lee (1988) used a computer dating service metaphor to help describe pragma. For example, if you went to a dating service, you might indicate that you are looking for a petite brunette who is Jewish, likes sports, and has a stable job. Or you might request a college-educated male who is older than you, has a good sense of humor, and wants a large family. In either case you would have specified the vital statistics that are most important to you. The pragmatic lover chooses these vital statistics based on both personal preferences and compatibility issues. Overall, this style of love is characterized by "a common-sense, problem-solving approach to life and love" (Taraban et al., 1998, p. 346).

Pragma combines elements of both storge and ludus. As Lee (1988) explained, storge comes into play because pragmatic lovers are looking for a compatible partner. Furthermore, for pragmatic lovers physical attraction usually is far less important than shared values and goals (although attractiveness is often on the pragmatic lover's "laundry list" of vital characteristics). Undertones of the ludus style also are evident in many pragmatic lovers, who typically avoid emotional risk taking and commit to a relationship only after careful thought and considerable time. Finally, it is important to note that pragmatic love is highly rational, based on empirical knowledge. For example, when pragmatic lovers are considering marriage, they might make a list of pros and cons before deciding whether to "take the plunge." If love is based only on practical concerns, however, it is likely to be lifeless and dull. Some level of intimacy and/or passion is required to put the spark into a relationship. For pragmatic lovers intimacy and passion sometimes develop after practical concerns have laid the foundation for the relationship.

Differences Due to Sex and Culture   Lee's original work, as well as subsequent research, suggests that the tendency to identify with the various love styles differs somewhat depending on sex and culture. Hendrick and Hendrick (1986) found that women tend to score higher in storge, mania, and pragma than men, while men score higher in ludus. These findings for storge and pragma are in line with other research showing women to be more rational lovers, who are choosier about their partners and value similarity and companionship. However, the finding for mania is somewhat contradictory to the research on jealousy, which has shown that men and women tend to feel similar levels of jealousy. However, jealous women focus more on emotional issues than do men, while jealous men focus more on sexual issues (see Chapter 13). The finding that men tend to identify more with ludus is consistent with research showing that men are generally more uncommitted to relationships than are women. But studies have also found that men tend to fall in love faster than do women (Huston, Surra, Fitzgerald, & Cate, 1981; Kanin, Davidson, & Scheck, 1970) and that they usually say "I love you" first in heterosexual romantic relationships (Owen, 1987; Tolhuizen, 1989). Together these seemingly inconsistent findings suggest that, although men may hesitate to make a strong commitment, when they do fall in love they do it more quickly and emotionally than do women.

As noted previously, some types of love tend to be experienced similarly across different cultures. For example, Jankowiak and Fischer (1992) tested the idea that romantic (or erotic) love is a product of Western culture. Contrary to this idea, they found romantic love to exist in 147 of the 166 cultures sampled. Based on this data, Jankowiak and Fischer suggested that romantic love is nearly universal. Companionate love also appears to cross cultural boundaries, with many different peoples embracing the warmth and security that friendship-based love offers. There are some cultural differences in love styles, however. People from cultures that endorse arranged marriages believe more strongly in pragmatic love than do cultures in which people choose to marry for love alone. In arranged marriages the parents and/or community often match their children based on perceived compatibility and an equitable exchange of resources.

The musical *Fiddler on the Roof* tells the story of three young Jewish sisters who decide to flaunt tradition by choosing romantic love over pragmatic love. At the beginning of the film, viewers are introduced to Yente, the matchmaker, whose job it is to arrange good marriages within her small community. Yente arranges a marriage between the oldest sister, Tzeitel, and a rich widower. However, Tzeitel rebels and eventually marries her true love, a poor young tailor, which lays the groundwork for the younger sisters to also marry men of their choosing. This is not to say, however, that arranged marriages do not succeed. In fact, some research suggests that arranged marriages actually have a higher success rate than love matches, perhaps because the community supports such marriages and the spouses share strong common goals and values. At one point in *Fiddler on the Roof*, the parents of the three sisters contemplate their own marriage, asking whether they truly love each other. It becomes clear to them that, after 25 years of marriage, which included raising a family and persevering through the bad times, they love each other very much. As this scene illustrates, the practical love that is characteristic of many arranged marriages can blossom into love that includes romance and deep friendship. Indeed, people from cultures endorsing arranged marriages may find it hard to believe that people in the West would trust ephemeral states such as romantic or sexual attraction as the basis of a long-term relationship.

Agapic love is also likely to differ across cultures. In the United States and other Western cultures, such as Australia, Great Britain, Canada, and the Netherlands, people are highly individualistic. In these cultures individuals are more likely to strive for personal goals. As Lustig and Koester (1993) put it, "Individualism is characterized by the key words *independence, privacy, self*, and the all-important *I*" (p. 89). For people in individualistic cultures, agapic love may be seen as too all-consuming, smothering, and other oriented. However, people in collectivist cultures—such as parts of South America, including Venezuela and Colombia, and parts of Asia, including Hong Kong and Taiwan—are likely to be more amenable to agapic love (Hofstede, 1982). Individuals in collectivist cultures value interpersonal contact and togetherness, and, given a choice, they would rather engage in behavior that benefits others than behavior that benefits only themselves.

Sternberg's Triangular Theory of Love

While Lee focuses primarily on stylistic differences in love, Robert Sternberg's (1986, 1987, 1988) triangular theory of love focuses on how three components of love—intimacy, passion, and commitment—work together to create different types of love. Specifically, Sternberg theorized that different love relationships are characterized by varying amounts of these three components. For some couples intimacy is dominant, with commitment and passion playing supporting roles. For other couples there may be lots of passion and intimacy but little commitment. As we will see, there are eight potential combinations of intimacy, passion, and commitment. Sternberg also made predictions about how intimacy, passion, and commitment change as relationships develop, as well as the degree to which each component is under our control. Box 6.2 provides a scale by which you can determine what your love triangle looks like.

Intimacy: The "Warm" Component   Of the three sides of Sternberg's (1986) triangle, intimacy is seen as the most foundational to love. This does not mean that intimacy is always a part of love, but rather that it is most often the central component within love relationships. Intimacy is based on feelings of emotional connection and closeness, and has therefore been called the "warm" or "affective" component of love. The close, connected feelings that people experience when having intimate conversations or exchanging hugs with loved ones exemplify this interpersonal warmth (Andersen & Guerrero, 1998a).

Sternberg theorized that intimacy is moderately stable over the course of a relationship. However, he made an important distinction between latent and manifest intimacy. **Latent intimacy** refers to internal feelings of closeness and interpersonal warmth, which are not directly observable by others. This type of intimacy is what we feel inside. **Manifest intimacy** refers to external behavioral

BOX 6.2 PUT YOURSELF TO THE TEST

What Does Your Love Triangle Look Like?

To determine what your love triangle looks like, rate yourself on each of these statements according to the following scale: **1 = Not at all . . . 5 = Moderately . . . 9 = Extremely**

	Not at All		Extremely
1. I view my relationship with my partner as permanent.	1 2 3 4 5 6 7 8 9		
2. My relationship with my partner is very romantic.	1 2 3 4 5 6 7 8 9		
3. I have a relationship of mutual understanding with my partner.	1 2 3 4 5 6 7 8 9		
4. I am certain of my love for my partner.	1 2 3 4 5 6 7 8 9		
5. I receive considerable emotional support from my partner.	1 2 3 4 5 6 7 8 9		
6. I adore my partner.	1 2 3 4 5 6 7 8 9		
7. I find myself thinking about my partner frequently during the day.	1 2 3 4 5 6 7 8 9		
8. I am committed to maintaining my relationship with my partner.	1 2 3 4 5 6 7 8 9		
9. My partner is able to count on me in times of need.	1 2 3 4 5 6 7 8 9		
10. Just seeing my partner is exciting for me.	1 2 3 4 5 6 7 8 9		
11. I find my partner very physically attractive.	1 2 3 4 5 6 7 8 9		
12. I idealize my partner.	1 2 3 4 5 6 7 8 9		
13. I have confidence in the stability of my relationship with my partner.	1 2 3 4 5 6 7 8 9		
14. I feel emotionally close to my partner.	1 2 3 4 5 6 7 8 9		
15. There is something almost magical about my relationship with my partner.	1 2 3 4 5 6 7 8 9		
16. I expect my love for my partner to last for the rest of my life.	1 2 3 4 5 6 7 8 9		
17. I give considerable emotional support to my partner.	1 2 3 4 5 6 7 8 9		
18. I can't imagine ending my relationship with my partner.	1 2 3 4 5 6 7 8 9		
19. I have decided that I love my partner.	1 2 3 4 5 6 7 8 9		

To find the triangle for your relationship, add your responses to items 3, 5, 9, 14, and 17, and divide by 5; this is your *intimacy* score. Next, add your responses to items 2, 6, 7, 10–12, and 15, and divide by 7; this is your *passion* score. Finally, add your responses to items 1, 4, 8, 13, 16, 18, and 19, and divide by 7; this is your *commitment* score. The closer each score is to 9, the higher the component.

Source: This scale is adapted from Acker and Davis's (1992) abbreviated Triangular Theory of Love Scale.

manifestations of affection and closeness, such as disclosing intimate feelings to a partner or spending extra time together. This type of intimacy is what we show to others. According to Sternberg (1986), latent intimacy is likely to increase but then reach a plateau as a relationship develops. For example, a dating couple may feel increasingly close as the two people get to know each other during the initial stages of their relationship. If the couple marries, this high level of latent intimacy is likely to stay fairly constant unless the spouses become dissatisfied with the relationship. Manifest intimacy, by contrast, is likely to grow during the initial stages of a relationship but then to decline over time.

Research has shown some support for Sternberg's predictions. Acker and Davis (1992) sampled a group of noncollege couples to see how the three components of the love triangle change over time and across relational stages. They found that couples in serious dating relationships reported feeling more intimacy than did couples in casual dating relationships. Intimate feelings were measured with questionnaire items such as "I feel emotionally close to my partner" (see Box 6.2). Thus, as couples became more serious, the partners' feelings of intimacy and closeness increased. However, consistent with Sternberg's (1986) predictions, Acker and Davis (1992) also found that behavioral (or manifest) intimacy decreased as relationship length increased. In other words, partners who had been together for a long time tended to show relatively low levels of behavioral intimacy. Behavioral intimacy was measured with items such as "I share my inner feelings with my partner" and "I make a special point of spending some time alone with my partner." Guerrero and Andersen (1991) reported similar findings for intimacy and touch. They unobtrusively observed couples in movie theater and zoo lines and recorded how many times partners touched each other. They found that, although people seriously dating and engaged couples touched the most, spouses felt just as close to each other as did daters. Therefore, even though married couples used less touch to manifest their intimacy, they still experienced very high levels of latent intimacy.

According to the triangular theory of love, intimacy is moderately controllable. This means that people have some control over their intimate feelings, but not to a great extent. An example may help illustrate this point. Imagine that you have been on two or three dates with a fun, attractive person to whom you feel an emotional connection. However, you discover that this person has very different values than you do. Perhaps your date wants to move to New York City to pursue a career on Wall Street, whereas you prefer the simple country life and hate the big city. Perhaps your date is not interested in starting a family for a long time, whereas you are ready to settle down, get married, and raise a couple of children. Although you feel an emotional connection to this person, you may decide to spend less time with her or him so that you won't develop any further attachment. Of course, it is hard to turn off one's emotions, so you might find yourself drawn to this person despite your intention to maintain an emotional distance.

Passion: The "Hot" Component   As we shall see, it is even harder to control the passionate part of a relationship. According to Sternberg (1986, 1988), passion is the "hot" component of love that consists of motivation and arousal. However, passion is not limited to sexual arousal. It also includes motivational needs for affiliation, control, and self-actualization. Thus, parents can feel a passionate love for their children without experiencing any form of sexual arousal. For instance, parents might feel passionately happy when their children achieve success in school or sports, and they may be passionately motivated to help their children succeed in life. In romantic relationships, however, passion is usually experienced primarily as sexual attraction and arousal.

According to the triangular theory of love, passion usually plays an important role in the initial stages of romantic relationships. Infatuation, for example, occurs when two people experience high degrees of passion before they get to know each other well enough to develop high levels of intimacy or commitment. Thus, passion draws people together and is a primary source of initial romantic attraction. Over time, however, it is difficult to sustain high levels of passion. Passion requires energy and excitement, and is draining and perhaps even stressful to maintain throughout a long-term relationship. Therefore, Sternberg (1986) predicted that passion and romance would be high during the initial stages of relationships but would then decrease as the relationship became more predictable and less arousing. This is not to say that long-term romantic relationships are devoid of passion. As Sternberg (1986) suggested, highly committed couples are likely to cycle back and forth in terms of passion. A romantic weekend away or a candlelight dinner followed by stargazing in a hot tub can provide an important passionate spark to a long-term relationship. Sternberg's point is that these types of events occur less often in developed relationships because it is hard to sustain a very high level of passion all of the time.

The research on how passion changes over the course of a relationship has been somewhat mixed, but overall it is generally consistent with Sternberg's predictions. According to Acker and Davis (1992), people feel and desire less passion as they grow older, which suggests that passion may become less integral to love as people age and as their relationships mature. Interestingly, however, Acker and Davis found that women felt less passion the longer they were in a relationship but that men did not vary in passion based on relationship length. In other words, women were more passionate in new relationships, whereas men showed fairly high levels of passion regardless of whether the relationship was new or old. In another study, Hatfield and Sprecher (1986a) found that college-aged couples reported an increase in passion during the early stage of relationships and then a leveling off, rather than a decline, in passion as the relationship stabilized. The duration of these relationships, however, was relatively brief. Emmers and Dindia (1995) had people report the amount of touch that commonly occurred in their romantic relationships. Similar to Guerrero and Andersen's (1991) findings, they found that couples reported experiencing the most touch in the intermediate stages of romantic relationships. Once relationships stabilized, a leveling-off effect occurred. Together these studies suggest that passion may increase rapidly in new relationships, level off for a while, and then decrease a bit over time.

As this discussion suggests, it can be very hard to control the passionate aspect of love. This component is based on arousal, and because arousal is associated with a physiological response, passionate feelings are difficult to control. You may have experienced times when you wished you could feel passion for someone but could not muster anything more than feelings of friendship. For example, one of our students once told us about a time when she and her male best friend had sat together in her bed talking comfortably all night. At one point they wondered out loud why they had never gotten together romantically. After all, they had a great relationship; they always had fun together, never fought, found each other attractive, and had been friends for a long time. In fact, their friendship had lasted longer than any of their romantic relationships. After some further discussion, they decided that their relationship simply did not have a romantic spark. They felt more like sister and brother than lovers, and even though it would be great to have passion as well, it just wasn't there. You may have also experienced the opposite phenomenon—wanting to feel less passionate about someone. You might feel passion for someone who is happily married to another person, someone who has repeatedly rejected you, or someone whom you know will be "bad" for you in the long run. But you cannot turn off those passionate feelings.

Commitment: The "Cool" Component   The third component of Sternberg's (1986, 1988) love triangle is commitment/decision. This component refers to the decision to love someone and the commitment to maintain that love. Because commitment is based on cognition and decision making, Sternberg referred to it as the "cool" or "cold" component. Commitment is undoubtedly an important part of love for many people. In a study by Fehr (1988), college-aged students were asked to rate how closely various words or phrases, such as "affection" and "missing each other when apart," relate to love. In this study, trust was rated as most central to love. Interestingly, however, of the 68 words and phrases Fehr listed, commitment ranked 8th overall, suggesting that it is highly central to love. The other two components of the triangular theory of love were also important, although less central, with intimacy ranking 19th and sexual passion rating 40th. Fehr (1988) also had college-aged students rate words and phrases describing the concept of commitment. Loyalty, responsibility, living up to one's word, faithfulness, and trust were the top five descriptors of commitment, suggesting that commitment involves being there for someone over the long haul.

Of the three components of the love triangle, commitment is also the most stable over time. In long-term relationships commitment typically builds gradually and then stabilizes. Acker and Davis (1992), for example, found that couples in more advanced relational stages reported more commitment. Commitment also appears to play an important role in keeping a relationship satisfying and stable. In Acker and Davis's study, intimacy, passion, and commitment were all related positively to satisfaction, but commitment, followed by intimacy, was the strongest predictor of satisfaction. Hendrick et al. (1988) conducted a study to determine whether commitment, relational satisfaction, or investment of time and effort was the best predictor of relational stability. They examined dating couples at the beginning and end of a 2-month period and found that commitment was the best predictor of whether couples would still be together at the end of the 2 months. Thus, commitment is not only a stable factor within many love relationships but also a stabilizing force within these relationships.

Of the three components of the triangular theory, commitment/decision is the most controllable. In other words, people have more conscious control over commitment than intimacy or passion (Sternberg, 1986). When people commit to a relationship, they have made a cognitive choice to maintain their love and build an enduring bond. Highly committed individuals are also likely to devote much time and effort to their relationships, and these investments help keep the relationship going (Rusbult, 1983). If people decide that they are no longer committed to a relationship, these investments will stop. Thus, people have a fairly high degree of conscious control over the commitment decision, as well as the decision whether to engage in behaviors that reinforce commitment.

Different Types of Love   Just as Lee argued that the primary styles of eros, storge, and ludus can be combined in different ways to create various love styles, Sternberg (1986, 1988) theorized that the three components of the triangle can be combined to create eight different types of love, including nonlove and liking. In this system **liking** is conceptualized as high in intimacy and low in passion and commitment. Notice that this conceptualization is similar to Davis's, in which friendship is based on comfortable feelings of intimacy, understanding, and acceptance, and love is based on these feelings plus caring and passion. Thus, passion and commitment may help separate liking from loving. Box 6.3 shows how the eight types of love differ in passion, commitment, and intimacy.

Two types of love contain passion but not commitment and often occur in the early stages of romantic relationships (Sternberg, 1988). In some ways these two types of love are similar to Lee's (1973) eros style. **Infatuation** is based on high levels of passion and low levels of both commitment and intimacy. When people become infatuated with someone, they usually do not know the person very well. Nonetheless, infatuated individuals idealize the objects of their affection and imagine that their lives would be wonderful if they could develop a relationship with the person whom they idolize. Because infatuation is based on the "hot" component of the love triangle, not surprisingly infatuated individuals often fall in and out of love quickly, as their passion heats up and then cools down. **Romantic love,** by contrast, is usually a bit more enduring. In this type of love, passion and intimacy are high, but commitment is still low. Romantic love often characterizes initial stages of dating relationships, when two people are sexually attracted to each other and feel an intimate connection but have not yet fully committed themselves to the relationship.

Companionate love, like Lee's storge love, is based on high levels of intimacy and commitment but low levels of passion. Love between family members and between friends often fits this description, as does love between romantic partners who have been together for a long time. **Empty love,** by contrast, characterizes relationships that are high in commitment and low in both passion and intimacy. Some long-term relationships may also fall here. For instance, if partners no longer feel attached to each other but stay together for religious reasons or because of the children, their love might be characterized

BOX 6.3 HIGHLIGHTS

Different Love Triangles

According to Sternberg's triangular theory of love, different types of love are based on the various combinations of intimacy, passion, and commitment. Using your scores from the love triangle test (see Box 6.2), you can determine what type of love best characterizes your present or past romantic relationship. A low score is represented by a minus sign; a high score is represented by a plus sign. Of course, your score may fall somewhere in between two or more types.

Types of Love	Intimacy	Passion	Commitment
Nonlove	−	−	−
Liking	+	−	−
Infatuation	−	+	−
Empty love	−	−	+
Romantic love	+	+	−
Friendship love	+	−	+
Fatuous love	−	+	+
Consummate love	+	+	+

as empty. In other cases empty love can characterize the beginning of a relationship. Arranged marriages sometimes begin with empty love because the spouses do not know each other well enough to have developed intimacy. Similarly, some pragmatic lovers may begin their relationships with empty love, particularly if they chose their partner based on vital statistics that were unrelated to physical appearance and attraction. In these relationships intimacy and passion may emerge later.

Within the United States **fatuous love,** which is characterized by high levels of passion and commitment but low levels of intimacy, is somewhat rare. This may appear odd at first. Why would people commit to someone if they did not feel emotional closeness and interpersonal warmth? Sometimes people meet, fall in love, and get married before really getting to know each other. Some long-term affairs can also be characterized by fatuous love. The individuals involved in the affair may feel more emotional intimacy with their spouses than with their lovers yet sustain an exciting, passionate, committed relationship with each other. Within Western cultures these types of arrangements were more acceptable in the past—especially for men. In fact, research reported in the History channel's documentary *The History of Sex* shows that until the 20th century men often were expected to have extramarital affairs. In Victorian England, for instance, women were taught that sex was something that good mothers and wives did not enjoy, and that sex should only be engaged in occasionally for purposes of procreation with one's spouse. Men, by contrast, were allowed to enjoy sex and taught to distinguish the kind of relations they had with their wives from those with their mistresses.

These types of arrangements, as well as open marriages in which both the wife and husband can have extramarital affairs, are still accepted in some cultures today (Altman & Ginat, 1996). In fact, in some cultures wives can easily disregard the importance of their husband's long-term mistresses because they know that the mistresses do not have the same intimate connection with their husbands that they do. In cultures that allow multiple husbands or wives, fatuous love may also surface fairly often. For example, when husbands have more than one wife, the wives often form very close, intimate friendships with one another rather than with the husband (Altman & Ginat, 1996). They are committed to their husband and possibly passionate toward him, but they feel more emotionally connected to one another than to him. In the PBS series *The Human Sexes,* anthropologist Desmond Morris reported that in some tribal cultures women with high social and economic status act as the head of household, acquiring both husbands and wives, and giving their name to all the children produced within their household. In this system the female head of household is committed to all of those under her, but she is likely to have stronger physical and/or emotional relationships with certain husbands and wives than others. Morris reported that in other cultures fatuous love is common in male-female relationships because true intimacy is only believed to be possible in same-sex relationships. Within these cultures people are committed to and sexually active with their spouses, but they engage in more acts of intimacy, such as hugging, holding hands, and disclosing personal information, with same-sex partners who are either friends or lovers.

While most Americans do not desire fatuous love, they believe strongly in **consummate love.** This type of love, which includes all three components of the triangle—intimacy, passion, and commitment—is held up as the ideal standard within American culture. Think about our fairy tales: The man and woman meet, fall madly in love, and live happily ever after; their relationship has it all! Some relationships are able to achieve this state, at least for a time, but this type of love may be hard to sustain. Most happy relationships will be characterized by some degree of intimacy, passion, and commitment (Acker & Davis, 1992), but it is unrealistic to expect these components to be high all of the time.

Different Perspectives on Triangles   Finally, to fully understand Sternberg's triangular theory of love, it is important to recognize that the love triangles can be viewed from different vantage points (Acker & Davis, 1992; Sternberg, 1987). First, every individual has her or his *actual triangle,* or perception of the type of love felt. Second, each person perceives that her or his partner sees their love in a particular way; this is the *perceived partner triangle.* Finally, both partners in any relationship have a *desired triangle* that represents what an ideal partner would think and feel. To illustrate, let's take a look at a fictional long-term dating relationship between Jamal and Dawn. Jamal might feel consummate love toward Dawn (his actual triangle), yet Dawn might think that Jamal feels only companionate love (her perceived partner triangle). To Dawn, Jamal might not seem as romantic and passionate as he once was, even though he still feels generally high levels of passion toward her. In this case there is likely to be a discrepancy between Dawn's desired triangle and her perceived partner's triangle. Discrepancies such as these are bound to occur, and small deviations are usually not a problem. If these discrepancies are large, however, the relationship is likely to be dissatisfactory (Acker & Davis, 1992; Sternberg, 1987). Thus, it is important for partners to have realistic expectations about love and to realize that they might not always perceive each other's feelings correctly.

Marston and Hecht's Love Ways

A third system for categorizing love was developed by Marston, Hecht, and their colleagues (Hecht, Marston, & Larkey, 1994; Marston & Hecht, 1994; Marston, Hecht, Manke, McDaniel, & Reeder, 1998; Marston, Hecht, & Robers, 1987). Marston and Hecht were particularly interested in determining how people experience and communicate love. Specifically, they looked at physiological and behavioral responses to love, with behavior encompassing both verbal and nonverbal communication.

To lay a foundation for their system of categorization, they conducted interviews to determine the types of feelings and behaviors that occur when people experience love (Marston et al., 1987). First, they asked people to describe the kinds of physiological changes that occur when they are in love. The most common response was that people feel more energetic and emotionally intense when in love. People also reported feeling (1) beautiful and healthy, (2) warm and safe, (3) nervous, as manifested by butterflies or knots in the stomach, (4) stronger than normal, and (5) less hungry, with a marked loss of appetite. Next, the researchers asked, "How do you communicate love to your partner?" The top five responses were (1) saying "I love you" to the partner, (2) doing special things for the partner, (3) being supportive, understanding, and attentive, (4) touching the partner, and (5) simply being together. Of these, saying "I love you" was the most common response, with 75% of respondents mentioning it. The researchers also asked, "How does your partner communicate love to you?" The top five responses were similar to those listed above. Saying "I love you" again emerged as the most common answer, with 70% of the participants mentioning this strategy. The next most common responses were showing love through touch and sexual contact, being supportive, doing favors or giving gifts, and engaging in behaviors that show togetherness. Other less frequently mentioned behaviors included communicating emotion, engaging in eye contact, and smiling. Together these findings show that love is communicated and received in a variety of ways but that verbally telling our partners that we love them is a particularly important way of expressing love.

Marston and his colleagues argued that love consists of a set of interdependent thoughts, feelings, attitudes, and behaviors, and that the subjective experience of love can change in importance throughout the relationship. They also suggested that relational partners can have similar or complementary styles, and that the degree of similarity versus complementarity often changes as partners adapt to each other (Marston & Hecht, 1994). Therefore, love experiences are unique at any given time and for any given person or relationship. Nonetheless, Marston et al. (1987) found that the physiological and behavioral responses to love could be grouped into seven categories or **love ways,** with these love ways representing the experiences of over 90% of lovers:

1. **Collaborative love:** Love is seen as a partnership that involves mutual support and negotiation, increases energy, and intensifies emotion.
2. **Active love:** Love is based on activity and doing things together. It also involves feelings of increased strength and self-confidence.
3. **Intuitive love:** Love is a feeling that often is communicated through nonverbal behavior such as touch and gaze, and experienced through physical reactions such as feeling warm all over, feeling nervous, and losing one's appetite.
4. **Committed love:** Love is based on commitment and involves experiencing strong feelings of connection, spending time together, and discussing the future.
5. **Secure love:** Love is based on security and intimacy. It is experienced through feelings of safety and warmth, and communicated through intimate self-disclosure.
6. **Expressive love:** Love is shown through overt behavior. It involves doing things for the partner and saying "I love you" frequently.
7. **Traditional romantic love:** Love involves togetherness and commitment. When people are in love they feel beautiful and healthy.

Understanding each other's love style may help partners maintain a happy relationship. Marston and Hecht (1994) gave some specific advice for managing love styles in ways that maximize relational satisfaction. First, they suggested that people recognize that their partner's love style might be different from their own. For example, if you express love through public affection, you should not necessarily expect your partner to do the same. In fact, your partner might dislike showing affection in public and prefer to cuddle in private. Second, people should be careful not to overvalue particular elements of their love way. For example, if you are an intuitive lover and the relationship develops to a point at which you no longer feel butterflies in your stomach and your appetite returns, you should not worry that you no longer love your partner as long as you are still experiencing love in other ways. Finally, people should avoid statements like "If you really loved me, you'd tell me more often" and instead focus on the various other ways that the partner does display his or her love. Remember that any two people bring different expectations about love to the relationship. The key may be to appreciate what each partner brings to the table, rather than wishing that the table was set in a different way.

Attachment Theory

So far, we have shown that scholars classify love in many different ways. Lee's six styles of love are based largely on stylistic and perceptual differences. Sternberg's types of love are based on various combinations of intimacy, passion, and commitment. Marston and Hecht's seven love ways are based on how people experience and express love through verbal and nonverbal communication. Attachment theorists take yet another approach in studying love. According to attachment theorists such as Hazan and Shaver (1987), love is best conceptualized as a process of attachment, which includes forming a bond and becoming close to someone. The theory also explains how **mental working models** (cognitive perceptions) guide how people interact with others. Based on these mental working models, people develop different attachment styles, experience different emotions, and display different behaviors. One unique aspect of the attachment perspective is that it takes a social-developmental approach, stressing how interactions with others affect people's attachment style across the life span.

An **attachment** is an affectional bond or relatively enduring tie "in which the partner is important as a unique individual, interchangeable with none other" (Ainsworth, 1991, p. 38). In other words, the relational partner has an irreplaceable position in someone's social network or memories, perhaps as a best friend, a first love, or a spouse. Being attached to someone involves having an emotional and cognitive connection to that person, which includes feelings of comfort and security. Ainsworth (1991) distinguished "attachments" from "relationships" in three ways. First, relationships are dyadic while attachments are situated within an individual's thoughts and feelings. Second, relationships can be short- or long-lived, but attachments are, by definition, enduring. For example, close childhood friends often live on in one another's memory despite the absence of a friendship in adulthood. These memories provide evidence that an attachment, or cognitive connection, was formed. Third, attachment is one of several components that helps define the nature of a relationship, with those relationships characterized by high levels of attachment likely to be the most influential within an individual's social network. In this section we describe some general ideas related to attachment theory, as well as discuss specific attachment styles.

The Propensity for Forming Attachments

Originally, attachment theory was studied within the context of child-caregiver relationships (Ainsworth, 1969; Ainsworth, Blehar, Waters, & Wall, 1978; Ainsworth & Wittig, 1969; Bowlby, 1969, 1973, 1980). Later, researchers extended the theory to include adult romantic relationships (Hazan & Shaver, 1987). Although parent-child and romantic relationships have received the most attention, attachment theory is applicable to all types of close relationships. Ainsworth (1989, 1991) listed participants in familial relationships (parent-child, siblings, grandparent-child), friends, and sexual partners as likely candidates for attachment relationships. Because people usually want to be part of a social group and to be loved and cared for by others, attachment theorists believe that people have a natural tendency to try to develop close relational bonds with others throughout the life span.

In childhood the need to develop attachments is an innate and necessary part of human development (Ainsworth, 1991). According to Bowlby (1969, 1973, 1980), attachment is an essential component within a larger system that functions to keep children in close proximity to caregivers. This proximity protects children from danger and provides them with a secure base from which to explore their world. For example, a toddler may feel free to try out the slides and swings at the playground because he or she knows that a caregiver is close by to act as a secure base in case he or she gets hurt or needs help. Exploration of the environment eventually leads to self-confidence and autonomy. Thus, one goal of the attachment system is to give children a sense of security and independence. Another goal is to help children develop a healthy capacity for intimacy. Children learn to trust and depend on those who care for them but to be wary of strangers.

In adult romantic relationships the type of attachment an individual feels for a partner helps define the type of relationship that person desires. For example, some people might want a relationship that is low in commitment and emotionally reserved, while others might desire relationships that are highly committed and emotionally charged. Bowlby (1977) and Ainsworth (1989, 1991), who pioneered research on child-caregiver attachments, both believed that attachment typifies intimate adult relationships, with Bowlby (1977) arguing that attachment is characteristic of all individuals from the cradle to the grave. The type of attachment individuals form depends on their cognitive conceptions of themselves and others. These cognitions, or mental working models, influence orientations toward love, intimacy, and interpersonal interaction in adult relationships.

Mental Working Models

Early interaction between children and their primary caregivers sets the stage for later attachments by shaping children's mental working models of "self" and "others." Mental working models can be thought of as generalized schemata or cognitive representations of both oneself and potential relational partners that reflect an individual's past experiences in close relationships and help him or her understand the world (Bowlby, 1973; Bretherton, 1988; Collins & Read, 1994). Models of both self and others fall along a positive-negative continuum. A positive self model is "an internalized sense of self-worth that is not dependent on ongoing external validation" (Bartholomew, 1993, p. 40). Thus, individuals who hold positive self models view themselves as self-sufficient, secure, and lovable. Those holding negative self models see themselves as dependent, insecure, and unworthy of love and affection. Positive models of others reflect expectations concerning how supportive, receptive, and accepting others are, as well as how rewarding it is to participate in an intimate relationship.

Individuals with positive mental working models of others see relationships as worthwhile and tend to possess "approach" orientations toward intimacy. Individuals with negative mental working models of others see relationships as relatively unrewarding and tend to possess "avoidance" orientations toward intimacy.

The idea that mental models are "working" implies that, although somewhat stable over time, new experiences can modify and/or alter existing cognitive perceptions of self and others. According to Bowlby (1977), the quality of the child-caregiver relationship first shapes these internal representations of self and others. In fact, Bowlby's research suggests that the first 2 to 3 years of life are especially critical in developing these mental models. By the time a baby is about 6 weeks old, he or she already shows a preference for the primary caregiver—usually the mother. For example, if a 2-month-old baby is crying, she might be best comforted by her mother. At around 14 to 20 months old, toddlers are usually attached to their mothers and feel separation anxiety when they leave. At this time babysitters may have trouble with their charges, who often become fairly distressed when they realize their mother, who functions as their secure base, is not around. One of us had an experience like this when babysitting a friend's child. The little boy, who was about 1½ years old, was fine right after his parents left. However, an hour later he began searching the house for his mother. When he could not find her, he stood at the window calling, "Mommy, mommy!" and looking for her. Eventually he settled down and watched a cartoon on television, but he clearly had experienced a bout of separation anxiety.

Most children emerge from the first 2 years of life with secure, healthy attachments to caregivers (Ainsworth et al., 1978; Bowlby, 1969). If this is the case, they have developed positive mental models of both themselves and others. However, not all children are so lucky. About 30% of children develop negative mental models of themselves and/or others. Often these children were neglected, received inconsistent care, or did not have their needs met. Based on these types of interactions, they may have trouble trusting others, and they may feel that they would have received the care they needed if they weren't such "bad" kids. Clearly these types of thoughts can affect a child's self-esteem.

Attachment Styles

Bowlby (1969, 1973, 1977) believed that people's early attachments with caregivers set the stage for adult attachments with friends, lovers, and their own children. In fact, Bowlby considered mental models of self and others to be the cornerstones of personality. Depending on individuals' configurations of mental working models—that is, the "mix" of how positive or negative their models of self and other are—they develop different "attachment styles." An **attachment style** can be defined as a social interaction style that is consistent with the type and quality of relationship one wishes to share with others, based on working models of self and others (Bartholomew, 1990). Social interaction styles include one's own communication style, the way one processes and interprets others' behavior, and the way one reacts to others' behavior (Guerrero & Burgoon, 1996). Because these styles are guided by differences in mental working models, they are also characterized by differences in (1) self-perceptions, (2) orientations toward relationships, and (3) expectations about relationships and relational partners (Bartholomew, 1990, 1993).

Children's Attachment Styles   Early work on both child-caregiver and adult romantic relationships concentrated on identifying different attachment styles. Within the child-caregiver literature, Ainsworth and her colleagues (Ainsworth, 1969, 1982, 1989; Ainsworth & Eichberg, 1991; Ainsworth et al., 1978; Ainsworth & Wittig, 1969) delineated three types of infant attachment: secure, avoidant, and anxious-ambivalent (with the latter category sometimes referred to as "resistant"). The majority of children fall into the secure category. **Secure** children tend to have responsive and warm parents, to receive moderate levels of stimulation, and to engage in synchronized interaction with their caregivers. The "goodness of fit" between the caregiver and the child is crucial. A caregiver may need to adjust her or his style of interaction to accommodate the child. Thus, one child may need a lot of cuddling and reassurance while another may prefer to be left alone. This helps explain why children from the same family environment may develop different attachment styles. Children who develop secure attachments to a caregiver are more likely to feel free to explore, to approach others, and to be positive toward strangers than are insecure types. Secure children are also likely to protest separation and then to show happiness when reunited with their caregivers. These children tend to develop positive mental models of self and others.

The two insecure attachment types—avoidant and anxious-ambivalent—often develop in response to dysfunctional child-caregiver communication or to the absence of a good fit between the caregiver's style and the child's needs. **Avoidant** children tend to have caregivers who are either insensitive to their signals or are trying too hard to please. In addition, avoidant children are often either over- or understimulated, which leads to physiological arousal and defensiveness. In short, their expectations are not being met, and they tend to hold fairly negative models of others as being unable to give them what they need. These children stay within themselves, explore their environments infrequently, and are seldom positive toward strangers. They also tend not to protest separation from caregivers.

Children who develop **anxious-ambivalent** attachment styles tend to be the product of inconsistent behavior by caregivers, who may be responsive at times and unresponsive at others. Sometimes caregivers are preoccupied with problems of their own, such as relational conflict, divorce, or substance abuse. Inconsistent interaction patterns cause these children to develop self models of doubt, insecurity, and uncertainty. Anxious-ambivalent children often are tentative when exploring their environment in the presence of their caregivers and fearful of exploration if alone. These children also tend to fear strangers. They protest separation from caregivers vehemently, yet are both relieved and angry when the caregiver returns. This contradiction is reflected in their label—they

BOX 6.4 HIGHLIGHTS

Three Boys at a Playground

Based on the descriptions of these three boys' behavior, who is secure, who is anxious-ambivalent, and who is avoidant?

Brandon: Brandon plays alone in a corner in a sandbox. He seems oblivious to the other children around him and instead concentrates on building a sand castle. When he gets sand in his eye, he uses the corner of his T-shirt to try to wipe his eye clean. He does not ask for help from his caregiver; nor does he acknowledge his caregiver's presence very much. When another child approaches him and asks if he can help build the castle, Brandon says he'd rather do it himself.

Bobby: Bobby is playing on the swings. A group of children join him, and they all take turns pushing one another. When Bobby is swinging particularly high, he calls out to his caregiver, "Look at me! See how high I'm going?" At one point Bobby gets going too high and fast, so he asks his caregiver to help him slow the swing down. Once the swing's motion is back under his control, he goes back to playing with the other children and no longer needs the caregiver.

Brent: Brent is playing on the slide. He is nervous about hurting himself, so he asks his caregiver to wait and catch him at the bottom of the slide. He is also a little nervous about playing with the other children, and he gets angry if someone cuts in front of him to use the slide. When Brent skins his knee on the side of the slide, he begins crying and asking his caregiver for help. Brent decides the slide is not really much fun after all, and he asks his caregiver to carry him home.

Note: Brandon is probably avoidant, Bobby is probably secure, and Brent could well be anxious-ambivalent.

---

are anxious upon separation and ambivalent when the caregiver returns. Sometimes these children develop positive models of others because they do receive some comfort and security from caregivers. However, they often see the "inconsistency" in the caregiver's behavior as more their "fault" than the caregiver's, resulting in more negative models of self than others. Box 6.4 gives examples of all three attachment styles.

Adult Attachment Styles Attachment styles also affect adult relationships. Hazan and Shaver (1987) delineated three distinct adult attachment styles that parallel those found in the child development literature. In their three-category system Hazan and Shaver conceptualized love as an attachment process that is "experienced somewhat differently by different people because of variations in their attachment histories" (p. 511). Using Ainsworth et al.'s (1978) three attachment styles as a guide, Hazan and Shaver (1987) proposed that adults can have secure, avoidant, or anxious-ambivalent attachments to their romantic partners. Secures are comfortable getting close to and depending on romantic partners, and seldom worry about being abandoned. Avoidants are uncomfortable getting close to or depending on romantic partners and feel nervous if others try to become too close to them. Finally, anxious ambivalents want to be close to

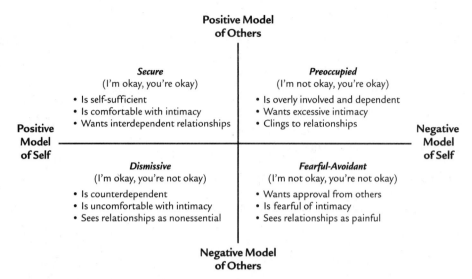

Positive Model of Others

Secure
(I'm okay, you're okay)
- Is self-sufficient
- Is comfortable with intimacy
- Wants interdependent relationships

Preoccupied
(I'm not okay, you're okay)
- Is overly involved and dependent
- Wants excessive intimacy
- Clings to relationships

Positive Model of Self

Negative Model of Self

Dismissive
(I'm okay, you're not okay)
- Is counterdependent
- Is uncomfortable with intimacy
- Sees relationships as nonessential

Fearful-Avoidant
(I'm not okay, you're not okay)
- Wants approval from others
- Is fearful of intimacy
- Sees relationships as painful

Negative Model of Others

FIGURE 6.2 Bartholomew's Four Attachment Styles *Source:* Adapted from Guerrero (1996).

their romantic partners but find it difficult to get as close as they want. As Hazan and Shaver (1987) put it, anxious ambivalents "want to merge completely with another person, and this desire sometimes scares people away" (p. 515). Thus, secures desire and can easily maintain intimacy, avoidants shy away from intimacy, and anxious ambivalents crave excessive amounts of intimacy.

Research has supported these associations between intimacy and attachment style. Secures have been found to be moderately open and self-disclosing, and to strive for interdependence with their partners. By contrast, avoidants tend to be underinvolved and autonomous, while anxious ambivalents tend to be overinvolved, demanding, and dependent (Collins & Read, 1990; Feeney & Noller, 1991). Thus, if interdependence is portrayed as a spider's web, secures would create intimacy webs that are intertwined, avoidants would keep their webs relatively separate, and anxious ambivalents would build webs filled with heavy entanglements.

A few years after Hazan and Shaver published their ground-breaking work, Bartholomew (1990) proposed a four-category system of attachment. She argued that the working mental models a person holds about self and other combine to produce four, rather than three, attachment styles: secure, preoccupied, dismissive, and fearful-avoidant; Figure 6.2 depicts these four styles.

Secures have positive models of themselves and others ("I'm okay and you're okay"). The secures in Bartholomew's system are essentially the same as those described by Hazan and Shaver. They feel good about themselves and their relationships, and they display "high self-esteem and an absence of serious interpersonal problems" (Bartholomew, 1990, p. 163). These individuals have the capacity for close, fulfilling relationships. They are likely to have realistic expectations, to be satisfied with their relationships, and to be comfortable depending on others and having others depend on them. Secures are also flexible in communicative situations (Bartholomew, 1990) and display high levels of social skill (Guerrero & Jones, 2000). In general, their communication tends to be pleasant, attentive, and expressive (Guerrero, 1996), and they smile at, laugh with, and touch their romantic partners more than do individuals with other attachment styles (Tucker & Anders, 1998). It is also important to note that when secures experience distress they are usually able to express their negative feelings appropriately and to seek support from others (Feeney, 1995; Simpson & Rholes, 1994).

Preoccupieds, who are fairly similar to anxious ambivalents in other systems, have positive models of others but negative models of themselves ("You're okay but I'm not okay"). Perhaps these individuals can best be described in terms of their overdependence on relationships. Bartholomew (1990), for example, argued that preoccupieds are characterized by "an insatiable desire to gain others' approval and a deep-seated feeling of unworthiness" (p. 163). As such, preoccupieds are likely to approach others readily and "to reach out to others in an attempt to fulfill dependency needs" (Bartholomew, 1990, p. 165). Their relational identities often are much stronger than their self-identities; they need to have a relationship with someone to feel worthwhile. In fact, preoccupieds report feeling lost and unable to cope without a close relationship. They also are likely to cling to their relationships in times of trouble and to resist any attempts by a partner to de-escalate or terminate close relationships. In terms of their communication style, preoccupieds tend to be pleasant, attentive, and expressive (Guerrero, 1996), although there are exceptions to this pattern. Preoccupieds can disclose too much and be overly expressive. For example, they may disclose intimate information too quickly and have trouble controlling their emotional expressions (Bartholomew & Horowitz, 1991; Guerrero & Jones, 2000; Mikulincer & Nachshon, 1991). Research has also shown that preoccupieds display dominant, demanding behavior in an attempt to hang onto their relationships or to change their partners (Bartholomew & Horowitz, 1991; Guerrero & Langan, 1999). Finally, preoccupieds feel intense negative affect during stressful situations and have difficulty coping with their distress (Simpson, 1990).

Fearful avoidants have negative models of both themselves and others ("I'm not okay and you're not okay"). Some of the avoidants in Hazan and Shaver's system fall in this category, as do a few of the anxious ambivalents, particularly when they have negative views of both others and themselves. The key characteristic of fearful avoidants is that they are afraid of hurt and rejection, perhaps because they have experienced painful relationships in the past. Fearful avoidants usually want to depend on someone but find it difficult to open up to others. As Bartholomew (1990) put it, fearful avoidants "desire social contact and intimacy, but experience pervasive interpersonal distrust and fear of rejection" (p. 164). Fearful avoidants tend to avoid social situations and potential relationships because of this fear of rejection. Even when in relationships, they tend to be hesitant to communicate emotions or to initiate escalation of the relationship. Bartholomew (1990) noted the paradoxical nature of fearful avoidants' actions and desires: By refusing to open themselves up to others, they undermine their chances for building the very type of trusting relationship they desire. Their communication style reflects their fear and lack of trust. Guerrero (1996) found that fearful avoidants were less fluent and used larger proxemic distances than individuals with other attachment styles.

Dismissives have positive models of themselves but negative models of others ("I'm okay but you're not okay"). Many of the avoidants in Hazan and Shaver's system would fall here. Dismissives can best be characterized as counterdependent. In other words, they are so self-sufficient that they shun close involvement with others. Some researchers suggest that counterdependence is a defensive strategy that allows people to feel good about themselves without opening themselves up to the criticisms and scrutiny of others. Dismissives neither desire nor fear close attachments, but rather lack the motivation to build and maintain intimate relationships (Bartholomew, 1990). They place a much higher value on autonomy than on relationships and tend to focus on less personal aspects of their lives, such as careers, hobbies, and self-improvement (Bartholomew, 1990). In terms of their communication style, dismissives generally exhibit less disclosure, conversational involvement, and affection than do individuals with the secure or preoccupied style (Bartholomew & Horowitz, 1991; Guerrero, 1996). Dismissives also are seen as fairly dominant or controlling, and they tend to interrupt their partners more than do those with other attachment styles (Guerrero & Langan, 1999). When dismissives experience emotional distress, they often deny their feelings and insist on handling their problems without help from others (Bartholomew, 1993). As Simpson and Rholes (1994) put it, dismissives "distance themselves from others emotionally. Over time they come to see themselves as fully autonomous and immune to negative events" (p. 184).

The Reinforcement Effect and Critical Life Events

Perhaps one of the most interesting aspects of attachment styles is that they are self-reinforcing (Bartholomew, 1993). In other words, if people act in ways that are consistent with their attachment style, their partners will react to them in ways that reinforce their views of self and others. For example, because secures are self-confident and readily approach others, they are more likely to make friends and develop relationships, which leads them to feel even better about themselves and others. Preoccupieds, by contrast, are continually reaching for higher levels of intimacy in their relationships. Perhaps you have had a partner like this—someone who wanted to meet your family right away, told you how much she or he loved you on the third date, or wanted to move in with you after a few dates. A common reaction to these premature declarations of love and commitment is to try to de-escalate the relationship, which only makes the preoccupied person work even harder to try to keep the partner close. This process reinforces that individual's negative model of self ("My partner doesn't love me as much as I love her") and positive model of others ("Everything would be great if only I could get him to love me"). Fearful avoidants suffer from similarly paradoxical interaction patterns. More than anything else, fearful avoidants need to build a secure, happy relationship to help them feel better about themselves and others. However, their fear of pain and rejection keeps them from reaching out to others and developing the kind of intimate relationship that would bring them out of their protective shells. Dismissives display similarly negative self-reinforcing patterns. If dismissives continually avoid highly committed relationships and refuse to ask others for help and support, they reinforce their view that other people are not necessary and that they should rely only on themselves. They miss the opportunity to discover ways in which committed relationships can enrich, rather than impede, personal satisfaction.

Because attachment styles can be self-reinforcing, they are fairly stable over time. However, it is important to note that people's attachment styles can change based on new experiences with others. While early interactions with caregivers may have the most power to create mental working models of self and others, later life experiences can also have an effect. For example, some research suggests that, if a child develops a close, positive friendship with a peer, this friendship can undo some of the damage caused by a bad parental attachment (Sullivan, 1953). Other research has shown that stressful life experiences, such as a painful divorce or relational breakup, or the death of a loved one, can affect people's attachment styles, usually making them more insecure (Shaver, Hazan, & Bradshaw, 1988). For example, one of our students once told us that he was secure until he caught his girlfriend of nearly 5 years in bed with another man. As would be expected, he said he had trouble trusting future girlfriends. Eventually he found a woman whom he called "the right person," and he once again built a happy and trusting relationship. In addition to changing over time, attachment styles may change somewhat depending on the type of relationship. For example, many people have secure relationships with family members and friends but are fearful or preoccupied with their romantic partners.

Finally, it is important to keep in mind that most people are not completely secure, preoccupied, fearful-avoidant, or dismissive. As Figure 6.2 suggests, most people do not hold perfectly positive or negative models of self or others. Instead, most people fall somewhere in the middle. Based on how positive or negative your models of self and others are, you will fall in a different place on Bartholomew's model. For instance, you might fall in the secure category but still be fairly close to the preoccupied category, or you might fall on the line between the fearful-avoidant and dismissive styles. Your partner is also unlikely to identify with a single attachment style perfectly. Moreover, the interaction between your two styles is likely to produce a unique set of behaviors. As with the love styles, the attachment styles reflect some important differences in how people approach close relationships, but it is crucial to see ourselves and others as complex individuals who do not always fit neatly into one category.

Conclusion

People approach loving relationships in many different ways. Every person has a special set of perceptions, expectations, and preferences that contribute to her or his styles of loving and attachment. When two people's styles interact within the context of a close relationship, an even more unique pattern emerges. Thus, partners should realize that what works in one of their relationships might not necessarily work in others and that it is difficult for two people to fully meet each other's expectations. Relational partners should also try to help each other grow as individuals. For example, preoccupied individuals may need to make an effort to give their partners more space, while dismissive individuals may need to strive to show more intimacy. At the same time, individuals in relationships with people who are preoccupied or dismissive should be patient and understanding, rather than demanding more or less intimacy than their partners are comfortable giving.

Several other issues related to love are elaborated on in other chapters. For example, Chapter 7 focuses specifically on one component of love—sexuality and passion, while Chapter 10 focuses on intimacy. Finally, it is important to note that love is not always a happy experience. Sometimes the object of our affection rejects us, and sometimes we feel guilty when we have to tell an admirer that we are not interested in him or her. This sad situation, which is referred to as "unrequited love," was discussed in Chapter 5.

Whether you are in a happy love relationship, are still trying to find a loving partner, or do not feel a need to develop many loving relationships, this chapter should give you a deeper appreciation for the unique way you think about and communicate love. At the beginning of this chapter, we tried to define love by contrasting it with friendship, in part because there is no simple answer to the seemingly straightforward question, What is love? Although we read about love in poems and novels, hear about love in songs and talk shows, and see love in films and television shows, it is a complex, highly variable phenomenon that defies simple definition. Indeed, instead of simply asking what love is, it may be more appropriate to ask, What is love to me and to my partner, and how does love function in the unique relationship we share?

Discussion Questions

1. How would you distinguish love from liking?
2. Do you think people's love styles change throughout their lives? If so, what factors do you think account for this change? How might culture affect people's love styles?
3. According to attachment theory, parent-child interaction forms the basis for personality development, including the capacity to have close, intimate adult relationships with others. To what extent do you agree or disagree that early interaction with parents shapes a person's life?

The Closest Encounter
Sexual Interaction

In the classic novel *Fanny Hill,* written more than 250 years ago, John Cleland's female character describes that timeless moment of sexual ecstasy: "We continued for some instants, lost, breathless, senseless of everything and in every part but those favorite ones of nature, in which all that we had enjoyed of life and sensation was now totally concentered." Human beings are sexual creatures. Sex is a powerful drive and a reinforcing behavior for nearly all of us. If humans lacked sex drive and if sex were not pleasurable, we would be unlikely to reproduce, and the human race would have become extinct thousands of years ago.

In this chapter we focus on sexual behavior as an important aspect of human relationships. In particular, we examine communication related to the initiation and refusal of sexual activity, coercion and harassment, and safe sex. Although many intimate relationships are platonic, some of our closest encounters are sexual, including romances and marriages. Much of the research in this area has focused on differences in sexual attitudes, preferences, and behaviors between men and women in heterosexual relationships, although some research has examined how sex functions in same-sex relationships. Thus, as you read this chapter, keep in mind that some of the research has a heterosexual bias. In addition, the majority of research reported here focuses on the attitudes and behaviors of couples living in the United States. In other parts of the world and other cultures, sexual attitudes and behaviors may be more or less rigid. Finally, keep in mind that an examination of the physiology of sex and sexual desire per se is beyond the scope of this chapter, although excellent books on these topics are available if you would like more information (see Rathus, Nevid, & Fishner-Rathus, 1993; Regan & Berscheid, 1999).

Sex in Relationships

Research has shown that sexual interaction, which includes physical contact such as intimate kissing and touching, and sexual intercourse, is usually a vital part of dating and marital relationships. Although most people experience some ambivalence about sexual involvement in premarital relationships (O'Sullivan & Gaines, 1998), some sexual involvement is typical in most dating relationships. For most people sex, attraction, desire, romance, and love are closely inter-twined. In this section we examine differences in sexual interaction based on the type of relationship, sex and gender, and sexual orientation.

Sex in Short-Term and Early Dating Relationships

Short-term sex occurs when a couple has sex once or a limited number of times without ever developing an emotionally intimate relationship. Most short-term sex occurs in the form of one-night (or one-day) stands. Contrary to the stereo-type that only men seek short-term sexual relationships, research shows that both men and women may engage in short-term mating strategies. Many of the motivations for short-term sexual relationships are similar for men and women: sexual desire, sexual experimentation, physical pleasure, and alcohol or drug use. However, men are more likely to use short-term sex to enhance their status, whereas women are more likely to use it as means of trying to establish a long-term commitment (Regan & Dreyer, 1999). For many men the ideal short-term mate is physically attractive, but men are willing to compromise on other dimensions such as intelligence and status. For women the ideal short-term partner is physically attractive, somewhat older, more experienced, and interpersonally responsive (Regan, 1998b). Women are much less likely than men to compromise on these standards.

Situational variables affect short-term mating strategies as well. In a creative study Pennebaker and his colleagues (1979) showed that people in bars do indeed get more attractive as closing time nears. At three preselected times researchers approached college students in bars and asked randomly selected men and women to evaluate the attractiveness of potential opposite-sex partners. Sure enough, as closing time neared, the perceived attractiveness of opposite-sex patrons increased while evaluations of same-sex patrons remained the same (Pennebaker et al., 1979).

Although one-night stands are not uncommon, premarital sex typically occurs within dating relationships between people who share some level of emotional intimacy. In dating relationships people become sexually involved for a variety of reasons including sexual attraction, sexual arousal, and desire for more relational intimacy (O'Sullivan & Gaines, 1998). Situational factors, such as drinking alcohol or going to the senior prom, can also prompt sexual involvement (Sprecher & McKinney, 1993). Research has revealed that among dating couples sexual satisfaction is an important component of relational satisfaction. The correlation between relational satisfaction and sexual satisfaction is very high for both men and women (Byers, Demmons, & Lawrence, 1998), although, of course, many other factors contribute to relational satisfaction, such as commitment, love, and compatibility. Research has shown that if the relationship is satisfying and if neither partner feels coerced or obligated to have sex, their first experience of sexual intercourse usually has a positive effect on the relationship (Cate, Long, Angera, & Draper, 1993). This is not to say that sex always makes a relationship better. But these findings do suggest that high-quality sexual interaction can contribute to a good relationship.

Sex in Marriage and Other Long-Term Relationships

In long-term love relationships, physical contact, including sexual contact, is very important. "Romantic lovers . . . seek to spend time with and maintain physical contact with the loved object; specifically they hold, touch, caress, kiss, make love with and smile at the partner" (Regan & Berscheid, 1999, p. 122). Buss (1988b) argued that sexual intimacy is the sine qua non (essential component) of heterosexual love and evolved to keep mates interested in one another. Buss (1994) illustrated the importance of couplehood when he argued that "tremendous benefits flow to couples who remain committed. From this unique alliance comes the efficiency of acquiring a complementary set of skills, a division of labor, a sharing of resources, a unified front against mutual enemies, . . . a stable home environment for rearing children, and a more extended kin" (p. 122).

Research has shown that in long-term romantic relationships sexual satisfaction is very important, even though it may not be quite as important as it is in dating relationships. In long-term romantic relationships the association between relational satisfaction and sexual satisfaction is still high (Lawrence & Byers, 1995), although not as high as in dating relationships. Couples who are happy with their sex lives also report being happier in the relationship overall. Lawrence and Byers also reported that men and women find a variety of sexual activities equally important in contributing to long-term sexual satisfaction.

According to research, both men and women view sexual desire as important to achieving true romantic love (Regan, 1998a; Regan & Berscheid, 1999; Sternberg, 1987). A study by Sprecher and Regan (1996) showed that people who reported high levels of sexual desire in their relationships also tended to report high levels of excitement and love. Interestingly, the positive association between sexual satisfaction and relational satisfaction has also been obtained in a sample from the People's Republic of China, suggesting the cross-cultural strength of this association (Reined, Byers, & Pan, 1997). Indeed, when students in the United States were asked to list the persons whom they sexually desired and the persons with whom they were in love, 85% of the persons named appeared on both lists (Berscheid & Meyers, 1996).

Selection criteria for a long-term romantic partner differ from those for a first date or short-term sexual encounter. Both men and women place a higher value on qualities such as interpersonal skill, emotional stability, responsiveness, and family orientation, and less value on physical attraction, in long-term as opposed to short-term relationships (Regan, 1998b). The bottom line, however, is this: In long-term relationships "sexual desire is a distinguishing feature and a prerequisite of the romantic love experience" (Regan & Berscheid, 1999, p. 126). In short-term sexual encounters, by contrast, sexual desire is often present without love or intimacy.

Sex and Gender Differences

Men and women both strive for good relationships, of which sex is an important part, but they are not identical in their sexual inclinations and behaviors. The reproductive roles of men and women are quite different, and sexual behavior and mate selection strategies are quite distinct as well. Biologically women expend a much greater investment of time and resources in becoming a parent. For women reproduction involves finding a mate, having sex, going through pregnancy and childbirth, nursing and nurturing the baby, and in most cases raising the child to adulthood. For men only finding a mate and having sex are biological imperatives. Of course, most men stay with their mate during pregnancy and help to raise their offspring. But this is a choice made by responsible men. As the large number of single moms and deadbeat dads indicates, some men make little investment in their offspring.

Of course, having sex does not necessarily mean having babies. Indeed, most couples conscientiously avoid pregnancy during their sexual encounters. Having a baby is a huge commitment of time, money, and resources. Most couples have sex on many occasions, but only a few of these sexual encounters are intended to produce offspring. Instead, sex is usually about pleasure, commitment, and closeness. The biological imperative of reproduction that makes humans so sexual is deeply ingrained, and for most people, sexual desire leads to frequent sexual encounters. Reproduction is far less necessary.

It is likely that both biology and socialization explain a primary difference between men and women: Women are more likely to be attracted to men who are relationally oriented and emotionally connected, and who show tenderness and intimacy with them. Men are more likely to experience sexual desire in response to sexy looks, erotic situations, and a variety of friendly social behaviors (Cupach & Metts, 1995). In fact, both men and women believe that males are more sexual (Regan & Berscheid, 1995). Many studies have reported that women's sexual desire is more dependent on feelings and the type of relationship they share with the partner, whereas men's desire is more influenced by physical attraction, sexual pleasure, and erotic qualities (Regan & Berscheid, 1995, 1999). Interestingly, the first act of sexual intercourse between two people usually has a much more positive effect on the relationship from the vantage point of women than men, assuming that the sex was a voluntary act reflecting love and/or commitment (Cate et al., 1993).

Recent research suggests that the female sex drive is much more socially flexible, adaptable, and responsive than the male sex drive, which is more predictable and consistent, less shaped by cultural forces, and somewhat stronger (Baumeister, 2000). This is compatible with evidence that the female sex drive is highly variable; that is, some women seem to do fine without sex, while other women are highly sexual. Baumeister (2000) made a strong case that women are much more sexually flexible than men are and adapt more easily to changing relational circumstances. He cited numerous studies that report high variation in sex drive across time for individual women. For example, a woman may have a stronger sex drive when she is in an intimate (or potentially intimate) relationship than when she is not involved with anyone. Men, by contrast, seem to have a more consistent sex drive that operates regardless of their relational involvement with someone. Evidence for this sex difference also comes from a variety of indirect sources. For instance, subscriptions to magazines such as *Playboy* and *Penthouse* far outnumber subscriptions to publications such as *Playgirl*. Of course, the popularity of Viagra suggests that men's sex drives are also somewhat variable, although not as variable as women's.

Female sexuality is also more varied across different sociocultural settings than is male sexuality. Baumeister (2000) cited ethnographic studies that report much greater cross-cultural variation in sexual behavior for females than for males. For example, in some cultures it is okay for women to have premarital sex while in others it is not. Many studies also show that women are more likely to hide their true sexual attitudes than are men. For example, women are more likely to exaggerate their level of sexual satisfaction to please their partners. In addition, women sometimes hesitate to reveal or express their full sexuality for fear of being seen as "easy." As traditional gender roles continue to break down, however, women may feel freer to take a more proactive, rather than reactive, stance when it comes to sexual interaction.

Men and women also think about sex differently. First, men have greater expectations for sex on dates than do women (Mongeau & Johnson, 1995); that is, they are more likely to anticipate and hope for more sexual activity than are women. Second, research suggests that men think about sex more often than do women. Some research has even shown that males think about sex every few seconds (Byers, Purden, & Clark, 1998). Also quite common, for both men and women, are sexually intrusive thoughts that are unwanted, sudden, involuntary, and often obsessive. One study found that 88% of men and 81% of women have sexually intrusive thoughts (Byers et al., 1998). Among the most common of these thoughts, for both men and women, were having sex in a public place, having sex with an authority figure, and being surrounded by people when naked. In the Byers et al. study, men were more likely than women to have thoughts related to sexual fantasies, whereas women were more likely than men to have thoughts about being sexually victimized.

Sex in Gay and Lesbian Relationships

A significant minority of people are simply not attracted to members of the opposite sex, but rather have same-sex attractions. Many homosexuals describe early recollections of same-sex attraction and a clear sense that they were different from the majority as early as the preschool years (Rathus et al., 1993). This is consistent with research suggesting that throughout the world most gay men and lesbians experience some degree of gender nonconformity as children (Crooks & Baur, 1999).

Because men and women differ in their sexual attitudes and behaviors (as described above), it seems likely that relationships between lesbians, gay men, and heterosexuals also differ. Of course, homosexual relationships, whether male or female, also differ from heterosexual relationships in many ways. Some of these differences stem from the fact that, despite increasingly progressive attitudes about homosexuality and bisexuality in the United States, these types of relationships still are not as readily accepted or understood by society at large as are heterosexual romantic relationships. Growing up gay in a largely heterosexual world is not easy, and the most severe problems typically arise in connection to reactions of the society or peer groups rather than from being gay. Adolescence is a tough time for all young people, as indicated by the high teenage suicide rate. And the rate is even higher for gay teens, who may need counseling as they adjust to their sexual orientation and to the attitudes of those around them.

Sex in Lesbian Relationships   Lesbian couples are likely to have sex less frequently than heterosexual dating or married couples. Most lesbian couples also have sex less frequently than do men in gay relationships (Blumstein & Schwartz, 1983). Blumstein and Schwartz's research also suggested that around 75% of lesbian couples are monogamous and that monogamy is an extremely important component contributing to a satisfying relationship for lesbians. Lesbians may also develop sexual relationships more slowly than other couples for at least two reasons. First, women are taught to be protective about sex in that they are more selective in choosing sexual partners than are men. Second, women are socialized to take a reactive as opposed to a proactive role in sexual situations; men are expected to initiate sexual activity, and women are expected to act as gatekeepers who decide whether sexual activity will take place. Lesbians must renegotiate these gender roles so that they feel comfortable initiating sex. There is also mounting evidence that women simply do not have as strong a sex drive as men (Baumeister, 2000; Julien, Bouchard, Gagnon, & Pomperleau, 1992). Like heterosexual women, lesbians prize physical contact, such as hugging, cuddling, and touching, and are much more likely to consider these ends in and of themselves rather than a prelude to sex (Blumstein & Schwartz, 1983). According to Blumstein and Schwartz, women need affection even more than sex, although heterosexual women adapt to male sexuality and treat hugging and snuggling as a prelude to sex rather than an end in itself.

As many as 25% of lesbians actually are married to men (Rathus et al., 1993). Some of these lesbians may be bisexual, others may be testing their potentially heterosexual orientation, and still others may be concealing their homosexual orientation. According to Bell and Weinberg (1978), relational satisfaction is low in such marital relationships, and almost all end in separation or divorce.

Over 75% of lesbians have had at least one sexual encounter with a man (Reinisch & Beasley, 1990). Interestingly, research suggests that women are more sexually variable or adaptable than men and have an easier time accepting various sexual orientations and conditions, including abstinence (Baumeister, 2000). Many lesbians have long-term homosexual relationships. One study revealed that the average length of a steady relationship for lesbians is about 4 years (Reinisch & Beasley, 1990).

Sex in Relationships Between Gay Men   According to the latest Kinsey report, although about one third of all men have engaged in homosexual behavior at one time in their lives, only about 8% have had exclusively gay relationships for 3 or more years, and only 4% have been exclusively gay throughout their lives. About two-thirds of gay men have had sex with a woman, and 10–15% may be more accurately viewed as bisexual (Reinisch & Beasley, 1990).

On average, gay men have a higher number of sex partners than lesbians and heterosexuals, and gay men also engage in sex more often than any other group (Blumstein & Schwartz, 1983). Since women often act as sexual gate-keepers, the absence of a woman in a relationship probably reduces restraint and increases sexual frequency. Gay men are also more likely than lesbians or heterosexuals to be in nonmonogamous relationships. In 1983, Blumstein and Schwartz reported that 82% of the gay men in their nationwide survey said they were nonmonogamous. Despite this, long-term relationships among gay men are much more common than the media would have us believe. The most recent Kinsey data suggest that virtually all gay men have had a steady, highly committed relationship that lasted 1 to 3 years (Reinisch & Beasley, 1990). Furthermore, some evidence suggests that gay men, like heterosexual men and women, have become more monogamous since the AIDS epidemic first emerged in the 1980s (Sprecher & Regan, 2000).

Gay men may have difficulty negotiating sexual initiation precisely because it is typically a male prerogative. In other words, some gay men resent the other male's continual initiation and refuse to exert control, which can lead to conflicts. However, gay men have more sex than other couple types since either partner can feel free to initiate sex (Blumstein & Schwartz, 1983). Kissing seems to be a primarily female behavior and is most likely in lesbian relationships, moderately likely in heterosexual relationships, and least likely in gay relationships between men (Blumstein & Schwartz, 1983).

Sexual Attitudes

Deciding if and when to have sex with someone is a highly personal choice that is influenced by a wide variety of factors, including levels of commitment and passion, alcohol consumption, and moral values. Sexual behavior is strongly related to people's attitudes. People may be born with a number of sexual feelings, preferences, and proclivities, but virtually all of their attitudes and beliefs about sex are learned. For example, a person might be physically aroused and curious when thinking about having sex for the first time, but moral attitudes and beliefs might stop her or him from acting on the impulse to have sex.

Developing Sexual Attitudes and Beliefs

Research has shown that sexual attitudes and knowledge come from a variety of sources including culture, mass media, parents, peers, and past relationships (Andersen, 1993). Together, these factors influence not only sexual attitudes but also sexual behavior.

Culture Culture is a primary influence on relational and sexual attitudes. Andersen (1998a) argued that "the most basic force that molds and shapes human beings, other than our membership in the human race itself, is culture. Culture is such a pervasive influence it is often confused with human nature itself" (p. 48). Culture is highly resistant to change, and people will adopt the values and attitudes of their parents and their culture unless very strong forces come into play. Children of immigrants, for example, are caught between two sets of cultural values—those of their parents and those of their peers. Sexual attitudes change slowly across each generation and still show cultural influences after a 100 or more years of cultural assimilation.

Research has shown that in the United States African Americans have the most permissive sexual attitudes, followed by whites, while people from Asian, Latino, and Middle Eastern cultures have the most conservative sexual orientations (Sprecher & McKinney, 1993). Among white Americans, particularly women, and to a lesser degree among African Americans, talking about sexual intimacy is quite common and is believed to be the heart and soul of a good relationship (Crooks & Baur, 1999). By contrast, Asian Americans and Hispanic Americans tend to be more reluctant to discuss their sexual relationship. White Americans and African Americans also tend to focus more on their individual sexual needs, whereas Asian Americans are more other oriented. In interethnic couples these differences require considerable understanding and adaptation by the partners.

The Mass Media One important source of information about sex is the mass media. According to Andersen (1993), "An abundance of mass media research has suggested that media—television in particular—provides prototypic family, sex-role, and relationship information that children imitate and incorporate into their cognitions and behaviors through the modeling process" (p. 5). These media effects are both consistent and pervasive. Research has shown that 29% of interactions on prime-time television shows contain verbal references to sexual issues that emphasize male sexual roles and a recreational rather than a procreational orientation toward sex (Ward, 1995). Most of these interactions depict sex as a competition and equate masculinity with being sexual. The media also influences "sexual scripts" for communicating about sex, which we will discuss later in this chapter.

In addition to television and film, magazines are an important source of information about sex and sexual issues. Starting in 1953 with the publication of *Playboy*, Americans were introduced not only to open nudity on conventional newsstands but perhaps more importantly to the "playboy" philosophy that rejected any limits on sexual expression, condoned any form of consensual sex, and was highly critical of the institution of marriage (D'Emilio & Freedman, 1988). Similarly, with the publication of Helen Gurley Brown's *Sex and the Single Girl* in the early 1960s, young women were urged to reconsider the taboo against premarital sex. These two publications illustrate the impact the media can have on sexual attitudes. Sexual material on the Internet is the most recent concern of parents, educators, and politicians. However, research on its effects is scant at this time. Cybersex may be a negative influence with increasingly bizarre or violent effects, or it may be a harmless form of safe sex with beneficial cathartic effects.

Parents   Children learn about sex and relationships from their parents in both indirect and direct ways. Indirectly parents serve as an example for children. For instance, if the parents are affectionate toward each other, children likely will expect their own romantic relationships to include both affection and sex. Parents can also teach their children about sex directly, often by having the sometimes dreaded "sex talk." Direct parent-child communication about sex is very important. Studies have shown that children are somewhat more likely to delay sexual activity and to use contraception when their parents have talked with them about sex (Fox, 1981). Yet most research suggests that many teenagers are uncomfortable when their parents discuss sex with them, primarily because the parents somewhat defensively issue commands or warnings rather than frankly discussing sexual thoughts and feelings (Brock & Jennings, 1993; Philliber, 1980; Rozema, 1986).

In most families, parents and children do not discuss sex very often. According to Warren's (1995) review of studies by Warren and Neer, only about 10–15% of American families have any kind of ongoing discussions about sex. Often, parents discuss sex with their children once or twice in the form of a sex talk and then simply ignore the topic. However, it is extremely important for children to feel free to initiate discussion about sex when they are experiencing sexual feelings or have questions about sexuality. Within the family teens report being most comfortable talking to a same-sex parent or older sibling about sex (Guerrero & Afifi, 1995b), and mothers and daughters are more likely to talk about sex than are fathers and sons (Philliber, 1980). Discussions about sex are most effective when they are integrated into family discussions well before a child is 16 years old (Warren, 1995). Box 7.1 gives recommendations for how parents can talk effectively to their teens about sex.

Peers   Peer groups have considerable influence on sexual beliefs and attitudes. Rogers (1995) showed that most diffusion of information about a variety of topics, including sexually related ones, occurs interpersonally between people who are highly similar to one another. Sprecher and McKinney (1993) summarized a series of studies showing that peers have a much stronger influence on people's sexual standards than do parents. Male adolescents are notorious for inculcating in other males attitudes regarding what constitutes a physically attractive woman and what is masculine behavior, as well as the value of sexual conquests. Females share all manner of relational and sexual information with one another regarding male attractiveness, birth control methods, and the quality of individual males as potential mates. Although these stereotypes of heterosexual men and women are often exaggerated, they illustrate that both men and women talk about sex with their peers. It is also important to note that many sexual attitudes and behaviors are modeled by friends and then imitated. Friends provide relational prototypes regarding appropriate sexual behavior.

BOX 7.1 HIGHLIGHTS

Ten Tips for How Parents Should Talk to Their Children About Sex

Clay Warren, a communication researcher who has conducted many studies on family sex communication, makes the following recommendations to parents who want to engage in effective communication about sex with their children.

1. **Start talking.** Most parents find it difficult to talk about sex with their children, but the more they initiate discussion about sex, the easier it becomes to talk about it.
2. **Continue talking.** Once discussions about sex are initiated, children expect to hear more. Parents should make an effort to continue talking about sex in more specific detail as their children mature.
3. **Start early.** Discussions about sex should start well before a teen is 16 years old. Early adolescence is often a good time to initiate sex talks. Once children are in their midteens, they may have outgrown the need to talk about sex with their parents and instead rely more on peers.
4. **Involve both parents if the family has two parents.** If both parents are actively involved in the communication process, neither one bears the pressure or responsibility alone. Also, teenagers may be more comfortable discussing certain issues with one parent and other issues with the other parent.
5. **Talk to both sons and daughters.** Some research suggests that parents are more likely to talk to their daughters than sons. This double standard needs to be broken so that females do not always bear the sexual responsibility in teen relationships. It is important for both boys and girls to understand the consequences of sexual activity.
6. **Establish a mutual dialogue.** When parents talk *to* rather than *with* their children about sex, the children are less satisfied with the information they receive. It is important that children feel free to initiate discussions about sex and to ask questions.
7. **Create a supportive environment.** Communication should be open and comfortable rather than defensive. Parents are often tense when discussing sex with their children. Instead, they should be relaxed and open.
8. **Use positive forms of nonverbal communication.** Nonverbal behavior is especially crucial in creating a supportive environment. Behaviors such as a relaxed posture, smiling, vocal warmth, and head nods can all help ease the tension.
9. **Remember that discussing sex does not promote promiscuity.** Knowing this fact might help ease some of the stress parents feel. Many studies have shown that talking about sex and sex-related topics such as contraception does not promote promiscuity. In fact, talking about these issues within the context of a broader discussion of sexual values might even reduce promiscuity.
10. **Don't leave the talking to someone else.** If parents are not successful in influencing their children's sexual attitudes, someone else will be. It might be a boyfriend, girlfriend, peers, teachers, or even the media. Adolescents have questions that need to be answered. If they cannot find the answers at home, they will seek them elsewhere.

Source: Adapted from Warren (1995).

As Andersen (1993) stated, "Relationships are highly salient, and information from close friends provides us with powerful schemata" (p. 7).

Past Relationships   Many attitudes about sex result from prior relational experiences. According to attachment theorists, people's past relationships help refine the way they think about current relationships. For example, people who have learned to trust others and to be comfortable with closeness tend to be more monogamous in their sexual relationships (Simpson & Gangestad, 1991). Moreover, having a partner who provides consistent, loving physical contact helps build an individual's self-esteem and sets up positive expectations for future relationships (Hazan & Zeifman, 1994). Some research also suggests that people who are uncomfortable with closeness and have had unsatisfying sexual relationships in the past will be more likely to desire short-term, casual sex than committed relationships (Brennan & Shaver, 1995; Stephan & Bachman, 1999). Additionally, people who have been hurt in past love relationships are less likely to experience highly passionate or obsessive love in the future (Stephan & Bachman, 1999). Together these findings suggest that people who have had positive sexual experiences in committed relationships are most likely to expect future relationships to be monogamous and sexually satisfying.

Past relationships affect sexual attitudes in other ways as well. Once people have had sex for the first time, they are more likely to have sex on subsequent occasions—assuming that the sex was voluntary and enjoyable. Similarly, determining if and when to have sex for the very first time is often a very difficult decision. People often wait until they are in a committed relationship and feel personally ready. Before having sex many people also deal with issues such as fear of sexually transmitted diseases (STDs) and pregnancy (Sprecher & McKinney, 1993). However, once a person has had sex, it usually becomes easier to decide whether to have sex in the future, with most people waiting to have sex until the relationship becomes intimate and committed (Sprecher & McKinney, 1993).

Finally, past sexual relationships can affect attraction. Sprecher and Regan (2000) reviewed research on the association between a person's sexual history and her or his desirability as a long-term romantic partner. They concluded that, "in general, research indicates that low to moderate levels of current or past sexual activity and the restriction of sexual activity to committed relationships are more likely to increase one's desirability as a partner than is a history of many sexual partners or casual sexual activity" (p. 219).

Social Norms and Changing Sexual Attitudes

In addition to culture, the media, family, peers, and past relationships, social norms have considerable influence on people's sexual attitudes. Attitudes toward sexuality, particularly premarital and female sexuality, became increasingly permissive and liberal in the United States during the 20th century (Sprecher & McKinney, 1993). Throughout most of the century, premarital sex was considered unacceptable, particularly for women. But "premarital sexual activity has become normative for today's youth. Rates of sexual intercourse for teens have increased dramatically" since the early 1960s (Christopher & Roosa, 1993, p. 111). Thus, in 1990 the average age of first sexual intercourse was between 16 and 17 years of age (Reinisch & Beasley, 1990), although first intercourse at an older age has been associated with higher levels of achievement and social adjustment. Before the sexual revolution of the 1960s and early 1970s, the primary value was sexual abstinence. Typically both men and women abstained from sex until marriage, or else the "double standard" prevailed—premarital sex was acceptable for men but not for women. The sexual double standard has not entirely disappeared, but it has diminished dramatically (Sprecher & McKinney, 1993).

The revolution in sexual attitudes that began in the 1960s was due to a number of factors. The 1960s was a revolutionary era for all types of values, including those associated with politics, the environment, civil rights, and women's rights. In this period issues in and images of sexuality were widely depicted in the mass media through magazines, books, and movies, and to a lesser degree, television. Perhaps the biggest factor was the birth control pill—the first simple and effective technology that permitted sex without reproduction. For the first time in human history, women could have sexual relationships without risking pregnancy. Several scholars have suggested that the sexual revolution of the 1960s and 1970s was mainly a change in women's values, with men remaining much the same (Baumeister, 2000; Ehrenreich, Hess, & Jacobs, 1986). Since the early 1980s, however, people in the United States have seen some movement back to more conservative sexual attitudes (Sprecher & McKinney, 1993), in part because of AIDS and other dangerous and sometimes incurable STDs. Nonetheless, teens and young adults are much more sexually active now than they were before the sexual revolution of the 1960s.

Sex experts have identified three types of sexual attitudes held by people today (Sprecher & McKinney, 1993). Some people have a **procreational orientation,** which reflects the belief that producing offspring is the primary purpose of sexual intercourse. Other people have a **relational orientation,** which holds that sexual intercourse is a way of expressing love and affection, and developing greater relational intimacy. Still others have a **recreational orientation,** viewing sex as a primary source of fun, escape, excitement, or pleasure. The procreational orientation, the position taken by most major religions, is associated with traditional, conservative cultural values. The relational orientation, which is equated with moderate sexual values, is widespread in the United States. People with this orientation disapprove of casual sex but usually approve of premarital sex in the context of a committed or loving relationship. The recreational orientation is a sexually liberal view holding that sex is appropriate between consenting adults.

Of course, these orientations are not mutually exclusive; many people's sexual attitudes are some combination of procreational, relational, and recreational. Indeed, most married couples in the United States embrace elements of all three values within their relationship at different times. By contrast, attitudes toward premarital sex vacillate between the relational and recreational orientations but are rarely procreational. Research has shown that couples are much more likely to endorse increased sexual activity, including sexual intercourse, as the relationship becomes closer (Sprecher, McKinney, Walsh & Anderson, 1988). As Figure 7.1 shows, in 1989 only 28% of subjects endorsed sexual intercourse on a first date while 82% of subjects endorsed sexual intercourse for engaged couples. Judging by their behavior, for several decades people in the

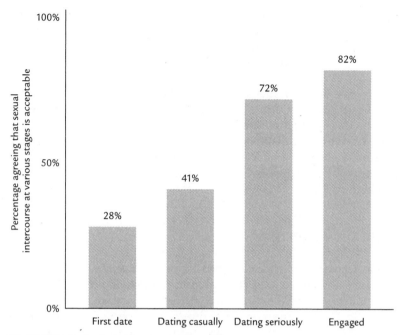

FIGURE 7.1 Attitudes Toward Sexual Intercourse, 1989
Source: Adapted from Sprecher et al. (1989).

United States have subscribed primarily to a relational orientation through the practice of **serial monogamy** (Christopher & Roosa, 1991; Rathus et al., 1993; Sorensen, 1973). In other words, couples are sexually active only with each other (monogamy) and do not engage in other sexual relationships until the current relationship ends. They may, however, move through a series of such relationships.

While much of the research has focused on the dark side of premarital sex, such as disease, pregnancy, and abortion, positive outcomes also occur. Most premarital sex takes place in an intimate and committed relationship that provides support and often leads to marriage (Christopher & Roosa, 1991). In fact, early research showed that serial monogamists overwhelmingly loved each other and had healthy, caring sexual relationships (Sorensen, 1973). Moreover, serial monogamists had the highest school grades, were most likely to use birth control, enjoyed sex more, and were generally better adjusted than were either promiscuous adventurers or virgins.

Although most college students are sexually experienced, some choose to remain virgins. In a study of the sexual behavior of college students at a major university, Sprecher and Regan (1996) found that 11% of men and 13% of women reported that they were virgins, although virtually all of the virgins reported experiencing sexual desire. Of course, the percentage of students who are virgins likely will differ at various colleges and universities. In Sprecher and

Regan's study, reasons for being a virgin included the absence of a long-term or love relationship, fear of negative consequences such as pregnancy or STDs, personal beliefs and values, and feelings of inadequacy and/or insecurity. All of these factors were stronger for women than for men. Virgins reported a mixture of pride and anxiety about their status, although positive emotions outweighed negative ones. Women were more likely to be proud and happy about keeping their virginity, while men were more likely to be embarrassed about it. The men and women who were virgins for religious or moral reasons were the most positive about their status, and the men who reported abstaining from sex because they were not in love also felt positive about themselves. Feelings of insecurity or inadequacy were negatively associated with positive feelings about being a virgin.

Communication Patterns

As discussed earlier, sex is an important part of many different kinds of romantic relationships. So how do couples use communication to move their relationships from platonic to sexual? Research on courtship patterns and sexual scripts gives some insight. The literature on courtship focuses specifically on how romantic couples develop their relationships through flirtation and increased sexual involvement. The literature on sexual scripts examines the types of communication people typically use to initiate and refuse sex at various stages in relationships.

Courtship and Flirtation

When people flirt, they typically use indirect communication strategies to convey their interest and attraction, especially when they are in the early stages of a relationship. Nonverbal displays of flirtation are more common than verbal displays. For example, gazes, smiles, warm vocal tones, and close distancing are key flirtatious behaviors (Givens, 1978, 1983; Moore, 1985; Muehlenhard, Koralewski, Andrews, & Burdick, 1986). Indirect nonverbal cues are often used because they provide some protection from potential rejection. That is, the other person can simply ignore these cues without having to verbally reject the flirtatious person. Or the flirtatious person can deny that he or she was flirting, and simply say that he or she was trying to be friendly. Sometimes, of course, direct verbal strategies are used, such as telling people they look sexy or talking about sex. These more direct strategies, however, are more likely to be used after two people have already established a romantic relationship.

Scheflen's (1965, 1974) model of the courtship process sought to explain how various nonverbal behaviors unfold over time to signal availability and sexual interest. Scheflen's model included five stages, with the earlier stages characterized by the most indirect communication. The courtship behaviors in this model often reflect attentiveness, approachability, and submissiveness. Thus, potential partners must gain one another's attention and signal that they

What nonverbal behaviors are these two people using to show their interest in one another?

are available or approachable for communication. Submissive behaviors that communicate a desire for intimacy are particularly useful during the courtship process because they are seen as a nonthreatening, playful way of conveying sexual interest. Some submissive behaviors, such as stroking someone's hair in a comforting way, also mirror those used in parent-child relationships to convey caring and intimacy.

The Attention Stage   The goal of the first stage in Scheflen's model is simply to secure the other person's attention and to present oneself in the best possible light. This can be done in a number of ways and can include either strategic or accidental communication. For example, two people might accidentally bump into each other and feel an instant attraction, or one person might purposely bump into the other as a way of securing attention. Throughout history people have practiced the art of gaining attention as a precursor to courtship. In 19th-century America, for instance, it was common for women to drop something, such as a glove or handkerchief, in front of a man whom they wanted to get to know. The man, if polite, would be obliged to retrieve the dropped item and to turn his attention to the woman. Similarly, men commonly asked to be formally introduced to a woman, often by a relative or friend, before pursuing a conversation. Today, the rules guiding the attention stage are less clearly defined. Any place where singles gather, we are likely to see a variety of attention-getting strategies, such as positioning oneself in a potential partner's view and trying to catch someone's eye. Typically the behaviors used in this stage are indirect and submissive. These behaviors include demure glances, tentative smiles, anxious movement such as twisting the ring on one's finger, and primping behavior such as fixing one's hair, applying lipstick, or straightening one's tie.

The Courtship Readiness Stage   In this stage, sometimes referred to as the "recognition stage," the person initiating the flirtation determines whether the other person is approachable and available for interaction. If friendly overtures are met with a cold stare or annoyed glance, or are simply ignored, the courtship process usually will cease. Similarly, if the object of someone's affection is busy interacting with other people, the suitor will probably hesitate to approach unless he or she receives a fairly clear signal of interest. Of course, if the person shows some interest, the courtship process is likely to move forward. Typical behaviors during this stage include more sustained mutual gaze and smiling, raised eyebrows, more direct body orientation, head tilts in the direction of the other person, and nervous laughter. However, these behaviors are still somewhat ambivalent and timid because individuals are still uncertain about whether the other person is attracted to them. More primping behavior also tends to occur in this stage, with people tucking in their stomachs, arranging their clothing and hair, and wetting their lips as they prepare to approach one another.

The Positioning Stage   At this point the dyad has made initial contact. If the two people continue to be attracted to each other, they will engage in a series of positioning behaviors that indicate continued availability for interaction while signaling to others that they are, at least temporarily, a "couple" and so should be left alone. Close distancing and face-to-face body orientation are typical at this stage, as are forward leans. Partners gaze and smile at each other and tend to show high levels of interest and animation through gestures and expressive voices. If the setting is quiet, the two people may lower their voices to draw each other closer. The communication between the two people also tends to become more synchronized; that is, turn taking becomes smoother, and partners engage in similar behaviors such as crossing their legs. Although there is a marked increase in the intimacy of communication at this stage, some submissiveness and ambiguity still remain. For example, if the partners gaze for too long into each other's eyes, they might feel embarrassed, avert their eyes, and laugh nervously.

The Invitations and Sexual Arousal Stage   If the two people are mutually attracted, at some point they are likely to move into the fourth stage—sexual intimacy. The beginning of this stage is marked by the first implicit invitation for touch and sexual contact. For example, a woman might put her hand on her partner's knee while watching a movie to see how he or she responds. Other more subtle signs of intimacy include grooming the partner, performing carrying and clutching activities, and acting sexually provocative (Burgoon, Buller, & Woodall, 1996; Givens, 1978; Scheflen, 1965). Grooming behaviors include tucking the tag from someone's clothing back inside the collar and pushing a stray strand of hair out of someone's eyes. Carrying and clutching behaviors include carrying someone's bags or books, holding hands, and leaning on someone's arm for support. Sexually provocative actions include dancing in a suggestive way, revealing body parts by unbuttoning one's shirt or crossing one's leg to expose more thigh, and touching the partner in intimate places.

The Resolution Stage If the invitation is accepted and sexual intercourse occurs, the partners have reached the final stage. Of course, determining whether the invitation is accepted is not always easy, especially if the behaviors used in the sexual arousal/invitations stage were somewhat indirect and ambiguous. When people move through the courtship stages rapidly, the intent of both partners might be unclear. Perhaps one person is merely being friendly while the other is interested in having sexual relations. Some studies have shown that men are more likely than women to see flirtatious behaviors as seductive, whereas women often see these same behaviors as ways of being friendly and expressing innocent attraction (Abbey, 1982, 1987; Abbey & Melby, 1986). To complicate matters even further, research has shown that people flirt for a variety of reasons, only one of which is to signal sexual interest. For example, people may flirt because they see it as innocent fun, they want to make a third party jealous, they want to develop their social skills, or they are trying to persuade someone to do something for them (Afifi, Guerrero, & Egland, 1994; Egland, Spitzberg, & Zormeier, 1996; Koeppel, Montagne-Miller, O'Hair, & Cody, 1993). Thus, when someone is flirting with you, he or she may or may not be showing sexual interest.

In longer courtships couples may spend considerable time in the sexual arousal/invitations stage, with sexual intimacy increasing slowly over time. These partners are more likely to be direct about their intentions, but misunderstandings can still occur. Sometimes one person is ready to have sex before the other, and one partner may view intimate touch as a way to express closeness while the other sees it as a prelude to sex. Partners must negotiate if and when sex occurs, often through both verbal and nonverbal communication. If one or both of the partners does not want to have sex, the first four of Scheflen's stages are referred to as **quasi-courtship** rather than courtship. Misinterpretation of flirtatious cues is likely given that the first three or four stages often look the same regardless of whether they are quasi-courtship or true courtship stages.

It is important to note that these courtship stages provide only a rough guide for how people signal romantic interest and increase sexual involvement. Couples are unique and progress at different speeds. A relatively small number of couples have sex on a first date or shortly after the partners meet, but most couples wait until some level of intimacy has developed before having sex. Christopher and Cate (1985) identified four types of couples. **Rapid-involvement couples** have high levels of physical arousal and have sex on the first date or shortly thereafter. For these partners, sexual intimacy often precedes psychological intimacy. **Gradual-involvement couples** let sexual involvement increase gradually as the relationship develops and becomes more psychologically intimate. The level of sexual involvement reflects the stage of the relationship, with sexual involvement increasing as the partners move from a first date, to a casually dating relationship, to a more serious, committed relationship. **Delayed-involvement couples** wait until the two people consider themselves to be a committed couple to become sexually involved. For them psychological intimacy precedes sexual intimacy. **Low-involvement couples** usually wait to have sex until the partners are engaged or married. Research suggests that most couples in the United States define themselves as falling under either the gradual- (31%) or delayed-involvement (44%) category, with around 17% identifying themselves as low involvement and only 7% classifying themselves as rapid involvement (Christopher & Cate, 1985; Sprecher & McKinney, 1993). These findings correspond with research showing that most people have a relational orientation toward sex.

Sexual Scripts

Scripts are social information that is deployed in everyday interaction. Cultural and societal forces define with whom, when, where, and in what relationships sexual behavior may appropriately be initiated and conducted (Regan & Berscheid, 2000). Thus, what is normal or appropriate in one culture or group may not be typical in another. **Sexual scripts** most often revolve around the initiation and acceptance or refusal of sexual advances.

As noted previously, research has shown that the traditional sexual script in North American society casts men as initiators and women as gatekeepers who decide whether to refuse or accept sexual invitations (Byers, 1996). This type of sexual script is particularly normative in new or casual relationships. As Hinde (1984) commented, men seek to propagate widely while women seek to propagate wisely. However, research indicates that both men and women are quite comfortable asking for dates and initiating sexual interaction (Kelly & Rolker-Dolinsky, 1987), although many women believe that their sexual initiatives might threaten men. In well-developed relationships, however, women are more likely to initiate sexual interaction.

Negotiating sexual activity in a developing relationship can be difficult because both individuals have multiple goals including managing impressions, providing relational definitions, satisfying their sexual desire, following their sexual standards or morals, and avoiding disease or pregnancy (Cupach & Metts, 1993). As noted previously, most attempts to initiate sexual activity are subtle and indirect, and are communicated through nonverbal behavior and flirtation (Andersen, 1999). Sometimes, however, friendly behaviors, particularly those by women, are misinterpreted by men as sex-initiating behaviors. To avoid sexually coercive situations (discussed later in this chapter), individuals need to verbally articulate their disinterest, and their partners need to respect their wishes.

Initiation Strategies Many different scripts and persuasive strategies are used by men and women to initiate dating and sexual relationships. These strategies typically fall into five categories: (1) hinting and indirect strategies, (2) expressions of emotional and physical closeness, (3) pressure and manipulation, (4) antisocial acts, and (5) logic and reasoning (Christopher & Frandsen, 1990; Edgar & Fitzpatrick, 1988, 1993).

For something as emotionally sensitive and ego involved as sexual relations, hinting and indirect strategies are very useful. Many conversations are full of indirect communication such as compliments, sexual innuendo, and hints. Such ploys are safe because if the partner does not respond sexually, little face is lost. As Edgar and Fitzpatrick (1988) noted, when one person wants to have sex, the situation can be emotionally charged, and an opportunity to save face is always welcome. Many indirect strategies are nonverbal and correspond to those discussed earlier in the context of flirtation and courtship.

Both men and women are most comfortable with sexual involvement if emotional and physical closeness is present; this is particularly true for women. Establishing a close relationship and sending reassuring relational messages can result in increased sexual activity in a relationship (Christopher & Frandsen, 1990). For example, doing special things for your partner, telling your partner how much you like her or him, flattering your partner, and sharing time and space with him or her are important ways of enhancing emotional closeness and initiating sexual activity.

Another common sexual influence tactic is logic and reasoning, which involves persuading someone that it is in her or his best interests to become sexually involved. This often takes the form of appeals to logic, appeals to compromise on the timing or degree of sexual involvement, and the use of reasoning to overcome a partner's concerns (Christopher & Frandsen, 1990). For example, if someone is afraid of getting pregnant and/or contracting an STD, the partner might make reassuring statements about the effectiveness of birth control and suggest that they both get tested for STDs before having sex. Christopher and Frandsen found that these types of tactics are associated with greater sexual activity in a relationship over the long term, although they may limit or postpone sexual involvement in the short term.

Not surprisingly men are more likely to use pressure and manipulation to gain sexual compliance than are women (Christopher & Frandsen, 1990). This strategy encompasses a wide variety of coercive tactics, such as repeated requests for sex, threats to break off or de-escalate the relationship, the use of drugs or alcohol to reduce resistance to sex, and outright deception. However, these tactics seldom increase the frequency of sexual activity in a relationship (Christopher & Frandsen, 1990) and can lead to relational dissatisfaction and/or de-escalation.

Evidence suggests that antisocial acts are also usually unsuccessful in initiating sex in a relationship (Christopher & Frandsen, 1990). This strategy encompasses a wide assortment of tactics including trying to make the partner jealous, pouting or holding a grudge to try to get one's way, and sexually harassing someone. Such acts may lead to relational termination and even legal action in some cases.

Refusing and Accepting Sexual Invitations   The power to refuse and regulate sex is primarily a woman's prerogative. Men are relatively poor at turning down sex and have few refusal strategies, and women are likely to regard men's refusals as insincere, unexpected, and upsetting (Metts, Cupach & Imahori, 1992). Of course, this does not imply that women have license to ignore men's refusals; men should be taken every bit as seriously as women when they decline to have sex. Still, throughout the world women are more judicious, less casual, and more prudent in their selection of mates than are men (Buss, 1994).

Research suggests that women are well prepared with sexual compliance–resisting scripts and use a variety of resistance strategies (Metts et al., 1992). Women frequently use indirect strategies because these are perceived as polite; however, more direct strategies seem to be more effective for avoiding unwanted sex. Moreover, most men have experience receiving sexual rejection messages and find them relatively predictable and not particularly disconcerting (Metts et al., 1992). This is useful information for women who use indirect strategies to refuse sex when they are worried about hurting the partner's feelings. Not only are direct strategies more effective, but they are unlikely to be taken personally by men.

Research has shown that in steady dating relationships the majority of sexual initiations by both men and women are accepted by their partner (Byers, 1996). In Byers' study only about 20% of initiations were refused by the partner, and this figure was the same for men and women. These data suggest that sex in steady dating relationships is not adversarial and that, contrary to the stereotype, women are more likely to be facilitators of sexual interaction than gatekeepers once the relationship has developed. In investigating sexual activity among heterosexual daters over a 1-month period, Byers and Lewis (1988) found that nearly half of the couples reported disagreements caused by the man's desire to increase sexual involvement. However, disagreements only occurred during 7% of all the dates. Thus, although disagreements about sex did occur once in a while over the course of a month, most dates were free of such disagreements.

Once sexual activity becomes fairly regular, shared dyadic scripts emerge to guide sexual interaction. In well-developed relationships women feel freer to initiate touch and other forms of affection and sexual behavior (Cupach & Metts, 1993; Guerrero & Andersen, 1991). In fact, Brown and Auerbach (1981) found that wives increased their initiation of sexual activity by about 1% per year of marriage.

Saying no to sex in a long-term relationship is particularly problematic and should be done tenderly and supportively with clear verbal communication. Research has shown that most refusals are done verbally and that the best refusals maintain both the relationship and the partner's face (Cupach & Metts, 1991). For example, telling your partner that you are "really tired" or "not feeling well" is better than saying that you are not feeling much sexual desire for him or her at the moment. When refusals are accompanied by assurances of future activity ("We'll have more time for each other this weekend"), they are also accepted more gracefully.

Sexual Coercion and Harassment

Most people associate sex with pleasure, intimacy, relational closeness, and desire. However, sex has its dark side as well. Negative aspects of sex include sexual dysfunction, sexual abuse, rape, sexual coercion, and sexual harassment. In this section we focus on coercion and harassment because communication is at the heart of these two types of problematic interaction.

Sexual Coercion

Sexual coercion occurs when one individual pressures, compels, or forces another to engage in sexual activity. Studies show that various methods of sexual coercion are considered unacceptable by the vast majority of men and women, with verbal pressure the least unacceptable and physical force the most unacceptable (Struckman-Johnson & Struckman-Johnson, 1991). Verbal persuasion is the most common method of coercion (Murnan, Perot, & Byrne, 1989). In general, women find sexual coercion to be less acceptable than do men (Christopher, Owens, & Strecker, 1993; Struckman-Johnson & Struckman-Johnson, 1991). Moreover, coercive strategies are generally unsuccessful in gaining sexual compliance (Christopher & Frandsen, 1990).

Sexual coercion is far too common. Research has shown that in the vast majority of sexually coercive situations a man is the perpetrator and a woman is the victim. For example, over 50% of college women report having been the victim of some form of sexual coercion (Byers, 1996), and over 95% of all women report having engaged in some form of unwanted sexual activity (Muehlenhard & Cook, 1988). In another study 22% of college women reported having been forced to engage in sexual intercourse, and in other studies 35–46% of women reported having unwanted sex as a result of sexual persuasion or coercion, typically from a partner the woman knew fairly well (Byers, 1996; Muehlenhard & Cook; 1988; Murnan et al., 1989). However, women report experiencing sexual coercion on only about 7% of all dates (Byers & Lewis, 1988). In yet another study 50% of college women reported that they had engaged in at least one unwanted sexual activity (ranging from hugs to sexual intercourse) over a 2-week period, with 20% of the women engaging in unwanted sexual intercourse (O'Sullivan & Allgeier, 1998). Sometimes women have unwanted sex to please their partners; other times they are pressured or forced to have sex.

The most common responses of women to sexual coercion are either no response or a strong verbal response. In the vast majority of situations in which men pursue sex and women refuse, the men halt their sexual advances (Byers, 1996). Approximately 15% of the time, however, the man does not believe the woman's refusal really means no (Byers & Wilson, 1986). In these cases the man perceives that when the woman says no she is offering only token resistance (Muehlenhard & Cook, 1988). Men should not try to second-guess a woman's motivation for saying no. As Andersen (1999) stated: "Sexual harassment or date rape can result from ignoring these explicit verbal cues in favor of nonverbal cues that seem positive and encouraging. We should all be aware: 'Stop' means stop and 'no' means no" (p. 210).

However, token resistance is used at times, which complicates this issue further. In fact, both men and women commonly use token resistance strategies, and contrary to the stereotype men are more likely to use them than women (O'Sullivan & Allgeier, 1994). These are dangerous strategies because they are potentially confusing. As noted previously, a sexual initiator should not ignore a request to stop. If, however, an initiator has learned that stop does not always really mean stop, "real" requests to stop may be ignored, leading to problems ranging from relational disagreements to charges of sexual assault. Thus, it is best to stop and ask for clarification if you think your partner might be engaging in token resistance. Unless your partner explicitly changes the no into a yes, you should avoid any further sexual activity. Similarly, research has shown that men often do not perceive indirect resistance messages on the part of women as real resistance (Motley & Reeder, 1995). Indeed, based on this research Motley and Reeder suggested that women need to be much more direct in communicating sexual resistance and that men should listen more carefully to try to understand women's resistance messages.

Women sometimes fail to send sexual resistance messages because they fear the relational consequences of turning down their partner (Motley & Reeder, 1995). But the reality is, men rarely disrupt or terminate a relationship because a woman resists sexual escalation. In fact, Motley and Reeder found that men rarely are hurt, offended, or angered when women use direct sexual resistance messages, although women erroneously think that men will be offended and de-escalate the relationship if they resist (Motley & Reeder, 1995). For their part women rarely are turned down in their attempts to sexually escalate a relationship, and they are more likely to be hurt and upset if they are turned down. They project these feelings onto men who do not share their hurt and anger over being sexually rejected. Many men have considerable experience with sexual rejection and have learned coping strategies to deal with rejection short of relational de-escalation or breakup.

In about 10% of sexually coercive situations, the woman is the aggressor and the man is the target. Among college students about one third of all men reported an episode of pressured or forced sex since the age of 16 (Byers, 1996; Struckman-Johnson & Struckman-Johnson, 1994), and in the vast majority of these cases, the perpetrator of coercion was a woman. O'Sullivan and Allegier (1998) reported that during a 2-week period 26% of college men engaged in an unwanted sexual act and almost 9% had unwanted sexual intercourse. Struckman-Johnson (1988) found that 16% of the men in her sample reported an incident of forced sexual intercourse. Muehlenhard and Cook (1988) studied over 1,000 men and women in introductory college psychology courses and found that more men (62.7%) than women (46.3%) reported having unwanted sexual intercourse. Although men generally have less negative reactions to being the target of coerced sexual encounters than do women, one fifth of the men in a study by Struckman-Johnson and Struckman-Johnson (1994) had a strong negative reaction to the experience.

Women are not very sensitive to male refusals to have sex. O'Sullivan and Byers (1993) found that, when met with a refusal to have sex, 97% of women still tried to influence the man to have sex. Women are not used to being refused, and they find such refusals unpredictable, constraining, and uncomfortable (Metts et al., 1992). But women get a lot of practice saying no and so develop good scripts to resist sexual persuasion and coercion. Men, by contrast, may have neither experience in nor well-developed scripts for saying no and often think it is unmanly to refuse sex (Metts et al., 1992). They also engage in unwanted intercourse due to peer pressure, inexperience, sex-role concerns, and popularity factors (Muehlenhard & Cook, 1988). Of course, men and women often experience ambivalence about having sex, so some of these cases of unwanted sex probably represent situations in which mixed feelings were present.

Sexual Harassment

Sexual harassment occurs when inappropriate sexual comments or requests create a hostile work or school environment or when a person feels pressure to have sex or suffer negative consequences. This form of harassment is all too common in the workplace and among some friends and acquaintances (Fairhurst, 1986; Keyton, 1996). Although men do sometimes experience sexual harassment, research indicates that women experience it much more. In fact, studies suggest that one out of every two working women is sexually harassed at some time (Swan, 1997). In a study by Hesson-McInnis and Fitzgerald (1997) of 4,385 women employed by the federal government, 1,792 reported being sexually harassed at least once over the past 2 years. This problem may be even worse for minority women. Hargrow (1997) found that over 80% of the working African American women she surveyed reported experiencing some form of sexual harassment. Sexual harassment is a serious problem that negatively affects job satisfaction, health, and psychological well-being (Glomb et al., 1997).

Describing the behaviors that constitute sexual harassment is complicated. What some people see as harassment, others might see as sexy or innocent fun. Moreover, women sometimes perceive behaviors to be more sexually harassing than do men, especially if they have recently entered the workforce (Booth-Butterfield, 1989). In any case, research suggests that certain verbal and nonverbal behaviors should be avoided. Dougherty, Turban, Olson, Dwyer, and Lapreze (1996) noted that some behaviors, such as making lewd comments or grabbing someone's breasts or buttocks, are blatantly harassing. Gutek, Morasch, and Cohen (1983) found that touch behavior (operationalized as a pat on the bottom) and verbal comments about another person's body were both perceived as harassing, although touch was perceived even more negatively than verbal comments. Similarly, Marks and Nelson (1993) found that potentially inappropriate touching by professors was seen as more harassing than inappropriate verbal comments.

Less sexually oriented forms of touch, such as on the shoulder or around the waist, are not perceived to be as harassing as verbal comments. For example, Doughtery et al. (1996) compared people's interpretations of potentially harassing situations involving touch behavior (putting an arm around a female coworker's shoulder) and verbal behavior (asking a female coworker how her love life was and if she'd had any exciting dates lately). They found that the verbal comment was perceived as more harassing than the touch to the shoulder.

In another study Lee and Guerrero (in press) compared types of touch to determine which were perceived as most harassing. They excluded blatantly harassing touches such as grabbing breasts or buttocks or kissing someone on the mouth and instead focused on more ambiguous forms of touch. Of the eight types of touch they studied, touching the face was perceived as most harassing, followed by arm around the waist. Lee and Guerrero theorized that these types of touch, because they invade people's personal space, are particularly threatening. Furthermore, the face is an especially vulnerable part of the body, and letting someone touch it requires trust. Interestingly, not everyone saw these types of touch as harassing. In fact, while about one third of the participants "agreed strongly" that face touch was sexually harassing, another one third "disagreed strongly." This finding suggests that some forms of touch are seen as harassing by some people but not others, which could lead to confusion and misunderstanding.

When people encounter sexual harassment, they can respond using passive, assertive, or retaliatory strategies. **Passive responses,** which are also referred to as indirect strategies, involve ignoring the harassment or appeasing the harasser. **Assertive responses** involve telling the harasser to stop the behavior with statements such as "Please stop bothering me," "I'm not interested in you that way," "I'm seeing someone else so I'd appreciate it if you'd stop asking me out," and "Your behavior is inappropriate and unprofessional." Assertive responses also involve issuing warnings, such as threatening to talk to the harasser's supervisor. Finally, **retaliatory responses** involve punishing or getting revenge on the harasser, usually by harassing him or her back, making derogatory comments about the harasser to others, or getting him or her in trouble.

Unfortunately, there is not always an effective way of responding to sexual harassment. Swan (1997) found that people who viewed their sexual harassment experiences as highly upsetting were most likely to use various types of coping responses. When people used assertive strategies, they reported feeling a little better about their jobs and themselves. By contrast, when people used passive or retaliatory strategies, they reported feeling even worse. Retaliatory responses were related to diminished job satisfaction, and passive responses were related to diminished job satisfaction and psychological well-being. But some studies also have shown that assertive strategies can sometimes exacerbate the problem (Schneider, Swan, & Fitzgerald, 1997). Bingham and Burleson (1989) found that, although sophisticated verbal messages were perceived to be more effective at stopping sexual harassment than unsophisticated verbal messages, neither type of message was particularly effective. Because sexual harassment often involves a power imbalance, it is a particularly difficult situation. If the victim uses passive strategies, she or he remains powerless, and the harassment is likely to continue. But if the victim uses direct strategies, the powerful person might resent being told how to act and retaliate by demoting the victim or making the work environment even more unpleasant. In any event, research suggests that assertive strategies are most effective. If these strategies do not work, the victim may need to talk with the harasser's supervisor.

Sexual Satisfaction: Misconceptions and Realities

People living in the United States consider themselves sexually knowledgeable and skilled, but research paints a somewhat different picture. What people learn about sex is often haphazard, unreliable, stereotypic, and incomplete (Strong, DeVault, & Sayad, 1999). In the fall of 1989 the Kinsey Institute tested the basic sexual knowledge of a representative sample of nearly 2,000 adults living in the United States (Reinisch & Beasley, 1990). Unfortunately they failed miserably. Applying a standard grading scale, 55% would have failed, 27% would have received a D, and less than 1% would have received an A (Reinisch & Beasley, 1990). As this study suggests, most people think they know more about sex than they really do.

To be a good partner in a romantic, sexual relationship, it is important to be knowledgeable about sexual interaction. A detailed description of the many topics associated with human sexuality is beyond the scope of this book, and we recommend a college course in human sexuality if you want to supplement what you learn in this chapter. Here, we will merely try to correct a few common misconceptions about the connections between sexual interaction and sexual satisfaction.

One misconception is that sexual intercourse is necessary for sexual satisfaction. The reality is that many forms of sexual interaction without sexual intercourse can be highly satisfying to both partners. Indeed, safe sex practices include a new form of sexual interaction called "outercourse" that involves minimal person-to-person contact and no exchange of bodily fluids. Furthermore, for some people sexual intercourse alone does not provide satisfaction. Shows of affection such as holding hands, cuddling, and kissing are just as important as, and in some cases even more important than, sexual intercourse for certain people.

A second misconception is that in an intimate heterosexual relationship women should not initiate sexual interaction because men will see them as easy and unfeminine, and it will undermine the traditional male role. The reality is that the vast majority of men, particularly those under age 40, think it is not only acceptable for women to initiate sex but highly desirable (Reinisch & Beasley, 1990). Nonetheless, as the misconception would suggest, nearly half of all wives rarely or never initiate sexual interaction (Reinisch & Beasley, 1990). When women do initiate sex, they often do it more subtly than males, so men need to tune in to these subtle cues and be responsive. Of course, men should not assume that every indirect cue is a signal that the woman wants to have sex. Once partners learn each other's signals for sexual initiation, the signal can be nonverbal and implicit. If a woman (or a man) is not comfortable asking for sex, special signals can be used such as lighting a candle, drinking wine, or playing romantic music in the bedroom (Reinisch & Beasley, 1990).

A third misconception is that heterosexual couples are more satisfied with sexual interaction than are gay or lesbian couples. The reality is that the sex lives of heterosexuals, gay men, and lesbians are different in many respects, but all couples generally report having satisfying sex lives. In fact, a study by Masters and Johnson (1979) revealed that gay and lesbian partners rated the *subjective* quality of their overall sexual experiences higher than did heterosexual couples, perhaps because they better understood each other's sexual needs (see also Crooks & Baur, 1999). Subjective quality was defined in terms of more psychological involvement, total body contact, enjoyment of sexual activities, and responsiveness to the sexual needs of the partner.

A fourth misconception is that men and women are equally aroused by the sight of nudity and by visual eroticism. The reality is that, while each is potentially arousing to members of both sexes, men are visually aroused more than are women. For example, seeing one's partner in sexy clothing is often more of a turn-on for men than for women. Conversely, women are much more aroused by touch than are men, particularly in nonsexual areas. Thus, cuddling and foreplay are often important precursors to sexual intercourse for women. In sexual areas of the body, both men and women are highly arousable. Heterosexual couples, in particular, need to understand that what arouses each partner personally might not necessarily be as arousing for the other partner. Both partners should adapt to each other's arousal needs.

A fifth misconception is that men enjoy sexual intercourse more than women do. The reality is that among heterosexual couples men and women both enjoy sexual intercourse. In fact, contrary to the stereotype, some research suggests that women may actually enjoy intercourse more than do men (Blumstein & Schwartz, 1983). In close, committed relationships, it is likely that women particularly enjoy sexual intercourse because of the extreme intimacy and closeness it reflects. Although some women may not want to have sex as often as men, when they do have high-quality sex they report finding it extremely pleasurable.

A sixth misconception is that the most important predictor of sexual satisfaction is how often a couple has sex. The reality is that the frequency with which a couple has sex is not as important as the quality of the sex and the match between two people's needs for sexual activity (Brehm, 1992; Sprecher & Regan, 2000). Couples who have more sex do tend to report more sexual and relational satisfaction (Blumstein & Schwartz, 1983), but this may be because partners who are in intimate, caring relationships and who are sexually compatible find sex more pleasurable and therefore have sex more often. When partners have similar attitudes about sex, they are also happier with their sex lives. Thus, if they believe that cuddling is more important than sex, they might have sex less often than a couple who believes that sex is the ultimate expression of intimacy; yet both couples would be satisfied. Some support for this line of reasoning also comes from studies comparing heterosexual couples to gay and lesbian couples. On average gay men place a higher value on sex than do heterosexuals, and heterosexuals place a higher value on sex than do lesbians. These values are reflected in behavior. Rosenzweig and Lebow (1992) found that almost half of gay men reported having sexual relations at least three times a week, while only about one third of heterosexual couples reported having sex that often. Among lesbian couples only about one fifth reported having sex three times a week or more. According to other studies, lesbians spend more time cuddling than do heterosexuals or gay men (Blumstein & Schwartz, 1983). Yet, as discussed previously, relational partners in heterosexual, gay, and lesbian relationships report roughly equal levels of overall sexual satisfaction.

A seventh misconception is that sexual satisfaction is the best predictor of relational satisfaction. The reality is that there is a fairly strong association between sexual satisfaction and relational satisfaction. In other words, people who report being happy with their sex lives are also likely to report being happy with their relationships. However, sexual satisfaction is not the *best* predictor of relational satisfaction in most relationships. As Sprecher and Regan (2000) put it, "Neither the quality nor the quantity of sex might be as important as other nonsexual forms of intimacy in the prediction of relationship satisfaction including expressed affection and supportive communication" (p. 223). These authors also noted that sexual dissatisfaction and incompatibility by themselves are usually not enough to destroy an otherwise close, caring, and healthy relationship. Only when these sexual problems are "symptomatic of other relational problems" are they likely to lead to conflict and possibly relational termination (p. 223). The message here is clear—sexual satisfaction is an important part of romantic relationships, but other factors, such as love, supportiveness, and compatibility, are usually even more important.

In addition to being knowledgeable about sex, it is important for partners to communicate about sex with each other. Some relational partners consider sex to be a taboo topic and so do not talk about their sexual desires and preferences with each other (Baxter & Wilmot, 1985). Yet studies suggest that communication about sex is very important. Frank, Anderson, and Rubinstein (1979) found that about one half of the husbands and three fourths of the wives they studied reported having some sexual difficulty in their marriages, and that these difficulties were exacerbated by poor communication skills. Cupach and Comstock (1990) examined the associations among sexual communication, sexual satisfaction, and overall relational satisfaction. They found that good communication about sex leads to greater sexual satisfaction, which in turn contributes to more relational satisfaction. As we discuss next, communication about safe sex is also crucial.

Communication and Safe Sex

The safest form of sex in relationships is no sex at all. Abstinence is the surest way to avoid unwanted pregnancy, AIDS, and other STDs. But total abstinence from sex throughout one's life is quite rare and precludes having both offspring and romantic relationships. Thus, additional safe sex practices are imperative.

Many publications now give excellent advice for safe sex and AIDS prevention (Center for Disease Control, 1996; Larkin 1998; Rathus et al., 1993; Student Health Services, 1998). These publications give recommendations for keeping oneself and one's partner safe from STDs. Box 7.2 summarizes these recommendations. For more information about HIV/AIDS, contact your campus health service or county health department. They have HIV/AIDS prevention information and information on testing, condom use, and safe, somewhat risky, and very risky practices.

Communication is an essential ingredient in promoting safe sex. Obviously, unsafe sex can occur with any partner, even one you know well. So it is always best to be proactive about safe sex with every partner. This requires communicating with partners about past sexual experiences and talking about safe sex practices such as those listed in Box 7.2. Unfortunately many people are complacent when they have sex with someone they know well (Hammer et al, 1996; Rosenthal, Gifford, & Moore, 1998). Specifically, they believe that being well acquainted with someone means that they must be free of STDs. Worse yet, many sexually active people believe that they can tell if a partner is lying to them about safe sex behaviors. In actuality, research has shown that people cannot tell when someone is lying about his or her sexual behavior or HIV status (Swann, Silvera, & Proske, 1995). Particularly dangerous is the truth bias whereby individuals tend to assume that people they like are telling them the truth (see Chapter 13).

Another danger is that people often avoid using condoms even though they know that condoms help prevent STDs. Many couples decline to use condoms because they limit spontaneity and reduce sensation (Hammer et al., 1996). But about one third of the males in Hammer et al.'s study reported that sharing the act of putting on a condom can actually bring the couple closer and even be arousing.

Even though logic suggests that people should use condoms to prevent STDs, in real relationships factors other than logic influence condom use. Managing identity, not wanting to seem promiscuous, not wanting to destroy a romantic moment, not liking the feel of condoms, believing a partner is "safe"— all are important in decision making regarding whether to use condoms (Afifi, 1999; Galligan & Terry, 1993). Galligan and Terry (1993) found that knowledge of the risk reduction effects of condom use was a major motivator for people to use them. However, women were less likely to want to use a condom when they feared it would destroy the romance of the moment. Afifi (1999) reported that, when attachment to a partner is high and partners worry that suggesting condom use will be perceived as reflecting a lack of trust, the probability of condom use is decreased. Of course, suggesting condom use may not always be perceived negatively by one's partner; rather, it may be seen as a sign of caring and of responsibility.

These findings underscore the importance of communication; partners should have a frank discussion of safe sex before becoming sexually involved. Interestingly, almost any communication strategy increases the likelihood of condom use, but discussing pregnancy prevention or suggesting condom use

BOX 7.2 HIGHLIGHTS

Safe Sex Practices

Practicing safe sex can save your life. Here are some tips for staying safe:

1. **Practice abstinence.** Although complete abstinence is unlikely for most adults, nearly 10% of the college-age population are virgins who have had no high-risk sexual activity (Rathus et al., 1993). Abstinence is the most effective policy when it comes to preventing STDs.

2. **Avoid high-risk sex.** HIV and other STDs are transmitted through the exchange of bodily fluids. Intercourse is particularly dangerous. A single episode of unsafe sex with an HIV-positive person puts you at risk for contracting the virus. Multiple unsafe sex episodes put you at even greater risk (Hammer, Fisher, Fitzgerald, & Fisher, 1996).

3. **Use condoms.** During sexual intercourse a new latex condom offers good protection from the transmission of HIV. Old condoms and "off brand" condoms offer poor protection because they may break or leak. Condoms made from animal membranes (skins) are porous and offer less protection against AIDS transmission. Although condoms do not offer complete protection, recent studies have shown that when condoms are used properly they are highly successful in preventing HIV/AIDS even with an infected partner (Center for Disease Control, 1996).

4. **Get tested.** If you are uncertain whether you have been exposed to HIV, get tested. Only about 1% of those who are tested show the presence of HIV, so the test is likely to relieve you of concern that you have the virus. And if you are HIV positive, you need to get treated immediately. With the proper treatment many people who are HIV positive live many symptom-free years and even decades. Your campus health center or county department of health typically does HIV tests that are either anonymous or confidential. Also, an HIV home test kit has recently been developed.

5. **Limit your partners.** Another effective preventive technique is to limit yourself to a single partner who was previously a virgin, has been strictly monogamous, or has been tested for HIV since her or his last sexual encounter with another person. Remember, when you have sex with your partner, you are exposing yourself to risk from every person who has had sex with your partner in the past.

6. **Know your partners.** A partner whom you know, respect, and trust is the safest kind of person with whom to have a sexual relationship. Today there is great risk associated with having sex with a new acquaintance, with someone whose sexual history you do not know, or with someone you do not trust. Research has shown that many people find it difficult to bring up the topic of safe sex and condom use during a sexual encounter with a new acquaintance (Rosenthal et al., 1998). Of course, people who hold that belief are literally risking their lives.

7. **Avoid intoxication.** Research has shown that binge drinkers engage in more sexual activity with a wider variety of partners (Mongeau & Johnson, 1995) than do heavy drug users. Studies also have shown that people are most likely to lapse in their safe sex practices when they are under the influence of alcohol and other drugs. More than one third of the participants in one study said that they had failed to use condoms on one or more occasions due to the use of drugs or alcohol (Hammer et al., 1996).

8. **Be honest.** It is essential that you report any unsafe sex outside your relationship to your partner so that appropriate steps can be taken. Of course, telling your partner about past sexual experiences or recent infidelities can be uncomfortable and even harm your relationship. However, in the long run it is better to warn your partner of possible dangers than to save yourself from potential discomfort or conflict.

"just to be safe" are the most effective strategies, probably because talking about AIDS can make people uncomfortable (Reel & Thompson, 1994). Interestingly, research has shown that general discussions about AIDS do not promote safe sex. By contrast, discussing the specific sexual history of the partners, negotiating monogamy, and requesting that the partner use a condom can promote safe sex (Cline, Freeman, & Johnson, 1990). Cline et al. (1990), however, found that those who discuss safe sex are only a little more likely to engage in safe sex practices than are those who do not. Therefore, it is crucial that partners do more than talk about safe sex practices; they must also take appropriate action to protect themselves.

Conclusion

Sex is a vital part of most romantic relationships. Partners who have similar sexual attitudes and high-quality sexual interaction are likely to be satisfied with their sex lives. Sexual satisfaction is associated with relational satisfaction, although it is important to remember that other factors, such as affection, love, and compatibility, are even more important. Partners who are able to communicate about sex with each other are generally happier in their sex lives and their overall relationship. Similarly, partners who are knowledgeable about sex are generally happier with their sex lives.

Communicating about sex is a complicated and risky enterprise, especially in developing relationships. People often communicate sexual desire through indirect behaviors such as hinting and flirtation. Sometimes these same behaviors are used to show friendliness rather than sexual interest, so misinterpretation can occur. Sexual initiation strategies that rely on pressure, manipulation, or antisocial behaviors are coercive and should be avoided. In the beginning of relationships, men and women usually play different roles in the sexual initiation process, with men more likely to be the initiators and women more likely to be gatekeepers. Socially accepted scripts for sexual communication are typically followed in the early stages of relationships. However, as the relationship develops, women usually feel freer to initiate sex. Unique, idiosyncratic sexual scripts then replace socially normative scripts for sexual communication. There are also sex differences in attraction and, in particular, in the resources men and women find desirable in mates. These differences are discussed in Chapter 8.

Finally, communication plays an important role in prompting people to engage in safe sex so they avoid STDs and other negative consequences, such as an unplanned pregnancy. Parents should talk to their children in a supportive, nondefensive manner rather than issuing warnings. Partners should also talk to each other openly about their past sexual experiences and the need to practice safe sex. However, it is important to remember that safe sex *talk* is not enough; safe sex *behaviors* can save lives.

Discussion Questions

1. In this chapter we presented data suggesting that most couples wait until some emotional intimacy has developed before engaging in sex. We also reported a study indicating that around 10–15% of college students are virgins. Based on the conversations you have had with friends, do you think these numbers hold true for your school? Why might these estimates differ depending on the group of people tested?

2. Based on what you learned in this chapter, what strategies would you use to protect yourself from sexual coercion or harassment? Why do you think people misinterpret supposed sexual cues so often?

3. Why do you think people practice unsafe sex even though they know the risks involved? What communication strategies might partners use to ensure that they engage in safe sex?

All Relationships Are Not Created Equal

Social Exchange, Equity, and Commitment

Have you ever been in a relationship in which you thought you were not "getting a fair deal"? Perhaps you thought you were putting more into the relationship than your partner. Or perhaps you thought that your partner was getting all the rewards while you were paying all the costs. If this type of imbalance describes any of your past or present relationships, you are not alone. One important aspect of successful relationships is that the partners perceive that they are obtaining valuable resources from each other and that those resources are distributed equitably. It is also important that both partners invest in the relationship. Like a seesaw that is too heavy on one side, if one partner is putting more effort into the relationship and still getting less out of it, this person will feel weighted down and as a result the relationship could come crashing down. Indeed, in some ways, relationships are like balancing acts. Both partners need to give and take in a fair manner.

In this chapter we examine four theories that focus on this delicate balancing act. First, we discuss social exchange theory, which explains how costs and rewards work in conjunction with other factors to affect relational satisfaction and commitment. Second, we look at the investment model, which is an extension of social exchange theory and which emphasizes the role that commitment plays in maintaining relationships. Third, we discuss equity theory, which focuses on whether rewards and costs are distributed fairly between relational partners. Finally, we review literature related to social evolutionary theory, which predicts that sex differences in sexual attraction and mate selection have evolved due to the different roles that men and women play in reproduction and parenting.

Social Exchange Theory

Social exchange theory, which has also been called interdependence theory, is based on the general principle that people want their rewards to outweigh their costs. Using accounting as an analogy, people want to maximize their "profits"

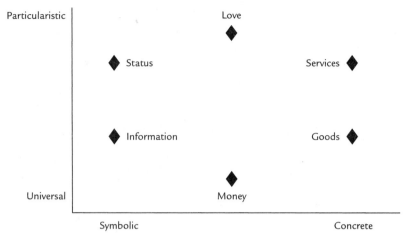

FIGURE 8.1 Foa and Foa's Resource Model

and minimize their "losses" in relationships (Blau, 1964; Homans, 1961, 1974; Thibaut & Kelley, 1959). Rewards and costs are weighed against each other, against people's standards and expectations for relationships, and against the alternative rewards and costs that people could have in other relationships or on their own. When these comparisons are favorable, people are generally satisfied with and committed to their relationships. In this section we examine the various components of social exchange theory.

Rewards and Costs

People bring a plethora of resources to relationships. Foa discussed six different resources that vary based on particularism versus universalism and concreteness versus symbolism: love, services, goods, money, information, and status (1971; Foa & Foa, 1980). When a resource is **particularistic,** it is important to receive it from a particular person. By contrast, it does not matter who supplies us with a **universal** resource. As shown in Figure 8.1, love is highest in particularism; that is, receiving love from a stranger or a disliked person is not very valuable to most people, but receiving love from a relational partner is usually very valuable and rewarding. By contrast, money is low in particularism. Thus, most people care far less about who their employer is than they do about getting paid for the work they do. Resources are **concrete** if they are tangible and **symbolic** if they are abstract. Goods and services are especially concrete because they include tangible products, objects, materials, or activities that usually involve another person engaging in labor (Foa, 1971). By contrast, status and information are more symbolic, or abstract, commodities.

All six of the resources discussed by Foa can play important roles in relationships, and all can be considered either rewards or costs. Indeed, Sprecher (1998b) defined **rewards** as "exchanged resources that are pleasurable and gratifying" and **costs** as "exchanged resources that result in a loss or punishment"

(p. 32). Love, which includes feelings and expressions of affection and closeness, is rewarding when it is reciprocated but punishing when it is unrequited. A partner who has high social status typically is rewarding, whereas a partner with low social status whom others dislike usually is costly. Similarly, a partner who has few debts and good financial prospects is more rewarding (at least in terms of money) than a partner who has heavy debts and who has just lost her or his job. Indeed, it might be very costly to support such a partner.

Research suggests that love, information, and services may be particularly important resources in close relationships. In one study, participants read a description of the types of resources that friends exchanged. When friends were described as exchanging love and services, they were rated as close (Tornblom & Fredholm, 1984). Another study compared casually involved couples with intimately involved couples. For the intimately involved couples the exchange of love and information was related to higher relational satisfaction (Lloyd, Cate, & Henton, 1982).

Another way to think of rewards and costs is that they can fall into four broad categories: emotional, instrumental, social, and opportunity. Emotional rewards include positive feelings such as love, warmth, happiness, and caring; emotional costs include negative feelings such as anger, hurt, stress, and fear of abandonment. Instrumental rewards and costs revolve around tasks. For example, if you have a partner who manages the household finances well, you enjoy an instrumental reward. By contrast, if you do the majority of the housework while your partner watches television, you incur an instrumental cost. Examples of social rewards include engaging in fun activities with someone and meeting interesting or high-status people through your association with your partner. Examples of social costs might include having to attend your partner's boring company picnic and being embarrassed when your partner criticizes you in front of others. Finally, being in relationships provides people with some opportunities while taking away others. For instance, if you move in with your partner, the two of you will be able to afford a nicer home than either of you could obtain alone. In this case being with your partner might give you the rewarding opportunity to purchase the home of your dreams. But if you have to quit your job and move across country to remain with your partner, you have given up the opportunity to advance in a particular organization, which is an opportunity cost. It is also important to note that when a romantic relationship is exclusive, both people give up the opportunity to pursue relationships with other people.

In every relationship, whether it is between friends, romantic partners, family members, coworkers, or employees and their supervisors, there are both rewards and costs. According to social exchange theory, people mentally account for rewards and costs so they can evaluate the outcome of their relationship as either positive or negative. When rewards outweigh costs, the outcome is positive; when costs outweigh rewards, the outcome is negative. Put another way, rewards minus costs equal the outcome ($R - C = O$). To illustrate, suppose that Carla perceives that she is receiving 20 rewards and 10 costs in her relationship with Tara. According to social exchange theory, Carla will have a positive outcome ($20 - 10 = +10$). But if Carla perceives that she is receiving 10 rewards and 20 costs, the outcome will be negative ($10 - 20 = -10$). Of course, rewards and costs are very hard to quantify, and some rewards and costs are more important than others. The important point here is that people mentally compare costs and rewards to determine whether they are in a positive or negative relationship.

Comparison Level (CL)

Knowing whether the relationship has a positive or negative outcome is not enough. Some people expect highly rewarding relationships, so the outcomes have to be particularly positive for them to be happy. But other people expect their relationships to be unrewarding, so a slightly positive outcome, or even an outcome that is not as negative as expected, might be all that is needed to make them happy.

To account for the influence of expectations, social exchange theory includes the concept of **comparison level (CL),** which involves the expectation of the kinds of outcomes a person thinks he or she should receive in a relationship (Thibaut & Kelley, 1959). This expectation is based on the person's past relational experiences and on her or his observations of other people's relationships. For example, if Su-Lin has had really good relationships in the past, and her parents and friends all tend to have happy relationships, she is likely to have a high comparison level. Thus, if she is in a relationship in which the rewards outweigh the costs, but not enough to exceed her comparison level, she likely will be dissatisfied. Again, a numeric example might help clarify this concept. Suppose that Miguel expects his rewards to outweigh his costs by about 3 to 1, but in his current relationship he perceives that he is receiving only 2 rewards for every cost. Even though Miguel's relationship has a positive outcome, because he is getting more rewards than costs, the outcome still does not meet his expectation. Therefore, he is likely to be dissatisfied with his relationship.

The opposite can be true when a person has a low comparison level. For example, if Cassie thinks a current relationship has 5 rewards and 10 costs, she will have a negative relational outcome (of -5 if we quantify it). However, Cassie has had horrible relationships in the past, and she expects that to receive 5 rewards she normally has to incur at least 20 costs. In this case her outcome of -5 actually is better than her low comparison level of -15, so she should be fairly satisfied with her relationship.

As these examples suggest, people will be satisfied when their outcomes meet or exceed their comparison levels. This can be written as an equation: satisfaction equals the outcome minus the comparison level ($S = O - CL$). Thus, the comparison level and the outcome work together to predict whether people will be satisfied with their relationships (Sabatelli, 1984).

Comparison Level of Alternatives (CL-Alt)

Although satisfaction and commitment often go together, it is possible for people to be in satisfying relationships that are uncommitted or in committed relationships that are unsatisfying. You can probably think of relationships that fit these categories. Perhaps you know someone who does not seem to want to commit to a relationship even though he or she seems happy. Perhaps you also know someone who seems to be stuck in a relationship that has no future and is unsatisfying. The **comparison level of alternatives (CL-Alt)** helps to explain these situations.

CL-Alt refers to the types of alternatives that a person perceives he or she has outside of a current relationship (Thibaut & Kelley, 1959). Alternatives might include pursuing other relationships or being on one's own. Some people perceive that they have many good alternatives. Perhaps many other attractive people would be interested in them, and perhaps they would be happier alone than in their current relationship. But other people might have poor alternatives. Perhaps they are dependent on their partner for financial support and cannot afford to leave the relationship, or they can envision no attractive alternative relationships, or they perceive themselves as unlovable and think that if they leave their partner they will be alone for the rest of their lives.

When people have good alternatives, they tend to be less committed to their relationships. By contrast, when people have poor alternatives, they tend be highly committed to their relationships. A simplistic example of the way alternatives function might be observed during the month before the senior prom. Suppose that Kelly, a high school senior, has been dating Kyle for the past year. She is considering breaking up with him sometime before they both leave for college, but she is not sure when. If Kelly thinks that two or three boys she finds attractive are likely to ask her to the prom, she might break up with Kyle sooner (assuming that going to the prom is important to her). But if Kelly thinks that no one "better" than Kyle is going to ask her to the prom, she is likely to stay with him, at least temporarily.

On a more serious note, some individuals stay in unsatisfying and even abusive relationships because they have poor alternatives. For example, a man might decide that it is better to stay in his unhappy marriage rather than risk losing custody of his children. In a study on predictors of divorce, people reported being much more likely to leave their spouses when they had appealing alternatives (Black, Eastwood, Sprenkle, & Smith, 1991). Research also suggests that abused women who are dependent on their husbands for financial support are more likely to stay in their abusive relationships (Pfouts, 1978; Rusbult & Martz, 1995). These women, many of whom have little education, few work skills, and no means of transportation, often see their abusive relationships as a better alternative than being poor, hungry, and unable to support their children (Rusbult & Martz, 1995).

The Combined Influence of CL and CL-Alt

Whereas CL is a measure of satisfaction, CL-Alt is a measure of dependency and (at least temporary) commitment. These two factors combine to create different types of relationships, as shown in Figure 8.2. Here are examples for each of the boxes in Figure 8.2:

Alternatives Are:

	Poor	Good
The Relationship: Meets or Exceeds CL	*Box 1: Joe* Satisfied Committed	*Box 2: Kristen* Satisfied Uncommitted
Fails to Meet CL	*Box 3: Caroline* Dissatisfied Committed	*Box 4: Charles* Dissatisfied Uncommitted

FIGURE 8.2 **The Combined Influence of CL and CL-Alt**

Box 1: The Committed and Satisfying Relationship. Joe perceives Darren to be the best relational partner he has ever had. He is more considerate and caring than all of his past boyfriends, and they also have a lot in common. Therefore, Joe's relationship exceeds his comparison level, and he is very satisfied. Furthermore, Joe cannot imagine being with anyone who makes him happier than Darren. When he considers his alternatives (which he rarely does), he thinks he is better off staying with Darren than pursuing a new relationship. Joe tells Darren, "I love you. Let's make our relationship exclusive."

Box 2: The Uncommitted but Satisfying Relationship. After her divorce Kristen was really depressed. She thought dating would be really difficult, and she didn't think she'd ever find anyone she liked. Then she met Tim, who exceeded her expectations in nearly every way. He was easy to talk to, fun to be with, and very attractive. He definitely made her happy. Lately, however, several other attractive men have shown an interest in Kristen, and she wonders if it would be a mistake to "settle" for the first man to come along after her divorce. She tells Tim, "I really want to keep seeing you, but I think we should both see other people as well."

Box 3: The Dissatisfying but Committed Relationship. Caroline and Diana are partners who have been living together for almost a year. When they first moved in together, everything was great. But in recent months they have started arguing more, and they seem to be drifting apart. Sometimes Caroline dreads coming home at night because she is so worried that they will argue. Diana no longer meets her expectations; Caroline has been in happier relationships than this. Yet Caroline feels trapped. She has not met anyone else she is remotely interested in dating, and she is terrified of being alone. She hopes that despite her unhappiness things will eventually get better, so she says to herself, "I'll stick it out a little while longer—at least until something better comes along."

Box 4: The Dissatisfying and Uncommitted Relationship. Charles feels that his relationship with Elise is at a standstill. At first Elise seemed like the perfect woman—intelligent, fun loving, easygoing, and beautiful. Six months into their relationship, however, Charles started focusing on Elise's flaws. Elise seems to use her intelligence to try to prove that she is always right, and she never wants to do anything fun anymore. In fact, Charles can think of many past girlfriends with whom he had much more fun. Lately Charles has noticed that a coworker he finds more attractive than Elise has started to pay extra attention to him. He is sure she will accept if he asks her out. Charles tells Elise, "I'm sorry but I don't think this is working out anymore. I think we need to break up."

As these four types of relationships illustrate, CL and CL-Alt work together to predict the type of relationship people share. Some people stay in unhappy relationships because they do not have better alternatives, while others leave happy relationships to pursue even more appealing alternatives. Indeed, Donovan and Jackson (1990) argued that social exchange theory "may well be the theory most frequently used to explain the cause of divorce" (p. 24).

The Investment Model

The investment model is an extension of social exchange theory. In the original **investment model,** Rusbult (1980, 1983) theorized that CL-Alt, relational satisfaction, and investment size affect commitment. Commitment, in turn, determines whether people stay together or break up. Later Rusbult and her colleagues developed an expanded investment model that focused on relational maintenance (Rusbult, Drigotas, & Verette, 1994). According to this expanded model, commitment has a profound influence on whether people use positive, relationship-maintaining behaviors and survive the problems, conflicts, and temptations that threaten their relationships. In this section we discuss both the original and expanded versions of the investment model.

The Original Investment Model

Within the investment model relational satisfaction is seen as a product of the choices and behaviors that *both* people in the relationship make. Consistent with other social exchange models, this model suggests that, when relationships are characterized by behavior that is rewarding and fulfills expectations, satisfaction is likely. But satisfaction is only part of the story. According to the investment model, commitment is influenced not only by level of satisfaction but also by the quality of alternatives and the investments that people put into their relationships. Figure 8.3 depicts the components of this model.

Investments are "resources that become attached to a relationship and would decline in value or be lost if the relationship were to end" (Rusbult et al.,

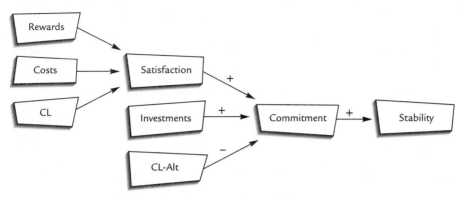

FIGURE 8.3 Rusbult's Original Investment Model

1994, p. 119). Investments can be classified as either intrinsic or extrinsic (Rusbult, 1983). **Intrinsic investments** are those that are put directly into the relationship, including time, effort, affection, and disclosure. **Extrinsic investments** are resources or benefits that are developed over time as a result of being in the relationship, such as material possessions, enmeshment within a common social system, and an identity that is attached to being in a relationship. People put more investments into relationships to which they feel a strong commitment (Matthews, 1986). These investments then make it difficult to walk away from a relationship, which strengthens commitment even more. If two people do end a highly invested relationship, they probably will feel that all the time and effort they put into their relationship was a waste of time. They also might feel that they now have to start over, find someone new, and make adjustments to their identity and social image. These challenges make the prospect of ending a long-term, committed relationship a daunting one.

The basic idea behind the investment model is that satisfaction (which is influenced by rewards, costs, and comparison level), quality of alternatives, and investment size work together to produce commitment (as shown in Figure 8.3). When satisfaction and investments are high, and the quality of alternatives is low, people are likely to be highly committed to their relationships. By contrast, when satisfaction and investments are low, and the quality of alternatives is high, people are likely to be highly uncommitted to their relationships.

Rusbult et al. (1994) noted that a high level of commitment can be good or bad. High commitment can keep a satisfying relationship strong, but it can also trap people in unsatisfying relationships—especially if their alternatives are poor. Therefore, according to the investment model, satisfaction and commitment are related but distinctly different. Several studies have supported the ideas behind the investment model. These studies have shown that investments and the quality of alternatives influence whether people are committed to and stay in their relationships with friends and romantic partners (Drigotas & Rusbult, 1992; Duffy & Rusbult, 1986; Rusbult, 1980, 1983), as well as whether people stay at their jobs (Farrell & Rusbult, 1981; Rusbult & Farrell, 1983).

FIGURE 8.4 Rusbult's Model of Responses to Dissatisfaction

For example, Rusbult (1983) looked at dating relationships over a 7-month period. She found that daters who reported increases in satisfaction and investment, as well as decreases in the quality of alternatives, were the most committed to their relationships. These people were also likely to be together at the end of the 7-month period. By contrast, daters who reported decreases in satisfaction and investment, as well as increases in the quality of alternatives, tended to experience less commitment and to voluntarily leave the relationship sometime during the 7-month period.

Another study examined abusive relationships by interviewing women at shelters (Rusbult & Martz, 1995). Women who went back to their abusive partners usually had large investments in the relationship and low-quality alternatives. Women in this situation may believe that it is better to stay in the relationship than to be alone or to move on to another, potentially worse, relationship. They may be dependent on their partner for financial resources and/or self-esteem. They also may not want to face the possibility that they have put a lot of time and effort into a bad relationship. Therefore, they may work even harder to improve their relationship by trying to change their own and their partner's behavior. This continuous investment, however, keeps them trapped within the dissatisfying relationship. Thus, while high levels of investment keep people in relationships, it does not always ensure that relationships are satisfying.

Even partners in satisfying, highly committed relationships can go through periods of dissatisfaction, conflict, and interest in high-quality alternatives. Rusbult (1987; Rusbult & Zembrodt, 1983) suggested that people in dissatisfying relationships have four general options: exit, neglect, voice, and loyalty. As Figure 8.4 shows, each of these responses is defined by whether it is constructive or destructive and whether it is passive or active. **Exit** behaviors include actions such as threatening to break up, moving out of the house, and getting a divorce. **Neglect** behaviors involve standing by and letting conditions in the relationship get worse—for example, ignoring the partner, spending less time together, treating the partner poorly, and avoiding any discussion of relational problems. Partners who use **voice** attempt to improve conditions in the relationship by

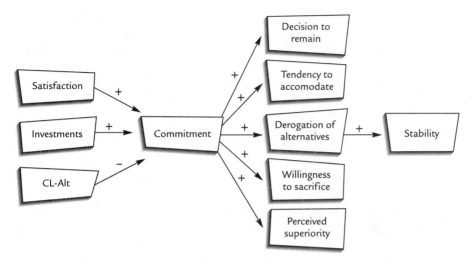

FIGURE 8.5 Rusbult's Expanded Investment Model
of Relationship-Maintaining Behavior

engaging in activities such as discussing problems in a polite manner, seeking help from others, and changing negative behavior. Partners who use **loyalty** optimistically wait for positive change by hoping that things will improve, standing by the partner during difficult times, and supporting the partner in the face of criticism. Partners who use voice and/or loyalty generally put themselves in a better position to maintain their relationships and get through relational problems than do those who use exit or neglect behaviors.

The Expanded Investment Model

An expanded version of the investment model (Rusbult et al., 1994) takes the original model a step further by suggesting that people in highly committed relationships get through difficult times by employing five types of prorelationship behavior, as shown in Figure 8.5: (1) deciding to remain in the relationship, (2) accommodating the partner, (3) derogating alternatives, (4) being willing to sacrifice, and (5) perceiving relationship superiority.

Deciding to Remain   The first and perhaps most important step is the decision to remain in the relationship. People who choose the exit or neglect responses have often stopped believing in the relationship. Without a commitment by the partners to stay in the relationship and work through problems, the relationship is unlikely to survive.

Accommodating the Partner   If the partners do decide to remain in the relationship, they must find a way to cope with their dissatisfaction. Often this requires making accommodations for the sake of the relationship. Rusbult,

Johnson, and Morrow (1986) conducted a study to see how the exit, voice, loyalty, and neglect responses work to help couples deal with relational problems and restore satisfaction. Their research showed that when both partners refrain from using exit or neglect behaviors, the relationship is likely to get back on track. Rusbult and her colleagues referred to this as the **good manners model** of couple functioning. Simply put, people who use less destructive responses and exhibit polite, positive communication report having more positive experiences in their relationships. This may seem obvious, but research has shown that it is easier said than done. Often people's first reaction when they are feeling hurt or dissatisfied is to retaliate against their partner. Rusbult and her colleagues (1994) summarized this **accommodative dilemma** in this way:

> The simple message in this body of research is straightforward: Partners should retain their good manners even during dissatisfying incidents—or perhaps especially during dissatisfying incidents—and would do well to behave constructively under all circumstances. Unfortunately, partners do not behave well under all circumstances. And when a partner engages in exit or neglect responses, the individual is faced with a dilemma: being treated in an inconsiderate manner generates a natural impulse to behave inconsiderately in turn (i.e., to fight fire with fire). . . . These findings suggest that accommodation is experienced as a costly or effortful reaction; that is, accommodating rather than retaliating when a partner behaves poorly is not the individual's immediate response inclination. However, accommodation is clearly in the best interest of the relationship. (pp. 126–127)

Research on the investment model shows that highly committed couples are better able to resist the inclination to retaliate, and the partners accommodate for the sake of the relationship.

Derogating Alternatives   Commitment also leads people to derogate their alternatives. In other words, committed people tend to find reasons to downgrade potential alternative partners. For example, in a study by Johnson and Rusbult (1989), when highly committed individuals were matched up with attractive partners via computer-assigned dates, they found ways to derogate their computer dates, especially if they were highly attractive! Imagine, for example, that Gabrielle and Joshua are engaged to be married. Gabrielle hears that a very handsome, successful acquaintance of hers named Aaron is distressed about her upcoming marriage because he is in love with her. According to the expanded investment model, if Gabrielle is highly committed to her fiancé, she will find fault with Aaron. She might say and think things like "He's probably got a really big ego," "He's not really as attractive as everyone says," and "Joshua will be more successful than Aaron in the long run."

Being Willing to Make Sacrifices   People in highly committed relationships are also more willing to make sacrifices for each other. Sacrifices can be thought of as special types of investments that involve putting aside one's own immediate self-interest and focusing on the best interests of the relationship. The willingness to make sacrifices has been found to be an important factor in maintaining high-quality relationships. As discussed in Chapter 9, supportiveness is a powerful maintenance behavior: We feel close to those who listen to our problems and help us through crisis situations. In fact, Burleson and Samter (1994) found that college students see their closest friends as a significant source of comfort, encouragement, and social support. Willingness to sacrifice is also important because it is difficult for two people to get everything each one wants within the constraints of the relationship. For example, spouses have to make hard decisions regarding their careers, children, and so forth. If the wife's new promotion means that the family will have to move somewhere that is unappealing to the husband, the couple will have to make some type of compromise or sacrifice. Or, if the husband wants to have only one child and the wife wants at least three, something will have to give. In short, because both people cannot always have everything their own way, it is essential that relational partners be willing to sacrifice their own preferences for the overall good of the relationship.

Perceiving Relationship Superiority   Relational partners who are highly committed to each other perceive their relationship to be superior to other relationships. This can be thought of as a "relationship-enhancing illusion" (Rusbult et al., 1994, p. 129). For highly committed relationships "the grass is rarely greener" on the other side. Rusbult et al. (1994) summarized research showing that people tend to see their own relationships as having more positive and fewer negative characteristics than the relationships of others. This bias is particularly strong in highly committed relationships. People might say and think things like "We give each other a lot more freedom than most couples do" and "Our relationship doesn't have as many problems as the average relationship has." This type of thinking leads to positive attitudes about the relationship and sets the tone for behaving constructively and making more accommodations and sacrifices. In relationships that are low in commitment and satisfaction, such positive thinking is less likely; the "grass on the other side" may indeed seem greener!

The investment model has proven to be a powerful theory for explaining the role that commitment plays in the process of relational maintenance. Two people are most likely to become committed to each other when they are satisfied with the relationship, have low-quality alternatives, and have made sizable investments. Once a couple is highly committed, the relationship is maintained through several types of prorelationship activities, including remaining in the relationship through good times and bad, accommodating the partner by resisting the urge to retaliate, derogating alternatives, being willing to sacrifice for the good of the relationship, and perceiving the relationship to be superior to the relationships of others. These forces combine to help maintain the relationship.

Equity Theory

Like social exchange theory and the investment model, equity theory has been used to explain why some couples are more satisfied with their relationships than others. **Equity theory** focuses on examining relational partners to determine whether the distribution of resources is fair (Deutsch, 1985). Equity is measured by comparing the ratio of contributions and benefits for each person. The key word here is "ratio." Partners do *not* have to receive equal benefits (such as receiving the same amount of love, care, and financial security) or make equal contributions (such as investing the same amount of effort, time, and financial resources) as long as the ratio between these benefits and contributions is similar. For example, if Neil puts more effort into the relationship than Renee but also gets more benefits than she does, their relationship is probably still equitable. But if Neil receives fewer benefits than Renee even though he puts more into the relationship, the relationship is inequitable.

Principles of Equity Theory

Equitable relationships are characterized by more satisfaction and commitment than inequitable relationships, largely because people feel distress when inequity is perceived to exist (Adams, 1965; Walster, Berscheid, & Walster, 1973; Walster, Walster, & Berscheid, 1978). Indeed, Walster, Walster, and Traupmann (1978) found that individuals who perceived their dating relationships to be equitable reported being happier and more content than those who perceived their dating relationships to be inequitable. Equity theory revolves around four major principles that help explain this association between equity and relational satisfaction (Walster, Walster, & Berscheid, 1978):

1. Individuals try to maximize their outcomes so that relational rewards outweigh relational costs.
2. People in groups and dyads will develop rules for distributing resources fairly.
3. Within groups and dyads, people will reward those who treat them equitably and punish those who treat them inequitably.
4. When individuals are in inequitable relationships, they will experience distress. This distress will lead them to try to restore equity, such that the more distress they experience, the harder they will try to alleviate that stress.

Consequences of Inequity

When relationships are inequitable, one individual is overbenefited and the other is underbenefited (Walster, Walster, & Berscheid, 1978). The **overbenefited individual** receives more benefits and/or makes fewer contributions than does his or her partner, so that the ratio between them is unbalanced. In simple terms, this person is getting the "better deal." The **underbenefited individual,** by contrast, receives fewer benefits and/or makes greater contributions than does her or his partner, so that the ratio between them is not balanced. This person is getting the "worse deal." When *actual* inequity exists, one person is always underbenefited and the other person is always overbenefited. However, perception does not always match reality. Because people tend to overestimate their own contributions to relationships, both dyadic members might think they are underbenefited even though this is not actually the case. For example, in a study by Ross and Sicoly (1979), husbands and wives rated the degree to which they had responsibility for various activities, such as caring for the children, washing the dishes, and handling the finances, on a scale from 0 (no responsibility) to 150 (complete responsibility). Thus, if a husband and wife split the task of doing the dishes evenly, both should have rated their responsibility at the 75-point midpoint. However, the results suggested that 73% of the spouses overestimated the amount of work they did; when their ratings were summed and averaged across all the activities, they totaled over 150 points. Apparently a lot of dishes were being cleaned twice! As this example illustrates, relational partners might both *perceive* themselves to be underbenefited; but in reality it would be impossible for both people to be getting a "worse deal" than the other.

According to equity theory, whether people are over- or underbenefited, they experience increases in distress and decreases in satisfaction and happiness (Walster, Walster, & Berscheid, 1978). Of course, underbenefited individuals experience a different kind of stress than overbenefited individuals. As you might suspect, underbenefited individuals are usually more distressed than overbenefited individuals (Austin & Walster, 1974). When people are underbenefited, they tend to feel cheated, used, and taken for granted, and they experience anger and/or sadness (Walster, Walster, & Traupmann, 1978). Men may be particularly likely to be angry when they are underbenefited, while women may be especially likely to be sad and disappointed (Sprecher, 1986).

Although overbenefited individuals tend to experience less distress than their underbenefited counterparts, they sometimes experience guilt. Women, in particular, seem likely to feel guilty when they are overbenefited (Sprecher, 1986; Walster, Walster, & Traupmann, 1978). This may be because women are taught to be the "relational keepers," and thus to put considerable effort into their relationships. People who perceive themselves to be overbenefited may also feel smothered and wish that their partner would spend less time doing things for them.

A good example of this is provided in the movie *The Joy Luck Club,* based on Amy Tan's novel of the same name. One of the characters is first presented as an independent young woman named Rose. In fact, her independence is one of the qualities that is attractive to her future husband when they first meet. Over time, however, Rose starts catering to her husband's wishes so much that she stops expressing her own thoughts and opinions. Her husband wants her to do less for him and more for herself, but eventually they separate. Even after they separate, Rose continues to give more than she receives—she even bakes her husband his favorite peanut butter pie the day they are going to discuss their divorce. This is a particularly interesting case of inequity because the husband, who is clearly overbenefited in terms of objective resources, ends up perceiving his excessive benefits as a cost, which leads him to resent and eventually leave his wife.

Of course, some overbenefited men and women feel quite content with their relationships, and not guilty at all (Hatfield, Greenberger, Traupmann, & Lambert, 1982; Traupmann, Hatfield, & Wexler, 1983). Most people may need to be highly overbenefited (like Rose's husband) before they experience distress, while being less underbenefited typically leads to anger and frustration. In any case, if equity is not achieved (or at least not perceived to exist), feelings of anger, sadness, and guilt are likely to pervade the emotional fabric of the relationship.

Again, numeric examples might help clarify how equity theory works. Suppose that Katie receives 25 benefits for every 5 contributions she makes to her relationship with Christian. This means that Katie has a benefit-contribution ratio of 25:5. Christian has a ratio of 50:10. Is their relationship equitable or inequitable? Because both Katie and Christian are receiving 5 benefits per contribution, their relationship is equitable, and they are likely to be happy. Notice that for the relationship to be equitable Katie and Christian do not have to be receiving the exact same number of benefits, nor do they have to be making the same number of contributions. Instead, the ratios between each's benefits and contributions must be the same.

Now imagine that Donna has a benefit-contribution ratio of 60:20 compared to Wayne's benefit-contribution ratio of 40:10. Because these ratios are different, Donna and Wayne have an inequitable relationship. Can you tell who is over-benefited and who is underbenefited? According to equity theory, even though Donna is receiving more overall benefits than Wayne, she is underbenefited. Donna receives only 3 benefits for each contribution she makes. In comparison, Wayne receives 4 benefits for each contribution he makes. As the under-benefited party, Donna is likely to feel angry and sad. Wayne might feel some guilt, although he would be more likely to do so if he were a woman and if the inequity were greater—that is, if the ratios were further apart. Of course, because Donna and Wayne are both receiving a high level of benefits versus contributions, and the difference between their ratios is small, they might perceive the relationship to be fair and satisfying even though, from an objective standpoint, it is somewhat inequitable.

Ways to Reduce Distress in Inequitable Relationships

So what happens when relational partners experience inequity and distress? According to Walster, Walster, and Berscheid (1978), they will be motivated to reduce inequity and the accompanying distress. There are three general ways to do this. First, people can attempt to restore **actual equity** through some behavioral change. For example, as the overbenefited partner, Wayne might work a little harder to contribute to the relationship, whereas Donna, as the underbenefited partner, might do less relational work. Alternatively, Donna might influence Wayne to change, perhaps by asking him to increase what he contributes to the relationship. Second, people can attempt to restore **psychological equity.** Recall that equity is "in the eye of the beholder" in that perceptions are as important as actions. To restore equity, Donna might reassess what she puts into and gets out of the relationship, and decide that she is receiving more benefits than she thought. Donna might also reassess Wayne's situation and conclude that he is actually putting more effort into the relationship than she thought. These types of mental adjustments can help people restore equity. Third, people can simply end the relationship. In *The Joy Luck Club* Rose's husband starts pursing this option. However, before they divorce, Rose decides to restore actual equity by decreasing her contributions and demanding more benefits. In essence, she tells her husband that she now realizes her self-worth and will no longer be a doormat. After actual equity is restored, the couple reunites—in line with both equity theory predictions and the typical Hollywood happy ending.

Equity and Relational Maintenance

As with the investment model, some research on equity theory has focused on relational maintenance. In general, this research shows that couples in equitable relationships engage in more friendly, constructive behavior than those in inequitable relationships (Canary & Stafford, 1992, 1993). In a study of married couples, Canary and Stafford (1992) found that wives' perceptions of equity (or inequity) were associated with differences in maintenance behavior. In particular, wives who perceived themselves to be in equitable relationships reported that both they and their husbands used more positivity, openness, and assurances than wives who perceived themselves to be either under- or overbenefited. **Positivity** involves making interactions pleasant and enjoyable by engaging in behavior such as acting cheerful and optimistic and complimenting the partner. **Openness** involves disclosing personal information, as well as engaging in more routine, mundane talk. **Assurances** involve making statements that show commitment to the relationship, such as talking about the partners' future together. (These maintenance behaviors are discussed in more detail in Chapter 9.)

Under- and overbenefited wives may report using less maintenance behaviors for different reasons. Underbenefited wives may be trying to reduce their contributions so that the relationship becomes more equitable, or they may engage in less maintenance because they are angry with their partners. By contrast, wives might perceive themselves as overbenefited at least partially because they engage in lower levels of maintenance. However, it is important to keep in mind that Canary and Stafford's study did not determine whether the perception of inequity causes less relational maintenance or whether less relational maintenance leads to perceptions of inequity.

Canary and Stafford's study also looked at husbands' perceptions of equity. Underbenefited husbands reported that their wives used less positivity, offered fewer assurances, and shared fewer tasks than did overbenefited husbands and husbands in equitable relationships. This finding is consistent with equity theory principles in that husbands are likely to perceive themselves as underbenefited when their wives are not contributing to the relationship by using high levels of maintenance.

This study, when combined with the research on emotional reactions to inequity, suggests that equitable relationships might be satisfying for at least two reasons. First, they are less distressing than inequitable relationships. Second, people in equitable relationships may engage in more positive behavior that helps maintain the relationship.

Of course, some relationships can be equitable without being particularly rewarding. For instance, Kurt might have a benefit-contribution ratio of 15:30 while Gretchen has a benefit-contribution ratio of 10:20. Both individuals are getting 1 benefit for every 2 contributions they make, so the relationship is equitable. But do Kurt and Gretchen have a satisfying relationship? The answer seems to be yes and no. They might be satisfied in that both are getting a fair deal but dissatisfied because they are not maximizing their rewards, which, as discussed previously, is the first principle of equity theory.

To be highly satisfied a couple should have an equitable relationship in which rewards outweigh costs. In fact, studies by Cate and his associates showed that the overall level of reward value associated with a relationship is more important than equity (Cate & Lloyd, 1988; Cate, Lloyd, & Henton, 1985; Cate, Lloyd, & Long, 1988). Some level of inequity might be inconsequential if both partners are receiving high levels of rewards. Thus, relationships that are characterized by equity and more rewards than costs are likely to be satisfying. Relationships that are inequitable with rewards outweighing costs should also be satisfying, especially if the rewards are high and the inequity is fairly small. By contrast, relationships that are equitable with costs outweighing rewards are likely to be fair but somewhat dissatisfying. Finally, inequitable relationships in which costs outweigh rewards will be the least satisfying.

Equity in the Division of Household Labor

As equity theory suggests, most people say that they want relationships that are fair and equitable (Steil, 2000). When it comes to achieving a fair division of labor, however, research suggests that equity is hard to obtain. Indeed, many studies have been conducted applying some of the principles from equity theory to the "fair" division of household chores. According to this research, when it comes to household work, women are typically underbenefited and men are typically overbenefited. In fact, according to Steil's (2000) careful review of the literature, working women do about two thirds of the household chores and even more of the child care. You might think that working women would do less household chores than nonworking women because their husbands would help more. However, Berk (1985) found that men in dual-career couples spend only 4 more minutes a day engaged in household tasks than do men in traditional single-career relationships. Even among dual-career partners who report splitting household tasks evenly, women still do far more in terms of caring for children (Rosenbluth, Steil, & Whitcomb, 1998). The situation is no better for wives who earn more than their husbands. In fact, Biernat and Wortman (1991) found that men actually do less household chores when their wives earn more than they do, perhaps because they see their wives as highly capable of handling multiple tasks or because they are resentful.

Ironically, although women usually air their relational grievances to their husbands (Gottman & Carrere, 1994), in the case of unfair division of household labor they are often silent (Thompson & Walker, 1989). Unless their share of household work exceeds the two thirds mark, they typically do not feel that the division of labor is unfair, nor do they complain. Steil (2000) labeled this problem "the paradox of the contented wife" (p. 127). Women want equality, yet even when they are aware that they do more household tasks than their husbands, they report having fair, equitable, and satisfying relationships. Perhaps this is because of societal expectations regarding gender roles.

Even though women are fairly satisfied in marriages in which inequities (up to the two-thirds share mark) occur, working mothers become less satisfied as the gap between their husband's and their own share of the housework tasks widens (Barnett & Baruch, 1987; Staines & Libby, 1986). At this point women begin to feel underbenefited. Based on these findings, Gottman and Carrere (1994) made the following recommendation: Most men need to do more housework, care for their children more, and show their wives more affection and appreciation if they want their wives to be truly happy.

Unlike their heterosexual counterparts, most gay and lesbian partners do roughly the same amount of household tasks. Peplau and Spalding (2000) provided a comprehensive review of the literature on the division of labor in homosexual households. In their review they noted that most gay men and lesbians are in dual-career relationships, "so that neither partner is the exclusive breadwinner and each partner has some measure of economic independence. The most common division of labor involves flexibility, with partners sharing domestic activities or dividing tasks according to personal preferences" (p. 117). Kurdek (1993a) compared the division of household labor in heterosexual, gay male, and lesbian couples. Consistent with other research, he found that women did a larger portion of household work than did men in heterosexual relationships. Gay men and lesbians were more likely to do an equal amount of household tasks. But whereas the gay men divided the chores up so that each man routinely did certain tasks more than the others, the lesbians tended to share tasks, often by doing chores together. Thus, opposite-sex couples might take a lesson from same-sex couples when it comes to sharing household chores in a fair, equitable manner.

Social Evolutionary Theories

Social exchange theories, including the original theory, the investment model, and equity theory, have been applied to a wide assortment of relational phenomena, such as satisfaction, commitment, and the fair distribution of resources and household labor. Social evolutionary theorists, by contrast, have taken a social exchange perspective to describe a more specific phenomenon—sex differences in sexual attraction and mating behavior (Buss, 1994; Buss & Kenrick, 1998; Trost & Alberts, 1998). According to this perspective, people's preferences for mates evolved in ways consistent with the biological imperative to reproduce. As such, men look for mates who are fertile and will be good mothers, while women look for mates who have the necessary resources to be good fathers and providers. A woman, however, should be choosier than a man when it comes to a finding a mate because her investment, in terms of pregnancy and child care, will typically be higher than his.

Social evolutionary theories of sexual attraction and mating also emphasize the importance of the **pair bond** (Kenrick & Trost, 1987, 1989). In other words, men and women evolved to pair up with one another so that by working together they could ensure the survival of the species. Kenrick, Groth, Trost, and Sadalla (1993) put it this way: Potential partners "seek and value mates that would (in our ancestor's time) have been related to (a) the likely possession of adaptive genes that might directly promote the survival of offspring and (b) the capacity and inclination to contribute tangible resources that could help the offspring survive" (p. 951). Thus, according to social evolutionary theory, resource exchange involves trading assets that will help a couple ensure the survival of their children. These evolutionary processes supposedly are driven by unconscious impulses that have evolved across the millennia.

Before discussing some of the specific studies used to test this evolutionary perspective, it is important to note that the theory is controversial, partly because it is new and people do not yet understand all its nuances. Some people have criticized the theory because it cannot be tested directly. That is, researchers cannot change evolutionary history to provide a comparison point, nor can they bring people into a research laboratory and manipulate their genes. Others have criticized the theory for being outdated. For example, the "money-for-beauty trade" discussed in some of the literature suggests that in the dating marketplace men trade financial resources for beauty, while women trade their looks for money (Murstein, 1972). Because most women in the 21st century are educated and capable of supporting themselves financially, the money-for-beauty trade may not be nearly as relevant as it was in previous generations when women could not own property and most did not attend college. Nonetheless, if social evolutionary theory is correct, these genetic predispositions are a function not of changing economic conditions, but of thousands of years of evolution.

The theory has been criticized as well for providing men with a convenient excuse for promiscuous behavior and infidelity, and for ignoring cultural and social forces that shape behavior. Indeed, people might claim that they could not help being unfaithful because it is "in their genes." Evolutionary theory should be used not as an excuse for bad behavior by either men or women, but as an explanatory force for understanding sex differences. In addition, the importance placed on the pair bond in social evolutionary theory actually suggests that both men and women bring considerable resources to monogamous relationships. This leads to another criticism of evolutionary theory—that it does not explain sexual attraction among gay men or lesbians who cannot reproduce. Finally, people sometimes have problems with the idea that their genes have considerable influence on their behavior. Social evolutionary theory, however, does not completely discount the importance of socialization. Indeed, when behaviors are socially adaptive, evolutionary theorists predict that they are more likely to evolve.

Despite criticisms and controversies, social evolutionary theory has a long history in the field of social psychology. In the 1990s researchers in the field of communication also started recognizing that biology and evolution might play important roles in shaping human behavior (Andersen, 1998b; McCroskey, 1997; Trost & Alberts, 1998). In this section we look at how these forces might influence sexual attraction and mating behavior.

Sex Differences in Sexual Attraction

Sexual attraction, which was defined in Chapter 3 as the desire to engage in sexual activity (which may or may not include intercourse) with a person, is an ubiquitous human experience. Although sexual desire and sexual attraction can be suppressed, most people experience sexual desire and are, at least occasionally, sexually attracted to other individuals. While some adults do abstain from sex for periods of time, most do not (Blumstein & Schwartz, 1983; Sprecher & Regan, 1996). The human sex drive is powerful and can be suppressed only with considerable difficulty, although women's sex drive is more variable and contextually driven than men's (Baumeister, 2000). According to evolutionary theories, the human sex drive is an innate, biological drive that serves to ensure reproduction and to maintain dyadic relationships between sexual partners.

Social evolutionary theorists believe that men and women are generally most attracted to potential mates who show signs of physical health, sexual maturity, and reproductive potential, and who are therefore capable of passing "good" genetic material on to their offspring (Buss & Kenrick, 1998). However, because men and women play different roles in the reproductive process, they should differ to some extent in the qualities they look for in a mate.

A huge body of research has shown that similarity produces attraction. As discussed in Chapter 3 and as Box 8.1 suggests, similarities in wealth, age, physical attractiveness, political beliefs, educational level, personal habits, religion, and a host of other factors typically increase attraction. Research has even shown that romantic partners are more sexually similar than randomly paired individuals (Cupach & Metts, 1995).

One exception to this rule is that women traditionally have tended to be attracted to somewhat older men and men to somewhat younger women. Social exchange models and cultural sex norms usually are used to explain this finding. A series of studies by Kenrick and Keefe (1992) suggested that these may be biologically based sex differences that have evolved over thousands of generations. Social evolutionary theory predicts that males would select sexually mature but youthful females to maximize their reproductive potential. Young males, however, would not prefer younger females because they would gain no reproductive advantage. Young females would prefer older men because of their greater resources such as physical strength and economic well-being. And as men age they should prefer progressively younger women, whereas as women age they should show less age preference.

Kenrick and Keefe (1992) tested this hypothesis in a series of studies. Specifically they looked at (1) want ads in singles' magazines and an elite intellectual

BOX 8.1 HIGHLIGHTS

Social Exchange in the Dating Marketplace

Consider the following fictional personal advertisements, which are similar to what you will find in newspapers across the United States:

Single Hispanic Woman, 28, 5'4" tall, petite brunette with green eyes and beautiful complexion, physically fit and athletic: Seeks Single or Divorced Man (any race) who is 28 or older, 5'10" or taller, well educated and financially secure, and likes children. Prefer nonsmoker who likes sports and only drinks socially.

Divorced White Male, 45, 6'4" tall, 220 lbs., dark curly hair and mustache, successful professional, likes country music, picnics, and baseball games: Seeks Woman, 35–45, who enjoys the same and is college educated. Looking for friendship, romance, and maybe even more.

Single White Female, 33, tall, brunette, nonsmoker, world traveler: Seeks Single White Female, 25–35, who is affectionate and easygoing, loves animals, and likes to travel to exotic destinations. If you are looking for a true companion and soulmate, who knows, maybe we'll connect.

Personal advertisements such as these, although typical, may appear quite superficial to you. However, they illustrate how social exchange operates in the dating marketplace. People look to exchange certain resources for other resources that they value. For some people there are even minimum "resource requirements," such as being a nonsmoker, college educated, or a certain age or height. Cameron, Oskamp, and Sparks (1977) examined personal advertisements such as these and suggested that they read like the New York Stock Exchange, with potential partners seeking to "strike bargains which maximize their rewards in the exchange of assets" (p. 28).

publication, (2) the current marriage records in two U.S. cities, (3) marriage records from 1923, (4) personal ads in Germany and Holland, and (5) Philippine marital statistics prior to World War II. Across all these samples Kenrick and Keefe confirmed this evolutionary hypothesis. However, it is important to note that this age difference often is small and that *both* men and women are waiting longer to get married now than in previous decades. According to data on first marriages from the U.S. Census Bureau, in the 1950s and 1960s the average woman married before her 21st birthday, while the average man married at around age 23, often after finishing college and starting a career. In the 1990s the average woman married at about age 24 and the average man married at about age 26. Still, when there is an age difference of 5 years or more between a husband and wife, the wife is much more likely to be the younger spouse.

If sex differences in mate selection are truly universal characteristics of men and women, then the same pattern of sex differences should show up in various cultures. According to social evolutionary theory, regardless of culture men should prefer characteristics associated with high reproductive capacity such as good looks, an hourglass body shape, youthfulness, and chastity. Singh (1993), for example, showed that men preferred women of average to below average weight and with hourglass figures (hip-to-waist ratios of .70) across two cultural groups. By contrast, women should prefer characteristics associated with resource acquisition in potential mates, such as a masculine body type, ambitiousness, industriousness, and good financial prospects. In a study of 37 cultures, from Zulus to Poles and from Canadians to Japanese, Buss (1989) uncovered just such a pattern. Likewise Singh (1995) showed that women prefer men with a masculine shape (a waist-to-hip ratio of .90 is best), moderate weight, and higher financial status. For whatever reason, resources such as status, dominance, and material possessions appear to be very important for women's attraction to men but less important for men's attraction to women.

Apparently, however, if they have to choose between the two characteristics, women value men with good personalities more than they value men with wealth. Cunningham, Barbee, Graves, Lundy, and Lister (1996), for example, found that women were more likely to report that they would have sexual intercourse with a nice, moral, wealthy man than with a nice, moral, middle-class man but would be unwilling to have sex with a man who was unfriendly and immoral regardless of his wealth. According to evolutionary theory, women should be attracted to men who will provide resources such as long-term emotional and financial support, so an unfriendly and immoral man would be unacceptable.

The Parental Investment Model

The evolutionary perspective also explains the influence of personality on long-term attraction. Having the ability to reproduce is not enough. Couples must also be able to care for their offspring to ensure survival. According to the **parental investment model**, men and women (like other mammals) fulfill different reproductive functions and make different investments in their children (Trivers, 1985). **Parental investment** refers to any resources that a parent devotes to her or his children at the cost of investing the resource elsewhere (Daly & Wilson, 1983). As new parents find out, raising a child takes considerable time, effort, and sacrifice. These parents forgo sleep and arrange their schedules around the needs of their children. Money that a couple could have spent on a vacation or new car might be placed in a child's college fund, and romantic nights out might become scarce. Thus, having a mate who is patient, willing to make sacrifices, and loyal to the family is a valued commodity.

According to the investment model, women make particularly costly investments in parenting because of pregnancy and nursing. Additionally, women are usually the primary caregivers for their children. Men, by contrast, have the option of investing minimally in their offspring simply by providing their genes. Although most men do invest heavily in their offspring, they still do not invest as much as women. As noted previously, among married couples with children, women typically handle more than two thirds of the child care responsibilities. In addition, most single-parent families are headed by women, which underscores the increased parental investment that often is shouldered by women. Although some men remain heavily invested in their children's lives after a divorce, many men gradually reduce their investments once they move out of the family home (Pearson & Thoennes, 1990; Seltzer, 1991).

Kenrick and his colleagues extended this line of reasoning by proposing the **relationship-qualified parental investment model** (Kenrick et al., 1993; Kenrick, Sadalla, Groth, & Trost, 1990). According to this model, various stages of relationships are characterized by different configurations of rewards and costs. In casual dating relationships that do not involve sex, the partners will be relatively unconcerned about resources connected to parental investment. However, if the relationship becomes more serious, issues related to parental investment will become more salient for both men and women. However, women will be choosier than men when deciding whether to have a one-night stand or a brief sexual liaison with someone because women (at least historically) risk pregnancy and the resulting costs.

Based on the relationship-qualified investment model, Kenrick and his associates (1990, 1993) tested for sex differences in attraction at different relational stages. Specifically, participants in these studies rated the *minimum* levels of physical attractiveness, dominance, status, and intelligence (among other characteristics) that they would seek in a person they would go on a date with, have sex with, date steadily, and marry. Consistent with social evolutionary theory, women were choosier than men on all characteristics except for physical attractiveness.

One of these studies (Kenrick et al., 1993) also included ratings of minimum characteristics needed for people to engage in one-night stands. As noted previously, social evolutionary theorists predict that women will be particularly choosy when engaging in one-night stands because of the risks associated with getting pregnant and not having the emotional support of a committed partner. Men, by contrast, will be particularly unselective because they have a low-cost opportunity to have sex. Kenrick et al.'s study supported this sex difference in selectiveness. That is, when rating potential partners for one-night stands, women were nearly as choosy as they were when rating potential partners for committed relationships, whereas men's level of choosiness dropped to its lowest point in every category except for physical appearance. The difference here was particularly striking when the results for intelligence were analyzed. Women reported that a man would have to be above average in intelligence if they were to consider having a one-night stand with him. Men, by contrast, reported that they would consider having a one-night stand with a woman who was below average in intelligence. However, both men and women desired marital partners who were well above average in intelligence, suggesting that both sexes are the most selective when it comes to choosing a long-term mate.

In sum, social evolutionary theory predicts that potential mates exchange resources at least partially based on their drive to reproduce and to care for their offspring. These evolutionary processes have evolved over many millennia and continue to evolve today. In the 21st century, as men and women bring new resources to the "marketplace," it is likely that different attributes will be seen as attractive, and new socially adaptive preferences may slowly emerge as humans continue to evolve.

Conclusion

People exchange resources with one another in all types of relationships. Parents provide children with love and a secure home, and children give their parents affection and feelings of self-worth. Friends exchange companionship and do favors for one another, and romantic partners exchange financial resources, household responsibilities, and love. Social exchange is even part of work relationships, wherein employers provide rewards such as praise and raises, and subordinates contribute productivity and loyalty to the company (Farrell & Rusbult, 1981).

Sometimes resources are exchanged in ways that are fair and equitable. Other times resources are unbalanced so that one person is underbenefited and the other is overbenefited. Relationships characterized by equity have a better chance of achieving happiness than do those marked by inequity, perhaps because partners in equitable relationships experience less distress, and perhaps because they use more maintenance behaviors. For relationships to be satisfying, it is also important that a partner meets or exceeds a person's comparison level. People in equitable relationships may be more committed, although investment size and quality of alternatives are better predictors of commitment than equity. The more people invest in their relationships and the poorer their alternatives, the more committed they are likely to be.

Research suggests that, even though people want to have equitable relationships, true equity is hard to achieve. The division of household labor provides one compelling example of this problem; working women typically do about two thirds of the household work. In Chapter 11 we discuss equity issues related to power and resources. The research reported there suggests that people in egalitarian relationships are more satisfied than are those in more traditional, less balanced relationships. Such findings provide further evidence that a fair exchange of contributions and benefits within a relationship is healthy.

Social evolutionary theory, although controversial, is supported by a considerable body of research on sex differences showing that, although both men and women are attracted to good-looking people, physical attractiveness is especially important for males. By contrast, financial prospects appear to be a more valued resource when women are choosing mates. But these sex differences may be getting smaller in the 21st century because women are much more financially independent. In addition, with the widespread use of birth control, women are much more in control of their reproductive capacity. Only over time will social evolutionary theorists be able to see if these changes affect sex differences in sexual attraction and mating behavior. For now, however, it is safe to say that regardless of sex differences both men and women prefer relationships that are rewarding and fair. So, the next time you think that you are not "getting a fair deal" in one of your relationships, we hope that this chapter will give you some insight into the causes of and possible remedies for your distress.

Discussion Questions

1. Most partners overestimate the contributions they make in comparison to the other person. To what extent might you do (or not do) this? How can this overestimation be corrected? (If you want to determine whether you or your partner or roommate are overestimating your contributions, list 10 household chores, and then independently write down what percentage of the time you believe you do each of them. If your estimates add up to over 100%, either one or both of you are overestimating your contribution.)
2. Why do you think working women still do two thirds of the household work, and, perhaps more importantly, why don't most women complain until their share of the work exceeds this two-thirds mark?
3. As stated in this chapter, some people consider social evolutionary theory to be a controversial theory. What do you think?

Staying Close

Maintaining Intimate Relationships

In fairy tales everyone lives "happily ever after," as if happiness was bestowed upon them almost magically. In real life, however, there is no magic recipe for a happy relationship. As we shall see in this chapter, maintaining relationships requires effort and perseverance. The road to a successful relationship often contains rough spots and detours, but "staying on course" and maintaining important relationships is a worthwhile endeavor. In fact, research has shown that having a close relationship is a key determinant of overall happiness (Hatfield, 1984). People who have trouble maintaining close relationships with others often are lonely and depressed, and they may even doubt their self-worth (Segrin, 1998). Married people tend to report being happier and more satisfied with their lives than do single people (Cargan & Melko, 1982), yet nearly half of the marriages in the United States end in divorce (Cherlin, 1983; Phillips, 1988).

So what is the secret to maintaining healthy, happy relationships? Although no magic formula exists, the research on relational maintenance provides us with some important information on the kinds of behaviors that are associated with relational satisfaction and longevity. The literature also provides information on ways of dealing with common relational tensions, such as between the desire for intimacy and the desire for independence and self-sufficiency. In this chapter we look at three areas of research related to maintenance. First, we discuss specific types of behaviors people use to maintain a variety of close relationships, including those between romantic partners and those between friends. Second, we look at barriers to relational dissolution. Finally, we focus on dialectics theory, which describes how people cope with common relational tensions.

Definitions of Relational Maintenance

People maintain all kinds of things. They take their cars in for routine maintenance service and repair mechanical problems when they occur. They maintain their homes by keeping them clean, mowing the lawn, trimming the hedges, painting the walls, and so forth. They maintain their good images at work by trying to be punctual, professional, and well organized. Similarly, people often try to maintain their relationships with others through contact and communication.

Obviously, maintaining a relationship is far more challenging for most of us than maintaining a car or a home. **Relational maintenance** refers to a number of different processes or goals, but Dindia and Canary (1993) identified four common components of relational maintenance. First, relational maintenance involves keeping a relationship in existence. Think of all the people to whom you send holiday cards once a year. Although you might not have much, if any, contact with many of these people over the course of a given year, the exchange of greeting cards helps you to maintain your relationships with them.

Second, relational maintenance involves keeping a relationship in a specified state or condition, or at a stable level of intimacy, so that the status quo is maintained (Ayres, 1983). For example, if Brooke and Kim are best friends, Brooke might feel threatened if Kim starts spending excessive amounts of time with her new boyfriend. Brooke might work to keep her friendship with Kim as close as it was before the new boyfriend came along. In other cases people might work at keeping a relationship from becoming *more* intimate. For instance, if Adam and Kory have been good friends for a long time, and Adam suddenly starts showing an unwanted romantic interest in Kory, Kory is likely to work to keep the relationship from becoming more intimate. To paraphrase an old saying, Kory might not want a potential romance to ruin a good friendship.

Third, relational maintenance involves keeping a relationship in satisfactory condition. For example, dating and married couples often try to rekindle the romance in their relationships to keep them satisfying. Friends might plan a weekend ski trip together if they feel they need to catch up with each other and have some fun. As this chapter will show, the use of maintenance activities can help dyadic partners to sustain mutually satisfying relationships. Feelings of liking, loving, respect, and commitment are all related to keeping both partners satisfied.

Fourth, relational maintenance involves keeping a relationship in repair. The idea here is that the dyad works to *prevent* problems from occurring and to *correct* problems when they do occur. For example, if Jennifer knows that Laura gets easily irritated in restaurants that are bright, noisy, and crowded, she might choose a quiet place to meet for dinner. If Steve and Blake start bickering about who is doing a larger share of the household chores, it might be time for them to sit down and negotiate a fair division of labor. Wilmot (1994) referred to the process of restoring a relationship to satisfactory condition as **relational rejuvenation.**

As Dindia and Canary (1993) stated, these four components of relational maintenance overlap. An important part of keeping a relationship satisfying is preventing and correcting problems, and an important part of keeping a relationship in existence is keeping it satisfying. In a broad sense, relational maintenance can be defined as keeping a relationship at a desired level (Canary & Stafford, 1994). Sometimes this involves keeping a relationship from becoming too intimate; other times it involves keeping a relationship high in satisfaction and low in problems. Notice also that this definition does not necessarily mean that a relationship remains at the same level of intimacy over time. As people's desires change, the way they define and maintain their relationships also changes. Therefore, maintenance is a dynamic process that involves continually adjusting to new needs and demands.

Behaviors Used to Maintain Relationships

Now that we have defined relational maintenance, you might be wondering *how* people maintain their relationships. Scholars began addressing this important question in the 1980s (Ayres, 1983; Bell, Daly, & Gonzalez, 1987; Dindia & Baxter, 1987; Duck, 1988; Shea & Pearson, 1986). Since then, much has been learned about the behaviors that people use to maintain their relationships. From this emergent body of literature, at least three general principles about maintenance behavior can be drawn.

Principle 1: *A variety of strategic and routine behaviors are used to maintain relationships.*

Canary and Stafford (1994) made an important distinction between strategic and routine maintenance behavior. **Strategic maintenance** involves enacting behaviors that are specifically and intentionally designed to maintain your relationship. For example, if you have an argument with your best friend, you might eventually call your friend with the intent of apologizing and repairing the situation. On Mother's Day you might send your mom a bouquet of flowers so that she knows you are thinking of her. If you live far away from a loved one, you might call her or him once a week at a designated time to keep in touch. These types of actions are deliberate and intentionally designed to help you maintain a positive relationship with someone.

Routine behaviors are less strategic and deliberate. They are used without the express purpose of maintaining the relationship, yet they still help people preserve their bonds with one another. For example, roommates might share the household responsibilities as a matter of routine or habit. One roommate might do the grocery shopping, pay the bills, and vacuum and dust the apartment, and the other might water the plants, clean the bathroom, and do the cooking. They might alternate doing dishes, and they might each do their own laundry. This system of sharing responsibilities helps ensure that the household runs smoothly, which helps maintain a satisfying roommate relationship. Similarly, a couple may routinely discuss the events of the day over the dinner table and spend time together watching favorite television programs or engaging in certain activities, such as jogging or playing tennis. Although these behaviors are not strategically designed to help partners maintain their relationship, chatting and spending time together is likely to help keep their relationship close. In fact, Duck (1994) argued that routine talk is at the heart of relational maintenance. Thus, maintaining a relationship does not always require "work." Sometimes maintenance rests in the seemingly trivial behaviors that people enact rather mindlessly on a day-to-day basis.

Of course, the line between strategic and routine maintenance behaviors is sometimes blurred. The same behavior can be strategic in some situations and routine in others. For example, holding your romantic partner's hand at the movie theater might be part of a habitual routine; you might always hold your partner's hand in this situation. After an argument, however, reaching for your partner's hand might be a strategic move designed to make things better by restoring intimacy to the relationship. Strategic maintenance behaviors may be used when people are trying to prevent a relationship from becoming too intimate, escalate or de-escalate the level of intimacy in the relationship, or restore intimacy to or repair a relationship. Both routine and strategic behaviors can contribute to relational maintenance in terms of keeping the relationship close and satisfying.

So what are the primary behaviors that people use to help maintain their relationships? Various researchers have come up with different lists of behaviors. Ayres (1983) focused on behaviors that function to keep a relationship at a given level of intimacy. He found three primary maintenance strategies: (1) **avoidance,** which involves avoiding talk or activities that might change the relationship; (2) **balance,** which involves reciprocating favors and emotional support levels; and (3) **directness,** which involves explicitly informing the person of a desire not to change the relationship. Dindia (1989) investigated maintenance strategies used by married couples. She found three general strategies: (1) **prosocial,** which refers to positive behaviors such as talking about the relationship and listening to each other; (2) **romantic,** which refers to behaviors that are affectionate, spontaneous, and fun, such as expressing affection nonverbally; and (3) **antisocial,** which refers to behaviors that are coercive, such as trying to manipulate or control the partner.

Stafford and Canary (1991) asked dating and married couples what the partners did to maintain their relationships and keep them satisfying. Five primary maintenance strategies emerged: positivity, openness, assurances, social networks, and task sharing. However, Canary and Stafford (1994; Canary, Stafford, Hause, & Wallace, 1993) later argued that these five behaviors may represent only *positive* strategies used by romantic couples. Thus, they sought to develop a category system that would include *negative* behaviors (like Aryes' avoidance strategy and Dindia's antisocial strategy) and be applicable to other relationships, such as those between friends, family members, and coworkers. Therefore, Canary et al.'s (1993) study examined a number of additional strategies, including avoidance, antisocial behavior, supportiveness, joint activities, and mediated communication. Other researchers (Afifi, Guerrero, & Egland, 1994; Dainton & Stafford, 1993) have also found that dating couples, married couples, and friends all use these additional behaviors. A summary of the most common relational maintenance behaviors reported in the literature is found in Box 9.1. As this list clearly shows, people use a wide variety of routine and strategic behaviors to maintain their relationships, and communication plays an essential role in the maintenance process.

In addition to using the maintenance behaviors listed in Box 9.1, Haas and Stafford (1998) found that gay and lesbian couples use some unique strategies to maintain their relationships. For example, gay and lesbian partners reported that it is important to live and work in environments that are supportive and not judgmental of their relationships. Similarly, gay and lesbian partners emphasized the importance of being "out" in front of their social networks. Spending time with friends and family members who recognize and accept their relationship was mentioned as a key relational maintenance behavior, as was being able to introduce each other as "my partner." Some gay and lesbian couples also reported modeling their parents' relationships or considering themselves to be similar to heterosexual couples in some respects. Specifically, gay and lesbian couples tended to see their relationships as similar to heterosexual relationships in terms of commitment and communication, but dissimilar in terms of nonconformity to sex-role stereotypes. Some people also mentioned that it would be helpful if gay and lesbian couples had the same legal rights as heterosexual couples.

Most of the behaviors listed in Box 9.1 are likely to be used to repair relationships, as well as to maintain relationships that are already in satisfactory condition. For example, if you feel that you are beginning to drift away from a close friend, you might call your friend on the phone (mediated communication) and plan to get together over the weekend (joint activities). If you did or said something hurtful to your sibling, you might be especially pleasant and complimentary (positivity) the next time you see her or him. In addition to the behaviors listed in Box 9.1, Dindia's (1994; Dindia & Baxter, 1987) research has revealed several behaviors that are particularly relevant for repairing relationships. First, **metacommunication,** or discussions about the relationship, is used more frequently when people want to repair or rejuvenate relationships than when they simply want to maintain them (Dindia & Baxter, 1987; Wilmot, 1994). This may be because people need to negotiate new relational rules and to fix relational problems in order to effectively repair the relationship. Dindia (1994) also reported that **changing behaviors** the partner viewed as undesirable and admitting fault and **apologizing** were frequently used when people want to repair or rejuvenate relationships (see also Wilmot, 1994).

Principle 2: People in relationships characterized by high levels of maintenance tend to stay together longer and be more satisfied.

As discussed previously, people have a wide assortment of maintenance behaviors at their disposal. But how effective are these behaviors in maintaining relationships? There is no easy answer to this question. All relationships are

---

BOX 9.1 HIGHLIGHTS

Common Relational Maintenance Behaviors

Behavior	Definition	Examples
Openness and routine talk	Talking and listening to one another	Using self-disclosure Talking about the relationship Sharing secrets Listening to each other Asking how each other's days went
Positivity	Making interactions pleasant and enjoyable	Giving compliments Acting cheerful and optimistic Accommodating each other's wishes
Assurances	Giving each other assurances about commitment	Assuring each other that you still care Showing commitment Talking about the future together
Supportiveness	Giving each other social support and encouragement	Encouraging each other Giving comfort Making sacrifices for each other Being there in times of need
Joint activities	Engaging in activities and spending time together	Going places and "hanging out" together Visiting each other's homes Exercising or playing a sport together
Task sharing	Performing routine tasks and chores relevant to the relationship together	Sharing the household responsibilities Helping each other with homework or work-related tasks Planning finances together
Romance and affection	Revealing positive, caring feelings for each other	Saying "I love you" Sending flowers Giving nonverbal signs of affection such as hugs and kisses Flirting Having a romantic dinner Sending sentimental cards Having sex

different, and what works well for one relationship might be ineffective in another. However, research has shown that many of the maintenance behaviors listed in Box 9.1 may help people sustain long-term, satisfying relationships.

If relational partners use maintenance behaviors frequently, are they more likely to sustain their relationships? If they fail to use maintenance behaviors, will the relationship fall apart? A study by Guerrero, Eloy, and Wabnik (1993) addressed these questions by investigating whether constructive maintenance strategies, such as positivity, assurances, openness, task sharing, and social net-

Behavior	Definition	Examples
Social networking	Spending time with each other's social network	Accepting each other's friends Going to family or work functions together Spending time with mutual friends Acting as a couple in front of others
Mediated communication	Using cards, letters, phone calls, and technology	Writing letters Calling each other once a week Sending birthday and holiday cards Sending photos or videos Corresponding via e-mail
Avoidance	Evading the partner, certain situations, or certain issues	Avoiding bothering each other when busy Planning separate activities Respecting each other's privacy Failing to discuss issues that cause conflict
Antisocial	Using behaviors that are coercive or unfriendly	Acting moody to scare each other away Kicking the other under the table to stop her or him from saying something Making each other feel jealous or guilty Initiating an argument Crying or pouting to get attention
Humor	Using inside jokes, humor, and sarcasm	Having funny nicknames for each other Laughing together Teasing each other good-naturedly
Balance	Keeping the relationship fair and equitable	Putting similar levels of effort into the relationship Returning favors Receiving equivalent rewards from being in the relationship Reciprocating each other's positive behaviors

works, help predict whether a couple will stay together or break up. In this study college-age daters were followed over an 8-week period. The study showed that people who reported using more maintenance behaviors at the beginning of the study were more likely to have become more serious or stayed at the same intimacy level by the end of the 8 weeks. Those who reported using low levels of maintenance behavior were likely to have de-escalated or terminated their relationships by the end of the 8 weeks. This illustrates that high levels of maintenance behavior can help keep relationships together.

People who use high levels of maintenance behavior also appear to be more satisfied with their relationships. Vangelisti and Huston (1994) defined relational satisfaction as the "pleasure or enjoyment" that people derive from their relationships (p. 173). Thus, not surprisingly, positive, pleasant forms of maintenance behavior are associated with relational satisfaction (Bell, Daly, & Gonzalez, 1987). Several specific maintenance behaviors appear to be particularly important to relational satisfaction. These include spending time together, communicating with each other, being positive and using assurances, and sharing tasks in a fair manner. Sexual compatibility and the ability to influence decision making also have been found to have a positive impact on satisfaction.

Spending time together, whether it involves sharing tasks, engaging in joint activities, social networking, or merely talking, is associated with relational satisfaction. Reissman, Aron, and Bergen (1993) reviewed literature showing that the amount of time spouses spend together is positively related to marital satisfaction because time together creates feelings of companionship and cohesion while opening the lines of communication. Other studies on both dating partners and spouses have found that sharing tasks is related to strong feelings of satisfaction and intimacy (Canary & Stafford, 1994; Guerrero et al., 1993).

Positivity and assurances are also related to satisfaction in close relationships (Dainton, Stafford, & Canary, 1994; Stafford & Canary, 1991). Positivity, which includes being cheerful and optimistic, and complimenting and encouraging the partner, is likely to enhance the atmosphere in the relationship. No one likes to be around someone who is always complaining and never has anything nice to say. People like to be around others who are fun and who make them feel good about themselves. Compliments and encouragement might even lead to higher levels of self-esteem, which could increase a person's satisfaction with her- or himself and with the relationship. Of course, no one can be cheerful and complimentary all the time. Everyone has their bad moods and criticisms. The key is to make sure that pessimism and complaints are the exception while optimism and praise are the rule (Gottman, 1994).

Like positivity, assurances are likely to make a person feel good about her- or himself and the relationship. Assurances include behaviors such as telling people how much you love and care about them, and letting them know that you expect the relationship to be a lasting one. These types of assurances are likely to reduce uncertainty about the future of the relationship and thereby make people feel secure.

An important study by Vangelisti and Huston (1994) further illustrated how various types of behavior are associated with relational satisfaction. These researchers examined data from a longitudinal study of newlyweds over the first 2 years of their marriages. The newlyweds were contacted three times—after they had been married 3 or less months, and then shortly after their first and second wedding anniversaries. The researchers found that spouses generally became less satisfied over time, possibly due to couples having unrealistic expectations at the beginning of their marriages. However, couples who were happy with certain areas of their married lives tended to be more generally satisfied with their relationships. For both husbands and wives, the areas of

Sharing tasks in a fair manner is an important way to maintain relationships.

"communication" and "influence" were very important. Communication referred to how well the spouses could talk to each other, while influence referred to the amount of input spouses had in making joint decisions. For wives, four other areas were related to satisfaction at one time or another over the first 2½ years of their marriages: (1) sex, (2) fair division of labor, (3) time spent with the spouse, and (4) time spent with friends and family. These findings suggest that communication-related maintenance behaviors such as being open and having a "voice" in the decision-making process are strongly related to marital satisfaction. For wives, being sexually compatible, sharing tasks in an equitable manner, engaging in joint activities with the spouse, and social networking also appear to be particularly important.

Principle 3: *Various types of relationships require different types of maintenance.*

Although people generally use more maintenance behaviors in satisfying than unsatisfying relationships, some relationships require less maintenance behaviors than others. Furthermore, because relational maintenance involves keeping a relationship in a desired state or level of intimacy, people use maintenance behaviors to accomplish different goals in different relationships. Maintenance behaviors reflect the type and degree of intimacy felt within a relationship at a given time. Therefore, you are likely to use different types of maintenance behavior with friends than with lovers, and with people you are extremely close

---

Can Relationships Go into "Cruise Control"?

Once you are in a committed, long-term relationship, do you still have to work hard to maintain your relationship, or can you go on "cruise control"? This is a complicated question that relational maintenance researchers are still trying to answer. Some researchers take a centrifugal perspective while others take a centripetal perspective (Canary & Stafford, 1994; Duck, 1988).

According to the **centrifugal perspective**, people must work actively to maintain their relationships. Without maintenance, relationships will deteriorate. Think of your car. It might be running great now, but if you never change the oil or check the coolant, it probably won't last very long. Researchers taking the centrifugal perspective see relationships the same way. If you don't put time and energy into maintaining them, they will eventually fall apart.

Researchers taking a **centripetal perspective** believe that people in close, committed relationships stay together unless something pulls them apart. According to this view, there are barriers that prevent people from leaving committed relationships. Unless some outside force makes it easier to break through the barriers, or some problem becomes so big that the couples cannot handle it, people will stay with their current partners. It is almost like driving in cruise control. You can relax until something unexpected (like an animal running across the road) happens. For example, a married couple might be content together until one spouse finds a more appealing partner and has an affair. The affair forces the couple out of its routine and has the power to tear the relationship apart.

In this book we take the position that highly committed relationships do run on cruise control some of the time, but that periodic maintenance is necessary to keep them healthy and to adjust to changing needs and demands. Thus, in this chapter we review literature on behaviors that help people stay together, as well as barriers that keep relationships from falling apart.

---

to versus those whom you are just getting to know. You are also likely to use different types of maintenance at different stages in the same relationship because of your changing needs and goals. Box 9.2 addresses the issue of whether relationships can go into "cruise control" and still prosper.

Maintenance Behavior in Various Types of Relationships

Most of the research on relationship type differences in maintenance behavior has concentrated on romantic relationships and friendships. Therefore, in this section we focus on these two types of relationships, as well as on how people in long-distance relationships maintain their relationships.

Maintenance Behavior in Romantic Relationships

Close romantic relationships are often high in both emotional and sexual intimacy, and the maintenance behaviors that romantic partners use reflect this special type of intimacy. Maintenance behaviors involving romance and affection are usually highest in romantic relationships, although people do show affection to their friends. Openness, assurances, and positivity also seem to be used more in romantic relationships than in other types of relationships (Canary et al., 1993). In addition, romantic partners who are living together use a variety of routine maintenance behaviors, including task sharing, joint activities, and routine talk, more than most friends do.

Some studies have compared the maintenance behaviors of married and dating couples. For example, Dainton and Stafford (1993) found that spouses shared more tasks than daters, probably because they live together. Daters, however, engaged in more mediated communication, such as calling each other on the phone, exchanging cards and letters, and so forth. Again, this could be due to the fact that most married couples live together while most dating couples do not.

Maintenance behavior also differs depending upon the *stage* of the romantic relationship. Stafford and Canary (1991) compared couples at four stages: casually dating, seriously dating, engaged, and married. They found that (1) married and engaged couples reported using more assurances and task sharing than did dating couples, (2) engaged and seriously dating couples reported using more openness and positivity than married or casually dating couples, and (3) married couples reported using the most social networking. These results make sense. As couples become more committed, partners may feel freer to give each other assurances, and they may, by necessity, share more tasks. Similarly, couples may need to integrate social networks as the relationship becomes more committed and people come to view the two individuals as a "couple." However, openness and positivity may peak before romantic partners become fully committed. Once couples are married, the spouses may not feel the need to disclose their innermost feelings all the time, in part because they have already told each other so much about themselves. Spouses may also express more negativity once they have the security of marriage. When spouses are still in the "honeymoon stage," they are more likely to be on their best behavior and to "put on a happy face." Also, the daily interaction that comes from living together makes it difficult for married couples to be positive all of the time. Criticisms, complaints, and conflict are likely to occur, even in the best of relationships.

Finally, it is important to note that some evidence suggests that people put more effort into maintaining romantic relationships than family or friend relationships (see Canary et al., 1993). This may be because we expect the most from our romantic relationships (Phillips, 1988). Our romantic partners are supposed to excite us, comfort us, and love us unconditionally. We are also taught that romantic relationships require a spark to get started and that the spark needs to be rekindled from time to time.

Maintenance Behavior in Friendships

Even though our friendships are extremely important (Fehr, 1996), we don't work as hard to maintain friendships as we do romantic relationships. Perhaps this is because we take a more casual approach to our friendships. In fact, Brehm (1992) claimed that we appreciate our friends the most in their absence!

Fehr's (1996) book on friendship summarized how friends maintain their relationships. She suggested that three maintenance behaviors are particularly important in friendships: openness, supportiveness, and positivity. Afifi et al. (1994) found that all three of these behaviors are associated with relational closeness in friendships. Several studies have shown that openness, which includes both routine talk and intimate self-disclosure, is the cornerstone of good friendships (Canary et al., 1993; Rose, 1985; Rosenfeld & Kendrick, 1984). In fact, Afifi et al. (1994) found that, of all the maintenance behaviors they studied, having frequent intimate conversation was the most important predictor of relational closeness for male friends. For female friends reciprocity or similarity of intimate disclosure was most important, followed by supportiveness and positivity.

Same-Sex Friendships   Many studies have compared, directly or indirectly, how female versus male friends maintain their relationships. One common finding is that women tend to "talk" more while men tend to "do" more (Barth & Kinder, 1988; Sherrod, 1989). Wright (1982) referred to women's friendships as "face to face" because of the focus on communication, and he referred to men's friendships as "side by side" because of the focus on activity. This sex difference, albeit small, appears early in life and extends to mediated communication. A study by Crockett, Losoff, and Peterson (1984), for example, found that 85% of eighth-grade girls reported talking to their friends on the phone every day as opposed to only 50% of the boys. In a study by the Annenberg Public Policy Center, researchers asked 10- to 17-year-old children what activity would be hardest to give up for a week (APPC Research Reports, 1997). Over 35% of the girls said that it would be most difficult to give up talking on the telephone. In fact, giving up telephone talk was the top answer for girls, surpassing other activities such as listening to music, playing sports, and watching television. By contrast, over 41% of the boys reported that it would be most difficult to cease playing sports for a week. Only 6.5% of the boys felt that giving up telephone talk would be the most difficult.

However, the "talking" versus "doing" distinction does not mean that men are insensitive clods who never communicate their thoughts and feelings to one another. Nor does it mean that women sit around all day chatting endlessly. Research shows that both men and women value intimate talk in their relationships (Afifi et al., 1994; Monsour, 1992; Parks & Floyd, 1996) but that women disclose to one another a little more. Similarly, both men and women value spending time with one another, even though men tend to engage in more focused activities than do women. Fehr (1996) reviewed research showing that men and women spend similar amounts of time with their friends. The difference is that men engage in more activities, such as playing sports. In other words, women get together more often "simply to talk and spend time in one another's company," whereas men get together more often to do something specific, like surf, play golf, or watch a movie. Of course, sometimes men get together just to talk, and sometimes women get together to play sports. In short, the difference between men's and women's activities is subtle rather than dramatic.

Friendships between men and women also differ somewhat in emotional supportiveness and affection. Fehr (1996) summarized research showing that women's friendships are characterized by more emotional support than men's friendships, although both men and women give one another social support at times. Afifi et al. (1994), for example, reported that female friends are more positive and supportive than male friends, although this sex difference is small. Fehr (1996) also summarized research showing that female friends are generally more nonverbally affectionate than male friends. This is true for elementary school–aged children (Thorne & Luria, 1986), university students (Hays, 1985), and elderly adults (Roberto & Scott, 1986). From a young age girls tend to be socialized to be more affectionate toward their friends than boys are. For example, girls often comb one another's hair, sit so that their arms are touching, and hold hands while skipping or running. By contrast, except in the context of sports, boys rarely touch one another, especially once they reach first grade. Similarly, adult women are more likely to hug one another and kiss cheeks than are male friends, especially in the United States and other Western cultures. Male friends show affection in other ways though, particularly through humor and shared activities (Fehr, 1996).

Together the research suggests that there are some sex differences in how men and women maintain their friendships. However, these differences are *not* dramatic; men and women are generally more similar than dissimilar, and when differences are found, they tend to be very small (Andersen, 1998b; Canary & Hause, 1993). We all want good friends whom we can talk to, do things with, and turn to in times of trouble, regardless of whether we are female or male. In fact, both men and women see their friendships as one of the most important sources of happiness in their lives (Fehr, 1996; Rawlins, 1992). Box 9.3 examines the issue of whether men and women really are from "different planets."

Cross-Sex Friendships   As more and more women enroll in college and enter the workplace, the opportunity for men and women to become close friends is increasing. Cross-sex friendships can be very rewarding (Werking, 1997). Both men and women like to get the perspective of the "other sex," and many people perceive cross-sex friendships as fun and exciting. Often, however, cross-sex friendships can be confusing and ambiguous. Think about your friends of the opposite sex. Do you sometimes wonder if they are physically attracted to you? Do you wonder what it would be like to get involved with them romantically? If one or both of you are heterosexual, these types of questions are likely to surface, even if only in your mind.

As a result of this ambiguity, cross-sex friends often face special challenges. O'Meara (1989) discussed four particular challenges that men and women face when they want to be "just friends" with one another. The first is the **emotional bond challenge.** Men and women are socialized to see one another as potential romantic partners rather than platonic friends. This can lead to uncertainty regarding whether cross-sex friends have romantic feelings for each other. It may also be confusing to feel close to opposite-sex friends without also feeling

BOX 9.3 HIGHLIGHTS

Are Men and Women Really from Different Planets?

If you watch television talk shows, you have probably been introduced to the idea that men and women are very different from each other and that these differences can cause relational problems. For example, Deborah Tannen's popular 1990 book *You Just Don't Understand: Women and Men in Conversation* is built around the idea that boys and girls grow up in different cultures, with girls learning to communicate in ways that are confirming and create intimacy, and boys learning to communicate in ways that enhance independence and power. According to Tannen, women and men have difficulty communicating with one another because of "cultural misunderstanding." John Gray's 1992 best-seller, *Men Are from Mars, and Women Are from Venus*, takes this argument a step further by conceptualizing men and women as inhabitants of different planets. As he put it, "Men and women differ in all areas of their lives. Not only do men and women communicate differently but they think, feel, perceive, react, respond, love, need, and appreciate differently. They almost seem to be from different planets, speaking different languages and needing different nourishment" (p. 5). According to Gray, these "interplanetary differences" are responsible for all the problems that people have in their opposite-sex relationships.

Most relationship researchers, however, do not take a position as extreme as Gray's. Some take a position similar to Tannen's in that they believe a **different cultures perspective** can help explain communication differences between men and women (see Wood, 1994, 1996). According to this view, boys and girls grow up primarily playing in same-sex groups. Therefore, they learn different sets of rules and values, leading to distinct communication styles. Some researchers, however, disagree with the different cultures perspective (Dindia, 1997). Instead, they believe that men and women are remarkably similar and that sex differences are small. These researchers are quick to point out that boys and girls grow up in a similar cultural environment, interacting with a variety of people, including teachers, and family members, of both sexes. As Dindia has put it, "Men are from North Dakota, and women are from South Dakota."

What do you think? Andersen (1998b) summarized his take on the debate as follows:

> The actual research on sex differences has led to one major, overall conclusion: Men and women are far more similar than different. They are not from different metaphoric planets or cultures. They are all earthlings with goals, hopes, dreams, emotions, fears, and communication behaviors that are a whole lot more similar than they are different. Of course, South Dakotans probably believe that North Dakotans are from another planet. From close range, differences are more obvious than similarities and they are certainty more newsworthy and sensational! From any vantage point other than Dakota, North and South Dakotans look pretty similar. (p. 83)

romantic toward them. For example, people sometimes have trouble understanding why they can't seem to fall in love with that man or woman who is such a nice person and good friend.

Second, cross-sex friendships are often faced with the **sexual challenge.** In the movie *When Harry Met Sally*, Harry says that men and women cannot be friends because the "sex thing" always gets in the way. Although Harry's statement is a bit extreme, it is true that cross-sex friends (particularly if both are heterosexual) are likely to think about sexual issues related to each other. This is especially true for men. Several studies have shown that men tend to see their female friends as potential sexual partners more often than do women (Abbey, 1982; Abbey & Melby, 1986; Shotland & Craig, 1988).

A third challenge in some cross-sex friendships is the **equality challenge.** Although women have made significant progress in areas such as education, business, and politics, some people still hold the traditional attitude that men should have higher status and wield more power than women. Inequality in such things as status and power can be a barrier in cross-sex friendships because putting similar levels of effort into the friendship, sharing tasks in a fair manner, and having the ability to influence one another are important components within friendships. To illustrate, suppose that Connie and Richard are colleagues working for a large corporation. They see each other 5 days a week and develop a close friendship. They spend time with each other's families and support each other at work. Then Richard suddenly receives a promotion and becomes Connie's boss even though he is less qualified than she is. It is easy to see how this new status differential could disrupt their friendship. Even though Connie might be happy for Richard, she is also likely to be upset about the unfairness of the situation and to feel awkward working under him.

The fourth challenge in cross-sex friendships is the **public presentation challenge.** People often assume that there is something romantic or sexual going on when they see opposite-sex friends spending a lot of time together (Werking, 1997). Therefore, cross-sex friends are likely to be particularly careful about how they present their relationship to others. Cross-sex friends may be asked to explain the nature of their relationship to others. If you have a close cross-sex friend, you can probably relate to this. Have people ever asked you questions such as "Are you really just friends?" or "Do you love her or him?" or "Have you ever slept together?" Romantic partners may also be suspicious and jealous of your close cross-sex friends.

Some scholars have criticized O'Meara's four challenges for being applicable only to cross-sex friendships between heterosexuals. However, with the possible exception of the equality challenge, which may apply best to female-male friendships, these challenges are also applicable to homosexual same-sex friends. In addition, when one friend is homosexual and the other is heterosexual, these challenges may apply regardless of whether the friends are of the same or the opposite sex.

In cross-sex friendships that include at least one heterosexual partner, these challenges can make relational maintenance a complex and delicate matter (Werking, 1997). A study on relational maintenance by Chavez and Guerrero (1999) took into account the emotional and sexual challenges faced by cross-sex friends. Specifically, Chavez and Guerrero examined four types of cross-sex friendships that differ in terms of romantic intent. Individuals in the **strictly platonic** group said that neither they nor their partner wanted the friendship to become romantic. Individuals in the **mutual romance** group said that both they and their partner wanted the friendship to become romantic. Individuals in the **desires-romance** group said that they wanted the friendship to become romantic but their partner wanted it to stay platonic. Finally, individuals in the **rejects-romance** group said that they wanted the friendship to stay platonic but their partner wanted it to become romantic.

As this study showed, the people in these four groups used different relational maintenance behaviors. Those in the mutual romance group used the most maintenance behaviors. In particular, they reported engaging in the most joint activity and task sharing, as well as the most self-disclosure, relational talk, positivity, and flirtation. Those in the desires-romance group also reported relatively high levels of joint activity, task sharing, positivity, and flirtation, but they used relatively low levels of self-disclosure and relational talk. In fact, people who desired romance but believed that their friend did not were the least likely to report talking about the relationship with their friend, perhaps because they feared rejection and worried that confessing their feelings could jeopardize the friendship. Together these results suggest that people who want their friendships to turn romantic are most likely to use high levels of maintenance behavior when they believe that their friend returns their romantic feelings. If they think that their friend does not return their feelings, they are likely to try to spend time with the person and to be positive and flirtatious, but they might avoid discussing their romantic intentions with him or her.

Individuals in the strictly platonic and rejects-romance groups may also behave strategically. In the Chavez and Guerrero study these individuals reported the least joint activity and flirtation. This suggests that individuals who want to keep the relationship platonic tend to refrain from flirting with each other, perhaps so as not to lead each other on. They may also limit their public appearances by showing up at parties separately and engaging in less joint activity in public settings. This may be a way of managing O'Meara's public presentation challenge. In other words, if the friends limit the amount of time they spend together, others are less likely to see them as a potentially romantic couple. As a whole, this study suggests that cross-sex friends do indeed use maintenance behaviors strategically to help them turn some friendships into romances and to help them keep other friendships platonic.

The Special Case of Long-Distance Relationships (LDRs)

Most people have been in at least one long-distance romantic relationship (LDR), and virtually everyone has been in an LDR of some sort, whether it be with a friend or family member. With more individuals pursuing higher education, more couples having dual professional careers, and more people immigrating to the United States, the number of romantic relationships in which the two members are separated by large distances is increasing. In 1987, Stafford, Daly, and Reske estimated that one third of dating couples in the United States were separated by sufficient distance to make frequent face-to-face interaction difficult. If you have been in one of these relationships, you know the challenges that they pose, particularly in terms of relational maintenance. How can couples stay close if the partners are unable to engage in many of the maintenance behaviors discussed in this chapter? When separated, people in LDRs cannot show each other nonverbal affection, share activities or tasks, or engage in the same type of daily routine talk that couples in proximal relationships can. Yet many long-distance couples maintain happy relationships.

Indeed, contrary to the old adage "Out of sight, out of mind," most research suggests that LDRs may be just as satisfying, close, and nurturing as more proximal relationships (Rohlfing, 1995; Van Horn et al., 1997). In fact, some studies suggest that individuals in LDRs are happier and are more "in love " with their partners than are people in proximal relationships (Stafford & Reske, 1990). Stafford and Reske also reported that people in LDRs idealize their partners more and are more likely to believe that the relationship will end in marriage than are people in proximal dating relationships. This may seem counterintuitive at first, but when you consider that people in LDRs usually care about each other a great deal before separating, these findings begin to make sense. Moreover, partners in LDRs are likely to think about how great their lives would be if they could be with their partners, and when they do spend time together they are likely to be on their best behavior and to engage in high-quality activities and communication. For these reasons people in LDRs are likely to idealize their partners (Stafford & Reske, 1990); in this case, "Absence indeed makes the heart grow fonder."

Three specific aspects of the communication landscape of LDRs help account for this increased idealization. First, staying in contact through mediated communication is a primary maintenance behavior in LDRs. People in LDRs rely on the phone and letters, and more recently e-mail, to communicate with each other. However, these forms of mediated communication may offer a skewed perception of the partners' communication styles. For example, a partner likely will pick up the phone when he or she feels like talking, something over which the partner has almost complete control. Moreover, if one partner calls but the other partner is not in the mood to talk, he or she can simply decline to pick up the phone or ask the partner if he or she can call back at another time. One of our students discussed how she sent videotapes to her long-distance boyfriend. She admitted to cutting out scenes in which she did not think she looked her best and to rehearsing her monologue so that she said exactly the right things. Such control over communication is unlikely in proximal relationships, in which relational partners are typically in face-to-face contact on a regular basis.

Second, people in LDRs may use more positivity and avoidance than couples in proximal relationships. Specifically, those in LDRs may hesitate to bring up sensitive or problematic issues during their phone conversations because they may feel that such issues should be discussed face-to-face or because they prefer to end the conversation on a positive note. As a result, sensitive, relationally important topics often do not get discussed, and couples instead focus on positivity. Indeed, Van Horn et al. (1997) found that members of LDRs disclose less to their partners than do members of proximal relationships. Alternatively, such topics may get discussed during weekend visits, a time when the partners appear particularly attractive, which leads to the third reason that heightened idealization may occur in LDRs.

Individuals in LDRs typically are on their best relational behavior when they are together. They plan shared activities more carefully, work hard to treat each other in a fair and equitable manner, and try to look especially attractive to each other. People in LDRs often prepare well in advance for the weekend visit and present an image of themselves that may not be consistent with the day-to-day reality of their lives. Dinner reservations are made, work calendars are cleared, and plans with friends and family are often suspended so the partners can spend quality time alone. Partners in proximal relationships seldom make such accommodations for each other.

As a result of these differences in communication and behavior, not surprisingly partners in LDRs have a heightened belief that their partners are ideal. However, these idealized images can lead to difficulties when the relationship becomes proximal. Suddenly the once seemingly perfect partner needs to study or write a report for work when the other partner wants to spend quality time together, and the sensitive issues that were never discussed over the phone lead to conflict in face-to-face interaction. Thus, partners in LDRs may need to work to keep their expectations realistic so that they are not disappointed once the relationship becomes proximal. In sum, the good news is that LDRs are as stable and satisfying, and perhaps more emotionally intense, than are proximal relationships (Van Horn et al., 1997). The bad news is that partners in LDRs need to ensure that their positive perceptions of each other are not a function of idealization. Perhaps this is the biggest challenge facing long-distance partners who wish to maintain their relationships.

Barriers to Relational Dissolution

Thus far we have looked at the various types of maintenance behaviors that people use to keep their relationships stable, satisfying, and rewarding. In this section we examine how barriers keep relationships from falling apart. **Barriers** can be thought of as all the forces that stop people from terminating a relationship. As Johnson (1982) has stated, "People stay in relationships for two major reasons: because they want to; and because they have to" (pp. 52–53). Attraction, relational satisfaction, love, and other rewards make people want to stay in relationships. Social pressures, financial considerations, and the fear of being alone are factors that make people feel that they have to stay in a relationship, whether they want to or not.

Researchers have identified many different barriers to relational dissolution. Attridge (1994) grouped these barriers into two overarching categories: (1) internal psychological barriers and (2) external structural barriers. **Internal psychological barriers** are personal factors that keep people from ending a relationship; **external structural barriers** are outside forces that keep people in a relationship together.

Internal Psychological Barriers

Commitment, obligation, and investments keep people together and act as internal psychological barriers. For example, if you are highly committed, you might see yourself as a failure if you can't somehow make the relationship work. In a similar vein you might have a strong sense of personal obligation to your partner. Perhaps your partner has been there for you through hard times. If your partner now needs you, you will feel obligated to stay in the relationship and work through problems. In a long-term, committed relationship, you are also likely to have made considerable personal investments that are irretrievable. These investments may include time and effort, as well as sacrifices such as not pursuing a career opportunity or an attractive alternative relationship.

Strong religious or moral beliefs might also act as barriers that keep people in relationships, and especially marriages. Some people believe that marriage is sacred and that divorce is not an option. In fact, Attridge (1994) reviewed research showing that, the more religious people were, the less likely they were to divorce. People who reported that they never attended church were two to three times more likely to divorce than were people who reported attending church at least once a week.

Another internal psychological barrier revolves around people's conceptions of themselves. Some people see their relationships as an important part of their self-identity. For example, a married man might think of himself as a good husband and father. His roles as husband and father are entwined within his broader image of himself as an accountant, son, Democrat, and so forth, but they are nonetheless likely to be central roles. Thus, if his marriage ends and he has to move out of the family home, he will have to adjust his view of himself. Self-identity is also connected to how partners reflect upon each other. For example, if you are married to an attractive, popular, successful person, you will lose the "reflected glory" of being with that person if you separate. The bottom line here is that, the more central the relationship is to a person's self-identity, the more difficult it is to end the relationship.

The final internal psychological barrier identified by Attridge (1994) is parental obligations. The presence of children has been shown to help keep relational partners together. Attridge reviewed research showing that couples without children may be as much as six times more likely to divorce than couples with two children. Moreover, as the number of children increases, the likelihood of divorce decreases (see also Greenstein, 1990). Some couples may even postpone a divorce until the spouses believe the children are old enough to handle it. Some couples with children are reluctant to divorce because the spouses remember how devastated they were when their own parents divorced. Interestingly, the presence of children also usually leads to an increased financial burden for divorced couples, which is related to one of the external structural barriers that we discuss next.

External Structural Barriers

Financial considerations are among the most important external structural barriers. Married couples, as well as some cohabitors, have to resolve a myriad of financial issues in order to end their relationships. Many couples cannot afford two separate mortgages so they must sell their home and move into less luxurious accommodations. Couples also may have joint savings accounts and credit cards that need to be changed to separate accounts. Possessions can also act as barriers. It is often difficult to decide who should keep joint possessions such as furniture, exercise equipment, CD collections, computers, and so forth. Separation can also lead to increased financial obligations if alimony and/or child support payments must be made. And, of course, one spouse may be financially dependent upon the other—typically the wife because, unfortunately, women still tend to earn less money than men, even for the same work (Greenstein, 1990). Greenstein (1990) reported that women are less likely to divorce if they are financially dependent on their husbands. Greenstein found that women who earned less than 25% of their household income were least likely to divorce, while women who earned more than 75% of their household income were most likely to divorce. All of these considerations—household income, possessions, alimony, child support, and financial dependency—make it costly, in more ways than one, to end the relationship.

For married couples the legal process also acts as an external structural barrier to relational dissolution. Depending on the state in which they reside, the legal process can be relatively easy or difficult, but the fact remains that spouses have to go through some formal process to divorce. This process may cause them to stop and think before ending the relationship. In fact, some spouses go through marriage counseling en route to a divorce, only to find that they would rather stay together after all. Interestingly, some states have drafted legislation to try to make it more difficult to obtain a divorce. The reasoning is that, if the legal process is more time consuming and draining, spouses might try harder to work their problems out before filing for a "quickie divorce."

Finally, a number of social pressures act as external structural barriers to ending relationships. People's relationships are embedded in a larger social structure that includes their families and friends, and sometimes their communities and churches. The breakup of a long-term relationship often leads to disruption of the larger social network. For example, common friends may feel uncomfortable inviting both members of the estranged couple to a party. Members of the social network might also exert pressure on the couple to stay together. For example, parents and church officials might urge them to try harder to work out their problems.

The Dialectical Perspective

Clearly, many factors are relevant to maintaining close relationships. The road to a happy relationship is not always smooth, and partners do not always travel in the same direction or at the same pace. Every relationship experiences ups and downs, and no relationship stays the same from start to finish. The dialectical perspective captures the dynamic nature of relationships and describes some of the common tensions, or ups and downs, that relational partners experience.

According to the **dialectical perspective** (see Baxter & Montgomery, 1996), relationships are never completely stable, but instead are constantly changing. As Baxter (1994) stated, "A healthy relationship is a changing relationship in which a stable state is nonexistent" (p. 234). Think about your close relationships. Wouldn't it be boring if they were always the same? Wouldn't you expect your partner to be somewhat different in several years than he or she is

	Dialectic of Integration-Separation	Dialectic of Stability-Change	Dialectic of Expression-Privacy
Internal	Connection-autonomy	Predictability-novelty	Openness-closedness
External	Inclusion-seclusion	Conventionality-uniqueness	Revelation-concealment

FIGURE 9.1 Baxter's Dialectical Tensions

today? Of course you would. Relationships, like people, are constantly changing as goals and needs are reevaluated and redefined. Thus, the dialectical perspective holds that relationships are *managed* rather than simply *maintained*. Put another way, dialectical tensions are never solved; instead, successful couples learn how to best cope with these tensions within the ever-changing context of their relationships.

A **dialectical tension** can be thought of as a push-and-pull toward two seemingly contradictory needs. In other words, people want two things that are both important yet are opposites. Fehr (1996) described the tug-of-war reflected in dialectical tensions this way: "We have to juggle our need for dependence with our need to be independent; wanting to be completely open versus wanting to protect ourselves by not revealing everything; wanting to have a lot in common, but not so much that the relationship feels boring and predictable" (p. 156). If two people can juggle these competing needs successfully, they will be more likely to sustain a happy and healthy relationship.

In this section we look at Baxter's (1988, 1990, 1993) dialectics theory and at some additional dialectical tensions discussed in Rawlins' (1989, 1992) important work on friendship.

Baxter's Dialectics Theory

Baxter (1993) proposed three major dialectical tensions: integration-separation, stability-change, and expression-privacy, with the first of these seen as the primary dialectic. Each of these dialectical tensions has both an internal and an external manifestation, as Figure 9.1 shows. **Internal manifestations** refer to the tensions experienced between relational partners, including how they communicate with one another. **External manifestations** refer to the tensions between a couple and other dyads or society, including how the couple presents itself to others.

Integration-Separation   The dialectic of **integration-separation** refers to the tension between social integration and social division. That is, people want to feel that they are a part of something larger than themselves, but they also want to be self-sufficient. The internal manifestation of this dialectic is the **connection-autonomy** tension. This is the tension between the desire to be close to the relational partner (connection) and the need to be independent (autonomy). Chances are, you have seen these tensions at work within your own relationships. You might have declared that you wanted more freedom or were feeling smothered. If so, you were experiencing the need for autonomy. Alternatively, you might have told your partner that you need more attention and affection, which would indicate that you were not experiencing enough connection at a given time.

The external manifestation of the integration-separation dialectic is the **inclusion-seclusion** tension. This is the tension between the amount of time partners spend with other people in their social network (inclusion) and the amount of time they spend doing things only with each other (seclusion). One of our students gave a great example of this external contradiction. After graduation, she and her fiancé were moving to Boulder, Colorado, where she had landed a job. Neither of them knew anyone in Colorado, which scared them because, at least initially, they would not have any friends or family with whom they could get together on a regular basis. At the same time, however, they both thought it would be nice to have some time alone for a while, without any interference from friends or family.

Stability-Change   The second major dialectical tension is **stability-change.** The idea behind this dialectic is that people want security and continuity on the one hand, and excitement and discontinuity on the other. The internal manifestation of this dialectic is the **predictability-novelty** tension. That is, people want some predictability in their relationships: They want to know that their partner will be there for them, and they necessarily establish routines and relational rules, such as eating dinner together in the evenings or making sure to call if they will be home late. However, people also want some novelty, excitement, and spontaneity in their relationships. As the saying goes, "Variety is the spice of life." Interestingly, boredom is one of the top reasons couples give for breaking up (Hill, Rubin, & Peplau, 1976), suggesting that excitement is indeed important in relationships. A study by Reissman et al. (1993) also confirmed the importance of excitement. In this study, couples who were told to engage in exciting activities once a week reported more satisfaction than couples who engaged in pleasant but routine activities.

The external manifestation of stability-change is the **conventionality-uniqueness** tension. The idea here is that people want to conform to societal standards and be accepted by society, so they sometimes act in conventional, predictable ways. For example, in the United States many couples strive for the "American dream" of home ownership, children, and a good job. However, couples also feel a need to see themselves as special and unique, and so they sometimes act in unconventional, unpredictable ways. For example, a couple might go against the norm by deciding not to have children or even by doing something as trivial as celebrating a holiday in a unique manner, such as decorating a cactus instead of a traditional tree for Christmas.

Expression-Privacy   The third and final major dialectical tension is **expression-privacy.** This dialectic reflects the need to be heard by others versus the need to keep some information private. The internal manifestation of this dialectic, the **openness-closedness** tension, refers to how much partners tell each other. They feel a push-and-pull regarding how much information they should disclose to each other (Petronio, 2000). On the one hand, they have a natural inclination to share their thoughts and feelings with the person to whom they feel closest; on the other, they feel a need to keep some things private and to protect themselves from judgment or criticism. You have probably felt this tension in your own relationships. You might have wondered how many details about your past relationships you should divulge to your current romantic partner. Or you might have wondered whether you should tell your partner about some of your biggest fears and insecurities.

The external contradiction, the **revelation-concealment** tension, refers to what partners tell other people about their relationship. For example, you might feel torn between a desire to tell your best friend about the big fight you had with your romantic partner and the need to keep the information to yourself. You would like to elicit support and comfort from your friend, but at the same time you would like to protect your romantic partner from the ill feelings that could result from your revelation.

Ways of Managing Dialectical Tensions   The next part of Baxter's theory addresses how couples manage the dialectics described above. There are four general ways of managing dialectical tensions: selection, separation, neutralization, and reframing (Baxter, 1990). **Selection** involves deciding to value one side of the dialectic more than another. For example, partners might decide that it is very important to be open and honest with each other and not to keep any secrets. The potential problem with this type of strategy is that the partners sacrifice one need in favor of the other, and the other need does not go away.

Separation involves favoring each side of the dialectic at different times. There are two specific ways of accomplishing this. First, couples can use **cyclic alternation** by moving from one side of the dialectic to the other in a cyclical fashion. For example, when partners start feeling disconnected from each other, they might plan a romantic getaway. Conversely, if they start feeling smothered, they might spend a day apart. Another way of accomplishing separation is through **topical segmentation,** which involves emphasizing different sides of the dialectic depending on the topic or context. For example, a couple might decide to reveal positive information about their relationship to others but to conceal negative information. Within their own relationship the partners might decide to be open with each other on most topics but to avoid discussions about politics and in-laws. Couples using topical segmentation might also decide to keep certain activities separate (such as playing golf or shopping with friends) while engaging in others together (such as going to a favorite restaurant).

Neutralization occurs when couples avoid fully engaging either side of the dialectic. There are two strategies for accomplishing neutralization. The first, **moderation,** involves striving to reach a "midpoint" such that couples engage both sides of the dialectic, but only to a certain extent For example, couples might try to be moderately open, affectionate, and conventional. Second, couples can use **disqualification,** which involves striving to be ambiguous so that neither side of the dialectic is engaged. Often this includes tactics such as changing the topic or avoiding an issue. For example, you might change the subject every time someone asks you how your relationship is going. Or you might avoid engaging in behavior that is either too predictable or too novel.

The final general way of managing dialectical tension is through **reframing,** a sophisticated strategy that involves adjusting perceptions of dialectics so that they seem complementary rather than contradictory. For example, partners might realize that, if they share everything with each other all the time, soon there will be nothing new to share. They might also realize that, if their lives become too enmeshed, they will lose their individual identity, and that, if they are always surprising each other, their novel behavior will eventually become predictable. For example, the first time you receive flowers or a gift from a romantic partner, it probably is a pleasant surprise. However, if your partner starts to bring you something every weekend, it will stop being a surprise and start becoming dull and predictable. These examples illustrate that the different sides of the various dialectics do not necessarily have to be seen as opposing. In fact, Allen et al. (1995) found that people often see the two sides of each dialectic as related rather than separate, even though they are opposing. All in all, reframing is an effective strategy because partners no longer need to worry if the other person temporarily seems unaffectionate, inattentive, or boring.

Other strategies are also effective, depending on the needs of a couple at a given time. Baxter's (1990) research showed that the most frequent way couples managed the autonomy-connection dialectic was through cyclic alternation. To manage the predictability-novelty and openness-closedness dialectics, couples used topical segmentation most frequently. This study also showed that reframing and topical segmentation may be better strategies than selection or disqualification, perhaps because the latter two strategies don't allow relational partners to fulfill needs related to one or both sides of a given dialectic. For example, if you select the connectedness side of the dialectic, you are ignoring your need for autonomy. If you select disqualification, you are ignoring the needs on both sides of the dialectic. Ignoring these needs will not make them disappear.

The research on dialectics also suggests that relational partners who are satisfied with their relationships find a way to balance their needs for seemingly contradictory sides of each dialectic. Baxter and Simon (1993) found that when people saw their relationships as more autonomous than connected, they reported more satisfaction if their partners tried to increase contact. They also found that spontaneous, romantic efforts were especially appreciated when relationships were seen, at least for the time being, as predictable rather than novel. Finally, avoidance of discussion about the relationship was seen as particularly negative when people saw their relationships as closed rather than open. This research suggests that satisfied couples are able to adjust to the changing needs within their relationships.

Rawlins' Dialectical Tensions

Although applicable to a variety of relationships, Baxter's work on dialectics has focused primarily on romantic relationships. Researchers have also looked at dialectics within the context of friendships (Bridge & Baxter, 1992; Rawlins, 1989, 1992, 1994). In particular, Rawlins' (1992) investigation of friendship took a dialectical perspective. He argued that six main dialectical tensions characterize friendships, as well as other types of relationships. As you shall see, two of these dialectics—independent-dependent and expressive-protective—are similar to those identified by Baxter.

The **independent-dependent** dialectic, like Baxter's connection-autonomy dialectic, refers to the tension between wanting the freedom to pursue individual activities and depending on someone for help and support. For example, suppose Marianne is having trouble in her Spanish class, while her good friend Denise is at the top of the class. Marianne might feel tension between wanting to handle the problem herself and wanting to go to her friend for help. Moreover, if Denise offers her help without being asked, Marianne might feel conflicting emotions. That is, she might be hurt that Denise didn't think she could manage the problem on her own, but she might also feel grateful that she can rely on Denise to help her.

The **expressive-protection** dialectic is similar to Baxter's openness-closedness dialectic. After interviewing pairs of close friends, Rawlins (1983a, 1983b) concluded that this was a central tension in many friendships. In order for a friendship to be close, people must disclose personal information. However, if friends disclose too much, they open themselves up to potential criticism and rejection (see also Chapter 5). For instance, if Paul tells Vince that he can't swim because he's afraid of water, Vince could make fun of him or embarrass him by telling other people. This example illustrates that although friends feel a need to confide in one another, they also feel a need to protect themselves.

The remaining four dialectics are different from those proposed by Baxter. The **judgment-acceptance** dialectic involves being able to accept a friend for who she or he is versus feeling free to offer criticism and advice. This is a common tension. Imagine that a good friend of yours has been at the same dead-end job for 2 years after graduation. Should you accept that your friend isn't very ambitious, or should you suggest that your friend go out and look for something better? You avoid insulting your friend if you do the former, but in the long run you might help your friend if you do the latter. The choice is indeed a dilemma.

The **affection-instrumentality** dialectic refers to whether friends focus more on their feelings of warmth and positive regard for one another or on instrumental tasks and benefits. Rawlins (1992) framed this dialectic in terms of dealing with the tension between seeing the friendship as the goal and seeing it as the way to achieve other goals. In other words, is the friendship the endpoint or is it the means to some other end? Some friendships are clearly instrumental. For example, you might choose your study partners based on who is intelligent and gets good grades in school. However, close friendships often are characterized by both affection and instrumental benefits. For example, you might want to develop a friendship with someone not only because that person is nice but also because he or she is smart and can help you with things. However, if you feel that a friend is taking advantage of you by asking for too much help and too many favors, you might question whether this person likes you or merely likes what you can do for her or him. Rawlins also suggested that there is a sex difference in which side of this dialectic men and women value more. Men appear to value instrumentality more, while women value affection more. Still, both sexes are likely to feel tension because they want both types of benefits from their friendships. This shows that both sides of this dialectic are important.

The **public-private** dialectic involves how the relationship is negotiated in public and in private. Rawlins (1992) argued that all friendships are negotiated primarily in private, yet some aspects of the relationship are made public. For example, you might call your friend silly nicknames like "bubblehead" or "monkey face" in private but not in public. You might also intentionally keep some details of your friendship private. Rawlins believed that some features of this tension are particularly important in adolescence when teenagers are concerned with popularity. For example, if you invite someone who is unpopular over to your house, you might not divulge this information to the other kids at school. But if the homecoming king and queen come over, you'd likely tell everyone. This tension can be particularly important in many cross-sex friendships. People might keep the intimate feelings they have for a close cross-sex friend private, even if those feelings aren't romantic, so that other people in the social network don't get the wrong impression.

Finally, the **ideal-real** dialectic reflects the tension between what the relationship "ought to be" and what the relationship "really is." People wish for the ideal friendship, but most people also know that the ideal relationship is a fantasy and that no friend is perfect. In high school some kids wish they could be friends with a particular student who is especially popular, athletic, talented, beautiful, and so forth. However, their "real" friends will have a mix of characteristics, some positive and some negative. Because people tend to make social comparisons, there is sometimes a tension between the ideal relationships they desire and the actual relationships they have with others. There may also be tension between trying to live up to idealistic expectations and wanting to be oneself.

It is important to note that although Rawlins' work focuses on friendships, his dialectical perspective also can be applied to relationships between coworkers, family members, and romantic partners. In fact, Rawlins (1992) argued that people consider some coworkers to be both colleagues and friends. Similarly, people often regard their family members and lovers as very special close friends. Rawlins also argued that the dialectical tensions experienced by friends vary over the course of the life span. For example, the adolescent years are usually marked by tension in the private-public and acceptance-judgment dimensions because of the focus on popularity during this life stage.

Conclusion

Keeping a relationship satisfying and preventing a relationship from ending are complicated processes, as anyone who has been through a relational breakup knows. People must put some effort into their relationships if they want them to last. This involves engaging in constructive maintenance behaviors and managing dialectical tensions effectively. Forces such as investment, internal psychological barriers, and external structural barriers also help keep relationships together.

Other issues relevant to relational maintenance were not discussed in this chapter. For example, Chapter 8 focused on how rewards, equity, commitment, and investment levels all influence whether couples stay together. In addition, as discussed in Chapter 14, how people manage interpersonal conflict is a key factor determining how satisfying and long-lasting a relationship is. And, as discussed in Chapter 13, how couples handle relational events such as jealousy, infidelity, and deception can also influence whether they stay together or break apart.

At this point, however, you should realize that relationships cycle through periods of highs and lows, and that by engaging in effective communication you can get through the lows if both you and your partner value the relationship. As Wilmot (1994) argued, the ebb and flow of relational closeness is a *normal* process. When things are not going well, it is a signal that a change needs to be made so that the relationship can be rejuvenated. This is comforting! An argument might help solve a problem, and a temporary feeling of being smothered by the relationship might lead to some valued time alone. Of course, some relationships never rejuvenate and instead decline. The question then becomes, How do some people sustain or recapture that "loving feeling"? We hope that this chapter has helped you begin to answer this question.

Discussion Questions

1. In this chapter we discussed sex differences in relational behaviors such as self-disclosure and sharing activities. Do you agree with our conclusion that, although some sex differences exist, they are actually quite small? What do your everyday experiences tell you about sex differences in relational maintenance behaviors?
2. Which of the following statements do you think is truer—"Relationships stay together unless something tears them apart" or "Relationships require effort or else they fall apart"?
3. Based on the information in this chapter, what five pieces of advice do you think would be most important to share with someone who wanted to maintain her or his relationship?

10

Communicating Closeness

Intimate Interaction

As Prager (2000) observed, "If intimacy is one of the most often discussed aspects of personal relationship functioning, then there are good reasons. It is predictive of the highest levels of satisfaction, love, and trust as well as the primary reward of closeness" (p. 22). Intimate interactions involve a special type of communication that takes place in our closest relationships. These interactions occur among close friends, within closely knit families, between romantic partners, and within many marriages. In everyday language, however, not everyone uses the term *intimate* to characterize her or his closest relationships. Instead, people may refer to intimate relationships as close, affectionate, warm, friendly, cozy, liking, caring, bonded, warm-hearted, convivial, compassionate, and even loving. In fact, research shows that the most common term people use for intimate relationships is *close* relationships (Parks & Floyd, 1996).

In their discussion of the "Bright Side of Relational Communication," Andersen and Guerrero (1998a) stated that intimate relationships are the foundation of our lives. As they put it:

> Almost without exception, our relationships with friends and loved ones are the cornerstone of our lives and our emotional well-being. The warm feelings of an intimate conversation, a reassuring hug, seeing a close friend after a long absence, or sharing joy with one's family are experiences each of us has had. Indeed, the brightest side of life's experiences often occurs in close intimate relationships during the exchange of warm, involving, immediate messages. (p. 303)

In this chapter we look at the feelings, behaviors, and relational qualities that contribute to the experience of intimacy. First, we define intimacy and discuss its importance across the life span. Second, we discuss nonverbal and verbal behaviors that reflect intimacy and interpersonal warmth, as well as the ways people communicate social support and comfort. Third, we review two interpersonal theories that focus on the exchange of intimate behavior: Reis and Shaver's intimacy process model, and Andersen's cognitive valence theory. Finally, we examine sex differences in intimacy.

Defining Intimacy

Intimacy refers to the special relational states and interactions that occur in close relationships, characterized by feelings of warmth, trust, and deep friendship. For many people intimacy is synonymous with sexual involvement; however, that is *not* the meaning of intimacy we intend in this chapter. Sex can be intimate or impersonal, although the best sexual encounters certainly are intimate ones for most people. To use a thermal metaphor: If sexual encounters are hot, then intimate interactions are best characterized by warmth (Sternberg, 1987). And according to Sternberg (1987), "Over the long term maintaining intimacy—communication, sharing, support and the like—is more important than maintaining passion" (p. 222). Thus, having dinner with an old friend, going to your son's graduation, chatting with your significant other by the fireplace with a glass of wine, telling your best friend about your new love— these are intimate encounters.

These intimate encounters have a quality that everyday interactions between strangers and acquaintances usually lack. Sternberg (1987) suggested that intimacy comprises feelings of warmth, trust, and happiness that typically are present only in close relationships. Among the many hundreds of people you meet at school, at work, in clubs and organizations, through your family, and through acquaintances and friends, you will build intimate relationships with only a few. Moving a relationship from impersonal to intimate is a fragile process (Andersen, 1998a). Many factors—such as cultural or personality differences, inappropriate behavior, loss of trust, lack of attraction, and lack of similarity, to mention just a few—can throw a relationship off track and prevent it from becoming a special, intimate one.

Intimacy comes in a variety of forms and contexts (Acitelli & Duck, 1987; Andersen, 1999). Indeed, Prager (1995) described intimacy as a multifaceted concept that encompasses certain types of feelings, interactions, and relationships. To illustrate the many facets of intimacy, Prager (p. 18) gave the following examples:

> Jorge feels a rush of warmth and love when he looks at Mariano. (Intimacy involves an emotion.)
>
> Jerry holds his infant close and strokes his skin. (Intimacy involves tender physical contact.)
>
> Yan Chang tells Alice a secret, and Alice promises not to reveal it to anyone. (Intimacy involves sharing private information.)
>
> Kareem is married to Aretha. (Intimacy involves a kind of relationship.)
>
> Marta knows that when Dwight purses his lips and looks away, he's feeling nervous. (Intimacy reflects how well two people know each other.)

Wilma and Betty reminisce about their many shared experiences. (Intimacy involves a kind of interaction.)

Felicia caresses Alex. (Intimacy involves sexual contact.)

Mark feels close to Greg while they are fishing in silence. (Intimacy requires no communication.)

Marion stands close enough to Edward for him to feel her breath on his face. (Intimacy reflects how two people occupy space together.)

Intimate Feelings

The feelings two people have for each other are the foundation of intimate relationships. These feelings are variously described as warmth, love, connectedness, bondedness, emotional connectedness, and affection. Andersen and Guerrero (1998a) argued that feelings of warmth that occur in the presence of a friend, close relative, or relational partner are at the heart of intimate relationships. In marital relationships emotional intimacy is connected to every other kind of intimacy: social, sexual, intellectual, and recreational (McCabe, 1999). These feelings may accompany a hug from a close friend, a talk with a lover, or a holiday celebration with the family.

Partners in close relationships commonly experience a number of positive emotions when interacting with or thinking about each other. Guerrero and Andersen (2000) described a cluster of interpersonal emotions, including love, passion, warmth, and joy, that are related to affection. **Love** is an inherently relational emotion that is evoked in relationships with others and is associated with an intense desire to maintain closeness (Aron & Aron, 1986; Shaver, Morgan, & Wu, 1996). **Passion** is sometimes conceptualized as part of love between romantic partners (Sternberg, 1986, 1988), although others see passion as encompassing feelings of attraction and sexual arousal. **Interpersonal warmth** is another inherently relational emotion that people experience as a sense of pleasantness, contentedness, and intimacy during interactions with relational partners, such as friends, lovers, and family members (Andersen & Guerrero, 1998a). Finally, **joy** (or happiness) often is an interpersonal emotion because it is commonly experienced after receiving praise from others or from being the object of love, affection, and/or admiration (Schwartz & Shaver, 1987). When partners frequently experience these types of emotions in connection with each other, they tend to feel closer and to be happier with their relationship (Feeney, Noller, & Roberts, 1998; Prager & Buhrmester, 1998).

Intimate Interactions

Intimate interactions are characterized by certain kinds of nonverbal and verbal communication, as we discuss later in this chapter. Such intimate behaviors are often called **immediacy behaviors**—actions that signal warmth, communicate availability, decrease psychological and/or physical distance, and promote involvement (Andersen, 1985). As Andersen (1999) noted, "Immediacy behaviors are foundations by which intimate interactions and intimate relationships are created and sustained" (p. 219). However, immediacy behaviors such as making eye contact, smiling, and using a pleasant tone of voice are important in nonintimate relationships as well. Consequently, while immediacy behaviors are essential components of intimate interaction, they are not enough by themselves. Intimate interactions also (1) are unique, (2) contain depth, (3) exist over time in that they have a history and a future and are marked by rituals, (4) involve the exchange of very high levels of positive emotions, and (5) are characterized by high levels of listening and understanding.

Uniqueness Unlike many short-term relationships, interactions in intimate relationships are unique. Knapp (1983) argued that when we first meet people our communication tends to be scripted. In other words, we use conventional language that is widely understood. However, as a relationship becomes close, Knapp suggested, two people develop a more idiosyncratic style of communication that reflects the unique characteristics of their personalities and the relationship they share. A study by Hopper, Knapp, and Scott (1981) revealed that couples do indeed use unique forms of communication in their relationships. For example, one couple reported that twitching their noses signaled "You're special" while another reported that twisting their wedding rings meant "Don't you dare do or say that!" Every close relationship produces intimate interactions that have a unique flavor.

Close relationships are also unique in that they are irreplaceable. Hendrick and Hendrick (1992) maintained that intimacy "is characterized by genuineness and an absence of 'role' relationships" (p. 166). Thus, if someone can instantly replace one intimate relationship with another, it probably was not very intimate after all. But the intimate interactions individuals share with their boyfriend or girlfriend, their best friend, and their mother or father are not the same. Intimate interactions are characterized by special forms of communication that individuals can share only with certain others with whom they have a great deal of trust and closeness. Think of a dark family secret, a sexual interaction you had with a relational partner, or a disclosure from a close friend about his or her sexual identity. With how many people could you share this information? Probably very few. Intimate relationships are special and relatively rare, although people often have numerous intimate interactions within their special relationships.

Depth Intimate interactions are deep rather than superficial connections. They are characterized by the sharing of time and space, touch, and in-depth self-disclosure not found in other relationships. Later in this chapter we will explore some of the nonverbal and verbal behaviors that lead to deep interactions. In intimate relationships partners "can communicate deeply and honestly . . . sharing innermost feelings" (Sternberg, 1987, p. 333). Self-disclosure plays a critical role in relationship development because, as people become closer, they share their innermost thoughts and feelings (see Chapter 5). In their social penetration theory Altman and Taylor (1973) proposed that building an intimate relationship is dependent upon breaking through a superficial layer of information and finding out what goes on inside someone's head and heart. Only by sharing personal information, thoughts, and feelings can two people get to know each other well enough to develop a close, intimate relationship.

Of course, self-disclosure is not the only way that a couple can communicate depth. Sometimes relational partners sit in silence, but their nonverbal behaviors show that they are connected in an intimate rather than superficial way. For example, a couple driving across town might hold hands and snuggle while listening to romantic music on the radio, and two close friends might smile and laugh together during certain scenes while watching their favorite movie (which they have seen together many times). Such interaction shows that nonverbal communication, and even silence, can communicate that two people share a deep connection with each other.

Time and Repeated Interaction   Intimate interactions rarely arise out of thin air. They typically occur in relationships that have developed considerably and between people who have sustained the relationship across multiple episodes and interactions. Intimate communication occurs in interaction sequences that may unfold over months, years, and even decades. Miller, Cody, and McLaughlin (1994) illustrated this point when they explained: "It is very likely that high intimacy not only reflects a particular set of qualities of the relationship (emotional attachment and so on) but also reflects a greater number of shared situations; nonintimates communicate in a limited range of events while intimates experience more situations together as well as a wider range of them" (p. 183).

Research has shown that total time spent with a relational partner is predictive of higher relational satisfaction in both marital and dating relationships (Egland, Stelzner, Andersen, & Spitzberg, 1997). As Andersen (1999) stated, "Although many parents tell their children they love them, they proceed to spend time on dozens of activities while spending little time with their children. Not surprisingly, many of these children feel unloved despite their parents' words" (p. 64). In a society in which "time is money" and time "spent" with others is precious, not surprisingly time together is an important index of relational intimacy. Some people believe that quality of time is more important than quantity of time. This is probably true, although people have more opportunities to spend quality time together when they are in frequent contact with one another.

Werner, Altman, Brown, and Ganat (1993) have shown that relationships are characterized by recurring and unique events, called **rituals,** that define and shape the relationship. Rituals such as annual birthday celebrations, anniversaries, and holidays spent together are important to virtually all relationships (Werner et al., 1993). For example, Braithwaite and Baxter (1995) showed that the renewal of wedding vows by married couples serves to establish commitment and continuity in marital relationships. Rituals are an important foundation for intimacy because they create simultaneous, intimate experiences for the relational partners and provide the basis for relational growth through shared experiences. Cultural holidays such as Christmas, Yom Kippur, or Ramadan solidify relationships by embedding them in a larger cultural context and infusing them with communal and spiritual meaning.

Positive Affect   High levels of positive emotional exchange characterize intimate interactions. While negative communication is common in many intimate exchanges (see Chapters 13 and 14), in general intimacy is fostered by a higher ratio of positive to negative behaviors. Feeney et al. (1998) reviewed several studies showing that happy couples report much "higher rates of positive behaviors in their daily interactions with their partners" and that "more than three-quarters of couples . . . identified positive intimate behaviors as crucial to maintaining satisfaction in their relationships" (pp. 480–481).

The expression of positive emotions such as love, passion, warmth, and joy is particularly important in communicating affection. A diary study by Prager and Buhrmester (1998) showed that high levels of positive affect characterize the most fulfilling and satisfying relationships for both men and women. Similarly, Guerrero and Andersen (2000) argued that using friendly, constructive forms of communication probably help maintain relationships because they are accompanied by and lead to positive affect. For example, complimenting your partner, showering your partner with affection, and making sacrifices for your partner are maintenance behaviors that are likely to make your partner *feel* good and therefore to strengthen the intimate bond that you share. Gottman and Levenson (1992) recommended that couples use at least five positive statements for every one negative statement, suggesting that positive affect must outweigh negative affect if a dyad is to be happy (see also Chapter 14).

Listening and Understanding   Being listened to and feeling understood also are essential to intimacy. Prager and Buhrmester (1998) found that for both men and women having a partner who listens and is understanding is very important for relational satisfaction and need fulfillment. Another study found that, among a large set of communications variables, perceived understanding was the best predictor of relational satisfaction (Egland et al., 1997). This study also found that a listener's ability to "back channel" (by saying "uh huh" and nodding in the appropriate places), actively listen, and show nonverbal immediacy were important predictors of perceived understanding. These types of behaviors help validate the partner's thoughts and feelings.

A number of specific verbal behaviors such as self-disclosure and nonverbal communication behaviors such as touch have been associated with intimacy. We will learn more about these behaviors later in the chapter.

Intimate Relationships

Relational intimacy occurs when both partners feel close, connected, or deeply caring toward each other. Relational intimacy is a function of repeated intimate interactions that foster and display relationship development (Montgomery,

1988; Prager, 2000). Montgomery (1988) maintained that people actively search for intimacy, and, "as sure as intimacy is the goal of this search, communication is its method" (p. 347). As Prager (1995) stated, "At its simplest level, an intimate relationship is one in which intimate interactions occur on a regular and predictable basis" (p. 23).

Throughout the millennia humans have had relationships characterized by solidarity and cooperation. These bonds, which have existed for centuries in tribes, villages, communities, and organizations, are characteristic of every human society (Brown, 1991). Throughout history societies have achieved intense solidarity in relatively small groups that tend to be isolated from one another (Gadlin, 1977). For example, in colonial America, intimacy was a function of the community and the family, and the result of proximity rather than personal choice (Gadlin, 1977). Some people attribute the loss of these deep, intimate group connections to the breakdown in social order that characterizes modern, urban, industrial society (Bendix, 1968; Goodman, 1960; Sennett, 1970; Whyte, 1957).

The creation of groups such as fraternities and sororities, sports teams, bowling leagues, bridge clubs, and service organizations is, in part, a search for institutions that will provide close, intimate interaction in our lives. In an individualistic country like the United States, voluntary associations have always filled a relational void. People become involved in organizations such as the Girl and Boy Scouts, the Sierra Club, and Toastmasters (a public speaking group), as well as attending church and serving as volunteers. Within these institutions intimate relationships can be forged and solidified.

Ultimately, however, intimate relationships cannot be institutionalized. They are unique, caring relationships, and although people might attempt to institutionalize their relationships by actions such as getting married or joining a sorority or fraternity, such actions are meaningful at an intimate level only if they reflect a close, internal bond. Put another way, marriage certificates or club membership cards are meaningless symbols if they are not connected to close, intimate relationships. Sternberg (1987) summarized 10 characteristics that promote closeness, connectedness, and bondedness. You can use this list to ascertain the intimacy level of some of your relationships. To what degree do you do the following?

Desire to promote the welfare of your partner

Experience happiness and good times with your partner

Feel respect and high regard for your partner

Know you can count on your partner when the "chips are down"

Have a mutual understanding with your partner

Readily share yourself and your possessions with your partner

Receive emotional support from your partner

Give emotional support to and make sacrifices for your partner

Communicate deeply, honestly, and intimately

Value your partner

The Importance of Intimacy

From infancy until death, intimate attachments are a vital part of life. Ainsworth (1989) described how intimate, secure attachments provide the basis for strong, trusting adult relationships (see Chapter 6 on attachment). Having close, secure relationships is associated with happiness and both mental and physical health.

Happiness

Intimate relationships are exceedingly beneficial in our lives. As Baumeister and Leary (1995) suggested, "Happiness in life is strongly correlated with having some close personal relationships. Research suggests that it does not seem to make a great deal of difference what sort of relationship one has, but the absence of close bonds is strongly linked to unhappiness, depression and other woes" (p. 56). In marriage intimacy has been found to be highly beneficial in maintaining a satisfying relationship. Acker and Davis (1992) reported that intimacy was associated with higher levels of both passion and commitment in marital relationships. For most people intimate relationships are the greatest source of satisfaction in their lives. In fact, according to Shaver, Schwartz, Kirson, and O'Connor (1987), people experience the most happiness when they feel loved and accepted, and when they receive affection and praise from others. Research has even shown that babies are happiest when they are interacting with people who love and care for them. For example, Magai and McFadden (1995) summarized over a century of research on what causes infants to display joy. They reported that babies tend to look happiest when they see a parent's face, when their limbs are lightly and playfully shaken, when they are tickled or hear someone singing, and when someone opens a curtain around the cradle. Thus, for both children and adults, intimate social interaction is an essential ingredient in the recipe for a happy life.

Mental Health

Research also has shown that healthy, intimate relationships are vital to mental and emotional well-being (Guerrero, 2000). Children who grow up with parents who are "absent" emotionally due to mental problems, chemical dependency, or marital problems are unlikely to trust others, are more prone to mental problems of their own, and are less likely to form healthy relationships (Vangelisti & Sprague, 1998). There is a moderately strong relationship between interpersonal rejection and depression that is probably mutually causal (Segrin, 1998). In other words, depression contributes to rejection and loneliness, but being rejected and lonely also contributes to depression. A number of studies have

Intimacy is important for healthy child development.

shown that clinically depressed individuals often do not form intimate relationships and that other people view these individuals as somewhat hostile and/or difficult to be around (Segrin, 1998). Intimate relationships both promote mental health and are enabled by good mental health.

Physical Health

Intimate relationships have been found to promote good health for a number of reasons. Studies have shown that married people live longer and suffer less ill health than do single people. Partners provide social support and get medical attention for their loved ones. But the effect of intimate relationships goes beyond that. Prager (1995) observed that "intimate relationships seem to buffer people against the pathogenic effects of stress. In the face of stressful life events, people who have intimate relationships have fewer stress-related symptoms, faster recoveries from illness, and a lower probability of relapse or recurrence than those who do not have intimate relationships" (p. 1). Moreover, social networks that provide social support seem to have salutary effects on health (Cunningham & Barbee, 2000). People who feel accepted and supported by others are more likely to stay active and healthy than are people who are depressed or lonely, in part because they are more likely to engage in enjoyable activities with members of their social network (Guerrero, 2000). In sum, intimacy has many positive effects on people's lives. But how do people use communication to create intimacy? Next we examine specific nonverbal and verbal behaviors that are associated with intimacy.

Nonverbal Intimacy

According to Montgomery (1988), "The nonverbal mode of expression appears to be more closely linked to relational quality than the verbal mode" (p. 348). Similarly, Prager (2000) suggested that "nonverbal behavior contributes substantially to people's intimate experiences. The influence of nonverbal behavior is probably due to its relatively involuntary character. People's facial expressions, voice tones, postures and gestures can reveal unspoken emotions and intentions and can override efforts at impression management" (p. 232). Clearly, nonverbal communication is an important component within close relationships. In this section we focus on nonverbal behaviors that can be used to convey involvement and warmth. Andersen (1985) referred to these behaviors as *nonverbal immediacy cues.* As you read this section, keep in mind that nonverbal behaviors are often processed as a **gestalt** (Andersen, 1985, 1999). In other words, rather than focusing on single behaviors, people usually take the whole package of nonverbal behaviors into consideration when assigning meaning. Also keep in mind that nonverbal communication is interpreted within a broader social context. For example, eye contact can reflect intimacy in one situation but intimidation in another situation. Similarly, a smile might be perceived as friendly in one context and condescending in another.

Visual or Oculesic Behaviors

Eye behavior, or **oculesics,** is essential in establishing interpersonal intimacy. The eyes have been said to be "the windows to the soul," and eye contact is widely recognized as an invitation to communicate (Andersen, 1999). Increased eye contact has been widely recognized as a sign of intimacy and attraction (Andersen, 1985; Exline & Winters, 1965). People engage in the highest levels of eye contact with friends, dating partners, and people they like (Coutts & Schneider, 1976; Exline & Winters, 1965). Romantic partners, in particular, appear to use high levels of eye contact to communicate intimacy (Guerrero, 1997). During intimate interaction eye contact is a sign of attentiveness and connection.

One interesting, although somewhat obscure, oculesic behavior is pupil dilation. You might be aware that pupils dilate in low light, but did you also know that pupils dilate in response to any stimuli people find interesting or attractive (Hess, 1965; Hess & Goodwin, 1974)? Moreover, people are more attracted to individuals with dilated pupils. In an imaginative study Hess and Goodwin (1974) showed people two virtually identical pictures of a mother holding her baby; however, in one photo the eyes were retouched to appear dilated while in the other photo they were constricted. Overwhelmingly the subjects reported that the mother with the dilated pupils seemed to love her baby more. Interestingly, few subjects identified the eyes as the source of the attributions, which suggests that pupil dilation is processed as an intimacy cue but at very low levels of awareness. Of course, low light, candle-lit dinners, and dusk have always been associated with romance and intimacy, perhaps in part due to subtle cues like pupil dilation.

Spatial or Proxemic Behaviors

The way people use space in interpersonal communication, or **proxemics,** signals how intimate the relationship is. Years ago, Hall (1968) identified four distance zones as a function of types of interpersonal interaction. He called the closest of these zones, from touch to 18 inches, "intimate distance." The only people permitted into this zone are those with whom we have intimate relationships, such as our children, our closest friends, our family members, and our romantic partners. The other three zones—"personal" (1½–4 feet), "social" (4–10 feet), and "public" (over 10 feet)—are used for less intimate relationships.

When our intimate zone is invaded by someone who is not a close friend or romantic partner, we react with a series of defensive or compensatory behaviors (Andersen, 1985, 1998b; Burgoon, Stern, & Dillman, 1995). These defensive behaviors include reducing eye contact, drawing back, using arms or objects as buffers, and literally giving the person the cold shoulder by turning away.

Intimacy is also communicated proxemically via body angle. Facing someone directly is very intimate, while sitting or standing at a 45-degree angle is less intimate, and positioning oneself side by side with another person is even less intimate. Turning one's back on someone is the opposite of intimate. Interestingly, women are more likely to use a direct, face-to-face body orientation than men (Guerrero, 1997); this is one of several ways that women seem to be more nonverbally intimate than men.

Face-to-face communication between people who are very different heights can be difficult. For example, when a 6-foot adult communicates with a child, a person in a wheelchair, or a 5-foot person, he or she is attempting to communicate on a different physical plane. Research has shown that communicating on the same eye-to-eye plane increases perceptions of intimacy (Andersen, 1985; Brown, 1965). Andersen and Andersen (1982) suggested that getting into the same physical plane is essential for early elementary school teachers to create rapport with their young students. Intimacy can be increased by sitting, reclining, or kneeling when height discrepancies inhibit interaction. Thus, the 6-foot adult can increase intimacy simply by putting her- or himself on the same physical plane, and shorter individuals can engage in behaviors to raise themselves. For example, toddlers are often placed in high chairs so they are face-to-face with the rest of the family at the dinner table.

Tactile or Haptic Behaviors

Physical contact, or **haptics,** is central to the notion of intimacy. People's most intimate relationships, such as those between parents and children, childhood friends, and romantic partners, are characterized by high levels of touch. Andersen (1985) observed that, "although dependent on cultural norms and the interpersonal relationship, normative touch is usually perceived as a warm, intimate behavior" (p. 10). Touch is an important sign of relational intimacy. In a study of airport arrivals and departures, Heslin and Boss (1980) found a strong association between the amount of tactile intimacy, recorded by observers, and the intimacy of the relationship, as reported by couples. Another study found that observers perceived higher levels of intimacy for touching couples than for nontouching couples (Kleinke, Meeker, & LaFong, 1974). Similarly, Guerrero and Andersen's (1991) study of couples' tactile communication in theater and zoo lines revealed that high levels of touch were associated with an intimate and accelerating relationship. Emmers and Dindia (1995) found that this was true for private touch as well. Andersen (1999) concluded: "The highest frequency of touch occurs in intimate relationships at intermediate or escalating levels of acquaintance" (p. 48).

Research has shown that a fundamental aspect of what people think of as intimate interaction involves physical contact (Monsour, 1992), particularly for romantic partners and female friends. It is also true for females in their closest cross-sex relationships even if their friend is not a romantic partner. While same-sex touch is less common among men in the United States, many men do express intimacy tactilely. For example, gay men who are involved romantically touch each other frequently. Although heterosexual men touch one another relatively infrequently, they still engage in roughhousing, physical contact during sports and sports celebrations, high fives, and chest bumps—all of which communicate intimacy with a masculine flavor.

Body Movement or Kinesics

Kinesics comprises body movements such as smiling, inclusive and expressive gestures, nodding, open body postures, and bodily relaxation. Emotions typically are revealed through facial expressions although they may also be manifested bodily and/or vocally. Research has shown that one of the primary components of relational intimacy is emotional expressiveness (Monsour, 1992). Relationships become more intimate when people express positive emotions about themselves, their partner, and the relationship.

The smile is a primary vehicle for the establishment of close relationships. Over several decades researchers have found that the frequency and intensity of smiling is the single best predictor of interpersonal intimacy and warmth (Argyle, 1972; Bayes, 1970; Reece & Whitman, 1962). Smiles are a universal sign of positive affect that signal approachability and availability for communication.

Open body positions free of obstruction by objects or limbs also are associated with greater intimacy. People are most likely to cross their arms, hide their face, or stand behind objects when they lack trust, feel vulnerable, and do not want to interact. Morris (1977) suggested that these "barrier signals" communicate avoidance and defensiveness in interpersonal interaction. Beier and

Sternberg (1977) reported that "close" couples used more open leg positions than did couples who were less close or who were experiencing conflict.

Like great dancers intimate couples demonstrate high levels of coordinated movement, called **body synchrony.** The good "vibes" resulting from smooth interaction with and adaptation to one's partner are a vital part of relational intimacy (Morris, 1977). As Andersen (1999) noted, "Although most synchronous patterns are reciprocal, some are not. Some are complementary: one person gives a back rub, and the other receives it; one person discloses, and the other listens and nods attentively" (p. 223). It is not just reciprocity that promotes intimacy; it is the smooth synchronization of behavior, whether complementary or reciprocal, that produces and characterizes relational intimacy.

Vocalic or Paralinguistic Communication

Words have meaning, but variations in pitch, volume, rate, and tone of voice are perhaps more important than the actual words uttered. These nonverbal elements of the voice, called **vocalics** or **paralinguistics,** have important effects on intimacy. Studies have shown that shifts in vocal pitch, rate, amplitude, and duration are associated with interpersonal affect (Beebe, 1980; Scherer, 1979). For example, voices that are warm and expressive reflect interpersonal intimacy.

Certain vocalic behaviors, like baby talk, produce uniquely high levels of intimacy. Adults frequently use baby talk, a high-pitched, highly varied imitation of children's speech, to communicate with infants and small children (Andersen, 1999). Baby talk includes real words ("You're a little sweetie") and nonsense sounds ("kutchy-kutchy-koo"). Such talk has been found to aid the development of conversational skills, as well as closer, more intimate parent-child relationships (Ferguson, 1964). Research also suggests that baby talk should be stopped once a child begins talking. Interestingly, lovers sometimes employ baby talk during their most intimate interactions, perhaps because intimate behaviors related to courtship are often submissive, nonthreatening, and childlike (see Chapter 7).

Chronemic Behaviors

The way people use time, or **chronemics,** communicates a lot about their relationships. In North America and much of Europe time is a precious commodity that can be spent, saved, wasted, or invested as though it were money. Studies show that chronemic cues are part of the intimacy exchange process (Andersen, 1984). Spending time with another person sends the message that the person is important and reflects a desire for interpersonal closeness. Egland, Stelzner, Andersen, and Spitzberg (1997) found that the best way to signal closeness and intimacy in a relationship is by spending time with one's partner. Similarly, being on time, waiting for a late partner, sharing conversation time, and devoting time to work on the relationship all play a role in the communication of intimacy.

Verbal Intimacy

Humans are talkative creatures. Although nonverbal communication may be the essence of an intimate relationship, talk is extremely important as well. Several types of verbal behaviors are critical to intimate relationships, including self-disclosure, verbal responsiveness, relationship talk, and relational language.

Self-Disclosure

Communicating openly about one's feeling and beliefs is called **self-disclosure** (see Chapter 5). Among the many verbal behaviors that create and sustain relational intimacy, self-disclosure is probably the most important (Derlega, Metts, Petronio, & Margulis, 1993). In fact, when Monsour (1992) asked people what intimacy meant to them, the most common response was self-disclosure. Research has shown that most definitions of intimacy include verbal self-disclosure, and this is true for males and females in both same-sex and opposite-sex relationships (Monsour, 1992; Parks & Floyd, 1996).

Self-disclosure figures prominently in all of the basic theories of relational development and closeness, including social penetration theory and Knapp's coming-together stages (see Chapter 5). Studies consistently have found that self-disclosure is necessary for intimate relationships. As we will learn later in this chapter, although both females and males enjoy self-disclosure and find it important to the development of intimacy, females disclose somewhat more than males. But self-disclosure is extremely important in both male and female friendships. For example, Afifi and Guerrero (1995) reported that self-disclosure was the strongest predictor of relational closeness for both men and women friends. Couples' interpersonal needs are most likely to be satisfied when the partners disclose actively and listen to each other's self-disclosure (Prager & Buhrmester, 1998).

Of course, self-disclosure is not always a positive thing. Studies have shown that excessive self-disclosure, too much negative self-disclosure, and poorly timed self-disclosure do not lead to intimacy (Bochner, 1984; Parks, 1982). For example, revealing a history of psychological counseling on a first date and always disclosing negative health information are ineffective ways to develop an intimate relationship.

However, research also has shown that well-developed intimate relationships often are a good place to disclose negative emotions. Once people develop a highly intimate relationship, they feel safe to disclose negative feelings and emotions (Metts & Bowers, 1994). This is somewhat paradoxical because in the early stages of a relationship people tend to be cheerful and positive and to put on their "best face" (Guerrero & Andersen, 2000). As Metts and Bowers (1994) argued, "Intimacy is, by definition, a state of openness and familiarity. It is the domain in which the prescription for positive emotion is suspended. In theory, a sign of intimacy is that individuals can feel and express negative emotion" (p. 535). Ironically, too much expressed negative emotion can lead to relational dissatisfaction and to a loss of intimacy, but some expression of negative emotion indicates that a relationship is open and comfortable (Guerrero & Andersen, 2000). Particularly damaging to relational intimacy are reciprocal spirals of negative disclosure of emotion. Relationships in which partners reciprocate the disclosure of emotions such as dissatisfaction, anger, jealousy, insecurity, and loneliness can damage a relationship. Gottman (1982) has shown that the ability to de-escalate negative affect is important to relational satisfaction.

Verbal Responsiveness

Verbal or conversational responsiveness, or **altercentrism** (as opposed to egocentrism), is an important part of intimacy. When people are altercentric, they listen carefully to their partner rather than focusing on their own thoughts and needs. The behavior of the listener is vital to the creation of intimacy. For example, intimacy is facilitated by the knowledge that your partner is listening to you, understands your feelings, and perhaps empathizes with you (Egland et al., 1997). Responsiveness also validates the discloser's thoughts and feelings. Indeed, responsiveness may be what makes the process of disclosure so intimate. As Prager (2000) argued, in an intimate interaction "the behavior of the listener/responder is as important as that of the discloser" (p. 233). In an intimate interaction the listener should be attentive to what the partner has said, respond appropriately and acceptingly, and show that she or he cares about the partner and her or his message.

Relationship Talk

People's communication about their feelings regarding the relationship is very important to the establishment of intimacy. Statements such as "I love you," "I value our friendship," "We always have a good time together," and "I hope our friendship never ends" are important symbols of relational intimacy (Andersen, 1998a; King & Sereno, 1984). Statements like these represent turning points that can lead to increased closeness and a more intimate relationship definition. But they can also frighten or intimidate a person who does not share that relationship definition or who is not ready for that level of intimacy. Similarly, talk about the future of the relationship can create perceptions of greater intimacy. For example, romantic partners might start making plans for next summer or talk about what they might name their future children. Such talk clearly implies a long-term commitment to the relationship, which reinforces intimacy. However, as with declarations of love or liking, talk about the future of the relationship can scare partners away if they do not share the same level of commitment.

Relational Language

Relational language, or **verbal immediacy**, is a function of several stylistic features of language used in close relationships (see Andersen, 1998a). Inclusive pronouns ("we" as opposed to "you and I") are perceived by interactants as indicating more relational intimacy (Weiner & Mehrabian, 1968). Prager (1995) suggested that more immediate pronoun use ("this" and "these" versus "that" and "those"), adverb use ("here" versus "there"), and verb tense (present versus past), as well as the use of the active as opposed to the passive voice, all contribute to greater verbal immediacy and relational intimacy. Bradac, Bowers, and Courtwright (1979) maintained that verbal immediacy builds positive relationships even as positive relationships lead to more verbal immediacy.

Casual forms of address ("Pat" as opposed to "Dr. Knight") also imply a more intimate relationship (King & Sereno, 1984), as do nicknames (Bell, Buerkel-Rothfuss, & Gore, 1987; Hopper, Knapp, & Scott, 1981). Using inappropriately informal names or disliked nicknames, however, is not a way to establish a positive intimate relationship. For example, calling your boss "Bud" when he prefers "Mr. Johnson" or calling your date by a derogatory nickname such as "big butt" or "booger" is not an effective way to build a strong relationship. Personal idioms, by contrast, can be a way to express intimacy and closeness in a relationship. Special greetings, secret nicknames, sexual euphemisms, mild teases, and unique labels for the relationship often are a source of intimacy (Bell et al., 1987; Hopper et al., 1981). Of course, the use of some of these terms in a public setting may be a source of embarrassment and cause a loss of relational intimacy.

The language partners use to refer to each other suggests a certain public, relational image that is an index of the intimacy between them. For example, cohabitors may describe themselves along a continuum that includes roommate, friend, boy/girlfriend, and partner—which signals increasing levels of relational intimacy. Similarly, when you refer to someone as your "best friend" in public, this label sends a strong message of intimacy. In romantic relationships the first time relational partners refer to each other as "boyfriend" or "girlfriend" in public often represents a turning point in the relationship. The intimacy level of the relationship is now made clear to others, suggesting that the two people have a special bond and are dating each other exclusively.

Comfort and Social Support

Another important way that people communicate intimacy is by showing that they are there for relational partners in times of distress. As discussed in Chapter 9, making sacrifices for one another and providing social support are key ways of increasing intimacy and maintaining relationships. People feel distress in reaction to a wide variety of situations. In Jones's (2000) study of distressing events among college students, the following were most frequently described as distressing: problems in a romantic relationship, college performance (grades), friend/roommate problems, family problems, work-related stress, family illness, death, and personal illness/injury.

As you might suspect, many of the nonverbal intimacy behaviors discussed previously are important in the comforting process. Dolin and Booth-Butterfield (1993) investigated nonverbal behaviors related to comforting by asking students how they would react nonverbally if their roommate was distressed because of a recent relational breakup. The students reported that they would use the following behaviors most frequently:

Hugs (reported in 41.9% of the accounts): giving the person a whole body hug or hugging him or her around the shoulder

Close proxemic distancing (40.9%): sitting down next to the person or leaning closer

Facial expression (38.7%): looking empathetic, sad, or concerned

Attentiveness (37.7%): listening carefully and nodding as the person talked about the distressing event

Increased miscellaneous touch (34.4%): using all forms of touch other than hugs or pats, such as holding the person's hand or stroking his or her hair

Pats (26.9%): using short, repetitive movements such as patting the distressed person's arm or shoulder

Eye contact (23.7%): looking directly at the distressed person, particularly while he or she was talking

In addition to these behaviors, Dolin and Booth-Butterfield found a few other nonverbal comforting strategies that were reported less often. Some students described behaviors related to weeping, such as crying with the distressed person or offering a "shoulder to cry on." Some said that they would engage in emotional distancing behavior, such as trying to remain uninvolved, getting comfortable, or fixing a cup of coffee. Presumably these strategies would keep the individual from experiencing too much negative affect while talking to the distressed person. Other students reported that they would engage in instrumental activities, such as getting the distressed person a tissue or making him or her something to eat. Still others indicated that they would show concern through warm vocal tones and empathetic gestures. For example, if the distressed person was angry, the individual in the comforting role might clench her or his fist to mirror the distressed person's anger.

Research also suggests that verbal strategies are important in the comforting process. In particular, messages that are person-centered seem to help people alleviate distress (Applegate, 1980; Burleson, 1982). **Person-centered messages** acknowledge, elaborate on, and validate the feelings and concerns of the distressed person. Comforting messages can be ranked as high or low in quality based on how person-centered they are (Applegate, 1990; Burleson, 1982, 1984; Jones, 2000). Highly person-centered messages help the distressed person gain a perspective on his or her feelings by placing them in a broader context. These messages also legitimize the distressed person's feelings. Suppose, for example, that Lauren gets a C on a psychology exam even though she studied diligently. If you were using a highly person-centered message, you might say something like, "It sure must be frustrating to study hard for a test and then get a C. In fact, that really surprises me because you are smart. Don't you think you'll do better on the next test now that you know the type of questions your professor asks?" Notice that the highly person-centered response conveys understanding ("It sure must be frustrating") and support ("You are smart") while also helping the distressed person to think about the event in a different way (perhaps as a learning experience).

Moderately person-centered messages also acknowledge the distressed person's feelings, but they do not help the distressed person contextualize or elaborate on his or her feelings as well as do highly person-centered messages. For example, you might tell Lauren, "I'll bet the test was really hard, and I'll bet most people got C's or worse, so you shouldn't feel that bad." Or you might say, "It's only one test. You'll do better on the next one. Let's go see a good movie— that will help get your mind off this." Notice that these messages provide neat, easy explanations and solutions that do not allow for much elaboration. These types of messages, which are frequently used by people in the comforter's role, provide support that is okay, but not great.

Finally, messages that are low in person-centeredness (sometimes called position-centered messages) implicitly or explicitly deny the legitimacy of the distressed person's feelings, sometimes by blaming the distressed person for the situation and other times by changing the topic or the focus. For example, you might tell Lauren, "It's only one test. You shouldn't make such a big deal out of it." Worse yet, you might say, "I'm sure some people got A's, so you really don't have anyone to blame but yourself. Maybe psychology is just hard for you to understand." You might also start talking about yourself: "I got a C on a test the other day, too. It was a real bummer, but that's life. Hey, do you want to get some lunch or something?"

As you might suspect, several studies have shown that people who use highly person-centered messages provide the best comfort and are perceived the most positively (Burleson & Samter, 1985a, 1985b; Jones, 2000; Jones & Burleson, 1997). In particular, research has shown that highly person-centered messages are perceived as the most appropriate, effective, helpful, and sensitive. These messages are likely to be effective in expressing care and concern, but perhaps more importantly they might help the distressed person to reevaluate the situation so that the event seems less distressing (Burleson & Goldsmith, 1998; Jones, 2000).

Of course, when comforting someone, it is important to use both verbal and nonverbal strategies. Jones (2000) investigated whether both nonverbal intimacy behaviors and verbal person-centeredness influenced the quality of comforting behavior. She trained people to enact high, moderate, and low levels of nonverbal intimacy and person-centeredness, and then had them listen and react to people's distressing stories. She found that both nonverbal intimacy behaviors and person-centeredness had strong effects on comforting quality. When distressed people interacted with someone who used high levels of nonverbal intimacy and high levels of person-centeredness, they reported feeling the best. When high person-centered messages were paired with low levels of nonverbal intimacy, or conversely, when low person-centered messages were paired with high levels of nonverbal intimacy, overall comforting quality decreased substantially. Not surprisingly, comforters who used low levels of both nonverbal intimacy and person-centeredness were least effective at alleviating distress.

Thus, if you want to do a good job comforting someone, you should pay attention to both your verbal and nonverbal behavior. It is also important to let the distressed person talk rather than changing the topic or focusing the discussion on yourself. When people can freely disclose their distressing circumstances to others, it helps them vent their negative emotion and possibly think through and reassess the problem, which can contribute to psychological and physical well-being (Burleson & Goldsmith, 1998; Pennebaker, 1989; Pennebaker, Colder, & Sharp, 1990).

Theories of Intimate Interaction

To truly understand how intimacy functions in close relationships, it is important to consider how partners initiate and respond to intimate behavior. In this chapter we focus on two theories that explain how intimacy is exchanged between two people: (1) the intimacy process model and (2) cognitive valence theory. Both of these theories provide snapshots of the intimacy development process. That is, they freeze the interaction at a given stage, often referring to person A and person B in an effort to analyze the complex processes that occur during intimacy development. In actual communication two interactants play both roles during interactions, so keep this limitation in mind as you read about each of the theories.

The Intimacy Process Model

One model of the process of intimate transactions is Reis and Shaver's (1988) **intimacy process model,** shown in Figure 10.1. In this model Person A is the individual who discloses intimate information or engages in intimate behavior, and Person B is the individual who receives and responds to the increased intimacy. To help illustrate the five components of this model, we will refer to Person A as Allison and Person B as Brittany.

The Motives, Fears, and Goals of Person A   Research has shown that two forces independently determine affiliative behavior: approach and avoidance (Mehrabian & Ksionzky, 1974). It is perfectly possible to simultaneously feel *both* a strong motivation to increase intimacy and a need to avoid increased intimacy. For example, Allison may seek the friendship and affection of Brittany but fear the commitment and involvement that the relationship could entail (Reis & Shaver, 1988).

Verbal Disclosure or Emotional Expression by Person A   Although Allison has a mixture of motives, needs, goals, and fears, she begins the process of

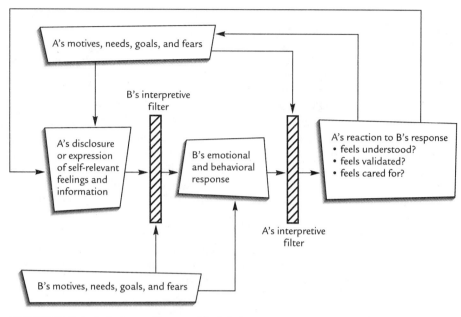

FIGURE 10.1 **Intimacy Process Model** *Source:* Reis and Shaver (1998).

engaging in verbal disclosure or nonverbal expression to Brittany. Early in a relationship these intimacy behaviors are not entirely intentional, but they nonetheless begin the process of intimacy development. Particularly important is disclosure of personal desires, fantasies, anxieties, and emotions rather then merely facts (Reis & Shaver, 1988). Such verbal disclosures and nonverbal expressions of emotion or social attraction are valuable because they get the intimacy process going and give Brittany a chance to validate and accept these emotions or expressions.

The Motives and Interpretive Filter of Person B   Brittany is now in a position to respond to Allison's increase in intimacy, probably with a similar mixture of positive and negative emotions. Brittany may want to make a good friend, like Allison, or fear involvement with a new person. Brittany might worry that a new friendship with Allison will interfere with other relational commitments, or she might be afraid of hurting Allison, or she might fear a loss of autonomy— the list of possible negative emotions and concerns is virtually endless (Reis & Shaver, 1988). Brittany also has a set of personality and situational filters through which she interprets Allison's behavior. Expectations and schemata actively influence perceptions and evaluations of the other person's behavior.

Person B's Responses to Person A's Expression of Intimacy   According to Reis and Shaver's (1988) model, Brittany's response to Allison's behavior is as important as Allison's behavior itself. Appropriate and accepting responses enhance feelings of connectedness, whereas nonresponses or negative responses serve to maintain the distance between the interactants and thwart the intimacy development process. Thus, intimacy takes two people. Brittany has the power to work with Allison to develop a close friendship, but she also has the ability to prevent the friendship from developing.

Person A's Interpretive Filter and Reactions to Person B's Response   Although researchers could objectively describe Brittany's response as accepting or rejecting, in real interactions the outcomes are never so simple (Reis & Shaver, 1988). Brittany's reaction passes through Allison's interpretive filter, which may include Allison's perception of whether Brittany valued her communication and was authentic in her response, as well as whether Allison has a general predisposition to see intimacy in others' behavior. Allison's reaction is crucial. If Allison responds positively to Brittany, then a cycle of intimacy has started. Of course, it may or may not be sustained through subsequent interactions. The final step of this model reinforces the idea that intimacy is created through a series of moves and countermoves, and that the perceptions and interpretations of these moves are as important as the moves themselves.

Cognitive Valence Theory (CVT)

Cognitive valence theory (CVT) seeks to explain the intimacy process by combining verbal and nonverbal intimacy behaviors, interpersonal perception, physiological arousal, social cognition, and relational outcomes in a single unified theory (Andersen, 1985, 1989, 1998a). CVT is depicted in Figure 10.2. As with the intimacy process model, CVT emphasizes how people respond to increases in intimacy behavior. Again, we will illustrate the components of the theory using Allison and Brittany.

Behavior   All intimate relationships begin with one person increasing intimacy via nonverbal or verbal communication (see the Behavior column in Figure 10.2). As Andersen (1998a) explained, "Relationships do not occur in the absence of human contact. They begin, develop, thrive and disengage as communicative acts" (p. 40). Thus, Allison would try to develop a closer relationship by increasing the intimacy level of an interaction through verbal or nonverbal communication. As noted previously, Allison would have a variety of verbal behaviors at her disposal, including self-disclosure, personal forms of address, and expressions of relational closeness such as telling Brittany that she really admires her and would like to get to know her better. Usually nonverbal communication plays a big role in the initiation of intimacy, so Allison also might engage in behaviors like smiling, making eye contact, touching, or standing close to Brittany. CVT holds that all intimate relationships begin with the initiation of immediate or intimate communication behaviors by one or both people in a potential relationship.

Perception   Of course, such behaviors by themselves do not increase intimacy; these behaviors must be noticed by one's partner (see the Perception column in

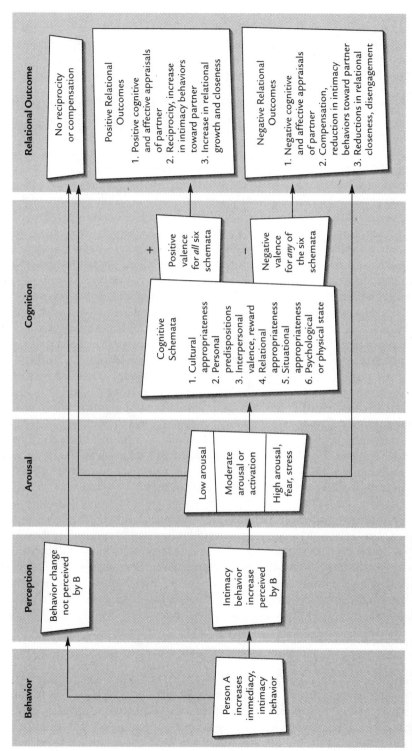

FIGURE 10.2 Cognitive Valence Theory

Figure 10.2). According to Andersen (1989), "The expression of intimacy by one person has no communicative significance if it is not perceived by one's relational partner" (p. 8). Such perceptions do not need to be conscious, but they must register in the mind of the receiver. Words spoken to no ear and smiles perceived by no eye do not communicate and have no chance of increasing intimacy. So, if Allison smiles and discloses to Brittany, but Brittany has her mind on something else, Allison's attempt to increase intimacy will fail (at least temporarily).

Arousal   However, if Brittany notices Allison's change in behavior, she is likely to respond physiologically, and possibly cognitively and behaviorally. Nonverbal intimacy behaviors are stimulating and increase physiological arousal (see the Arousal column in Figure 10.2). In his summary of 24 studies on the relationship between immediacy behaviors and arousal, Andersen (1985) concluded, "The research generally supports a positive relationship between immediacy and increases in arousal" (p. 15). More recent research has confirmed that increases in multichanneled immediacy behavior (such as more eye contact, smiles, and touch) increase physiological arousal (Andersen, Guerrero, Buller, & Jorgensen, 1998). For example, if a threatening-looking stranger stares at you with a menacing facial expression, you will experience very high arousal and look to flee. Many studies have shown that rapid arousal increases are aversive and frightening (see Andersen, 1999, for a summary). As a consequence, CVT predicts that negative relational outcomes will occur when arousal levels are very high. By contrast, if your best friend says "hi" to you on the way to class, no arousal will occur because this behavior is highly routine and represents no real increase in intimacy. The most interesting reactions occur in relation to moderate increases in intimacy. For example, when an attractive person in class smiles at you or when your friend discloses important information, moderate arousal occurs. Moderate arousal has been shown to stimulate cognitive processes, which in turn produce your reaction to your partner.

Cognition   For the sake of our example, let's imagine that Allison's friendly behavior leads Brittany to experience a moderate level of arousal. If this is the case, CVT predicts that Brittany's response to Allison's behavior will be contingent on how she cognitively appraises the situation. Specifically, CVT suggests that Brittany will employ knowledge structures called **cognitive schemata** to make sense of Allison's change in behavior. Figure 10.2 shows six of the most commonly studied cognitive schemata (see Andersen, 1993, 1998a, 1999, for a detailed discussion of these schemata); the following list outlines the key features of each:

1. **Culture.** Andersen (1999) argued that "culture is such a basic and invisible force it is often confused with human nature itself" (p. 231). We determine if something is appropriate in our culture, and that gives us a basis for reacting to it. For instance, kissing the wife of a friend goodbye would be appropriate in the United States but not in Arab countries. If a behavior

is appropriate, it can be positively valenced; if the behavior is culturally inappropriate, it will be negatively valenced. Within American culture Allison's smile and self-disclosure would probably be perceived as appropriate and so would be positively valenced. However, if Allison's self-disclosure was inappropriately intimate and/or negative, it could be valenced negatively.

2. **Personality.** Our personal predispositions make up personality. People differ in their sociability, extroversion, and attitudes toward touch, and in the degree to which they approach or avoid new experiences or sensations (see Andersen, 1993, 1998a). For example, a hug or an intimate disclosure may be appreciated by one person but not by another. Thus, people will valence the same behavior differently based on their personality. If Brittany is an outgoing, friendly person, she might welcome Allison's self-disclosure. However, if Brittany is shy and introverted, she might be nervous and uncomfortable hearing something personal about Allison. In the former case, Brittany would likely react positively to Allison's self-disclosure; in the latter, she would likely react negatively.

3. **Rewardingness.** The degree to which we find someone rewarding influences how we react to their increases in intimacy behavior. Rewardingness, which has also been called interpersonal valence, refers to the degree to which we find someone attractive. Recall from Chapter 3 that people can be attractive based on physical attributes (such as how beautiful they are or what clothes they wear), social qualities (such as how friendly they are), and instrumental qualities (such as how good they are at performing certain tasks). In general, people who are physically attractive, have high social standing, possess positive personality traits, and are similar to ourselves are highly rewarding. Thus, who actually instantiates an intimacy behavior is crucial. Andersen (1993) noted that "positive perceptions of another person's values, background, physical appearance and communication style are the primary reasons why we initiate and maintain close relationships" (p. 25). For example, a touch from someone you dislike is judged very differently from a touch from your highly attractive date. Similarly, if Brittany likes Allison and thinks she is a fun person, she is likely to react positively when Allison increases intimacy. By contrast, if Brittany thinks Allison is a pest who is no fun to be around, she is likely to react negatively.

4. **The relationship.** The most important valencer of a person's intimate behavior is one's relationship with that person (see Andersen, 1998a, 1999). People are able to easily classify their relationships with others as friend, coworker, best friend, lover, fiancée, parent, boss, roommate, and so on. Thus, too much touch or too much self-disclosure on a first date is usually a turnoff, yet the same amount of touch or self-disclosure from a fiancée would be warmly accepted. In the right relationship almost any immediate behavior will be valenced positively. In the wrong relationship such intimacy will be negatively valenced and cause negative relational outcomes.

So, if Brittany knows Allison from biology class and sees her as a potential friend, she will probably be open to increases in intimacy. But if Brittany does not know Allison at all and Allison suddenly starts disclosing information to her, Brittany is likely to react negatively.

5. **The situation.** The situation or the context in which intimacy behavior occurs is vital to the relational outcome (Andersen, 1993). Intimacy in the classroom, boardroom, bathroom, and bedroom produces distinctly different reactions. Some settings, such as living rooms, Jacuzzis, and hotel rooms are highly conducive to intimacy. Some situations are highly formal, and intimacy would be limited to handshakes or polite smiles. Passionately kissing your date goodnight in a private place has entirely different connotations than engaging in the same behavior in front of your parents. The bottom line is this: Intimacy must be situationally appropriate. If Allison increases intimacy with Brittany in a quiet place during a private conversation, her self-disclosure is likely to be regarded positively. But if she increases intimacy while Brittany is in the middle of an important conversation with her boyfriend, her self-disclosure is likely to be regarded negatively.

6. **Temporary states.** Everyone has bad days and good days—intellectually, emotionally, and physically. Temporary states are short-term internal conditions that make individuals feel and react differently at various times (Andersen, 1993). Many things affect a person's temporary state or mood, including having a fight with the boss, being criticized (or complimented) by a friend, getting a bad night's sleep, partying too much, and receiving a pay raise. A classic example of negative-state valencing is a person's response to an affectionate spouse: "Not tonight, dear, I have a headache." Negative physical or emotional states generally lead to negative valencing of intimate behavior, whereas positive states generally lead to positive valencing. Therefore, Brittany is more likely to react positively to Allison's increase in intimacy if she is alert, feeling well, and in a good mood.

Relational Outcomes   Earlier we noted that relationships are fragile and that few relationships reach intimacy. CVT provides one explanation for why this is so. Negative valancing for *any* of the six cognitive schemata can result in negative relational outcomes. When intimacy increases are valenced negatively, a host of negative outcomes follow, including appraising one's partner negatively, reducing intimacy behaviorally (perhaps by moving away), and perhaps even disengaging from the relationship. Positive valencing of the intimacy behavior, by contrast, results in more positive appraisals of one's partner, reciprocity of intimacy behaviors, and greater relational closeness and intimacy. Thus, increasing intimacy behavior is not without risk, but the benefits can outweigh the potential costs if a more enjoyable, close relationship is desired. Allison's attempts to become friends with Brittany might result in rejection, but Allison could also end up developing a rewarding relationship with a new friend.

Sex Differences in Intimacy

If Allison and Brittany were opposite-sex friends, they might be more likely to express intimacy in different ways. This is not to say that we should assume that Allison and Brittany are similar just because they are both women; indeed, personality differences may make Allison and Brittany quite dissimilar. Furthermore, it should not be presumed that men and women are completely different. Rather, men and women may achieve intimacy in somewhat different ways, but the important point is that men and women are far more similar than different in the ways they achieve intimacy in both same-sex and opposite-sex relationships.

Sex Differences in Relational Importance

Intimate relationships are extremely important to both men and women. However, a considerable body of literature suggests that relationships may be somewhat more important to women than to men. The landmark study of couples in the United States by Blumstein and Schwartz (1983) revealed that women are the primary keepers of the relationship. This means that women are more likely to do relational work such as performing relational maintenance behaviors and initiating discussion of relationship issues. In addition, men are less monogamous and are more likely to have more sexual partners than women. Comparisons of heterosexual couples with gay male and lesbian couples confirm this fact by revealing that lesbians are the most loyal, heterosexuals are in the middle, and gay men are least relationally loyal. In sum, men are more likely to "search for variety while women prefer a special relationship" (Blumstein & Schwartz, 1983, p. 279). In general, women are the keepers of fidelity and the protectors of the relationship (Blumstein & Schwartz, 1983). Women also cultivate more numerous and deeper relationships than do men. According to Verhoff, Young, and Coon (1993), "Women more than men rely on and invest in relationships in addition to marriage for defining themselves" (p. 449). Perhaps this is due to a combination of the biological predisposition of women to bear, nurse, and nurture children (Andersen, 1998b) and the fact that men are socialized into task relationships and away from purely interpersonal ones. As more women enter the workplace, it will be interesting to see if their relational orientation decreases or is imported into the workplace.

Sex Differences in the Development of Intimacy

Certainly both men and women have the potential to develop highly intimate relationships. Despite popular literature suggesting that men and women are from different planets, research has shown that men and women are far more similar than different. As noted in Chapter 9, according to Dindia, a more apt metaphor than "men are from Mars, women are from Venus" is "men are from North Dakota, women are from South Dakota" (Wood & Dindia, 1998). Even in the area of relational intimacy, men and women are far more similar than different. Males and females overwhelmingly believe that emotional communication is more important in the development of intimacy than are instrumental or task-oriented skills (Burleson, Kunkel, Samter, & Werking, 1996). Perhaps surprisingly, this appears to be true in male-male relationships as well as male-female and female-female relationships. As Burleson et al. (1996) discovered, "Affectively oriented communication skills appear to be important for both genders in the conduct of intimacy—regardless of whether intimacy is realized in same-sex friendship or opposite-sex romances" (p. 218). Some recent studies have shown no difference in intimacy levels for men and women. A study of intimacy in married Canadian couples showed almost identical intimacy levels for males and females for all types of intimacy (McCabe, 1999).

Despite the considerable similarity in intimacy levels between males and females, some literature has reported that females are more intimate than males. For example, one study noted that girls have more intimate relationships than boys (Meurling, Ray, & LoBello, 1999). Others claimed that girls show more trust and loyalty, more dependence on friends, and a greater tendency to discuss their relationships with friends (Muerling et al., 1999; Sharabany, Gershoni, & Hoffman, 1981). In addition, girls are more understanding with their friends, offer more benefits to their friends, and are generally perceived as more rewarding to friends than are boys. But boys' friendships are more extensive than girls' friendships and often incorporate large play groups and playground activities and games rather than the closer, more intimate dyadic and small-group relationships that characterize girls.

The finding that females have more intimate relationships with one another than do males may be due to the fact that researchers have employed a "feminine" definition of intimacy. Most of the data on the differences in intimacy between men and women comes from a body of literature claiming that in the United States women disclose more than men (Floyd, 1995). But disclosure is only one type of intimacy. Parks and Floyd (1996) pointed out that for decades scholars have thought of intimate relationships as emotional, feminine, and affectionate rather instrumental, masculine, and logical. Because men's relationships are somewhat lower in emotional expression and self-disclosure, men were thought not to have very intimate relationships. However, there is little actual evidence for a sharp difference in male and female intimacy. Parks and Floyd (1996) found no support for the hypothesis that women are more likely than men to label their relationships as intimate.

Men may have somewhat different ways of communicating intimacy than women. Sharing adventures, telling stories, doing physical labor, working on a joint project, taking a fishing trip, serving in the army—all are experiences that are very intimate in their own way. We are not saying that women do not engage in these activities—they do, just not quite as often as men. Floyd (1995) suggested that men's intimacy primarily comes from shared interests and activities. These more action-oriented behaviors may be a valid path to high levels of intimacy just as self-disclosure or emotional expression are. Traditionally, research has found that males find intimacy in recreational activities such as playing or watching sports and engaging in projects and task-related activities. Floyd (1995) found that among college students males are more likely than females to create intimacy through shaking hands, drinking together, and talking about sex. Women, by contrast, are most likely to experience intimacy in sharing time, using expressive nonverbal and verbal communication during conversations, expressing liking or love for one another, hugging, discussing personal problems, talking about fears, and shopping (Floyd, 1995; Helgeson, Shaver, & Dyer, 1987; Monsour, 1992).

Conclusion

As this chapter has emphasized, people communicate intimacy in a number of different ways. The literature reviewed in this chapter provides several hints for how to establish and promote intimacy. First, listen and look. Real connection is impossible without communication, and communication requires both a sender and a receiver. If you listen carefully to a partner and observe her or his nonverbal behavior, intimacy is far easier to achieve. Second, plan activities. Many people, particularly men, like activity during relational interaction, so find activities you have in common, and engage in activities your partner likes even though you have never tried them before. Third, avoid evaluating your partner. People like to be accepted, not criticized, so keep judgments to a minimum, especially when comforting your partner. Fourth, talk about your relationship. As intimacy increases, it may be important to define where you are in your relationship. Saying "I love you," giving rings, and planning a future together are important turning points. Avoid making such moves too early in the relationship, or they may scare your partner off, but do not put off relational communication indefinitely, either. Fifth, balance negative emotions and disclosures with positivity. Relationships are a safe haven in which the negative side of your life can be revealed, but negativity must be balanced with positivity or an intimate partner might begin to view you and the relationship in purely negative terms. When your partner shares negative, distressing events with you, respond with nonverbal intimacy behaviors and highly person-centered messages if you want to provide high-quality comfort.

As the theories presented in this chapter suggest, intimacy is created by two people through a series of moves and countermoves. One person alone cannot create an intimate interaction; "it takes two to tango." It is also important to remember that intimate interaction occurs within a larger context. As cognitive valence theory predicts, factors such as culture, context, temporary moods and states, personality, the partner's level of rewardingness, and, of course, the relationship can all influence whether intimacy moves are accepted or rejected. We hope that this chapter, as well as the chapters on relationship development and maintenance, will help you improve your intimate communication so that your attempts to develop new and closer relationships are more effective.

Discussion Questions

1. Think about the five most intimate moments you have ever shared with others. What communication qualities made these moments special?
2. Which of the theories presented in this chapter do you think best captures the process of intimate interaction? What aspects of the intimacy process model and cognitive valence theory did you most like and/or dislike?
3. If you want to give friends and loved ones effective social support, what should you say and do? What might you avoid saying or doing?

Power Plays

The Politics of Close Relationships

11

The mathematician and philosopher Bertrand Russell (1938) once remarked, "The fundamental concept in social science is Power in the same sense that Energy is the fundamental concept in Physics" (p. 10). And the historian Lord Acton (1887) famously observed, "Power corrupts and absolute power corrupts absolutely" (p. 335). It has also been said that power abhors a vacuum, and close relationships are no exception. Power exists in all relationships: Someone takes the initiative to start a relationship, or decides how to spend money, or initiates sex, or accepts or rejects the initiation, or takes out the garbage and cleans the bathroom. At some level politics and power exist in every friendship, romance, marriage, and family. In this chapter we examine how issues of power, control, and influence play out in close relationships. First, we define power and outline seven principles of power. Next, we review the literature on influence goals, and examine specific verbal tactics and nonverbal behaviors related to power. Finally, we discuss the "politics" of power by focusing on issues of power and equality in families.

Defining Power and Related Terms

Power generally refers to an individual's ability to influence others to do what he or she wants (Berger, 1985; Henley, 1977), as well as a person's ability to resist the influence attempts of others (Huston, 1983). People often exert power by controlling valuable resources (Ellyson & Dovidio, 1985). In relationships people can control resources in several different ways. First, relational partners can grant or withhold resources, such as money and possessions, affection, sex, and time spent together (Fitzpatrick & Badzinski, 1985). For example, Vince might give his partner extra affection as a way to reinforce her positive behavior and withhold affection to punish her negative behavior. Second, power is part of the decision-making process when relational partners determine how to spend valuable resources such as time and money. For example, relational partners exercise power when they distribute tasks such as washing the dishes, balancing the checkbook, and doing the driving on a road trip. Relational partners also exercise power when they decide what type of car to buy, how to spend their time together, and where to go on vacation. As these examples illustrate, in interpersonal relationships power reflects the ability to affect the behavior, emotions, or decisions of one's partner (Berger, 1985).

Power is a basic feature of relationships because humans want to control their lives and be their own free agents. **Agency** is that unique, empowering quality of experience in which a person masters the surrounding environment, including social interaction and relationships (McAdams, 1985). This is why people often feel the need to "change" their relational partners so they fit their conceptions of how a perfect partner should behave. However, uncontrolled agency leads to conquest and dominance. Ideally, power motivates, energizes, and enables a person without diminishing or enslaving other people. Negative forms of power, such as harassment or coercion, almost always destroy intimacy and produce unstable and dissatisfying relationships. The key to using power productively is for both partners to use their influence for the good of the relationship and to keep the decision-making process fair and equitable. In other words, both people in a relationship should have a voice.

To have this voice, relational partners can wield power by engaging in dominant behaviors and/or persuasion. **Dominance** refers to the display or expression of power through behavior (Burgoon, Buller, & Woodall, 1996). As we will discuss in this chapter, dominant behaviors include verbal communication such as commands and other "one-up" messages ("WE are going to MY family's house for Thanksgiving this year"), as well as nonverbal communication such as looming over someone while maintaining high levels of eye contact. However, using a particular type of behavior does not determine whether someone is dominant. Instead, "dominance is determined by the subservient or submissive responses of others. It is not dominance unless it works" (Burgoon et al., 1996, p. 306). So, if the demand to spend Thanksgiving with your family is met with a response such as "I'm not going—you can go by yourself," or if the strategy of standing over someone while maintaining steady eye contact fails to intimidate, dominance has not occurred.

Dominant behaviors often are used to try to influence or persuade others. **Social influence** involves changing someone's thoughts, emotions, or behaviors (Burgoon et al., 1996). Sometimes social influence is the result of strategic communication, whereby one person actively uses communication to try to change the other person's attitudes, beliefs, feelings, or behaviors. In other cases indirect influence occurs. For example, Courtney might emulate Joan's behavior because she respects and admires her. Thus, dominant behaviors can be part of the social influence process, although they do not necessarily have to be. The person who ultimately affects a change in the other person has wielded power, either directly or indirectly.

Power Principles

Whether power is exercised through dominance or more subtle forms of influence, it occurs within a social and relational context. In this section we discuss seven principles of power that describe how power functions within our interactions with others.

Principle 1: *Power is a perception*.

As suggested earlier, people can engage in powerful communication, but if others do not perceive them as powerful, their behavior is not dominant. This highlights the point that others are powerful only to the extent that we believe them to be powerful. Some people have objective power but still have trouble influencing others. **Objective power** is the authority associated with factors such as position, strength, weaponry, and wealth. For example, presidents, defensive lineman, nuclear powers, and millionaires have objective power, but they have real power only if other people perceive and believe in their power and are influenced by these perceptions. If people with objective power are not respected by others, their attempts to turn objective power into real power are likely to fail.

The opposite can occur as well. That is, some people become highly influential and powerful even though they do not engage in much dominant behavior. The lives of people such as Mahatma Gandhi, Martin Luther King, and Mother Teresa suggest that people of humble means and little objective power still can be very influential and wield real power when they stand for something in which large groups of people believe. Similarly, our relational partners can only be as powerful (or as powerless) as we perceive them to be, regardless of their level of objective power.

The way people perceive themselves also is important. For example, thinking that you are powerful does not ensure that you will be powerful, but thinking you are powerless virtually guarantees that you will be powerless. People who are confident and appear self-assured are more likely to influence others than are people who lack confidence and seem unsure of themselves (Burgoon et al., 1996). Moreover, people who perceive themselves as powerless sometimes get trapped in bad relationships because they do not have the confidence to assert themselves and try to change the situation.

Principle 2: *Power exists in relationships*.

Power is always an interpersonal concept, and an individual cannot be powerful without someone else being less powerful. Moreover, power is always a joint perception of self and other. Thus, you are more powerful if you and your partner act in accordance with the belief that you are powerful. However, this power can be shared through the exertion of mutual power over each other in a relationship (Berger, 1985). Indeed, in many close and happy relationships

Sometimes people who have little objective power and use messages of peace rather than aggression are highly influential.

partners allow considerable influence and control of each other at different times in various arenas. For example, in a single day a wife may influence her husband to invest in a certain stock and meet her at a particular restaurant for dinner, while he may decide what movie they see that night and which babysitter to call.

In close relationships influence is inevitable and even desirable. Partners who exercise little influence over each other may not really be a couple, but simply strangers in the same household. This is because partners in close couples are interdependent, with the actions of one person affecting the actions of the other. As we will see throughout this chapter, the way in which power is exercised and communicated is crucial. When partners perceive that power is fairly distributed and that they are receiving adequate resources from each other, they are more likely to experience relational satisfaction (see Chapter 8).

Principle 3: *Power is about resources.*

People bring a variety of resources to their relationships. Most early research on power focused on money and social standing as powerful resources (Berger, 1980), and when resources are defined in this way, men typically have more power than women. Of course, the gap between men's and women's earnings is narrowing. Today more women than men are graduating from college, and most of these women are pursuing well-paying careers. As women increasingly bring these resources to relationships, their level of power in the financial arena will increase.

Income also appears to be an important source of power for gay men. Studies have shown that in gay relationships the man who is older and earns more money typically has more power (Blumstein & Schwartz, 1983; Harry, 1984; Harry & De Vall, 1978). For lesbians as well, some research has shown that the woman who earns more has more power (Caldwell & Peplau, 1984; Reilly & Lynch, 1990), but Blumstein and Schwartz's extensive study found no differences in power based on income. Instead, lesbians reported that it was important for both partners to earn money so that neither partner would be financially dependent on the other.

Of course, money is only one of many resources that people bring to relationships. In fact, Berger (1980) criticized the research on power in families for focusing too much on income and social prestige. He argued that many other resources, such as affection, communication skill, and a sense of humor, are exchanged in relationships. Similarly, McDonald (1981) discussed five bases of resource power:

1. **Normative resources.** These resources are connected to family or societal definitions of authority. For example, in traditional marriages husbands are expected to have primary responsibility for supporting the family financially, while wives are expected to have primary responsibility for the household and children. Based on these expectations, husbands and wives would have power in different domains. Of course, in nontraditional marriages normative resources would be distributed in more unique ways.

2. **Affective resources.** These resources are connected to the level of involvement, affection, and dependence that characterize people's relationships with others. Being able to give love and care to a relational partner is a valued resource. Some scholars suggest that sex is another type of affective resource (Schwartz, 1994).

3. **Personal resources.** These resources are connected to people's personality characteristics. Factors such as interpersonal skill, role competence, physical attractiveness, and a sense of humor can all be valuable assets within relationships.

4. **Cognitive resources.** These resources are connected to the insights people have. Insight can be gained through intelligence, awareness, or life experiences. People with high levels of cognitive resources can think through problems logically and can contribute to good decision making.

5. **Economic resources.** These resources are connected to money and possessions. When one relational partner earns more money and/or has more valuable possessions than the other, or when one partner controls more of the finances, he or she has more economic power.

When resources are defined more broadly, women wield considerable power in their relationships. Gottman and Carrere (1994) argued that in public interactions, or interactions with strangers, men typically act more dominant and are more influential than women. However, in private interactions, especially with relational partners, women typically are more dominant and influential. As Gottman and Carrere put it, "Women's public tentativeness and deference, the acceptance of a subordinate role, and politeness in stranger groups does not hold in marriages" (p. 211). In close relationships women have considerable influence in that they confront conflict more readily, and are more demanding, expressive, and even coercive (Gottman, 1979). Thus, women are *not* passive in marriages, as gender stereotypes may suggest.

Principle 4: *Power is related to scarce or valued resources.*

The association between resources and power underlies this **scarcity principle,** according to which people have the most power when the resources they possess are scarce or in high demand. This is easily illustrated in workplace relationships. As individuals move toward the "top of the ladder," there are fewer people in higher roles. For instance, there may be many midlevel managers, a few senior managers, three vice presidents, and only one president and CEO. The higher status positions are scarcer or harder to obtain.

Similarly, some resources are scarcer than others in relationships. For example, you may be able to date several different people, but if you are in love with only one of them, that person will have the most power. Of course, a scarce resource leads to power only if it is highly valued within a relationship. For one person money and position may be important, so a partner who is rich and successful might be seen as possessing a scarce and valuable resource. For another person religious beliefs and family values might be perceived as scarce and valuable resources that are important for a relational partner to possess.

The principle of scarcity is also related to the quality of alternatives a person has. According to social exchange theory, "alternatives" refers to the types of relationships and opportunities people could have if they were *not* in their current relationship (see Chapter 8). Take two dating partners, Tyreke and Keisha, as an example. If Tyreke is being pursued by several people he finds attractive while all of Keisha's alternative relational partners are unappealing, Tyreke will have more power in the relationship than Keisha. This is because Tyreke could obtain valuable resources such as affection from other people while Keisha could not.

Principle 5: *Power can enable or disable.*

People can use power to hone their skills and to achieve success. Power is part of the human spirit that infuses us with agency and potency. However, excessive power or frequent use of power plays often cripple close relationships. No one likes to be dominated or manipulated, and people respond to such power plays with resistance, stubbornness, and defiance (McAdams, 1985). As we will learn later, large power discrepancies in a relationship tend to be unhealthy. Overall, research has shown that men with very high power needs frequently have problems in love relationships, and both men and women with high power needs have less intimate friendships (McAdams, 1985).

Interestingly, research also suggests that some insecure individuals try to use dominant behavior to change their relationships. When these power plays fail, these people become even more insecure about themselves and their relationships. For example, research on attachment suggests that preoccupied individuals (those who perceive themselves negatively but perceive their relational partners positively) often try to change their partner's behavior in an effort to improve their relationships. They might make demands on their partner, such as insisting that they spend more time together, be more committed, or show more affection (Guerrero & Langan, 1999). However, preoccupied individuals usually are not seen as very powerful, so their demands often are met with resistance and their power plays often fail, leaving them even more vulnerable and powerless.

Principle 6: *The person with less to lose has greater power.*

The example of a preoccupied person trying desperately to gain power but never succeeding helps illustrate the **principle of least interest** (Safilios-Rothschild, 1970; Waller & Hill, 1951). Thus, if you are in love with your partner but your partner is not in love with you, your partner has more power. Similarly, if you are worried that your partner might leave you or that you care more for your partner than she or he cares for you, your partner is likely to be much more powerful than you. In such cases there is an inverse relationship between how strongly you feel about your partner and how much relational power you have. When the less interested partner makes requests, such as asking for money or sexual favors, the more interested partner is likely to comply rather than risk losing the relationship. By contrast, when the more interested partner makes a demand or request, the less interested partner knows that she or he does not have to give in to maintain the relationship.

Research on heterosexual dating couples and lesbian couples has confirmed the principle of least interest (Caldwell & Peplau, 1984; Peplau & Campbell, 1989; Sprecher & Felmlee, 1997). Sprecher and Felmlee found that the partner who was less emotionally involved in the relationship had greater power. This relationship held true whether the more emotionally invested partner was a man or a woman. Sprecher and Felmlee also found that in general men are less emotionally invested in their relationships than women, which suggests that the balance of power favors men in heterosexual romantic couples when the principle of least interest applies. In lesbian relationships, Caldwell and Peplau found that women who were more committed and involved in the relationship than their partners tended to have less power.

Principle 7: The person with more power can make and break the rules.

According to the **prerogative principle,** the person with more power can violate norms, break relational rules, and manage interactions. This principle operates in a variety of relationships. In organizations people who have higher status and power usually can arrive to a meeting late without penalty, while subordinates are often reprimanded. Similarly, high-status individuals, such as presidents and CEOs, can wear casual dress when they want (Burgoon et al., 1996). In families, parents may be able to eat while sitting on the new leather sofa in the living room, but children might be told to eat their food in the kitchen or at the dining room table. In romantic relationships the person who cares the least may be able to get away with arriving late for dates, forgetting birthdays or anniversaries, or even dating other people.

The more powerful person also has the prerogative to manage both verbal and nonverbal interactions. For example, powerful individuals can initiate conversations, change topics, interrupt others, and terminate discussions more easily than can less powerful individuals. Verbal power often is evident in organizational settings. For instance, if you are in a hurry to get home and you run into the CEO on your way to the parking lot, you are likely to stop and talk if he or she initiates a conversation. But if you run into a coworker or subordinate, you are more likely to brush the person off. The same type of dynamic holds true in personal relationships. In high school the more popular kids often get to decide where to go and what to talk about, with the less popular kids following their lead. In romantic relationships the person with the most power may decide which relational topics can be discussed and which are taboo.

The power prerogative is evident in nonverbal behavior as well (Andersen, 1999; Burgoon et al., 1996). Take touch as an example. Think about interactions between teachers and students, superiors and subordinates, or lawyers and clients. Who has the prerogative to initiate touch in these relationships? Research suggests that the teachers, superiors, and lawyers will be most likely to initiate touch because they typically have more power in these relationships. By contrast, if the students, subordinates, or clients initiate touch, it will be perceived as inappropriate. Some research also suggests that in heterosexual romantic relationships men typically have more power in the initial stages of the relationship. As a result, they have the prerogative to ask the woman out and to initiate behavior such as hand-holding and sex. For example, Guerrero and Andersen (1994) found that men were more likely than women to initiate touch in casual dating relationships but that women tend to initiate touch more than men in married relationships.

Together these seven principles of power suggest that power is negotiated by relational partners based on their perceptions of each other and the characteristics of their relationship. In close relationships partners often share power, with each person exerting influence at certain times and accommodating the partner's wishes at other times. Thus, designating one person as "powerful" and the other as "powerless" often can be misleading. Next we examine some of the goals relational partners have when they are trying to influence each other.

Interpersonal Influence Goals

Most communication is influential. Thus, when we ask someone to do us a favor, when we advertise a product, or when we campaign for a political office, we are trying to influence people's attitudes and change their behavior. Other times we try to resist such influence. This is particularly true in close relationships—for example, when parents try to prevent their kids from smoking, dating partners initiate or refuse sexual involvement, and spouses influence each other about when and whether to have children or to buy a new house. As Dillard (1989) stated, "Close personal relationships may be the social arena that is most active in terms of sheer frequency of influence attempts" (p. 293). Most interpersonal influence attempts are goal driven. In other words, people enact influence attempts to try to achieve particular goals (Berger, 1985). Dillard's (1989) research suggests that most influence goals fall into the six categories described here.

Making Lifestyle Changes

The most frequent kind of influence attempt in close relationships involves the desire to change the behavior patterns of a partner, friend, or family member, which Dillard (1989) called giving advice about lifestyles. Examples of these types of influence goals might include trying to prevent conflict between your partner and your friends, trying to get your spouse to buy a computer for the family, getting a close friend to terminate a romantic relationship that you think is bad for her, convincing your brother not to move to Ohio for a job, and persuading a friend to reconcile differences with his parents. In addition to being the most common kinds of influence attempts in relationships, influence attempts that revolve around lifestyle changes are also some of the most important. Dillard's (1989) research indicated that lifestyle change messages are usually logical, positively presented, and direct.

Gaining Assistance

A more mundane but nonetheless important kind of influence attempt involves gaining assistance. Examples of these influence attempts might include getting your spouse to type your term paper, getting a friend to drive you to another city to see your girlfriend, borrowing money from your parents, and getting the university to accept your petition for readmittance. These influence attempts may be less significant than lifestyle changes, but they are still personally and relationally important. For example, when romantic partners, friends, or family members assist you, their actions say something powerful about your relationship with them—namely, that they are willing to aid and support you. Messages designed to gain assistance are often indirect rather than direct. Thus, when people attempt to gain assistance, they may do so through the use of hints or suggestions (Dillard, 1989). Instead of saying, "Get me a blanket and a bowl of popcorn," the person might hint by saying, "I'm kind of cold and hungry. I could really use a blanket and some popcorn."

Sharing Activities

A critical type of relational influence attempt involves offers to share time and space (see Egland, Stelzner, Andersen, & Spitzberg, 1997). As discussed in Chapter 9, shared activities play a critical role in helping people to maintain a variety of different relationships. Joint activities enable people to spend time together, show common interests, enjoy companionship, and develop a sense of intimacy. Shared activities may be a particularly important form of intimacy in male friendships because men disclose personal information to one another somewhat less often than do women. Examples of these influence attempts might include going out on a date together, running or biking together, taking a vacation together, or spending the night together. Many of these activities reflect serious attempts to increase the closeness of a relationship, and if the other person agrees to the persuasive overture the relationship can escalate. This is particularly true of activities that require people to spend time together, especially time alone together, and activities that signal commitment or exclusivity, such as going to a romantic partner's home for Thanksgiving. Sometimes requests for shared activity are direct, but more often they are indirect and appeal more to emotion than logic (Dillard, 1989).

Changing Political Attitudes

Some people are more political than others, but nearly everyone gets involved in political issues at one time or another. Convincing someone to take a stand, support a cause, or join a movement are all acts of political persuasion. Examples of these influence attempts might include talking someone out of joining a union, persuading someone to vote for a student initiative or particular candidate, getting someone to register to vote, or convincing someone to boycott a sexist movie. We all engage in these activities occasionally, but sometimes they are particularly important to our relationships. For example, if you become very active in a cause, you might want your close friends or romantic partner to join you in that cause. By participating with you, they show their support and attitudinal alignment, which can contribute to relational satisfaction. When relational partners seek to change each other's political attitudes, they often use indirect appeals for involvement that are low in coerciveness so that they will not threaten each other's autonomy (Dillard, 1989).

Giving Health Advice

One of the most important reasons for exerting power and influence in close relationships is to help partners improve their mental and physical health. For example, we persuade our romantic partners to get more exercise or to take vitamins. We advise friends to abandon abusive relationships, and we tell our teenage brothers or sisters to drive carefully and to party safely. We tell a troubled colleague to seek counseling, and we recommend that a sick friend go to the doctor. Of course, the way people give health advice may make a difference in terms of whether the advice is followed. If the persuader is too judgmental or demanding, the receiver may resist exercising, refuse to seek help, or rebel by engaging in dangerous behavior. Simple messages that express concern without being critical may be best. Dillard (1989) found that most messages aimed at giving health advice are direct and logical.

Changing Relationships

A common form of influence among close friends is relationship advice. For example, we may suggest that a friend dump her unfaithful boyfriend, or ask a friend to join our church community, or suggest to a romantic partner that we "just be friends." Because the stakes are so high, such influence attempts can be problematic, and whether they are accepted or not, they signal major changes in a relationship. Think about times when you wanted to change either your own or a friend's relationship. Maybe you wanted a platonic friendship to turn romantic but were afraid that communicating your romantic desire might ruin your friendship. Or perhaps you were afraid to give relational advice to a friend because you thought that you might get caught in the middle. The prototypical example of this is when you see a friend's romantic partner out with someone else. If you tell your friend what you saw, your friend might side with her or his partner and accuse you of being jealous or making things up. But if you keep silent, your friend might be more hurt in the long run. As these examples suggest, giving relational advice can be a tricky proposition. When people try to influence others to change their relationships, they usually use direct communication, logical appeals, and large amounts of positivity (Dillard, 1989).

Verbal Power Ploys

Traditionally, power and persuasion have been thought of as verbal activities. But in reality communication that is powerful and persuasive consists of a combination of verbal and nonverbal cues. In this section we examine aspects of verbal power ploys; in the next section we consider power associated with nonverbal communication.

Verbal Influence Strategies

Research has shown that relational partners can choose from an assortment of strategies that help them influence each other. These strategies are often called compliance-gaining (Miller & Boster, 1988; Miller, Boster, Roloff, & Siebold, 1977; Wiseman & Schenck-Hamlin, 1981) or influence (Falbo & Peplau, 1980) strategies. Skilled communicators have a diverse arsenal of strategies at their disposal. In given situations they select the strategies that are most likely to be influential for particular people and purposes. However, research has shown that people in more stable and equitable relationships use fewer overall strategies than do people in unstable and inequitable relationships (Aida & Falbo, 1991), presumably because there is less that they want to change. Here we discuss some of the most common verbal influence strategies.

Direct Requests   One of the most obvious interpersonal influence strategies is the direct request (Wiseman & Schenck-Hamlin, 1981), which is also known as the simple request or asking (Falbo & Peplau, 1980). Indeed, research has shown that this is the most common strategy for both men and women, and that it is most likely to be used by a person who feels powerful and supported (Sagrestano, 1992). Examples of direct requests include asking your boyfriend or girlfriend, "Could you turn down the stereo, please?" or saying, "I really wish you wouldn't swear in public." Although these are not very sophisticated or strategic messages, they are usually very effective, particularly in relationships with high levels of mutual respect and closeness. Indeed, in a study of unmarried heterosexual and gay couples, Falbo and Peplau (1980) found that the most satisfied couples typically use direct strategies. Similarly, in a study of married couples, Aida and Falbo (1991) found that satisfied couples used more direct and fewer indirect strategies than did unsatisfied couples.

Bargaining   This strategy involves agreeing to do something for someone if they do something for us. In addition to bargaining (Falbo & Peplau, 1980; Howard, Blumstein, & Schwartz, 1986), this type of influence attempt has been called promising (Miller et al., 1977; Wiseman & Schenck-Hamlin, 1981) and the quid-pro-quo strategy. For example, if one partner agrees not to watch football on Sunday if the other gives up smoking, each partner is giving up something in return for a concession by the other. Sometimes individuals using the bargaining strategy to persuade a partner will recall past favors or debts owed by the partner (Wiseman & Schenck-Hamlin, 1981). For example, before she asks for a favor, Shana might remind her younger sister of all the times she helped her with her homework. Other times people using the bargaining strategy reward their partner prior to a persuasive request; this is called pregiving (Miller et al., 1977). For instance, Karim might clean up the apartment before asking his roommate for an extension on the rent money he owes. Interestingly, Howard et al. (1986) found that more occupationally and relationally equal couples tended to bargain more than did unequal ones. In unequal relationships the person with more power does not need to bargain to get what he or she wants, while the person with less power does not have as many resources at her or his disposal to use in the bargaining process.

Aversive Stimulation   Also called the negative affect strategy (Falbo & Peplau, 1980), aversive stimulation (Miller et al., 1977; Wiseman & Schenck-Hamlin, 1981) involves whining, pouting, sulking, complaining, crying, or acting angry until the person gets her or his way. The idea here is that the receiver will get so tired of the aversive behavior that he or she will comply merely to stop it. This strategy is not very sophisticated and is often thought of as childish because it is so widely employed by toddlers and small children. Although this strategy often is effective, individuals who use it may be seen as spoiled or immature, and other people will avoid them if they use this strategy frequently. In fact, Sagrestano (1992) reported that people perceived aversive stimulation as the second most negative and unpleasant power strategy among the 13 strategies she tested (withdrawal, which we will discuss shortly, ranked first).

Ingratiation   Often called positive affect (Falbo & Peplau, 1980), liking (Miller et al., 1977), ingratiation (Wiseman & Schenck-Hamlin, 1981), "kissing up," or "sucking up," this strategy involves using excessive kindness to get one's way. A husband buying his wife flowers before asking for forgiveness or an athlete continually complimenting her coach are examples of ingratiation strategies. The person using the ingratiation strategy wants to be perceived as friendly and likable so that the other person will want to be helpful and compliant. Of course, ingratiation strategies can backfire if the person using them is perceived as insincere. Canary and Cody (1994) discussed the concept of **illicit ingratiation,** which occurs when a person acts nice merely to gain compliance. Illicit ingratiation can be persuasive only if it is seen as honest rather than manipulative.

Hinting   Called indirect requests, suggesting (Falbo & Peplau, 1980), or hinting (Wiseman & Schenck-Hamlin, 1981), this strategy involves implying a request without ever coming right out and stating one. For example, a wife who mentions to her husband how nice it would be to go on a vacation might be hinting that she wants to go somewhere special for their anniversary. A person who complains about how little privacy she has might be suggesting to her roommate that her boyfriend should not be around all the time. Although this is a polite strategy, its effectiveness depends on the perceptiveness of one's relational partner. If the partner does not pick up on the hint, this strategy will fail. In other cases, the partner might understand what the sender is hinting at but ignore the request nonetheless. When the request is made in such an indirect manner, some of the partner's responsibility for responding is diminished.

Moral Appeals   These compliance-gaining messages, which are also called positive and negative altercasting (Miller et al., 1977), take one of two forms. Positive moral appeals suggest that a good or moral person would comply with the request ("A good daughter would remember to visit her parents once a week"). Negative moral appeals suggest that only bad or immoral people would fail to comply ("Only an inconsiderate boyfriend would stop taking his girlfriend out to dinner"). Both positive and negative moral appeals associate certain behaviors with the basic "goodness" of the receiver. For these strategies to work, the receiver must want to make a positive impression and to look "good" or "moral" in the sender's eyes. Such a strategy also ties into an individual's identity as a basically good person. As discussed in Chapter 2, people generally prefer to act in ways that are consistent with their positive self-identities. So, if you see yourself as a good daughter or son, or a considerate boyfriend or girlfriend, you might be more likely to comply in response to the moral appeals just described. Sometimes moral appeals are called "esteem" strategies (Wiseman & Schenck-Hamlin, 1981), as when, for example, you remind your roommate of how thoughtful it would be to go to the store on the way home or to leave for a while when your fiancé is visiting.

Manipulation   This set of strategies involves attempts to make the partner feel guilty, ashamed, or jealous until the sender gets her or his way (Guerrero, Andersen, Jorgensen, Spitzberg, & Eloy, 1995; Wiseman & Schenck-Hamlin, 1981). Examples of this strategy might include making a relational partner feel guilty for going on vacation without you or feel ashamed for flirting with other people. Suggestions that alternative partners are available are also highly manipulative and threatening, and can occasionally be an effective manipulation strategy based on jealousy. For instance, if your partner is not spending enough time with you at a party, you might flirt with someone in the hope that your partner will get jealous and be more attentive to you. Of course, such strategies can backfire because people do not like to be manipulated. Manipulative strategies can also be thought of as a special kind of aversive stimulation. As mentioned earlier, strategies that cause people to experience negative affect often are seen as childish. Moreover, instead of stopping the offending behavior, some people avoid the person administering the aversive stimulation as a way of alleviating negative affect. So, when you start flirting with someone at a party, your partner simply might ignore you or leave with someone else rather than giving you the attention you want.

Withdrawal   Closely related to both aversive stimulation and manipulation are a set of strategies called distancing, avoidance (Guerrero et al., 1995), withdrawal (Falbo & Peplau, 1980), or passive aggression, whereby people give their partners the silent treatment, ignore them, or otherwise limit communication with them. A young woman in one of our classes gave a good example of how withdrawal can be used as an influence strategy. She had been dating her fiancé for 6 years and thought she would be getting an engagement ring for Christmas. When she failed to receive a ring, she gave her fiancé the silent treatment until he asked what was wrong; eventually he bought her the ring. Of course, this might not be the best way to become engaged. Over time, she might begin to wonder whether he would have proposed if she had not influenced him in this way. Furthermore, this strategy does not always work. Sometimes the partner gets used to being ignored or grows tired of dealing with negativity and moves on. In fact, Sagrestano (1992) found that people perceived withdrawal as the most negative of the 13 power strategies she examined. Still, the withdrawal strategy can be effective. Sometimes people might be hesitant to bring up a sensitive subject, and by withdrawing they can let the partner be the one who initially asks, "What's wrong?" and starts the conversation.

Deception. Some people use lies and deception as a compliance-gaining strategy (Wiseman & Schenck-Hamlin, 1981). People may make false promises, such as saying that they will do something in exchange for compliance, when they actually have no intention of doing so. People may also exaggerate or make up information to try to gain compliance. For example, a teenager who wants his curfew extended might tell his parents that all of his friends get to stay out past midnight when only a handful of them actually do. Aside from the ethical issues associated with this strategy, it is a risky relational maneuver. Discovery of deception may result in a loss of trust and the general deterioration of the relationship (see Chapter 13). Even if the relationship survives the discovery of deception, the partner may become suspicious and guarded, making it difficult for the deceiver to successfully gain compliance later.

Distributive Communication With distributive strategies, people attempt to blame, hurt, insult, or berate their partner, sometimes in an effort to gain compliance (Guerrero et al., 1995; Sillars, Colletti, Parry, & Rogers, 1982; Wiseman & Schenck-Hamlin, 1981). These strategies are sometimes called bullying (Howard et al., 1986). For example, Danielle might be upset because Todd lost his ATM card and she is afraid someone will gain access to their bank account. She might call him "careless" and "irresponsible" and question how he could possibly have misplaced his card. Tactics such as these usually are ineffective and often lead to escalated conflict (see Chapter 14) and relational deterioration. Todd might retaliate by reminding Danielle that she recently lost her car keys and he had to drive 45 miles out of his way to give her his key. Instead of changing Todd's behavior, Danielle now finds herself defending her own actions. In line with this example, Howard et al. (1986) reported that, contrary to some stereotypes, both men and women and both masculine and feminine people are likely to use distributive strategies.

Threats The use of threats, such as threatening to walk out on the partner, failing to cooperate with the partner until he or she gives in, or promising to withhold resources such as money or information, are usually ineffective. Howard et al. (1986) found that asserting authority through the use of self-serving threats was used equally by men and women. People also engage in mock violence or issue violent warnings, acting as if they are going to hurt their partner but then not doing so. For example, a girl might make a fist and shake it in front of her brother's face without hitting him to illustrate what might happen if he does not stop teasing her.

Strategy Selection

Research has shown that people use more sophisticated and diverse compliance gaining strategies in close relationships because they know their partners well and understand the types of strategies that work best with them (Miller & Boster, 1988). Of course, when close relational partners are familiar with each other's compliance-gaining strategies, they may also develop effective ways to resist persuasion.

Considerable portions of compliance-gaining routines are probably not mindful or well planned at all, but rather are relatively mindless and habitual. In most persuasive situations people fall back on familiar scripts and may not have the communication skills to apply clever new persuasive strategies (Miller & Boster, 1988). Likewise, in the best relationships, characterized by high levels of satisfaction and equality, both men and women are more likely to use less sophisticated, more direct strategies (Aida & Falbo, 1991; Falbo & Peplau, 1980). Readily doing favors and granting requests may be part of the recipe for keeping relationships happy.

Relational Control Moves: One-Ups and One-Downs

One classic method of determining power and control in relational communication was developed by Rogers and her associates (Rogers & Farace, 1975; Rogers & Millar, 1988). In any conversation messages can be coded as exerting dominance and control (a one-up message), relational deference or acceptance (a one-down message), or neutrality (a one-across message). The focus is on the *form* of the conversation rather than the *content*. Consider the following interaction between two teenage sisters:

> MARISSA: You've been on the phone for an hour—get off! (one-up)
>
> NICOLE: Okay. (one-down)
>
> MARISSA: Now! (one-up)
> [Nicole tells her friend she will call her later and hangs up.]
>
> MARISSA: Thank you. (one-down)
>
> NICOLE: Ask a little more nicely next time. (one-up)

Coding a person's verbal behavior can reveal whether he or she is domineering or submissive. Researchers can also look at how the behavior of one partner impacts the relationship. For example, Rogers and Millar (1988) reported that when wives were domineering both husbands and wives tended to experience less relational satisfaction. More significantly, by looking at patterns of one-up and one-down messages, we can determine the nature of the relationship between two people. This coding method represented a major conceptual breakthrough. A pair of utterances, called a **transact,** can be coded as symmetrical or complementary. If people engage in a pattern in which one person uses mostly one-ups and the other person uses mostly one-downs, the pattern is **complementary.** If both people use the same moves, it is **symmetrical.** When two people repeatedly use one-up moves, the pattern is termed **competitive symmetry.** When two people repeatedly use one-down moves, the pattern is termed **submissive symmetry.** A considerable portion of conversation is neu-

---

BOX 11.1 HIGHLIGHTS

Examples of Transacts

Complementarity

A: What do you want to do tonight? (one-down)
B: Let's go see that new movie I told you about. (one-up)

A: When are you making dinner? (one-up)
B: I'll get started right now. (one-down)

Competitive Symmetry

A: You need to take out the trash. (one-up)
B: You need to do the dishes. (one-up)

Submissive Symmetry

A: What should we watch on TV tonight? (one-down)
B: I don't know. You decide. (one-down)

Neutral Symmetry

A: It sure is cold out today. (one-across)
B: It is supposed to snow. (one-across)

Transition*

A: I wish you would stop talking about work all the time. (one-up)
B: Did you see Ken's new car? (one-across)

A: I wonder if there are any tickets left for the game. (one-across)
B: If you want to go, we can go. (one-down)

*Transitions include all combinations of one-across messages paired with one-up or one-down messages, regardless of order.

---

tral in terms of control. When both partners exchange these one-across messages, the pattern is termed **neutral symmetry.** And when a one-up or one-down message is paired with a one-across message, a **transition** has occurred. Box 11.1 gives examples of these five patterns. Research has shown that spouses who report dyadic inequality in their marriages have higher proportions of competitive symmetry (Rogers & Millar, 1988).

Of course, some interactions do not fall neatly into one of these categories. Take the interaction between Marissa and Nicole. At the beginning of the interaction, Marissa is the more dominant sister, but by the end of the interaction, Nicole asserts herself. Thus, some scholars have argued that transacts do not reveal much relational information by themselves. It is important to consider the nonverbal components and the context as well when interpreting one-up and one-down statements. A statement such as "You sure are in a good mood today" could be interpreted as a one-down or one-across message in some cases, but as a one-up message if delivered using a sarcastic tone of voice.

Powerful and Powerless Speech

Researchers have also identified the characteristics associated with powerful speech. Speakers who use **powerful speech** focus mainly on themselves rather than others, dominate conversations, redirect the conversation away from topics others are discussing, and interrupt others (Fitzpatrick & Badzinski, 1985).

Research suggests that men are somewhat more likely than women to use certain forms of powerful speech. For example, Falbo and Peplau (1980) found that women used more indirect strategies such as hinting, whereas men used more direct strategies such as open communication. Moreover, women were more likely to use unilateral strategies such as pouting or negative affect, whereas men were more likely to use bilateral strategies such as debate or negotiation.

It is also important to note that the differential use of strategies appears to be less a function of sex or gender than one of powerlessness. Cowan, Drinkard, and MacGavin (1984) found that both men and women tend to use more indirect and unilateral strategies when communicating with a power figure. By contrast, both females and males tend to be more direct and bilateral when communicating with a power equal. Kollock, Blumstein, and Schwartz (1985) found that the more powerful person in the relationship tends to interrupt her or his partner more, regardless of sex or sexual orientation. Moreover, whether men or women use more powerful verbal behavior depends on the topic. A study by Dovidio, Brown, Heltman, Ellyson, and Keating (1988) revealed that on traditionally male topics, such as working on a car, men engage in more verbal power strategies, such as speech initiation and total time speaking. However, women use more of these verbal power strategies when discussing traditionally female topics such as cooking or raising children.

Some studies have also found that women use more **powerless speech** than men (Giles & Wiemann, 1987). Powerless speech occurs when people use tag questions and hedges. Tag questions involve asking people to affirm that you are making sense or that they understand you. For example, you might ask, "You know what I mean, don't you?" Hedges refer to statements that give the sender or receiver an "out." Statements such as "I'm not sure this is right but . . ." and questions such as "You did say you'd help me with this, didn't you?" exemplify hedges. Although studies show that women use these forms of powerless speech more often than do men, studies also suggest that perhaps these forms of speech are not always submissive. Sometimes women use tag questions and hedges in creative ways to get more information, accomplish goals, and improve their relationships (Giles & Wiemann, 1987). For instance, if Raquel notices that Luis seems reluctant to help her decorate the house for a birthday party she is giving for one of their mutual friends, she might hedge by saying, "You did say you would help me get everything ready, didn't you?" Such a hedge might function to remind Luis of a promise he made without making Raquel sound pushy or ungrateful. As this example illustrates, knowing that women use more forms of so-called powerless speech does not paint the whole picture. It is also important to consider what impact these forms of speech have on the relationship.

Nonverbal Positions of Power

Verbal communication carries many messages of power, but nonverbal communication is an even richer source of power messages. The animal kingdom is full of dominance displays, power structures, and pecking orders. Competition for mates, food, and territory is fierce and can be deadly. Animals developed numerous power cues that establish dominance hierarchies without the need for continual deadly combat, and these pecking orders are all established nonverbally. Humans have even more complex power structures, and these are mostly nonverbal in nature (Andersen, 1999). Power is communicated through many different channels of nonverbal communication. As you read through our list of nonverbal behaviors, keep in mind that the context and the relationship between people help determine if these behaviors are perceived as powerful.

Physical Appearance

Before a word is ever uttered, people make judgments about power from others' physical appearance. Formal, fashionable, and expensive dress is indicative of power (Andersen, 1999; Bickman, 1974; Morris, 1977). Molloy (1976) argued that in most business organizations employees must "dress for success" with the traditional dark solid or pinstriped suit. Similarly, heavy polished shoes, as well as the latest aerobic or basketball shoes, are major status symbols that connote power (Andersen, 1999; Mehrabian, 1976). Women's clothing, once inflexibly prescribed, is now quite varied. Women can dress informally or formally, in modest or sexy attire, and in a feminine or masculine style. Men's clothing, by contrast, is proscribed more rigidly and generally must be modest, masculine, and appropriate to the occasion (Kaiser, 1997). However, despite the variability of women's clothing, when women violate norms by dressing in attire that is perceived as too trendy, sexy, or masculine, they often are perceived more negatively than men are when they violate clothing norms. Uniforms can convey the power associated with a task or occupation (surgeon, police officer), or they can convey powerlessness because they strip away individuality and other status symbols (fast food worker, exterminator) (Joseph & Alex, 1972). Color also makes a difference. Black athletic uniforms, for instance, may be associated with power and aggression (Frank & Gilovich, 1988).

Height is also related to power. Fair or not, tall individuals are generally perceived as more powerful and confident than short individuals (Andersen, 1999; Burgoon et al., 1996). This is why powerful people are often seated in elevated positions. For example, kings and queens sit on thrones, and judges often sit above the courtroom. By contrast, people bow to show submission. In interpersonal interactions, people can exercise power by looming over someone who is seated (Andersen, 1999). Height differentials are also related to the use of space. For example, moving in close while looming over someone is often perceived as intimidating.

Spatial Behavior

The study of interpersonal space and distance (proxemics) has revealed that the way we use space reflects and creates power in interpersonal relations. Invading someone's space and "getting in someone's face" are powerful and intimidating behaviors. In the United States most people interact at about arm's length, but powerful people, such as superiors communicating with subordinates, or parents talking to children, and people with dominant personalities are afforded the right to invade another's space (Henley, 1977; Remland, 1981). Subordinates, by contrast, must respect the territory of their superiors. As the prerogative principle suggests, powerful individuals can violate personal space norms by invading other people's space or by remaining spatially aloof. These violations, in turn, are viewed as dominance displays by others (Burgoon & Dillman, 1995).

A higher status person can give another the "cold shoulder" by adopting an indirect body orientation and not facing that person. For example, the wife who reads the paper during a conversation with her husband or the teenager who won't even look at his parents when they are talking to him might be seen as powerful but also as rude. Body orientation often interacts with another form of nonverbal communication, eye behavior, to create messages of power.

Eye Behavior

The study of eye behavior (oculesics) has revealed a number of behaviors associated with power, including staring, gazing while speaking, and failing to look when listening. People who are perceived as powerful are also looked at more by others. Eye contact is a critical nonverbal behavior; face-to-face communication is almost impossible in its absence (Andersen, 1999). While eye contact is usually an affiliative and friendly behavior, staring is powerful, rude, and intrusive (LaFrance & Mayo, 1978). People who use high levels of gaze while speaking are perceived as very powerful, particularly if they also use low levels of gaze while listening. To illustrate, try talking to someone without breaking eye contact or blinking; your interaction partner will find you very serious and dominant.

Many people avert eye contact during conversation, which reduces other people's perception of their power. Similarly, excessive blinking is perceived as an indication of weakness and submission (Mehrabian, 1971). By contrast, listening inattentively is interpreted as both rude and powerful. Exline, Ellyson, and Long (1975) computed a **visual dominance ratio** that is a function of the time spent looking while speaking divided by the time spent looking while listening. If a person has a high visual dominance score in a typical dyadic interaction, it is an excellent indication that he or she is perceived as powerful in that relationship.

Body Movements

The study of body movements (kinesics) has revealed that several different body positions, facial expressions, and gestures communicate power and status. More expansive body positions, with arms and legs apart and away from the body, convey considerable power (LaFrance & Mayo, 1978; Remland, 1982). Similarly, the hands-on-hips position communicates dominance. Superiors have the latitude to sprawl and even to get into another person's personal space (Andersen, 1999). Powerful people can lean back to relax or lean forward to make a point; submissive people usually must remain still and attentive.

Some facial expressions, such as a deep frown or a scornful sneer, are highly dominant and even threatening. A jutting jaw, narrowed eyes, and a face reddened with anger are additional facial expressions that send powerful messages of dominance (Andersen, 1999; Henley, 1977). Smiling is a submissive, appeasing gesture in both humans and other primates designed to convey the lack of a threat to and power over others (Andersen & Guerrero, 1998b). Women smile more and by doing so send friendly but submissive messages (Andersen, 1999). Smiling women are more likely to be interrupted by their interaction partner than are either unsmiling women or men (Kennedy & Camden, 1983).

Gestures, especially grand, sweeping gestures and those directed toward another person, are associated with power. Purposeful, nonanxious gestures communicate power and confidence. Pointing at someone or wagging one's finger in the face of an interaction partner is a powerful but somewhat hostile move (Remland, 1981; Scheflen, 1972). Such gestures are intrusive acts, much like invading another person's space or, as we discuss next, brashly or rudely touching another person

Touch

The study of interpersonal touch (haptics) has shown that, while touch is usually an affectionate, intimate behavior, it can also be used to display one's power (Andersen, 1999). First, the initiation of touch is perceived as more dominant than receiving or reciprocating touch (Major & Heslin, 1982), because the person who initiates touch is controlling the interaction. Among casual daters men are more likely to initiate touch, presumably because social norms dictate that men have the prerogative to try to escalate intimacy in the early stages of relationships. Women, however, initiate touch more often in marital relationships (Guerrero & Andersen, 1994; Stier & Hall, 1984). Guiding another person through a door, physically restraining an individual, and touching someone in an intimate place are all indicative of high power (Andersen, 1999). But caution is advised; charges of sexual harassment and even sexual assault can be the consequences of excessive or inappropriate touch (Lee & Guerrero, in press). While early research (Henley, 1977) indicated that touch was a highly dominant, powerful behavior, more recent research suggests that touch is more likely to be interpreted as affiliative rather than dominant (Andersen, 1999; Burgoon & Dillman, 1995; Stier & Hall, 1984). When touch is perceived as harassing, the sender sometimes means to send a message of affiliation, but the touch is instead seen as dominant and inappropriate by the receiver.

The Voice

The content of spoken words are the subject of verbal communication, but voice tones and intonations are in the realm of nonverbal communication. This area of study associated with vocal characteristics is called vocalics or paralinguistics. Social status can be detected from one's voice fairly accurately (Harms, 1961; Moe, 1972), with higher class speakers having clearer articulation and sharper

enunciation of consonants. Similarly, listeners can make fairly accurate judgments about people's levels of dominance by listening to samples of their voices
(Scherer, 1972). In general, louder, deeper, and more varied voices are perceived
as more dominant (Andersen, 1999). However, recent research suggests that for
male speakers higher pitched voices are sometimes rated as more dominant
(Tusing & Dillard, 1999) and that for both men and women both louder and
slower speech rates are viewed as more dominant than softer or faster speech
rates. When people are making an important point, they might vary their pitch
and talk slowly but loudly and deliberately. Other research suggests that moderately fast voices are perceived as reflecting confidence and power because
they suggest that the speaker knows what he or she is talking about and does
not need time to think (Burgoon et al., 1996).

Time

The study of the interpersonal use of time (chronemics) has revealed that the
way people employ time tells a lot about how powerful and dominant they are.
Waiting is the fate of the powerless, as people are generally waiting for the
powerful. The powerless wait in long lines for welfare checks and job interviews
while the rich and powerful have reservations and can relax in luxurious
lounges on the rare occasions when they must wait (Henley, 1977). Doctors are
notorious for exercising their power prerogative to keep patients waiting, and
many executives let people "cool their heels" as a power ploy before negotiating
a business deal. Keeping relational partners waiting may be a bad idea because
it signals their lack of importance and could be perceived as inconsiderate.

Spending time with relational partners is one of the most meaningful signs
of love and also shows that a relationship is important. Egland et al. (1996)
found that, among all the behaviors that convey understanding, equality, and
intimacy, spending time together is the most important. Conversely, people who
spend little time with children, friends, or spouses are communicating that the
relationship is of little importance to them.

Artifacts

Artifacts are the ultimate status symbols. Having a big house, luxury cars, and
expensive toys are signs of power, particularly in our status-conscious, materi-
alistic society. Some status symbols are subtle, such as the largest office, the
reserved parking space, and the most expensive and slimmest briefcase (Korda,
1975). Similarly, giving gifts to loved ones that are expensive, unique, or rare is
a sign of their status and importance in your life.

Family Politics

Power is part of the fabric of most family relationships. Although equality is
often the goal, parents sometimes have more knowledge than do their children,
and one spouse sometimes has more financial resources than the other. In this

section we outline some of the main power issues that surface in parent-child relationships and in romantic relationships.

Parent-Child Relationships

Parents need power. No one believes that a 2-year-old is capable of making important decisions. Parents must control the behavior of their young children, but control should be inversely related to age. Clearly the youngest children need the most control. Teenagers still need considerable control and guidance, but parents are kidding themselves if they believe they can start to become strong parents during the teen years. Attempts to crack down on an unruly teen who has no moral foundation will usually result in conflict and defiance. A strong foundation laid in early childhood helps children to become good decision makers and responsible teens. Indeed, the whole enterprise of parenting involves the gradual relinquishing of authority, from total control over an infant or toddler to minimal control over a young adult. As Gibran (1923) said of children, "Your children are not your children. They come through you but not from you. And though they are with you, yet they belong not to you. You are the bows from which your children as living arrows are sent forth. Let your bending in the archer's hand be for gladness" (pp. 18–19).

Gibran's quote highlights two junctures at which power can be an important component characterizing parent-child relationships: (1) at the beginning, when parents are raising infants and very young children, and (2) during the teenage years, when children often assert their independence. Although parents need to control young children, they certainly are not the only agents of influence in early parent-child interactions. As anyone who has seen a mother trying desperately to calm a crying infant or a father trying to get his toddler to eat her vegetables can attest, young children can have a huge impact on their parents' behavior. Yingling (1995) put it this way: "That parents influence their infants is beyond dispute, but infants' influence on parents has begun to receive attention as well. . . . At some point in the first year, infants begin to recognize the power of their interactive behaviors to influence the primary relationship. However, interactive effects begin even before that recognition" (p. 35). Without even meaning to, newborns get their parents to feed them in the middle of the night, change their diapers around the clock, and soothe them when they are upset. As infants get older, they learn to manage social interactions through crying, cooing, and smiling, and by the time they are toddlers, they are particularly good at using the word "no" to assert themselves (Lewis & Rosenblum, 1974).

Of course, parents use much more sophisticated influence strategies than their children. Many of these parental influence strategies are aimed at reinforcing positive behavior or punishing negative behavior. Research on reinforcement strategies and discipline techniques gives us some insight into how parents can influence their children's behavior. As this research shows, parents can influence children as much through affection as punishment (Becker, 1964).

Reinforcement and Punishment   There is a long history of research on **reinforcement theory,** also called **operant conditioning** (Skinner, 1953). This theory suggests that people have three major ways of encouraging positive behavior and discouraging negative behavior: (1) positive reinforcement, (2) negative reinforcement, and (3) punishment. **Positive reinforcement** involves doing something positive to reward someone who does something "good." For example, if Carrie does well on a math test, her parents might post the test on the refrigerator and tell her how proud they are of her. **Negative reinforcement** involves taking away something negative as a reward for good behavior. In this case Carrie's parents might reward her for doing well on her math test by telling her that she does not have to do the dishes, her usual evening chore, for the rest of the week. **Punishment** involves responding to bad behavior by imposing negative consequences—introducing some kind of punishment and/or taking away something that is positive. Thus, if Carrie did poorly on her math test, her parents might insist that she study an extra half hour after school for a week (imposing a negative consequence) instead of spending time playing with her friends after school (taking away a positive activity).

Of course, parents are not the only people who use these types of reinforcement and punishment strategies. Husbands and wives routinely reinforce each other's positive behaviors every time they exchange a kiss for a kind word or do the other person's chores to thank them for driving the children to school. Spouses also punish each other's negative actions by engaging in behaviors such as holding grudges or withdrawing affection. To the extent that these types of reinforcement and punishment behaviors help shape future actions, they function as influence strategies within a wide variety of relationships.

Influence Through Discipline   In parent-child relationships, parents also exert influence through the use of discipline, which may involve using punishment strategies and/or attempting to get a child to understand why a particular behavior is wrong. Baumrind (1971, 1991) and Hoffman (1980) described general parenting styles for disciplining children. Baumrind found three styles: authoritarian, permissive, and authoritative; Hoffman focused on two general philosophies of parenting: power assertive and inductive.

According to Baumrind, **authoritarian** parents are demanding, directive, and nonresponsive. They are demanding and directive because they want to control their children's behavior so that it conforms to strict standards of order. They monitor their children's behavior carefully to ensure that they are meeting these standards. These parents are nonresponsive in that they expect their children to obey them without question. Authoritarian parents also believe that they do not need to explain the reasons behind their disciplinary action to their children—their word is "law" and is not to be questioned.

Permissive parents, by contrast, are undemanding and nondirective, but also responsive. These parents relinquish most of their authority and let their children regulate their own behavior in most situations. When they do punish their children, they are lenient. Permissive parents try to be responsive to their children by showing them support and giving them encouragement. Unlike the authoritarian parent, who acts like a dictator, the permissive parent acts more like a friend.

The **authoritative** style blends aspects of the authoritarian and permissive styles. These parents are demanding and directive, but also responsive. Authoritative parents have clear standards and expectations for how their children should behave, and these standards are communicated to the children in terms they can understand. These parents set limitations, but they also allow their children some freedom and privacy. Authoritative parents are responsive in that they generally avoid harsh punishments and focus instead on reasoning with their children and providing support. The authoritative parent is more like a benevolent teacher than either a dictator or friend.

Hoffman's (1980) work on parental styles of discipline produced similar findings. The first of Hoffman's two styles, **power assertion,** is similar to the authoritarian style. Parents with the power assertion philosophy believe that they should be in complete control and so should be able to demand compliance without having to explain why. The prototypical dialogue that characterizes this style is when a parent issues a directive ("You cannot go to Alicia's party"), the child asks for an explanation ("Why not?"), and the parent asserts authority without giving an explanation ("Because your father and I say you can't go—that's why not"). Power assertion strategies can also include threats, spankings or other physical punishment, and harsh verbal reprimands.

Hoffman also described an inductive philosophy to parental discipline that is similar to the authoritative style. When parents use **induction,** they believe that it is critical that they provide their children with reasons for their disciplinary actions. They give their children explanations for their decisions in the hope that the children will eventually learn how to make good decisions on their own. For example, if Eve was told that she could not go Alicia's party, her parents would explain why. Perhaps Eve's parents know that Alicia's parents will not be home and that some of the kids are planning to bring beer, or perhaps Eve had violated her curfew the last three times she went to a party. In any case, Eve's parents would explain their thinking, and Eve would have the opportunity to reason with them.

As Box 11.2 suggests, scholars generally regard the authoritative or inductive style of discipline as the best. Burleson, Delia, and Applegate (1992) argued that discipline strategies that are **reflection enhancing** are particularly effective. Such strategies, which involve explanation and reasoning, encourage children to reflect on their misconduct, including how their actions affect themselves and others over time. Several studies have also suggested that children who are disciplined using the authoritative or inductive style have higher self-esteem, are more morally mature, engage in more prosocial and cooperative behavior, show greater communication competence, and are more accepted by their peers than are children who are disciplined using other styles (Baumrind, 1991; Buri, Louiselle, Misukanis, & Mueller, 1988; Burleson et al., 1992; Hart, DeWolf, Wozniak, & Burts, 1992; Hoffman, 1970; Kennedy, 1992). These findings hold for both preschoolers and teenagers.

Of course, authoritarian or power assertive strategies might be necessary in some cases. Steinmetz (1979) found that power strategies often lead to more rapid compliance than do inductive strategies. Similarly, studies have shown

BOX 11.2 HIGHLIGHTS

Discipline Strategies

When it comes to disciplining children, experts in the social science and medical fields appear to agree that explanation and inductive techniques are superior to power assertion strategies. Here is the American Academy of Pediatrics position on spanking: "[We strongly oppose] striking a child. If the spanking is spontaneous, parents should later explain calmly why they did it, the specific behavior that provoked it, and how angry they felt. They might apologize to their child for their loss of control, because that usually helps the youngster understand and accept the spanking" (Shelov, 1998, p. 286). Eisenberg, Murkoff, and Hathoway (1996) took a similar stand, stating that spanking and other punitive measures have never been effective discipline strategies. Instead of learning to differentiate right from wrong, children merely learn how to avoid getting punished. Moreover, when children are disciplined using power strategies, it "denies them the chance to learn alternative, less hurtful, routes to dealing with anger and frustration" and "represents an abuse of power" (Eisenberg et al., 1996, p. 339). As these authors argue, there should be a fair distribution of rights in parent-child relationships, with parents teaching their children to make good choices rather than forcing them to act a certain way.

that power assertive strategies are efficient when parents are seeking immediate, short-term compliance (Grusec & Kuczynski, 1980; Kuczynski, 1984). Thus, when a mother is worried that her son might hurt himself by crossing the street without looking or by using drugs, an authoritarian strategy might be most effective in the short term, with inductive explanations given later.

Separation and Individuation As children grow older and become more independent, a moral foundation based on explanations and reasoning rather than commands will help them make better decisions. Such a foundation is particularly important during the adolescent years when teenagers become more independent and sometimes rebel against their parents' authority. Several studies have shown that by their early teens most children depend more on their friends than their parents when it comes to making decisions and asking for advice (Hamm & Hoving, 1971; Steinberg and Silverberg, 1986; Utech & Hoving, 1969). Similarly, children yield much less to their parents and insist on making their own decisions much more often when they reach midadolescence (Steinberg, 1981). The teenage years serve as a transition period between the time when young children are heavily dependent on their parents and the time when teenagers become responsible, independent young adults. Scholars have referred to this transition period as a process of **separation and individuation** whereby teenagers distance themselves, either somewhat or completely, from their parents and develop an individual identity apart from the family structure (Guerrero & Afifi, 1995b).

During this transition period some form of power struggle between parents and teenagers is almost inevitable. Teenagers often are ready to express their independence before parents are ready to relinquish authority or before the teens are ready to make responsible adult decisions. This can lead to a period of "storm and stress" characterized by emotional distance between parents and children, as well as increased conflict (Kidwell, Fischer, Dunham, & Baranowski, 1983; Paikoff & Brooks-Gunn, 1991; Steinberg, 1987). Researchers have also found that parent-child interaction during the teen years is often marked by less warmth (Paikoff & Brooks-Gunn, 1991; Steinberg, 1981), more interruptions by the child (Jacob, 1974), and less communication (Guerrero & Afifi, 1995b).

Of course, some adolescent-parent relationships are stormier than others. If children gradually show that they are responsible enough to make their own decisions and parents gradually relinquish authority, the transition from child to young adult can be marked by more cooperation and mutual respect than rebellion. Indeed, Hill and Holmbeck (1986) argued that adolescence is a time of family regrouping, as parents and teenagers renegotiate rules and role relationships. Hill and Holmbeck also argued that the process of separation and individuation does not preclude close relationships between parents and children. Instead, this period of transition often leads to a redefinition of the parent-child relationship, from an authority-based relationship characterized by unequal power to one characterized by mutual friendship and respect. Indeed, Grotevant and Cooper (1985) found that by age 17 most teens had begun renegotiating relational rules and roles with their parents. The key to a successful transition lies partially with the parents, who need to let adolescents become more individuated while still providing a supportive and caring environment (Campbell, Adams, & Dobson, 1984; Papini, Sebby, & Clark, 1989; Sabatelli & Mazor, 1985).

Marriages and Other Close Relationships

The power structure within marriages and other close relationships is influenced by societal norms, as well as the individual attributes of the relational partners. In this section we discuss power from a societal standpoint by examining the "pitfalls of patriarchy" and then examine how power functions within traditional versus egalitarian marriages.

The Pitfalls of Patriarchy   Traditionally, relationships, just like families and societies in general, have been male-dominated in most cultures. Such relationships are based on power discrepancies that almost guarantee problems. Men with very high power motivation often have problems in love relationships and have lower marital satisfaction and intimacy (McAdams,1985). Women in such relationships may feel trapped, resentful, or hostile.

Today most of our students say that they believe marriages should be equal. However, several factors suggest that most marriages still are not equal. Several decades ago Rodman (1972) suggested that the United States was in a period of **transitional egalitarianism.** According to Rodman, in traditional patriarchic societies men are automatically afforded more social status and more power to control resources—especially money. By contrast, in truly egalitarian societies power is not dependent on who controls resources or who has more social standing. Instead, power is equally distributed between relational partners, who negotiate a fair distribution of resources. Rodman's research suggested that the United States was in transition between patriarchy and egalitarianism. Like people in patriarchic societies, people in the United States tended to associate power with resources such as money, possessions, and high-status careers. However, unlike people in patriarchic societies, people in the United States believed that either the wife or the husband could control these resources. To be a truly egalitarian society like Sweden or Denmark, people in the United States would need to separate power from resources (Rodman, 1972).

Several factors suggest that the United States is still in a transitional period. In the year 2000, television shows such as *Who Wants to Be a Millionaire* and *Greed* were among the highest rated programs on television, which highlights the importance that society still puts on resources such as money. Moreover, at the turn of the millennium, most wives in the United States still earned less money than their husbands (around 76 cents to a dollar), which tipped the power balance in the male's favor. Research by Sprecher and Felmlee (1997) has also shown that, while most relationships are balanced in power between the partners, when an imbalance exists it is likely to favor the man. Moreover, a study by Rosenbluth, Steil, and Whitcomb (1998) on dual-career couples suggested that, even when a wife earns more money than her husband, she still typically has less power. In this study 17% of the sample consisted of couples in which the wife earned more than the husband, but within these couples none of the husbands or wives saw the woman's careers as "primary" or "most important."

While it may be inevitable that one partner has more occupational status or income than the other, what is critical is how the power is exercised and how the money gets spent. In Blumstein and Schwartz's (1983) survey of 10,000 couples in the United States, satisfaction was related to equal control over money, and not to how much money individuals or couples earned. Similarly, later work by Schwartz (1994) suggested that couples are much more satisfied when the partners have an egalitarian rather than a traditional relationship.

Traditional Versus Egalitarian Relationships   Relationships are complex, and maintaining any long-term relationship is difficult (see Chapter 9). Although there is no one formula for an ideal romantic relationship, evidence suggests that peer relationships characterized by respect and relative equality are healthier, more satisfying, and more likely to succeed. This is true for both friendships and dating relationships (Roiger, 1993). However, equality may be harder to achieve in marriages than in many friendships or dating relationships because spouses typically share money and possessions and have to divide household chores. As discussed in Chapter 8, this division is not usually equitable; most working married women in the United States are still responsible for around two thirds of household chores and an even larger percentage of child care. Trying to find a fair way to share resources and divide labor can lead to power struggles within even the best of marriages. When studying this issue, social scientists have described two different types of marriages: traditional and egalitarian (Steil, 2000).

According to Steil (2000), "Traditional marriages are based on a form of benevolent male dominance coupled with clearly specialized roles. Thus, when women are employed, the responsibility for family work is retained by the women, who add the career role to their traditionally held family role" (p. 128). Of course, some women in traditional marriages are not employed or only work part time, so that they can devote considerable time to managing the house and raising the children.

Some couples are very happy in traditional marriages (Fitzpatrick, 1988). However, in the 21st century, most women are not satisfied with traditional gender roles, and dual-career households are the rule rather than the exception. In dual-career marriages (as well as other close relationships in which people live together), partners need to negotiate roles related to household responsibilities rather than relying on traditional gender roles. Thus, although various types of marriages can be rewarding and fulfilling, research suggests that today the best chance for happiness resides in marriages in which the balance of power is nearly equal (Aida & Falbo, 1991; Schwartz, 1994; Steil, 2000; Thompson & Walker, 1982). In egalitarian marriages, also called peer marriages or role-sharing marriages (Schwartz, 1994), "Both spouses are employed, both are actively involved in parenting, and both share in the responsibilities and duties of the household" (Steil, 2000, p. 128).

Egalitarian marriages are often more intimate and committed than traditional marriages. Most egalitarian marriages are deep and true friendships, as well as romances. Emotionally bonded spouses are likely to achieve equality in their relationships. Research conducted in Scandinavia by Thagaard (1997) showed that "close emotional ties between spouses are linked to the interpretation of the relationship in terms of equality. The perception of equality is based on the ability to influence the relationship beginning with one's own values" (p. 373). Aida and Falbo (1991) found that partners in egalitarian marriages used fewer dominant power strategies than partners in traditional marriages, perhaps because they could influence each other without resorting to power moves. When they want to influence each other, partners in equal, independent relationships are likely to use more diverse and more egalitarian influence strategies than are traditional couples (Witteman & Fitzpatrick, 1986). Partners in traditional, unequal couples, by contrast, are more likely to use blatant power strategies such as verbal aggression or constraints and less likely to use compliance-gaining strategies.

Inequality in some relationships is associated with poorer mental health. Among couples with troubled marriages, inequality is likely to be associated with depression symptoms in the less powerful partner (Bagarozzi, 1990). Couples in troubled marriages characterized by an equal power structure are far less likely to have either partner show severe mental or emotional problems. Halloran (1998) suggested that inequality in close relationships is a cause of both depression and low-quality marriages. Moreover, this pattern leads to a vicious cycle. As one spouse becomes depressed, the other spouse must take over more control of the family, leading to greater inequality.

Equality in marriage does not simply "happen." It takes commitment on the part of both partners. As Schwartz (1994) observed, "Social forces and psychological processes tenaciously maintain marriage along the old guidelines. Women still look to men to provide larger and more predictable income that establishes the family's social class and creature comforts" (p. 8). Several forces conspire against equality. At the turn of the century women in the United States still earned less than 80% of what men earn, creating a power discrepancy and dependence on the part of many wives. Childbearing typically impacts a woman's career and earning power more than her husband's. Perhaps even more importantly, in terms of household labor, most so-called egalitarian relationships are not really so equal after all. As reported in Chapter 8, in heterosexual relationships women still tend to do much more of the household work than men, even when both relational partners are working. Additionally, centuries of hierarchical relationships do not disappear overnight, nor do the power structures that exist in most families. While great progress has been made in elevating the status of women, sources of inequality still exist that will take additional years and effort to break down.

Conclusion

Power and influence are present in almost every human relationship. Whether you are trying to persuade your roommate to take out the trash, asking your child to be home at a certain time, or deciding if and when you should marry your dating partner, some level of interpersonal influence is occurring. Power is a perception. But people do not automatically have power; rather, power is granted to people. Resources such as money, social standing, and love give people the ability to be powerful, especially when these resources are scarce, but ultimately people are only as influential as others let them be.

In relationships people can assert power and try to influence others using a variety of verbal and nonverbal strategies. Generally people who have a large assortment of influence strategies at their disposal and who know how to select the most appropriate strategies in a given situation are the most effective at persuasion. Power is also tied to issues of authority and equality. Parent-child relationships are initially marked by child dependence and parental authority. Gradually, however, parents relinquish control and children assert their independence—a process that prepares children to be responsible young adults. In marriage the husband typically has more concrete resources (such as income and occupational status) than the wife, which can reduce her power base. Both men and women, however, are usually happier in egalitarian marriages than in traditional marriages.

Issues of power and equality certainly are important in relationships. As discussed in Chapter 8, relationships function best when people are receiving more rewards than costs and when they feel that they are being treated fairly. Thus, not surprisingly, when Peplau and Cochran (1980) asked gay men, heterosexuals, and lesbians about the ideal power structure in their relationships, all three groups thought it was important to have an egalitarian relationship. Achieving equality, however, is a difficult task. Partners need to value the different resources they bring to the relationship equally. They need to have the power to influence decisions without getting their way at the expense of the partner. And they need to divide up household tasks and responsibilities in ways that are fair to both partners. Power and influence are important components in any healthy relationship, but too much power can destroy an otherwise happy relationship.

Discussion Questions

1. Think about the three most powerful famous people you have heard of. Now think about the three most powerful people you have known personally. What characteristics make (or made) these individuals powerful?
2. In this chapter we discussed Rodman's work from the 1970s, which showed that the United States is in a transitional period but is not yet an egalitarian society. Do you think the United States has made progress in this area? Why or why not?
3. In this chapter we discussed a number of strategies people use to gain compliance in their relationships. Which persuasive strategies do you think are most effective? Why?

Getting Too Close
for Comfort
Privacy in Relationships

In *A Tale of Two Cities*, Charles Dickens wrote, "A wonderful fact to reflect upon, that every human creature is constituted to be that profound secret and mystery to every other." Indeed, no matter how much people talk to one another, they can never know each and every thought and feeling that passes through one another's minds and hearts. This is why communication is so critical to human relationships—it helps people bridge the wide gap between them to cocreate meaning and to reach understanding. However, there are times when people would rather not cross that bridge, preferring to keep their thoughts and feelings private and to preserve some of the mystery about which Dickens so eloquently marveled.

Think about this for a moment. Can you remember a time when you were upset because your privacy had been violated? Can you recall instances when you made it a point *not* to tell someone something or when you were angry with yourself for revealing too much information? Several studies have shown that the times people seek privacy and/or avoid sharing information with others are just as important to personal and relational health as disclosure and connectedness. Parks (1982) was one of the first to recognize this. He argued that the ideology of complete intimacy is overrated—that too much openness can be smothering and that sometimes people need privacy. Rosenfeld (2000) echoed this sentiment when he stated, "Self-disclosure is a scary notion! It can explain our existence, reveal who we are to ourselves and others as we disclose and engage in an act of 'becoming,' and, more fundamentally, *allow* us to exist in the world" (p. 4). It is no wonder, then, that people value their privacy. Yet too much privacy can be problematic, too. Most people also need a sense of connection with others.

In this chapter we review some of the research on the importance of privacy in our relationships with others. First, we examine communication boundary management (CBM) theory, which explains how people manage information in ways that maintain privacy (Petronio, 1991). Second, we discuss privacy violations, including obsessive relational intrusion. Finally, we use the framework of CBM to discuss patterns of topic avoidance and secret-keeping in relationships.

Communication Boundary Management (CBM)

Communication boundary management (CBM) theory helps explain how individuals cope with the need to maintain privacy boundaries (Petronio, 1991). The theory is rooted in the assumption that people set up **boundary structures** as a way to control the risks inherent in disclosing private information. These boundary structures are based on two elements associated with private information: ownership and permeability. First, when people feel that they have **ownership** over information, they believe that they also have the "right" to control who has access to it. For example, if Daunte thinks that the details of his divorce are private information that he owns, he will be upset if one of his friends starts telling people stories about the breakup of his marriage. The courts are filled with cases in which this battle over information ownership is being waged. For example, movie stars and other celebrities have sued the tabloid press for using their words or images without permission. Second, for each piece of private information, a strict set of rules governs who can access it. In other words, the information people own comes with varying **levels of permeability.** For example, you may feel that it is acceptable to share certain information with your parents and siblings but no one outside the immediate family, and other information with your best friend but not your family. In this sense each piece of private information differs in the extent to which the boundaries of access are permeable.

Once boundary structures are set, rules are established for managing the information within the boundaries. These rules are guided by three principles (Petronio, 1991), which we will discuss next.

Principle 1: *Rules are influenced by several factors.*

At least five factors influence the rules for communication boundary management: culture, personality, the relationship, sex/gender, and needs/motivation. First, each culture has different rules regarding privacy and self-disclosure. For example, some cultures have relatively loose rules regarding what topics are appropriate to discuss with strangers; other cultures are more restrictive. Second, personality variables such as extroversion/introversion, expressiveness, shyness, and social skills are all important. Some people are highly self-disclosive and expressive, whereas other people are much more private. Third, a host of relational factors, such as attraction, closeness, and relationship type (friends versus coworkers), impact the dynamics of privacy and self-disclosure. As mentioned in Chapter 5, people tend to disclose more with individuals they like than with those they dislike. Fourth, sex and gender differences, although usually small, can nonetheless influence privacy boundaries. As discussed previously, women's rules for disclosing sometimes differ from men's, and women tend to disclose a little more than men, particularly on intimate topics. Finally, individuals' needs and motivations can affect how they manage privacy boundaries. For instance, people who are motivated to make friends may disclose more than those who are motivated to accomplish a task, and people who worry about getting hurt or rejected might avoid too much self-disclosure. Through these criteria for rule formation, people determine when, where, and to whom they disclose information.

Principle 2: Successful boundary management often requires cooperation between people.

People often must involve others in their information boundary management. For example, secrets held by an entire family require that all family members agree to keep the relevant information private, which means that they must coordinate their boundary structures and rules on that particular issue. In a similar vein, a married couple may decide to refrain from discussing pregnancy plans in front of others. Coming to this agreement requires a degree of boundary coordination between the spouses. To help maintain coordinated boundary structures, people usually develop sanctions that penalize group or dyad members for violating the boundary structure (Petronio, 1991). The importance of boundary coordination becomes especially salient when the information is revealed to someone who previously was not a part of the group with access to the secret. For example, a family secret may be divulged to the fiancée of one of the family members. The addition of a new member into the secret-keeping group necessitates additional boundary structure coordination, and the boundary structure and rules must often be made explicit to the new member.

Principle 3: Stress creates boundary turbulence.

Boundary turbulence occurs when boundary structures come under stress or threat, forcing renewed boundary management (Petronio, 1991). In other words, there are situations in which old boundary structures may need to be either fortified or renegotiated. For example, when people's lives change, topics previously avoided (such as the future of the relationship) may become acceptable topics (such as after a marriage proposal). Similarly, once a previously held boundary structure is violated (such as when a secret is first disclosed), a radical change in the nature of the newly formed structure may occur (such as the once-secret information becoming a commonplace disclosure).

These principles form the basis of the boundaries that shape who discloses what, when, and to whom (Petronio, 2000). As a theory CBM is framed around the assumptions that (1) individuals erect informational boundaries to control the degree of autonomy and vulnerability they experience when disclosing and receiving private information, (2) boundaries are more tightly managed with private information than with other types of information that are less risky to individuals, and (3) boundary rules are used to determine when, with whom, and how much private information is disclosed, as well as how to respond to balance personal autonomy with relational intimacy. In sum, Petronio (2000) argued that people's need to maintain privacy leads them to create boundaries that guide their communication behavior. These boundaries are often revised to adjust to changing circumstances, but their continual management allows people to balance their needs for privacy with their coexisting needs for self-disclosure and connection. Next, we review research on privacy seeking that further emphasizes the delicate balance that people attempt to strike between autonomy and connectedness.

Negotiating Privacy Boundaries in Relationships

The struggle for privacy emerges in many different relationships, including those between friends, romantic partners, and coworkers. Much of the research in this area, however, has focused on privacy in family relationships, particularly those between parents and children (Guerrero & Afifi, 1995b). Big "Stay Out" signs often adorn the doors of teenagers' rooms, sending a clear message of the desire for privacy. Frequently, parents and children do not view privacy issues in the same way. As they move closer to adulthood, teenagers may believe they have a right to be independent and to maintain their privacy, but parents may believe that their teens still need guidance and protection. In this sense the boundary coordination rules in families can be highly complex, and their negotiation can be very difficult. What is considered private information and private behavior becomes a topic of heated debate in some families, especially ones in which teenage sons and daughters are asserting their independence.

Children react to privacy violations in various ways depending on the circumstances, but they are particularly likely to be resentful of privacy violations once they are adults and have left home. Once children have "left the nest," privacy violations by the parents reflect a failure to recognize the children's "right" to independence at a time when their sense of autonomy is beginning to flourish (McGoldrick & Carter, 1982). Indeed, the consequences of such privacy violations are potentially severe, but how common are they, and what form do they take?

To answer these questions, Petronio and Harriman (1990) asked students to describe ways that their parents invade their privacy and their reaction to these privacy violations. All of the students were able to describe at least one example, and 96% of them described at least three such incidences, suggesting that privacy violations by parents are a fairly typical occurrence for college students. Eight types of parental privacy violations were reported: (1) asking personal questions about the student's life, (2) giving unsolicited advice, (3) making unsolicited remarks about the student's life, (4) opening the student's mail without permission, (5) going through the student's belongings without permission, (6) entering the bathroom without knocking, (7) eavesdropping on face-to-face conversations with others, and (8) using a second telephone line to listen in on a phone conversation without permission.

As you might suspect, some of these violations are more severe than others. Petronio and Harriman grouped the violations into two general types: (1) **subversive invasion tactics,** which are used to violate children's privacy without their prior knowledge or permission (eavesdropping, opening mail, going through personal things), and (2) **direct invasion tactics,** which include more overt violations of privacy with no attempt by the parents to hide their actions (giving unsolicited advice, asking personal questions). Not surprisingly, the students in Petronio and Harriman's study reported that subversive invasion tactics were considerably worse than direct ones.

According to Petronio and Harriman (1990), young adults react to parental privacy invations in at least seven ways: They (1) show disappointment, (2) ask the parents to stop invading their privacy, (3) make the parents feel guilty, (4) confront the parents with evidence, (5) use a pay phone to make personal calls, (6) hide personal belongings, and (7) meet friends outside the home. As you may already have noticed, these reactions differ along two general lines: They are either confrontational, in the sense that the child openly challenges the guilty parent (asking the parent to stop the privacy violation, confronting the parent with evidence), or (2) they are evasive, in the sense that the child changes her or his behavior to protect privacy but does not discuss it directly with the parents. Petronio and Harriman found that students were more likely to react in a confrontational manner in response to subversive invasions. In other words, they were more likely to directly challenge their parents when they caught their parents secretly trying to invade their privacy than when their parents invaded their privacy by asking questions or giving unsolicited advice.

Privacy violations and related responses have a strong impact on the parent-child relationship. Privacy invasion, especially when subversive and when followed by a confrontational response, was generally associated with less trust and a decrease in the perceived quality of the parent-child relationship (Petronio & Harriman, 1990). However, sometimes privacy violations increased openness in parent-child relationships (probably by forcing the discussion of issues that would otherwise have been ignored). In sum, subversive boundary violations can have long-term effects on the parent-child relationship.

Privacy is important in other relationships as well. Our need to maintain privacy and to control information about ourselves is evident in many of the things we do. Think about some of the actions you take to let people know that they have entered your "domain" (whether it be your room, your office, or even your car). Or think about some of the ways you behave to show people that you want to be left alone, even if you are in the midst of others. If you can imagine yourself doing these things, you certainly are not alone. Several scholars have studied the ways people try to create their private space and communicate their needs for privacy (Burgoon, Buller, & Woodall, 1996; Buslig, 1999). For example, people erect fences around their houses and put partitions between office cubicles. Doors are perhaps the most obvious architectural way that people regulate privacy. Think of the difference between professors who have "open-door policies" and those who do not. Those who have such policies are signaling a willingness to forgo some of their privacy needs and, in doing so, appear much more accessible than those who protect their privacy needs by closing their office doors. People also signal their degree of privacy needs by the way they arrange furniture. Again, think about professors' offices. Some professors have their office set up so that during meetings students sit on one side of the desk and they sit on the other, thereby maximizing privacy boundaries. Other professors sit with no desk between them and their students, thereby minimizing privacy boundaries and creating a greater sense of closeness. Other forms of privacy management are less subtle. For example, Buslig (1999) reported that college students sometimes hang markers on the outside of their doors (such as tying a scarf around the door knob) to indicate that they are "entertaining" a boyfriend or girlfriend and want privacy. A desire for privacy is communicated in other subtle nonverbal ways, such as reducing eye contact, increasing conversational distance, and using less alert or positive facial expressions (see Burgoon et al., 1996). Indeed, we spend much of our time signaling to others, often unconsciously, the degree of privacy we need and, in so doing, managing our privacy boundaries.

One of the most difficult aspects in gaining privacy is that the need for privacy is often interpreted as a desire to separate from others (see Mehrabian, 1981). For example, it is sometimes hard to separate a partner's request for some alone time from a desire to distance her- or himself from you. Similarly, if your spouse or roommate retreats into another room for an extended period of time and refuses to talk to you about something that is bothering her or him, you might interpret this as a violation of marriage or friendship rules that call for openness. Of course, as discussed in previous chapters, the need for privacy is completely normal and, in fact, is critical to healthy relationships (Baxter & Montgomery, 1996). As dialectics theory suggests, people have needs for both autonomy and connection, and for both expression and privacy. Still, the reality is that communicating privacy needs, especially in relationships, can be difficult. Therefore, relational partners often do not express their privacy needs directly. For example, you may communicate that you are upset when your partner departs for a weekend trip, but not that you are also looking forward to the time alone afforded by his or her absence.

Of course, if people simply wait until they happen to be separated from friends and loved ones to have time alone, they might not have enough private time. Therefore, it is important for people to communicate their privacy needs on a day-to-day basis. Although few scholars have investigated the ways that people seek privacy in relationships, Buslig and Burgoon (2000) recently conducted a study that did exactly that. They studied both privacy protection (attempts to protect privacy prior to intrusion) and privacy restoration (attempts to restore privacy after it was violated). Whether people were trying to protect or restore their privacy, they were more likely to use indirect than aggressive strategies. In fact, only 16% of the participants in Buslig and Burgoon's study reacted to privacy violation or its potential by aggressively demanding privacy, and those people were more often reacting to strangers than to friends. When people did react aggressively with friends, they often paid a price by experiencing a decrease in the quality of the relationship. Curiously, though, people who responded the least aggressively to privacy violation or its potential were also least satisfied with the outcome. So, as discussed in Chapter 2 on identity management, if a strategy is too indirect, people do not "get the hint," and the

---

BOX 12.1 HIGHLIGHTS

Types of Obsessive Relational Intrusion (ORI)

Cupach and Spitzberg surveyed 876 people to determine the types of ORI behaviors they had experienced. Some of the behaviors they found are listed below, along with the percentage of people who reported experiencing these types of ORI.

Called and argued with me (73%)
Called and hung up when I answered (70%)
Constantly asked for "another chance" (64%)
Watched or stared at me from a distance (62%)
Made exaggerated claims about her or his affection for me (61%)
Drove by my house or work (57%)
Used third parties to spy or keep tabs on me (55%)
Performed large favors for me without my permission (52%)

Spread false rumors about me to my friends (49%)
Left notes on my car windshield (45%)
Sent me unwanted cards or letters (42%)
Increased contact with my family members to stay connected to me (37%)
Went through private things in my room (34%)
Physically shoved, slapped, or hit me (32%)
Made obscene phone calls to me (30%)
Damaged my property or possessions (26%)
Forced me to engage in unwanted sexual behavior (16%)
Called radio station and devoted songs to me (15%)
Cluttered my e-mail with messages (11%)
Broke into my home or apartment (8%)

Source: Spitzberg and Cupach (1998).

---

attempt to protect or restore privacy goes unheeded. By contrast, more direct, aggressive strategies can be face threatening and relationally damaging, but they are also more likely to "get the job done." A strategy that is somewhere in the middle—direct but not aggressive—may work best.

Obsessive Relational Intrusion (ORI)

In some cases people continue to invade other people's privacy even when the other person clearly wants to be left alone. This is often the case when people use **obsessive relational intrusion (ORI),** defined as repeated invasion of one's privacy boundaries (Cupach & Spitzberg, 1998). ORI occurs when someone uses intrusive tactics to try to get closer to someone else. For example, in Chapter 5 we discussed situations of unrequited love, wherein one person (the would-be lover) is interested in another person who does not return her or his affection (the rejector). Some would-be lovers use ORI, as do some people after a relational partner breaks up with them. Episodes of ORI typically increase in intensity as the object of attention tries to fortify her or his privacy boundaries—for example, by taking pains to avoid the pursuer. Box 12.1 contains a sample of ORI behaviors.

As Box 12.1 suggests, ORI encompasses a wide variety of behaviors, although some are more severe than others. ORI sometimes escalates to stalking, wherein someone repeatedly harasses another person in a way that threatens her or his safety (Meloy & Gothard, 1995). In fact, we hear about sensational cases of ORI and its severest form, stalking, in the media, and the negative impact ORI can have on its victims is evident in many of these stories. The death of Princess Diana is one tragic example of what can happen when a person is pursued relentlessly by others. Ordinary people who are not famous also experience ORI. In fact, in 1993 Cohen estimated that approximately 200,000 people in the United States were being stalked, a figure that likely has increased since then.

At its basic level ORI reflects one person's interest in establishing a relationship with someone who does not share that desire (see Cupach & Spitzberg, 1998). This imbalance in relational interests sometimes leads pursuers to use all possible means of contacting the individual in the hopes of winning the person over. According to Cupach and Spitzberg's (1998) review, the types of behaviors that constitute ORI episodes vary dramatically and range from mildly intrusive (receiving unwanted gifts, being pestered for a date), to moderately intrusive (being spied on, having false rumors spread about you to friends), to very intrusive (having your home invaded, being verbally threatened or physically assaulted). But all of these behaviors cause an unwanted loss of privacy and autonomy.

Even when pursuers do not physically harm their targets, the psychological consequences for these targets can be devastating. The most obvious consequence of ORI episodes is the extreme and repeated experiences of fear associated with the target's loss of control over his or her physical and psychological privacy (Mullen & Pathe, 1994). This fear often results in the target making drastic attempts to regain this privacy, including equipping house and car with alarm systems, changing phone numbers and addresses, and even changing jobs. In fact, Wallace and Silverman (1996) argued that the effects of stalking are often similar to those experienced by victims of posttraumatic stress disorder.

Unfortunately, efforts to cope with ORI are rarely fully successful. Burgoon et al. (1989) discussed four broad categories of strategies that individuals use to cope with privacy violations. First, people can use **interaction control,** such as showing disinterest in the interaction and ending conversations prematurely. Second, people can use **blocking and distancing** behaviors. For example, you might place physical barriers between yourself and the pursuer, or you might increase the physical distance between the two of you. You might also avoid going to places where the pursuer might be. Third, people can use **assertive strategies,** such as expressing anger or directly asking the pursuer to leave. Finally, people can use **violence and threats,** such as enacting or threatening to enact violence against the perpetrator. In some cases of ORI, people might also take legal action by obtaining restraining orders, calling the police for protection, or suing the pursuer.

Thus far, no studies have investigated which of these strategies are used most often and most successfully by ORI targets. However, Burgoon et al. (1989) have reported that victims of privacy invasions are hesitant to use any of these strategies and instead try to deal cognitively with the loss of privacy control. Of course, in the context of ORI episodes, the target of pursuit may fear that these coping responses might worsen the problem. Future research needs to investigate whether such a fear is justified and which strategies are most likely to successfully end the ORI and help people regain control over their privacy boundaries.

Topic Avoidance

So far, we have discussed how people react to privacy violations that are either mild or highly intrusive. Many of the strategies we discussed were reactive rather than proactive. One proactive way to maintain privacy is to engage in topic avoidance. **Topic avoidance** occurs when a person deliberately decides to avoid disclosing information on a particular subject. Sometimes topic avoidance occurs regardless of the context or the person with whom one is talking. For example, there might be certain topics that you keep completely private and do not disclose to anyone—perhaps a particularly embarrassing moment or painful failure. More often, however, topic avoidance is specific to the situation or the person with whom one is talking. For example, there might be a topic that you refuse to discuss with your parents but would readily discuss with a friend. Conversely, you may keep some information about your family secret from your social network. Indeed, research suggests that some topic avoidance is common in all types of close relationships. Baxter and Wilmot (1984), in one of the first published studies on topic avoidance, found that over 95% of the college students in their study could name at least one topic that they considered to be "taboo" or off limits in their friendships or dating relationships. Subsequent research has revealed that individuals use topic avoidance to maintain control over information across a wide variety of relationships, from stepfamilies (Golish & Caughlin, 2000), to sibling relationships (Guerrero & Afifi, 1995a), to same- and cross-sex friendships (Afifi & Guerrero, 1998).

Commonly Avoided Topics

Although people can avoid talking about almost anything, some topics are more likely to be avoided than others. Guerrero and Afifi's (1995a, 1995b) summary of the available research revealed six general topics that are commonly avoided in close relationships:

1. **Relationship issues.** This category includes past negative relational behavior (past conflicts) and current and future relationship issues (relationship norms, the state of the relationship, the future of the relationship, the amount of attention to the relationship). People typically avoid relational issues such as past conflicts or infidelities to curtail further disagreement. They also avoid discussing the state and future of the relationship if they are still trying to sort out their feelings or are not ready to commit fully to the relationship.

2. **Negative experiences/failures.** This category includes past experiences that may be considered socially unacceptable or were traumatic, such that reliving the experience through disclosure would be distressing, unpleasant, and/or embarrassing. People avoid some of these topics, such as failing a test or being fired from a job, to save face. People avoid other topics, such as being a victim of abuse or losing a loved one to cancer, because they are too painful and distressing.

3. **Romantic relationship experiences.** This category includes past or present romantic relationships, dating patterns, and partners. For example, some spouses avoid discussing old boyfriends and girlfriends or ex-spouses. Some people also report keeping the details of their current romantic relationship hidden from friends or family members who are disapproving.

4. **Sexual experiences.** This cateogry includes past or present sexual activity, sexual preferences, and/or sexual likes and dislikes. For instance, teens and young adults might not want to talk about their sexual experiences with their parents. People also might avoid discussing past sexual experiences with current romantic partners. And they might avoid discussions about sexual orientation and past homosexual or heterosexual encounters, such as a lesbian preferring not to talk about a past sexual encounter with a man.

5. **Friendships.** This category includes current friendships with others, the qualities of the friendship, and the activities engaged in together. Some people avoid talking about a friendship when the person they are talking with disapproves of or is critical of a particular friend. People also may avoid talking about the activities they engage in with their friends. For example, teens often keep the details of their activities with friends hidden from their parents, and even adults report intentionally concealing information, such as going on a ski trip with a group of friends, from someone who might feel left out or jealous.

6. **Dangerous behavior.** This category includes behaviors that are potentially hurtful to oneself. Teenagers are perhaps most likely to avoid this topic when interacting with their parents. That is, they might avoid any mention of using drugs or alcohol, staying out late in a dangerous area, hitch-hiking, and other potentially harmful behaviors to protect themselves from criticism or punishment. Romantic partners also report concealing some forms of dangerous behavior from each other. For example, a husband might not tell his wife that he was out bungee jumping if he knows that she will get upset.

Although these topics do not represent all the possible issues that may be avoided in relationships, they are the ones that most commonly emerged in the research. Given that most studies in this area have been conducted using college students, adolescents, and young married couples, they likely underrepresent some of the topics avoided by older adults. Still, the categories are general enough to adequately represent the range of possible topics. It is important to keep in mind, though, that the specific topics in each general category are likely to change even as relationships change. For example, money and in-laws may be two specific relationship issues that are particularly avoided in marital relationships but not at all in parent-child relationships. Of course, in every relationship a unique set of topics is likely to be avoided. For example, two sisters may talk about almost any topic freely but avoid politics because they know that they are on opposite sides of the political spectrum and will only argue about these issues.

Some research does suggest that certain types of relationships may be more fraught with informational boundary management than others. Unfortunately, no study has compared all relationships against one another on the amount of topic avoidance, but studies have shown differences in the amount of topic avoidance within certain sets of relationship types. For example, Golish and Caughlin (2000) found that children in stepfamilies avoided discussing issues with their stepparent more than with their natural father and with their natural father more than with their natural mother. Guerrero and Afifi (1995a) found that adolescents and young adults avoided discussing negative life experiences and dating experiences with their parents more than with their siblings, and avoided sexual discussions with opposite-sex family members more than with same-sex ones. Thus, a teenage boy is more likely to talk about sex with his older brother or father than with his mother or sister, while a teenage girl is more likely to talk to her older sister or mother. Finally, Afifi and Guerrero (1998) found that individuals avoided discussions of negative life experiences and relationship issues with male friends more than with female friends, and avoided topics related to dating and sexual experiences when with cross-sex friends more than when with same-sex friends. The "state of the relationship" also appears to be a particularly taboo topic in relationships between heterosexual cross-sex friends when the romantic intentions of one (or both) of the partners are unclear. In sum, people do appear to have relationship-specific concerns that lead them to avoid particular issues most often in certain types of relationships.

Reasons for Topic Avoidance

Research has also examined *why* people avoid talking about certain topics. Afifi and Guerrero's (2000) summary of the literature suggests that there are three general motivations for topic avoidance, with specific motivations underlying each. Each of these motivations helps people to define their informational boundaries.

Relationship-Based Motivations Paradoxically, people can use topic avoidance to strengthen or to disengage from a relationship. In fact, contrary to research conducted in the 1970s and early 1980s that touted the benefits of complete openness and self-disclosure, more recent studies on topic avoidance suggest that one of the most important reasons for maintaining individual boundaries around information is a concern for maintaining the relationship (Afifi & Guerrero, 2000; Parks, 1982). In fact, Baxter and Wilmot (1985) found that the desire for **relationship protection** was the single biggest motivator leading to the decision to avoid discussing a particular issue with a relational partner. Similarly, Hatfield (1984) and Rosenfeld (1979) noted that fear of abandonment often explained someone's decision to avoid certain topics. In other words, people may avoid talking about their past or any other topics that they think reflect negatively upon themselves if they are worried that their current dating partner will disapprove and leave them.

This motivation is not restricted to romantic relationships, however. Guerrero and Afifi (1995a) found that individuals were more likely to be driven by a desire to protect the relationship when avoiding topics with their parents, as opposed to their siblings. In an extension of this research, Golish and Caughlin (2000) found that relationship protection was more often a reason underlying avoidance with stepparents than with fathers, and with fathers than with mothers. Finally, Afifi and Guerrero (1998) found that males were more likely than females to claim relationship protection as a reason for topic avoidance in their friendships and that people avoided certain topics with male friends more than with female friends because of that same concern. So, although relationship protection is an important reason underlying decisions to avoid disclosure, it seems especially relevant to some relationships.

In contrast to the desire to protect and sustain the relationship, some people avoid discussing certain topics in hopes of destroying the relationship or preventing it from becoming closer. This motivation has been labeled **relationship destruction** or **relationship de-escalation** (Afifi & Guerrero, 2000). Although much less work has focused specifically on this motivation, several lines of research support the idea that people use topic avoidance to terminate a relationship or to prevent it from becoming more intimate. For instance, during the breakup stages of relationships, one of the partners may distance her- or himself from the other by shutting down communication and keeping information that was previously shared private (see Chapter 15). Another way to think about this motivation is how it works when someone you dislike wants to become friends with you. You might strategically avoid discussing personal topics with this person so that intimacy cannot develop.

As dialectics theory would suggest, people sometimes feel competing tensions to maintain a certain level of closeness in a relationship but to also prevent the relationship from becoming closer. For example, have you ever been in a relationship in which you wanted to remain just a friend but the other person wanted to become a romantic partner? One way of preserving the friendship is to avoid discussing any topics that may lead to "relational talks" or otherwise give the person an opportunity to express her or his interest in advancing the relationship. You might worry that discussing the relationship could harm your friendship by making communication awkward or by forcing you to reject your friend. Notice that in this case topic avoidance may actually serve a dual motivation: (1) preventing friendship from turning romantic and (2) preserving the friendship itself.

Individual-Based Motivations   People also avoid discussing certain issues to protect themselves. In Chapter 2 we talked about the importance that people place on protecting their public identities. Literally hundreds of studies have shown that people work hard to project and maintain a certain image. As a result, not surprisingly, one of the main reasons people avoid discussing certain issues is that disclosure on certain topics may simply make them "look bad." Afifi and Guerrero (2000) labeled this motivation **identity management.** In fact, across four studies, spanning sibling relationships, parent-child relationships, stepparent-child relationships, friendships, and dating relationships, this fear of embarrassment and criticism, fueled by feelings of vulnerability, was the leading reason given for topic avoidance (Afifi & Guerrero, 1998; Guerrero & Afifi, 1995a, 1995b; Hatfield, 1984). Together, these studies suggest that the primary reason people choose to avoid discussing certain issues is the fear that disclosure will threaten their identities. Apparently people decide that it is better not to talk about something if it might make others see them in a negative light. If a person's identity is on the line, disclosure oftentimes is not worth the risk.

Besides this concern over public identity, people may avoid certain topics as a way to maintain their privacy. This motivation, which has been termed **privacy maintenance,** is rooted in individuals' needs for privacy and autonomy (Afifi & Guerrero, 2000). Earlier we discussed the importance of privacy maintenance in people's lives. One way that people maintain privacy is avoiding disclosure about certain topics. As we noted, this sort of privacy maintenance is especially common in families, in which teenage sons and daughters create their own identity in large part by refusing to share certain information about themselves with their parents. This enables the teenagers to maintain the privacy boundary that is so crucial for them. Of course, this desire for privacy appears in other relationships as well. For example, you may become annoyed with a friend who wants to know all the details about your romantic relationship or who is constantly asking you how well you did on exams and term papers. In response, you may refuse to answer your friend's questions and avoid bringing up any related topics in the future as a way to protect your privacy.

Information-Based Motivations   The final set of reasons that people choose to avoid disclosure has to do with the information they expect to receive from the other person. In particular, people may choose to avoid disclosure because they suspect that the other person will find the disclosure trivial, not respond in a helpful way, or lack the requisite knowledge to respond. Afifi and Guerrero (2000) labeled these types of motivations **partner unresponsiveness.** For example, if you have a problem for which you need advice, but you think your friend will be unable to provide you with much help or will not care enough to really listen to you, you will likely avoid discussing that problem with your friend. Studies have found that people are especially likely to avoid discussing problems with men for this reason (Afifi & Guerrero, 1998; Guerrero & Afifi, 1995a, 1995b). In fact, a study by Burke, Weir, and Harrison (1976) found that 23% of wives, compared to only 10% of husbands, avoided disclosure because of a belief that their spouse would be unresponsive. This finding is consistent with some research on social support, which shows that women generally are better listeners than men (Derlega, Barbee, & Winstead, 1994).

BOX 12.2 HIGHLIGHTS

Examples of Different Motivations for Topic Avoidance*

Relationship-Based Motivations

Relationship protection. A member of a cross-sex friendship discussed avoiding talk about the "state of the relationship" by stating that, "if you bring that stuff back up, you don't know what it's going to cause, you know . . . so it's safer to just avoid it . . . safer on the relationship."

Relationship destruction. A 15-year-old girl wrote the following account: "My mom remarried about a year ago. I don't like my stepdad at all. He is always trying to act like my real dad and boss me around. I resent this. He will *never* be my dad. I already have a dad. I really hate it when he tries to get all close to me by asking about my life. He'll try to cozy up to me and ask all about my friends and stuff like he's my buddy or something. I make sure I don't tell him *anything* but he never gets the hint."

Individual-Based Motivations

Identity management. A college student wrote the following about her actions on a first date. "He asked about school and started talking about grades and stuff. I tried to switch the topic because I am not a very good student and I didn't want him to think I'm dumb or something."

Privacy maintenance. A 17-year-old girl wrote this account: "My mom wants me to tell her everything. She thinks she has to know everything about me all the time. I get sick of it. Sometimes I want to tell her it's just not her business. I am almost an adult. I have my own life. I need my privacy."

Information-Based Motivations

Partner unresponsiveness. A college student wrote this account: "My husband sometimes asks me about school, but I know that he is only asking out of politeness. He is not really interested and doesn't really understand what it is like to go back to school when you are in your 40s. Once when I was stressed out about a final, he told me it was 'only an exam.' Since then, I haven't talked about school with him much at all."

Futility of discussion. A 17-year-old boy wrote the following: "It is a total waste of time to talk to my dad about my SAT scores. We have been over it a million times and no matter how much we talk about it, it doesn't change anything. My college applications are in and I'm going to have to live with my score."

*These are actual accounts written by people who reported topic avoidance (see Afifi & Guerrero, 2000; Afifi, Guerrero, & Egland, 1994).

People also engage in topic avoidance when they believe that talking about a particular topic would be futile or a "waste of their time." Afifi and Guerrero (2000) labeled this motivation **futility of discussion.** Although this motivation has received less attention than the others discussed here, it may play an important role in people's decisions to withhold information. Believing that a partner or friend is so entrenched in her or his position as to make discussion meaningless certainly will motivate topic avoidance, but it may also be especially detrimental to relational success.

Collectively, these motivations account for many of the reasons that people maintain strict information boundaries within their relationships with others; Box 12.2 gives real-life examples of each. Next, we turn to a specific form of topic avoidance that has received considerable attention from researchers and therapists: secrets.

Secrets

Secrets are defined as the intentional concealment of information (Vangelisti & Caughlin, 1997). Research suggests that almost everyone keeps some sort of information secret (Vangelisti, 1994; Wegner, 1992), but not all secrets are highly relevant to relationship success. Secrets differ dramatically in content and may have positive or negative effects on close relationships. For example, you may keep secret the surprise birthday party you are planning for your best friend, the vacation plans you have made for yourself and your romantic partner, or a gift you purchased for your child. These are relatively positive examples of secret-keeping. But you may also conceal more negative types of information, such as a one-night stand you had, a socially stigmatized illness you have, your alcoholic father's behavior, your violent past, or a wish for harm to come to someone you hate.

Despite the diversity of secrets that people keep and the variety of relationships in which secrets occur, most of the research in this area has focused on family secrets, perhaps because these are often relevant in therapy (for a review see Brown-Smith, 1998). Researchers have addressed several questions relevant to secret-keeping: (1) What are the types and features of family secrets? (2) Are there any benefits to keeping information secret, or are secrets always harmful to a relationship? and (3) What leads people to tell secrets, and what are the consequences of doing so? In this section we will review studies that provide answers to these and similar questions related to the impact of secrets on families and other relationships.

Features and Types of Family Secrets

Although secrets could be classified in many different ways, Karpel (1980) discussed three forms of secrets particularly relevant to family units. These three forms essentially differ in the complexity of the required boundary coordination (to use CBM terminology). The first form of secrets described by Karpel are **whole-family secrets,** which are held by the entire family and kept from outsiders. For example, the entire family may be aware of a parent's abusive behavior but may keep that information from everyone outside the family. Indeed, Armstrong (1978) described a common tendency to keep a child's sexual abuse secret from all those outside the immediate family. Karpel's (1980) second form of secrets, labeled **intrafamily secrets,** occurs when some family members are aware of certain information and keep it from other members. For instance, two brothers who are aware that their sister violated her curfew might intentionally conceal this information from their parents. Or a sexually abusive father may tell the abused child to "keep it our little secret," thereby hiding the abuse from other family members (Cottle, 1980). Karpel's (1980) third form of secrets, **individual secrets,** occurs when information is held by a single individual and kept secret from other family members, as when a son hides his homosexuality from family members. Individual secrets may or may not be shared with people outside of the family. So the gay son might be comfortable "coming out" to his close friends but not to his family.

Another way to classify secrets is not by the degree of boundary coordination they necessitate, but by the content of the information. Vangelisti (1994) conducted the first investigation into the content of family secrets. She asked undergraduate students to describe, if possible, any secrets they held in their family, including one whole-family secret, one intrafamily secret, and one individual secret. An amazing majority were able to think of at least one example of each type. Specifically, 97% were able to describe a whole-family secret, 99% had an intrafamily secret they could recount, and 96% had an individual secret they kept. Keep in mind that Vangelisti asked only about secrets held within the family unit. Imagine what her results would have been if she had opened it up to secrets of any sort, in any relationship type. Obviously, secret-keeping is commonplace.

To follow up on this research, Vangelisti and Caughlin (1997) conducted two additional studies that focused exclusively on whole-family secrets. They surveyed over 700 students and again found that almost all (98%) could describe a family secret they were keeping. One of their goals was to determine which types of secrets were most often kept within family boundaries. Perhaps surprisingly, secrets involving finances, which include issues related to money, business holdings, and other assets owned by family members, were by far the most often kept secrets by families, followed by substance abuse, and then premarital pregnancy. While the latter two topics are the kinds of issues that often come to mind as secrets, many people may not think of family finances as secretive, yet they obviously are. Of course, even though family finances were mentioned most often, they might not be very emotionally charged secrets. The high percentage of people identifying family finances as their family secret may reflect the fact that those individuals are not holding any family-related information that anyone would consider particularly threatening. Indeed, unless secrets about family finances involve bankruptcy, they may not be highly face threatening. Instead, family finances may be considered "not anyone else's business" and not be disclosed as a way to maintain family privacy. Still, the fact that family finances are such a common secret is worth noting and emphasizes the degree to which we consider financial affairs private.

Negative Consequences of Secrets

Besides examining what topics families keep secret, scholars have studied some of the consequences keeping family secrets have for family and personal well-being, and some of the reasons people maintain these secrets. Research on the consequences of family secrets comes mostly from studies conducted to help professional counselors. Therapists often are asked to assist families in which the communication boundaries created by secrets have negatively impacted family dynamics. As such, the impact of family secrets is particularly relevant for them.

The movie *Very Bad Things* illustrates the potentially devastating effects of secret-keeping, albeit in a humorous and exaggerated manner. The plot concerns how a group of friends tries to keep the accidental murder of two acquaintances secret. As the story unfolds, the anxiety caused by the need to keep the information private becomes so severe, and the relationships among the friends deteriorate so rapidly, that they start murdering one another. A somewhat similar story line can be found in the movie *A Simple Plan,* although this time with more familial involvement. In this case two brothers and their friends are trying to keep secret the discovery of a large sum of money. Again, the anxiety caused by the secret-keeping is so severe that it destroys the various relationships and leads to murder. Indeed, the impact of secret-keeping is a plot underlying many movies, almost all of which imply very negative consequences.

Although murder may be an extreme result of the anxiety caused by secret-keeping, the available research on the familial effects of secret-keeping does suggest that family secrets often influence the family unit in a negative way. In fact, there appear to be at least six ways that secrets harm the family.

Consequence 1: Secrets can create power imbalances. Given that knowledge often is equated with power, family members who know the secrets have power over those who do not (Imber-Black, 1993). This information is likely to make another family member or the entire family vulnerable, and its revelation may be very harmful to that individual or to the family as a whole. As a result, the typical power structure in families, especially as it relates to the traditional power of parents over children, may be irreversibly altered, changing the family dynamics forever (Brown-Smith, 1998). For example, imagine a child having information about a parent's adulterous affair and essentially holding that parent hostage with that information. Any disciplinary power that the parent has over that child is undermined by the fear that the secret will be disclosed.

Consequence 2: Secrets create stress and lead to unpleasant interaction. Maintaining a family secret will likely increase anxiety during family interactions, making such interactions unpleasant and counterproductive (Brown-Smith, 1998). This increased anxiety may be caused by (1) fear that the secret will be disclosed, (2) efforts to avoid topics remotely related to the secret, or (3) the shame and guilt associated with the secret. Anxiety is especially likely to result if the secret involves other members of the family. For example, two brothers who recently vandalized school property and are keeping the incident secret from their parents may experience considerable anxiety when the family sits together at the dinner table. First, each may be fearful that the other will disclose the episode. As noted before, boundary coordination becomes increasingly difficult if the secret is shared by more than one person. Second, any topic related to school may spark an anxious reaction and will likely be avoided, making for awkward family interactions. Finally, the brothers may experience a high degree of guilt that significantly increases their overall level of anxiety. And the situation will be even worse if the brothers are constantly reminded of the incident by each other's presence.

Consequence 3: Secrets encourage concealment of relational problems. Often, hiding a secret from others requires the secret-keepers to put on an "air" that everything is fine and that the secret-keepers share a happy relationship. This pretense can cause relational stress (Karpel, 1980). In the movie *Very Bad*

Things, one of the friends who took part in the murders is getting married, and with his friends he has to attend his rehearsal dinner. Not only does the groom have to appear calm, but he and his friends also have to act as if they are enjoying their time together—an impression that is difficult to project given the anger they are experiencing toward one another. In perhaps a more sobering example, children who are the victims of sexual abuse by a parent often feel pressure to act happy with that parent when in the presence of other family members. Obviously, the effort it takes to project these *fake* feelings hinders development of healthy familial relationships.

Consequence 4: Secrets encourage deception.   The need to keep secrets often results in the spinning of lies to cover up the information. The consequence often is a web of deception that must be continuously tended. Another movie example helps illustrate how easily secrets and lies can spin out of control. In the comedy *Don't Tell Mom the Babysitter Is Dead,* a teenage girl named Sue Ellen and her younger brother are left to fend for themselves when their mother goes on an extended trip, their babysitter dies, and they run out of money. Sue Ellen poses as a woman in her mid-20s and submits a fake resume (which she copied from a book) to a fashion firm, where she lands a job. Throughout the movie Sue Ellen and her brother try to keep the secret that she is really only a high school student. To avoid being discovered, she repeatedly has to lie. She tells her boss and coworkers that her brother is her son, creates a fictional ex-husband, and lies to a potential teenage boyfriend about what she does during the day. Eventually her lies are uncovered, but to her surprise and delight, almost everyone is understanding and forgiving. In real life, however, deception does not always have a happy ending. In fact, deception is often perceived to be a serious relational transgression that erodes trust (see Chapter 13).

Consequence 5: Secrets change communication by decreasing breadth.   The communication boundaries necessitated by secret-keeping often shape the entire terrain of the communication landscape. In other words, the desire to keep certain information secret shapes much of what is and is not acceptable to discuss. Topics become off limits for discussion because of their proximity to the secret. For example, if a couple is secretly being treated for infertility, they might avoid discussing topics related to children and pregnancy with family members who could question them and possibly uncover their secret. Besides creating anxiety, this shaping of acceptable topics for discussion can impact the normal functioning of family relationships by restricting the breadth of self-disclosure, especially if multiple secrets are being kept. As discussed in Chapter 5, breadth refers to the variety of topics that people feel free to discuss. Given the importance of disclosure for relational growth, excessive topic avoidance, motivated by the desire to keep certain information secret, will undoubtedly harm the family relationships.

Consequence 6: Secrets can lead to patterns of "split loyalty."   Finally, secrets often create what Karpel (1980) called a "split loyalty pattern." Secret-keepers are often put in a bind of having to choose between being loyal to other secret-holders or being loyal to friends or family members who may be hurt by not knowing the secret. For example, a son may be torn between wanting to keep his mother's sexual affair secret and to disclose the information to his father. Such split loyalties can also occur outside the family. For example, if you know that your best friend, Chris, is a recovering alcoholic, and another friend of yours, Katelyn, is going to drive with Chris to and from a party, you might have to decide whether to warn Katelyn about Chris's past drinking problem. Should you help maintain Chris's positive identity by keeping the alcoholism secret, or should you protect Katelyn by giving her information that might help her determine whether it is safe to drive with Chris? These split loyalties can create lose-lose situations, ruin relational dynamics, tear families apart, and destroy friendships.

Positive Functions of Secrets

The negative effects of family secrets are most relevant to intrafamily secrets. Whole-family secrets, by contrast, may be immune to some of the effects because the secret is known to all family members. As a result, the familial power structure will likely remain stable, anxiety levels within the family will likely not be high, and some of the other negative effects may dissipate. The same could be said for friendship groups. As long as everyone in the group knows the information, secret-keeping is not very problematic. Indeed, research by Vangelisti (1994) and Vangelisti and Caughlin (1997) seems to support this conclusion. Students in these studies reported that the existence of family-wide secrets often improved relationships, perhaps by creating a special bond between members who were trusted to keep secrets. Thus, secret-keeping can sometimes be beneficial rather than harmful to relationships.

The studies by Vangelisti suggest that family members keep secrets for at least five different reasons. Most of these motivations stem from a desire to maintain family connections or protect the family or individual family members from harm. First, secret-keeping can promote bonding by increasing family cohesiveness. Second, secret-keeping can protect people from negative evaluation. In this case a secret is kept as a way to protect the family as a whole, or individuals within the family, from "looking bad." Third, secrets can function to maintain relationships by helping family members avoid stress. For example, talking about a family member's illness with people outside of the family might be stressful, and this additional stress could spill over into the family environment. Fourth, secrets can function to preserve privacy. This motivation is fueled by the belief that the secret represents private information that is not relevant to outsiders, thereby motivating family members to keep the secret. For example, if you think that the amount of money your family has in the bank is no one's business but your family's, you are not likely to divulge this information to anyone. Finally, people keep secrets as a matter of defense. Specifically, people are motivated to defend the family or its members from malicious uses of information. For example, another reason for keeping a family's bank balance a secret is to protect the family from requests to borrow money.

As these five motivations illustrate, family members keep secrets for reasons ranging from a desire to maintain the family bond to a desire to protect the family from harm—hardly the sort of negative image that people often associate with the maintenance of family secrets. In fact, much as research has linked identity management to topic avoidance, Vangelisti (1994) found that the most common reason given for keeping a family secret is to protect the family from negative evaluation by others. This desire to protect the family's image accounted for approximately 40% of the reasons that individuals gave for maintaining family secrets. Perhaps more important, the students in Vangelisti's (1994) study reported that they kept secrets as a way to benefit another person or other people, regardless of whether the secrets were whole-family secrets, intrafamily secrets, or individual secrets. So, at least in Vangelisti's study, participants believed that family secrets were kept for good reasons. Of course, the fact that family members feel that they are keeping a secret for a good reason does not preclude them from also believing that secret-keeping is hurting family relationships. In other words, family members may decide to keep the father's past illegal activity a secret from others because its revelation would harm the father's image, but they may also be fully aware that the secret is creating strain on the family's relationship with others.

In sum, the research on family secrets suggests that secret-keeping can have both positive and negative consequences for relationships. Several studies have shown that families that keep a secret are often more cohesive than those that do not (for a review see Brown-Smith, 1998; Vangelisti & Caughlin, 1997). But other studies have shown that family satisfaction and trust decreases as the number of secrets being held in a family increases (Afifi, 2000; Vangelisti & Caughlin, 1997). The positive or negative effects of family secrets depend heavily on features related to the actual information being kept secret and the complexity of the boundary coordination. In families whose cohesiveness increases with the maintenance of a secret, the secret serves as a bond that ties the family together and reinforces family members' ability to work together toward a mutual goal—keeping the information secret. Family members may also be pleasantly surprised by the ability of certain family members to keep quiet about private information (such as a pending move) and develop newfound respect for them. However, if the secret information is negative and causes stress within the family, trust and satisfaction are likely to decrease. In addition, whole-family secrets may be associated with cohesion, whereas intrafamily and individual secrets may be associated with stress and dissatisfaction.

Thought Suppression and Hyperaccessibility

The mixed effects found within families are also evident in research on secret-keeping outside the family context. Wegner and his colleagues have conducted several interesting studies on the effects of secret-keeping on individuals (for a review see Wegner, 1989, 1992). Wegner focused on how keeping information secret influences people's thought patterns. More specifically, he was interested in how the desire to suppress certain thoughts affects people. Because secrets require people to avoid disclosing information to others, people often try to suppress the information and thoughts related to that secret. The reasoning here is that, if people suppress thoughts about a secret, they will be less likely to disclose secret information because it will not be "on their minds." However, thought suppression is not usually successful, and it can even backfire. The strong impact of thought suppression can be illustrated by a simple example: DO NOT THINK OF PINK ELEPHANTS. Now that you have been asked not  to think about pink elephants, you will probably have pink elephants on your mind as you read this section. The simple request that people suppress a thought about a particular thing, regardless of how innocent the request or how irrelevant the thing, has been shown to increase their thinking about it. In fact, that information is often *all* they can think about! For example, in the first of Wegner's studies to examine the effect of thought suppression, Wegner, Schneider, Carter, and White (1987) asked students not to think of a white bear and then had them ring a bell every time they thought of the bear. Rather than suppress the thought of the white bear, a completely irrelevant piece of information and a harmless request, the students, on average, thought of the bear more than once per minute over a 5-minute period. Several subsequent studies not only have confirmed this finding but have shown the reverse effects of thought suppression to be even stronger than initially thought. The conclusion from these studies is that suppressed information, of which secrets are one type, produce **hyperaccessibility** of the thought (see Wegner, 1992). In other words, the desire to suppress the thought does the exact opposite, bringing it to the forefront of our thoughts and thus making it "hyperaccessible."

Studies of secret relationships and crushes also show that information people are trying to suppress can be hyperaccessible. For instance, if Rachel has a crush on her best friend's boyfriend, Justin, she might want to keep her feelings secret. Yet the more she tries to forget about her feelings for Justin, the more he will be in her thoughts. Moreover, attempts at suppressing thoughts and the resulting hyperaccessibility of those thoughts seem to influence people's attraction to others. Wegner, Lane, and Dimitri (1994) conducted several studies to test the effect of secrecy on obsessive thinking. They predicted that secret relationships would be the subject of obsessive thoughts precisely because people try to keep them secret. In their first study the researchers asked people to identify up to five of their past "significant relationships" and to rate them on several aspects, including how secretive each relationship was and how much they still thought about each relational partner. Their results showed that people were more preoccupied with secret relationships than with relationships that were out in the open; that is, secret relationships were *still* invading their thoughts much more than were relationships that had no secret aspects to them.

In another study by Wegner et al. (1994), four unacquainted students reported to a research laboratory. The researchers paired them into two cross-sex teams, sat the members of the two teams around a table, and had them play a card game. Unbeknownst to Team B, the members of Team A (a randomly selected pair of male-female strangers) had previously been told to get an edge in the game by keeping their feet in contact under the table at all times, as a signaling device. They had then been instructed either to keep that tactic a secret from Team B or to tell Team B what they were doing. After the 10-minute game was completed, Team A members rated their attraction to each other. Consistent with what Wegner et al. had predicted, those who kept their foot contact secret were more attracted to their card-playing partner than were those who did not, despite everything else being equal. Thus, people who hold secrets may feel more connected and more attracted to one another than those who do not. This finding may partly explain the initial success but frequent eventual failure of secret office romances. The secrecy "fans the flames of desire." The coworkers find themselves always thinking about each other, and their attraction to one another increases. But once they decide to "come out" with the information about their relationship, and the relationship is no longer secret, they suddenly find that they are not thinking about each other as much, and their attraction dissipates.

Studies have also examined *why* thought suppression leads to hyperaccessibility. Imagine that Dylan is trying to keep his romantic relationship with a coworker secret. Wegner (1992) described the resultant cognition along these lines: First, Dylan plans to distract himself from thoughts about the relationship so that he will not think about it at work (attempts at thought suppression). Next, he tries to think of something else, such as the project that is due next week. So he starts thinking in earnest about the project, but soon thoughts about his partner pop in his head—perhaps about how the project will take time away from that relationship. Dylan continues to think about the relationship for a while. Even though he is trying to suppress it, it is hard to get it out of his head, so he shifts tactics and tries to think about something else, such as his mother's birthday party next week. But whatever Dylan thinks about, the same cycle kicks in, as he thinks about how he wishes he could bring his romantic partner to his mother's party. In sum, he keeps going back to the thought he is trying to ignore.

This cycle occurs because two cognitive processes kick in as soon as you try to suppress information (Wegner & Erber, 1992). The first process is a **controlled distracter search.** This process is a conscious attempt to search for thoughts that will distract you from the thought you want to suppress. Your mind scours for things to distract you from that thought, but at the same time your mind is going into a protective mode, unconsciously scanning your thoughts for any sign of that unwanted thought. This process is called the **automatic target search.** Paradoxically, that unconscious search to zap the unwanted thought out of your mind actually impels your mind to find it, and the thought intrudes into the distracter search, making you think of it.

But is this hyperaccessibility permanent? Don't those thoughts eventually fade? According to Wegner et al. (1987), the hyperaccessibility of the suppressed thought does minimize over time if you remove yourself from contact with the relevant information or secret. But the thoughts come back with a vengeance at first contact with anything that reminds you of the information or secret. For example, children who are sexually abused may eventually stop thinking about the "secret" if they are separated from the abusing parent for long enough, but the thoughts will come flooding back as soon as the possibility of a reunion with the parent is mentioned.

This "rebound" effect may also make it difficult for infidelity to remain a secret in relationships. The unfaithful person may be away from her or his partner at work long enough to successfully suppress the thought of infidelity, but seeing the partner or lover will immediately serve as a reminder of the thought that he or she is trying to suppress. The hyperaccessibility of the thought will then make it difficult for the unfaithful person to keep the infidelity a secret. As a result of repeatedly thinking about the affair, the unfaithful person may also experience more guilt about the affair and/or anxiety about being caught.

These effects can be explained by the fever model of self-disclosure (Stiles, 1987; Stiles, Shuster, & Harrigan, 1992). According to this model, people who are distressed about a problem or who think about a problem a lot are much more likely to reveal thoughts and feelings about the problem than are those who are not experiencing as much anxiety about an issue. In sum, if given the opportunity, people who are feeling highly anxious about something are likely to disclose a lot more about it than people who are not. This model, when combined with Wegner's research on the hyperaccessibility of secrets, may explain why people often reveal secrets to others. Their hyperaccessibility (especially during times when the secret information is "rebounding") makes the level of stress and anxiety so high that individuals have to find an outlet. The result frequently is the selection of someone they consider to be a confidant.

Revealing Secrets

In addition to hyperaccessibility, Derlega and Grzelak (1979) noted five other reasons people eventually reveal private information: (1) to achieve catharsis, (2) to clarify their own interpretation of events, (3) to get validation from others that they are still a good person, (4) to make the relationship closer, or (5) to control others. Each of these reasons has very different consequences—positive and negative.

Positive Consequences of Revealing Secrets   Although it is impossible to say with certainty when someone should or should not disclose a secret, Kelly and McKillop (1996) made several recommendations for when to do so. Their review of the relevant research led them to identify three reasons people might want to consider revealing secrets. Specifically, they suggested that disclosing a secret might have positive consequences if it: (1) reduces psychological and/or physical problems, (2) helps deter hyperaccessibility, and/or (3) leads to resolution of secrets.

First, there is considerable evidence that secret-keeping is stressful and wears on secret-keepers, both psychologically and physiologically (see Pennebaker, 1990). For example, Spiegel (1992) has found that individuals with life-threatening illnesses who reveal private information in therapy sessions have a longer life expectancy than those who do not. Pennebaker's research on social support also suggests that the mere act of disclosing distressful information can make people feel better.

Second, as noted previously, keeping information secret makes secrets especially salient. As Wegner et al. (1994) put it, "The secret must be remembered, or it might be told. And the secret cannot be thought about, or it might be leaked" (p. 288), thus creating the two conflicting cognitive processes discussed earlier. Disclosing the secret frees the secret-keeper from having to suppress it and makes it no longer hyperaccessible, thereby decreasing anxiety.

Third, without disclosing the secret, secret-keepers cannot work toward a resolution. Sharing the information with others may provide the individual with insight into the secret and allow her or him to regain a much-needed sense of control over life events (see Pennebaker, 1990). The secret-keeper often has an unbalanced view of the situation and may benefit from the perspective of the recipient of the disclosure. For example, Silver, Boone, and Stones (1983) found that female victims of incest who were able to reveal the secret to a confidant were much more likely to feel better about themselves and their lives than those who were unable to do so.

Negative Consequences of Revealing Secrets   These positive consequences of revealing a secret should be weighed against three possible negative consequences. Specifically, Kelly and McKillop (1996) suggested that people might consider keeping a secret if revelation would (1) elicit a negative reaction from the listener or (2) help a person maintain a privacy boundary; and Petronio (1991) suggested that people might decide to keep secrets if revealing private information (3) would be seen as a betrayal by others.

First, given the typically negative nature of secrets, there is always a possibility that the recipient of the information will react with disapproval or shun the discloser. In fact, Lazarus (1985) reported that confidants often distance themselves following the disclosure of a secret. And Coates, Wortman, and Abbey (1979) showed that people who disclose secret problems to others are considered less attractive than those who suppress such disclosure. When people have kept negative information to themselves as a way to manage their identities, they are especially likely to put stock in the listener's reaction when they finally reveal the secret. Disconfirming reactions may worsen what is likely an already diminished sense of self.

Work on disclosure of abuse makes this point especially well. Dieckman (2000) interviewed female victims about their decision to tell others about their abuse. Her interviews highlighted the difficulty associated with disclosure and the importance of the response. Victims of abuse often are hesitant to tell others about their experience because they fear being perceived as "weak" or being ridiculed for staying in the relationship. Indeed, Crocker and Schwartz (1985) found that many people responded to disclosures of abuse by telling the discloser that they "would never put up with that kind of treatment" and asking them why they "didn't just leave." Since victims typically disclose past abuse for the purpose of self-expression or validation, responses like those noted by Crocker and Schwartz can diminish the discloser's ability to cope with the situation. Rather than helping disclosers, such responses often lower their self-esteem and discourage future disclosure. Their already low sense of self falls even lower because the response they feared the most—ridicule—is the response they received. Worse yet, the discloser might decide to keep the information secret once again, rather than risking more ridicule. As this example illustrates, the listener's response to sensitive self-disclosure is of paramount importance. (See Chapter 10 for specific information on how you can give effective social support to others.)

Second, preserving personal boundaries is critical to people's identities. Indeed, it is the essence of the communication boundary management theory discussed in this chapter. To the extent that secrets make up part of the personal boundaries of individuals, secret-keeping may help people maintain a sense of independence. Some scholars have even argued that secret-keeping serves a developmental function by helping people manage their personal identity (Hoyt, 1978). By contrast, revealing the secret erodes the personal boundaries being tightly held by the secret-keeper. In a related vein, keeping secrets greatly increases a person's control over the information. By contrast, the decision to disclose a secret requires boundary coordination and leaves the individual vulnerable to betrayal of confidences. The information is no longer solely the person's own, and he or she has less control over how the information is spread.

Third, sometimes secrets are shared between two or more people, and revealing the secret to someone outside the dyad or group will be seen as a betrayal. Indeed, research reported in Chapter 13 suggests that betraying confidences is one of the most common relational transgressions in friendships, romantic relationships, and family relationships. If a confidence has been betrayed, revealing a secret often has a significant cost. Trust is eroded, and future self-disclosures from the person who feels betrayed are less likely. As such, another negative consequence of revealing secrets may be severe sanctions by other secret-keepers. To ensure that a member of a group of secret-keepers is not tempted to disclose the secret, groups will often make explicit boundary rules or threaten individuals with severe penalties for revealing the secret (Petronio, 1991).

The diversity of potential positive and negative consequences make it difficult to determine when to disclose a secret and when not to do so. Kelly and McKillop (1996) developed a decision-making model for revealing secrets that takes into account the primary consequences associated with the revelation of individually held secrets; Figure 12.1 shows the model. In a similar vein, Petronio (1991) noted that the answers to five questions typically determine what people will disclose and to whom they will disclose it: (1) How badly do you need to reveal the information? (2) What do you think will be the outcome of the disclosure? (3) How risky will it be to tell someone the information? (4) How private is the information? and (5) How much control do you have over your emotions? These questions reflect a variety of issues raised in this chapter, as well as capturing the essence of Kelly and McKillop's model. Clearly, then, issues of anxiety, hyperaccessibility, and informational control play a key

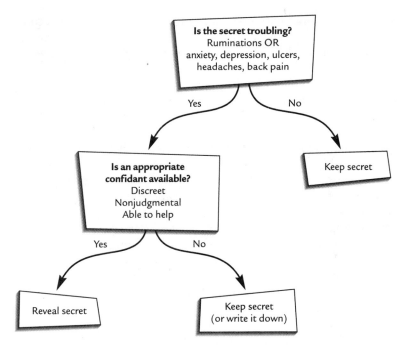

FIGURE 12.1 Decision-Making Model for Revealing Secrets
Source: Kelly and McKillop (1996).

role in determining whether the revelation of secrets is likely to produce positive or negative outcomes.

Conclusion

In this chapter we reviewed many studies showing the impact of privacy boundaries on our relationships and day-to-day lives. By contrast, Chapter 5 highlighted the many ways in which privacy loss through self-disclosure affects our relationships. Together, these chapters provide a peek into the dialectical struggles between openness and closedness that shape our lives. People need both privacy and expression. Managing privacy boundaries to accommodate both of these needs is a delicate process.

This process can be even more delicate and complex in the context of close personal relationships, because many people subscribe to an ideology of intimacy. In other words, many people think that openness is the hallmark of close relationships and that any attempts to maintain privacy will hinder the development and maintenance of intimacy. The research in this chapter, however, paints a very different picture. Individuals need privacy as well as connection. Relational partners who are always together and constantly sharing every bit of information with each other may lose their individual identities and become engulfed by the relationship. Thus, the hallmark of satisfying relationships may be the maintenance of individual identities in the midst of a close, connected relationship.

Discussion Questions

1. In this chapter we discussed several studies suggesting that most close relational partners consider certain topics to be "taboo" and keep certain secrets from each other. Based on your personal experiences, do you agree or disagree? What types of topics are taboo in your relationships?
2. On television and in the news, we often hear about cases involving obsessive relational intrusion and/or stalking. Have you or people you have known ever experienced this problem? What strategies might you use to stop such behavior?
3. How hard is it for you to keep a secret? Do you agree with the idea that attempts to suppress thoughts about it actually make it harder to keep the secret?

Relational Transgressions

Hurting the Ones We Love

Close your eyes for a moment and imagine what ideal relationships with romantic partners, friends, and family would be like. When you thought about your ideal romantic relationship, did you envision bright, sunny days filled with picnics by the lake or long walks hand in hand on the beach? When you thought about your ideal family relationships, did you envision "perfect" parents who would always give you the "right" advice and unconditional emotional and financial support? And when you thought about the ideal friend, did you envision someone who would always be loyal and would drop everything to be by your side in times of need? These types of idealized images are perpetuated in the media, romance novels, and fairy tales, but they are seldom seen in real life.

In the real world, even the closest and happiest relationships contain some "dark" and challenging moments. The romantic partner you love may stop packing the picnic basket and start spending less time with you and more time at work. Your parents may be unsupportive of your romantic relationship or career. Or your best friend may seem to have forgotten you after meeting a new love interest. Increasingly, relationship researchers have begun focusing on issues such as these, which represent part of the "dark side" of relationships (Cupach & Spitzberg, 1994; Spitzberg & Cupach, 1998). In this chapter we focus on one particular part of this dark side: relationship transgressions. In Chapter 14 we focus on another element of the dark side: conflict.

Relational transgressions occur when people violate implicit or explicit relational rules (Metts, 1994). In other words, people have expectations for how a "good" romantic partner, close friend, or family member should act. For example, many people believe that romantic partners should be sexually and emotionally faithful. Many people also expect their romantic partners and friends to be honest with them, and to protect them by keeping secrets. When people violate these standards of faithfulness, loyalty, and honesty, a relational transgression has occurred. In this chapter we examine three of the top issues associated with relational transgressions: infidelity, jealousy, and deception. We then discuss how people deal with relational transgressions through forgiveness and remedial behavior. We begin, however, with a more specific description of relational transgressions in general.

The Nature of Relational Transgressions

Relational transgressions are hurtful. As Dowrick (1999) put it, "It is one of life's most terrible ironies that betrayal can be as connective as love. It can fill your mind and color your senses. It can keep you tied to a person or to events as tightly as if you were bound, back to back—or worse, heart to heart. The person you want to think of least may become the person you think of constantly" (p. 46). Metts (1991) surveyed college students regarding what types of behaviors and attitudes they considered to be relational transgressions in their romantic relationships. The top three transgressions were (1) having sex with someone else, (2) wanting to or actually dating others, and (3) deceiving others. Similarly, Roscoe, Cavanaugh, and Kennedy (1988) asked undergraduates to describe unfaithful behaviors in dating relationships. The majority of these students (56.9%) saw dating or spending time with another person as an unfaithful act. Sexual intercourse with someone else (41.9%), sexual interactions that included behaviors such as flirting with or kissing someone else (39.8%), keeping secrets from the partner (17.1%), becoming emotionally involved with someone else (10.2%), and betraying the partner's confidence (3.3%) were also seen as unfaithful acts by some of the participants. A study by Jones and Burdette (1994) on acts of betrayal yielded similar results, with participants identifying extramartial affairs, lies, betrayed confidences, and two-timing as primary types of betrayal.

As these studies suggest, unfaithfulness, disloyalty, and/or dishonesty are at the heart of many relational transgressions. Indeed, Metts (1994) argued that the prototypical relational transgression involves some kind of third-party involvement, such as becoming sexually or emotionally involved with someone else, betraying a confidence, or being too jealous or possessive. Dishonesty is also commonly seen as a transgression (Jones & Burdette, 1994; Metts, 1994; Roscoe et al., 1988). In short, most people expect their relational partners to be loyal and honest. When they are not, a rule has been violated and a transgression has occurred.

Transgressions often have negative consequences for relationships. In Jones and Burdette's (1994) study, 93% of people who had been betrayed by their partners said that their relationships had been harmed as a result of the transgression. Davis and Todd (1985) found that individuals who reported relational violations in their friendships felt less acceptance of, respect for, and trust in their friends. Similarly, Wiseman (1986) argued that, after people are betrayed by a friend, they often recast the friend's entire personality to frame her or him in a more negative light.

Infidelity

Of the various types of betrayal discussed here, infidelity often is perceived as the most hurtful. In fact, in romantic relationships the prototypical transgression involves both sexual and emotional infidelity. **Sexual infidelity** refers to "sexual activity with someone other than one's long-term partner" (Shackelford & Buss, 1997, p. 1035). In its most extreme form sexual infidelity involves having sexual intercourse, but other extradyadic sexual activity, such as kissing and petting, also qualifies as forms of sexual infidelity. Although most people in the United States disapprove of sexual infidelity (Weinbach, 1989; Weis & Slosnerick, 1981), several studies have indicated that extradyadic affairs are fairly common (see, for example, Thompson, 1984). Gass and Nichols (1988) estimated that nearly 7 out of 10 husbands and 5 out of 10 wives have at least one sexual extramarital relationship at some point during their marriages. Extradyadic sexual activity ranging from intercourse to kissing also appears to be common in serious dating relationships. In Hansen's (1987) research, 70.9% of men and 57.4% of women reported engaging in some type of sexual activity outside their current dating relationships.

When sexual infidelity is coupled with emotional infidelity, it can be particularly devastating. **Emotional infidelity** refers to emotional involvement with another person, which leads one's partner to channel "emotional resources such as romantic love, time, and attention to someone else" (Shackelford & Buss, 1997, p. 1035). Although scholars typically have defined emotional infidelity in the context of romantic relationships, friends may also experience this type of infidelity. For instance, people often feel left out when a good friend goes skiing with a group of coworkers. In this case the friend has taken away valuable resources (such as time spent engaging in fun activities) and given them to other people.

Reasons for Infidelity

Given the prevalence of sexual and emotional infidelity, it is important to ask *why* people engage in acts of infidelity in the first place. Most research in this area has centered on sexual infidelity. As we might expect, dissatisfaction with the current relationship is the most frequently cited reason for sexual infidelity (Hunt, 1974; Sheppard, Nelson, & Andreoli-Mathie, 1995). In fact, in Roscoe et al.'s (1988) study on dating relationships, 43.5% of respondents listed dissatisfaction with the relationship as a force contributing to sexual infidelity, making it the top reason cited. Other research suggests that boredom, or the need for excitement and variety, contributes to infidelity (Johnson, 1972; Wiggins & Lederer, 1984). In Roscoe et al.'s (1988) study, boredom was the second most frequently cited reason for sexual infidelity. Other fairly common reasons for sexual infidelity include wanting to feel attractive or enhance one's self-esteem (Elbaum, 1982; Johnson, 1972; Wiggins & Lederer, 1984), trying to get revenge after experiencing jealousy or anger (Greene, Lee, & Lustig, 1974; Johnson, 1972;

Roscoe et al., 1988), and being sexually incompatible with the primary partner (Buunk, 1980; Roscoe et al., 1988).

Although research has examined the causes of emotional infidelity only indirectly, there are hints in the literature as to what precipitates this type of extradyadic involvement. For example, in the family literature research suggests that when a baby enters a family the baby's father and siblings may become jealous of the attention that the new family member receives from the mother. As Dunn and Kendrick (1982) reported, mothers spend significantly less time communicating with first-born children after a second child arrives. Similarly, people often report feeling jealous when a friend starts spending less time with them and more time with a new friend or romantic partner. In both cases the transfer of time and attention to someone else leads to a form of emotional infidelity. Thus, one cause of emotional infidelity might be competition from others for a person's time and energy. When people are dissatisfied with the communication and support they receive in their current relationships, they may also turn to someone else for comfort and emotional involvement, leading to emotional infidelity.

Behavioral Cues to Infidelity

While any of the reasons just given might make people worry that their partner could be unfaithful either sexually or emotionally, researchers have uncovered some specific behavioral cues that trigger suspicion about infidelity. In particular, a study by Shackelford and Buss (1997) looked at cues to both sexual and emotional infidelity. In this study undergraduate students were asked to describe the cues that would lead them to suspect that their partners were (1) being sexually unfaithful (sexual infidelity) and (2) falling in love with someone else (emotional infidelity). Fourteen types of behavior were found to trigger suspicion. As can be seen in Box 13.1, some of these cues were associated more with suspicions of sexual infidelity, while others were associated more with suspicions of emotional infidelity. When the partner acted apathetic or referred to and spent more time with another person, people suspected sexual and emotional infidelity about equally.

It is important to note that some of the behaviors that trigger suspicion about infidelity seems to be the opposite of those that people use to maintain their relationships. For instance, apathetic communication involves shutting off communication and spending less time together. As discussed in Chapter 9, self-disclosure, routine talk, and time spent together are key behaviors that help keep a relationship satisfying. Another set of behaviors that triggers suspicion about infidelity—passive rejection—involves acting rude and inconsiderate, which is the opposite of the maintenance strategy of positivity, which focuses on being cheerful, optimistic, and polite around the partner. Another cue to infidelity is reluctance to spend time together, which involves strategies that function to keep social networks separate rather than integrated. As discussed in Chapter 9, integrating social networks is an important part of relational maintenance. Thus, when people feel that their partners are no longer working to

BOX 13.1 HIGHLIGHTS

Cues to Infidelity

Behaviors Leading Primarily to the Suspicion of Sexual Infidelity

Behavior	Definition	Examples
Physical signs of disinterest in sexual exclusivity	You indirectly find out from your partner that she or he has had sex with someone else	Your partner smells like he or she had sex with someone else Your partner suddenly does not want to have sex anymore Your partner says she or he wants to have sex with other people
Revelations of sexual infidelity	You witness or are told directly that your partner is having sex with someone else	You walk in on your partner in bed with someone else Your partner confesses to having an affair Someone says he or she has been having sex with your partner
Changes in routine and sexual behavior	You notice that your partner's actions are different from usual	Your partner's clothing style suddenly changes Your partner starts trying new and unusual positions during sex Your partner sleeps more than normal
Increased sexual interest/ exaggerated displays of affection	You notice that your partner seems more interested in sex and shows more affection than usual, probably as a compensatory strategy	Your partner says "I love you" more than she or he used to Your partner talks about sex more often Your partner starts acting overly affectionate
Sexual disinterest/ boredom	You notice that your partner seems less interested and excited about sex	Your partner acts like he or she is merely "going through the motions" when having sex Your partner seems less sexually aroused Your partner wants to have sex for a shorter duration than normal

Behaviors Leading Primarily to the Suspicion of Emotional Infidelity

Behavior	Definition	Examples
Relationship dissatisfaction/ loss of love	Your partner reveals that she or he is no longer in love with you and wants to pursue other alternatives	Your partner breaks up with you Your partner starts suggesting that you both see other people Your partner says he or she does not love you anymore
Emotional disengagement	Your partner seems to be distancing her- or himself from you emotionally	Your partner starts forgetting special dates like your birthday or anniversary Your partner doesn't say "I love you" as much as he or she usually does Your partner doesn't respond when you say "I love you"

(continued)

Behavior	Definition	Examples
Passive rejection/ inconsiderate behavior	Your partner reveals her or his lack of emotional connection through passive acts rather than direct rejection	Your partner starts acting rude toward you Your partner stops saying "I love you" Your partner is less loving and gentle when having sex with you
Angry, critical, and argumentative communication	Your partner is uncharacteristically angry, critical, or argumentative when with you	Your partner starts looking for reasons to start an argument with you Your partner becomes critical or angry over little things Your partner is less forgiving when you make mistakes
Reluctance to spend time together	Your partner starts to spend less time with you and to separate her or his social network from yours	Your partner doesn't want to go out on dates with you as much as usual Your partner stops inviting you to spend time with her or his friends and family
Reluctance to talk about a certain person	Your partner seems reluctant or nervous to talk about a particular person	Your partner changes the topic when a certain person's name comes up in conversation Your partner acts nervous when a certain person's name is mentioned
Guilty and anxious communication	Your partner acts like he or she has done something wrong	Your partner is unusually forgiving and apologetic Your partner won't look you in the eyes Your partner acts as if she or he feels guilty after engaging in sexual activity with you

Behaviors Leading to the Suspicion of Both Sexual and Emotional Infidelity

Behavior	Definition	Examples
Apathetic communication	Your partner seems to be putting less effort into the relationship	Your partner doesn't disclose or share emotions with you as much as usual Your partner spends less time on her or his physical appearance before seeing you Your partner says he or she is too tired to have sex
Increased contact with and reference to a third party	Your partner seems to be focusing more time and attention on another person	Your partner accidentally calls you by someone else's name Your partner starts spending more time with someone else Your partner starts wearing something belonging to another man or woman

Source: Adapted from Shackelford and Buss (1997).

maintain the relationship, they may suspect this lack of effort is due to emotional or sexual infidelity.

Responses to Infidelity

Now that you have learned about the different types of behavior that trigger suspicions about infidelity, you might wonder how people act once they suspect that their partners are being unfaithful. Buunk's (1995) work on reactions to extradyadic sex gives us at least a partial answer to this question. Buunk found that people generally respond to sexual infidelity in one of three general ways. First, people can use **angry retreat.** Here, individuals who suspect or confirm sexual infidelity might feel so much anger and betrayal that they turn away from their partner emotionally and physically, seek revenge (perhaps by having an affair of their own), or terminate the relationship. Second, people can use **accommodation,** which involves adapting to the situation by expressing loyalty, trying to understand the partner, and perhaps forgiving the partner. Third, people can use an **assertive response,** whereby they seek to protect themselves and voice their feelings and concerns. Examples of assertive responses include demanding that the partner stop seeing other people, having the partner be tested for HIV, asking the partner to wear condoms during intercourse (Buunk & Bakker, 1997), and renegotiating relational rules and boundaries.

Buunk and Bakker (1997) used equity theory to try to determine the conditions under which people might use each of these three behavioral responses to infidelity. According to this study, people were most likely to use angry retreat and/or assertiveness when they were somewhat committed and satisfied but had good alternatives outside the relationship. Additionally, when people thought they might be likely to have an extradyadic affair themselves, they were highly unlikely to use angry retreat. Accommodation, by contrast, was most likely when people were highly committed, highly satisfied, and had made investments in the relationship. The most important of these factors appears to commitment, which makes sense given that people who are highly committed to their relationships are probably the most likely to try to work through relational problems such as infidelity.

Sex Differences in Infidelity

Research has also examined sex differences in reactions to perceived and actual infidelity. A considerable portion of the research in this area takes a social evolutionary perspective (Buss, 1989, 1994). According to this perspective, men and women react to emotional and sexual infidelity differently because they have different priorities related to survival needs. Men should be more worried about sexual infidelity because they are concerned with paternal certainty, whereas women should be more worried about emotional infidelity because they are more concerned with protecting resources (see Chapter 7).

Some research has indirectly supported the ideas behind social evolutionary theory. Studies have found that men show greater psychological and physiological distress when they imagine their partner engaging in sexual infidelity, whereas women display more distress when they imagine their partner engaging in emotional infidelity (Buss, Larsen, Westen, & Semmerlroth, 1992; Wiederman & Allgeier, 1993). Similarly, in studies on whether they would be more upset if their partner was emotionally or sexually unfaithful, men identified sexual infidelity as the most important predictor of jealousy, whereas women identified emotional infidelity (Trost & Alberts, 1998). However, some studies have found that, when people are asked to rate how upset they would be if their partner was sexually versus emotionally involved with someone, both men and women were more upset when sexual intercourse had occurred as opposed to emotional involvement only (Parker, 1994). Men, however, were even more upset than women. Together these studies indicate that the most devastating effects occur when people suspect or confirm *both* sexual and emotional infidelity. However, men may be more upset than women when their partners have emotionally meaningless one-night stands, whereas women may be more upset than men when their partners have an emotionally meaningful but nonsexual relationship with someone else.

There may also be sex differences in how people perceive possible cues to infidelity and how they respond to those cues. In Shackelford and Buss's (1997) study, women were more likely than men to see suspicious behaviors as indicative of infidelity (see Box 13.1). Perhaps this is because American men are somewhat more likely than women to have extradyadic affairs (Sprecher & McKinney, 1993) or because women are better encoders of information than are men (Burgoon, Buller, & Woodall, 1996). Buunk and Bakker's (1997) study also revealed that women might respond to infidelity with angry retreat and assertion more than men. This study did not find a sex difference for accommodation, although other research has shown that women are more likely to forgive men for sexual infidelity than vice versa.

Jealousy

When people suspect or discover infidelity, jealousy is a common reaction. Interestingly, jealousy is often the *result* of a relational transgression such as a partner having an affair or spending extra time with someone else. But jealousy is also seen as a transgression *in its own right* when a partner's suspicions are unwarranted. For example, if Sabrina has been completely faithful to Tyler, but Tyler nonetheless acts possessive and accuses her of seeing other people, she might be upset with his behavior. To Sabrina, Tyler's lack of trust may very well be seen as a relational transgression.

Characteristics of Jealousy

This example highlights an important point about jealousy—that jealousy can be a reaction to an *imagined* threat or to an *actual* threat. There are also different types of jealousy. **Romantic jealousy** occurs when a relational partner worries that a potential rival might interfere with the existence or quality of his or her romantic relationship. As White and Mullen (1989) put it, this perceived threat "is generated by the perception of a real or potential romantic attraction between one's partner and a (perhaps imaginary) rival" (p. 9). **Sexual jealousy** is a particular form of romantic jealousy whereby an individual worries that a rival is having or wants to have sex with her or his partner.

There are also more general forms of jealousy, including jealousy over time or social position. Jealousy over time occurs when people worry that someone or something is taking a relational partner away from them. Friends can experience this type of jealousy. For example, if your best friend starts spending more time with a new friend or romantic partner than with you, you might become jealous. Notice that in this type of situation the quality or quantity of the time you spend with your friend has been threatened by a third party. Similarly, you might feel jealous if your romantic partner starts spending extra time at work. In this case your partner's job, rather than a third party, is interfering with your relationship. The basic premise, however, is similar—someone or something is threatening the quality and/or quantity of time you spend with a person you care about.

Jealousy over social position is a little different. With this type of jealousy you might worry that someone else will replace you as your friend's "best friend." Jealousy over position can also occur in romantic relationships, in families, and in the workplace. For instance, a child might worry that a new baby sister will replace her as "Daddy's little girl" and an employee might worry that the smart young woman who just graduated from Harvard and joined the firm might replace him as "the bright new star" in the company.

Jealousy has also been distinguished from two related constructs: envy and rivalry (Bryson, 1977; Guerrero & Andersen, 1998a; Salovey & Rodin, 1986, 1989). Jealousy occurs when people worry that they might lose something they value, such as a good relationship or high-status position, due to interference from someone. The prototypical jealousy situation involves fearing that someone will "steal" a romantic partner away. Envy, by contrast, occurs when people want something valuable that someone else has. Prototypical envy situations involve feelings of resentment toward someone who seems to have a better life, often because he or she has stronger relationships, is better looking, is intelligent, and talented, or has more stature, money, or possessions. Rivalry occurs when two people are competing for something that neither one of them has. A prime example of rivalry involves siblings who are competing to be seen as "best" in the eyes of their peers, parents, and other adults (Dunn, 1988a, 1988b). Another common example of rivalry is found in organizational settings in which coworkers are competing for promotions. As these examples illustrate and Figure 13.1 shows, jealousy, envy, and rivalry are differentiated by who possesses the desired relationship or commodity.

The following situation is a further example of the differences between jealousy, envy, and rivalry. Jan and Susan are both in love with Craig. Craig recently met Susan at a party and found her attractive, but he has been in a serious dating relationship with Jan for 2 years and wants to marry her. Would

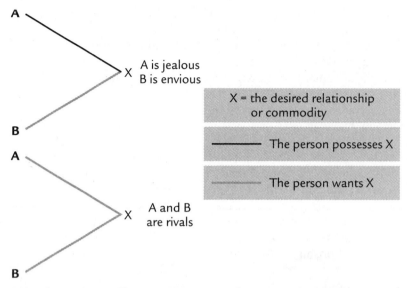

FIGURE 13.1 **Differences Between Jealousy, Envy, and Rivalry Based on Possession of a Desired Relationship or Commodity**

Jan and Susan be experiencing jealousy, envy, or rivalry? According to the definitions given here, if Jan started worrying that Susan could damage her relationship with Craig, she would be jealous. This is because Jan is the one who possesses a relationship with Craig, and so she is the one with something to lose. Susan, for her part, likely would be envious of Jan's relationship with Craig. Since she does not have a relationship with him, she has something to gain. Now let's imagine that Jan perceives Susan to be more intelligent and beautiful than she is. If this was the case, Jan might experience envy as well as jealousy because she would not only worry that Susan could steal Craig away but also might wish that she were as smart and pretty as Susan.

What if Jan and Craig eventually broke up and a new woman, Rochelle, came on the scene to compete with Susan for Craig's affection? In this case Susan and Rochelle probably would experience rivalry because neither has a romantic relationship with Craig yet, but both desire one. Susan and Rochelle also might experience envy if they admire certain characteristics about each other. As this example shows, jealousy, envy, and rivalry often coexist within the same set of relationships. Nonetheless, the remainder of this section will focus specifically on how people experience and express romantic jealousy.

Experiencing Romantic Jealousy

When people perceive a third-party threat to their romantic relationship, they are likely to experience a number of thoughts and emotions. On the cognitive side, jealous individuals typically make appraisals regarding the source and severity of the threat. On the emotional side, jealous individuals tend to experience a cluster of jealousy-related emotions.

Jealous Thoughts   White and Mullen (1989) described primary and secondary cognitive appraisals that tend to occur as jealous feelings develop. **Primary appraisals** involve general evaluations about the existence and quality of a rival relationship, including how much of a threat the third party is. At this stage people ask themselves questions such as, "Is my partner really seeing someone else?" "Does my partner love this person instead of me?" and "Was it a one-night stand, or is it a long-running affair?" For example, Nathan might notice that his girlfriend, Lily, has been spending more time than usual with her co-worker Ben. Nathan sees how Ben looks at Lily and decides that Ben wants to be more than just friends with her, but he also thinks that nothing has happened between them yet. These judgments help Nathan assess the severity of the threat.

Next, White and Mullen suggested that jealous individuals make secondary appraisals to help them plan coping strategies. **Secondary appraisals** involve more specific evaluations of the jealousy situation, including possible causes and outcomes. White and Mullen described four types of secondary appraisal that people use to gather information and interpret the situation. First, jealous people assess motives. If, for example, you think that your romantic partner is seeing someone else, you might try to determine *why* this is happening. Is your partner bored with you? Is the other person so attractive that your partner could not resist temptation?

Second, jealous people compare themselves to the rival. At this point, for example, you might worry that the rival is a more sensitive and caring person than you are, even though you think that you are better looking and more intelligent. If you perceive that the rival is "better" than you, the level of threat will increase. Conversely, if you perceive that you are better than the rival, the level of threat might decrease, even though your self-esteem might be shaken because your partner is attracted to someone whom you perceive to be rather unappealing.

Third, jealous people evaluate their alternatives. For example, if you are worried that you could lose your partner to a rival, you will start to think about alternatives. Are there other people you would like to date? Would you rather be on your own than in a relationship with someone who is unfaithful? Or do you want to stay with your partner if at all possible? These questions would help prepare you for a possible breakup or reconciliation.

Finally, jealous people assess their potential loss. For example, if the relationship does end due to interference from a rival, how would you feel? Would you be sad and lonely, or would you be glad to get out of a bad relationship before investing too heavily in it?

According to White and Mullen, jealous individuals make these types of appraisals so that they can plan coping strategies and assess outcomes. For example, if you decide that your partner is interested in the rival because he or she is more sensitive and considerate than you, you might compensate by being especially nice and caring. If your partner responds favorably by spending more time with you and less time with the rival, you will likely continue these behaviors. But if your behavior change does not have the desired effect, you are likely to try a different strategy. By contrast, if you decide that you have good alternatives and are not that emotionally attached to your partner anymore, you might terminate the relationship. If you do not miss the partner much after breaking up, you would probably conclude that you made the right decision.

Jealous Emotions   In addition to making various types of cognitive appraisals, jealous individuals usually experience a combination of emotions. The emotions most central to jealousy are probably fear and anger (see Guerrero & Andersen, 1998a, 1998b; Sharpsteen, 1991). People are jealous because they fear losing their relationships, and they are often angry at their partner for betraying them. Sometimes jealous individuals are also angry at the rival, particularly if the rival is someone they know; other times they feel irritated or annoyed but not really angry (Guerrero & Yoshimura, 1999).

Research also suggests that jealousy is initially experienced as a heightened state of arousal (Pines & Aronson, 1983) or a "jealousy flash" (Ellis & Weinstein, 1986). A jealousy flash occurs when a person suddenly perceives a third-party threat, and this threat triggers a strong and immediate physiological response. Jealous individuals experiencing this flash often report feeling flushed, anxious, afraid, angry, and/or confused, with some combination of these occurring in a short time span.

As this research suggests, jealousy is often marked by a variety of emotions beyond fear and anger. Indeed, some scholars have argued that jealousy is a unique emotion because it is connected to a distinctive cluster of emotions (Fitness & Fletcher, 1993; Sharpsteen, 1991). In addition to fear and anger, White and Mullen (1989) listed sadness, guilt, envy, and sexual arousal as emotional components of the jealousy experience. Sadness occurs near the end of some jealousy episodes when people are feeling sad and lonely because a breakup seems inevitable or has recently occurred (Sharpsteen, 1991). Sometimes jealous individuals feel guilty because they wrongly accused their partners of misdeeds; other times they feel guilty because they think that something negative about them caused the partner to become interested in someone else. For example, a jealous husband might think that if he had paid more attention to his wife she might not have been attracted to someone else. As noted previously, envy can be part of the jealousy experience, especially when the rival has certain positive qualities that the jealous person does not possess. Sometimes jealousy leads to increased passion and sexual arousal, because the thought of someone else engaging in sexual activity with one's partner can be highly arousing. Think about how you might feel if you saw someone flirting with your romantic partner. The fact that someone else sees your partner as attractive might make you feel passionate toward her or him.

In addition to passion, some research suggests that jealousy may be related to other positive emotions such as love and appreciation (Guerrero & Andersen,

1998b; Trost & Yoshimura, 1999). Pines (1992) suggested that, when people take their partners for granted, seeing that someone else regards the partner as desirable might make the jealous person appreciate the partner more. Pines also argued that jealousy can lead partners to reexamine their relationship, to feel more passionate and loving toward each other, to become more committed to the relationship, and to work harder to maintain the relationship. Other researchers have argued that jealousy is closely related to love because people would not get jealous if they did not care about their partners. Ciabattari (1988) even suggested that jealousy is born of love, while envy is born of hate and resentment. As Salovey and Rodin (1985) stated, "Jealousy can be a reasonable and healthy emotion. Sometimes the irrational feelings of jealousy can be taken as signs of caring and devotion, rather than as possessiveness and insecurity" (p. 29).

Communicative Responses to Jealousy

Just as jealousy can involve a wide range of thoughts and emotions, so, too, can jealousy be expressed in a diverse assortment of behaviors. Guerrero and her colleagues have conducted several studies to determine the different ways that people communicate when feeling jealous (Guerrero, 1998; Guerrero & Andersen, 1998b; Guerrero, Andersen, Jorgensen, Spitzberg, & Eloy, 1995). These researchers have described 14 communicative responses to jealousy, which are summarized in Box 13.2. The most common responses are negative affect expression, integrative communication, and distributive communication (Guerrero et al., 1995).

Research suggests that people use different communicative responses to jealousy based on their personal and relational goals (Bryson, 1977; Guerrero & Afifi, 1998, 1999). Guerrero and Afifi's work suggests that jealous individuals often have one or more of six goals in mind when communicating their feelings: (1) maintaining the relationship, (2) maintaining or repairing self-esteem, (3) reducing uncertainty about the primary relationship, (4) reducing uncertainty about the rival relationship, (5) retaliating against the partner, and (6) reassessing the relationship. When people want to maintain their relationship, they report using reactions such as integrative communication and compensatory restoration (Guerrero & Afifi, 1998). Jealous individuals also report using integrative communication when they want to reduce uncertainty about the primary relationship, whereas they report using surveillance and rival contacts when trying to reduce uncertainty about the rival relationship (Guerrero & Afifi, 1999). When people wish to maintain their self-esteem, they report denying their jealous feelings to protect their images. A number of different retaliation tactics have also been reported, including manipulation attempts (such as counterjealousy and guilt inductions), distributive communication, and active distancing (see Box 13.2). Finally, although people react in many different ways when they want to reassess their relationships, jealous individuals who have this goal might avoid communicating their jealousy until they have had time to think things through.

BOX 13.2 HIGHLIGHTS

Communicative Responses to Jealousy

Behavior	Definition	Examples
Negative affect expression	Nonverbal expressions of jealousy-related affect that the partner can see	Acting anxious when with the partner and rival Appearing hurt Wearing facial "displeasure" Crying in front of the partner
Integrative communication	Direct, nonaggressive communication about jealousy with the partner	Disclosing jealous feelings to the partner Asking the partner probing questions Trying to reach an understanding with the partner Reassuring the partner that they can "work it out"
Distributive communication	Direct, aggressive communication about jealousy with the partner	Accusing the partner of being unfaithful Being sarcastic or rude toward the partner Arguing with the partner Bringing up the issue over and over again to "bombard" the partner
Active distancing	Indirect, aggressive communication about jealousy with the partner	Giving the partner the "silent treatment" Storming out of the room Giving the partner cold or dirty looks Withdrawing affection and sexual favors
Avoidance/ denial	Indirect, nonaggressive communication that focuses on avoiding the jealousy-invoking issue, situation, or partner	Denying jealous feelings when confronted by the partner Pretending to be unaffected by the situation Decreasing contact with the partner Avoiding jealousy-invoking situations
Violent communication	Threats or actual physical violence against the partner	Threatening to harm the partner if she continues to see the rival Scaring the partner by acting as if he was about to hit her Roughly pulling him away from the rival Pushing or slapping him
Signs of possession	Public relationship displays so people know the partner is "taken"	Putting an arm around the partner and saying "she's taken" Constantly introducing the partner as "my girlfriend" Telling potential rivals that they plan to be married Kissing the partner in front of potential or actual rivals

Behavior	Definition	Examples
Derogating competitors	Negative comments about potential rivals to the partner and to others	"Bad-mouthing" the rival in front of the partner and her friends Telling the partner that the rival was a "ladies man" who would hurt her Expressing disbelief that anyone would be attracted to the rival
Relationship threats	Threats to terminate or de-escalate the primary relationship or to be unfaithful	Threatening to end the relationship if the partner continued to see the rival Threatening infidelity Telling the partner that they should both start dating other people if he continued to do so with others
Surveillance/ restriction	Behavioral strategies designed to find out about or interfere with the rival relationship	Spying or checking up on the partner Looking through the partner's belongings for evidence of a rival relationship Pressing the redial button to see whom the partner phoned last Restricting the partner's access to rivals at parties
Compensatory restoration	Behavior aimed at improving the primary relationship and/or making oneself more desirable to compensate for one's shortcomings	Sending the partner flowers or gifts Keeping the house especially clean and nice Trying to present oneself as "better" than the rival Trying to appear more physically attractive Reading a self-help book on jealousy and love relationships
Manipulation attempts	Moves to induce negative feelings in the partner and/or shift responsibility for communicating about the problem to the partner	Flirting with others to make the partner jealous Inducing guilt Calling the partner's "bluff" by daring him to break up and go off with the rival Bringing the rival's name up in conversation to check for a reaction Asking a friend to talk to the partner about the situation
Rival contacts	Direct communication with the rival about the jealousy situation or rival relationship	Telling the rival to stop seeing the partner Informing the rival that the partner is in another relationship Saying something "mean" to the rival Asking the rival about the relationship without revealing her "identity" as the girlfriend
Violent behavior toward objects	Violence toward objects, either in private or in the presence of others	Slamming doors Breaking dishes Throwing the partner's possessions out of the house Throwing the partner's makeup across the room

Source: Adapted from Guerrero and Andersen (1998b); examples from actual accounts by jealous individuals, as reported in Guerrero et al.'s (1995) qualitative data.

Jealousy and Relational Satisfaction

Although jealousy can be a sign of love and attachment, it can also be both a symptom and a cause of relational distress. In fact, research has shown that jealous thoughts and feelings generally are associated with relational dissatisfaction (Andersen, Eloy, Guerrero, & Spitzberg, 1995; Buunk & Bringle, 1987; Guerrero & Eloy, 1992; Salovey & Rodin, 1989). However, jealousy is experienced in many relationships that remain satisfying. The trick seems to be to manage jealousy in a productive way such that the jealous individual shows care and concern without seeming overly fearful, aggressive, or possessive.

Among the many communicative responses to jealousy listed in Box 13.2, only three appear to be associated with relational satisfaction: integrative communication, negative affect expression, and compensatory restoration. All of the other responses usually make the problem worse, although some studies have shown that manipulation attempts such as the counterjealousy induction can be effective under certain circumstances (Buss, 1988a). Integrative communication involves talking about jealousy in a constructive manner, often by disclosing feelings and renegotiating relational rules and boundaries. Rusbult and Buunk (1993) suggested that this type of communication is critical for maintaining relationships after jealousy is felt. Similarly, Afifi and Reichert (1996) found a positive association between integrative communication and relational satisfaction.

Negative affect expression may also be an effective way to communicate about jealousy, but only if it is used in conjunction with integrative communication. Andersen et al. (1995) found that jealous individuals reported the most relational satisfaction when they used *both* integrative communication and negative affect expression. Integrative communication alone was not as effective as this combination, and negative affect expression could actually *reduce* relationship satisfaction when used alone or with other strategies. Andersen and his colleagues concluded that people who engage in constructive communication about jealousy while expressing their emotions openly and honestly probably come across as sincerely hurt yet rational and in control. Furthermore, the honest expression of negative emotion may cause the partner to feel empathy for the jealous individual, which could lead to positive outcomes.

In some cases compensatory restoration may also be associated with relational satisfaction. Individuals who try to improve themselves and their relationships may become more desirable to their partners. Indeed, Buss (1988a) reported that strategies such as demonstrating love and caring for one's partner were highly effective in keeping couples together after jealousy had occurred. However, it is important to recognize that too much compensatory restoration can make a person seem desperate and overly eager to please, which can have detrimental effects on the relationship. As Guerrero (1998) put it, "When used too dramatically, compensatory restoration behaviors may be viewed as desperate attempts to win back the partner, and these attempts could cause the partner to feel engulfed and retreat" (p. 23).

The partner of the jealous person can also use certain types of communication to improve the situation (Andersen, Spitzberg, & Guerrero, 2000). Sometimes the jealous person has nothing to worry about, because the partner has been faithful and is not interested in anyone else. If this is the case, the partner can reassure the jealous person by expressing love and commitment. The partner might also calmly explain and/or justify any actions that led the partner to feel jealous. If some of the actions were inconsiderate (perhaps the partner spent most of the night talking to someone else at a party they went to together), the partner might apologize. But if the partner thinks that the jealous person is overreacting or being overly possessive, he or she might try to renegotiate relational boundaries while reassuring the partner.

Other times the partner has indeed been unfaithful and/or been attracted to someone else. If this is the case, the partner should be honest with the jealous person while trying not to hurt her or him further. If the partner wants to maintain the relationship, apologizing and asking for forgiveness or renegotiating relational boundaries may be appropriate. Andersen et al. (2000) listed nine integrative behaviors that both partners can use to communicate about jealousy effectively:

1. **Emotional disclosure:** calming telling your partner that you are angry, upset with, or hurt by her or his actions

2. **Questioning:** calmly asking your partner if your jealous emotions are justified, or asking the jealous person what caused her or him to feel this way

3. **Confrontation and explanation:** in a nonthreatening fashion, telling your partner why you feel the way you do or why you behaved in a certain way

4. **Open discussion:** talking with your partner to come to an understanding about jealous feelings and behavior, as well as issues of trust and possessiveness

5. **Reassurance:** comforting your partner by offering assurances that she or he has no basis for feeling jealous

6. **Humor:** joking about the jealousy-evoking situation to relieve tension (although this strategy usually is effective only when used by the jealous person)

7. **Relationship talk:** getting your partner to describe and disclose her or his jealous thoughts and feelings, as well as renegotiating relational rules and boundaries, such as issues of exclusivity

8. **Apology:** apologizing for unfounded jealous feelings or jealousy-inducing behaviors, and possibly asking for forgiveness

9. **Concession:** agreeing with or validating your partner's feelings and observations, and possibly admitting blame

Sex Differences in Jealousy

Both men and women get jealous, but there seem to be subtle differences in *why* they get jealous, how they *feel* when they are jealous, and how they *communicate* their jealous feelings. As discussed earlier in this chapter, both men and women tend to become jealous and upset when their partners have been sexually unfaithful, but men seem to get even more upset than women. Conversely women seem to get more jealous than men when their partners have been emotionally (but not sexually) unfaithful.

Research findings on sex differences in jealousy situations are mixed, but some studies suggest that women experience more sadness, anxiety, and confusion than men, perhaps because they blame themselves for the situation more often (Bryson, 1976). Women may also feel a stronger sense of betrayal than men. By contrast, men have been found to deny jealous feelings and to focus on bolstering their self-esteem more than women (Buunk, 1982; White, 1981). These differences are small, but they suggest that women are somewhat more focused on the relationship, whereas men are more focused on individual concerns.

Sex differences in communicative responses to jealousy are more consistent, although these differences also are relatively small. Jealous women report using integrative communication, expressing negative affect, enhancing their appearance, and using counterjealousy inductions more often than do jealous men (Buss, 1988a; Guerrero & Reiter, 1998). As White and Mullen (1989) concluded, jealous women are "more oriented toward solving relationship problems or directly expressing their emotions" than are men (p. 129). For their part, jealous men are more likely to contact the rival, restrict the partner's access to potential rivals, and give gifts and spend extra money on the partner than are jealous women (Guerrero & Reiter, 1998). Buss (1988a) explained these findings by suggesting that from an evolutionary perspective men are likely to "guard" their mates by restricting their access to other males. Buss also suggested that jealous men give gifts and money as a way of showing that they have more valuable resources than do rivals. Some research also suggests that jealous men engage in dangerous behaviors, such as getting drunk or engaging in promiscuous sex with others, more often than do jealous women (see White & Mullen, 1989).

Deception

Like jealousy, deception is a primary relational transgression that often leads to feelings of betrayal and distrust (O'Hair & Cody, 1994). Deception also violates both relational and conversational rules. Research suggests that most people expect friends and loved ones, as well as strangers, to be truthful most of the time. In fact, McCornack (1992) argued that expecting others to be truthful is one of the basic features of conversations (see also Grice, 1989). If people did not accept that most conversations are truthful, talking to others would simply be too difficult and nonproductive. Think about this for a moment: If you were always suspicious and had to question the veracity of every statement you heard, it would be virtually impossible to get to know people.

On a given day, however, it is highly likely that you or someone you are talking to will engage in some form of deception. In fact, in a study conducted by Turner, Edgley, and Olmstead (1975), people were asked to keep a log of their conversations. Remarkably, only one third of these conversations were completely truthful. This does not mean that someone will blatantly lie to you in two out of every three conversations you have. Deception actually includes a variety of statements and nonstatements that serve to distort or omit the truth. Buller and Burgoon (1994) defined **deception** as intentionally managing verbal and/or nonverbal messages so that a target will believe or understand something in a way that the deceiver knows is false. Notice that *intentionality* is part of this definition. For example, if you truly believe that the big basketball game between your college and a rival school starts at 6:00 p.m. when it really starts at 7:00 p.m., it would not be deception if you told your friend the incorrect time. Instead, this type of misinformation might be termed a *mistake.* But when people intentionally mislead others or conceal or misrepresent the truth, deception has occurred.

Types of Deception

Research suggests that there are at least five types of deception: lies, equivocations, concealments, exaggerations, and minimizations. **Lies,** which are also called falsifications or fabrications, involve making up information or giving information that is the opposite of (or at least very different from) the truth (Ekman, 1985). For example, if you are single and someone you do not find attractive approaches you at a bar and asks if you are married, you might say that you are. If the unattractive stranger then asks how long you have been married, you might give more false information by saying something like, "Oh, Pat and I have been married for a couple years now, and we're really happy."

Another form of deception, **equivocation** or evasion (Bavelas, Black, Chovil, & Mullett, 1990; O'Hair & Cody, 1994), involves making an indirect, ambiguous, and perhaps contradictory statement. The prototypical example of equivocation involves people's physical appearance. For instance, suppose your friend asks you if he looks fat after putting on 10 pounds over the winter break. You might answer by saying that most people put on a little weight over the holidays, so it's not a big deal. Notice, however, that you did not really answer the question. Similarly, suppose your friend asks you how her new hairstyle (which you hate) looks. Instead of saying, "You look like a French poodle" (which is what you really think), you might say, "It's the latest style." Again, you did not answer the question directly. Furthermore, in both cases the statements you made might very well be true when considered apart from the context. That is, you might really believe that people tend to gain weight over the holidays and that your friend's new hairstyle is the latest fashion, but in the given context they mislead your friends regarding your true feelings.

Concealment or omission is yet another form of deception (Buller & Burgoon, 1994; O'Hair & Cody, 1994; Turner et al., 1975). The key here is that people omit information they know is important or relevant to a given context. For example, if Tracy asks Serena if she has seen her ex-boyfriend, Garrett, lately, Serena might respond, "Yes, I saw him at the game last night." Although Serena's response is true, she purposely omits the fact that she saw Garrett with a date because she thinks that information will make Tracy feel bad. Other times concealment involves engaging in behavior that helps hide relevant information. A good example of this is found in the 1980 Academy Award winner for best picture, *Ordinary People*. In this movie Conrad quits his high school swim team but continues coming home at the same time each evening as if he had been at practice. His mother hears that he quit the team from a friend at the supermarket. She then confronts Conrad, who insists that he never lied about it—he just didn't tell her. The mother fires back that every time he came home at the usual time he was deceiving her.

A fourth form of deception involves **exaggeration** or overstatement (O'Hair & Cody, 1994; Turner et al., 1975). When people exaggerate, they stretch the truth a little—often to make themselves look better or to spice up a story. The prototypical example of exaggeration involves job interviews, in which people often make their skills and experiences sound better than they actually are. For instance, in a job interview Emilio might be asked, "How much experience do you have using videotaped material to create Web pages?" Emilio might reply, "I have a lot of experience pulling various pictures off videotapes and creating collages out of them for Web pages" when in fact he has done this only a few times.

Finally, **minimizations** or understatements are the opposite of exaggerations. When minimizing, people downplay aspects of the truth. As with exaggerations, people often use minimizations to make themselves look better. People also use minimizations when they want to avoid getting in trouble or taking too much blame. For instance, Sam may tell Heather that he ran into his ex-girlfriend and they had a casual chat, when actually they had lunch together and talked for an hour. Or Ian might tell his parents that he did not do quite as well as he wanted to on his midterm exams when he actually failed them.

Motives for Deception

People engage in deception for a variety of reasons. Metts (1989; Metts & Chronis, 1986) described three major motivations for deception in close relationships. First, relational partners have **partner-focused motives,** such as using deception to avoid hurting the partner, to help the partner maintain his or her self-esteem, to avoid worrying the partner, and to protect the partner's relationship with a third party. For example, if you say that your best friend's new hairstyle looks great when you really think it looks awful, your deceptive behavior probably has a partner-focused motive. Sometimes partner-motivated deception is seen as socially polite and relationally beneficial. Indeed, *not* engaging in deception when you hate your friend's new hairstyle might violate relational expectations and hurt your friend's feelings.

Second, people deceive one another due to **self-focused motives,** such as wanting to enhance or protect their self-image, or wanting to shield themselves from anger, embarrassment, criticism, or other types of harm. So, if Emilio exaggerates his qualifications during a job interview, or Conrad fails to tell his mother that he quit the swim team because he thinks he will be punished, they have a self-focused motive. This type of deception is usually perceived as a much more serious transgression than partner-focused deception because the deceiver is acting for selfish reasons rather than for the good of the partner or the relationship.

Finally, people may have **relationship-focused motives** for deceiving a partner. Here the deceiver wants to limit relational harm by avoiding conflict, relational trauma, or other unpleasant experiences. For example, you might not tell your current romantic partner about some of your past sexual experiences because you think that it will lead to a hurtful discussion that could harm your relationship. Notice that in this case, as well as in other cases involving relationship-focused motives, partner- and self-focused motivations may also come into play. By avoiding conversations about past sexual experiences, you might also be protecting yourself from negative judgments while protecting your partner from feeling hurt and jealous. The key, however, is that you are using deception primarily to protect the relationship, rather than only to protect either yourself or the partner.

Sometimes, relationally motivated deception is seen as beneficial within a relationship. Other times, however, such deception only complicates matters. Metts (1994) used the following excerpt from an advice column to illustrate how deception can make a bad situation even worse:

> Dear Abby: My husband and I were planning a 40th anniversary celebration, but I called it off 3 months ago when I learned from someone that my husband had had an affair with a young woman while he was stationed in Alameda, California, during World War II. The affair lasted about a year while he was waiting to be shipped out, but never was. When I confronted him with the facts, he admitted it, but said it was "nothing serious.". . . I am devastated. I feel betrayed, knowing I've spent the last 47 years living with a liar and a cheat. How can I ever trust him again? The bottom has fallen out of my world. (p. 217)

In this situation, even if the deception was motivated by relational concerns, such as wanting to avoid conflict and perhaps even divorce, it compounded the problem in the long run. As Metts (1994) observed, "In this case, the act of infidelity is only the first blow; the 37 years of omission is the second, and probably more devastating, hit" (p. 217).

Effects of Familiarity on Deception Detection

As you read the letter about the husband who cheated on his wife, you might have wondered how he got away with deceiving her for so long. You might think that there must have been clues that he had had an affair or that he was concealing something from her. In reality, however, it is very difficult to detect deception in everyday conversations with relational partners unless one partner says something that is blatantly false or that contradicts information the other partner knows. This is not to say that most people can successfully deceive their partners all the time. Indeed, it is difficult to hide serious relational transgressions such as infidelity over a long period. However, in day-to-day conversations about relatively minor issues, deception often occurs without one partner suspecting that anything is amiss.

Deception is difficult to detect in close relationships for at least two reasons. First, people have truth biases. In other words, people expect family members, friends, and lovers to be honest with them, so they enter conversations without suspicion and do not look for deceptive behavior. McCornack and Parks (1986) argued that this truth bias makes close relational partners overly confident of the truthfulness of each other's statements, causing them to miss much of the deception that occurs.

Even in the face of seemingly deceptive information, relational partners can be influenced by the truth bias. For example, one of the authors of this book helped run an experiment on deception in which friends engaged in an interview. The friend who was assigned to be the interviewee was instructed to lie in response to some questions and to tell the truth in response to others. The interviewer, who did not know that the interviewee had been instructed to lie on some questions, later rated her or his friend's answers on a variety of attributes, including truthfulness. The truth bias was evident in many of these interactions. As a case in point, one of the interviewees lied and said "no" when asked if he usually went out of his way to help other people in need. The interviewer looked at him in disbelief and said, "Yes, you do. Just the other day you stopped and helped those teenagers who were stranded at the side of the road—you stopped and put the spare tire on their car." The interviewee paused and then said, "Yeah, but I hadn't changed a tire in a while, and I wanted to make sure I could still do it." Amazingly, when the interviewer later recorded how truthful he thought his friend's answer was, he marked "very truthful." This example shows how the truth bias works. We expect and look for honesty in our friends and loved ones, even if it sometimes means having to reevaluate our initial suspicions of deception.

The second reason close relational partners might have trouble detecting deception is that the deceiver may try to control his or her nervous behaviors so as to appear friendly and truthful. Several prominent deception researchers have demonstrated that, regardless of whether they are interacting with friends or strangers, deceivers try to control their behavior so that they seem honest (see Ekman & Friesen, 1969; Zuckerman, DePaulo, & Rosenthal, 1981). However, this may be particularly true for close relational partners, who have more to lose if the deception is discovered. Indeed, Buller and Aune (1987) found that when people deceived friends and romantic partners they became friendlier and showed less anxiety as the interaction progressed than when they deceived strangers. Buller and Aune concluded that people tried harder to look truthful when deceiving relational partners, in part by "putting on a happy face" and hiding nervousness.

Detection of deception is also difficult because there are no completely reliable indicators of deception. Although deception is often accompanied by behaviors such as speech hesitations and body shifts, these behaviors can indicate general anxiety, shyness, or discomfort in addition to deception (Burgoon,

Buller, & Woodall, 1996). Also, stereotypic behaviors such as eye behavior are often controlled during deception. Thus, when people lie to you, they know to look you straight in the eye, which makes eye contact an unreliable cue for detecting deception (Hocking & Leathers, 1980). Perhaps the most reliable method for detecting possible deception is to compare a person's normal, truthful behavior with her or his current behavior. If the person's behavior is noticeably different—either more anxious or more controlled—*perhaps* deception is occurring. There is *not*, however, a fool-proof method for detecting deception.

Because comparing "normal" behavior to deceptive behavior is important in the deception detection process, close relational partners have one big advantage over strangers when it comes to determining whether their partners are lying to them—they have knowledge of the partner's typical communication style. Burgoon and her colleagues (1996) called this type of knowledge **behavioral familiarity.** Close friends, family members, and romantic partners are familiar with one another's honest behavior; therefore, deviations from this behavior can tip them off that something is amiss. A study by Comadena (1982) found results consistent with the theory that behavioral familiarity gives people an advantage in detecting deception. Specifically, Comadena found that friends and spouses are better at detecting deception than are acquaintances. However, Comadena also found that friends are superior to spouses at uncovering deception, giving support to the idea that truth biases can blind people to deception cues in very close relationships. Other researchers (Buller, Strzyzewski, & Comstock, 1991; McCornack & Parks, 1986) have also found support for the truth bias in close relationships. Burgoon et al. (1996) summarized the research in this area as follows:

> Your intimate partners and close friends may be successful when deceiving you because you are likely to believe their messages. If, however, contextual cues are present that warn you about possible deception, you may be able to detect it because you are familiar with their truthful behavior—although suspicion may cause you simply to seek cues confirming their truthfulness rather than cues that would uncover deceit. (p. 447)

Of course, if your partner routinely deceives you without your knowledge, you might not really know what her or his truthful behavior looks like. This would make it even harder to detect deception.

Repairing the Damage

After a relational transgression has been discovered, partners have two basic choices: (1) They can end the relationship, or (2) they can work to repair the damage. As we discuss in Chapter 15, issues related to jealousy, infidelity, and deception, along with other relational transgressions, often are cited as the cause of relational breakups. Yet many romantic couples and friends survive and even thrive after experiencing transgressions. Doing so, however, is a challenging enterprise. Fincham (2000) used the metaphor of "kissing porcupines" to describe this challenge:

> Imagine two porcupines huddled together in the cold of an Alaskan winter's night, each providing life-sustaining warmth to the other. As they draw ever closer together the painful prick from the other's quills leads them to instinctively withdraw—until the need for warmth draws them together again. This "kiss of the porcupines" is an apt metaphor for the human condition, and it illustrates two fundamental assumptions . . . humans harm each other and humans are social animals. (p. 2)

As Fincham put it, acceptance of these two assumptions results in the following challenge: "how to maintain relatedness with fellow humans in the face of being harmed by them" (p. 2). In this section we focus on two bodies of literature that offer insight into how people face this challenge and repair their relationships after experiencing hurtful transgressions. Specifically, we look at work in the areas of forgiveness and remedial strategies.

Forgiveness

In some ways it would be easier if people could "forgive and forget," and simply get on with their lives after relational transgressions occur. Forgiveness, however, is not always an easy process, nor should it be. The transgressor has to prove to the offended party that he or she is sorry and will not engage in untoward actions in the future. As Fincham (2000) argued, forgiveness is a complicated process that does not occur immediately; instead, "The decision to forgive starts a difficult process that involves conquering negative feelings and acting with goodwill toward someone who has done us harm. It is this process, set in motion by a decision to forgive, that makes statements like 'I'm trying to forgive you' meaningful" (p. 9). It is also important to recognize that forgiving and forgetting are two different things. People may be able to forgive their partners for engaging in negative behavior, but they may not forget the partner's actions or the hurt that they experienced. If, however, forgiveness is granted after relational rules and boundaries are renegotiated, the relationship may have new life.

Forgiveness is difficult. As discussed in Chapter 14, people have a natural tendency to retaliate by matching negative behavior with more negative behavior when they are hurt or to avoid future hurt by withdrawing from the person who has committed offensive behavior. In other words, people have an innate tendency to protect themselves either by fighting back or by leaving, which is sometimes referred to as the **fight-or-flight** tendency. Forgiveness requires that a person resist these retaliatory and withdrawal tendencies, and instead move toward reconciliation. Indeed, McCullough, Worthington, and Rachal (1997) defined **forgiveness** as a state of motivational change that involves inhibiting relationally destructive behavior and instead behaving constructively toward the person who committed the offense. As Freedman and Enright (1996) stated,

"There is a decidedly paradoxical quality to forgiveness as the forgiver gives up the resentment, to which he or she has a right, and gives the gift of compassion, to which the offender has no right" (p. 983). Fincham (2000) also made the important point that forgiveness is contingent not only on the hurt person's change in motivation but also on the offending person's change in behavior. If a person does not believe that her or his partner will change the hurtful behavior, that person is unlikely to be forgiving.

When partners wish to stay together after transgressions have occurred, forgiveness appears to be very important. North (1987), who was one of the first scholars to conceptualize forgiveness in the context of repairing damaged relationships, believed that partners who do not forgive will repeatedly focus on the negative actions that haunted the relationship in the past. By contrast, partners who have the ability to forgive tend to be more satisfied with their relationship (Nelson, 1993). Similarly, Emmers and Canary (1996) found that college-age couples perceived apologies and forgiveness to be important ways of repairing a relationship after a transgression had occurred.

Three factors in particular appear to make it more likely that forgiveness will be granted following a relational transgression. First, the offending partner must apologize and admit responsibility (Darby & Schlenkler, 1982; Hargrave, 1994; McCullough et al., 1997; Weiner, Graham, Peter, & Zmuidinas, 1991). Sincere apologies can lead the injured party to perceive the offender as a generally good and thoughtful person despite the transgression. Second, if the offended partner experiences empathy, forgiveness is more likely. Interestingly, apologies might lead to empathy in some cases. When the offender apologizes and admits guilt, the injured party may empathize since both relational partners now feel negative affect. For example, you might be upset because your best friend lied to you, but after your friend admits making a mistake and confesses to feeling guilty and ashamed, you might start feeling badly for your friend despite your initial anger. As McCullough et al. (1997) put it, "Empathy for the offender [leads to] an increased caring for the offending partner that overshadows the salience of the offender's hurtful actions" (p. 333). Of course, if the offender's actions are extremely hurtful, empathy might not be forthcoming, and an apology might never be accepted. Thus, a third factor affecting forgiveness is the severity of the transgression. When the offense is severe, forgiveness is less likely (Bennett & Earwaker, 1993; Girard & Mullet, 1997).

The relationships between apologies, empathy, forgiveness, and behavior were studied by McCullough and his colleagues (1997). These researchers used two studies to test the model of forgiveness depicted in Figure 13.2. According to their model, forgiveness was most likely when apologies led the hurt person to experience empathy for the offending person. Forgiveness then led to an increase in positive, conciliatory communication and a decrease in avoidance and retaliatory communication. As they predicted, the researchers found strong positive associations between apologies and empathy, and between empathy and forgiveness. Their studies also showed that people who forgave their partners reported using more positive behavior and less negative behavior and withdrawal. In a later study, McCullough and his colleagues (1998) found that

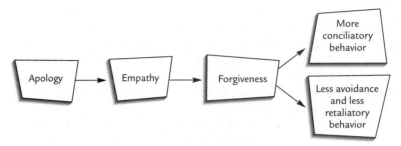

FIGURE 13.2 Model of the Forgiveness Process

partners in close relationships were more likely to apologize for their transgressions and to develop empathy for the offending partner.

A study by Kelley (1998) examined the motivations behind and strategies and consequences of forgiveness across a variety of relationships, including those between friends, romantic partners, family members, and coworkers. Participants in this study wrote three personal narratives about a time when they had either asked for or granted forgiveness. Kelley found that people had five main motives for granting forgiveness. First, in 44% of the narratives on forgiving someone, people said that they forgave the other person after reframing the situation so that the transgression seemed less severe. For example, they came to understand why the transgressor had behaved in a certain way or realized that the transgressor had not intended to hurt them. In 35% of the accounts, forgiveness was granted because people wanted to repair their relationship. For instance, Winona might have forgiven Cheyenne because they had been friends since elementary school, or Joey might have forgiven Jackie because the transgression was not severe enough to let it destroy the relationship. In 31% of the accounts, people reported that they forgave their partners because they acted in ways that showed remorse and/or accepted responsibility, such as apologizing for their actions. In 21% of the accounts, the motivation for forgiving the partner was to restore well-being to the hurt person or the partner. Kelley gave the following excerpts from one of the narratives: "I began to realize that this anger was not only torturing him, but myself as well. It was eating me up inside and making me more of an angry person. Why should I suffer for what he has done?" (p. 264). Finally, love was mentioned as a motivation behind forgiveness in 15% of the accounts.

Kelley's study also examined the ways that people communicate forgiveness. The most common strategy was to directly address the issue with the offender. The prototypical direct strategy is simply to tell the offender, "I forgive you." Other times the hurt person might tell the offender that he or she understands. The second most common strategy was to indirectly communicate forgiveness to the offender. This can be accomplished by returning to normal behavior, acting as if the transgression never happened, and/or showing affection. Some people also reported that forgiveness was never verbally granted, but that there was an implicit understanding that one partner forgave the other. A final way of communicating forgiveness involved setting forth conditions. Here the hurt person forgives the offender but only on the condition that the behavior stops and/or will not happen in the future. For example, one of the participants in Kelley's study wrote about forgiving an alcoholic father this way: "I told him I would accept his apology; however, we both knew that there was the stipulation that he stay off the booze" (p. 264).

Finally, it is important to note that the consequences of forgiveness are not always positive. Although research has shown that partners who forgive each other are more likely to stay together and have happier relationships, this is not always the case. In Kelley's (1998) study 40% of the narratives included a description of relational consequences. Of these, 72% described how the relationship had changed in some way after the transgression and subsequent forgiveness, with the other 28% reporting that the relationship had returned to "normal." However, when relationships changed, they did not always change for the better. In fact, of the people who reported that their relationships had changed, 36% said that the relationship had deteriorated, 32% that it had strengthened, and 29% that it had worsened or improved but that the rules and expectations had changed. This finding suggests that forgiveness can help heal a relationship, but it cannot always save it. As one of the participants in Kelley's study said, "I apologized and asked him to forgive me and he did . . . we were still friends, but not as good of friends" (pp. 264–265). Furthermore, in some cases it may be better *not* to save the relationship. For instance, people who forgive too readily might stay in abusive relationships rather than leaving their partners (Katz, Street, & Arias, 1995).

Making Amends: Remedial Strategies

Thus far, we have looked at repair from the hurt party's perspective by focusing on issues related to forgiveness. But what if you are the transgressor and you want to save your relationship? The answer to this question is far from simple; you cannot erase your offense with a magic wand, and your relationship might never again be the same even if your partner forgives you. As Kelley's (1998) research showed, even when forgiveness is secured, the relationship might still deteriorate, and sometimes a transgression is so severe that the hurt partner is unwilling or unable to grant forgiveness. Research on ways of managing discovered deception (Aune, Metts, & Hubbard, 1998), giving accounts for sexual infidelity (Mongeau, Hale, & Alles, 1994), dealing with social predicaments (Cupach, 1994), and seeking forgiveness (Kelley, 1998), however, suggests that people often use remedial strategies to try to remedy the situation. **Remedial strategies** represent attempts to correct problems, restore one's positive face, and repair the relationship. Some of the most common remedial strategies are discussed next.

Apologies/Concessions Apologizing and admitting guilt is one of the most obvious and frequently used remedial strategies. As noted earlier, apologies can increase empathy while showing that the transgressor is willing to take responsibility for her or his actions. In fact, in Mongeau et al.'s (1994) study on responses to infidelity, concessions emerged as the most effective strategy for repairing relationships. Apologies, however, are effective only if they are perceived to be sincere. Moreover, if an apology and accompanying confession are offered after someone is accused of a transgression, the apology is not as effective as it would have been if it had been offered before accusations were made. Of course, many people do not want to apologize and admit guilt if their partner does not know about the transgression (Mongeau & Schulz, 1997). But if they wait until the partner accuses them, their apology might be seen as a response to being caught rather than an admission of guilt. Apologies can vary from a simple statement such as "I'm sorry" to more elaborate forms of apology that include expressing guilt and remorse, derogating oneself, promising to make up for the bad behavior, and promising never to engage in the transgression again (Cupach, 1994; Schlenker & Darby, 1981). Darby and Schlenker (1982, 1989) have shown that when people have committed severe transgressions elaborate apologies are more successful than simple ones.

Excuses/Justifications When transgressors try to explain *why* they engaged in an untoward act, they are using excuses or justifications to account for their behavior. When transgressors use **excuses,** they try to minimize responsibility for their negative behavior by focusing on their inability to control their own actions or by shifting the blame to others (Aune et al., 1998; Cupach, 1994; Mongeau & Schulz, 1997). A transgressor offering an excuse might say, "I couldn't help it," or "I didn't mean to hurt you." In the case of jealousy or infidelity, the transgressor might blame the rival for "tricking" her or him into engaging in flirtatious or sexual behavior. When transgressors use **justifications,** by contrast, they try to minimize the negative implications of the transgression by denying that their behavior was wrong or that the transgression was severe (Aune et al., 1998; Cupach, 1994; Mongeau & Schulz, 1997). Here the transgressor admits to wrongdoing but claims that the negative behavior was not really so bad. For example, a man who has been caught lying might justify his behavior by saying, "It was only a white lie; it didn't hurt anyone," and a woman who has betrayed a friend's confidence by disclosing a secret might say, "Everyone would have found out eventually anyway."

Refusals With excuses and justifications the transgressor admits some degree of responsibility for her or his actions. However, with refusals transgressors argue that they should not be held accountable for their behavior or that a transgression never occurred. Some scholars have discussed refusals as a special type of excuse, in that if the excuse is good enough the transgressor may feel that he or she should not have to take the blame and even that a relational rule has not been broken. For example, even if you are angry because your partner has been spending extra time with her or his friends lately, your partner may feel that he or she has done nothing wrong and has a right to spend time alone or with friends. In this case your partner might refuse to take any blame because he or she does not see the behavior as a transgression. This example illustrates the complexity of relational transgressions—what is perceived as a transgression by one party might not necessarily be perceived as a transgression by the other. Not surprisingly Mongeau et al. (1994) found refusals to be an ineffective remedial strategy that was likely to aggravate rather than repair the relationship.

Appeasement/Positivity   Different types of appeasement behaviors have appeared in the literature on remedial strategies. For instance, Kelley (1998) found that people seeking forgiveness often used ingratiation strategies. Aune et al. (1991) found that people who were caught deceiving used soothing strategies, as well as relational rituals designed to appease the target and relational work aimed at reaffirming or strengthening the relationship. With all of these strategies, the transgressor seeks to "make up" for the untoward behavior by being particularly nice and helpful. Aune et al.'s (1998) study suggests that transgressors using the appeasement/positivity strategy might engage in behaviors such as complimenting the partner more, trying to be more attentive to the partner, spending more time with the partner, saying "I love you" more often, buying the partner gifts and flowers, and making concessions ("You are completely right and I am completely wrong").

Avoidance/Evasion   This strategy, which has also been called "silence," involves efforts to avoid discussing the transgression. Transgressors who use this strategy often report that talking about the problem only makes it worse and that it is better to let the transgression fade into the background of the relationship and be minimized (Aune et al., 1998). Transgressors using this strategy might also refuse to give an explanation for their behaviors. If avoidance/evasion is used after an apology has been made and forgiveness has been granted, it may be an effective strategy. However, if avoidance/evasion is the primary strategy used, the problem might be left unresolved and could resurface in the future. Because relational transgressions often lead to relational change, which sometimes includes the altering of rules and boundaries, avoidance/evasion may not be a particularly effective strategy in the long run. Indeed, Mongeau et al. (1994) found that avoidance (or silence) was an ineffective strategy for repairing relationships after infidelity had occurred.

Relationship Talk   This strategy involves talking about the transgression within the larger context of the relationship. Aune et al. (1998) discussed two specific types of relationship talk. The first, which they termed **relationship invocation,** involves expressing attitudes or beliefs about the relationship, or using the qualities of the relationship as a backdrop for interpreting the transgression. For example, transgressors might say, "Our relationship is strong enough to survive this," or "I love you too much to lose you over something like this." The second type of relationship talk, **metatalk** (Aune et al., 1998), involves explicitly discussing the transgression's effect on the relationship. For instance, after one member of a dating couple starts seeing someone else, the partners might renegotiate the rules about the exclusivity of their relationship. They might also discuss the future of the relationship.

Conclusion

In a perfect world people would never hurt one another. But the world is full of imperfect people leading imperfect lives. Coping with relational transgressions and hurt feelings is a difficult challenge that many relational partners face. Sometimes the damage from infidelity, deception, or other transgressions is too great, and the relationship ends. Other times, like Fincham's kissing porcupines, people decide to draw back together despite the pain, hoping that they will not be "pricked" again.

When coping with transgressions, it is important for partners to weigh the severity of the crime against the degree to which they value the relationship. When the transgression destroys trust in a relationship, the relationship probably cannot recover. However, many transgressions can be worked out by renegotiating the rules and boundaries of the relationship or by offering apologies and explanations for one's actions. For example, a jealous husband might discover that his wife is completely committed to him and is only friends with a perceived rival, and a woman who has been lied to by a friend might find out that the deception was meant to protect her rather than hurt her.

In this chapter we focused on two processes that sometimes follow relational transgressions: (1) granting forgiveness and (2) using remedial strategies. Sometimes, however, transgressions are followed by conflict and even violence. As you will see in the next chapter, jealousy is one of the top catalysts for violence in relationships prone to aggression. We hope this chapter showed you that, if you want to repair your relationship after transgressions have occurred, there are a number of nonviolent strategies that you can use to express your feelings and try to get the relationship back on track. A transgression can be a bump in the relationship road or a detour sign; it depends on the severity of the offense, the strategies used to cope with the problem, and the willingness or unwillingness of the hurt party to forgive the transgressor.

Discussion Questions

1. If your long-time relational partner were unfaithful, do you think you would leave your partner or try to work things out? If you think that "it depends," what does it depend on? Do you think men and women are socialized to react differently to sexual infidelity? Is there still a "sexual double standard" when it comes to infidelity?
2. Think about the last time you or someone you know was jealous. Which of the communicative responses to jealousy did you or the person you know use? Did these responses make the situation better or worse?
3. Under what circumstances, if any, do you think it is okay to deceive a friend or relational partner? When would you feel betrayed if your friend or partner deceived you?

When People Disagree

Interpersonal Conflict

Think about all the positive and negative experiences you have had with close friends, family members, and romantic partners. As you reflect on these experiences, can you think of a close relationship that has not included some level of conflict or disagreement? If you can, that relationship is the exception to the rule. Conflict is an inevitable part of close relationships. However, conflict does not necessarily have a negative effect on relationships. In fact, Gottman's (1979, 1994) research suggests that satisfied couples are actually more likely to discuss issues of disagreement, whereas dissatisfied couples are more likely to minimize or avoid conflict. By confronting issues of disagreement, relational partners can manage their differences in ways that enhance closeness and relational stability (Braiker & Kelley, 1979; Canary, Cupach, & Messman, 1995; Lloyd & Cate, 1985).

A study that examined the effects of a couple's "first big fight" also underscores the important role that conflict can play in relationship development. In this study Siegert and Stamp (1994) compared couples who broke up after their first big fight with those who stayed together. Partners who stayed together gained a greater understanding of their feelings for each other. They also felt that they could solve problems together and were confident that they would both be willing to make sacrifices for each other. By contrast, partners who broke up reported feeling confused or uncertain about their relationship after that first big fight. During the fight many of these people discovered negative information about their partners, and many felt that future interactions would be tense and uncomfortable. More than anything else, however, the way that the partners perceived and handled conflict predicted whether their first big fight would signal the end of their relationship or a new beginning. As this study showed, the way partners manage conflict is a much better predictor of relational satisfaction than is the experience of conflict itself.

When people think about having "conflict" in their relationships, they often imagine angry voices, name-calling, and relationship decline. However, people can engage in conflict by using positive forms of communication, such as collaboration and compromise. Voices can be calm, positions can be validated, and relationships can be strengthened instead of weakened. Conflict encompasses more than merely argument. Most scholars define **conflict** more broadly as disagreement between two interdependent people who perceive that they have incompatible goals (Cahn, 1992; Hocker & Wilmot, 1998). Because the two people are interdependent, this lack of compatibility can interfere with each person's ability to reach personal goals. Of course, some forms of incompatibility are more important than others. Hocker and Wilmot (1998) argued that incompatibility is most likely to lead to a struggle when rewards are scarce. In other words, conflict is most likely when incompatible goals are important to both people and those goals are hard to obtain.

In this chapter we examine several issues related to how people cope with disagreement in their relationships. First, we discuss common conflict issues in a variety of close relationships, including those between family members, friends, and romantic partners. Next, we turn our attention to how people communicate during conflict situations. Specifically, we focus on styles of conflict management, negative spirals, and rules for constructive conflict management.

Common Conflict Issues in Relationships

Most close relationships contain some level of conflict. In fact, Argyle and Furnham (1983) found that relational closeness and conflict were positively associated. In their study people rated different relationships in terms of how much conflict participants had and how emotionally close and connected they were. Argyle and Furnham found that the most conflict occurred in people's closest relationships. Thus, spouses reported the most closeness and the most conflict. Family relationships, such as those between parents and children or between siblings were also relatively high in both conflict and closeness. Conversely, relationships between neighbors were low in both conflict and closeness. In another study, Lloyd and Cate (1985) found that conflict increased as relational partners became more committed and interdependent. These studies make an important point—that conflict by itself is not associated with relational dissatisfaction. When people are in close relationships, they not only have more opportunities for conflict but also feel freer to express disagreement. Therefore, if you are living with siblings, parents, a spouse, a boyfriend or girlfriend, or a roommate, you have an increased opportunity to disagree with these people.

Although conflict is a part of many different types of relationships, most research has focused on conflict between parents and children or between romantic partners. Some research has also looked at conflict in friendships and sibling relationships. Canary et al. (1995) reviewed the research in each of these areas to determine some of the key issues that lead to conflict in various relationships. In this section we present some of their conclusions.

Conflict in Parent-Child Relationships

Most of the research on parent-child relationships has focused on children—from infants to adolescents—interacting with their parents. Little research has been done on the conflict patterns of parents and adult children, perhaps because conflict is usually less prevalent once a child "leaves the nest." For young children conflict with parents is part of the learning process (Canary et al., 1995). Young children develop social skills by learning appropriate ways to express disagreement, such as not raising their voices and asking politely. Conflict between parents and young children appears to be a frequent occurrence. For instance, Dunn and Munn (1987) studied interaction patterns between mothers and their 18- to 36-month-old children. They found disputes between toddlers and their mothers to occur around seven times per hour, with about half of these disputes being brief and the other half lasting longer and being more competitive. Disputes were most common with 2-year-olds, supporting the common belief that parents often have to deal with increased conflict when their children hit the "terrible twos."

However, research suggests that conflict remains prevalent in a parent-child relationship until the child reaches late adolescence (Paikoff & Brooks-Gunn, 1991). During adolescence conflict is often about parental influence and the teenager's emerging independence. Canary et al. (1995) discussed research suggesting that around 20% of parents and adolescents complain that they have too much conflict with one another. However, the frequency of conflict alone is not a good predictor of family stress. Parents and children who handle conflict constructively are much more likely to feel positive about their relationship, regardless of how frequently they engage in conflict.

Parents and children disagree about various issues, but most disagreements revolve around day-to-day events and reflect the struggle between the parents' desire to exert control and the child's need to gain independence. Canary et al. (1995) explained:

> Conflicts involving parent-child interactions typically reflect the routines of daily living. . . . During the child's early years, conflicts often concern possessions that symbolize the child's desire for social control; during adolescence, conflicts often concern lifestyle issues that symbolize the child's desire for personal control. Although both parents and children understand each other's positions, they often simply do not accept the legitimacy of these positions. (p. 75)

Thus, young children and parents argue most frequently about issues such as whether a child should get a new toy, eat her or his vegetables, or do her or his homework. Adolescents and their parents may argue most frequently about issues such as curfews, dating patterns, and privacy. In Eisenberg's (1992) study of conflict between parents and young children, many of these same issues surfaced. Specifically, Eisenberg found that parents and children typically argued about issues related to possession and rights (such as having to share a toy with a sibling or wanting to stay up late), caretaking (such as having to take a bath), hurtful behavior (such as not calling a sibling names), rules and manners (such as being polite and not talking back to one's parents), and assistance (such as demanding to be helped or left alone). Underlying all of these issues, however, are the deeper issues of social and personal control.

Conflict in Friendships and Sibling Relationships

As with parent-child relationships, conflict between young children and their peers is an important part of the social learning process. Canary et al.'s (1995) summary of the research suggests that the most frequent conflict issue for toddlers and preschoolers is the possession of objects. In fact, in a review of 20 studies, Hay (1984) found that 71% of conflicts between young children involved arguments about objects such as toys or food. As children reach elementary school age, conflict over objects decreases, although such conflict still occurs at times, especially between siblings who find it difficult to share possessions such as clothing and videotapes, as well as space (Arliss, 1993). In general, however, elementary school–age children appear to have more conflict over issues related to social conduct and norm violations. For example, Shantz (1993) found that conflict between 7-year-olds often started when one child teased the other, called the other names, or physically harmed the other. In addition, conflict was often instigated when one child violated the rules of the friendship, such as not inviting a classmate to a birthday party. Some children in Shantz's study also reported having conflict over facts and opinions, such as arguing about whose father was stronger. Studies on sibling conflict during the school-age years suggest that siblings compete with one another for many types of resources, but primarily for the attention of their parents (Dunn, 1983).

Conflict between adolescent friends becomes more sophisticated. Common conflict issues include friendship violations, norms for sexual behavior, differences in ideas and opinions, teasing/criticism, and annoying behavior (Canary et al., 1995; Laursen, 1989). However, conflict between adolescent friends is not as commonplace as is conflict between adolescents and their parents or siblings. During adolescence friendship formation and maintenance is of particular importance. Adolescent friends often are influenced fairly easily by one another, but they resist the influence attempts of parents, which can lead to conflict (Steinberg & Silverberg, 1986). Similarly, Arliss (1993) contended that "just as adolescence is a volatile period in the parent-child relationship, it is a stormy time for siblings" (p. 181). Same-sex siblings who are close in age are particularly likely to experience conflict during the teenage years, presumably because they are trying to assert their independence from one another. Issues of privacy, such as having one's own territory and personal space, can be a source of contention for brothers and sisters when they reach the teenage years (Dunn & Kendrick, 1982), and siblings are unlikely to compromise with one another. Instead, sibling conflict often ends in a standoff or in intervention by another family member or friend (Laursen & Collins, 1994).

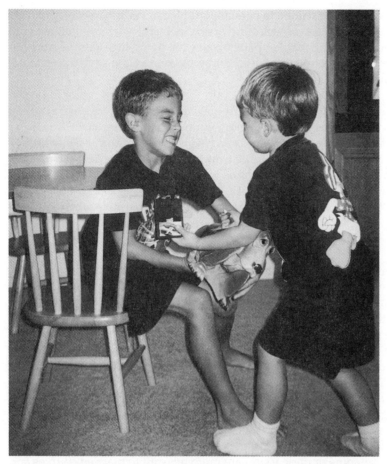

Conflict is inevitable even at an early age. For example, young children often have conflict over who gets to play with a particular toy.

Little research has been done on conflict in the context of adult friendships. However, what research there is suggests that adult friends do experience some conflict, although the conflict is usually less severe and less protracted than in relationships between romantic partners or family members. Although people tend to report the highest levels of satisfaction in their romantic relationships, the ratio of satisfaction (or enjoyment) to conflict is higher for friends than for romantic couples (Argyle & Furnham, 1983; Dykstra, 1990). In other words, romantic partners typically report high levels of both conflict and satisfaction, whereas friends typically report higher levels of satisfaction than conflict. Argyle and Furnham (1983) found that same-sex friends tended to have the most conflict when they were competing with one another over jobs, promotions, other friends, and dating partners. Cross-sex friends, by contrast, reported having the most conflict over issues related to personal problems. The most severe conflicts in friendships appear to revolve around acts of betrayal, such as violating confidences or deceiving a friend. Fehr (1996) gave the following example from her data to illustrate how betrayal can lead to severe conflict and even the termination of a friendship:

> My best friend and I were like sisters. We grew up together, we went to the same school and finished high school together. I was closer to her than anybody in my life. We did everything together. We dated different boys and shared our secrets, everything. I knew her like a book. But two years ago [it] all changed. She started to tell lies about me to my boyfriend, and we broke up. After a few weeks, I found out they were going out behind my back. I did talk to her since and she apologized. But I don't want to talk to her anymore. I am very sad because I love her. (p. 161)

Conflict in Romantic Relationships

Disagreement appears to be quite common in romantic relationships. Canary et al. (1995) summarized several studies that examined the frequency with which conflict occurs in dating and marital relationships. These studies suggest that most romantic couples have somewhere between 1 and 3 disagreements per week, with 1 or 2 disagreements per month being particularly unpleasant. Couples who are dissatisfied often experience much more conflict; one study found that distressed couples reported having 5.4 conflicts over a 5-day period (see Canary et al., 1995).

So what do romantic couples argue about? Research suggests that the most serious disagreements are related to the fair division of household labor, jealousy and possessiveness, sex, money and possessions, the social network (including in-laws), and children (Gottman, 1994; Mead, Vatcher, Wyne, & Roberts, 1990). Of course, some of these issues are more relevant to married couples and cohabiting couples than to dating partners who live apart. The fair division of household labor can be a particularly contentious issue for women in heterosexual relationships, given that working women still do about two thirds of the household work (see Chapter 8). Issues related to jealousy and possessiveness include conflict over spending time with a third party, not spending enough time together, and engaging in emotional or sexual infidelity. Partners in premarital relationships often disagree about when to first have sex, and those in all types of romantic relationships might disagree about how often to have sex, who should initiate sex, and what types of sexual behaviors are acceptable. Romantic partners often argue about money and possessions. For example, should they pool their money and have joint accounts, or should they keep their money and possessions separate? Financial issues are also a common source of contention if a couple breaks up. For example, how will money and possessions be divided? Finally, partners sometimes report disagreement over the social network and children. They might disagree about which partner's family to visit during holidays, whether a friend is trustworthy, and if, when, or how many children they want to have. They might also disagree about how to discipline a child, where a child should go to college, and so forth. Of course, people can argue about more than one of these issues at a time. For example, spouses might argue about whether they should lend money to the husband's brother, which would implicate both finances and the social network.

Although all these issues are commonly listed as causing conflict in romantic relationships, they represent only a small piece of the pie when it comes to the topics about which couples disagree. Rather than organizing conflict issues by topic, Braiker and Kelley (1979) discussed four levels of conflict. First, couples argue about specific, concrete behaviors such as whether to roll up the toothpaste container or how to properly clean the kitchen. Second, couples argue about relational rules and norms, such as forgetting someone's birthday or working late without informing the partner. Third, couples argue about personality traits. Perhaps Pamela thinks Brenda is too old-fashioned and set in her ways, and Brenda thinks Pamela is flighty and irresponsible. Finally, couples argue about the process of conflict itself, which can be termed **metaconflict.** People might accuse their partner of pouting, nagging, throwing a temper tantrum, not listening to them, fighting unfairly, and so forth. Because you are reading this book and learning about how to engage in constructive conflict, you might be at particular risk for using metaconflict. If you start telling your partner how he or she *should* be acting during an argument, your partner may very well resent your advice!

Conflict Styles

Regardless of the issue being discussed, people can handle conflict in various ways. Suppose that Mary and Doug catch their teenage daughter, Amanda, smoking after school with her friends. Because she is convinced that Amanda's friends are a bad influence on her, Mary wants to ground Amanda for a month, making her come home immediately after school. But Doug thinks that grounding will be more of a punishment for the parents than the child because Amanda will be around the house whining and complaining all the time. Instead, he proposes that they deduct the cost of a carton of cigarettes from Amanda's weekly allowance for the next 6 months. Mary objects, saying that she does not want Amanda to be motivated to change her behavior because of money. Both parents feel strongly that their punishment is best, leading to a disagreement. What conflict styles might Mary and Doug use to deal with this situation?

Considerable research has focused on the strategies or styles that people use to deal with conflict. Some of this research addresses conflict styles within organizations (Blake & Mouton, 1964; Putnam & Wilson, 1982; Rahim, 1986; Rahim & Bonoma, 1979); other research addresses conflict strategies used in relationships between friends, lovers, and roommates (Fitzpatrick & Winke, 1979; Klein & Johnson, 1997; Sillars, 1980).

Whether disagreement occurs within organizations or relationships, research suggests that conflict styles can be distinguished based on two dimensions: (1) concern for others and (2) concern for self. **Concern for others** involves

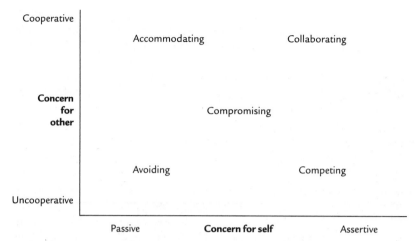

FIGURE 14.1 **Conflict Styles** *Source:* Adapted from Blake and Mouton (1964) and Rahim (1983).

wanting to get along with the partner and attempting to satisfy the partner's needs. The degree to which a person is (or is not) concerned with others can be defined in terms of a cooperative versus uncooperative dimension. That is, those who are highly concerned with the partner's interests are likely to be cooperative, whereas those who are not concerned with the partner's interests are likely to be uncooperative. **Concern for self,** by contrast, involves wanting to satisfy one's own interests. This concern is defined in part by an assertive versus passive dimension. To get what they want, individuals often have to be direct and assertive. But when people do not care about personal concerns, they can be indirect or passive without incurring costs. Of course, some people want to take control and achieve personal goals but find it difficult to speak up and be assertive. In such cases their concern for self is not manifested in their behavior.

When people's concerns for self and others are considered together, five conflict styles emerge, as shown in Figure 14.1 (Kilmann & Thomas, 1977; Rahim, 1986). These five styles are related to different patterns of attributions and outcomes, as discussed next.

The Competing Style

When people use the competing style, they are more concerned with their own interests than their partner's interests (Kilmann & Thomas, 1977). As such, the competing style is assertive and uncooperative (Blake & Mouton, 1964). This style has also been called distributive (Sillars, 1980), dominating (Rahim, 1986), controlling (Putnam & Wilson, 1982), and contentious (Klein & Johnson, 1997; Pruitt & Carnevale, 1993). As these labels suggest, people using the competing style try to control the interaction so that they have more power than their partner. They attempt to achieve a win-lose situation, wherein they win and their partner loses. Indeed, Papa and Canary (1995) framed the competing style as the **maximizing response** to conflict, because competition maximizes the importance of one's own needs at the expense (or minimization) of the other person's needs. In their attempts to achieve dominance, individuals using the competing style might make confrontational remarks, accusations, personal criticisms, threats, and antagonistic jokes. Other competitive tactics include name-calling, trying to prove that one partner is right and the other is wrong, and denying responsibility for any wrongdoing (Hocker & Wilmot, 1998).

For instance, if Mary and Doug both used the competing style in trying to decide how to punish Amanda, they might cling stubbornly to their own perspectives, with each arguing that their punishment is superior to the other's. Thus, Mary might accuse Doug of being too lazy to put up with Amanda when she is home all the time, and Doug might claim that Mary's past attempts at grounding Amanda have been unsuccessful. The conflict could very well escalate, with Mary and Doug yelling at each other and calling each other names. Even if one of them eventually yields, the desired win-lose outcome likely will be only temporary (Kilmann & Thomas, 1977). In the long run Mary and Doug's relationship could be harmed, leading to a lose-lose situation for both.

As this example illustrates, the competing style is usually associated with low levels of communication (Canary & Spitzberg, 1987, 1989, 1990; Gross & Guerrero, 2000; Sillars, 1980). People who use the competing style typically are ineffective in meeting their goals and inappropriate in their treatment of their partner. There are some exceptions to this, however. In relationships in which a power differential exists, such as those between managers and employees or between parents and children, certain competing strategies might be effective. For instance, if a manager needs her employees to work overtime to meet an important deadline, she might tell them that if they do not put in the work they risk losing their jobs. Similarly, if a father wants to prevent his son from engaging in dangerous behavior, he might force him to stay home while his friends attend a rowdy party. Thus, the competing style is sometimes useful when immediate compliance is necessary (Hocker & Wilmot, 1998). In most cases, however, the competing style leads to an escalation of conflict and only harms relationships.

Despite the fact that the competing style usually is ineffective and inappropriate, studies suggest that people use it more frequently than cooperative styles (Canary et al., 1995; Sillars, 1980). This might be because of negative spirals whereby aggression begets more aggression; that is, once one person uses a competitive tactic, the other person is likely to follow suit. (We discuss negative spirals in more detail later in this chapter.)

People might also be prone to using the competing style because of attribution biases. Attributions are the cognitive explanations that people have for their own behavior and the behavior of others. These attributions include determining why people engage in certain behaviors and who is to blame for negative behavior. In a study of college dormitory roommates, Sillars (1980) found that people's attributions were related to the types of conflict strategies they used. Individuals were especially likely to use the competing style when they saw their roommate as uncooperative and when they perceived the conflict to be mostly their roommate's fault. Given that people tend to overestimate the extent to which their partners are to blame for conflict (in comparison to themselves), it is not surprising that the competing style is used frequently. It is also important to note that, when two people blame each other for a given problem, both are likely to use competing strategies, and both are likely to cling stubbornly to the belief that they are right and their partner is wrong.

The Collaborating Style

When people use the collaborating style, they have dual concerns for themselves and for others (Blake & Mouton, 1964; Kilmann & Thomas, 1977). This style has also been called integrating (Rahim, 1986; Sillars, 1980), solution oriented (Putnam & Wilson, 1982), and problem solving (Klein & Johnson, 1997; Pruitt & Carnevale, 1993). As these labels suggest, the collaborating style focuses on cooperative problem solving that leads to a win-win situation. Individuals using this style are assertive and try to find new and creative solutions to problems by focusing on both their own needs and the needs of their partners. The collaborating style opens lines of communication, increases information seeking and sharing, and helps keep the relationship intact for future interaction (Hocker & Wilmot, 1998).

How might Mary and Doug use the collaborating style to manage their disagreement? First, they both need to stay open-minded and to look for merit in each other's opinions and suggestions. Rather than focusing on adopting one person's discipline plan over the other's, they should consider creative options that will satisfy both of them. For instance, Doug might discover that Mary's main motivation is to keep Amanda away from the "bad" crowd she has been spending time with lately. And Mary might discover that Doug's main objections to grounding are that Amanda will be moping around the house (which in the past has led them to give in and reduce the length of her grounding) and that grounding by itself will not teach Amanda anything about the bad effects of smoking. Doug might also realize that reducing Amanda's allowance by the cost of several cartons of cigarettes will only teach Amanda about the monetary cost associated with smoking, and not the health risks. After they reach an understanding about each other's concerns, Mary might suggest that Amanda volunteer some time after school at the local hospital, where she can help patients with lung cancer. Such a disciplinary action will keep Amanda away from her new friends (meeting Mary's needs) while also letting her go out of the house and teaching her about the risks associated with smoking (meeting Doug's needs). In fact, this new solution might very well address each of their concerns better than their original plans would have.

Because collaboration leads to a win-win outcome, it makes sense that people using the collaborating style are seen as highly competent. Indeed, Papa and Canary (1995) suggested that people who use the collaborating style engage in an **optimal response** to conflict. Thus, the collaborating style is both effective and appropriate in managing conflicts (Canary & Spitzberg, 1987, 1989, 1990). Gross and Guerrero (2000) argued that the collaborating style is competent because it gives each individual access to the partner's perceptions of incompatible goals, which allows disputants to reach an understanding and to coconstruct meaning. When such understanding occurs, problems can be defined, and a solution that integrates the goals and needs of both parties can be reached (Tutzauer & Roloff, 1988).

Despite the effectiveness and appropriateness of collaborating strategies, research suggests that collaboration is used less often than competition or avoidance (Canary et al., 1995; Sillars, 1980). Why would this be the case? There are at least five possibilities. First, once one partner uses a negative tactic, the natural tendency is for the other person to follow suit. In fact, researchers have found that people find it very difficult to engage in cooperative tactics once their partners become competitive (Gottman, 1994; Rusbult, Drigotas, & Verette, 1994). Second, it takes two people to collaborate. If one person is unwilling or unable to collaborate, the other person's attempts at collaboration will eventually fail, often leading to frustration (Hocker & Wilmot, 1998). Third, sometimes collaboration is not possible. For example, if a couple is arguing about whether to have children, there may not be a creative solution that satisfies both partners' needs. Fourth, collaboration is only possible when people have considerable time and energy to devote to problem solving (Hocker & Wilmot, 1998). Fifth, attribution biases may steer people away from collaboration. Sillars (1980) found that, when people blamed their roommates for the conflict, they were unlikely to use the collaborating style. This was especially true when they perceived the cause of the conflict to be based on stable personality factors, such as laziness, ignorance, or rudeness. Because individuals tend to blame other people more than themselves, collaboration is less likely than other strategies. Yet the research overwhelmingly indicates that the collaborating style is the most effective way to manage conflict.

The Accommodating Style

Like the collaborating style the accommodating style is cooperative, but unlike the collaborating style the accommodating style is indirect and passive (Blake & Mouton, 1964). Thus, the accommodating style is based on having a stronger concern for others than for oneself (Kilmann & Thomas, 1977). This style has also been labeled obliging (Rahim, 1986) and yielding (Klein & Johnson, 1997; Pruitt & Carnevale, 1993). Papa and Canary (1995) called the accommodating style a **sufficing response** to conflict. This type of response is adequate and comfortable; it does not cause further disagreement or escalations in conflict. However, the accommodating style involves glossing over differences, playing down disagreements, and trivializing conflict, which makes effective conflict management difficult. Hocker and Wilmot (1998) described several specific types of accommodating tactics, including putting aside one's own needs to please the partner, passively accepting the decisions the partner makes, making conciliatory statements, denying or failing to express one's needs, and explicitly promoting harmony and cooperation in a conflict episode.

Mary or Doug might engage in any or all of these tactics as part of an accommodating response. Suppose Doug decides to give in to Mary and ground Amanda. He might tell Mary that she is right, that he'll just have to deal with having Amanda at home, and that he loves his family and hopes that it all works out. Doug may accommodate for many different reasons. Perhaps he really does believe that Mary knows best when it comes to disciplining Amanda. Or perhaps he decides that it is not worth arguing over and he will simply let Mary have her way. Yet another possibility is that he feels threatened or coerced. Cloven and Roloff (1993) found that people are likely to avoid voicing their opinions and complaints when they feel powerless or fear that their partner will act aggressively toward them.

Because accommodation occurs for many different reasons, it can be perceived as both competent and incompetent (Gross & Guerrero, in press). Accommodating behaviors may be cooperative and appropriate when one person feels strongly about an issue and the other person does not. It cases such as this, it is appropriate for the person who feels less strongly to give in to her or his partner's wishes. Accommodating may also be an appropriate strategy when two people cannot agree but a decision needs to be made. For instance, if Mary and Doug are arguing over which of them is going to pick Amanda up after a party (each believes it is the other's turn), one of them might give in so that Amanda will have a safe ride home.

However, most research suggests that, although the accommodating style is sometimes appreciated by one's partner, it is generally ineffective (Papa & Canary, 1995; Gross & Guerrero, 2000). People who use the accommodating style are unlikely to reach their personal goals, which could put a strain on their relationship. According to Hocker and Wilmot (1998), people who use the accommodating style sacrifice their own needs for the needs of the partner, which puts them in a powerless position. Along the same lines, Cloven and Roloff (1993) discussed the "chilling effect," which occurs when there is a power imbalance in a relationship. The person who is less powerful may withhold expressing grievances because he or she is worried about negative relational consequences. Specifically, Cloven and Roloff found that people who are dependent on their relationships and/or who worry that their partners might respond with aggression are likely to withhold complaints. When this happens, problems are likely to remain unsolved. Moreover, when one partner uses accommodation, the decision-making process is one-sided, which reduces the possibility of developing a creative collaborative solution or compromise. Thus, on the surface it might seem that the accommodating style leads to a lose-win situation, with the accommodating person "losing" and the partner "winning." However, in the long run accommodation can lead to a lose-lose situation.

The frequency with which people use accommodating strategies is not yet clear. In his study of roommate conflict, Sillars (1980) examined the extent to which roommates reported using accommodating strategies (which he termed "yielding" strategies). Sillars had students recall all the disagreements they had with their roommate and then describe how they and their roommate communicated about the most significant of these disagreements. Sillars (1980) found that they rarely reported using accommodation. In fact, only 2% of the students in his sample reported using accommodating strategies during their most significant disagreement with a roommate. By contrast, Sillars found that 33% of students perceived their roommates to be accommodating during these same disagreements. Why was there such a discrepancy? Sillars suggested that the students did not use accommodation very often because they were reporting on a disagreement that was very significant to them. Their roommates, conversely, may not have seen these disagreements as very significant and so were more willing to concede the issue. This finding suggests that accommodating is more common when people do not care very much about an issue.

The Avoiding Style

The avoiding style is based on having little or no concern for oneself or others (Kilmann & Thomas, 1977). As such, it is uncooperative and indirect (Blake & Mouton, 1964). This style has also been called nonconfrontation (Putnam & Wilson, 1982), inaction (Klein & Johnson, 1997; Pruitt & Carnevale, 1993), and withdrawal (Hocker & Wilmot, 1998; Gottman, 1994). Avoiding occurs when people physically or psychologically remove themselves from the conflict scene, refrain from arguing, and refuse to confront their partners in any meaningful way. Papa and Canary (1995) called the avoiding style a **minimizing response** to conflict, because avoidance diminishes the importance of the conflict and the interests of both parties. People who use the avoiding style engage in behavior such as denying the conflict, being indirect and evasive, changing and/or avoiding topics, acting as if they don't care, making irrelevant remarks, and joking as a way to avoid dealing with the conflict (Hocker & Wilmot, 1998). Some avoiding behaviors are even more uncooperative. For instance, people might purposefully ignore the partner, hold a grudge, or administer the silent treatment (Guerrero, 1994).

Suppose Mary and Doug deal with their disagreement through avoidance. Neither of them wants to confront the issue, so they avoid talking about how to best handle the situation with Amanda. Perhaps they both punish Amanda their own way, without consulting the other, making Amanda suffer two punishments instead of one. Or perhaps they both decide not to do anything, letting Amanda "off the hook" for smoking. Either way, the use of avoidance leads to a lose-lose situation, with little being accomplished.

It is more likely, however, that one of the spouses will want to discuss the issue and the other will try to avoid it. For instance, Mary might approach Doug to discuss Amanda's punishment, and Doug might tell her he does not want to talk about it anymore. This will be very frustrating for both Mary and Doug. Mary wants to confront the issue, but she cannot do it alone, and Doug has to keep hearing about an issue he does not want to talk about. Consistent with this example, research has shown that women are more likely to confront conflict issues, and men are more likely to withdraw (Gottman, 1994).

Indeed, researchers have discussed a conflict sequence called the **demand-withdraw interaction pattern** (Gottman, 1994; Gottman & Levenson, 1988). This type of sequence occurs when one person wants to engage in conflict and the other wants to avoid it. This interaction pattern often escalates, with both partners experiencing considerable negative affect. Conflict engagers increase their demands for discussion as they become more desperate to confront and solve problems. At the same time, conflict avoiders become increasingly stubborn in their efforts to dodge discussion and to withdraw from an interaction that they perceive to be unpleasant and/or unnecessary. The demand-withdraw pattern of interaction is generally seen as a highly incompetent form of dyadic communication (Christensen & Shenk, 1991; Gottman & Levenson, 1988).

Not surprisingly, several studies have shown that the avoiding style is inappropriate and ineffective (Canary & Spitzberg, 1987, 1989, 1990; Gross & Guerrero, 2000). Despite the general ineffectiveness of avoidance, Sillars (1980) found that roommates reported using the avoiding style most frequently in their conflicts. Similarly, Roloff and Cloven (1990) found that 63% of college students reported withholding at least one complaint from their dating partners. There are, of course, some situations in which avoidance is appropriate. For example, suppose two brothers always disagree on political issues, because one brother is staunchly conservative and the other is extremely liberal. The brothers might "agree to disagree" and decide to avoid any future discussion of politics since it is futile to argue about their opposing views. Thus, in some situations the avoiding style can be used to acknowledge that a relationship is more important than a particular issue (Hocker & Wilmot, 1998). This type of situation, however, is the exception. In most cases, avoidance is an ineffective and inappropriate conflict strategy.

The Compromising Style

The compromising style is somewhat focused on the self and somewhat focused on others (Kilmann & Thomas, 1977; Rahim, 1986). As such, the compromising style is characterized by moderate levels of both cooperation and assertiveness (Blake & Mouton, 1964). When people compromise, they search for an intermediate position that satisfies some of their own needs and some of their partner's needs. However, compromise leaves some of both people's needs unmet, leading to a part-win/part-lose situation, or even a lose-lose situation. Indeed, people who compromise talk about "splitting the difference" and "meeting the partner halfway." The idea here is that people need to give up some of their own desires and goals in order to reach a solution that will meet at least some of their expectations. According to Hocker and Wilmot (1998), compromising behaviors include appealing to fairness, suggesting a trade-off, maximizing wins while minimizing losses, and offering a quick, short-term resolution to the conflict at hand.

Once again, let's turn to our example of Mary and Doug. How might they use the compromising strategy to manage their conflict? They could decide to ground Amanda for 2 weeks instead of a month and to deduct cigarette money from her allowance for 3 months instead of 6. This way, Mary and Doug both get to administer the punishment they perceive to be most appropriate, but neither gets to apply the punishment for the length of time they originally proposed. In short, they get to keep something but they also have to give up something. Notice that compromising usually involves modifying preexisting solutions, whereas collaborating involves creating new solutions.

Little research has been done on the compromising style. However, the available research suggests that the compromising style is generally perceived to be moderately appropriate and effective (Gross & Guerrero, 2000). Although this style is not as effective or appropriate as collaborating, there are situations in which compromising is the best option available. For example, if people have radically different goals and no viable solution exists that will satisfy both partners' needs, compromise might be a good choice (Gross & Guerrero, 2000). Similarly, when people are unable to come up with a creative new solution to a problem, compromise is a good alternative. Suppose a couple is arguing over whom to ask to be godparents for their son. The husband wants his sister and brother to be godparents, while the wife prefers her favorite aunt and uncle. Assuming that they want only two godparents for their son, the couple might decide to put names in a hat, with one slip of paper appointing the aunt and brother as godparents and the other slip designating the sister and uncle. Such a compromise is likely to be seen as fair by all parties. As Hocker and Wilmot (1998) described, most people perceive compromising to be a reasonable, fair, and efficient strategy for managing conflict, even though it requires some level of sacrifice and hampers the development of creative alternatives. To determine your own conflict style, complete the scale in Box 14.1.

Conflict Escalation and Negative Spirals

Although using strategies such as collaboration and compromise can help people deal with conflict more effectively, often conflict escalates into a negative spiral with both partners becoming increasingly angry. Several types of negative spirals can occur (Gottman, 1994; Christensen & Heavey, 1990; Pike & Sillars, 1985; Raush, Barry, Hertel, & Swain, 1974; Sillars & Wilmot, 1994). One of these spirals, the demand-withdrawal sequence, was discussed previously. In this sequence one partner wants to talk about the conflict issue, while the other partner continually withdraws. This leads to a vicious cycle, with one partner becoming more agitated because he or she cannot talk about the issue, vent frustration, and ultimately solve the problem, and the other partner becoming more irritated because he or she is continually being nagged about an issue that is perceived to be unimportant or unpleasant. Other couples engage in **double withdrawal sequences,** with both partners practicing aggressive avoidance. For example, after getting into an argument, Jenna might give Amber the "silent

BOX 14.1 PUT YOURSELF TO THE TEST

What Is Your Conflict Style?

Think about the last few times you and a relational partner disagreed. How did you behave? Use the following scale to determine your typical conflict style.

1 = Strongly disagree . . . 7 = Strongly agree

	Disagree					Agree	
1. I discuss the problem to try to reach a mutual understanding.	1	2	3	4	5	6	7
2. I stick to my argument until I prove my point.	1	2	3	4	5	6	7
3. I give in to my partner to keep my relationship satisfying.	1	2	3	4	5	6	7
4. I sometimes sacrifice my own goals so my partner can meet her or his goals.	1	2	3	4	5	6	7
5. I try to find a new solution that will satisfy all our needs.	1	2	3	4	5	6	7
6. I usually try to win arguments.	1	2	3	4	5	6	7
7. I do not like to talk about issues of disagreement.	1	2	3	4	5	6	7
8. I am willing to give up some of my goals in exchange for achieving other goals.	1	2	3	4	5	6	7
9. I try to get all my concerns and my partner's concerns out in the open.	1	2	3	4	5	6	7
10. I usually try to forget about issues of disagreement so I don't have to confront my partner.	1	2	3	4	5	6	7
11. I try to think of a compromise that satisfies some of both our needs.	1	2	3	4	5	6	7
12. I argue until my ideas are accepted.	1	2	3	4	5	6	7
13. It is important to get both our points of view out in the open.	1	2	3	4	5	6	7
14. I try to convince my partner that my position is right.	1	2	3	4	5	6	7
15. I try to meet my partner half way.	1	2	3	4	5	6	7
16. If the issue is very important to my partner, I usually give in.	1	2	3	4	5	6	7
17. I attempt to work with my partner to find a creative solution we both like.	1	2	3	4	5	6	7
18. I usually let my partner take responsibility for bringing up conflict issues.	1	2	3	4	5	6	7
19. I would rather not get into a discussion of unpleasant issues.	1	2	3	4	5	6	7
20. I avoid bringing up certain issues if my arguments might hurt my partner's feelings.	1	2	3	4	5	6	7
21. I might agree with some of my partner's points to make my partner happy.	1	2	3	4	5	6	7
22. I avoid talking with my partner about disagreements.	1	2	3	4	5	6	7
23. I try to find a "middle ground" position that is acceptable to both of us.	1	2	3	4	5	6	7
24. I try to influence my partner so he or she will see things my way.	1	2	3	4	5	6	7
25. I believe that you have to "give a little to get a little" during a disagreement.	1	2	3	4	5	6	7

To obtain your results, add your scores for the following items:

3, 4, 16, 20, 21   (accommodating)   _____
7, 10, 18, 19, 22   (avoiding)   _____

1, 5, 9, 13, 17	(collaborating)	_____
2, 6, 12, 14, 24	(competing)	_____
8, 11, 15, 23, 25	(compromising)	_____

Higher scores indicate that you possess more of a particular conflict style.

---

treatment." Amber might retaliate by ignoring Jenna and refusing to call her and apologize. Both Jenna and Amber might stubbornly refuse to approach each other, in part because they do not want to lose face. Of course, if this cycle continues, Jenna and Amber's relationship will end. Finally, some couples engage in **reciprocal negative behavior,** with both partners resorting to competitive behaviors, such as complaints, name-calling, and accusations. For example, Gottman (1979) found that dissatisfied couples were likely to engage in complaint-countercomplaint sequences. One relational partner might complain that they never spend enough time together, and the other might complain that when they do spend time together all the other partner does is complain about the relationship.

Although negative spirals are most predominant in dissatisfying relationships, even partners in satisfying relationships tend to respond to negativity with more negativity. On the surface this may seem somewhat counterintuitive. If people care about their relationships with each other, why don't they try to defuse a negative situation by reacting with positivity? Sometimes people do respond positively, but often they find it difficult to refrain from negativity because of the emotions they are experiencing, the attributions they make, or their lack of communication skill. Each of these explanations for conflict escalation are discussed next.

Emotional Flooding

During conflict situations negative emotions may become so intense that people automatically resort to the fight-or-flight response. Gottman (1994) discussed the concept of **flooding,** which occurs when people become "surprised, overwhelmed, and disorganized" by their partner's "expressions of negative emotion" (p. 21). When this happens, people typically experience high levels of physiological arousal (including increased heart rate and higher blood pressure), have difficulty processing new information, rely on stereotyped thoughts and behaviors, and respond with aggression (fight) or withdrawal (flight). Thus, flooding contributes to negative spirals that involve both negative behavior and avoidance.

Several behaviors are associated with flooding. According to Gottman's (1994) research, if your partner becomes defensive, stubborn, angry, or whiny, you are likely to experience emotional flooding. Other behaviors act as buffers against emotional flooding. Specifically, if your partner expresses joy, affection, or humor during the course of a conflict interaction, you are less likely to experience emotional flooding. Situational variables may also play a role. For instance, Zillman's (1990) work on the excitation transfer suggests that people who are highly aroused (due to either stress or physical exertion) before engaging in conflict are more likely to react with aggression, presumably because they are experiencing a form of emotional flooding.

Research also suggests that many of the behaviors commonly used during conflict situations provoke anger. Canary, Spitzberg, and Semic (1998) summarized research on factors causing anger in interpersonal relationships. Among the primary causes were threats to one's identity, physical and/or verbal aggression, frustration due to goal interference and feelings of powerlessness, a lack of equity or fairness, incompetent partner behaviors such as inconsideration or rudeness, and relationship threats such as jealousy or betrayal. When these issues surface in conflicts, people are likely to respond with anger, which, in turn, will contribute to heightened levels of physiological arousal and emotional flooding.

Attributions

People like to be able to explain the behavior of others, particularly during significant events such as conflict episodes. To do this, people make attributions. In their book on interpersonal communication, Fisher and Adams (1994) defined an **attribution** as "a perceptual process of assigning reasons or causes to another's behavior" (p. 411). This definition is in line with Heider's (1958) conception of people as "naive scientists" who study one another's behavior and make judgments about why they act the way they do. Later research by Kelley (1973) suggested that people make casual attributions based on at least three factors: (1) how internal or external a cause is to a person, (2) how stable or unstable a cause is, and (3) how global or specific a cause is. These three types of attributions have been found to influence how people respond to conflict.

The internal/external dimension refers to the extent to which a behavior is seen as typical or characteristic of a particular person. When people make internal attributions, they believe that the cause of another person's behavior is rooted in their personality. By contrast, when people make external attributions, they believe that the other person's behavior is caused by less personal, situational factors. For example, Tatiana might be upset because Dimitri forgot her birthday. She could attribute Dimitri's behavior to personality factors (Dimitri is forgetful, self-centered, and uncaring) or to situational factors (Dimitri has been preoccupied with problems at work). Interestingly, research suggests that we tend to attribute other people's negative behavior to internal, personality-related causes, and our own bad behavior to situational causes (Jones & Nisbett, 1972). This tendency has been called the **fundamental attribution bias.** In general, people appear to be harder on others than themselves. People are also harder on strangers and those they dislike than on friends and those they like. So, if you have a good relationship with your friend, you will be more likely to attribute her or his unsympathetic behavior to situational causes.

The second type of causal attribution relates to how stable versus unstable a cause is judged to be. In other words, does the behavior occur in a consistent manner over time, or is the behavior hard to predict? For example, you might figure out that your sister gets upset when you talk about your love life because she always seems to be in a bad relationship. Her consistently bad relationships will then become a stable cause for her reaction, and you might avoid discussing this topic with her. By contrast, your sister may become upset during some conversations about your love life but not others. In this case you might decide that her reactions are based on unpredictable causes, such as her current love interest, her changing mood, or even the weather.

The third type of causal attribution is based on how global versus specific a cause is predicted to be. When causes are perceived to be global, they apply to a wide variety of behaviors. For example, you might usually attribute all the nice things your partner does for you (cooking you dinner, complimenting your haircut, sending you romantic cards or flowers) as a sign of her or his love for you. However, sometimes a behavior is linked to a very specific cause. Perhaps you suspect that your partner is being extra nice to get you to do something for her or him, or is cooking you a special dinner because it is your birthday. Notice that these causes are specific to a certain behavior enacted at a certain time, whereas global causes are attributed to a wide variety of behaviors over time.

The types of attributions that people make about their relational partner's behavior can affect the satisfaction level of the relationship. Satisfied partners make relationship-enhancing attributions, whereas dissatisfied couples make distress-maintaining attributions (Bradbury & Fincham, 1990; Brehm & Kassin, 1990; Harvey, 1987; Holtzworth-Monroe & Jacobson, 1987). As Figure 14.2 shows, people in happy relationships tend to attribute negative behavior such as complaints, whining, and nagging to causes that are external, unstable, and specific; by contrast, people in unhappy relationships tend to attribute negative behavior to internal, stable, and global causes. Based on this reasoning, if Dwight calls Yolanda a rude name during a disagreement, Yolanda's attribution for Dwight's behavior will differ based on whether they are in a happy or unhappy relationship. If they are in a happy relationship, Yolanda might think, "He's just in a bad mood because of all the pressure he's been facing at work lately. He doesn't usually treat me this way." However, if the relationship is unhappy, Yolanda might think, "He's such a jerk. He always treats me with disrespect because he doesn't care about me anymore."

The attributional pattern is the opposite when people attribute causes to positive behaviors. Suppose Andrea goes out of her way to help Rebecca with an important project for work. If Andrea and Rebecca are in a happy relationship, Rebecca is likely to attribute her nice behavior to internal, stable, and global causes, such as that Andrea is an unselfish person who is always there to help when she needs her. Conversely, if they are in an unhappy relationship, Rebecca is likely to be suspicious and to attribute her nice behavior to external, unstable, and specific causes, such as that Andrea will expect a favor in return.

As these examples suggest, the attributions people have influence communication patterns. When we attribute people's negative behavior to external,

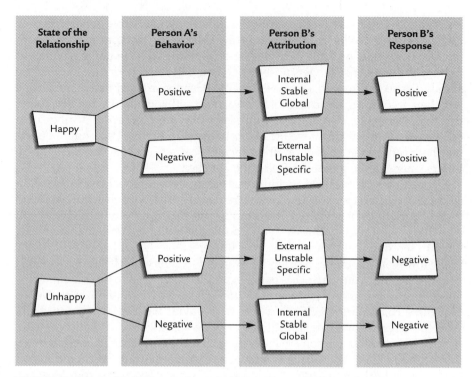

FIGURE 14.2 Attribution Patterns in Happy Versus Unhappy Couples

unstable, and specific causes, we are less likely to get upset and more likely to excuse their behavior and even to try to comfort them. But when we attribute people's negative behavior to internal, stable, and global causes, we are more likely to respond with negative behaviors and less likely to be forgiving. This can lead to negative spirals in dissatisfying relationships. Even when people in dissatisfying relationships do engage in positive behaviors, the attributions are negative, so partners still are likely to respond with negativity. Unless these attribution biases are corrected, dissatisfied couples will likely stay caught in a spiral of negative thoughts and behaviors.

Communication Skill Deficits

In addition to emotional flooding and cognitive attributions, some people simply do not have the behavioral skill to engage in constructive conflict. These individuals are likely to feel particularly helpless and defensive when attacked by others because they cannot respond effectively. Thus, they resort to aggressive behaviors or to withdrawal, which can contribute to negative spirals of behavior.

With the idea that communication skill deficits contribute to negative patterns of interaction in mind, Infante and his colleagues made an important distinction between argumentativeness and verbal aggressiveness (Infante, 1987; Infante, Chandler, & Rudd, 1989; Infante & Rancer, 1982). According to Infante, argumentativeness is an important social skill that helps people deal effectively with conflict. When people are unskilled in argument, Infante suggested, they will resort to aggression. **Argumentativeness** refers to a conflict style that focuses on logical argument and reasoning: People with an argumentative style confront conflict directly by recognizing issues of disagreement, taking positions on controversial issues, backing up claims with evidence and reasoning, and refuting positions that go against their own viewpoint. People who are skilled in argument do not have to resort to name-calling, accusations, or other negative tactics. Instead, they can present their positions in a skilled and convincing manner. Rather than attacking their partner, they attack their partner's position.

Verbal aggressiveness involves attacking the other person's self-concept, often with the intention of hurting the other person. Verbally aggressive people engage in such tactics as teasing, threatening, and criticizing the partner's character or appearance (Infante, Sabourin, Rudd, & Shannon, 1990). Partners in violent marriages are more likely to report high levels of verbal aggression and low levels of argumentativeness than are those in nonviolent marriages (Infante et al., 1989, 1990). Thus, an inability to express one's opinion through rational argument may be one cause of interpersonal violence.

The following example might help illustrate how difficult it is to deal with someone who is verbally aggressive. While watching a news report, Irene and Vanessa start discussing their differing opinions on affirmative action.

IRENE: I can't believe they are going to prohibit affirmative action at our university.

VANESSA: If you ask me, it's about time they did.

IRENE: You mean you are against affirmative action?

VANESSA: Let's put it this way: I think people should be admitted to universities based on their qualifications rather than their skin color.

IRENE: So you are a racist who hates minorities.

VANESSA: That's not true. I don't like discrimination in any shape or form. I just think that universities should make exceptions based on factors other than race. Poor white students are also disadvantaged. Maybe a policy that admits students based on where they rank in their particular high school would be fairer. That way, all students who are economically disadvantaged, including many minority students, would get help.

IRENE: And I suppose you think that white men are discriminated against too. I thought you were smarter than that. How can you be so gullible?

If you did not have a strong opinion about affirmative action policies in universities before reading Irene and Vanessa's comments, you might have been swayed more by Vanessa's arguments because they focused on her position rather than attacking Irene as a person. In other words, Vanessa used argumentative communication. By contrast, Irene used verbal aggression when she called Vanessa a racist, implied that she was unintelligent, and asked how she could be so gullible. If Irene had been the one to use argumentative communication, you might have been more persuaded by her argument. This example also illustrates how verbally aggressive communication can lead to negative spirals. Put yourself in Vanessa's place. If the conversation continued, and you kept being attacked personally, would you be tempted to retaliate by using verbal aggression yourself? Most people have a hard time remaining neutral in the face of personal attacks, partly due to emotional flooding.

Principles of Constructive Conflict Management

At the outset of this chapter, we stressed that conflict is not necessarily detrimental to relationships. In fact, conflict can help couples iron out problems and grow closer. What is important, however, is that couples handle conflict in a constructive manner, which can be difficult to do. As discussed previously, thoughts and emotions can interfere with people's ability to remain constructive during conflict. In addition, constructive conflict management requires considerable social skill. Relational partners must be able to adapt their conflict behaviors to a given situation. In some cases it may be best to confront conflict, and in other cases it may be better to avoid conflict or accommodate (Sillars & Weisberg, 1987). In this section we examine six interrelated principles of constructive conflict management.

Principle 1: *Stick to the topic.*

One of the most important principles of "fair fighting" is to stick to the current topic without bringing up past conflict issues or attacking the person. Researchers coined the term **gunnysacking** to describe the process whereby people store up old grievances and then bring them all up during conflict situations (Bach & Wyden, 1970). For example, roommates Don and Brett may be upset with each other on a daily basis for a number of minor infractions, such as leaving the air conditioner on with the windows open, eating each other's food without asking, or forgetting to give each other phone messages. Rather than discussing each of these issues when they surface, the roommates might place them in their "gunnysacks." Eventually, their gunnysacks might become so heavy that they overflow—usually during a conflict about another issue. So, although Don and Brett start arguing about the phone bill, they might soon get off track by hauling old issues out of their gunnysacks.

Related to the idea of gunnysacking is the idea of **kitchen-sinking** (Bach & Wyden, 1970). When people "throw everything but the kitchen sink" into their arguments, the conflict usually escalates and the original issue remains unsolved.

Kitchen-sinking often occurs when people experience emotional flooding or when they think they are losing an argument. When people get emotional during conflict situations, they sometimes think about all the negative, hurtful things that have happened in their relationships, and so they lash out at their partner. Similarly, when people think that they are losing an argument, they will sometimes shift to an issue that they know they can "win." Sometimes gunnysacking and kitchen-sinking go hand in hand. For example, suppose that in December Sean and Caitlyn had gotten into an argument because Sean thought Caitlyn had lost a Christmas check from his grandmother. Sean had called Caitlyn "irresponsible and unorganized" and accused her of "misplacing everything all the time." A month later Sean found the check tucked away in a small compartment in his briefcase; embarrassed, he apologized to Caitlyn. Now it is June, and Sean and Caitlyn are arguing because Caitlyn sent the mortgage payment a couple days late, and they had to pay a late fee. Caitlyn knows that this is her fault, so she diverts the topic by saying, "Yeah, Sean, but remember how *you* accused *me* of losing that check from your grandmother when it was really all *your* fault. You don't always handle money so well yourself." This leads to a shouting match, with both Sean and Caitlyn recalling past miscarriages of justice against each other.

Finally, sticking to the topic means attacking people's positions rather than attacking them personally or physically. As noted earlier, Infante's work on argumentativeness and verbal aggression suggests that people should focus on advancing and defending their positions rather than on attacking the person. In position-focused argument there is no room for name-calling, character assaults, or violence. There is also no room for **button pushing,** which occurs when people purposely try to hurt the partner by bringing up a taboo topic or insulting him or her in a way that they know will be especially hurtful. Like many other negative tactics used during conflict situations, people may resort to button pushing when they feel trapped and defensive. For example, if Nick starts complaining that Lisa does not have any self-control when it comes to spending money, Lisa might become hurt and defensive. If she knows that Nick is sensitive about his weight, she might retaliate by saying, "You are not one to talk about self-control. You cannot even control what you eat." Such a comment is likely to push Nick's buttons and to escalate the conflict. Instead of focusing on the original issue, Lisa and Nick might start hurling personal insults at each other.

Principle 2: Don't bring other people into the conflict.

It is also important to refrain from bringing other people into arguments unless it is absolutely necessary. Sometimes the conflict issue revolves around other people, such as when friends or in-laws are interfering with a married couple's relationship or when children are involved. In these cases other people are integral to the conflict. However, people often get brought into a conflict even when they are not part of the problem. For example, when Don and Brett are arguing about the phone bill, Don might make comments such as "Gary warned me that you would be hard to get along with as a roommate." Similarly, Sean might tell Caitlyn that "even your sister says you are not good at handling money." Such comments are particularly hurtful and hard for receivers to defend since they cannot immediately confront the person who supposedly made them (in these cases, Gary and Caitlyn's sister). This is why Johnson (1986) suggested that people "own" their own messages. In other words, if you are angry or bothered by something, talk about the way *you* feel rather than bringing other people's feelings and opinions into the argument.

Individuals bring third parties into their conflicts in at least three other ways. First, sometimes people badmouth the partner's friends or family by making comments such as "I guess your erratic behavior shouldn't surprise me—your whole family acts that way" or "the Smith temper comes through again—next you'll be slamming the door like your brother does." Statements like these make people particularly defensive. Not only do people have to defend themselves, but now they also have to defend their friends and/or family.

Second, individuals sometimes claim that other people would act in more positive ways than their partners. For instance, Dwain might compare Kendra to his ex-girlfriend by saying, "Tina would never act this way," or Manuela might tell her best friend that she is acting less mature than her 3-year-old daughter. Not only do these types of tactics bring other people into the argument, but they tend to push buttons and get the conflict off track.

Third, some people discuss their conflict with biased third parties, such as a best friend or family member. These friends and family members usually will be supportive of the person (Duck, 1988), perhaps assuring them that the problem is the partner's fault and not theirs. The drawback, however, is that talking to others about one's relationship problems can cause irreparable damage to the social network. For example, if Caitlyn calls her sister every time she and Sean argue, her sister is likely to develop a negative perception of Sean. Her sister might even tell the rest of Caitlyn's family that Sean is mistreating Caitlyn, which could cause friction between Sean and his in-laws. As this example suggests, it is usually best to keep conflict issues within a relationship or to consult an impartial third party. There are some exceptions, though. For instance, if someone is being physically or mentally abused, it is important to seek help from others.

Principle 3: Don't say things you don't mean.

In the heat of conflict, people often say and do things they do not really mean, especially when the situation is emotionally charged. People sometimes call each other names and make statements such as "I hate you" or "I wish I never met you." At the moment such statements may seem true because people are filled with so much negative emotion. However, when they calm down, they realize that they actually care deeply for each other. Other times people make these kinds of statements to get revenge. They know that they don't really hate the partner, but by saying "I hate you," they hope to hurt the partner the way they themselves feel hurt.

Sometimes people make empty relational threats. For instance, someone might say, "If you see her again, I'll break up with you," or "I can't stand this anymore; I want a divorce" when they actually have no intention of terminating the relationship. Such empty threats can have at least two negative consequences. First, if you do not follow through on these threats, you will lose face, and your partner might think you are bluffing some time in the future when you really are considering ending the relationship. As the old fairy tale tells us, it is not wise to "cry wolf" too many times! Second, if you threaten to leave your partner when you do not really intend to, you could actually be planting the seed for relationship termination. Some research suggests that people go through a cognitive process of psychological separation before terminating close, interdependent relationships (Duck, 1988). For instance, if you keep talking about leaving your partner, your partner will start thinking about what he or she would do without you. Your partner might even start to think about pleasant alternatives, such as other relationship possibilities. If this happens, you have moved the possibility of breaking up to the forefront of your partner's mind. Thus, empty relational threats are more likely to backfire than to solve problems.

One way to prevent saying things you do not mean is to avoid engaging in conflict when your emotions are piqued. Instead, wait until both you and your partner are calm before discussing issues of disagreement. Do not, however, put off conflict indefinitely. If necessary, you might have to schedule a time to talk about the issues that are bothering you. In the interim you might want to write down your feelings. One of our students once told us about a writing technique that she and her husband used when they were feeling really angry with each other. From their past experiences they knew there was a good chance that conflict would escalate if they confronted each other when their emotions were running high. So they decided to vent their negative emotions by going to different rooms and writing letters to each other. Later, after they had calmed down, they would each read the letters to themselves and decide whether to share them with the spouse. This student told us that neither of them ever ended up sharing the letters, but instead always tore them up. The letters were usually filled with things they did not really mean, such as exaggerations, name-calling, or empty threats. But these letters helped our student and her husband put their conflict issues in perspective and enabled them to move on and discuss their problems in a calmer fashion.

Principle 4: *Practice active listening*.

Regardless of the type of interaction, active listening can be a challenge, especially during conflict situations, when people can become defensive. Think about the last heated argument you had with someone. How carefully did you listen to what the other person had to say? If you felt attacked and/or became defensive, chances are that you did not really listen to the other person very carefully. Instead, you were probably thinking about what you would say next. Your mind may have been racing as you thought about ways to defend yourself, and your emotions may have been so turbulent that you became preoccupied with your own thoughts and feelings and "tuned the other person out." Ironically, if your partner was not practicing active listening either, all the counterarguments you spent so much time thinking about would never really be heard.

Active listening requires effort and concentration. The experts on listening and negotiation give the following advice for improving your skill (Stark, 1994; Steil, Barker, & Watson, 1983; Stiff, Dillard, Somera, Kim, & Sleight, 1988):

1. **Let your partner speak.** This means that you should refrain from arguing your case until your partner finishes stating her or his position. You should also avoid interrupting your partner. Finally, if you spend noticeably more time talking than your partner, this probably means that you need to talk less and encourage your partner to talk more.

2. **Put yourself in your partner's place.** If you are unmotivated to be a good listener, you are likely to be sidetracked. Therefore, you should enter a conflict situation with specific goals regarding what you would like to learn from your partner. It is usually particularly productive to focus on your partner's needs and motives. As Gottman (1994) emphasized, if people want to understand and empathize with each other, they need to create mental maps of each other's thoughts and feelings. By listening actively, people can see things from their partner's perspective.

3. **Don't jump to conclusions.** Even when people are trying to listen, they sometimes assume that they know what the partner will say or why they will say it. They then interpret the partner's statements in a way that is consistent with their preexisting beliefs. For example, a teenage girl we know once got into an argument with a male friend because he teased her about hanging out with college-age men. She assumed he was teasing her because he thought she was stuck up. But the girl's mother pointed out that this boy might actually be teasing her because he liked her and was jealous. This turned out to be the case, and a while later the two started dating. If the girl had not jumped to conclusions so quickly, they might have started dating sooner.

4. **Ask questions.** To really understand your partner's position, you should ask clarifying questions. For example, if Ross tells Nancy that he hates the way she acts when they are around their coworkers, Nancy might ask him to specify what behaviors he dislikes. Of course, her immediate reaction might be to defend her behavior, but it would be more productive for her to try to understand what specific behaviors bother Ross, and why.

5. **Paraphrase what your partner says.** Paraphrasing is an important technique that helps confirm that you have really heard what your partner is trying to tell you. When partners paraphrase, they summarize each other's

positions. For example, the teenage girl mentioned previously might have paraphrased her friend's argument by saying, "So you think I hang around with college guys because I'm too stuck up to be around high school boys." Then he might have corrected her by saying, "No, I don't think you're stuck up. I just wish you wouldn't hang around them so much." By paraphrasing, partners give each other the opportunity to correct misinterpretations and to further clarify their positions.

Principle 5: Avoid the "four horsemen of the apocalypse."

Gottman's extensive research on the causes of divorce suggests that four factors, which he termed the "four horsemen of the apocalypse," are critical in predicting whether couples will stay together. These four factors are complaints/criticisms, contempt/disgust, defensiveness, and stonewalling. Stonewalling occurs when a person withdraws from interaction and refuses to talk to the partner. Gottman (1994) proposed that the four horsemen of the apocalypse form a "cascade" or sequence, with complaining and criticizing leading to contempt, "which leads to defensiveness, which leads to listener withdrawal from interaction" (p. 110); Figure 14.3 depicts this process.

Complaints and Criticisms   The cascade starts when one person complains or criticizes. Gottman (1994) noted that some complaints can actually be healthy. If relational partners never complained, they would be unable to improve their relationships by changing problematic behavior. However, if complaints continue over long periods or if they turn into criticisms, Gottman's research suggests that the partner will start to feel contempt. The least threatening types of complaints are specific and focus on behaviors. Once complaints start to focus on aspects of a person's character, they turn into criticisms and are likely to lead to contempt.

People can complain in at least five different ways (Alberts, 1988, 1989). First, they can complain about **behavior.** For instance, you might tell your friend that you wish she wasn't always late. Notice that this type of complaint is specific in terms of the kind of action a person has to take to remedy the problem— in this case to start showing up on time. In addition, the focus is on the behavior, not the person. This type of complaint was by far the most common in Alberts' (1988) data. Second, people can complain about **personal characteristics** ("You are so inconsiderate and rude"). These types of complaints, which almost always constitute a character attack, occurred the second most frequently in Alberts' study. Third, people can complain about **performance.** In this case they dislike the way something is done ("You were supposed to put oil in the water before cooking the spaghetti"). This type of complaint can be frustrating because it implies that someone is not doing something the proper way. Fourth, people can complain about **personal appearance.** To illustrate this type of complaint, Alberts (1988) gave the following example from her data: "You have a fat butt and better lose weight" (p. 188). Clearly this type of complaint is also a

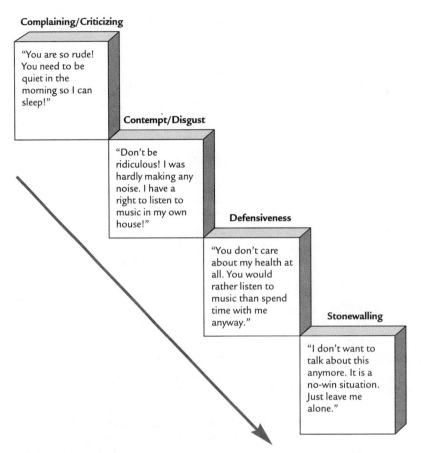

FIGURE 14.3 Gottman's Cascade Process of Relational Dissolution: The Four Horsemen of the Apocalypse

form of personal attack. Finally, people can make **metacomplaints,** which involve complaining about the partner's complaining behavior. For example, a wife might tell her husband to "stop nagging," or a husband might tell a wife to "quit whining and complaining." Alberts (1988) found that satisfied couples were more likely than dissatisfied couples to use behavioral complaints. Dissatisfied couples, by contrast, were more likely to use personal characteristic complaints.

Contempt and Disgust According to Gottman, complaints about a partner's personal characteristics or other types of criticism lead to contempt and disgust. These feelings are usually communicated to the partner. As Gottman (1994) put it, "Disgust typically is communicated by sounding fed up, sickened, and repulsed" (p. 25). For example, you might say, "I've had enough" or "I'm not going to take it anymore." When people who have been criticized feel disgust, they may be particularly prone to making both real and empty relational threats, such as threatening to leave the partner. Contempt is communicated in similarly negative ways. Gottman (1994) stated:

> Contempt is also easy to identify in speech. It involves any insult, mockery, or sarcasm or derision, of the other person. It includes disapproval, judgment, derision, disdain, exasperation, mockery, put downs, or communicating that the other person is absurd or incompetent. Three types of contempt are hostile humor, mockery, or sarcasm. In this form of contempt, there may be derision, a put down, or cold hate. There is often a definite sense of distance, coldness, and detachment in this category of behavior. (p. 25)

Defensiveness   People become defensive when they feel a need to defend themselves and ward off personal attacks. Gottman listed several communicative behaviors that are related to defensiveness, including denying responsibility for a problem, issuing countercomplaints, whining, making accusations, and reading minds. According to Gottman (1994), when a person begins mind-reading, this is a particularly good clue that he or she is becoming defensive. **Mind-reading** occurs when people assume that they know their partner's feelings, motives, and behaviors. Gottman (1994) gave the following examples to illustrate mind-reading: "You don't care about how we live," "You get tense in situations like this one," and "You have to spend whatever we save" (p. 25). Gottman also noted that mind-reading statements often include words like "always" or "never." As such, mind-reading violates two principles of fair fighting: (1) It often is based on jumping to conclusions, and (2) it usually is based on overgeneralizations.

Mind-reading is common within marital interaction, yet it is seldom accurate, and it usually escalates conflict (Gottman, 1994). Conversational data collected by Alberts and Driscoll (1992) on complaints help illustrate this point. In the following example Charles was upset because Cindy assumed that if he did a favor for her he would hold it against her in some way. He told her that he did not mind doing favors for her and would not expect anything in return. Eventually Charles said to Cindy, "When you tell me what I was going to say, it's almost always wrong. I mean it's wrong, and it's infuriating and it drives me nuts. Like you really know me so well, that you know exactly what I'm going to say. And it's never ever true. It's never the correct answer. It's what you want to believe I'm going to decide" (p. 404).

In addition to mind-reading, defensiveness may also be related to problems of **punctuation** (Watzlawick, Beavin, & Jackson, 1967). When people become defensive, they usually "punctuate" the cause of the conflict differently. The classic example of punctuation problems concerns the cycle of nagging and withdrawing. One partner might say, "I have to nag you all the time because you always withdraw," whereas the other partner might say, "I have to withdraw because you are always nagging me." Notice that each person blames the other for her or his behavior. Notice also that both statements contain the word "always," which can be problematic during conflict interaction.

Stonewalling   Stonewalling falls at the end of Gottman's cascade of negative conflict behavior. After people have been attacked, experienced contempt, and tried (often unsuccessfully) to defend themselves, they often **stonewall,** or withdraw from the interaction. At this point interaction seems futile. Partners no longer are trying to work problems out, as disagreements escalate into negative conflict interactions, and both partners are hurt and defensive. As mentioned previously, however, men tend to stonewall more frequently than women (Gottman, 1994). This often leads to the demand-withdrawal cycle discussed earlier, with wives insisting on talking about problems and husbands refusing to engage in such a dialogue. If stonewalling persists, Gottman's research suggests, relationships become stagnant and couples are likely to break up.

Principle 6: Respond with positive, validating messages.

Finally, it is important for partners to either prevent or halt the escalation of conflict by limiting the number of negative statements they make. In fact, according to Gottman's (1994) research, partners in happy relationships counterbalance every negative statement they make with around five positive statements. Gottman suggested that satisfied partners are better able to regulate their interaction. Successful regulation requires the effort of both partners—each must have the ability to respond to complaints and criticisms with more positive than negative messages. Dissatisfied partners, by contrast, find it difficult to regulate conflict interaction. One or both partners become emotionally flooded, and they respond to most statements negatively. Indeed, Alberts and Driscoll (1992) found that individuals in dissatisfying relationships were twice as likely as individuals in satisfying relationships to respond to complaints by denying the validity of the complaint or by escalating the hostility level of the interaction.

So how should people respond to complaints and criticisms? Alberts' (1988) work on conversational complaints helps answer this question. Imagine that Holly complains that Keith takes her for granted. How might Keith respond? According to Alberts (1988), Keith has five general options:

1. **Justifications/excuses:** providing a reason for his attitude or behavior (Keith tells Holly that it only seems that way because he is so comfortable around her.)
2. **Denial:** refusing to acknowledge the legitimacy of the complaint (Keith tells Holly, "I don't know why you would think that. I do a lot of things for you.")
3. **Agreement:** acknowledging that the complaint is legitimate, sometimes through an apology (Keith tells Holly, "I'm sorry about that. I should show you how much I care for you more often.")
4. **Countercomplaint:** responding to the complaint with another complaint (Keith tells Holly, "You take me for granted, too.")

5. **Pass:** ignoring or failing to respond to the complaint (Keith changes the topic by asking Holly if she wants to go out to see a movie this weekend.)

Alberts found that dissatisfied couples were more likely to engage in countercomplaints than were satisfied couples. A complaint-countercomplaint sequence is likely to start a negative spiral and to induce contempt. By contrast, satisfied couples were more likely to use agreements than dissatisfied couples. Alberts and Driscoll's (1992) data on conversational complaints show how agreement can help couples stick to the topic and reach an understanding. They gave an example of a man (we'll call him Aaron) who complains to a woman (we'll call her Beth) that he cannot find his possessions because she moves them when she cleans the house. The end of their conversation went this way:

AARON: But, I mean, it's not like you do it on purpose. It's because you're absent-minded.

BETH: Uh huh. Yeah.

AARON: And it's not like I don't do it either.

BETH: Yeah, I mean, I agree that things have to have their place . . . if you put them in their place, then you know where they are and it saves you a lot of worry.

AARON: Well, then, there's really no disagreement.

BETH: Yeah, that's the way things should be. It's just that sometimes we do things that are contrary to the things we agree on.

Notice that Aaron violated one of the rules of fair fighting by calling Beth "absent-minded." However, instead of responding to a personal attack with another personal attack, Beth expressed agreement (perhaps because she agreed that she did not do it "on purpose"). This led Aaron to admit that he sometimes does the same thing, which paved the way to ending the disagreement.

It takes considerable social skill and patience to respond to complaints and criticisms with positive or neutral statements. Indeed, it is easy to be nice when your partner is nice, but it is difficult to be nice when your partner is complaining or criticizing. As Rusbult et al. (1994) argued, people have a natural tendency to reciprocate negative, hurtful behavior. And once a negative cycle starts, it is hard to break. Therefore, if possible, you should try to prevent a negative spiral from starting in the first place.

Being able to respond to negativity with positivity appears to be one key to relational satisfaction. In one study, couples in which people were nice only when the partner was nice were more likely to separate either 1½, 2½, or 5 years later than were couples in which the two people were nice regardless of whether their partners were acting positively or negatively. As this study demonstrated, it is important for people to be positive when the partner is sad, angry, or inexpressive, as well as when the partner is happy. Gottman's (1994) recommendation

---

BOX 14.2 HIGHLIGHTS

Ten "Rules" for Fair Fighting

Based on the situation, there are various ways to manage conflict effectively. However, based on the research reviewed in this chapter, the following ten "rules" should serve people well in most conflict situations.

1. Avoid gunnysacking, or bringing in everything but the kitchen sink.
2. "Own" your thoughts and feelings, and do not bring other people into the conflict.
3. Attack positions, not people (no name-calling, button-pushing, or violence).
4. Avoid making empty relational threats.

5. If necessary, postpone conflict until your emotions cool down.
6. Practice active listening by trying to understand your partner's position.
7. Use behavioral complaints rather than personal criticisms.
8. Avoid defensiveness and mind reading.
9. Try to validate your partner's position by expressing agreement and positivity rather than stonewalling or escalating conflict.
10. For every one negative statement or behavior, use five positive statements or behaviors.

---

that couples counterbalance every one negative statement with five positive statements appears to be very sound advice. Box 14.2 lists some other rules and recommendations for fair fighting.

Conclusion

Conflict can be positive or negative. When differences are handled constructively, conflict can improve relationships by helping partners solve problems and understand each other better. However, engaging in constructive conflict is a complex social skill. Many people use competitive strategies and personal attacks, which can cause conflicts to escalate. Other people avoid conflicts, which in many cases allows the problem to get worse. Several types of negative spirals can develop within relationships. Some relational partners get caught in a demand-withdrawal cycle, others engage in dual withdrawal, and still others find themselves reciprocating each other's negative behavior. Because people often experience emotional flooding during conflict situations, it is difficult to stop these negative spirals from emerging.

Constructive conflict is a two-way street. It takes two people to collaborate or compromise. This is why it is critical that people refrain from responding to negative statements with more negativity. Instead, relational partners need to try to counter a negative statement with a positive or neutral statement. This probably makes a lot of sense to you, but it may nonetheless seem somewhat unrealistic. In fact, as you read through the six principles of constructive conflict and the more specific list of 10 rules of fair fighting, you probably thought they constituted good advice. However, you might also have thought that it would be very difficult to follow this advice in an actual conflict situation. Even if you have good intentions and know how you *should* act during a conflict situation, if your emotions are running high it will be difficult not to violate some of the rules and recommendations discussed in this chapter. If you find yourself engaging in some destructive tactics during conflict situations, do not panic— even experts in negotiation make mistakes. Recognizing these mistakes is the first step toward rectifying the problem.

Research suggests that conflict is heading in the wrong direction when the "four horsemen of the apocalypse" appear (Gottman, 1994). So, if you notice that your conflict interactions are characterized by a lot of personal criticism, contempt, defensiveness, and/or stonewalling, you would be well advised to try to use more constructive modes of conflict in the future. According to Gottman, your relationship could depend on dismounting the four horsemen.

Discussion Questions

1. Think about your long-term relationships. How often do you have disagreements with these relational partners? Did the number and types of conflict change as the relationship became more serious?
2. Do you tend to avoid or engage in conflict? Which of the five conflict styles discussed in this chapter best fits you?
3. When people are in the midst of interpersonal conflict, they often are flooded with emotions. This makes it difficult to "fight fairly." Which of the principles or rules for constructive conflict management do you think is most difficult to follow? Do you have any additional suggestions that might help your classmates learn to manage conflict in more constructive ways?

In the End

Relationship Disengagement and Termination

In Paul Simon's classic song "Fifty Ways to Leave Your Lover," listeners are told to "slip out the back, Jack, hop, off the bus, Gus," or "drop off the key, Lee" when they want to end relationships. Researchers who have been examining the ends of relationships for several decades can offer more sophisticated communication strategies. We have come to know a lot about how and why relationships end, as well as the central role played by communication before, after, and during relationship breakups.

In this chapter our goal is to give you a better understanding of the relational disengagement process. Think about the relationships in your own life that have come to an end. It is likely that some of them ended abruptly, whereas others disintegrated slowly. It is also likely that it was painful to end some relationships and a relief to end others. A variety of communication strategies may have been used to end the relationship, or one person may simply have said that it was over and walked away. Relational disengagement is a complex phenomenon. To help unravel this complexity, this chapter focuses on four areas of relational disengagement research. First, we examine the reasons relationships end. Second, we review models of the disengagement process. Third, we discuss 12 communication strategies people use to leave their partners. Finally, we take a look at the aftermath of relational disengagement.

Why Relationships End

All relationships end. Regardless of whether they are brief or close encounters, last 50 days or 50 years, or are friendships or marriages, all relationships end at one time or another. Conville (1991) suggested that "disintegration is everywhere. . . . Disintegration is a process that is triggered when the relationship is out of kilter" (p. 96). Baxter (1982) stated: "The breaking up of a relationship is a phenomenon known to most and dreaded by all. It accounts for some of our most intense and painful social experiences" (p. 223). The deep positive and negative feelings we experience in our relationships are connected: There are no highs without lows. Gibran (1923) described these two sides of love:

> When love beckons to you follow him, though his ways are hard and steep, and when his wings enfold you, yield to him, though the sword hidden among his pinions may wound you. And when he speaks to you believe in him, though his voice may shatter your dreams as the north wind lays waste the garden. Even as love crowns you so shall he crucify you. Even as he is for your growth so is he for your pruning. (p. 12)

The knowledge that relationships end, and frequently do so painfully, prevents some people from developing meaningful relationships. By denying themselves the opportunity to feel both the joys and the sorrows connected with relationships, these people miss an important secret of life: Not feeling anything at all may be worse than feeling bad. Avoiding relationships prevents them from experiencing the deepest involvements and emotions humans can have.

People become deeply enmeshed and involved in their close relationships (Baxter, 1982). Relationships exist in a web of close ties, emotional involvements, financial arrangements, sexual relations, friendship networks, possessions, memories, identities, families, and sometimes offspring. When a relationship dies many of these ties die as well. The emotional pain of relational loss is compounded by the loss of these other relationships, resources, and connections. Given how painful the end of relationships can be, you might wonder, Why then do relationships end? What are the common causes for relationship breakdowns? This section addresses this question.

General Pathways to Relational Endings

While slight differences exist in the way various types of relationships end, the research suggests that most couples, unmarried or married, straight or gay, show more similarity than difference in the way they break up. For example, research reveals few differences between heterosexual, gay, and lesbian couples in the origins or effects of relational breakups, or in the communication strategies used to terminate relationships and cope with relational loss (Kurdek, 1991). However, in their massive study of American couples, Blumstein and Schwartz (1983) were surprised to find that lesbians were most likely to break up, followed by gay men, followed by heterosexual cohabitors. Married couples were the most stable of these four couple types. While married couples were the most stable, when they did break up, they separated for many of the same reasons as did other couples.

Conscious Choice   Most breakups are a rational or strategic choice by one or both partners. In Baxter's (1984) study, about two thirds of all breakups were the choice of one partner and one third were a bilateral decision to terminate the relationship. The fact that most relationship breakups are driven by one partner is one reason breakups can be so painful. One person might want the relationship to continue, while the other person may feel guilty for terminating the relationship. As the popular saying goes, it takes two people to develop a relationship, but only one person to end it. Interestingly, summaries of research have shown that in marriages the wife is the "dumper" in about two thirds of the cases (Braver, Whitney, & Ng, 1993). Similarly, in a study of dating breakups, Hill, Rubin, and Peplau (1976) found that women were more likely to precipitate breakups than men.

Atrophy   Some relationships slowly wither away. This is particularly the case for friendships and some dating relationships, especially if they are long distance. Bonded and committed relationships are less likely simply to wither away. But research shows that even marriages suffer from atrophy and that marital happiness slowly declines over time (Sternberg, 1987). Marital partners rarely just disappear the way casual friends and even lovers do, partially because of barriers to disengagement such as children, intertwined social networks, and shared possessions and financial resources (see Chapter 9). Still, in marriages, like other relationships, feelings of intimacy may disappear as the relationship slowly atrophies.

Relationships experience atrophy for many reasons. Metts and Cupach (1986) found that many relationships terminate after the partners slowly drift apart. This could be due to different interests, decreased quality and quantity of communication, distance, reduced efforts to maintain the relationship, or competition from the hundreds of competing relationships in today's fast-paced world. In a study on people's accounts of relationship breakups, Owen (1993) found that many relationship breakups were characterized by atrophy or decay. Typical metaphors for relationship endings were "It was like a flower that blossomed and then withered," "I could see the relationship rot each day," and "The relationship faded into the sunset" (pp. 271–272).

Separation   The history of America has been the history of movement. Our ancestors emigrated from other lands, and Americans have always moved from state to state, farm to city, city to suburb, and job to job. Many of you went away to college and will move to another place when you graduate. In their study of turning points in romantic relationships, Bullis, Clarke, and Sline (1993) found that one of the most common turning points was physical separation, such as through extended vacations, distant schools, or job transfers. Although such actions were not the result of a breakup, they were often the turning point that eventually led to a breakup. Shaver, Furman, and Buhrmester (1985) reported that moving away to college was the cause for the decline of 46% of precollege romances. In some cases, it seems, "Absence does not make the heart grow fonder." Instead, "Out of sight means out of mind." When people are separated from one another for extended periods of time, they often make new friends and discover new interests. In his study of gay and lesbian relationships, Kurdek (1991) reported that frequent absence was the primary reason for breakups. The finding that separation often has negative effects on relationships corresponds with the attraction principle (discussed in Chapter 3), according to which geographical closeness and repeated interaction lead to liking and enhance feelings of intimacy.

BOX 15.1 HIGHLIGHTS

The Top 10 Reasons for Breakups in Marriages and Dating Relationships

Marital Relationships	Dating Relationships
1. Communication breakdown	1. Becoming bored with the relationship
2. Loss of shared goals or interests	2. Differences in interests
3. Sexual incompatibility	3. Desire to be independent
4. Infidelity and jealousy	4. Differences in background
5. Boredom/lack of excitement	5. Conflicting ideas about sex
6. Money and financial issues	6. Conflicting ideas about marriage
7. Conflicts about children	7. Living too far apart
8. Alcohol or drug abuse	8. Interest in someone else
9. Women's equality issues	9. Differences in intelligence
10. Conflict with or about in-laws	10. Pressure from parents

Source: Adapted from Safron (1979) and Hill, Rubin, and Peplau (1976).

Death   Perhaps the most difficult relational ending is the death of a spouse or primary partner. Because the average woman marries a man who is a couple of years older than her and then lives 6 to 8 years longer than her husband, widows outnumber widowers by a 10:1 ratio.

Research has shown that an important buffer in coping with the loss of a partner is the presence of a social support network (Prager, 1995). Likewise, research suggests that hospice workers are invaluable in providing comfort and support to the widow or widower (Zimmerman & Applegate, 1994). Unfortunately these authors also found that hospice workers with more training provided fewer person-centered comforting messages than newer, untrained hospice workers, suggesting a need for more communication training among hospice workers. Nonetheless, most people's experiences with hospices are far superior to those with the traditional medical establishment. It appears to be most important, however, for widows and widowers to have a close circle of friends and family around them.

Specific Reasons for Relationship Termination

For several decades scholars have been studying why and how relationships end. As Box 15.1 shows, relational researchers have repeatedly identified a number of themes or causes associated with relational breakups—both marital and dating. Poor communication is a common culprit. Indeed, several studies have found that the number one problem leading to divorce is poor communication

(Bradford, 1980; Cleek & Pearson, 1985; Parker & Drummond-Reeves, 1993), including too much communication, too little communication, low-quality communication, and communication that is too negative. A number of studies also have found that divorcing couples have less mutually constructive communication than nondistressed couples. Many other factors, such as sexual incompatibility, money, and equality issues can also lead to relationship termination. These different causes are discussed next.

Withdrawal   Withdrawal or "stonewalling" is often related to marital and premarital breakups. As discussed in Chapter 14, stonewalling occurs when individuals fail to discuss important issues with their partners (Christensen & Shenk, 1991; Gottman, 1993; Gottman & Levenson, 1992). Males have been found to use this type of dysfunctional communication more often than females (Clements, Cordova, Markman, & Laurenceau, 1997).

Several other studies have shown that withdrawal is a common reason for relationship breakups. Baxter (1986) found that lack of supportiveness, particularly lack of listening, was a major factor in over one fourth of the relational breakups she studied. Likewise, demand-withdrawal communication, whereby one person insists on more closeness and the other pulls away, is also associated with separation (Christensen & Shenk, 1991). Honeycutt, Cantrill, and Allen (1992) had disengaged couples recall and describe behaviors that aided in the process of relational disengagement. These behaviors included spending less time together, avoiding each other in public settings, and making excuses for not going out together.

Negative Communication   All couples have conflicts and disagreements. In fact, as dating partners become more loving and committed, conflict increases, presumably because of their increased interdependence (Lloyd & Cate, 1985). Research has shown that it is not primarily the presence or absence of conflict that determines whether a couple will be satisfied and stay together; it is how the partners deal with conflict that is more important (see Chapter 14). In a series of studies spanning 15 years, Clements et al. (1997) reported that in their earliest interactions partners who were destined to break up dealt with their disagreements in a negative and destructive fashion characterized by fights, name-calling, criticisms, and accusations. Research by Filsinger and Thoma (1988) found that negative communication during interpersonal interaction was predictive of disengagement 1½ years later. In a major statistical summary of the research on divorce, Karney and Bradbury (1995) reported that one of the most prevalent factors leading to divorce was negative behavior. One study found that a common path to relational disengagement was rules violation, whereby one partner engages in behavior inappropriate to the relationship (Metts & Cupach, 1986). For example, if relational partners have agreed not to swear at each other and to call when they are going to be late, repeated violations of these rules can lead to dissatisfaction and, perhaps, disengagement.

Although conflict increases as dating relationships become more committed, conflict rises even more for partners who are contemplating a breakup or have decided to terminate their relationships (Lloyd & Cate, 1985). These findings suggest that there may be an optimal level of conflict in a committed relationship beyond which the relationship is threatened. In other words, some conflict may be normal and even healthy for relationships. But high levels of conflict may be detrimental, particularly if issues of contention keep resurfacing because they have not yet been discussed in a constructive manner.

Increased negative emotional expression and decreased positive emotional expression also put couples at risk for dissolution (Gottman, 1993; Gottman & Levenson, 1992; Karney & Bradbury, 1995). Karney and Bradbury (1995) found that the reciprocity of negative behaviors was the most detrimental factor in a marriage. Surprisingly, Gottman (1993) reported that husbands' anger was unrelated to divorce. However, husbands who became defensive, showed contempt, and used stonewalling were more likely to divorce. Similarly, wives who criticized, became defensive, and showed contempt were more likely to see their relationships end. Honeycutt et al. (1992) reported that couples recalled various forms of aversive communication, such as arguing about little things, disagreeing, verbally fighting, criticizing the partner, and making sarcastic comments, as sets of behaviors that led to the breakup of their relationships.

Lack of Openness and Intimacy Open disclosure is very important for relationships. Partners who stayed together rather than breaking up reported much higher levels of self-disclosure early in their relationships (Berg & McQuinn, 1986). Sprecher (1987) found that dating couples who engaged in more self-disclosure were much more likely to be together 4 years later. Openness is particularly important to women. In Baxter's (1986) study, 31% of the women, as compared to only 8% of the men, mentioned lack of openness as a major factor in relational termination. In a study on memories of relationship breakups, Honeycutt and his colleagues (1992) reported that many people remember decreases in verbal and nonverbal intimacy as the starting point for relational decline. Couples at risk for eventual disengagement may stop expressing intimate feelings and decrease acts of physical intimacy such as hugs, kisses, and touches.

Lack of Similarity Despite the oft-repeated folk wisdom that "opposites attract," a more appropriate statement is that "birds of a feather flock together" (see Chapter 3). Dozens of studies show that the more two people have in common the more likely they are to stay together. Think of your close friends. Chances are that you have many things in common, including hobbies and interests, political opinions, and religious values. Similarities are also important in romantic relationships. Studies have shown that similarities in personality lead to longer relationships and fewer breakups. For example, spouses who are more alike in extraversion, attractiveness, and interest in art are less likely to divorce (Bentler & Newcomb, 1978). Similarly, Cody (1982) found personality incompatibility to be a major cause of relational breakups.

Lack of similarity in attitudes and interests, as well as differences in ethnic, religious, and socioeconomic backgrounds, can also precipitate relational breakups. Baxter (1996), in her study of heterosexual dating relationships, reported that the second most common reason for breakups was a discrepancy in beliefs, attitudes, and values, a factor mentioned by nearly one third of the respondents. Likewise, Metts and Cupach (1986) found that value dissimilarity was a common factor leading to relational disengagement. In their landmark statistical summary of factors leading to divorce, Karney and Bradbury (1995) concluded that attitude dissimilarity was one of the most important factors leading to both relational dissatisfaction and divorce.

Although many interethnic dating relationships and marriages are very successful and rewarding, some are at greater risk for breakups. This may be primarily due to the prejudicial influences of family, friends, and society in general (Williams & Andersen, 1998). Felmlee, Sprecher, and Bassin (1990) reported that a major predictor of breakups in dating relationships is differences in race or ethnicity. In a classic study on dating relationships, Hill et al. (1976) found that the fourth most important factor leading to breakups was differences in background. Similarly, although people who have a large age differential can have happy relationships, age differences are statistically related to breakups (Bentler & Newcomb, 1978).

Differences in educational background and intelligence may also pose problems for relationships. In Hill et al.'s (1976) study, differences in intelligence were among the top reasons for dating relationship breakup. Similarly, when one partner continues her or his education and the other partner does not, they sometimes find that they have less and less in common (Scott & Powers, 1978).

While some difference in interests is probably good for a relationship, in general common interests are more likely to lead to relational stability than are dissimilar interests. In Hill et al.'s (1976) study of dating relationships, the second biggest factor leading to breakups for both men and women was differences in interests. Similarly, Safron (1979) found that the second most important reason for marital breakups was loss of shared goals or interests.

Sexual Incompatibility Sex is a central feature of marriages, romances, and many dating relationships (see Chapter 7). Because sex is such a personal and important aspect of many relationships, it can lead to several types of problems. Relational partners may differ over the desired frequency of sexual relations, the type of sexual behaviors, the initiation of sex, and, of course, fidelity issues. During dating relationships, engagements, and marriages, and in straight and gay relationships, fighting about sex is associated with relational breakups (Blumstein & Schwartz, 1983), although there is little association between how much sex a couple has and how long the partners stay together. Apparently frequency is not as important as compatibility. In other words, some couples may be satisfied with less sex than others. The key is that both partners have similar sexual needs and desires.

Conflicting sexual attitudes was a common reason for premarital breakups in the Hill et al. (1976) study and for marital breakups in Safron's (1979) study. Similarly, sexual incompatibility was the fifth most important reason for divorce in Cleek and Pearson's (1985) study, and the second most important reason for gay and lesbian separations in Kurdek's (1991) study. Together these studies clearly show that sexual incompatibility is an important force that can lead to relationship breakups.

Sexual satisfaction is important in romantic relationships. In a major statistical analysis of the prior research on marital stability, Karney and Bradbury (1995) reported that sexual satisfaction was one of the most important factors in a stable marriage for both husbands and wives. Sexual dysfunction was a factor in the dissolution of 75% of marriages in one study (Bradford, 1980) and 60% of the marriages in another (Parker & Drummond-Reeves, 1993).

For women tenderness, communication, and intimacy are especially important parts of sexual satisfaction, and their absence during sex is associated with dissatisfaction and relational termination. For men physical attraction is an important part of sex, and absence of attraction may lead to male-initiated breakups. When men place great emphasis on physical attraction, their relationships are unlikely to survive past the first few years, because for these men the "grass is always greener elsewhere" (Blumstein & Schwartz, 1983).

Extramarital and extrarelational sex is often detrimental to a relationship and may lead to termination, although the reverse is sometimes true—that is, an unhappy relationship leads to extrarelational sex. For every type of couple, including gay and straight, the relationship is less likely to survive when one partner is having sex outside the relationship (Blumstein & Schwartz, 1983). Gagnon (1977) reported that nearly 40% of extramarital sexual relationships had an important effect on the decision to divorce, and 14–18% of the time these affairs had a major effect. Bradford (1980) reported that extramarital affairs were a factor in the breakups of 55% of the couples in his study. Parker and Drummond-Reeves (1993) reported that an extramarital affair was a factor for 25% of the divorced couples they studied. In Safron's (1979) study infidelity was the fourth most common reason for divorce. Cupach and Metts (1986) found that, while extrarelational affairs were a problem associated with breakups for both married and unmarried couples, affairs were a more salient concern for women than for men. They suggested that for men an affair is a form of self-gratification, whereas women see affairs as a violation of the relationship, and thus a more central cause of relationship disengagement.

Autonomy and Independence   Studies have repeatedly shown that wanting to maintain one's autonomy is a major reason for relationship disengagement. People often complain that the relationship is "smothering" or "suffocating" them and that they need their "space" and "freedom." In Hill et al.'s (1976) classic study, the third most important reason for termination of a dating relationship was the desire to be independent. Baxter (1986) reported that the most frequent reason for the breakup of a heterosexual dating relationship was the need for autonomy. Indeed, this was the primary reason for over one third of the respondents. Men reported lack of autonomy 24% of the time, but women listed it as a primary reason 44% of the time. Similarly, one of the five most common general issues leading to relational breakups in gay and lesbian couples was excessive fusion, which is a loss of individuality due to the relationship (Kurdek, 1991).

Interest in Someone Else   Rivals can be threats to relationships. Perhaps this is why jealousy is such a widespread emotion and a major cause of relational violence (see Chapter 13). Hill et al. (1976) reported that one of the top 10 reasons for terminating a dating relationship for both men and women was interest in someone else. Similarly, Metts and Cupach (1986) reported that one of the most common disengagement themes was third-party involvement, particularly for women. Failure to maintain loyalty and fidelity was a primary reason for terminating relationships in 16% of the accounts in Baxter's (1986) study on breakups. The availability of attractive alternative partners makes breakups of relationships more likely (Felmlee et al., 1990; Rusbult, Zembrodt, & Gunn, 1982). Interestingly, when people have few good prospects as alternative partners, they are more likely to stay with their current partner (Simpson, 1987). These findings correspond with social exchange theory principles (see Chapter 8). That is, people tend to be more committed to their relationships when the quality of alternative partners is low, and are less committed when the quality of alternative partners is high.

Boredom   The most important reason for relational breakups in Hill et al.'s (1976) study was boredom. Similarly, Safron (1979) found that boredom, or lack of excitement, was one of the top factors leading to divorce. In Safron's study many people indicated that the fun or excitement had gone out of the relationship. Nearly 10% of the participants in Baxter's (1986) study noted the absence of magic and romance as a primary cause for relational termination. Interestingly, this was a factor for 19% of the men but only 5% of the women, suggesting that men are less practical partners who may disengage if the magic is no longer there. Honeycutt et al. (1992) also reported that one of the most common thoughts that disengagers have about a relationship is that it has become boring. Our interpersonal relationships are one of our greatest sources of joy and excitement. Thus, when they begin to bore us, the end may be near.

Money   Money is a major problem in many relationships. Money was the sixth most important cause of divorce in Safron's (1979) survey of 730 marital counselors, the third most important factor in the divorces in one study (Bradford, 1980), and the fourth most important factor in the divorces in another study (Parker & Drummond-Reeves, 1993). Financial problems also can be a factor in gay and lesbian separations (Kurdek, 1991). Interestingly, few relational problems revolve around how much money a couple makes. Indeed, family income is not a correlate of personal or relational satisfaction.

According to Blumstein and Schwartz's (1983) landmark study of 10,000 U.S. couples, money management and the values surrounding spending and saving produce considerable turmoil for couples. Even long-standing couples are likely to break up if arguments about money continue to occur. Partners who pool their money are much more likely to stay together than those who do not. Arguments about income are a factor only for heterosexual couples (particularly when there is inequity in the amount of money that two people are contributing to the relationship) and is less important than money management issues.

Women's Equality Issues Because women have experienced relational inequality for so many years, equality issues are particularly important to them. In Safron's (1979) study, women's equality issues were the ninth most common reason cited for marital breakups. Likewise, in Baxter's (1986) study of heterosexual dating relational breakups, equity was a primary factor in the breakup for 17% of the women but only for 5% of the men. In Blumstein and Schwartz's (1983) landmark study of U.S. couples, a major factor in relational breakups revolved around men's opinions about working women. Specifically, if the man objected to the woman working, or if he was unhappy about her job, the couple was more likely to terminate their relationship.

Working women are also under considerable stress, especially if they have children and are trying to run a household. In the popular press this problem is referred to as the "superwoman syndrome." Women are supposed to do their jobs and then to go home and tend to their families and homes. Because women are expected to be the caregivers at home, they are constantly working—at the office and at home. Research has validated the existence of the superwoman syndrome. Hochschild (1997; Hochschild & Machung, 1989), for example, has shown that women typically do about 70% of the household chores. Moreover, only about 20% of dual-career couples report that a fair distribution of labor exists in their home. For the other 80% of couples, the woman is nearly always responsible for the majority of homemaking and childcare chores. When this type of inequity exists, it is often a primary source of tension in the relationship.

Alcohol and Drugs Alcohol and drugs play a role in many relational breakups. These problems were cited as the eighth most prevalent reason for divorce in the Safron (1979) study. Similarly, alcohol and drugs were reported to be a factor in 45% of the divorces in Parker and Drummond-Reeves' (1993) study. Alcohol and drugs may lead to violence, addiction, problems with the law, the squandering of money, and problems at work, any of which can greatly strain a relationship.

Research suggests that alcohol and drugs can also lead to codependency in relationships. Le Poire, Hallett, and Giles (1998), for example, argued that the partners of alcoholics and drug addicts often become **codependent,** letting their partner's behavior greatly affect their own behavior. Many codependents become obsessed with controlling their partner's negative behaviors and with nurturing the partner. According to Le Poire et al. (1998), codependents often show a mix of punishing and reinforcing behaviors. Sometimes they try to get their partner to stop using drugs or alcohol through punishment (verbal confrontation, threats to leave the relationship). Other times, however, they reinforce the partner's behavior by doing things such as keeping the children out of the way and taking care of the partner when he or she is ill. Although codependency may keep people in relationships for a while, in the long run codependent behavioral patterns may put considerable strain on relationships.

Social Networks   When friends and family disapprove of someone's partner, it can put pressure on a relationship. In fact, Felmlee et al. (1990) reported that the likelihood of relational breakup increased as people's social networks became more disapproving of the partner. Likewise, Sprecher and Felmlee (1992) found that it was important for women to have their parents be supportive of their dating relationships. When parents were supportive, the stability of the dating relationship increased; when they were unsupportive, a breakup was more likely. There is little evidence of the "Romeo and Juliet" effect, whereby parental prohibitions on the relationship actually increase relational strength and stability (see Chapter 3).

Developing new social networks that displace an existing network or strain the relationship is another common theme in relational disengagements (Metts & Cupach, 1986). Vaughn (1986) claimed that in many relationships partners separate physically by developing friendship networks that are disconnected from one another. In other words, the partners have separate friends who do not intermix. In Safron's (1979) study, in-laws were a major factor in the breakup of marriages. Likewise, in the Hill et al. (1976) study pressure from both the woman's and the man's parents regarding the relationship was a common cause of relational breakups. The lesson here seems clear: The more the social network disapproves of and interferes with the relationship, the harder it is for the couple to build and maintain a stable relationship.

Chronic Dissatisfaction   Research has shown that temporary dissatisfaction may cause couples to attempt to repair and maintain their relationship (see Chapter 9). However, a couple with a long history of dissatisfaction is more likely to be at risk for marital dissolution and divorce (Kurdek, 1993b). Similarly, dating couples experiencing chronic dissatisfaction are more likely to employ exit and neglect strategies that are detrimental to the relationship (Rusbult et al., 1982; see also Chapter 9). Exit strategies include breaking up, moving out, and getting a divorce; whereas neglect strategies include ignoring the partner, initiating new romantic relationships, and spending less time with the partner. Of course, chronic dissatisfaction may be related to the other factors (negative communication, inequity) discussed earlier in this section.

Models of the Disengagement Process

Now that you are aware of the many factors that contribute to relational breakups, you might be wondering *how* people go about ending their relationships. Researchers have tackled this question in two ways: (1) They have examined the general process by which relationships end, and (2) they have uncovered specific communication strategies that people use to terminate their relation-

Breakdown: Relationship dissatisfaction

Threshold: "I can't stand this anymore!!!"

Phase 1: The Intrapsychic Phase

Threshold: "I'd be justified in withdrawing."

Phase 2: The Dyadic Phase

Threshold: "I mean it!!!"

Phase 3: The Social Phase

Threshold: "It's now inevitable."

Phase 4: The Grave-Dressing Phase

FIGURE 15.1 Duck's Phase Model
of Relationship Dissolution

ships. We will examine the research in both of these areas, starting with the overall process of disengagement.

Researchers have created several models of how relationships come apart. Most of the thinking in this area has suggested that relationships pass through several phases—as if descending a staircase on their way from close, bonded relationships to breakups. These are stage model approaches to disengagement. Alternatively, we propose that many relationships go through sudden changes more akin to falling off a balcony than descending a flight of stairs. These are catastrophe theory approaches to disengagement.

Stage or phase theories suggest that breaking up is a process comprised of a series of steps that relational partners pass through as they disengage. The leading communication models of this type are Duck's phase model of relational dissolution and Knapp's reversal hypothesis.

Duck's Phase Model of Relational Dissolution

One of the foremost stage models of relational breakups is Duck's (1982, 1988) **phase model of relational dissolution,** depicted in Figure 15.1. The model conceives of breakups as a set of distinct but connected phases. It is important to note, however, that couples can go through several of these stages (particularly the first two) without proceeding to relational breakup. In fact, many couples recognize and resolve relational problems during the first two phases of Duck's model. But as couples reach and then proceed through the third phase, relationship dissolution becomes more likely.

One of the most elegant features of Duck's model is that it blends cognitive and behavioral factors. Each of the dissolution phases is preceded by a cognitive threshold (see Figure 15.1). These thresholds can be thought of as statements that represent the culmination of a person's thoughts at the end of each phase. These cognitive thresholds then propel the individual into the next phase. Sometimes, of course, partners do not reach these cognitive thresholds, but instead repair their relationships and return to a state of satisfaction. Duck's phases are described in more detail next.

The Intrapsychic Phase If people are dissatisfied with the relationship and reach the conclusion that they just can't stand it anymore, they move into the intrapsychic phase. In this first stage of relational dissolution, a relational partner begins to think and reflect about the negative aspects of the relationship, and contrasts these flaws with the cost of leaving the relationship. In some ways this phase involves determining one's own feelings about the relationship, as well as preparing to talk to the partner about problems. Sometimes individuals in this phase realize that their problems are not as bad as they originally thought. Other times, however, mulling about relational problems makes them worse rather than better (Cloven & Roloff, 1993). Vaughn (1986) claimed that "uncoupling begins with a secret. One of the partners starts to feel uncomfortable with the relationship" (p. 11). Dissatisfied partners face the dilemma of whether to discuss these feelings and thoughts with their relational partner. They may begin to hint about the problems to the partner, but more often they confide in a third party (Duck, 1988). A breakup is certainly not inevitable at this phase; often the partner is seeking to resolve the problems and maintain the relationship. However, when people get to the point where they believe that withdrawing from the relationship would be justified, they move into the next phase.

The Dyadic Phase In this phase dissatisfied partners begin to communicate about negative thoughts and feelings with each other. They also attempt to negotiate and sometimes reconcile the differences that could lead to a relationship breakup. Fights, arguments, and long discussions characterize this phase. According to Duck (1988), partners display uncertainty, oscillation, and hesitancy during this phase because of doubts over which path to take and because of the guilt, distress, and unpleasantness that would accompany a full-fledged breakup. In addition, some partners decide to use avoidance and withdrawal rather than communicating with each other during this phase. At the end of this phase, if people conclude that they are serious about the possibility of breaking up ("I mean it!"), they move into the third phase.

The Social Phase In this phase people begin talking to their social networks and investigating alternatives to the current relationship. They also attempt to save face and receive support by telling their side of the story to friends and family members. They develop a story to convince their network, and themselves, that they are doing the right thing (Duck, 1982). Often nonverbal behaviors such as looking depressed or sounding upset reveal to others that something is wrong in the relationship. Thus, the breakup initiator not only starts to complain publicly but also displays discontentment about the partner to others (Vaughn, 1986). Initially the individual's network may try to prevent a breakup, but when the outcome seems inevitable, they help him or her facilitate the breakup by providing interpersonal and emotional support and taking his or her side in any disputes. In addition, when members of the person's social network take their friend's side, it helps convince the breakup initiator that he or she is making the right decision. A word of caution is in order here, though: If people complain too loudly about their partners to others, the social network may have a hard time accepting them back into the fold if the partners change their minds and get back together. If, however, the partners decide to proceed ("It is now inevitable"), they move on to the final phase.

The Grave-Dressing Phase   After the breakup, emotional repair and relational realignment must occur. Often there is property to divide, children to deal with, and reputations to repair. Duck (1982, 1988) drew an analogy between erecting a burial monument and giving a eulogy, and the story that the separated parties begin to construct to help them save face and justify the breakup. Often the story is that, despite how good the two people were, the relationship was flawed from the start. Of course, not all former relational partners are this gracious toward each other. Sometimes partners continue to harbor ill will toward one another and to smear each other's names. Still, stories are a vital part of the psychology of breakups and the movement toward new relationships.

Knapp's Reversal Hypothesis: The "Coming-Apart" Stages

One of the earliest and most creative stage models of disengagement was Knapp's (1978) model of interaction stages, which later became known as the **reversal hypothesis.** Knapp posited that five stages characterize the "coming-apart" process: differentiating, circumscribing, stagnating, avoiding, and terminating; Box 15.2 traces a hypothetical couple as they pass through these stages. These stages are essentially the reverse of Knapp's stages of coming together discussed earlier in the book (see Chapter 5). Hence, this part of Knapp's model is called the reversal hypothesis.

Differentiating   This stage occurs when people begin to behave as individuals rather than as a couple. At this stage differences are emphasized at the expense of similarities. Partners may start doing things separately, and they may also argue about their differences. Of course, many relational partners go through the differentiation phase without proceeding toward relational termination.

BOX 15.2 HIGHLIGHTS

The Coming-Apart Stages: The Story of Randy and Rhonda

Randy and Rhonda met and proceeded to go through Knapp's coming-together stages (see Chapter 3). They fell in love and moved in together. However, it was not always smooth sailing for our hero and heroine, and soon they began a long climb down the stages of discontent.

1. **Differentiating.** Rhonda begins to feel smothered. She thinks that Randy always has to have things "his way," so she starts asserting herself more. When Randy wants to watch a particular television show, she quickly points out that the show is boring. When Randy wants to go rollerblading in the park, she tells him she would prefer to go hiking.

2. **Circumscribing.** Randy and Rhonda begin to feel disconnected, and this disconnection is reflected in their communication. The few conversations they have lack breadth and depth. For example, when Rhonda asks Randy how his day was, he replies that it was okay instead of launching into a discussion of the hard day he had. When Randy asks Rhonda if she is mad at him, she shrugs her shoulders and says, "No, not really."

3. **Stagnating.** Before long Randy and Rhonda completely stop talking to each other about their thoughts and feelings. Randy stops asking Rhonda what she wants to do, because he figures she'll simply tell him she'd rather be alone. Rhonda stops asserting herself because she thinks that Randy will merely ignore her ideas anyway and continue to do what he wants. The relationship is at a standstill.

4. **Avoiding.** Both Rhonda and Randy feel that the relationship is over. One day, Randy volunteers to move out at the end of the month. Rhonda agrees. Until then, Randy sleeps on the sofa. There is very little communication between Rhonda and Randy at this point, and they ignore each other as much as possible. Basically they are marking time until Randy can move out.

5. **Terminating.** Randy moves out of the apartment and starts spending time with a new group of friends from work. Rhonda removes reminders of Randy from the apartment. For example, she takes pictures of the two of them off of her dresser and puts them in a photo album. When Randy and Rhonda see each other at social functions, they feel a bit awkward. Both are trying to get on with their lives.

Sometimes people simply need to assert their individuality and autonomy. Extended differentiation, however, can lead couples to feel disconnected.

Circumscribing This stage occurs when communication becomes constricted in both depth and breadth. In other words, communication becomes superficial and is restricted to certain topics. In some ways the communication that takes place during this stage is similar to small talk, except that the communicators are using talk (and avoidance of talk) to distance themselves from each other instead of to learn more about each other. Communication can be constricted at any stage of a relationship. However, when partners begin to feel that they have nothing to talk about, it could be a sign that the relationship is declining.

Stagnating During the third stage the relationship seems to be at a standstill. Communication becomes tense and awkward, and the relationship is itself virtually a taboo subject. At this point people often feel that they already know what their partner will say or that the outcome of interaction will always be negative. Therefore, communication is seen as unproductive and unpleasant. Some couples who reach this stage eventually find a way to revive the relationship. Others, however, give up hope and, quickly or gradually, move to the next stage.

Avoiding   This stage is best characterized by physical separation. If possible, relational partners move into separate physical environments and try not to encounter each other. If physical separation is not possible, the partners simply ignore each other. For example, spouses who have young children and cannot afford to live apart might move into separate bedrooms until a more permanent solution can be reached. In any case, the goal in the avoidance stage is to achieve as much physical and psychological distance as possible.

Terminating   In this final stage relational partners end contact, and the relationship is over. Although the partners may quickly be able to separate from each other physically, it might take longer to separate psychologically. Individuals develop their own self-interests and social networks as a way of distancing themselves from their past relationship and moving on with their lives. If communication does occur at this stage, it is usually tense, awkward, and hesitant.

Knapp's model makes intuitive sense, but it has not been tested extensively. One study partially supported Knapp's reversal prediction regarding self-disclosure. Tolstedt and Stokes (1984) found that during breakups self-disclosure decreased in breadth and became more negatively valenced, consistent with Knapp's model. However, contrary to the reversal hypothesis, depth of disclosure actually increased. This may be because some couples have intense arguments and relationship discussions as they move toward relational termination. Other critics have argued that Knapp's model fails to accurately represent most breakups because it focuses almost exclusively on patterns of avoidance and distancing, rather than on conflict and relational discussion.

Catastrophe Theory

In many ways catastrophe theory is diametrically opposed to the stage models of relational disengagement. The stage models suggest that most deteriorating relationships follow a series of steps, akin to descending a staircase. However, many critics believe that these are artificial conceptualizations that fail to capture the actual nature of relational dissolution. First, many relational breakups skip steps. For instance, not every relationship goes through the stages of circumscribing or stagnation; some go straight to avoidance or termination. In the latest versions of the model (see Knapp & Vangelisti, 1996), the researchers address the process of skipping steps. Second, stages may occur nonlinearly, in various orders. For instance, termination may be followed by reconciliation, temporary bonding, stagnation, and then avoidance. Derlega, Metts, Petronio, and Margulis (1993) contended that cyclical movements characterize most relationships as they swing between periods of stability and change. Likewise, couples may go in and out of a stage several times before entering a stable period. Third, the stages of dissolution cannot simply be the reverse of the acquaintance process. Derlega et al. (1993) argued that during dissolution partners cannot "unknow" each other and are still very capable of predicting each other's behavior.

The **catastrophe model** of disengagement addresses some of these concerns. According to this model, relationships do not gradually unwind through stages of relational dissolution, but instead are characterized by sudden death (Davis, 1973). Like earthquakes along a silent fault line or like the violent wall next to the quiet eye of a hurricane, the stability of a relationship is shattered by a sudden cataclysmic event. Of course, fault lines are never completely silent, and impending hurricanes are accompanied by subtle signs such as falling air pressure and increased humidity. There are always signs of an impending relational catastrophe as well, but people fail to see them or deny them. As Vaughn (1986) stated, "Partners often report that they are unaware, or only remotely aware, even at the point of separation, that the relationship is deteriorating. Only after the other person is gone are they able to look back and recognize the signals" (p. 62).

Research has also found that many relationship breakups are precipitated by a critical incident that led to rapid disengagement (Baxter, 1984; Bullis et al., 1993; Cupach & Metts, 1986). These incidents ranged from the discovery of infidelity, to big arguments and physical violence, to a discovery of basic differences in values, such as the mundane reality that one partner hates pets and the other person loves them. In about 25% of the relationships in Baxter's (1984) study, partners reported that a single critical incident led to a breakup. Interestingly, Bullis et al. (1993) reported that few disengagements were intentional. Instead, disengagements often represented a nonstrategic turning point in relationships that happened relatively quickly, which is more in line with a catastrophe model of breakups than a stage model.

Even when no critical incident can be singled out, relationships sometimes dissolve very rapidly. Wilmot (1995) talked about the "point of no return" in every relationship, at which one or both of the partners knows for sure that it is over. Wilmot maintained that in these cases "sometimes people just disappear, without any warning or indication of their discomfort with the relationship" (p. 119). Similarly, Davis (1973) talked about sudden relational death, which occurs when a person abruptly decides the relationship is over, or falls in love with someone else, or suffers a trauma like partner abuse. According to Wilmot (1995), sudden death can be likened to an execution rather than a slow death of the relationship. The breakup often occurs without direct, face-to-face communication, but the person initiating the breakup may enlist the help of a friend to tell the partner that the relationship is over, or terminate the relationship via a letter or phone call.

Many events in nature are explained by catastrophe theory. This theory posits that events are discontinuous rather than following linear patterns (Isnard & Zeeman, 1976; Tesser & Achee, 1994). Sometimes human behavior, including the behavior of partners in relationships, will flow along a smooth, geometric plane. However, like hikers on a path next to a cliff, the relationship can slip off the edge of the plane to a completely different level, with catastrophic discontinuities for the relationship. Catastrophe theory has been successfully applied in many contexts, including mood changes, conflict during arguments, stock market behavior, and hostilities among nations (Zeeman, 1977). Relational researchers would be wise to use catastrophe theory to predict sudden death of relationships.

Of course, different relationships end in various ways. In a study of disengagement accounts, Baxter (1984) reported that in some relationships incremental problems gradually occurred while in others a critical incident led to a rapid breakup. Thus, the stage models and catastrophe theory help explain different types of breakups. The stage models are useful snapshots of the process of relational dissolution, especially if the process is more gradual. Stages help people understand what may be happening at a particular time as a relationship declines. Catastrophe theory, by contrast, is better equipped to explain rapid relational disengagement precipitated by one or more critical incidents.

A Dozen Ways to Leave Your Partner

People liberate themselves from relationships in a variety of ways. The strategies that people use to end relationships can be differentiated based on whether they are direct or indirect, and whether they are unilateral or bilateral (Baxter, 1982, 1984). Direct strategies rely primarily on face-to-face verbal communication, whereas indirect strategies involve more subtle, less direct forms of communication, including nonverbal communication. Unilateral strategies involve one person making the decision to break up, whereas bilateral strategies involve a joint decision to terminate the relationship.

More breakups are unilateral than bilateral, and more people end their relationships using indirect rather than direct strategies. Indeed, Baxter (1979b) found that 71% of all disengagement strategies reported in her study were indirect and implicit. Similarly, in her study of relationship disengagement accounts, Baxter (1984) found that 76% of couples employed indirect as opposed to direct communication strategies. In another study Baxter (1979a) found that when direct strategies were used they were more commonly unilateral "dumps" than negotiated dialogues. While most sex differences regarding breakups are minimal or nonexistent, Wilmot, Carbaugh, and Baxter (1985) reported that females are more likely to use direct strategies than males.

Although indirect strategies are used often to end both casual and close relationships, they are particularly likely to be used in casual relationships when couples have less to negotiate (Baxter, 1979b, 1984, 1992; Perras & Lustig, 1983; Thieme & Rouse, 1991; Wilmot, Carbaugh, & Baxter, 1985). Breakups are stressful, and disengagers try to minimize their pain and anxiety through indirect rather than direct communication. In light of the fact that "ending a relationship is perhaps one of the most face-threatening situations we encounter" (Cupach & Metts, 1994, p. 81), people are most likely to use indirect strategies that seem to minimize guilt and embarrassment.

Unfortunately, indirect strategies send neither clear nor kind messages. According to one study, only 22% of the recipients of indirect disengagement messages believed that the relationship was over (Baxter, 1984). Worse yet, relational partners were most likely to express regrets about the relationship when indirect rather than direct relational disengagement strategies were employed (Baxter, 1979b). Baxter (1979b) suggested that "hints" and other indirect relational disengagement strategies may actually create uncertainty, prolong the termination process, and be more painful for the participants.

Individuals can terminate their relationships using a single strategy or a complex array of both direct and indirect strategies. There is no set pattern. As you read through the following strategies, you will likely recognize some of them from your own relational breakups. We do not intend for this section to be a "how-to" guide for breaking up with relational partners. As the research presented in this chapter shows, breakups can be very emotionally distressing, and the strategies you use to end a relationship can contribute to that distress. We hope, however, that by learning about the ways that people break off relationships you will be better able to understand the disengagement process—and perhaps will be a little kinder and gentler the next time you find yourself initiating a breakup.

Strategies That Are Unilateral and Indirect

Avoidance The most common and perhaps least direct relational disengagement strategy is avoidance, whereby people literally "just slip out the back, Jack." A number of studies have reported avoidance as a primary disengagement strategy (Baxter, 1982; Cody, 1982; Perras & Lustig, 1992). Avoidance can range from complete evasion to decreased contact. Baxter (1979a) found decreased frequency of contact with a partner to be one of the two most common indirect disengagement strategies. In Baxter's (1984) study of disengagement accounts, 66% of the couples using indirect strategies reportedly used avoidance-based withdrawal strategies. Research has shown that avoidance tactics are especially likely when there is little likelihood of maintaining a friendship in the future, when intimacy is low, when there are fewer formal ties, and when the perceived faults of the partner are high (Banks, Altendorf, Greene, & Cody, 1987).

Not surprisingly, research shows that the avoidance strategy is a fairly ineffective way to end a relationship. Both parties experience a loss of face (Metts, 1997), and it is difficult for the former relational partners to experience closure. When avoidance strategies such as withdrawal are used, "the breakup is particularly dissatisfying for the disengager and the partner, even in low-level relationships" (Metts, 1997, p. 387). Several studies have found that avoidance strategies are the least effective, most protracted, and most distressing way to end a relationship (Baxter & Philpott, 1980).

Relational Ruses   Unfortunately, disengagers sometimes resort to strategies that are downright unethical. Relational ruses are a group of unethical strategies that involve manipulation and/or threats. In one of Baxter's (1982) studies, a common indirect communication strategy was labeled "manipulation attempts" and included behaviors such as leaking the impending breakup to a friend, asking a third party to break the news of the disengagement, or bullying the other person into a breakup. Fortunately manipulation is less likely to be used as a disengagement strategy in close relationships (Baxter, 1982). Research also has shown that relationships that are ended through manipulation are unlikely to evolve into cordial postromantic relationships, such as a friendship (Metts, Cupach, & Bejlovich, 1989).

Withdrawal of Supportiveness   A common disengagement strategy in romantic relationships is the withdrawal of social and emotional support. Gradually the disengager is less available to talk to, discuss problems with, and provide comfort and compassion. One study found that this was the most common relationship disengagement strategy in relationships of less than 2 years (Baxter, 1979b). As noted in Chapters 9 and 10, social support is an important part of close relationships. We expect our friends and loved ones to be there when we need them. If they are unavailable or refuse to make the effort to help us, their inaction sends an indirect but clear message that they no longer value the relationship.

Pseudo De-escalation   This strategy is a false declaration to the other party that the relationship would profit from some distance that masquerades as de-escalation, but is really disguised relational breakup (Baxter, 1985). In reality, this is a cover for the disengager's motivation to totally exit from the relationship. A person might say, "let's just put a little space into the relationship" or "let's just be friends for a while" when they really mean, "this relationship is over." The intent is often to let the other party down easily. However, even though this strategy may be more humane than the relational ruses described above, pseudo de-escalation is still essentially a deceptive, unethical behavior that shows little regard for one's partner. Baxter (1984) reported that this strategy comprised 22% of all indirect breakup strategies. However, she also found that pseudo de-escalation was highly ineffective since only 9% of the receivers of such a message got the clue that the relationship was actually over (Baxter,

1984). The rest of the participants harbored false hope that the relationship would eventually be revitalized.

Cost Escalation   When employing this strategy, disengagers are deliberately messy, obnoxious, rude, argumentative, or disloyal so that the partner comes to dislike them and becomes more amenable to a breakup. This strategy has been called cost escalation (Baxter, 1984; Thieme & Rouse, 1991) and Machiavellianism (Baxter 1979c; Perras & Lustig, 1982). In one account of a breakup, the dumper stated: "I thought I would be an 'asshole' for a while to make her like me less" (Baxter, 1985, p. 249). In another study cost escalation was found to be the most commonly used disengagement strategy, employed by 31% of the respondents (Thieme & Rouse, 1991). However, in Baxter's (1984) study cost escalation was employed by only 12% of the couples using indirect strategies. Ironically cost escalation can be beneficial in some breakups, especially if the "dumpee" is happy to break off the relationship after the costs have been escalated.

Strategies That Are Unilateral and Direct

The Direct Dump   The most common direct communication strategy is the simple statement that the relationship is over (Baxter, 1984; Thieme & Rouse, 1991). This strategy is sometimes called the open-and-honest approach, whereby someone forthrightly communicates her or his desire to end the relationship (Baxter, 1982; Perras & Lustig, 1982). Most commonly called the "fait accompli" approach (Baxter, 1979b, 1984), this tactic typically gives the partner no choice and little chance for a response. Often this strategy emphasizes the negative consequences of not breaking up, which helps the partner accept the breakup. Baxter (1984) reported that "fait accompli" resulted in 81% of the receivers of such messages accepting the breakup and offering no resistance, probably because of the perceived futility of countering such a direct message. Of course, it can also be disconcerting to be the recipient of the direct dump—to suddenly be told that the relationship is over and there's nothing you can do about it.

Dating Other People   Sometimes, rather than break up completely, a disengager recommends dating other people. This strategy, which is sometimes called negative identity management (Banks et al., 1987; Cody, 1982; Metts, 1997), imposes one person's solution on the other person, at the expense of the recipient's feelings. For example, the person initiating the breakup might say, "I told him that I was going to date other people and that he should also date other people." In this strategy the dumper at least has the class to communicate directly to his or her partner. However, even though this strategy is direct, its underlying meaning is less clear. Sometimes dating other people represents a temporary hiatus from an intense, intimate relationship that will rekindle. Often, however, this announcement is a disengagement message.

Justification   This strategy includes explanations for why the relationship is ending, why the partner is dissatisfied, and/or what changes have occurred in the individuals or in the relationship (Banks et al., 1987; Cody, 1982). Unlike the direct dump this strategy acknowledges the need to provide some rationale for the breakup to one's partner. It is an attempt to protect the face of both partners to some extent. This strategy is most likely to be used in highly intimate and committed relationships in which the friendship networks of the partners are highly overlapping (Banks et al., 1987). Justification is also more likely when the disengager feels that the rejected partner has many faults.

Research has shown that justifications are important to the rejected partner's ability to accept the end of the relationship. Thieme and Rouse (1991) found a significant association between the number of reasons given for a breakup and the rebuffed person's ability to accept the end of the relationship. Of course, if the justification focuses on the rejected individual's personal faults, hurt feelings and lowered self-esteem are likely to follow. But when justifications focus on the initiator of the breakup and general relationship issues, more positive outcomes are likely.

One particular type of justification that commonly occurs in dating relationships revolves around the desire for autonomy. Sometimes people feel they are becoming too dependent on each other and are losing their independence and individuality. As a result, they deescalate or disengage from the relationship using a strategy Cody (1982) called "relationship faults" or "appeals to independence." Often young lovers give this reason because they are not sure they are ready to settle down with one person just yet. Partners may also point to external factors, such as needing to concentrate more on school or one's career, as reasons for decreasing interdependence. This strategy is often less threatening than others because it is centered on the needs of the breakup initiator (for more space or freedom) and/or external events (such as school or work) rather than on the faults of the person who is being left. Often the reason for leaving the relationship is framed in situational terms—"At this point in my life I'm not ready to settle down yet" or "Right now I only have time for school."

The Relationship Talk Trick   Some disengagers talk about "problems" in the relationship as a guise for a relationship breakup. Baxter (1984) found that this strategy was incorporated in 27% of direct breakups. Sometimes this strategy is an honest attempt to discuss and solve problems in the relationship. More often, however, it is an insincere attempt to discuss problems and solutions in a manner that leads to the conclusion that the problems are insurmountable and justify a breakup. In other words, the breakup initiator intentionally structures the "relational talk" to show that the partners are better off going their separate ways. Like cost escalation this strategy can be hurtful in some instances but beneficial in others. If the person initiating the breakup can convince her or his partner that the relationship is not worth saving, both partners can walk away feeling that although they tried the relationship just could not be saved.

A Strategy That Is Bilateral and Indirect

In Baxter's research only one strategy emerged as both bilateral and indirect. This strategy is called fading away. Sometimes both people in a relationship recognize that the relationship is at a standstill, and they gradually drift apart and lose contact. This is very common in the case of friends who lose touch over the years (Baxter, 1979b). Fading away is also common when relational partners are separated from each other for long stretches of time. In long-distance relationships people sometimes come to feel like strangers due to the limited contact they have with one another. Words may not be necessary to end the relationship; instead, the couple may simply sense that it is over. For example, one of our students told the following story of her relational breakup:

> We only saw each other a couple times since moving away from our hometown to attend different colleges. At first, we called each other frequently, but over time the calls slowed down, and we seemed to have less and less to say to each other. After spending some awkward time together during Thanksgiving weekend, he drove me to the airport. When I left to board the plane, we hugged briefly, and it was clear that the relationship was not the same—it was over.

In some ways fading away is the antithesis of breakups that occur in a catastrophic fashion. With fading away there is no single incident leading to the breakup, but rather a slow and gradual descent.

Strategies That Are Bilateral and Direct

The Blame Game   In some cases conflict and dissatisfaction lead to a competitive blaming game that eventually results in relational breakup. In many cases cycles of negativity become a common pattern, with both partners dissatisfied and the relationship charged with negative emotion. When the partners try to talk about their problems, they end up complaining about and blaming each other rather than taking responsibility for their own actions. Eventually, when they agree to break up, they argue over the reasons and blame each other for the relationship's demise (Cody, 1982). Both may claim that the impending breakup is the other's fault, and both may feel justified in ending the relationship. In fact, partners who use the blaming strategy may set each other up so that leaving the relationship is the option that best helps them save face. In other words, it makes little sense to stay with a partner who is blameworthy, so the best option is to end the relationship. This type of strategy can be beneficial in that it provides both partners with a good reason to exit the relationship. However, breakups of this kind can be particularly messy, since conflict and disagreement are likely to prevail to the bitter end.

The Negotiated Farewell   Another common method of relational disengagement is negotiation based on positive, supportive communication. This method is usually called the positive tone strategy (Banks et al., 1987; Baxter, 1982; Cody,

	Unilateral	Bilateral
Indirect	Avoidance Relational ruses Withdrawal of supportiveness Pseudo de-escalation Cost escalation	The fadeaway
Direct	The direct dump Dates with other people The relationship talk trick Justifications	The blame game Negotiated farewell

FIGURE 15.2 Disengagement Strategies

1982; Perras & Lustig, 1982) or integrative communication (Metts, 1997). People using this strategy often have been together for a relatively long time but sense that problems cannot be resolved and that they would be better off if they parted. Some of these couples may also need to divide up possessions, negotiate child custody and financial issues, and determine how they can both reside comfortably within a joint social network. The key to the negotiated farewell is that both parties are willing to try to be fair to each other during the disengagement process (which is in direct contrast to the attitude of those playing the blame game). Often partners using the negotiated farewell tell each other that, even though the relationship is ending, they have no regrets about the time spent in the relationship and no hard feelings about the breakup. Sometimes appeals to fatalism are used ("It just wasn't meant to be"); other times the fairness approach is adopted ("If I stayed in this relationship it wouldn't be fair to you"). The goal of the negotiated farewell is to leave the relationship "well" rather than on a sour note. This strategy is most often used when there are high levels of relational intimacy and commitment, and the partners' interpersonal networks are overlapping (Baxter, 1982; Cody, 1982). As you might suspect, this is one of the least distressing ways to end a relationship. Figure 15.2 summarizes the various disengagement strategies.

Outcomes: The Results of Relationship Endings

Losing a relational partner can be a devastating experience. At the time of breakup the world looks bleak and there is little hope. While the experience is usually negative, most people do move on with their lives and eventually may find positive outcomes associated with the loss. In this section we discuss the emotional and relational outcomes that often follow (1) the death of a loved one and (2) the breakup of a close relationship.

Kübler-Ross's Stages of Coping with Death

In her classic book on death and grieving, Kübler-Ross (1969) advanced a chronological model of how individuals cope with death. Kübler-Ross maintained that when people lose a loved one they pass through five predictable stages: (1) denial, (2) anger and blame, (3) bargaining, (4) depression, and (5) acceptance. Some aspects of these stages are also relevant to relational breakups.

These five stages are so well known that they were featured in an episode of the popular sitcom *Frasier*. In fact, the names of the stages were flashed on the screen to introduce scenes. In this episode Frasier loses his radio job. At first he tells everyone that being a radio talk show host wasn't very important to him anyway (denial). Then he starts whining and throwing things around his apartment (anger and blame). Next, he starts promising to be a better son, brother, and friend if only he can get a good job again (bargaining). Finally, he resigns himself to the loss of his position as a popular Seattle radio personality (acceptance). The components of these stages are discussed in more detail next.

Denial   The news of our own imminent death or the loss of loved ones through death or breakup often results in disbelief and denial. The phone call informing people of their own terminal state or the death of a loved one is often met with "No, no" or "It can't be true," as they struggle to comprehend the loss. As time passes, this denial of relational loss usually fades, but many people still pretend the individual is not gone by doing things such as leaving all the departed person's belongings in her or his room or continuing to set an extra place at the dinner table. After breakups some people also refuse to believe the relationship is over and search for the slightest clue that their lover still wants them back. They might also keep the person's belongings around them, as well as photographs and other reminders of the relationship. Some divorced people even have trouble taking off their wedding rings. Of course, until the person stops denying the death of the relationship, healing cannot occur.

Anger and Blame   Since loss is so painful, it is natural to feel anger and to search for someone to blame. With death people may direct blame at the alleged cause of the person's death: cigarette companies, a drunk driver, a medical mistake, and so on. They may blame themselves or even God for the loss. In relationships people may blame a third party or even become angry or violent with the loved one or themselves, which are indications of how irrational they can become in this stage.

Bargaining   This phase involves promises to oneself, one's partner, or God about being a better person, trying harder, or living a healthier life. When people find out that a loved one is critically ill or dying, they often promise to treat the loved one better if he or she recovers. Bargaining can also occur after relational breakups. For example, if Brad is feeling especially depressed and lonely after his breakup with Emily, he might call Emily and tell her that he has changed and that all their previous problems will go away. Brad might also promise himself and his friends that he will get out of the house more and start meeting people, and he might ask the supreme being he believes in to give him a second chance with Emily or to help him find someone new. In exchange for these blessings, he may promise to be a better person and to pray more. As these examples illustrate, bargaining, like the previous phases, can be a completely irrational response to loss.

Depression   The loss of a relationship, like the impending loss of a loved one's life, can lead to extreme depression. Sadness, helplessness, and grief permeate one's life. The social support of loved ones and professional counseling can be of great benefit at this time. The experience of depression and sadness appears to be an essential step in coping with loss, but people deal with loneliness and depression in various ways. Rubenstein and Shaver (1982) proposed four categories of lonely behavior: (1) sad passivity, such as sleeping, crying, and moping around the house; (2) active solitude, such as getting involved in new projects, reading, playing music, and exercising; (3) social contact, such as communicating with a friend or loved one about one's problems; and (4) distractions, such as shopping, gambling, and spending money. Active solitude and social contact were found to be positive, constructive strategies for coping with loneliness and depression, whereas sad passivity and distractions seemed to make matters even worse.

Acceptance   The only way to get beyond death and/or relationship loss is to accept the relationship's end and get on with life as best one can. Of course, this may be more easily said than done. Acceptance of loss, particularly of death, does not have to be viewed as an insult to the dearly departed, nor should it be a happy time. Often during this time people are almost devoid of emotion (Kübler-Ross, 1969). It simply becomes too painful for them to experience feelings, so they shut their emotions down. This sense of emptiness, however, eventually subsides into a realization of the inevitable and a decision to go with the loss rather than fight against it. Happy memories of the person and/or the relationship can also help sustain the grieving person. Eventually this acceptance leads to the opening of new doors in life, often including the possibility of new relationships.

Negative Outcomes of Relational Breakups

Although most relational breakups are not as traumatic as the death of a loved one, they are usually characterized by some degree of distress. In fact, most short-term reactions to relationship breakup are negative. Relational partners often feel as if the world is about to end. Even some long-term negative consequences may persist.

Negative Emotions   One of the most common outcomes associated with a relational breakup is the presence of negative emotions. Indeed, a relational breakup is one of the most distressing, traumatic events we experience, particularly for the unwilling partner in the breakup. As Duck (1988) stated, "There is very little pain on earth like the pain of a long-term personal relationship that is falling apart" (p. 102).

Studies have shown that depression, anger, hurt, guilt, confusion, and frustration are common feelings during a relational breakup. In one-sided breakups a sizable majority of partners experience negative emotions, regardless of whether they initiated the breakup and whether they are female or male (Kurdek, 1991; Simpson, 1987; Ugbah & DeWine, 1986; Wilmot et al., 1985). In Owen's (1993) study of relationship accounts, respondents described breakups as emotional injuries: "He left a huge hole in my heart," "My heart felt like a dart board," and "I was torn to shreds." Contrary to intuition, research has found that men experience more emotional trauma than women after an unwanted breakup (Hill et al., 1976). This is not, however, to minimize women's distress after breakups. Studies have found that *both* sexes experience considerable emotional distress following an unwanted breakup (Wilmot et al., 1985); men simply seem to do so a little more intensely.

A variety of factors predict how much distress or depression people experience after a relational breakup. Research has shown that people are more depressed when their love for their partner was deep, when their partner was physically attractive, when they didn't want the relationship to end, and when their partner did want the relationship to end (Mearns, 1991). Other research has shown that people in a romantic relationship who felt emotionally close to their partner, had high levels of relational satisfaction, had dated for a long time, and had little control over the breakup were likely to experience the most distress following the breakup (Simpson, 1987; Frazier & Cook, 1993).

While distress typically is greater for the victim of an unwanted breakup, we should never underestimate the emotional distress experienced by the initiator of the breakup. Initiators may feel guilt, shame, embarrassment, stress, and ambivalence about the breakup. Also, they may repeatedly be reminded of the breakup by their social network and may have to provide numerous accounts and justifications for their actions.

Loneliness   The loss of a relationship is very likely to produce intense feelings of loneliness. In a study of gay and lesbian relationships, Kurdek (1991) found that loneliness was the second most common emotional reaction following a breakup. Moreover, a breakup is a double whammy: Not only have the partners lost one of the most important people in their lives, they have lost the person they would normally have turned to for comfort following such a loss.

It is natural for people to feel lonely after the breakup of a significant relationship. According to Segrin (1998), loneliness is the result of a discrepancy between one's actual and desired level of social interaction with others. When an intimate relationship ends, this discrepancy may increase. Suddenly there is a wider gap between how much intimacy someone wants and how much intimacy he or she is receiving. However, individuals are likely to feel less loneliness after a breakup if they are surrounded by friends and family members who care about them (Segrin, 1998).

Interestingly, loneliness can also be a motivation for breaking off a relationship. As discussed previously, people sometimes initiate breakups because they are dissatisfied or bored with their relationships. They long for the connection that they felt early in their relationships when they were first getting to know each other and everything was exciting and new. Breaking up an old relationship and searching for a new one that better fulfills one's needs is often an impetus for breakup. Indeed, one reason for divorce is the hope of finding a happier relationship, and most divorced people do remarry. Unfortunately, a divorce is even more likely in a second marriage (Argyle & Henderson, 1988).

Financial Consequences   Divorce or separation frequently turns into a financial disaster. The costs of maintaining dual residences, paying lawyers, and selling a large home quickly, to mention but a few problems, makes divorce one of the worst things that can happen to a couple from a financial standpoint. Single moms and "deadbeat dads" are a major source of poverty in this country. And men who pay alimony and child support often feel financially trapped (Hendrick & Hendrick, 1992); it is difficult to start a new family when the financial burdens of another family are still on one's shoulders.

Unfortunately, one factor keeping many long-term partners in negative and even abusive relationships is financial dependency (see Chapter 9). Just as with married couples, Kurdek (1991) found that one of the problems facing gay and lesbian couples after a breakup involved finances. Cohabitors, regardless of their sexual orientation, are particularly likely to experience financial difficulties as they move out of each other's homes and lives. Like emotional dependency, financial dependency often traps people in unhealthy relationships.

Effects on Children   What effect does the breakup have on the children of the divorcing couple? Sadly children seem to fare worse in divorced families than in families in which their parents were continuously and happily married. Amato and Keith (1991) published a statistical summary of prior research on the effects of parental divorce on children's well-being as adults. Based on information from 81,000 people, they reported that divorce is generally associated with a host of negative consequences. Adults from divorced homes are more likely to be depressed, less satisfied with life, less likely to have satisfying relationships, more likely to get divorced themselves, and more likely to have lower socioeconomic status, less income, and poorer physical health than adults from nondivorced families. The authors concluded: "These results lead to a pessimistic conclusion: the argument that parental divorce presents few problems for children's long-term development is simply inconsistent with the literature on this topic" (Amato & Keith, 1991, p. 54). The bad news is that these negative effects are consistent across dozens of studies. The good news is that the effects tend to be small, and when both parents maintain positive relationships with their children, the effects are smaller still. There is also some evidence that boys cope better if they live with their father and that girls cope better if they live with their mother (see Hendrick & Hendrick, 1992, for a summary). These gloomy findings notwithstanding, sometimes it is better for a child to suffer through a divorce than to live with parents who are constantly fighting (Booth & Edwards, 1989).

Health Consequences Studies have also shown that separation and divorce threaten people's health. Argyle and Henderson (1988) reported research showing that divorced people have a higher incidence of heart problems, cancer, liver disease, pneumonia, and a host of other diseases. Hendrick and Hendrick (1992) reported that divorce has been linked to a variety of emotional and physical disorders, psychiatric illness, suicide, and interpersonal violence. Similarly, the death of a partner can affect the grieving person's physical health. When people are depressed, stressed, and grieving, their bodies may be more susceptible to certain physical ailments, such as ulcers, heart problems, and even the common cold.

Healing After a Separation

Because relationship loss can be personally devastating, it is important to understand what factors influence recovery from the distress, loneliness, and depression that often accompanies a breakup. Mutually negotiated breakups result in the fewest bad feelings (Wilmot et al., 1985) and generally are the easiest to recover from. Recovery from a unilateral breakup is difficult or impossible when one person wants the relationship to continue (Frazier & Cook, 1993). Thus, if a relationship is really over, it is important to stop dwelling on it and to move on with one's life. Of course, this is more easily said than done. Research also suggests that breakups are more protracted and distressing when more indirect termination strategies are employed (Baxter & Philpott, 1980). It is more humane and honest to tell someone, in direct and positive terms, that the relationship is over. Only then can the recovery process begin.

Positive Outcomes of Relational Breakups

Despite the trauma associated with breakups, it is not uncommon for one or both partners to actually have positive feelings about a separation (Wilmot et al., 1985). One of the most common outcomes in Kurdek's (1991) study of gay and lesbian relationships was increased happiness following the breakup. Indeed, often it is a relief to be out of a bad or dangerous relationship. Sometimes a breakup can provide relief from relational ambiguity or conflict. Not infrequently a person moves on to a more satisfying relationship following a breakup. Kurdek (1991) reported that relief from conflict was one of the most common outcomes of separation in gay and lesbian relationships. In addition, Kurdek found that personal growth was the most commonly cited positive outcome of relational breakups. Of course, some relationships continue to be problematic after the breakup, especially if one person cannot let go.

Ending any relationship, especially a bad relationship, also represents an opportunity to form a new relationship. But many people make the mistake of leaping head first into a new relationship, which can land them in another relationship destined to fail. Thus, rapid expressions of love and affection in a new relationship are often a turnoff because people think that you cannot possibly like them that much yet (Sternberg, 1987) and that you are just using them to recover from your loss. Let any new relationships evolve slowly and naturally.

Conclusion

All relationships end, for a variety of reasons. Sometimes people make a conscious choice to end a relationship and take their lives in a new direction. Other times relationships slowly wither away, partners physically separate from each other due to school or career choices, or death occurs. In each case coping with the loss of a significant relationship is difficult.

Researchers have also identified various specific reasons for relational breakups. Often, communication is the culprit. Avoidance, negative communication, and lack of openness are three common communication problems that cause breakups. Dissimilarity and sexual incompatibility can also precipitate relational breakups, as can financial issues, inequity, and alcohol or drug abuse. The most common reason for the termination of dating relationships is boredom. People simply miss the excitement that once was present in their relationships but that somehow dimmed over time. Sometimes this boredom leads people to look elsewhere and to develop an interest in alternative partners. Still others feel smothered by their relationships and break up to achieve autonomy and independence.

Regardless of why a relationship ends, research has shown that people usually experience a host of negative outcomes following relational termination, including emotional and financial distress. If a person did not want the relationship to end, he or she might feel rejected and fearful of starting a new relationship. If a person initiated the relational breakup, he or she often feels guilt. The strategy that people use to end their relationships can make a difference. Direct strategies are usually preferred, especially if they include positive communication. Such strategies allow people to get over the breakup more quickly, which opens up the possibility of finding new partners and exploring uncharted relational territory.

Discussion Questions

1. How are the stage models developed by Duck and by Knapp similar and different? Which of these models describes the disengagement process better? Why?
2. Of the dozen specific breakup strategies mentioned in this chapter, which do you think are the least pleasant and/or ethical? In an ideal world, what strategies do you think people should use to end relationships?
3. How might you help a friend get over a relationship breakup or the death of a loved one?

References

Abbey, A. (1982). Sex differences in attributions for friendly behavior: Do males misperceive females' friendliness? *Journal of Personality and Social Psychology, 42,* 830–838.

Abbey, A. (1987). Misperceptions of friendly behavior as sexual interest: A survey of naturally occurring incidents. *Psychology of Women Quarterly, 11,* 173–194.

Abbey, A., & Melby, C. (1986). The effects of nonverbal cues in gender differences in perceptions of sexual intent. *Sex Roles, 15,* 283–298.

Aboud, F. E., & Mendelson, M. J. (1998). Determinants of friendship selection and quality: Developmental perspectives. In W. M. Bukowski & A. F. Newcomb (Eds.), *The company they keep: Friendships in childhood and adolescence* (pp. 87–112). New York: Cambridge University Press.

Acitelli, L. K., & Duck, S. W. (1987). Intimacy as the proverbial elephant. In D. Perlman & S. W. Duck (Eds.), *Intimate relationships: Development, dynamics, and deterioration* (pp. 297–308). Beverly Hills, CA: Sage.

Acker, M., & Davis, M. E. (1992). Intimacy, passion, and commitment in adult romantic relationships: A test of the triangular theory of love. *Journal of Social and Personal Relationships, 9,* 21–50.

Acton, L. (1887/1972). *Essays on freedom and power.* Gloucester, MA: Peter Smith.

Adams, J. S. (1965). Inequity in social exchange. In L. Berkowitz (Ed.), *Advances in experimental psychology* (Vol. 2, pp. 267–299). New York: Academic Press.

Afifi, T. (2000). *Family secrets: The impact on family cohesiveness.* Manuscript submitted for publication.

Afifi, W. A. (1999). Harming the ones we love: Relational attachment and perceived consequences as predictor of safe-sex behavior. *Journal of Sex Research, 36,* 198–206.

Afifi, W. A., & Burgoon, J. K. (1998). "We never talk about that": A comparison of cross-sex friendships and dating relationships on uncertainty and topic avoidance. *Personal Relationships, 5,* 255–272.

Afifi, W. A., & Burgoon, J. K. (2000). The impact of violations on uncertainty and the consequences for attractiveness. *Human Communication Research, 26,* 203–233.

Afifi, W. A., & Guerrero, L. K. (1995, June). *Maintenance behaviors in same sex friendships: Sex differences, equity and associations with relational closeness.* Paper presented at the meeting of the International Network on Personal Relationships, Williamsburg, VA.

Afifi, W. A., & Guerrero, L. K. (1998). Some things are better left unsaid II: Topic avoidance in friendships. *Communication Quarterly, 46,* 231–249.

Afifi, W. A., & Guerrero, L. K. (2000). Motivations underlying topic avoidance in close relationships. In S. Petronio (Ed.), *Balancing the secrets of private disclosures* (pp. 165–180). Mahwah, NJ: Erlbaum.

Afifi, W. A., Guerrero, L. K., & Egland, K. L. (1994, June). *Maintenance behaviors in same- and opposite-sex friendships: Connections to gender, relational closeness, and equity issues.* Paper presented at the annual meeting of the International Network on Personal Relationships, Iowa City, IA.

Afifi, W. A., & Metts, S. (1998). Characteristics and consequences of expectation violations in close relationships. *Journal of Social and Personal Relationships, 15,* 365–392.

Afifi, W. A., & Reichert, T. (1996). Understanding the role of uncertainty in jealousy experience and expression. *Communication Reports, 9,* 93–103.

Aida, Y., & Falbo, T. (1991) Relationships between marital satisfaction, resources, and power strategies. *Sex Roles, 24,* 43–56.

Ainsworth, M. D. S. (1969). Object relations, dependency, and attachment: A theoretical review of the infant-mother relationship. *Child Development, 40,* 969–1025.

Ainsworth, M. D. S. (1982). Attachment: Retrospect and prospect. In C. M. Parkes & J. Stevenson-Hinde (Eds.), *The place of attachment in human behavior* (pp. 3–30). New York: Basic Books.

Ainsworth, M. D. S. (1989). Attachments beyond infancy. *American Psychologist, 44,* 709–716.

Ainsworth, M. D. S. (1991). Attachments and other affectional bonds across the life cycle. In C. M. Parkes, J. Stevenson-Hinde, & P. Marris (Eds.), *Attachment across the life cycle* (pp. 33–51). New York: Tavistock/Routledge.

Ainsworth, M. D. S., Blehar, M. C., Waters, E., & Wall, S. (1978). *Patterns of attachment: A psychological study of the strange situation.* Hillsdale, NJ: Erlbaum.

Ainsworth, M. D. S., & Eichberg, C. (1991). Effects of infant-mother attachment of mother's unresolved loss of an attachment figure, or other traumatic experience. In C. M. Parkes, J. Stevenson-Hinde, & P. Marris (Eds.), *Attachment across the life cycle* (pp. 160–186). New York: Tavistock/Routledge.

Ainsworth, M. D. S., & Wittig, B. A. (1969). Attachment and the exploratory behaviour of one-year-olds in a strange situation. In B. M. Foss (Ed.), *Determinants of infant behavior* (pp. 113–136). London: Methuen.

Alain, M. (1985). Help-seeking and attractiveness in cross-sex dyads. *Canadian Journal of Behavioral Science, 17,* 271–275.

Albas, D., & Albas, C. (1988). Aces and bombers: The post-exam impression management strategies of students. *Symbolic Interaction, 11,* 289–302.

Alberts, J. K. (1988). An analysis of couples' conversational complaints. *Communication Monographs, 55,* 184–197.

Alberts, J. K. (1989). A descriptive taxonomy of couples' complaint interactions. *Southern Communication Journal, 54,* 125–143.

Alberts, J. K. & Driscoll, G. (1992). Containment versus escalation: The trajectory of couples' conversation complaints. *Western Journal of Communication, 56,* 394–412.

Allen, M., Berchild, J., Bernhart, K., Domain, M., Gilbertson, J., Geboy, L., Grob, L., Harris, W., Henry, L., Hoffman, L., Jones, M., Kuhn, J., Langan, E., Ling, P., & Sahlstein, E. (1995, November). *Dialectical theory: Testing the relationships between tensions and relational satisfaction.* Paper presented at the annual meeting of the International Communication Association, Chicago, IL.

Altman, I., & Ginat, J. (1996). *Polygamous families in contemporary society.* New York: Cambridge University Press.

Altman, I., & Taylor, D. A. (1973). *Social penetration: The development of interpersonal relationships.* New York: Holt, Rinehart & Winston.

Amato, P. R. & Keith, B. (1991). Parental divorce and adult well-being: A metaanalysis. *Journal of Marriage and the Family, 53,* 43–58.

Andersen, J. F. (1984, April). *Nonverbal cues of immediacy and relational affect.* Paper presented at the annual convention of the Central States Speech Association, Chicago, IL.

Andersen, P. A. (1982, November). *Interpersonal communication across three decades.* Paper presented at the annual convention of the Speech Communication Association, Louisville, KY.

Andersen, P. A. (1985). Nonverbal immediacy in interpersonal communication. In A. W. Siegman & S. Feldstein (Eds.), *Multichannel Integrations of Nonverbal Behavior* (pp. 1–36). Hillsdale, NJ: Erlbaum.

Andersen, P. A. (1989, May). *A cognitive valence theory of intimate communication.* Paper presented at the International Network on Personal Relationships Conference, Iowa City, IA.

Andersen, P. A. (1991). When one cannot communicate: A challenge to Motley's traditional communication postulates. *Communication Studies, 42,* 309–325.

Andersen, P. A. (1993). Cognitive schemata in personal relationships. In S. Duck (Ed.), *Individuals in relationships* (pp. 1–29). Newbury Park, CA: Sage.

Andersen, P. A. (1998a). The cognitive valence theory of intimate communication. In M. T. Palmer & G. A. Barnett (Eds.), *Progress in communication sciences: Vol. 14. Mutual influence in interpersonal communication: Theory and research in cognition, affect and behavior* (pp. 39–72). Stamford, CT: Ablex.

Andersen, P. A. (1998b). Researching sex differences within sex similarities: The evolutionary consequences of reproductive differences. In D. J. Canary & K. Dindia (Eds.), *Sex differences and similarities in communication* (pp. 83–100). Mahwah, NJ: Erlbaum.

Andersen, P. A. (1999). *Nonverbal communication: Forms and functions.* Mountain View, CA: Mayfield.

Andersen, P. A., & Andersen, J. F. (1982). Nonverbal immediacy in instruction. In L. L. Barker (Ed.), *Communication in the classroom: Original essays* (pp. 98–120). Englewood Cliffs, NJ: Prentice-Hall.

Andersen, P. A., Eloy, S. V., Guerrero, L. K., & Spitzberg, B. H. (1995). Romantic jealousy and relational satisfaction: A look at the impact of jealousy experience and expression. *Communication Reports, 8,* 77–85.

Andersen, P. A., & Guerrero, L. K. (1989, February). *Avoiding communication: Verbal and nonverbal dimensions of defensiveness.* Paper presented at the annual meeting of the Western States Communication Association, Spokane, WA.

Andersen, P. A., & Guerrero, L. K. (1998a). The bright side of relational communication: Interpersonal warmth as a social emotion. In P. A. Andersen & L. K. Guerrero (Eds.), *Handbook of communication and emotion: Research, theory, applications, and contexts* (pp. 303–329). San Diego, CA: Academic Press.

Andersen, P. A., & Guerrero, (1998b). Principles of communication and emotion in social interaction. In P. A. Andersen & L. K. Guerrero (Eds.), *Handbook of communication and emotion: Research, theory, applications, and contexts* (pp. 49–96). San Diego, CA: Academic Press.

Andersen, P. A, Guerrero, L. K., Buller, D. B., & Jorgensen, P. F. (1998). An empirical comparison of three theories of nonverbal immediacy exchange. *Human Communication Research, 24,* 501–535.

Andersen, P. A., Spitzberg, B. H., & Guerrero, L. K. (2000). Dealing with jealous people. In B. Gorden, C. Waugh, & L. Moore (Eds.), *Let's talk: A cognitive-skills exposure approach to interpersonal communication.* In press.

APPC research reports on children and television. Available at http://www.asc.upenn.edu/appc/ctv.

Applegate, J. L. (1980). Person-centered and position-centered teach communication in a day care center. *Studies in Symbolic Interactionism, 3,* 59–96.

Archer, J. (1989). The relationship between gender-role measures: A review. *British Journal of Social Psychology, 28,* 173–184.

Argyle, M. (1972). Non-verbal communication in human social interaction. In R. A. Hinde (Ed.), *Non-verbal communication* (pp. 248–268). Cambridge: Cambridge University Press.

Argyle, M., & Dean, J. (1965). Eye contact, distance, and affiliation. *Sociometry, 28,* 289–304.

Argyle, M., & Furnham, A. (1983). Sources of satisfaction and conflict in long-term relationships. *Journal of Marriage and the Family, 45,* 481–493.

Argyle, M., & Henderson, M. (1984). The rules of friendship. *Journal of Social and Personal Relationships, 1,* 211–237.

Argyle, M., & Henderson, M. (1985). The rules of relationships. In S. Duck & D. Perlman (Eds.), *Understanding relationships: An interdisciplinary approach* (pp. 63–84). London: Sage.

Argyle, M., & Henderson, M. (1988). *The anatomy of relationships.* London: Penguin Books.

Arliss, L. P. (1993). *Contemporary family communication: Messages and meanings.* New York: St. Martin's Press.

Armstrong, L. (1978). *Kiss daddy goodnight: A speak-out on incest.* New York: Doubleday.

Aron, A., & Aron, E. N. (1986). *Love as the expansion of self: Understanding attraction and satisfaction.* New York: Hemisphere.

Aron, A., & Aron, E. N. (1996a). Self and self-expansion in relationships. In G. J. O. Fletcher & J. Fitness (Eds.), *Knowledge structures in close relationships: A social psychological approach* (pp. 325–344). Mahwah, NJ: Erlbaum.

Aron, A., Aron, E. N., & Smollan, D. (1992). Inclusion of Other in the Self scale and the structure of interpersonal closeness. *Journal of Personality and Social Psychology, 63,* 593–612.

Aron, A., Paris, M., & Aron, E. N. (1995). Falling in love: Prospective studies of self-concept change. *Journal of Personality and Social Psychology, 69,* 1102–1112.

Aron, E. N., & Aron, A. (1996b). Love and expansion of the self: The state of the model. *Personal Relationships, 3,* 45–58.

Aronson, E., & Linder, D. (1965). Gain and loss of esteem as determinants of interpersonal attraction. *Journal of Experimental Social Psychology, 1,* 156–171.

Attridge, M. (1994). Barriers to dissolution of romantic relationships. In D. J. Canary & L. Stafford (Eds.), *Communication and relational maintenance* (pp. 141–164). San Diego, CA: Academic Press.

Aune, R. K., Metts, S., & Hubbard, A. S. E. (1998). Managing the outcomes of discovered deception. *Journal of Social Psychology, 138,* 677–689.

Austin, W., & Walster, E. (1974). Reactions to confirmations and disconfirmations of expectancies of equity and inequity. *Journal of Personality and Social Psychology, 30,* 208–213.

Ayres, J. (1983). Strategies to maintain relationships: Their identification and perceived usage. *Communication Quarterly, 31,* 62–67.

Bach, G. R., & Wyden, P. (1970). *The intimate enemy: How to fight fair in love and marriage.* New York: Avon Books.

Bagarozzi, D. A. (1990). Marital power discrepancies and symptom development in spouses: An empirical investigation. *American Journal of Family Therapy, 18,* 51–64.

Bandura, A. (1986). *Social foundations of thought and action: A social cognitive theory.* Englewood Cliffs, NJ: Prentice-Hall.

Banks, S. P., Altendorf, D. M., Greene, J. O., & Cody, M. J. (1987). An examination of relationship disengagement: Perceptions, breakup strategies and outcomes. *Western Journal of Speech Communication, 51,* 19–41.

Barnett, R., & Baruch, G. (1987). Mothers' participation in child care: Patterns and consequences. In F. Crosby (Ed.), *Spouse, parent, worker: On gender and multiple roles.* New Haven, CT: Yale University Press.

Barth, R. J., & Kinder, B. N. (1988). A theoretical analysis of sex differences in same-sex friendships. *Sex Roles, 19,* 349–363.

Bartholomew, K. (1990). Avoidance of intimacy: An attachment perspective. *Journal of Social and Personal Relationships, 7,* 147–178.

Bartholomew, K. (1993). From childhood to adult relationships: Attachment theory and research. In S. Duck (Ed.), *Learning about relationships* (pp. 30–62). Newbury Park, CA: Sage.

Bartholomew, K., & Horowitz, L. M. (1991). Attachment styles among young adults: A test of a four-category model. *Journal of Personality and Social Psychology, 61,* 226–244.

Bateson, G. (1951a). Conventions of communication. In J. Ruesch & G. Bateson (Eds.), *Communication: The social matrix of psychiatry* (pp. 212–227) New York: Norton.

Bateson, G. (1951b). Information and codification: A philosophical approach. In J. Ruesch & G. Bateson (Eds.), *Communication: The social matrix of psychiatry* (pp. 168–211). New York: Norton.

Baumeister, R. F. (1982). A self-presentational view of social phenomena. *Psychological Bulletin, 91,* 3–26.

Baumeister, R. F. (Ed.). (1986). *Public and private self.* New York: Springer-Verlag.

Baumeister, R. F. (2000). Gender differences in erotic plasticity: The female sex drive as socially flexible and responsive. *Psychological Bulletin, 126,* 347–374.

Baumeister, R. F., & Leary, M. R. (1995). The need to belong: Desire for interpersonal attachments as a fundamental human motivation. *Psychological Bulletin, 117,* 497–529.

Baumeister, R. F., & Wotman, S. R. (1992). *Breaking hearts: The two sides of unrequited love.* New York: Guilford.

Baumeister, R. F., Wotman, S. R., & Stillwell, A. M. (1993). Unrequited love: On heartbreak, anger, guilt, scriptlessness, and humiliation. *Journal of Personality and Social Psychology, 64,* 377–394.

Baumrind, D. (1971). Current patterns of parental authority. *Developmental Psychology Monographs, 4*(1).

Baumrind, D. (1980). New directions in socialization research. *American Psychologist, 35,* 639–652.

Baumrind, D. (1991). Parenting styles and adolescent development. In R. M. Leder, A. C. Petersen, & J. Brooks-Gunn (Eds.), *Encyclopedia of adolescence* (Vol. 2, pp. 746–758). New York: Garland.

Bavelas, J. B., Black, A., Chovil, N., & Mullett, J. (1990). *Equivocal communication.* Newbury Park, CA: Sage.

Baxter, L. A. (1979a). Self-disclosure as a relational disengagement strategy. *Human Communication Research, 5,* 215–222.

Baxter, L. A. (1979b, February). *Self-reported disengagement strategies in friendship relationships.* Paper presented at the annual convention of the Western Speech Communication Association, Los Angeles, CA.

Baxter, L. A. (1979c, November). *Relational closeness, relational intent and disengagement strategies.* Paper presented at the annual meeting of the Speech Communication Association, San Antonio, TX.

Baxter, L. A. (1982). Strategies for ending relationships: Two studies. *Western Journal of Speech Communication, 46,* 223–241.

Baxter, L. A. (1984). Trajectories of relationship disengagement. *Journal of Social and Personal Relationships 1,* 29–48.

Baxter, L. A. (1985). Accomplishing relational disengagement. In S. Duck and D. Perlman (Eds.), *Understanding personal relationships: An interdisciplinary approach* (pp. 243–265). London: Sage

Baxter, L. A. (1986). Gender differences in the heterosexual relationship rules embedded in breakup accounts. *Journal of Social and Personal Relationships, 3,* 289–306.

Baxter, L. A. (1988). A dialectical perspective on communication strategies in relationship development. In S. Duck (Ed.), *Handbook of personal relationships* (pp. 257–273). New York: Wiley.

Baxter, L. A. (1990). Dialectical contradictions in relationship development. *Journal of Social and Personal Relationships, 7,* 69–88.

Baxter, L. A. (1993). The social side of personal relationships: A dialectical perspective. In S. Duck (Ed.), *Understanding relationship processes* (pp. 139–165). Newbury Park, CA: Sage.

Baxter, L. A. (1994). A dialogic approach to relationship maintenance. In D. J. Canary & L. Stafford (Eds.), *Communication and relational maintenance* (pp. 233–254). San Diego, CA: Academic Press.

Baxter, L. A., & Bullis, C. (1986). Turning points in developing romantic relationships. *Human Communication Research, 12,* 469–493.

Baxter, L. A., & Montgomery, B. M. (1996). *Relating: Dialogues and dialectics.* New York: Guilford.

Baxter, L. A., & Philpott, J. (1980, November). *Relational disengagement: A process view.* Paper presented at the annual meeting of the Speech Communication Association, New York, NY.

Baxter, L. A., & Simon, E. P. (1993). Relationship maintenance strategies and dialectical contradictions in personal relationships. *Journal of Social and Personal Relationships, 10,* 225–242.

Baxter, L. A., & Wilmot, W. W. (1984). "Secret tests": Social strategies for acquiring information about the state of the relationship. *Human Communication Research, 2,* 171–201.

Baxter, L. A., & Wilmot, W. W. (1985). Taboo topics in close relationships. *Journal of Social and Personal Relationships, 2,* 253–269.

Bayes, M. A. (1970). An investigation of the behavioral cues of interpersonal warmth. (Doctoral dissertation, University of Miami, 1970). *Dissertation Abstracts International, 31,* 2272B.

Becker, W. C. (1964). Consequences of different kinds of parental discipline. In M. L. Hoffman & L. W. Hoffman (Eds.), *Review of child development research* (pp. 169–208). New York: Russell Sage Foundation.

Beebe, S. A. (1980). Effects of eye contact, posture and vocal inflection upon credibility and comprehension. *Australian scan: Journal of human communication, 7–8,* 57–70.

Beier, E. G., & Sternberg, D. P. (1977). Marital communication: Subtle cues between newlyweds. *Journal of Communication, 27,* 92–97.

Bell, A. P., & Weinberg, M. A. (1978). *Homosexualities: A study of diversity among men and women.* New York: Simon & Schuster.

Bell, R. A., & Buerkel-Rothfuss, N. L. (1990). S(he) loves me, s(he) loves me not: Predictors of relational information-seeking in courtship and beyond. *Communication Quarterly, 38,* 64–82.

Bell, R. A., Buerkel-Rothfuss, N. L., & Gore, K. E. (1987). "Did you bring the yarmulke for the cabbage patch kid?" The idiomatic communication of young lovers. *Human Communication Research, 14,* 47–67.

Bell, R. A., Daly, J. A., & Gonzalez, C. (1987). Affinity-maintenance in marriage and its relationships to women's marital satisfaction. *Journal of Marriage and the Family, 49,* 445–454.

Bellah, R. N., Madsen, R., Sullivan, W. M., Swidler A., & Tipton, S. M. (1985*). Habits of the heart: Individualism and commitment in American life.* New York: Harper & Row.

Bem, S. L. (1974). The measurement of psychological androgyny. *Journal of Consulting and Clinical Psychology, 42,* 155–162.

Bendix, R. (1968). *Tradition and modernity reconsidered.* Berkeley, CA: Institute of Industrial Relations.

Bennett, M., & Earwaker, D. (1994). Victims' responses to apologies: The effects of offender responsibility and offense severity. *Journal of Social Psychology, 134,* 457–464.

Bentler, P. M., & Newcomb, M. D. (1978). Longitudinal study of marital success and failure. *Journal of Consulting and Clinical Psychology, 46,* 1053–1070.

Berg, J. H., & McQuinn, R. D. (1986). Attraction and exchange in continuing and noncontinuing dating relationships. *Journal of Personality and Social Psychology, 50,* 942–952.

Berger, C. R. (1979). Beyond initial interaction: Uncertainty, understanding, and the development of interpersonal relationships. In H. Giles & R. N. St. Clair (Eds.), *Language and social psychology* (pp. 122–144). Oxford: Basil Blackwell.

Berger, C. R. (1985) Social power and interpersonal communication. In M. L. Knapp & G. R. Miller (Eds.), *Handbook of interpersonal communication* (pp. 439–499). Beverly Hills, CA: Sage.

Berger, C. R. (1986). Uncertain outcome values in predicted relationships: Uncertainty reduction theory then and now. *Human Communication Research, 13,* 34–38.

Berger, C. R. (1987). Communicating under uncertainty. In M. E. Roloff & G. R. Miller (Eds.), *Interpersonal processes: New directions in communication research* (pp. 39–62). Newbury Park, CA: Sage.

Berger, C. R. (1988). Uncertainty and information exchange in developing relationships. In S. Duck (Ed.), *Handbook of personal relationships* (pp. 239–256). Chichester, UK: Wiley.

Berger, C. R. (1993). Uncertainty and social interaction. In S. A. Deetz (Ed.), *Communication yearbook 16* (pp. 491–502). Newbury Park, CA: Sage.

Berger, C. R., & Bradac, J. J. (1982). *Language and social knowledge: Uncertainty in interpersonal relations.* London: Edward Arnold.

Berger, C. R., & Calabrese, R. J. (1975). Some explorations in initial interactions and beyond: Toward a developmental theory of interpersonal communication. *Human Communication Research, 1,* 99–112.

Berger, C. R., & Douglas, W. (1981). Studies in interpersonal epistemology III: Anticipated interaction, self-monitoring, and observational context selection. *Communication Monographs, 48,* 183–196.

Berger, C. R., & Kellermann, K. (1983). To ask or not to ask: Is that a question? In R. N. Bostrom (Ed.), *Communication Yearbook 7* (pp. 342–368). Newbury Park, CA: Sage.

Berger, C. R., & Kellermann, K. (1994). Acquiring social information. In J. A. Daly & J. M. Wiemann (Eds.), *Strategic interpersonal communication* (pp. 1–32). Hillsdale, NJ: Erlbaum.

Berk, S. (1985). *The gender factory.* New York: Plenum.

Berscheid, E., Dion, K., Walster, E., & Walster, G. W. (1971). Physical attractiveness and dating choice: A test of the matching hypothesis. *Journal of Experimental Social Psychology, 7,* 173–189.

Berscheid, E., & Meyers, S. A. (1996). A social categorical approach to questions about love. *Personal Relationships, 3,* 19–43.

Berscheid, E., & Peplau, L. A. (1983). The emerging science of relationships. In H. H. Kelley, E. Berscheid, A. Christensen, J. H. Harvey, T. L. Huston, G. Leaving, E. McClintock, L. A. Peplau, & D. R. Peterson (Eds.), *Close relationships* (pp. 1–19). Nee York: Freeman.

Berscheid, E., & Walster, E. H. (1969). *Interpersonal attraction.* Reading, MA: Addison-Wesley.

Berscheid, E., & Walster, E. H. (1974). A little bit about love. In T. L. Houston (Ed.), *Foundations of interpersonal attraction* (pp. 355–381). New York: Academic Press.

Bickman, L. (1974). The social power of a uniform. *Journal of Applied Social Psychology, 4,* 47–61.

Biernat, M., & Wortman, C. B. (1991). Sharing of home responsibilities between professionally employed women and their husbands. *Journal of Personality and Social Psychology, 60,* 840–860.

Bingham, S. G., & Burleson, B. R. (1989). Multiple effects of messages with multiple goals: Some perceived outcomes of responses to sexual harassment. *Human Communication Research, 16,* 184–216.

Black, L. E., Eastwood, M. M., Sprenkle, D. H., & Smith, E. (1991). An exploratory analysis of the construct of leavers versus left as it relates to Levinger's social exchange theory of attractions, barriers, and alternative attractions. *Journal of Divorce and Remarriage, 15,* 127–139.

Blake, R. R., & Mouton, J. S. (1964). *The managerial grid.* Houston, TX: Gulf.

Blanck, P. D. (Ed.). (1993). *Interpersonal expectations: Theory, research, and applications.* Paris: Cambridge University Press.

Blau, P. M. (1964). *Exchange and power in social life.* New York: Wiley.

Blumstein, P., & Schwartz, P. (1983). *American couples: Money, work, sex.* New York: Morrow.

Bochner, A. P. (1984). The functions of human communication in interpersonal bonding. In C. C. Arnold & J. W. Bowers (Eds), *Handbook of rhetorical and communication theory* (pp. 544–621). Boston: Allyn & Bacon.

Bochner, A. P. (1992). On the efficacy of openness in closed relationships. In M. Burgoon (Ed.), *Communication yearbook 5* (pp. 109–124). New Brunswick, NJ: Transaction Books.

Booth, A., & Edwards, J. N. (1989). Transmission of marital and family quality over the generations: The effect of parental divorce and unhappiness. *Journal of Divorce, 13,* 41–58.

Booth-Butterfield, M. (1989). Perceptions of harassing communication as a function of locus of control, work force participation, and gender. *Communication Quarterly, 37,* 262–275.

Bowers, J. W., & Bradac, J. J. (1984). Contemporary problems in human communication theory. In C. C. Arnold & J. W. Bowers (Eds.), *Handbook of rhetorical and communication theory* (pp. 871–892). Boston: Allyn & Bacon.

Bowlby, J. (1969). *Attachment and loss: Vol. 1. Attachment.* New York: Basic Books.

Bowlby, J. (1973). *Attachment and loss: Vol. 2. Separation.* New York: Basic Books.

Bowlby, J. (1977). The making and breaking of affectional bonds. *British Journal of Psychiatry, 130,* 201–210.

Bowlby, J. (1980). *Attachment and loss: Vol. 3. Loss, sadness, and depression.* New York: Basic Books.

Boyden, T., Carroll, J. S., & Maier, R. A. (1984). Similarity and attraction in homosexual males: The effects of age and masculinity-femininity. *Sex Roles, 10,* 939–948.

Bradac, J. J., Bowers, J. W., & Courtwright, J. A. (1979). Three language variables in communication research: Intensity, immediacy and diversity. *Human Communication Research, 5,* 257–269.

Bradac, J. J., Hosman, L. A., & Tardy, C. H. (1978). Reciprocal disclosures and language intensity: Attributional consequences. *Communication Monographs, 45,* 1–14.

Bradbury, T. N., & Fincham, F. D. (1990). Attributions in marriage: Review and critique. *Psychological Bulletin, 107,* 3–33.

Bradford, L. (1980). The death of a dyad. In B. W. Morse & L. A. Phelps (Eds.), *Interpersonal communication: A relational perspective* (pp. 497–508). Minneapolis, MN: Burgess.

Braiker, H. B., & Kelley, H. H. (1979). Conflict in the development of close relationships. In R. L. Burgess & T. L. Huston (Eds.), *Social exchange in developing relationships* (pp. 135–168). New York: Academic Press.

Braithwaite, D. O. (1995). Ritualized embarrassment at "coed" wedding and baby showers. *Communication Reports, 8,* 145–157.

Braithwaite, D. O., & Baxter, L. A. (1995). "I do" again: The relational dialectics of renewing marriage vows. *Journal of Social and Personal Relationships, 12,* 177–198.

Bratslavsky, E., Baumeister, R. F., & Sommer, K. L. (1998). To love or be loved in vain: The trials and tribulations of unrequited love. In B. H. Spitzberg & W. C. Cupach (Eds.), *The dark side of close relationships* (pp. 307–326). Mahwah, NJ: Erlbaum.

Braver, S. L., Whitley, M., & Ng, C. (1993). Who divorced whom? Methodological and theoretical issues. *Journal of Divorce and Remarriage, 20,* 1–19.

Brehm, J. W. (1966). *A theory of psychological reactance.* New York: Academic Press.

Brehm, S. S. (1992). *Intimate relationships* (2nd ed.). New York: McGraw-Hill.

Brehm, S. S., & Kassin, S. M. (1990). *Social psychology.* Boston: Houghton Mifflin.

Brennan, K. A., & Shaver, P. R. (1995). Dimensions of adult attachment, affect regulations, and romantic relationship functioning. *Personality and Social Psychology Bulletin, 21,* 267–283.

Bretherton, I. (1988). Open communication and internal working models: Their role in the development of attachment relationships. In R. A. Thompson (Ed.), *Nebraska Symposium on Motivation* (pp. 57–113). Lincoln: University of Nebraska Press.

Bridge, K., & Baxter, L. A. (1992). Blended friendships: Friends as work associates. *Western Journal of Communication, 56,* 200–225.

Brock, L. J., & Jennings, G. H. (1993). Sexuality education: What daughters in their 30s wish their mothers had told them. *Family Relationships, 42,* 61–65.

Brown, D. E. (1991). *Human universals.* Philadelphia: Temple University Press.

Brown, M., & Auerbach, A. (1981). Communication patterns in the initiation of marital sex. *Medical Aspects of Human Sexuality, 15,* 105–117.

Brown, P., & Levinson, S. (1987). *Politeness: Some universals in language usage.* Cambridge: Cambridge University Press.

Brown, R. (1965). *Social psychology.* New York: Free Press.

Brown-Smith, N. (1998). Family secrets. *Journal of Family Issues, 19,* 20–42.

Bryson, J. B. (1976). *The nature of sexual jealousy: An exploratory paper.* Paper presented at the annual meeting of the American Psychological Association, Washington, DC.

Bryson, J. B. (1977). *Situational determinants of the expression of jealousy.* Paper presented at the annual meeting of the American Psychological Association, San Francisco, CA.

Bryson, J. B. (1991). Modes of responses to jealousy-evoking situations. In P. Salovey (Ed.), *The psychology of envy and jealousy* (pp. 1–45). New York: Guilford.

Buller, D. B., & Aune, R. K. (1987). Nonverbal cues to deception among intimates, friends, and strangers. *Journal of Nonverbal Behavior, 11,* 269–290.

Buller, D. B., & Burgoon, J. K. (1994). Deception: Strategic and nonstrategic communication. In J. A. Daly & J. M. Wiemann (Eds.), *Strategic interpersonal communication* (pp. 191–223). Hillsdale, NJ: Erlbaum.

Buller, D. B., & Burgoon, J. K. (1996). Interpersonal deception theory. *Communication Theory, 6,* 203–242.

Buller, D. B., Strzyzewski, K. D., & Comstock, J. (1991). Interpersonal deception: I. Deceivers' reactions to receivers suspicious and probing. *Communication Monographs, 58,* 1–24.

Bullis, C., Clark, C., & Sline, R. (1993). From passion to commitment: Turning points in romantic relationships. In P. J. Kalbfleisch (Ed.), *Interpersonal communication: Evolving interpersonal relationships* (pp. 213–236). Hillsdale, NJ: Erlbaum.

Burgoon, J. K. (1978). A communication model of personal space violations: Explication and an initial test. *Human Communication Research, 4*, 129–142.

Burgoon, J. K. (1982). Privacy and communication. In M. Burgoon (Ed.), *Communication Yearbook 6* (pp. 206–249). Beverly Hills, CA: Sage.

Burgoon, J. K., Buller, D. W., & Woodall, W. G. (1996). *Nonverbal communication: The unspoken dialogue* (2nd ed.). New York: McGraw-Hill.

Burgoon, J. K. & Dillman, L. (1995). Gender, immediacy and nonverbal communication. In P. J. Kalbfleisch & M. J. Cody (Eds.). *Gender, power, and communication in human relationships* (pp. 63–81). Hillsdale, NJ: Erlbaum.

Burgoon, J. K., & Hale, J. L. (1984). The fundamental topoi of relational communication. *Communication Monographs, 51*, 193–214.

Burgoon, J. K., & Hale, J. L. (1987). Validation and measurement of the fundamental themes of relational communication. *Communication Monographs, 54*, 19–41.

Burgoon, J. K., & Hale, J. L. (1988). Nonverbal expectancy violations: Model elaboration and application to immediacy behaviors. *Communication Monographs, 55*, 58–79.

Burgoon, J. K., & Langer, E. (1995). Language, fallacies, and mindlessness-mindfulness. In B. R. Burleson (Ed.), *Communication yearbook 18* (pp. 105–132). Newbury Park, CA: Sage.

Burgoon, J. K., & Newton, D. A. (1991). Applying a social meaning model to relational message interpretations of conversational involvement: Comparing observer and participant perspectives. *Southern Communication Journal, 56*, 96–113.

Burgoon, J. K., Parrott, R., Le Poire, B. A., Kelley, D. L., Walther, J. B., & Parry, D. (1989). Maintaining and restoring privacy through communication in different types of relationships. *Journal of Social and Personal Relationships, 6*, 131–158.

Burgoon, J. K., Stern, L. A., & Dillman, L. (1995*). Interpersonal adaptation: Dyadic interaction patterns.* New York: Cambridge University Press.

Buri, J. R., Louiselle, P. A., Misukanis, T. M., & Mueller, R. A. (1988). Effects of parental authoritarianism and authoritativeness on self-esteem. *Personality and Social Psychology Bulletin, 14*, 271–282.

Burke, R. J., Weir, T., & Harrison, D. (1976). Disclosure of problems and tensions experienced by marital partners. *Psychological Reports, 38*, 531–542.

Burleson, B. R. (1982). The development of comforting communication skills in childhood and adolescence. *Child Development, 53*, 1578–1588.

Burleson, B. R. (1984). Comforting communication. In H. Sypher & J. L. Applegate (Eds.), *Communication by children and adults* (pp. 63–104). Beverly Hills, CA: Sage.

Burleson, B. R. (1998). Similarities in social skills, interpersonal attraction, and the development of personal relationships. In J. S. Trent (Ed.), *Communication: Views from the helm for the twenty-first century* (pp. 77–84). Boston: Allyn & Bacon.

Burleson, B. R., Delia, J. G., & Applegate, J. L. (1992). Effects of maternal communication and children's social-cognitive and communication skills on children's acceptance by the peer group. *Family Relations, 41*, 264–272.

Burleson, B. R., & Goldsmith, D. J. (1998). How the comforting process works: Alleviating emotional distress through conversationally induced reappraisals. In P. A. Andersen & L. K. Guerrero (Eds.), *Handbook of communication and emotion: Theory, research, contexts, and applications* (pp. 246–275). San Diego, CA: Academic Press.

Burleson, B. R., Kunkel, A. W., Samter, W., & Werking, K. J. (1996). Men's and women's evaluations of communication skills in personal relationships: When sex differences make a difference—and when they don't. *Journal of Social and Personal Relationships, 13*, 201–224.

Burleson, B. R., & Samter, W. (1985a). Consistencies in theoretical and naïve evaluations of comforting messages. *Communication Monographs, 52*, 104–123.

Burleson, B. R., & Samter, W. (1985b). Individual differences in the perception of comforting messages. *Central States Speech Journal, 36*, 39–50.

Burleson, B. R., & Samter, W. (1994). A social skills approach to relationship maintenance: How individual differences in communication skills affect the achievement of relationship functions. In D. J. Canary & L. Stafford (Eds.), *Communication and relational maintenance* (pp. 61–90). San Diego, CA: Academic Press.

Buslig, A. L. S. (1999). "Stop" signs: Regulating privacy with environmental features. In L. K. Guerrero, J. A. DeVito, & M. L. Hecht (Eds.), *The nonverbal communication reader: Classic and contemporary readings* (2nd ed., pp. 241–249). Prospect Heights, IL: Waveland Press.

Buslig, A. L. S., & Burgoon, J. K. (2000). Aggressiveness in privacy-seeking behavior. In S. Petronio (Ed.), *Balancing the secrets of private disclosures* (pp. 181–196). Mahwah, NJ: Erlbaum.

Buss, D. M. (1988a). From vigilance to violence: Tactics of mate retention in American undergraduates. *Ethology and Sociobiology, 9*, 291–317.

Buss, D. M. (1988b). Love acts: The evolutionary biology of love. In R. J. Sternberg & M. L. Barnes (Eds.), *The psychology of love* (pp. 100–117). New Haven, CT: Yale University Press.

Buss, D. M. (1989). Sex differences in human mate preferences: Evolutionary hypotheses tested in 37 cultures. *Behavioral and Brain Sciences, 12*, 1–49.

Buss, D. M. (1994). *The evolution of desire: Strategies of make selection.* New York: Basic Books.

Buss, D. M., & Kenrick, D. T. (1998). Evolutionary social psychology. In D. T. Gilbert, S. T. Fiske, & G. Lindsay (Eds.), *The handbook of social psychology* (4th ed., Vol. 2, pp. 982–1026). New York: McGraw-Hill.

Buss, D. M., Larsen, R. J., Westen, D., & Semmelroth, J. (1992). Sex differences in jealousy: Evolution, physiology, and psychology. *Psychological Science, 3,* 251–255.

Buunk, B. P. (1980). Extramarital sex in the Netherlands: Motivations in social and marital context. *Alternative Lifestyles, 3,* 11–39.

Buunk, B. P. (1982). Strategies of jealousy: Styles of coping with extramarital involvement of the spouse. *Family Relations, 31,* 13–18.

Buunk, B. P. (1995). Sex, self-esteem, dependency, and extradyadic experience as related to jealousy responses. *Journal of Social and Personal Relationships, 12,* 147–153.

Buunk, B. P., & Bakker, A. B. (1997). Responses to unprotected extradyadic sex by one's partner: Testing predictions from interdependence and equity theory. *Journal of Sex Research, 34,* 387–397.

Buunk, B., & Bringle, R. G. (1987). Jealousy in love relationships. In D. Perlman & S. Duck (Eds.), *Intimate relationships: Development, dynamics, and deterioration* (pp. 123–147). Beverly Hills, CA: Sage.

Byers, E. S. (1996). How well does the traditional sexual script explain sexual coercion? Review of a program of research. *Journal of Psychology and Human Sexuality, 8,* 7–25.

Byers, E. S., Demmons, S., & Lawrence, K. (1998). Sexual satisfaction within dating relationships: A test of the interpersonal exchange model of sexual satisfaction. *Journal of Social and Personal Relationships, 15,* 257–267.

Byers, E. S., & Lewis, K. (1988). Dating couples' disagreements over the desired level of sexual activity. *Journal of Sex Research, 24,* 15–29.

Byers, E. S., Purden, C., & Clark, D.A. (1998). Sexually intrusive thoughts of college students. *Journal of Sex Research, 35,* 359–369.

Byers, E. S., & Wilson, P. (1985). Accuracy of women's expectations regarding men's responses to refusals of sexual advances in dating situations. *International Journal of Women's Studies, 4,* 376–387.

Byrne, D. (1961). Interpersonal attraction and attitude similarity. *Journal of Abnormal and Social Psychology, 62,* 713–715.

Byrne, D. (1971). *The attraction paradigm.* New York: Academic Press.

Byrne, D. (1992). The transition from controlled laboratory experimentation to less controlled settings: Surprise! Additional variables are operative. *Communication Monographs, 59,* 190–198.

Byrne, D. (1997). An overview (and underview) of research and theory within the attraction paradigm. *Journal of Social and Personal Relationships, 14,* 417–431.

Byrne, D., & Clore, G. L. (1970). A reinforcement model of evaluative responses. *Personality: An International Journal, 1,* 103–128.

Cahn, D. (1992). *Conflict in intimate relationships.* New York: Guilford.

Caldwell, M., & Peplau. L. A. (1984). The balance of power in lesbian relationships. *Sex Roles, 10,* 587–600.

Cameron, C., Oskamp, S., & Sparks, W. (1977). Courtship American style: Newspaper ads. *Family Coordinator, 26,* 27–30.

Campbell, E., Adams, R., & Dobson, W. R. (1984). Familial correlates of identity formation in late adolescence: A study of the predictive utility of connectedness and individuality in family relationships. *Journal of Youth and Adolescence, 13,* 509–525.

Campbell, W. K. (1999). Narcissism and romantic attraction. *Journal of Personality and Social Psychology, 77,* 1254–1270.

Canary D. J., & Cody, M. J. (1994). *Interpersonal communication: A goals-based approach.* New York: St. Martin's Press.

Canary, D. J., Cupach, W. R., & Messman, S. J (1995). *Relationship conflict.* Thousand Oaks, CA: Sage.

Canary, D. J., & Hause, K. G. (1993). Is there any reason to research sex differences in communication? *Communication Quarterly, 41,* 129–144.

Canary, D. J., & Spitzberg, B. H. (1987). Appropriateness and effectiveness perceptions of conflict strategies. *Human Communication Research, 14,* 93–118.

Canary, D. J., & Spitzberg, B. H. (1989). A model of perceived competence of conflict strategies. *Human Communication Research, 15,* 630–649.

Canary, D. J., & Spitzberg, B. H. (1990). Attribution biases and associations between conflict strategies and competence outcomes. *Communication Monographs, 57,* 139–151.

Canary, D. J., Spitzberg, B. H., & Semic, B. A. (1998). The experience and expression of anger in interpersonal settings. In P. A. Andersen & L. K. Guerrero (Eds.), *Handbook of communication and emotion: Research, theory, applications, and contexts* (pp. 189–213). San Diego, CA: Academic Press.

Canary, D. J., & Stafford, L. (1992). Relational maintenance strategies and equity in marriage. *Communication Monographs, 59,* 243–267.

Canary, D. J., & Stafford, L. (1993). Preservation of relational characteristics: Maintenance strategies, equity, and locus of control. In P. J. Kalbfleisch (Ed.), *Interpersonal communication: Evolving interpersonal relationships* (pp. 237–259). Hillsdale, NJ: Erlbaum.

Canary, D. J., & Stafford, L. (1994). Maintaining relationships through strategic and routine interaction. In D. J. Canary & L. Stafford (Eds.), *Communication and relational maintenance* (pp. 3–22). San Diego, CA: Academic Press.

Canary, D. J., Stafford, L., Hause, K. S., & Wallace, L. A. (1993). An inductive analysis of relational maintenance strategies: Comparisons among lovers, relatives, friends, and others. *Communication Research Reports, 10,* 5–14.

Cantor, N., Mischel, W., & Schwartz, J. (1982). A prototype analysis of psychological situations. *Cognitive Psychology, 14,* 45–77.

Cappella, J. N. (1988). Personal relationships, social relationships and patterns of interaction. In S. Duck (Ed.), *Handbook of personal relationships: Theory, research and interventions* (pp. 325–342). Chichester, UK: Wiley.

Cargan, L., & Melko, M. (1982). *Singles: Myths and realities.* Beverly Hills, CA: Sage.

Cate, R. M., & Lloyd, S. A. (1988). Courtship. In S. Duck (Ed.), *Handbook of personal relationships* (pp. 409–427). New York: Wiley.

Cate, R. M., Lloyd, S. A., & Henton, J. M. (1985). The effect of equity, equality, and reward level on the stability of students' premarital relationships. *Journal of Social Psychology, 125,* 715–721.

Cate, R. M., Lloyd,. S. A., & Long, E. (1988). The role of rewards and fairness in developing premarital relationships. *Journal of Marriage and the Family, 50,* 443–452.

Cate, R. M., Long, E., Angera, J. J., & Draper, K. K. (1993). Sexual intercourse and relational development. *Family Relations, 42,* 158–164.

Center for Disease Control and Prevention. (1996, February). *Condoms and their use in preventing HIV infection and other STDs.* Rockville, MD.

Chaikin, A. L., & Derlega, V. J. (1974). Liking for the norm breaker in self-disclosure. *Journal of Personality, 42,* 117–129.

Chaiken, S. (1979). Communicator physical attractiveness and persuasion. *Journal of Personality and Social Psychology, 37,* 1387–1397.

Chavez, A. M., & Guerrero, L. K. (1999, February). *Relational maintenance in cross-sex friendships: Strategies that promote and discourage romantic involvement.* Paper presented at the annual meeting of the Western States Communication Association, Vancouver, BC.

Chelune, G. J., Rosenfeld, L. B., & Waring, E. M. (1985). Spouse disclosure patterns in distressed and nondistressed couples. *American Journal of Family Therapy, 13,* 24–31.

Cherlin, A. (1983). The trends: Marriage, divorce, remarriage. In A. S. Skolnick & J. H. Skolnick (Eds.), *Family in transition* (4th ed., pp. 128–137). Boston: Little & Brown.

Christensen, A., & Heavey, C. L. (1990). Gender and social structure in the demand/withdrawal pattern of marital conflict. *Journal of Personality and Social Psychology, 59,* 73–81.

Christensen, A., & Shenk, J. L. (1991). Communication, conflict, and psychological distance in nondistressed, clinical, and divorcing couples. *Journal of Consulting and Clinical Psychology, 59,* 458–463.

Christopher, F. S., & Cate, R. M. (1985). Premarital sexual pathways and relationship development. *Journal of Social and Personal Relationships, 2,* 271–288.

Christopher, F. S., & Frandsen, M. M. (1990). Strategies of influence in sex and dating. *Journal of Social and Personal Relationships, 7,* 89–105.

Christopher, F. S., Owens, L. A., & Strecker, H. L. (1993). An examination of single men's and women's sexual aggressiveness in dating relationships. *Journal of Social and Personal Relationships, 10,* 511–527.

Christopher, F. S., & Roosa, M. W. (1991). Factors affecting sexual decisions in premarital relationships of adolescents and young adults. In K. McKinney & S. Sprecher (Eds.), *Sexuality in close relationships* (pp. 111–133). Hillsdale, NJ: Erlbaum.

Ciabattari, J. (1988, December). Will the '90s be the age of envy? *Psychology Today,* pp. 47–50.

Cialdini, R. B. (1988). *Influence: Science and practice* (2nd ed.). New York: Harper Collins.

Clatterbuck, G. W. (1979). Attributional confidence and uncertainty in initial interaction. *Human Communication Research, 5,* 147–157.

Cleek, M. G., & Pearson, T. A. (1985). Perceived causes of divorce: An analysis of interrelationships. *Journal of Marriage and the Family, 47,* 179–183.

Clements, M. L., Cordova, A. D., Markman, H. J., & Laurenceau, J. (1997). The erosion of marital satisfaction over time and how to prevent it. In R. J. Sternberg & M. Hojjat (Eds.), *Satisfaction in close relationships* (pp. 335–365). New York: Guilford.

Cline, R. J. W., Freeman, K. E., & Johnson, S. J. (1990). Talk among sexual partners about AIDS: Factors differentiating those who talk from those who do not. *Communication Research, 17,* 792–808.

Clore, G. L., & Byrne, D. (1974). A reinforcement-affect model of attraction. In T. L. Huston (Ed.), *Foundations of interpersonal attraction* (pp. 143–170). New York: Academic Press.

Cloven, D. H., & Roloff, M. E. (1993). The chilling effect of aggressive potential on the expression of complaints in intimate relationships. *Communication Monographs, 60,* 199–219.

Coates, D., Wortman, C. B., & Abbey, A. (1979). Reactions to victims. In I. H. Frieze, D. Bar-Tal, & J. S. Carroll (Eds.), *New approaches to social problems* (pp. 21–52). San Francisco: Jossey-Bass.

Cody, M. (1982). A typology of disengagement strategies and an examination of the role intimacy and relational problems play in strategy selection. *Communication Monographs, 49,* 148–170.

Cohen, W. S. (1993). *Antistalking proposals* (Hearing before the Committee on the Judiciary, Publication No. J-103-5). Washington, DC: U.S. Government Printing Office.

Collins, N. L., & Miller, L. C. (1994). The disclosure-liking link: From meta-analysis toward a dynamic reconceptualization. *Psychological Bullentin, 116,* 457–475.

Collins, N. L., & Read, S. J. (1990). Adult attachment, working models, and relationship quality in dating couples. *Journal of Personality and Social Psychology, 58,* 644–663.

Collins, N. L., & Read, S. J. (1994). Cognitive representations of attachment: The structure and function of working models. In K. Bartholomew & D. Perlman (Eds.), *Attachment processes in adulthood: Advances in personal relationships* (Vol. 5, pp. 53–90). Bristol, PA: Kingsley.

Comadena, M. E. (1982). Accuracy in detecting deception: Intimate and friendship relationships. In M. Burgoon (Ed.), *Communication yearbook 6* (pp. 446–472). Beverly Hills, CA: Sage.

Conville, R. L. (1991). *Relational transitions: The evolution of personal relationships.* New York: Praeger.

Cooley, C. H. (1922). *Human nature and the social order.* New York: Scribner.

Cottle, T. J. (1980). *Children's secrets.* Reading, MA: Addison-Wesley.

Coutts, L. M., & Schneider, F. W. (1976). Affiliative conflict theory: An investigation of the intimacy equilibrium and compensation hypothesis. *Journal of Personality and Social Psychology, 34,* 1135–1142.

Cowan, G., Drinkard, J., & MacGavin, L. (1984). The effects of target, age, and gender on power use strategies. *Journal of Personality and Social Psychology, 47,* 1391–1398.

Crocker, J., & Schwartz, I. (1985). Prejudice and ingroup favoritism in a minimal intergroup situation: Effects of self-esteem. *Personality and Social Psychology Bulletin, 11,* 379–386.

Crockett, L., Losoff, M., & Peterson, A. C. (1984). Perceptions of the peer group and friendship in early adolescence. *Journal of Early Adolescence, 4,* 155–181.

Crooks, R., & Baur, K. (1999). *Our sexuality.* Pacific Grove, CA: Brooks/Cole.

Cunningham, J. D., & Antil, J. K. (1995). Current trends in marital cohabitation: In search of the POSSLQ. In J. T. Wood & S. Duck (Eds.), *Understudied relationships: Off the beaten track* (pp. 148–172). Thousand Oaks, CA: Sage.

Cunningham, M. R., & Barbee, A. P. (2000). Social support. In C. Hendrick and S. S. Hendrick (Eds.), *Close relationships: A sourcebook* (pp. 171–183). Thousand Oaks, CA: Sage.

Cunningham, M. R., Barbee, A. P., Graves, C. R., Lundy, D. E., & Lister, S. C. (1996, August). *Can't buy me love: The effects of male wealth and personal qualities on female attraction.* Paper presented at the annual meeting of the American Psychological Association, Toronto, Canada.

Cupach, W. R. (1994). Social predicaments. In W. R. Cupach & B. H. Spitzberg (Eds.), *The dark side of interpersonal communication* (pp. 159–180). Hillsdale, NJ: Erlbaum.

Cupach, W. R., & Comstock, J. (1990). Satisfaction with sexual communication in marriage: Links to sexual satisfaction and dyadic adjustment. *Journal of Social and Personal Relationships, 7,* 179–186.

Cupach, W. R., & Metts, S. (1986). Accounts of relational dissolution: A comparison of marital and non-marital relationships. *Communication Monographs, 53,* 311–334.

Cupach, W. R., & Metts, S. (1991). Sexuality and communication in close relationships. In K. McKinney & S. Sprecher (Eds.), *Sexuality in close relationships* (pp. 93–110). Hillsdale, NJ: Erlbaum.

Cupach, W. R., & Metts, S. (1994). *Facework.* Thousand Oaks, CA: Sage.

Cupach, W. R., & Metts, S. (1995). The role of sexual attitude similarity in romantic heterosexual relationships. *Personal Relationships, 2,* 287–300.

Cupach, W. R., & Spitzberg, B. H. (Eds.). (1994). *The dark side of interpersonal communication.* Hillsdale, NJ: Erlbaum.

Cupach, W. R., & Spitzberg, B. H. (1998). Obsessive relational intrusion and stalking. In B. H. Spitzberg & W. R. Cupach (Eds.), *The dark side of close relationships* (pp. 233–264). Mahwah, NJ: Erlbaum.

D'Emilio, J., & Freedman, E. B. (1988). *Intimate matters: A history of sexuality in America.* New York: Harper & Row..

Dainton, M., & Stafford, L. (1993). Routine maintenance behaviors: A comparison of relationship type, partner similarity and sex differences. *Journal of Social and Personal Relationships, 10,* 255–271.

Dainton, M., Stafford, L., & Canary, D. J. (1994). Maintenance strategies and physical affection as predictors of love, liking, and satisfaction in marriage. *Communication Reports, 7,* 88–98.

Daly, J. A., Hoggs, E., Sacks, D., Smith, M., & Zimring, L. (1983). Sex and relationship affect social self-grooming. *Journal of Nonverbal Behavior, 7,* 183–189.

Daly, J. A., & Kreiser, P. O. (1994). Affinity seeking. In J. A. Daly & J. M. Wiemann (Eds.), *Strategic interpersonal communication* (pp. 109–134). Hillsdale, NJ: Erlbaum.

Daly, M., & Wilson, M. (1983). *Sex, evolution, and behavior* (2nd ed.). Boston: Willard Grant Press.

Darby, B. W., & Schlenker, B. R. (1982). Children's reactions to apologies. *Journal of Personality and Social Psychology, 43,* 743–753.

Darby, B. W., & Schlenker, B. R. (1989). Children's reactions to transgressions: Effects of the actor's apology, reputation, and remorse. *British Journal of Social Psychology, 28,* 353–364.

Davidson, B., Balswick, J., & Halverson, C. (1983). Affective self-disclosure and marital adjustment: A test of equity theory. *Journal of Marriage and the Family, 45,* 93–102.

Davis, J. D., & Skinner, A. E. G. (1974). Reciprocity of self-disclosure in interviews: Modeling or social exchange? *Journal of Personality and Social Psychology, 29,* 779–784.

Davis, K. E., & Roberts, M. K. (1985). Relationships in the real world: The descriptive approach to personal relationships. In K. J. Gergen & K. E. Davis (Eds.), *The social construction of the person.* New York: Springer-Verlag.

Davis, K. E., & Todd, M. J. (1982). Friendship and love relationships. In E. E. Davis (Ed.), *Advances in descriptive pyschology* (Vol. 2, pp. 79–122). Greenwich, CT: JAI Press.

Davis, K. E., & Todd, M. J. (1985). Assessing friendships: Prototypes, paradigm cases, and relationship description. In S. Duck & D. Perlman (Eds.), *Understanding personal relationships: An interdisciplinary approach* (pp. 17–38). London: Sage.

Davis, M. (1973). *Intimate relations.* New York: Free Press.

DePaulo, B. M. (1992). Nonverbal behavior and self-presentation. *Psychological Bulletin, 111,* 203–243.

Derlega, V. J., Barbee, A. P., & Winstead, B. A. (1994). Friendship, gender, and social support: Laboratory studies of supportive interactions. In B. R. Burleson, T. L. Albrecht, & I. G. Sarason (Eds.), *Communication of social support: Messages, interactions, relationships, and community* (pp. 136–151). Thousand Oaks, CA: Sage.

Derlega, V. J., & Grzelak, J. (1979). Appropriateness of self disclosure. In G. L. Chelune (Ed.), *Self-disclosure: Origins, patterns, and implications of openness in interpersonal relationships* (pp. 151–176). San Francisco: Jossey-Bass.

Derlega, V. J., Harris, M. S., & Chaikin, A. L. (1973). Friendship and disclosure reciprocity. *Journal of Personality and Social Psychology, 9,* 277–284.

Derlega, V. J., Metts, S., Petronio, S., & Margulis, S. T. (1993). *Self-Disclosure.* Newbury Park, CA: Sage.

Deutsch, M. (1985). *Distributive justice: A social-psychological perspective.* New Haven, CT: Yale University Press.

Dieckman, L. E. (2000). Private secrets and public disclosures: The case of battered women. In S. Petronio (Ed.), *Balancing the secrets of private disclosures* (pp. 275–286). Mahwah, NJ: Erlbaum.

Dillard, J. P. (1989). Types of influence goals in personal relationships. *Journal of Social and Personal Relationships, 6,* 293–308.

Dillard, J. P., & Witteman, H. (1985). Romantic relationships at work: Organizational and personal influences. *Human Communication Research, 12,* 99–116.

Dindia, K. (1989, May). *Toward the development of a measure of marital maintenance strategies.* Paper presented at the annual meeting of the International Communication Association, San Francisco, CA.

Dindia, K. (1994). A multiphasic view of relationship maintenance strategies. In D. J. Canary & L. Stafford (Eds.), *Communication and relational maintenance* (pp. 91–112). San Diego, CA: Academic Press.

Dindia, K. (1997, November). *Men are from North Dakota, women are from South Dakota.* Paper presented at the annual meeting of the Speech Communication Association, Chicago, IL.

Dindia, K. & Allen, M. (1992). Sex differences in self-disclosure: A meta-analysis. *Psychological Bulletin, 112,* 106–124.

Dindia, K., & Baxter, L. A. (1987). Strategies for maintaining and repairing marital relationships. *Journal of Social and Personal Relationships, 4,* 143–158.

Dindia, K., & Canary, D. J. (1993). Definitions and theoretical perspectives on relational maintenance. *Journal of Social and Personal Relationships, 10,* 163–173.

Dion, K. K. (1972). Physical attractiveness and evaluations of children's transgressions. *Journal of Personality and Social Psychology, 24,* 207–213.

Dion, K. K. (1986), Stereotyping based on physical attractiveness: Issues and conceptual perspectives. In C. P. Herman, M. P., Zanna, & E. T. Higgins (Eds.), *The Ontario symposium: Vol. 3. Physical appearance, stigma, and social behavior* (pp. 7–21). Hillsdale, NJ: Erlbaum.

Dion, K. K., Berscheid, E., & Walster, E. (1972). What is beautiful is good. *Journal of Personality and Social Psychology, 24,* 285–290.

Disraeli, B. (1827/1969). *Vivian Grey.* London: Cassell.

Doelger, J. A., Hewes, D. E., & Graham, M. L. (1986). Knowing when to "second-guess": The mindful analysis of messages. *Human Communication Research, 12,* 301–338.

Dolin, D. J., & Booth-Butterfield, M. (1993). Reach out and touch someone: Analysis of nonverbal comforting responses. *Communication Quarterly, 41,* 383–393.

Donald, M. (1991). *Origins of the modern mind: Three stages in the evolution of culture and cognition.* Cambridge, MA: Harvard University Press.

Donovan, R. L., & Jackson, B. L. (1990). Deciding to divorce: A process guided by social exchange, attachment, and cognitive dissonance theories. *Journal of Divorce, 13,* 23–35.

Dougherty, T. W., Turban, D. B., Olson, D. E., Dwyer, P. D., & Lapreze, M. W. (1996). Factors affecting perceptions of workplace sexual harassment. *Journal of Organizational Behavior, 17,* 489–501.

Douglas, W. (1985). Anticipated interaction and information-seeking. *Human Communication Research, 12,* 243–258.

Douglas, W. (1990a). Uncertainty, information-seeking, and liking during initial interaction. *Western Journal of Speech Communication, 54,* 66–81.

Douglas, W. (1990b, November). *Uncertainty, information exchange, and social attraction during initial interaction.* Paper presented at the annual meeting of the Speech Communication Association, Chicago, IL.

Douglas, W. (1994). The acquaintanceship process: An examination of uncertainty, information seeking, and social attraction during initial conversation. *Communication Research, 21,* 154–176.

Dovidio, J. F., Brown, C. E., Heltman, K., Ellyson, S. L., & Keating, C. F. (1988). Power displays between men and women in discussions of gender-linked tasks: A multichannel study. *Journal of Personality and Social Psychology, 55,* 580–587.

Dowrick, S. (1999, March-April). *Utne Reader,* pp. 46–50.

Drigotas, S. M., & Rusbult, C. E. (1992). Should I stay or should I go? A dependence model of breakups. *Journal of Personality and Social Psychology, 62,* 62–87.

Driscoll, R., Davis, K. W., & Lipetz, M. E. (1972). Parental interference and romantic love. *Journal of Personality and Social Psychology, 24,* 1–10.

Duck, S. (1976). Interpersonal communication in developing acquaintances. In G. R. Miller (Ed.), *Explorations in interpersonal communication* (pp. 127–147). Beverly Hills, CA: Sage.

Duck, S. (1982). A topography of relational disengagement and dissolution. In S. Duck (Ed.), *Personal relationships 4: Dissolving personal relationships* (pp. 1–30). London: Academic Press.

Duck, S. (1988). *Relating to others.* Monterey, CA: Brooks/Cole.

Duck, S. (1994). Steady as (s)he goes: Relational maintenance as a shared meaning system. In D. J. Canary & L. Stafford (Eds.), *Communication and relational maintenance* (pp. 45–60). San Diego, CA: Academic Press.

Duffy, S., & Rusbult, C. E. (1986). Satisfaction and commitment in homosexual and heterosexual relationships. *Journal of Homosexuality, 12,* 1–23

Dunn, J. (1983). Sibling relationships in early childhood. *Child Development, 54,* 787–811.

Dunn, J. (1988a). Connections between relationships: Implications of research on mothers and siblings. In R. A. Hinde & J. Stevenson-Hinde (Eds.), *Relationships within families: Mutual influences* (pp. 168–180). New York: Oxford University Press.

Dunn, J. (1988b). Relations among relationships. In S. W. Duck (Ed.), *Handbook of personal relationships* (pp. 193–209). New York: Wiley.

Dunn, J., & Kendrick, C. (1982). *Siblings: Love, envy, and understanding.* Cambridge, MA: Harvard University Press.

Dunn, J., & Munn, P. (1987). Development of justification in disputes with another sibling. *Developmental Psychology, 23,* 791–798.

Dutton, D. G., & Aron, A. P. (1974). Some evidence for heightened sexual attraction under conditions of high anxiety. *Journal of Personality and Social Psychology, 30,* 510–517.

Dykstra, P. A. (1990). *Next of (non)kin.* The Netherlands: Swets & Zeitlinger.

Edgar, T., & Fitzpatrick, M. A. (1988). Compliance-gaining and relational interaction: When your life depends on it. *Southern Speech Communication Journal, 53,* 385–405.

Edgar, T., & Fitzpatrick, M. A. (1993). Expectations for sexual interaction: A cognitive test of the sequencing of sexual communication behaviors. *Health Communication, 5,* 239–261.

Egland, K. L., Spitzberg, B. H., & Zormeier, M. M. (1996). Flirtation and conversational competence in cross-sex platonic and romantic relationships. *Communication Reports, 9,* 105–118.

Egland, K. L., Stelzner, M. A., Andersen, P. A., & Spitzberg, B. H. (1997). Perceived understanding, nonverbal communication and relational satisfaction. In J. Aitken & L. Shedletsky (Eds.), *Intrapersonal communication processes* (pp. 386–395). Annandale, VA: Speech Communication Association.

Ehrenreich, B., Hess, E., & Jacobs, G. (1986). *Remaking love: The feminization of sex.* Garden City, NY: Anchor/Doubleday.

Eisenberg, A., Murkoff, H. E., & Hathaway, S. E. (1996). *What to expect the first year.* New York: Workman.

Eisenberg, A. R. (1992). Conflicts between mothers and their young children. *Merrill-Palmer Quarterly, 38,* 21–43.

Ekman, P. (1985). *Telling lies.* New York: Norton.

Ekman, P., & Friesen, W. V. (1969). Nonverbal leakage and clues to deception. *Psychiatry, 32,* 88–106.

Elbaum, P. L. (1982). The dynamics, implications, and treatment of extramarital sexual relationships for the family therapist. *Journal of Marital and Family Therapy, 7,* 489–495.

Ellis, C., & Weinstein, E. (1986). Jealousy and the social psychology of emotional experience. *Journal of Social and Personal Relationships, 3,* 337–357.

Ellyson, S. L., & Dovidio, J. F. (1985). Power, dominance, and nonverbal behavior: Basic concepts and issues. In S. L. Ellyson & J. F. Dovidio (Eds.), *Power, dominance, and nonverbal behavior* (pp. 1–27). New York: Springer-Verlag.

Emmers, T. M., & Dindia, K. (1995). The effect of relational stage and intimacy on touch: An extension of Guerrero and Andersen. *Personal Relationships, 2,* 225–236.

Emmers, T. M., & Canary, D. J. (1996). The effect of uncertainty reducing strategies on young couples' relational repair and intimacy. *Communication Quarterly, 44,* 166–182.

Epstein, S. (1973). The self-concept revisited: Or a theory of a theory. *American Psychologist, 28,* 404–416.

Exline, R. V., Ellyson, S. L., & Long, B. (1975). Visual behavior as an aspect of power role relationships. In P. Pliner,

L. Krames, & T. Alloway (Eds.), *Nonverbal communication of aggression* (pp. 21–52). New York: Plenum.

Exline, R. V., & Winters, L. C. (1965). Affective relations and mutual glances in dyads. In S. Tomkins & C. E. Izard (Eds.), *Affect, cognition, and personality.* New York: Springer.

Fairhurst, G. T. (1986). Male-female communication on the job: Literature review and commentary. In M. McLaughlin (Ed.), *Communication yearbook 9* (pp. 83–116). Beverly Hills, CA: Sage.

Falbo, T., & Peplau, L. A. (1980). Power strategies in intimate relationships. *Journal of Personality and Social Psychology, 38,* 618–628.

Farrell, D., & Rusbult, C. E. (1981). Exchange variables as predictors of job satisfaction, job commitment, and turnover: The impact of rewards, costs, alternatives, and investments. *Organizational Behavior and Human Performance, 27,* 78–95.

Feeney, J. A. (1995). Adult attachment and emotional control. *Personal Relationships, 2,* 143–159.

Feeney, J. A., & Noller, P. (1991). Attachment style and verbal descriptions of romantic partners. *Journal of Social and Personal Relationships, 8,* 187–215.

Feeney, J. A., Noller, P., & Roberts, N. (1998). Emotion, attachment and satisfaction in close relationships. In P. A. Andersen & L. K. Guerrero (Eds.), *Handbook of communication and emotion: Research, theory, applications and contexts* (pp. 273–505). San Diego, CA: Academic Press.

Fehr, B. (1988). Prototype analysis of the concepts of love and commitment. *Journal of Personality and Social Psychology, 58,* 281–291.

Fehr, B. (1996). *Friendship processes.* Thousand Oaks, CA: Sage.

Feingold, A. (1988). Matching for attractiveness in romantic partners and same-sex friends: A meta-analysis and theoretical critique. *Psychological Bulletin, 104,* 226–235.

Feingold, A. (1991). Sex differences in the effects of similarity and physical attractiveness on opposite-sex attraction. *Basic and Applied Social Psychology, 12,* 357–367.

Felmlee, D. (1995). Fatal attractions: Affection and disaffection in intimate relationships. *Journal of Social and Personal Relationships, 12,* 295–312.

Felmlee, D. H. (1998). "Be careful what you wish for . . .": A quantitative and qualitative investigation of "fatal attraction." *Personal Relationships, 5,* 235–254.

Felmlee, D. H., Sprecher, S., & Bassin, E. (1990). The dissolution of intimate relationships: A hazard model. *Social Psychology Quarterly, 53,* 13–30.

Ferguson, C. A. (1964). Baby talk in six languages. *American Anthropologist, 66,* 103–114.

Festinger, L., Schacter, S., & Back, K. (1950). *Social pressures in informal groups: A study of human factors in housing.* New York: Harper.

Filsinger, E. E., & Thoma, S. J. (1988). Behavioral antecedents of relational stability and adjustment: A five-year longitudinal study. *Journal of Marriage and the Family, 50,* 585–595.

Fincham, F. D. (2000). The kiss of the porcupines: From attributing responsibility to forgiving. *Personal Relationships, 7,* 1–23.

Fisher, B. A., & Adams, K. L. (1994). *Interpersonal communication: Pragmatics of human relationships* (2nd ed.). New York: McGraw-Hill.

Fitness, J., & Fletcher, G. J. O. (1993). Love, hate, anger, and jealousy in close relationships: A prototype and cognitive appraisal analysis. *Journal of Personality and Social Psychology, 65,* 942–958.

Fitzpatrick, M. A. (1988). *Between husbands and wives: Communication in marriage.* Newbury Park, CA: Sage.

Fitzpatrick, M. A., & Badzinski, D. M. (1984). All in the family: Interpersonal communication in kin relationships. In M. L. Knapp & G. R. Miller (Eds.), *Handbook of interpersonal communication* (pp. 687–736). Beverly Hills, CA: Sage.

Fitzpatrick, M. A., & Winke, T. (1979). You always hurt the one you love: Strategies and tactics in interpersonal conflict. *Communication Quarterly, 27,* 3–11.

Fletcher, G. J. O., & Fincham, F. D. (Eds.). (1991). *Cognition in close relationships.* Hillsdale, NJ: Erlbaum.

Floyd, K. (1995). Gender and closeness among friends and siblings. *Journal of Psychology, 129,* 193–202.

Floyd, K., Ramirez, A., & Burgoon, J. K. (1999). Expectancy violations theory. In L. K. Guerrero, J. A. DeVito, & M. L. Hecht (Eds.), *The nonverbal communication reader: Classic and contemporary readings* (2nd ed., pp. 437–444). Prospect Heights, IL: Waveland Press.

Foa, E. B., & Foa, U. G. (1980). Resource theory: Interpersonal behavior as exchange. In K. J. Gergen, M. S. Greenber, & R. H. Willis (Eds.), *Social exchange: Advances in theory and research* (pp. 77–140). New York: Plenum.

Foa, U. G. (1971). Interpersonal and economic resources. *Science, 171,* 345–351.

Folkes, V. S. (1982). Communicating the causes of social rejection. *Journal of Experimental Social Psychology, 18,* 235–252.

Folkes, V. S., & Sears, D. O. (1977). Does everybody like a liker? *Journal of Experimental Social Psychology, 13,* 505–519.

Fox, G. L. (1981). The family's role in adolescent sexual behavior. In T. Ooms (Ed.), *Teenage pregnancy in a family context* (pp. 73–130). Philadelphia: Temple University Press.

Frank, E., Anderson, C., & Rubinstein, D. (1979). Marital role strain and sexual satisfaction. *Journal of Consulting and Clinical Psychology, 217,* 1096–1103.

Frank, M. G., & Gilovich, T. (1988). The dark side of self- and social perception: Black uniforms and aggression in professional sports. *Journal of Personality and Social Psychology, 54,* 74–85.

Frazier, P. A., & Cook, S. W. (1993). Correlates of distress following heterosexual relationship dissolution. *Journal of Social and Personal Relationships, 10,* 55–67.

Freedman, S. R., & Enright, R. D. (1996). Forgiveness as an intervention goal with incest survivors. *Journal of Consulting and Clinical Psychology, 64,* 983–992.

Frey, L. R., Botan, C. H., Friedman, P. G., & Kreps, G. L. (1991). *Investigating communication: An introduction to research methods.* Englewood Cliffs, NJ: Prentice Hall.

Friedman, H. S., Riggio, R. E., & Casella, D. F. (1988). Nonverbal skill, personal charisma, and initial attraction. *Personality and Social Psychology Bulletin, 14,* 203–211.

Gadlin, H. (1977). Private lives and public order: A critical view of the history of intimate relations in the United States. In G, Levenger & H. L. Rausch (Eds.), *Close relationships: Perspective of the meaning of intimacy* (pp. 33–71): Amherst: University of Massachusetts Press.

Gagnon, J. H. (1979). *Human sexualities.* Scott, Forseman.

Gaines, S. O. (1995). Relationships between members of cultural minorities. In J. T. Wood & S. Duck (Eds.), *Understudied relationships: Off the beaten track* (pp. 51–88). Thousand Oaks, CA: Sage.

Galligan, R. F., & Terry, D. J. (1993). Romantic ideals, fear of negative implications and practice of safe sex. *Journal of Applied Social Psychology, 23,* 1685–1711.

Gass, B. Z., & Nichols, W. C. (1988). Gaslighting: A marital syndrome. *Contemporary Family Therapy, 10,* 3–16.

Gelles, R. J., & Cornell, C. P. (1990). *Intimate violence in families* (2nd ed.). Newbury Park, CA: Sage.

Gibran, K. (1923/1970). *The prophet.* New York: Knopf.

Gilbert, S. J. (1976). Self disclosure, intimacy, and communication in families. *The Family Coordinator, 25,* 221–230.

Gilbert, S. J., & Horenstein, D. (1975). The dyadic effects of self-disclosure: Level vs. valence. *Human Communication Research, 1,* 316–322.

Giles, H., & Wiemann, J. M. (1987). Language, social comparison, and power. In C. Berger & S. H. Chafee (Eds.), *Handbook of communication science* (pp. 350–384). Newbury Park, CA: Sage.

Girard, M., & Mullet, E. (1997). Propensity to forgive in adolescents, young adults, older adults, and elderly people. *Journal of Adult Development, 4,* 209–220.

Givens, D. B. (1978). The nonverbal basis of attraction: Flirtation, courtship, and seduction. *Psychiatry, 41,* 346–359.

Givens, D. B., (1983). *Love signals.* New York: Crown.

Glick, P. (1985). Orientation toward relationships: Choosing a situation in which to begin a relationship. *Journal of Experimental Social Psychology, 21,* 544–562.

Glomb, T. M., Richman, W. L., Hulin, C. L., Drasgow, F., Schneider, K. T., & Fitzgerald, L. F. (1997). Ambient sexual harassment: An integrated model of antecedents and consequences. *Organizational Behavior and Human Decision Processes, 71,* 309–328.

Goffman, E. (1959). *The presentation of self in everyday life.* Garden City, NY: Anchor/Doubleday.

Goffman, E. (1967). *Interaction ritual: Essays on face-to-face behavior.* New York: Pantheon Books.

Goffman, E. (1971). *Relations in public.* New York: Basic Books.

Golish, T. D., & Caughlin, J. P. (2000, November). *I'd rather not talk about it: Adolescents' and young adults' use of topic avoidance in stepfamilies.* Paper presented at the annual meeting of the National Communication Association, Seattle, WA.

Goodman, P. (1960). *Growing up absurd: Problems of youth in the organized society.* New York: Vintage Books.

Gottman, J. M. (1979). *Marital interaction: Experimental investigations.* New York: Academic Press.

Gottman, J. M. (1982). Emotional responsiveness in marital conversations. *Journal of Communication, 32,* 108–120.

Gottman, J. M. (1993). A theory of marital dissolution and stability. *Journal of Family Psychology, 7,* 57–75.

Gottman, J. M. (1994). *What predicts divorce? The relationship between marital processes and marital outcomes.* Hillsdale, NJ: Erlbaum.

Gottman, J. M., & Carrere, S. (1994). Why can't men and women get along? Developmental roots and marital inequities. In D. J. Canary & L. Stafford (Eds.), *Communication and relational maintenance* (pp. 203–222). San Diego, CA: Academic Press.

Gottman, J. M., & Levenson, R. W. (1988). The social psychophysiology of marriage. In P. Noller & M. A. Fitzpatrick (Eds.), *Perspectives on marital interaction* (pp. 182–200). Philadelphia: Multilingual Matters.

Gottman, J. M., & Levenson, R. W. (1992). Marital processes predictive of later dissolution: Behavior, physiology, and health. *Journal of Personality and Social Psychology, 63,* 221–233.

Gouldner, A. W. (1960). The norm of reciprocity: A preliminary statement. *Sociological Review, 25,* 161–178.

Gray, J. (1992). *Men are from Mars, women are from Venus: A practical guide to improving communication and getting what you want in your relationships.* New York: Harper Collins.

Greenblat, C. S. (1983). The salience of sexuality in the early years of marriage. *Journal of Marriage and the Family, 45,* 289–299.

Greene, B. L., Lee, R. R., & Lustig, N. (1974). Conscious and unconscious factors in marital infidelity. *Medical Aspects of Human Sexuality, 8,* 87–91.

Greenstein, T. N. (1990). Marital disruption and the employment of married women. *Journal of Marriage and the Family, 52,* 657–676.

Grice, H. P. (1989). *Studies in the way of words.* Cambridge, MA: Harvard University Press.

Griffit, W. (1970). Environmental effects on interpersonal affective behaviors: Ambient effective temperature and attraction. *Journal of Personality and Social Psychology, 15,* 240–244.

Gross, M. A., & Guerrero, L. K. (2000). Managing conflict appropriately and effectively: An application of the competence model to Rahim's organizational conflict styles. *International Journal of Conflict Management, 11,* 200–226.

Grotevant, H. D., & Cooper, C. R. (1985). Patterns of interaction in family relationships and the development of identity exploration in adolescence. *Child Development, 56,* 415–428.

Grusec, J. E., & Kuczynski, L. (1980). Direction of effects in socialization: A comparison of the parent's versus the child's behavior as determinants of disciplinary techniques. *Development Psychological, 16,* 1–9.

Gudykunst, W. B. (1988). Culture and the development of interpersonal relationships. In J. A. Anderson (Ed.), *Communication yearbook 12* (pp. 315–354). Newbury Park, CA: Sage.

Gudykunst, W. B. (1989). Uncertainty and anxiety. In Y. Y. Kim & W. B. Gudykunst (Eds.), *Theories in intercultural communication* (pp. 123–156). Newbury Park, CA: Sage.

Gudykunst, W. B., & Nishida, T. (1984). Individual and cultural influences on uncertainty reduction. *Communication Monographs, 51,* 23–36.

Guerrero, L. K. (1994). "I'm so mad I could scream": The effects of anger expression on relational satisfaction and communication competence. *Southern Communication Journal, 59,* 125–141.

Guerrero, L. K. (1995). Nonverbal communication: Themes and theories. In R. L. Hartman & L. A. Texter (Eds.), *Advanced interpersonal communication* (pp. 69–92). Dubuque, IA: Kendall/Hunt.

Guerrero, L. K. (1996). Attachment-style differences in intimacy and involvement: A test of the four-category model. *Communication Monographs, 63,* 269–292.

Guerrero, L. K. (1997). Nonverbal involvement across interactions with same-sex friends, opposite-sex friends, and romantic partners: Consistency or change? *Journal of Social and Personal Relationships, 14,* 31–59.

Guerrero, L. K. (1998). Attachment-style differences in the experience and expression of romantic jealousy. *Personal Relationships, 5,* 273–291.

Guerrero, L. K. (2000). Intimacy. In D. Levinson, J. Ponzetti, & P. Jorgensen (Eds.), *The encyclopedia of human emotions.* New York: Macmillan Reference Works.

Guerrero, L. K., & Afifi, W. A. (1995a). Some things are better left unsaid: Topic avoidance in family relationships. *Communication Quarterly, 43,* 276–296.

Guerrero, L. K., & Afifi, W. A. (1995b). What parents don't know: Topic avoidance in parent-child relationships. In T. J. Socha & G. H. Stamp (Eds.), *Parents, children,*

and communication: Frontiers of theory and research (pp. 219–246). Mahwah, NJ: Erlbaum.

Guerrero, L. K., & Afifi, W. A. (1998). Communicative responses to jealousy as a function of self-esteem and relationship maintenance goals: A test of Bryson's dual motivation model. *Communication Reports, 11,* 111–122.

Guerrero, L. K., & Afifi, W. A. (1999). Toward a goal-oriented approach for understanding communicative responses to jealousy. *Western Journal of Communication, 63,* 216–248.

Guerrero, L. K., & Andersen, P. A. (1991). The waxing and waning of relational intimacy: Touch as a function of relational stage, gender, and touch avoidance. *Journal of Social and Personal Relationships, 8,* 147–165.

Guerrero, L. K., & Andersen, P. A. (1994). Patterns of matching and initiation: Touch behavior and avoidance across romantic relationship stages. *Journal of Nonverbal Behavior, 18,* 137–153.

Guerrero, L. K., & Andersen, P. A. (1998a). The dark side of jealousy and envy: Desire, delusion, desperation, and destructive communication. In B. H. Spitzberg & W. R. Cupach (Eds.), *The dark side of relationships* (pp. 33–70). Mahwah, NJ: Erlbaum.

Guerrero, L. K., & Andersen, P. A. (1998b). The experience and expression of romantic jealousy. In P. A. Andersen & L. K. Guerrero (Eds.), *The handbook of communication and emotion: Research, theory, applications, and contexts* (pp. 155–188). San Diego, CA: Academic Press.

Guerrero, L. K., & Andersen, P. A. (2000). Emotion in close relationships. In C. Hendrick and S. S. Hendrick (Eds.). *Close relationships: A sourcebook* (pp. 171–183). Thousand Oaks, CA: Sage.

Guerrero, L. K., Andersen, P. A., Jorgensen, P. F., Spitzberg, B. H., & Eloy, S. V. (1995). Coping with the green-eyed monster: Conceptualizing and measuring communicative responses to jealousy. *Western Journal of Communication, 59,* 270–304.

Guerrero, L. K., & Burgoon, J. K. (1996). Attachment styles and reactions to nonverbal involvement change in romantic dyads: Patterns of reciprocity and compensation. *Human Communication Research, 22,* 335–370.

Guerrero, L. K., & Eloy, S. V. (1992). Jealousy and relational satisfaction across marital types. *Communication Reports, 5,* 23–31.

Guerrero, L. K., Eloy, S. V., & Wabnik, A. I. (1993). Linking maintenance strategies to relationship development and disengagement: A reconceptualization. *Journal of Social and Personal Relationships, 10,* 273–283.

Guerrero, L. K., & Jones, S. M. (2000, June). *Attachment-style differences in social skills: Through the eyes of a romantic partner and an observer.* Paper presented at the annual meeting of the International Communication Association, Acapulco, Mexico.

Guerrero, L. K., & Langan, E. J. (1999, February). *Dominance displays in conversations about relational problems: Differences due to attachment style and sex.* Paper presented at the annual meeting of the Western States Communication Association, Vancouver, BC.

Guerrero, L. K., & Reiter, R. L. (1998). Expressing emotion: Sex differences in social skills and communicative responses to anger, sadness, and jealousy. In D. J. Canary & K. Dindia (Eds.), *Sex differences and similarities in communication* (pp. 321–350). Mahwah, NJ: Erlbaum.

Guerrero, L. K., & Yoshimura, S. M. (1999, May). *General threat and specific emotions as predictors of communicative responses to jealousy.* Paper presented at the annual meeting of the International Communication Association, San Francisco, CA.

Gutek, B. A., Morasch, B., & Cohen, A. G. (1983). Interpreting social-sexual behavior in a work setting. *Journal of Vocational Behavior, 32,* 30–48.

Haas, A., & Sherman, M. A. (1982). Reported topics of conversation among same sex adults. *Communication Quarterly, 30,* 332–333.

Haas, S. M., & Stafford, L. (1998). An initial examination of maintenance behaviors in gay and lesbian relationships. *Journal of Social and Personal Relationships, 15,* 846–855.

Hale, J. L., & Burgoon, J. K. (1984). Models of reactions to changes in nonverbal intimacy. *Journal of Nonverbal Behavior, 8,* 287–314.

Hall, E. T. (1968) Proxemics. *Current Anthropology, 9,* 83–109

Halloran, E. C. (1998). The role of marital power in depression and marital distress. *American Journal of Family Therapy, 26,* 3–14.

Hamida, S. B., Mineka, S., & Bailey, J. M. (1998). Sex differences in perceived controllability of mate value: An evolutionary perspective. *Journal of Personality and Social Psychology, 75,* 953–966.

Hamm, N. H., & Hoving, K. L. (1971). Conformity in children as a function of grade level and real versus hypothetical adult and peer models. *Journal of Genetic Psychology, 118,* 253–263.

Hammer, J. C., Fisher, J. D., Fitzgerald, P., & Fisher, W. A. (1996). When two heads aren't better than one: AIDS risk behavior in college-age couples. *Journal of Applied Social Psychology, 26,* 375–397.

Hansen, G. L. (1987). Extradyadic relations during courtship. *Journal of Sex Research, 23* 382–390.

Hansen, J. E., & Schuldt, W. J. (1984). Marital self-disclosure and marital satisfaction. *Journal of Marriage and the Family, 46,* 923–926.

Hargrave, T. D. (1994). *Families and forgiveness.* New York: Brunner/Mazel.

Hargrow, A. M. (1997). Speaking our realities: From speculation to truth concerning African American women's experiences of sexual harassment. *Dissertation Abstracts International, 57*(7-B), 4707.

Harms, L. S. (1961). Listener judgments of status cues in speech. *Quarterly Journal of Speech, 47,* 164–168.

Harry, J. (1984). *Gay couples.* New York: Praeger.

Harry, J., & De Vall, W. B. (1978). *The social organization of gay males.* New York: Praeger.

Hart, C. H., DeWolf, D. M., Wozniak, P., & Burts, D. C. (1992). Maternal and paternal disciplinary styles: Relations with preschoolers' playground behavioral orientations and peer status. *Child Development, 63,* 879–892.

Harvey, J. H. (1987). Attributions in close relationships: Recent theoretical developments. *Journal of Social and Clinical Psychology, 5,* 420–434.

Hasart, J. K., & Hutchinson, K. L. (1993). The effects of perceptions of interpersonal attraction. *Journal of Social Behavior and Personality, 8,* 521–528.

Hatfield, E. (1984). The dangers of intimacy. In V. J. Derlega (Ed.), *Communication, intimacy, and close relationships* (pp. 207–220). New York: Academic Press.

Hatfield, E. (1988). Passionate and companionate love. In R. J. Sternberg & M. L. Barnes (Eds.), *The psychology of love* (pp. 191–217). New Haven, CT: Yale University Press.

Hatfield, E. (1999, August 20). Personal communication to Peter Andersen.

Hatfield, E., Cacioppo, J. T., & Rapson, R. L. (1994). *Emotional contagion.* New York: Cambridge University Press.

Hatfield, E., Greenberger, E., Traupmann, J., & Lambert, P. (1982). Equity and sexual satisfaction in recently married couples. *Journal of Sex Research, 18,* 18–32.

Hatfield, E., & Rapson, R. L. (1987). Passionate love: New directions in research. In W. H. Jones & D. Perlman (Eds.), *Advances in personal relationships* (Vol. 1, pp. 109–139). Greenwich, CT: JAI Press.

Hatfield, E., & Rapson, R. L. (2000, March 15). *Rosie.* Pittsburgh, PA: Sterling House.

Hatfield, E., & Sprecher, S. (1986a). Measuring passionate love in intimate relationships. *Journal of Adolescence, 9,* 383–410.

Hatfield, E., & Sprecher, S. (1986b). *Mirror, mirror . . . The importance of looks in everyday life.* Albany: State University of New York Press.

Hay, D. F. (1984). Social conflict in early childhood. In G. Whitehurst (Ed.), *Annals of child development* (Vol. 1, pp. 1–44). Greenwich, CT: JAI Press.

Hays, R. B. (1985). A longitudinal study of friendship development. *Journal of Personality and Social Psychology, 48,* 909–924.

Hazan, C., & Shaver, P. (1987). Conceptualizing romantic love as an attachment process. *Journal of Personality and Social Psychology, 52,* 511–524.

Hazan, C., & Zeifman, D. (1994). Sex and the psychological tether. In K. Bartholomew & D. Perlman (Eds.), *Advances in personal relationships* (Vol. 5, pp. 151–177). London: Kingsley.

Hecht, M. L. (1993). 2002—A research odyssey: Toward the development of a communication theory of identity. *Communication Monographs, 60,* 76–82.

Hecht, M. L., Collier, M. J., & Ribeau, S. (1993). *African American communication: Ethnic identity and cultural interpretations.* Newbury Park, CA: Sage.

Hecht, M. L., DeVito, J. A., & Guerrero, L. K. (1999). Perspectives on nonverbal communication: Codes, functions, and contexts. In L. K. Guerrero, J. A. DeVito, & M. L. Hecht (Eds.), *The nonverbal communication reader: Classic and contemporary readings* (2nd ed., pp. 3–18). Prospect Heights, IL: Waveland Press.

Hecht, M. L., Marston, P. J., & Larkey, L. K. (1994). Love ways and relationship quality in heterosexual relationships. *Journal of Social and Personal Relationships, 11,* 25–43.

Heider, F. (1958). *The psychology of interpersonal relations.* New York: Wiley.

Helgeson, V. S., Shaver, P., & Dyer, M. (1987). Prototypes of intimacy and distance in same-sex and opposite-sex relationships. *Journal of Social and Personal Relationships, 4,* 195–233.

Hendrick, C., & Hendrick, S. S. (1986). A theory and method of love. *Journal of Personality and Social Psychology, 50,* 392–402.

Hendrick, C., & Hendrick, S. S. (1990). A relationship specific version of the love attitude scale. *Journal of Social Behavior and Personality, 5,* 239–254.

Hendrick, S. S. (1981). Self-disclosure and marital satisfaction. *Journal of Personality and Social Psychology, 40,* 1150–1159.

Hendrick, S. S., & Hendrick, C. (1987). Love and sex attitudes: A close relationship. In W. H. Jones & D. Perlman (Eds.), *Advances in personal relationships* (Vol. 1, pp. 141–169). Greenwich, CT: JAI Press.

Hendrick, S. S., & Hendrick, C. (1992). *Liking, loving, and relating* (2nd ed.). Pacific Grove, CA: Brooks/Cole.

Hendrick, S. S., Hendrick, C., & Adler, N. L. (1988). Romantic relationships: Love, satisfaction, and staying together. *Journal of Personality and Social Psychology, 54,* 980–988.

Henley, N. M. (1977). *Body politics: Power, sex and nonverbal communication.* Englewood Cliffs, NJ: Prentice-Hall.

Hensley, W. E. (1994). Height as a basis for interpersonal attraction. *Adolescence, 29,* 469–474.

Heslin, R., & Boss, D. (1980). Nonverbal intimacy in arrival and departure at an airport. *Personality and Social Psychology Bulletin, 6,* 248–252.

Hess, E. H. (1965). Attitude and pupil size. *Scientific American, 212,* 46–54.

Hess, E. H., & Goodwin, E. (1974). The present state of pupilometrics. In M. P. Janisse (Ed.), *Pupillary dynamics and behavior* (pp. 209–246). New York: Plenum.

Hesson-McInnis, M. S., & Fitzgerald, L. F. (1997). Sexual harassment: A preliminary test of an integrative model. *Journal of Applied Social Psychology, 27,* 877–901.

Hewes, D. E., Graham, M. L., Doelger, J., & Pavitt, C. (1985). "Second-guessing": Message interpretation in social networks. *Human Communication Research, 11,* 299–334.

Hewitt, J., & Stokes, R. (1975). Disclaimers. *American Sociological Review, 40,* 1–11.

Higgins, R. L., & Berglas, S. (1990). The maintenance and treatment of self-handicapping: From risk-taking to face-saving—and back. In R. L. Higgins (Ed.), *Self-handicapping: The paradox that isn't* (pp. 187–238). New York: Plenum.

Hill, C. T., Rubin, Z., & Peplau, L. A. (1976). Breakups before marriage: The end of 103 affairs. *Journal of Social Issues, 32,* 147–168.

Hill, J. P., & Holmbeck, G. (1986). Attachment and autonomy during adolescence. In G. Whitehurst (Ed.), *Annals of child development* (vol. 3, pp. 145–189). Greenwich, CT: JAI.

Hinde, R. A. (1984). Why do the sexes behave differently in close relationships? *Journal of Social and Personal Relationships, 1,* 471–501.

Hochschild, A. (1997). *The time bind: When work becomes home and home becomes work.* New York: Metropolitan Books.

Hochschild, A., & Machung, A. (1989). *The second shift: Working parents and the revolution at home.* New York: Viking/Penguin.

Hocker, J. L., & Wilmot, W. W. (1998). *Interpersonal conflict* (5th ed.). Dubuque, IA: Brown & Benchmark.

Hocking, J. E., & Leathers, D.G. (1980). Nonverbal indicators of deception: A new theoretical perspective. *Communication Monographs, 47,* 119–131.

Hoffman, M. L. (1970). Power assertion by parents and its impact on the child. *Child Development, 31,* 129–143.

Hoffman, M. L. (1980). Moral development in adolescence. In J. Adelson (Ed.), *Handbook of adolescent psychology* (pp. 295–343). New York: Wiley.

Hofstede, G. (1982). *Culture's consequences* (abridged ed.). Beverly Hills, CA: Sage.

Hogg, M. A., & Hains, S. C. (1996). Intergroup relations and group solidarity: Effects of group identification and social beliefs on depersonalized attraction. *Journal of Personality and Social Psychology, 70,* 295–309.

Holtgraves, T. (1988). Gambling as self-presentation. *Journal of Gambling Behavior, 4,* 78–91.

Holtgraves, T., & Yang, J. (1990). Politeness as a universal: Cross-cultural perceptions of request strategies and inferences based on their use. *Journal of Personality and Social Psychology, 59,* 719–729.

Holtgraves, T., & Yang, J. (1992). Interpersonal underpinnings of request strategies: General principles and differences due to culture and gender. *Journal of Personality and Social Psychology, 62,* 246–256.

Holtzworth-Monroe, A., & Jacobson, N. S. (1987). An attributional approach to marital dysfunction and therapy.

In J. E. Madduz, C. D. Stolenberg, & R. Rosenwein (Eds.), *Social processes in clinical and counseling psychology* (pp. 153–170). New York: Springer-Verlag.

Homans, G. C. (1961). *Social behavior.* New York: Harcourt, Brace & World.

Homans, G. C. (1974). *Social behavior: Its elementary forms* (2nd ed.). New York: Harcourt, Brace & World.

Honeycutt, J. M., Cantrill, J. G., & Allen, T. (1992). Memory structure of relational decay: A cognitive test of the sequencing of de-escalating actions and stages. *Human Communication Research, 18,* 528–562.

Hoobler, G. D. (1999, June). *Ten years of personal relationships research: Where have we been and where are we going?* Paper presented at the annual meeting of the International Network on Personal Relationships, Louisville, KY.

Hopper, M. L., Knapp, M. L., & Scott, L. (1981). Couples' personal idioms: Exploring intimate talk. *Journal of Communication, 31,* 23–33.

Hosman, L. A., & Tardy, C. H. (1980). Self-disclosure and reciprocity in short- and long-term relationships: An experimental study of evaluational and attributional consequences. *Communication Quarterly, 28,* 20–30.

Howard, J. A., Blumstein, P., & Schwartz, P. (1986). Sex, power, and influence tactics in intimate relationships. *Journal of Personality and Social Psychology, 51,* 102–109.

Hoyle, R. H., Insko, C. A., & Moniz, A. J. (1992). Self-esteem, evaluative feedback, and preacquaintance attraction: Indirect reactions to success and failure. *Motivation and Emotion, 16,* 79–101.

Hoyt, M. F. (1978). Secrets in psychotherapy: Theoretical and practical considerations. *International Review of Psycho-Analysis, 5,* 231–241.

Hunt, M. (1974). *Sexual behavior in the 1970s.* New York: Playboy Press.

Huston, M., & Schwartz, P. (1995). The relationships of gay men and lesbians. In J. T. Wood & S. Duck (Eds.), *Understudied relationships: Off the beaten track* (pp. 89–121). Thousand Oaks, CA: Sage.

Huston, T. L. (1983). Power. In H. H. Kelley et al. (Eds.), *Close relationships* (pp. 169–219). New York: Freeman.

Huston, T. L., & Levinger, G. (1978). Interpersonal attraction and relationships. *Annual Review of Psychology, 29,* 115–156.

Huston, T. L., Surra, C. A., Fitzgerald, N. M., & Cate, R. M. (1981). From courtship to marriage: Mate selection as an interpersonal process. In S. Duck & R. Gilmour (Eds.), *Personal relationships: Developing personal relationships* (Vol. 2, pp. 53–88). London: Academic Press.

Imber-Black, E. (1993). Secrets in families and family therapy: An overview. In E. Imber-Black (Ed.), *Secrets in families and family therapy* (pp. 3–28). New York: Norton.

Infante, D. A. (1987). Aggressiveness. In J. C. McCroskey & J. A. Daly (Eds.), *Personality and interpersonal communication* (pp. 157–192). Newbury Park, CA: Sage.

Infante, D. A., Chandler, T. A., & Rudd, J. E. (1989). Test of an argumentative skill deficiency model of interpersonal violence. *Communication Monographs, 56,* 163–177.

Infante, D. A., & Rancer, A. S. (1982). A conceptualization and measure of argumentativeness. *Journal of Personality Assessment, 46,* 72–80.

Infante, D. A., Sabourin, T. C., Rudd, J. E., & Shannon, E. A. (1990). Verbal aggression in violent and nonviolent marital disputes. *Communication Quarterly, 38,* 361–371.

Isnard, C. A., & Zeeman, E. C. (1977). Some models from catastrophe theory in the social sciences. In E. C. Zeeman (Ed.). *Catastrophe theory: Selected papers 1972–1977.* Reading, MA: Addison-Wesley.

Jackson, L. A., & Ervin, K. S. (1992). Height stereotypes of women and men: The liabilities of shortness for both sexes. *Journal of Social Psychology, 132,* 433–445.

Jacob, T. (1974). Patterns of family conflict and dominance as a function of child age and social class. *Developmental Psychology, 10,* 1–12.

Jankowiak, W. R., & Fischer, E. F. (1992). A cross-cultural perspective on romantic love. *Ethnology, 31,* 149–155.

Janofsky, A. I. (1971). Affective self-disclosure in telephone versus face-to-face interviews. *Journal of Humanistic Psychology, 11,* 93–103.

Jellison, J. M., & Oliver, D. F. (1983). Attitudinal similarity and attraction: An impression management approach. *Personality and Social Psychology Bulletin, 9,* 111–115.

Jensen-Campbell, L. A., Graziano, W. G., & West, S. G. (1995). Dominance, prosocial orientation, and female preferences: Do nice guys really finish last? *Journal of Personality and Social Psychology, 68,* 427–440.

Johnson, D. J., & Rusbult, C. E. (1989). Resisting temptation: Devaluation of alternative partners as a means of maintaining commitment in close relationships. *Journal of Personality and Social Psychology, 57,* 967–980.

Johnson, D. W. (1986). *Reaching out: Interpersonal effectiveness and self-actualization* (3rd ed.). Englewood Cliffs, NJ: Prentice-Hall.

Johnson, M. L., Afifi, W. A., & Duck, S. (1994). *Social attraction on first dates: Is communication underrated?* Unpublished manuscript.

Johnson, M. P. (1982). Social and cognitive features of the dissolution of commitment to relationships. In S. Duck (Ed.), *Dissolving personal relationships* (pp. 51–73). New York: Academic Press.

Johnson, R. E. (1972). Attitudes toward extramarital relationships. *Medical Aspects of Human Sexuality, 6,* 168–191.

Jones, E., & Gallois, C. (1989). Spouses' impressions of rules for communication in public and private marital conflict. *Journal of Marriage and the Family, 51,* 957–967.

Jones, E. E., & Nisbett, R. E. (1972). *The actor and the observer: Divergent perceptions of the causes of behavior.* Morristown, NJ: General Learning Press.

Jones, E. E., & Wortman, C. (1973). *Ingratation: An attributional approach.* Morristown, NJ: General Learning Press.

Jones, S. M. (2000). *Nonverbal immediacy and verbal comforting in the social support process.* Unpublished doctoral dissertation, Arizona State University, Tempe.

Jones, S. M., & Burleson, B. R. (1997). The impact of situational variables on helpers' perceptions of comforting messages: An attributional analysis. *Communication Research, 24,* 530–555.

Jones, W. H., & Burdette, M. P. (1994). Betrayal in relationships. In A. L. Weber & J. H. Harvey (Eds.), *Perspectives on close relationships* (pp. 243–262). Needham Heights, MA: Allyn & Bacon.

Joseph, N., & Alex, N. (1972). The uniform: A sociological perspective. *American Journal of Sociology, 77,* 719–730.

Joshi, K., & Rai, S. N. (1987). Effect of physical attractiveness upon the inter-personal attraction of subjects of different self-esteem. *Perspectives in Psychological Research, 10,* 19–24.

Jourard, S. M. (1959). Self-disclosure and other cathexis. *Journal of Abnormal Social Psychology, 59,* 428–431.

Jourard, S. M. (1964). *The transparent self.* New York: Wiley.

Julien, D., Bouchard, C., Gagnon, M., & Pomperleau, A. (1992). An insider's view of marital sex: A dyadic analysis. *Journal of Sex Research, 29,* 343–360.

Kahneman, D., Slovic, P., & Tversky, A. (Eds.). (1982). *Judgment under uncertainty: Heuristics and biases.* Cambridge: Cambridge University Press.

Kaiser, S. B. (1997). *The social psychology of clothing: Symbolic appearances in context* (2nd ed.). New York: Fairchild Publications.

Kandel, D. B. (1978). Similarity in real life adolescent friendship pairs. *Journal of Personality and Social Psychology, 36,* 306–312.

Kandel, D. B., Single, E., & Kessler, R. C. (1976). The epidemiology of drug use among New York high school students: Distribution, trends, and change in rates of use. *American Journal of Public Health, 66,* 43–53.

Kanin, E. J., Davidson, K. D., & Scheck, S. R. (1970). A research note on male-female differentials in the experience of heterosexual love. *Journal of Sex Research, 6,* 64–72.

Karney, B. R., & Bradbury, T. N. (1995).The longitudinal course of marital quality and stability: A review of theory, method, and research. *Psychological Bulletin, 118,* 3–34.

Karpel, M. (1980). Family secrets. *Family Process, 19,* 295–306.

Katz, J., Street, A., & Arias, I. (1995, November). *Forgive and forget: Women's responses to dating violence.* Paper presented at the annual meeting of the Association for the Advancement of Behavior Therapy, Washington, DC.

Kellermann, K. A. (1991). The conversation MOP: II. Progression through scenes in discourse. *Human Communication Research, 17,* 385–414.

Kellermann, K. A. (1995). The conversation MOP: A model of patterned and pliable behavior. In D. E. Hewes (Ed.), *The cognitive bases of interpersonal communication* (pp. 181–224). Hillsdale, NJ: Erlbaum.

Kellermann, K. A., & Berger, C. R. (1984). Affect and the acquisition of social information: Sit back, relax, and tell me about yourself. In R. N. Bostrom (Ed.), *Communication yearbook 8* (pp. 412–445). Newbury Park, CA: Sage.

Kellermann, K. A., & Reynolds, R. (1990). When ignorance is bliss: The role of motivation to reduce uncertainty in uncertainty reduction theory. *Human Communication Research, 17,* 5–75.

Kelley, D. (1998). The communication of forgiveness. *Communication Studies, 49,* 255–271.

Kelley, H. H. (1973). The processes of causal attribution. *American Psychologist, 28,* 107–128.

Kelley, H. H. (1983). Love and commitment. In H. H. Kelley, E. Berscheid, A. Christensen, J. H. Harvey, T. L. Huston, G. Levinger, E. McClintock, L. A. Peplau, & D. R. Peterson (Eds.), *Close relationships* (pp. 265–314). New York: Freeman.

Kelley, H. H. (1986). Personal relationships: Their nature and significance. In R. Gilmour & S. Duck (Eds.), *The emerging field of personal relationships* (pp. 3–19). Hillsdale, NJ: Erlbaum.

Kelley, H. H., et al. (1983). Analyzing close relationships. In H. H. Kelley, E. Berscheid, A. Christensen, J. H. Harvey, T. L. Huston, G. Levinger, E. McClintock, L. A. Peplau, & D. R. Peterson (Eds.), *Close relationships* (pp. 20–67). New York: Freeman.

Kelly, A. E., & McKillop, K. J. (1996). Consequences of revealing personal secrets. *Psychological Bulletin, 120,* 450–465.

Kelly, K., & Rolker-Dolinsky, B. (1987). The psychosexology of female initiation and dominance. In D. Perlman & S. Duck (Eds.), *Intimate relationships: Development, dynamics and deterioration* (pp. 63–87). Newbury Park, CA: Sage.

Kennedy, C. W., & Camden, C. (1983). Interruptions and nonverbal gender differences. *Journal of Nonverbal Behavior, 8,* 91–108.

Kennedy, J. H. (1992). Relationship of maternal beliefs and childrearing strategies to social competence in preschool children. *Child Study Journal, 22,* 39–55.

Kenrick, D. T., Groth, G. E., Trost, M. R., & Sadalla, E. K. (1993). Integrating evolutionary and social exchange perspectives on relationships: Effects of gender, self-appraisal, and involvement level on mate selection criteria. *Journal of Personality and Social Psychology, 64,* 951–969.

Kenrick, D. T., & Keefe, R. C. (1992). Age preferences in mates reflect sex differences in human reproductive strategies. *Behavioral and Brain Sciences, 15,* 75–113.

Kenrick, D. T., Sadalla, E. K., Groth, G., & Trost, M. R. (1990). Evolution, traits, and the stages of human courtship: Qualifying the parental investment model. *Journal of Personality, 58,* 97–116.

Kenrick, D. T., & Trost, M. R., (1987). A biosocial theory of heterosexual relationships. In K. Kelley (Ed.), *Females, males, and sexuality: Theories and research* (pp. 59–100). Albany: State University of New York Press.

Kenrick, D. T., & Trost, M. R. (1989). Reproductive exchange model of heterosexual relationships: Putting proximate economics in ultimate perspective. In C. Hendrick (Ed.), *Review of personality and social psychology* (Vol. 10, pp. 92–118). Newbury Park, CA: Sage.

Keyton, J. (1996). Sexual harassment: A multidisciplinary synthesis and critique. In B. R. Burleson (Ed.), *Communication yearbook 19* (pp. 92–155). Thousand Oaks, CA: Sage.

Kidwell, J., Fischer, J. L., Dunham, R. M., & Baranowski, M. (1983). Parents and adolescents: Push and pull of change. In H. I. McCubin & C. R. Figley (Eds.), *Stress in the family: Coping with normative transitions* (pp. 74–89). New York: Brunner/Mazel.

Killworth, P. D., Bernard, H. R., & McCarty, C. (1984). Measuring patterns of acquaintanceship. *Current Anthropology, 25,* 381–397.

Kilmann, R. H., & Thomas, K. W. (1977). Developing a forced-choice measure of conflict-handling behavior: The "MODE" instrument. *Education and Psychological Measurement, 37,* 309–325.

Kilpatrick, S. D. (1995). *Turning points, uncertainty, and information search in dating relationships.* Unpublished master's thesis, University of North Carolina, Chapel Hill.

King, S. W., & Sereno, K. K. (1984). Conversational appropriateness as a conversational imperative. *Quarterly Journal of Speech, 70,* 264–273.

Klein, R. C. A., & Johnson, M. P. (1997). Strategies of couple conflict. In S. Duck (Ed.), *Handbook of personal relationships: Theory, research, and interventions* (2nd ed., pp. 267–486). New York: Wiley.

Kleinke, C. L., Meeker, F. B., & LaFong, C. (1974). Effects of gaze, touch, and use of name on evaluation of "engaged" couples. *Journal of Research in Personality, 7,* 368–373.

Knapp, M. L. (1978). *Social intercourse: From greeting to goodbye.* Boston: Allyn & Bacon.

Knapp, M. L. (1983). Dyadic relationship development. In J. Wiemann (Ed.), *Nonverbal interaction* (pp. 179–197). Newbury Park, CA: Sage.

Knapp, M. L., & Vangelisti, A. L. (1996). *Interpersonal communication and human relationships* (3rd ed.). Boston: Allyn & Bacon.

Koeppel, L. B., Montagne-Miller, Y., O'Hair, D., & Cody, M. (1993). Friendly? Flirting? Wrong? In P. J. Kalbfleisch (Ed.), *Interpersonal communication: Evolving interpersonal relationships* (pp. 13–32). Hillsdale, NJ: Erlbaum.

Kollock, P., Blumstein, P., & Schwartz, P. (1985). Sex and power in interaction: Conversational privileges and duties. *American Sociological Review, 50,* 34–46.

Korda, M. (1975). *Power: How to get it, how to use it.* New York: Ballantine Books.

Kornreich, J. (1999, June). On what date should you do it? *Cosmopolitan,* pp. 106–108.

Krueger, R. F., & Caspi, A. (1993). Personality, arousal, and pleasure: A test of competing models of interpersonal attraction. *Personality and Individual Differences, 14,* 105–111.

Kruglanski, A. W. (1990). Motivations for judging and knowing: Implications for causal attribution. In E. T. Higgins & R. M. Sorrentino (Eds.), *Handbook of motivation and cognition: Foundation of social behavior* (Vol. 2, pp. 333–368). New York: Guilford Press.

Kruglanski, A. W., Webster, D. M., & Klem, A. (1993). Motivated resistance and openness to persuasion in the presence or absence of prior information. *Journal of Personality and Social Psychology, 65,* 861–876.

Kübler-Ross, E. (1969). *On death and dying.* New York: Macmillan.

Kuczynski, L. (1984). Socialization goals and mother-child interaction: Strategies for long-term and short-term compliance. *Developmental Psychology, 20,* 1061–1073.

Kurdek, L. A. (1991). The dissolution of gay and lesbian couples. *Journal of social and personal relationships, 8,* 265–278.

Kurdek, L. A. (1993a). The allocation of household labor in gay, lesbian, and heterosexual married couples. *Journal of Social Issues, 49*(3), 127–139.

Kurdek, L. A. (1993b). Predicting marital dissolution: A 5-year prospective longitudinal study of newlywed couples. *Journal of Personality and Social Psychology, 64,* 221–242.

LaFrance, M., & Mayo, C. (1978). *Moving bodies: Nonverbal communication in social relationships.* Monterey, CA: Brooks/Cole.

Langer, E. J. (1989). *Mindfulness.* Reading, MA: Addison-Wesley.

Larkin, M. (1998). Easing the way to safer sex. *Lancet, 351,* 964–967.

Laursen, B. (1989). *Relationships and conflict during adolescence.* Unpublished doctoral dissertation, University of Minnesota, Minneapolis.

Laursen, B., & Collins, W. A. (1994). Interpersonal conflict during adolescence. *Psychological Bulletin, 115,* 197–209.

Lawrence, K., & Byers, E. S. (1995). Sexual satisfaction in long-term heterosexual relationships: The interpersonal exchange model of sexual satisfaction. *Personal Relationships, 2,* 267–285.

Lazarus, R. S. (1985). The trivialization of distress. In J. C. Rose & L. J. Solomon (Eds.), *Primary prevention of psychopathology: Vol. 8. Prevention in health psychology* (pp. 279–298). Hanover, NH: University Press of New England.

Lea, M., & Spears, R. (1995). Love at first byte: Building personal relationships over computer networks. In J. T. Wood & S. Duck (Eds.), *Understudied relationships: Off the beaten track* (pp. 197–233). Thousand Oaks, CA: Sage.

Lear, D. (1997). *Sex and sexuality: Risk and relationships in the age of AIDS*. Thousand Oaks, CA: Sage.

Leary, M. R. (1995). *Self-presentation: Impression management and interpersonal behavior*. Madison, WI: Brown & Benchmark.

Leary, M. R., & Kowalski, R. M. (1990). Impression management: A literature review and two-component model. *Psychological Bulletin, 107*, 34–47.

Lee, J. A. (1973). *The colors of love: An exploration of the ways of loving*. Don Mills, Ontario: New Press.

Lee, J. A. (1977). A typology of styles of loving. *Personality and Social Psychology Bulletin, 3*, 173–182.

Lee, J. A. (1988). Love styles. In R. J. Sternberg & M. L. Barnes (Eds.), *The psychology of love* (pp. 38–67). New Haven, CT: Yale University Press.

Lee, J. W., & Guerrero, L. K. (in press). Types of touch in cross-sex relationships between coworkers: Perceptions of relational and emotional messages, inappropriateness, and sexual harassment. *Journal of Applied Communication Research.*

Le Poire, B. A., Hallett, J. S., & Giles, H. (1998). Codependence: The paradoxical nature of the functional-afflicted relationship. In B. H. Spitzberg & W. R. Cupach (Eds.), *The dark side of relationships* (pp. 153–176). Mahwah, NJ: Erlbaum.

Levinger, G., & Senn, D. J. (1967). Disclosure of feelings in marriage. *Merrill-Palmer Quarterly, 13*, 237–249.

Levitt, M. J. (1991). Attachment and close relationships: A life span perspective. In J. L. Gerwitz & W. F. Kurtines (Eds.), *Intersections with attachment* (pp. 183–206). Mahwah, NJ: Erlbaum.

Levitt, M. J., Coffman, S., Guacci-Franco, N., & Loveless, S. C. (1994). Attachment relationships and life transitions: An expectancy model. In M. B. Sperling & W. H. Berman (Eds.), *Attachment in adults: Clinical and developmental perspectives* (pp. 232–255). New York: Guilford.

Lewis, M., & Rosenblum, L. A. (Eds.). (1974). *The effect of the infant on its caregiver*. New York: Wiley.

Livingstone, K. R. (1980). Love as a process of reducing uncertainty. In K. S. Pope et al. (Eds.), *On love and loving* (pp. 133–151). San Francisco: Jossey-Bass.

Lloyd, S. A., & Cate, R. M. (1985). The developmental course of conflict in dissolution of premarital relationships. *Journal of Social and Personal Relationships, 2*, 179–194.

Lloyd, S. A., Cate, R., & Henton, J. (1982). Equity and rewards as predictors of satisfaction in casual and intimate relationships. *Journal of Psychology, 110*, 43–48.

Lustig, M. W., & Koester, J. (1993). *Intercultural competence: Interpersonal communication across culture*. New York: Harper Collins.

Magai, C., & McFadden, S. H. (1995). *The role of emotion in social and personality development: History, theory, and research*. New York: Wiley.

Major, B., & Heslin, R. (1982). Perceptions of cross-sex and same-sex nonreciprocal touch: It is better to give than to receive. *Journal of Nonverbal Behavior, 6*, 148–162.

Marano, H. E. (1997, November/December). Gottman and Gray: The two Johns. *Psychology Today*, p. 28.

Marks, M. A., & Nelson, E. S. (1993). Sexual harassment on campus: Effects of professor gender on perception of sexually harassing behaviors. *Sex Roles, 28*, 207–217.

Marston, P. J., & Hecht, M. L. (1994). Love ways: An elaboration and application to relational maintenance. In D. J. Canary & L. Stafford (Eds.), *Communication and relational maintenance* (pp. 87–202). Orlando, FL: Academic Press.

Marston, P. J., Hecht, M. L., Manke, M., McDaniel, S., & Reeder, H. (1998). The subjective experience of intimacy, passion, and commitment in heterosexual loving relationships. *Personal Relationships, 5*, 15–30.

Marston, P. J., Hecht, M. L., & Robers, T. (1987). True love ways: The subjective experience and communication of romantic love. *Journal of Social and Personal Relationships, 4*, 387–407.

Masters, W. H., & Johnson, V. E. (1979). *Homosexuality in perspective*. Boston: Little, Brown.

Matthews, S. (1986). *Friendships through the life course: Oral biographies in old age*. Beverly Hills, CA: Sage.

May, J. L., & Hamilton, P. A. (1980). Effects of musically evoked affect on women's interpersonal attraction toward and perceptual judgments of physical attractiveness of men. *Journal of Social and Clinical Psychology, 6*, 180–190.

Mayback, K. L., & Gold, S. R. (1994). Hyperfeminity and attraction to macho and non-macho men. *Journal of Sex Research, 31*, 91–98.

McAdams, D. P. (1985). Motivation and friendship. In S. Duck & D. Perlman (Eds.), *Understanding personal relationships: An interdisciplinary approach* (pp. 85–105). London: Sage.

McAdams, D. P. (1988). Personal needs and personal relationships. In S. Duck (Ed.), *Handbook of personal relationships: Theory, research, and intervention* (pp. 7–22). New York: Wiley.

McCabe, M. P. (1999). The interrelationship between intimacy, relationship functioning, and sexuality among men and women in committed relationships. *Canadian Journal of Human Sexuality, 8*, 31–39.

McCornack, S. A. (1992). Information manipulation theory. *Communication Monographs, 59*, 1–16.

McCornack, S. A., & Parks, M. R. (1986). Deception detection and relationship development: The other side of trust. In M. L. McLaughlin (Ed.), *Communication yearbook 9* (pp. 377–389). Beverly Hills, CA: Sage.

McCroskey, J. C. (1997, November). *Why we communicate the ways we do: A communibiological approach.* Arnold distinguished lecture presented at the annual meeting of the National Communication Association, Chicago, IL.

McCroskey, J. C., Larson, C. E. & Knapp, M. L. (1971). *An introduction to interpersonal communication.* Englewood Cliffs, NJ: Prentice-Hall.

McCroskey, J. C., & McCain, T. A. (1974). The measurement of interpersonal attraction. *Speech Monographs, 41*, 261–266.

McCullough, M. E., Rachal, K. C., Sandage, S. J., Worthington, E. L., Brown, S. W., & Hight, T. L. (1998). Interpersonal forgiving in close relationships: II. Theoretical elaboration and measurement. *Journal of Personality and Social Psychology, 75*, 1586–1603.

McCullough, M. E., Worthington, E. L., & Rachal, K. C. (1997). Interpersonal forgiving in close relationships. *Journal of Personality and Social Psychology, 73*, 321–336.

McDonald, G. W. (1981). Structural exchange and marital interaction. *Journal of Marriage and the Family, 43*, 825–839.

McGoldrick, M., & Carter, E. (1982). The family life cycle. In F. Walsh (Ed.), *Normal family processes* (pp. 167–195). New York: Guilford.

Mead, D. E., Vatcher, G. M., Wyne, B. A., & Roberts, S. L. (1990). The comprehensive areas of change questionnaire: Assessing marital couples' presenting complaints. *American Journal of Family Therapy, 18*, 65–79.

Mearns, J. (1991). Coping with a breakup: Negative mood regulation expectancies and depression following the end of a romantic relationship. *Journal of Personality and Social Psychology, 60*, 327–334.

Mehrabian, A. (1971). *Silent messages.* Belmont, CA: Wadsworth.

Mehrabian, A. (1976). *Public places, private spaces.* New York: Basic Books.

Mehrabian, A. (1981). *Silent messages: Implicit communication of emotions and attitudes* (2nd edition). Belmont, CA: Wadsworth.

Mehrabian, A., & Ksionzky, S. (1974). *A theory of affiliation.* Lexington, MA: Lexington Books.

Meloy, J. R., & Gothard, S. (1995). Demographic and clinical comparison of obsessional followers and offenders with mental disorder. *American Journal of Psychiatry, 152*, 258–263.

Merton, R. K. (1948). The self-fulfilling prophecy. *Antioch Review, 8*, 193–210.

Metts, S. (1989). An exploratory investigation of deception in close relationships. *Journal of Social and Personal Relationships, 6*, 159–179.

Metts, S. (1991, February). *The wicked things you say, the wicked things you do: A pilot study of relational transgressions.* Paper presented at the annual meeting of the Western States Communication Association, Phoenix, AZ.

Metts, S. (1992). The language of disengagement: A face-management perspective. In T. L. Orbuch (Ed.), *Close relationships loss: Theoretical approaches* (pp. 111–127). New York: Springer-Verlag.

Metts, S. (1994). Relational transgressions. In W. R. Cupach & B. H. Spitzberg (Eds.), *The dark side of interpersonal communication* (pp. 217–240). Hillsdale, NJ: Erlbaum.

Metts, S. (1997). Face and facework: Implications for the study of personal relationships. In S. Duck (Ed.), *Handbook of personal relationships: Theory, research and interventions* (pp. 373–390). Chichester, UK: Wiley.

Metts, S., & Bowers, J. W. (1994). Emotion in interpersonal communication. In M. L. Knapp & G. R. Miller (Eds.), *Handbook of interpersonal communication* (2nd ed., pp. 508–541). Thousand Oaks, CA: Sage.

Metts, S., & Chronis, H. (1986, May). *An exploratory investigation of relational deception.* Paper presented at the annual meeting of the International Communication Association, Chicago, IL.

Metts, S., & Cupach, W. R. (1986, February). *Disengagement themes in same and opposite sex friendships.* Paper presented at the annual meeting of the Western Speech Communication Association, Tucson, AZ.

Metts, S., Cupach, W. R., & Bejlovich, R. A. (1989). "I love you too much to ever start liking you": Redefining romantic relationships. *Journal of Social and Personal Relationships, 6*, 259–274.

Metts, S., Cupach, W. R., & Imahori, T. T. (1992). Perceptions of compliance-resisting messages in three types of cross-sex relationships. *Western Journal of Communication, 56*, 1–17.

Metts, S., Sprecher, S., & Regan, P. C. (1998). Communication and sexual desire. In P. A. Andersen & L. K. Guerrero (Eds.), *Handbook of communication and emotion: Research, theory, applications, and contexts* (pp. 353–377). San Diego, CA: Academic Press.

Meurling, C. N., Ray, G. E., & LoBello, S. G. (1999). Children's evaluations of classroom friend and classroom best friend relationships. *Child Study Journal, 29*, 79–83.

Mikulincer, M., & Nachshon, O. (1991). Attachment styles and patterns of self-disclosure. *Journal of Personality and Social Psychology, 61*, 321–331.

Miller, G. R. (1976). *Explorations in interpersonal communication.* Beverly Hills, CA: Sage.

Miller, G. R., & Boster, F. (1988). Persuasion in personal relationships. In S. Duck (Ed.), *Handbook of personal relationships: Theory, research and interventions* (pp. 275–287). Chichester, UK: Wiley.

Miller, G. R., Boster, F., Roloff, M., & Siebold, D. (1977). Compliance-gaining message strategies: A typology and some findings concerning the effects of situational differences. *Communication Monographs, 44,* 37–51.

Miller, G. R., & Steinberg, M. (1975). *Between people: A new analysis of interpersonal communication.* Chicago: Science Research Associates.

Miller, L. C., Cody, M. J., & McLaughlin, M. L. (1994). Situations and goals as fundamental constructs in interpersonal communication research. In M. L. Knapp & G. R. Miller (Eds.), *Handbook of interpersonal communication* (pp. 162–198). Thousand Oaks, CA: Sage.

Miller, N. (1999, June). Get a guy by the 4th of July. *Cosmopolitan,* pp. 163–167.

Miller, R. S. (1996). *Embarrassment: Poise and peril in everyday life.* New York: Guilford.

Miller, S. M. (1987). Monitoring and blunting: Validation of a questionnaire to assess styles of information-seeking under threat. *Journal of Personality and Social Psychology, 52,* 345–353.

Miller, S. M., Brody, D. S., & Summerton, J. (1988). Styles of coping with threat: Implications for health. *Journal of Personality and Social Psychology, 54,* 142–148.

Mishel, M. H. (1981). The measurement of uncertainty in illness. *Nursing Research, 30,* 258–263.

Mishel, M. H. (1988). Uncertainty in illness. *Image: Journal of Nursing Scholarship, 20,* 225–232.

Mishel, M. H. (1990). Reconceptualization of the uncertainty in illness theory. *Image: Journal of Nursing Scholarship, 22,* 256–262.

Modigliani, A. (1968). Embarrassment, facework, and eye contact: Testing a theory of embarrassment. *Sociometry, 31,* 313–326.

Moe, J. D. (1972). Listener judgments of status in speech: A replication and extension. *Speech Monographs, 39,* 144–147.

Molloy, J. T. (1976). *Dress for success.* New York: Warner Books.

Mongeau, P. A., & Johnson, K. L. (1995). Predicting cross-sex first date sexual expectations and involvement: Contextual and individual difference factors. *Personal Relationships, 2,* 301–312.

Mongeau, P. A., Hale, J. L., & Alles, M. (1994). An experimental investigation of accounts and attributions following sexual infidelity. *Communication Monographs, 61,* 326–344.

Mongeau, P. A., & Schulz, B. E. (1997). What he doesn't know won't hurt him (or me): Verbal responses and attributions following sexual infidelity. *Communication Reports, 10,* 143–152.

Monsour, M. (1992). Meanings of intimacy in cross- and same-sex friendships. *Journal of Social and Personal Relationships, 9,* 277–295.

Montagu, A. (1971/1978). *Touching: The human significance of the skin.* New York: Harper & Row.

Montepare, J. M., & Vega, C. (1988). Women's vocal reactions to intimate and casual male friends. *Personality and Social Psychology Bulletin, 14,* 103–113.

Montgomery, B. M. (1988). Quality communication in personal relationships. In S. Duck (Ed.), *Handbook of personal relationships* (pp. 343–362). New York: Wiley.

Moore, M. M. (1985). Nonverbal courtship patterns in women: Context and consequences. *Ethology and Sociobiology, 6,* 237–247.

Morr, M. C., & Mongeau, P. A. (1998, November). *First date goals: Measurement and sex differences.* Paper presented at the annual meeting of the National Communication Association, New York, NY.

Morris, D. (1971). *Intimate behavior.* New York: Random House.

Morris, D. (1977). *Manwatching: A field guide to human behavior.* New York: Abrams.

Motley, M. T. (1990). On whether one can(not) communicate. An examination via traditional communication postulates. *Western Journal of Speech Communication, 54,* 1–20.

Motley, M. T. (1991). How one may not communicate: A reply to Andersen. *Communication Studies, 42,* 326–339.

Motley, M. T., & Reeder, H. M. (1995). Unwanted escalation of sexual intimacy: Male and female perceptions of connotations and relational consequences of resistance messages. *Communication Monographs, 62,* 355–382.

Muehlenhard, C. L., & Cook, S. W. (1988). Men's self-reports of unwanted sexual activity. *Journal of Sex Research, 24,* 58–72.

Muehlenhard, C. L., Koralewski, M. A., Andrews, S. L., & Burdick, C. A. (1986). Verbal and nonverbal cues that convey interest in dating: Two studies. *Behavior Therapy, 17,* 404–419.

Mullen, P. E., & Pathe, M. (1994). Stalking and pathologies of love. *Australian and New Zealand Journal of Psychiatry, 28,* 469–477.

Murnan, S. K., Perot, A., & Byrne, D. (1989). Coping with unwanted sexual activity: Normative responses, situational determinants, and individual differences. *Journal of Sex Research, 26,* 85–106.

Murstein, B. I. (1972). Physical attractiveness and marital choice. *Journal of Personality and Social Psychology, 22,* 8–12.

Nell, K., & Ashton, N. (1996). Gender, self-esteem, and perception of own attractiveness. *Perceptual and Motor Skills, 83,* 1105–1106.

Nelson, M. K. (1993). *A new theory of forgiveness.* Unpublished doctoral dissertation, Purdue University, West Lafayette, IN.

Newcomb, T. M. (1961). *The acquaintance process.* New York: Holt, Rinehart & Winston.

Norman, C., & Aron, A. (July, 1997). *Shared expansion experiences and relationship satisfaction.* Paper presented at the meeting of the International Network on Personal Relationships, Oxford, OH.

North, J. (1987). Wrongdoing and forgiveness. *Philosophy, 62,* 499–508.

O'Hair, D. H., & Cody, M. J. (1994). Deception. In W. R. Cupach & B. H. Spitzberg (Eds.), *The dark side of interpersonal communication* (pp. 181–213). Hillsdale, NJ: Erlbaum.

O'Meara, J. D. (1989). Cross-sex friendships: Four basic challenges of an ignored relationship. *Sex Roles, 21,* 525–543.

O'Sullivan, L. F., & Allgeier, E. R. (1994). Disassembling a stereotype: Gender differences in the use of token resistance. *Journal of Applied Social Psychology, 24,* 1035–1055.

O'Sullivan, L. F., & Allgeier, E. R. (1998). Feigning sexual desire: Consenting to unwanted sexual activity in heterosexual dating relationships. *Journal of Sex Research, 35,* 234–243.

O'Sullivan, L. F., & Byers, E. S. (1993). Eroding stereotypes: College women's attempts to influence reluctant male partners. *Journal of Sex Research, 30,* 270–282.

O'Sullivan, L. F., & Gaines, M. E. (1998). Decision-making in college student's heterosexual dating relationships: Ambivalence about engaging in sexual activity. *Journal of Social and Personal Relationships, 15,* 347–363.

Owen, W. F. (1987). The verbal expression of love by women and men as a critical communication event in personal relationships. *Women's Studies in Communication, 10,* 15–24.

Owen, W. F. (1993). Metaphors in accounts of romantic relationship terminations. In P. J. Kalbfleisch (Ed.), *Interpersonal communication: Evolving interpersonal relationships* (pp. 261–268). Hillsdale, NJ: Erlbaum

Paikoff, R. L., & Brooks-Gunn, J. (1991). Do parent-child relationships change during puberty? *Psychological Bulletin, 110,* 47–66.

Papa, M. J., & Canary, D. J. (1995). Communication in organizations: A competence-based approach. In A. M. Nicotera (Ed.), *Conflict and organizations: Communicative processes* (pp. 153–179). Albany: State University of New York Press.

Papini, D. R., Sebby, R. A., & Clark, S. (1989). Affective quality of family relations and adolescent identity exploration. *Adolescence, 24,* 457–466.

Parker, B. L., & Drummond-Reeves, S. J. (1993). The death of a dyad: Relational autopsy, analysis and aftermath. *Journal of Divorce and Remarriage, 21,* 95–119.

Parker, R. G. (1994, November). *An examination of the influence of situational determinants upon strategies for coping with romantic jealousy.* Paper presented at the annual meeting of the Speech Communication Association, New Orleans, LA.

Parks, M. R. (1982). Ideology of interpersonal communication: Off the couch and into the world. In M. Burgoon (Ed.), *Communication yearbook 5* (pp. 79–108). New Brunswick, NJ: Transaction Books.

Parks, M. R., & Adelman, M. B. (1983). Communication networks and the development of romantic relationships: An expansion of uncertainty reduction theory. *Human Communication Research, 10,* 55–79.

Parks, M. R., & Floyd, K. (1996). Meanings for closeness and intimacy in friendship. *Journal of Social and Personal Relationships, 13,* 85–107.

Patterson, M. L. (1983). *Nonverbal behavior: A functional perspective.* New York: Springer-Verlag.

Pearson, J., & Thoennes, N. (1990). Custody after divorce: Demographic and attitudinal patterns. *American Journal of Orthopsychiatry, 60,* 233–249.

Pennebaker, J. W. (1989). Confession, inhibition, and disease. In L. Berkowitz (Ed.), *Advances in experimental social psychology* (Vol. 22, pp. 211–244). San Diego, CA: Academic Press.

Pennebaker, J. W. (1990). *Opening up: The healing power of confiding in others.* New York: Morrow.

Pennebaker, J. W., Colder, M., & Sharp, L. K. (1990). Accelerating the coping process. *Journal of Personality and Social Psychology, 58,* 528–537.

Pennebaker, J. W., Dyer, M. A., Caulkins, R. S., Litowitz, D. L., Ackerman, P. L., Anderson, D. B., & McGraw, K. M. (1979). Don't girls get prettier at closing time? A country and western application to psychology. *Personality and Social Psychology Bulletin, 5,* 122–125.

Peplau, L. A., & Campbell, S. M. (1989). The balance of power in dating and marriage. In J. Freeman (Ed.), *Women: A feminist perspective* (4th ed., pp. 121–137). Mountain View, CA: Mayfield.

Peplau, L. A., & Cochran, S. D. (1980, September). *Sex differences in values concerning love relationships.* Paper presented at the annual meeting of the American Psychological Association, Montreal, Canada.

Peplau, L. A., & Spalding, L. R. (2000). The close relationships of lesbians, gay men, and bisexuals. In C. Hendrick & S. S. Hendrick (Eds.), *Close relationships: A sourcebook* (pp. 111–123). Thousand Oaks, CA: Sage.

Perras, M. T., & Lustig, M. W. (1982, February). *The effects of intimacy level and intent to disengage on the selection of relational disengagement strategies.* Paper presented at the annual meeting of the Western Speech Communication Association, Denver, CO.

Petra, R., & Petra, K. (1993). *The 775 stupidest things ever said.* New York: Doubleday.

Petronio, S. (1991). Communication boundary management: A theoretical model of managing disclosure of private information between marital couples. *Communication Theory, 1,* 311–335.

Petronio, S. (1994). Privacy binds in family interactions: The case of parental privacy invasion. In W. R. Cupach & B. H. Spitzberg (Eds.), *The dark side of interpersonal communication* (pp. 241–258). Mahwah, NJ: Erlbaum.

Petronio, S. (2000). The boundaries of privacy: Praxis of everyday life. In S. Petronio (Ed.), *Balancing secrets of private disclosure* (pp. 37–49). Mahwah, NJ: Erlbaum.

Petronio, S., & Harriman, S. (1990, October). *Parental privacy invasion: Tactics and reactions to encroachment.* Paper presented at the annual meeting of the Speech Communication Association, Chicago, IL.

Pfouts, J. H. (1978). Violent families: Coping responses of abused wives. *Child Welfare, 57*, 101–111.

Philliber, S. (1980). Socialization for childbearing. *Journal of Social Issues, 36*, 20–44.

Phillips, G. M., & Metzger, N. J. (1976). *Intimate communication.* Boston, MA: Allyn & Bacon.

Phillips, R. (1988). *Putting asunder: A history of divorce in Western society.* Cambridge: Cambridge University Press.

Pierce, C. A. (1996). Body height and romantic attraction: A meta-analytic test of the male-taller norm. *Social Behavior and Personality, 24*, 143–149.

Pike, G. R., & Sillars, A. L. (1985). Reciprocity of marital communication. *Journal of Social and Personal Relationships, 2*, 303–324.

Pines, A. (1992). *Romantic jealousy: Understanding and conquering the shadow of love.* New York: St. Martin's Press.

Pines, A. (1998). A prospective study of personality and gender differences in romantic attraction. *Personality and Individual Differences, 25*, 147–157.

Pines, A., & Aronson, E. (1983). Antecedents, correlates, and consequences of sexual jealousy. *Journal of Personality, 51*, 108–136.

Planalp, S., & Honeycutt, J. M. (1985). Events that increase uncertainty in personal relationships. *Human Communication Research, 11*, 593–604.

Prager, K. J. (1995). *The psychology of intimacy.* New York: Guilford.

Prager, K. J. (2000). Intimacy in personal relationships. In C. Hendrick & S. S. Hendrick (Eds.), *Close relationships: A sourcebook* (pp. 229–242). Thousand Oaks, CA: Sage.

Prager, K. J., & Buhrmester, D. (1998). Intimacy and need fulfillment in couple relationships. *Journal of Social and Personal Relationships, 15*, 435–469.

Pruitt, D. G., & Carnevale, P. J. (1993). *Negotiation in social conflict.* Pacific Grove, CA: Brooks/Cole.

Putnam, L. L., & Wilson, C. E. (1982). Communicative strategies in organizational conflicts: Reliability and validity of a measurement scale. In M. Burgoon (Ed.), *Communication yearbook 6* (pp. 629–652). Beverly Hills, CA: Sage.

Rahim, M. A. (1983). A measure of styles of handling interpersonal conflict. *Academy of Management Journal, 26*, 368–376.

Rahim, M. A. (1986). *Managing conflicts in organizations.* New York: Praeger.

Rahim, M. A., & Bonoma, T. V. (1979). Managing organizational conflict: A model for diagnosis and intervention. *Psychological Reports, 44*, 36–48.

Rankin, R. P., & Maneker, J. S. (1985). The duration of marriage in a divorcing population: The impact of children. *Journal of Marriage and the Family, 47*, 43–54.

Rathus. S. A., Nevid, J. S., & Fisher-Rathus, L. (1993). *Human sexuality in a world of diversity.* Boston: Allyn & Bacon.

Raush, H. L., Barry, W. A., Hertel, R. J., & Swain, M. A. (1974). Communication, conflict, and marriage. San Francisco: Jossey-Bass.

Rawlins, W. K. (1983a). Negotiating close friendships: The dialectic of conjunctive freedoms. *Human Communication Research, 9*, 255–266.

Rawlins, W. K. (1983b). Openness as problematic in ongoing friendships: Two conversational dilemmas. *Communication Monographs, 50*, 1–13.

Rawlins, W. K. (1989). A dialectical analysis of the tensions, functions, and strategic challenges of communication in young adult friendships. In J. A. Anderson (Ed.), *Communication yearbook 12* (pp. 157–189). Newbury Park, CA: Sage.

Rawlins, W. K. (1992). *Friendship matters: Communication, dialectics, and the life course.* Hawthorne, NY: Aldine de Gruyter.

Rawlins, W. K. (1994). Being there and growing apart: Sustaining friendships during adulthood. In D. J. Canary & L. Stafford (Eds.), *Communication and relational maintenance* (pp. 275–294). San Diego, CA: Academic Press.

Redmond, M. V., & Virchota, D. A. (1994, November). *The effects of varying lengths of initial interaction on attraction and uncertainty reduction.* Paper presented at the annual meeting of the Speech Communication Association, New Orleans, LA.

Reece, M. M., & Whitman, R. N. (1962). Expressive movements, warmth, and verbal reinforcement. *Journal of Abnormal and Social Psychology, 64*, 234–236.

Reel, B. W., & Thompson, T. L. (1994). A test of the effectiveness of strategies for talking about the effectiveness of condom use. *Journal of Applied Communication Research, 22*, 127–140.

Regan, P. C. (1998a). Of lust and love: Beliefs about the role of sexual desire in romantic relationships. *Personal Relationships, 5*, 139–157.

Regan, P. C. (1998b). What if you can't get what you want? Willingness to compromise ideal mate selection standards as a function of sex, mate value, and relationship context. *Personality and Social Psychology Bulletin, 24*, 1294–1303.

Regan, P. C., & Berscheid, E. (1995). Gender differences in beliefs about the causes of male and female sexual desire. *Personal Relationships, 2*, 345–358.

Regan P. C., & Berscheid, E. (1996). Beliefs about the state, goals and objects of sexual desire. *Journal of Marital and Sex Therapy, 22*, 110–120.

Regan P. C., & Berscheid (1999). *Lust: What we know about sexual desire*. Thousand Oaks, CA: Sage.

Regan, P. C., & Dreyer, C. S. (1999). Lust? Love? Status? Young adults' motives for engaging in casual sex. *Journal of Psychology and Human Sexuality, 11*, 1–24.

Reilly, M. E., & Lynch, J. M. (1990). Power-sharing in lesbian partnerships. *Journal of Homosexuality, 19*(1), 1–30.

Reined, C., Byers, E. S., & Pan, S. (1997). Sexual and relational satisfaction in mainland China. *Journal of Sex Research, 34*, 399–410.

Reinisch, J. M., & Beasley, R. (1990). *The Kinsey Institute report on sex: What you must know to be sexually literate*. New York: St. Martin's Press.

Reis, H. T., & Shaver, P. (1988). Intimacy as an interpersonal process. In S. Duck (Ed.), *Handbook of personal relationships* (pp. 367–389). New York: Wiley.

Reissman, C., Aron, A., & Bergen, M. R. (1993). Shared activities and marital satisfaction: Causal direction and self-expansion versus boredom. *Journal of Social and Personal Relationships, 10*, 243–254.

Remland, M. S. (1981). Developing leadership skills in nonverbal communication: A situational perspective. *Journal of Business Communication, 18*, 17–29.

Remland, M. S. (1982, November). *Leadership impressions and nonverbal communication in a superior subordinate situation*. Paper presented at the annual meeting of the Speech Communication Association, Louisville, KY.

Reyes M., Afifi, W., Krawchuk, A., Imperato, N., Shelley, D., & Lee, J. (June, 1999). *Just (don't) talk: Comparing the impact of interaction style on sexual desire and social attraction*. Paper presented at the joint conference of the International Network on Personal Relationships and the International Society for the Study of Personal Relationships, Louisville, KY.

Riordan, C. A., & Tedeschi, J. T. (1983). Attraction in aversive environments: Some evidence for classical conditioning and negative reinforcement. *Journal of Personality and Social Psychology, 44*, 683–692.

Roberson, B. F., & Wright, R. A. (1994). Difficulty as a determinant of interpersonal appeal: A social-motivational application of energization theory. *Basic and Applied Social Psychology, 15*, 373–388.

Roberto, K. A., & Scott, J. P. (1986). Friendships of older men and women: Exchange patterns and satisfaction. *Psychology and Aging, 1*, 103–109.

Robinson, T., & Smith-Lovin, L. (1992). Selective interaction as a strategy for identity maintenance: An affect control model. *Social Psychology Quarterly, 55*, 12–28.

Rodman, H. (1972). Marital power and the theory of resources in cultural context. *Journal of Comparative Family Stuides, 3*, 50–69.

Rogers, C. R. (1954). *Becoming a person*. Oberlin, OH: Oberlin College Press.

Rogers, E. M. (1995). *Diffusion of innovations* (4th ed.). New York: Free Press.

Rogers, L. A., & Farace, R. V. (1975). Analysis of relational communication in dyads: New measurement procedures. *Human Communication Research, 1*, 222–239.

Rogers, L. A., & Millar, F. E. (1988). Relational communication. In S. Duck (Ed.), *Handbook of personal relationships* (pp. 289–305). New York: Wiley.

Rohlfing, M. E. (1995). "Doesn't anybody stay in one place anymore?" An exploration of the understudied phenomenon of long-distance relationships. In J. T. Wood & S. Duck (Eds.), *Understudied relationships: Off the beaten track* (pp. 173–196). Thousand Oaks, CA: Sage.

Roiger, J. F. (1993). Power in friendship and use of influence strategies. In P. J. Kalbfleisch (Ed.), *Interpersonal communication: Evolving interpersonal relationships* (pp. 133–145). Hillsdale, NJ: Erlbaum.

Rollins, B., & Cammon, K. (1974). Marital satisfaction over the family life cycle: A reevaluation. *Journal of Marriage and the Family, 36*, 271–282.

Roloff, M. E., & Cloven, D. H. (1990). The chilling effect in interpersonal relationships: The reluctance to speak one's mind. In D. D. Cohn (Ed.), *Intimates in conflict: A communication perspective* (pp. 49–76). Hillsdale, NJ: Erlbaum.

Roscoe, B., Cavanaugh, L. E., & Kennedy, D. R. (1988). Dating infidelity: Behaviors, reasons, and consequences. *Adolescence, 89*, 36–43.

Rose, S. M. (1985). Same- and cross-sex friendships and the psychology of homosociology. *Sex Roles, 12*, 63–74.

Rosenberg, S., & Sedlack, A. (1972). Structural representations of implicit personality theory. In L. Berkowitz (Ed.), *Advances in experimental psychology* (Vol. 6, pp. 235–297).

Rosenbluth, P. C., Steil, J. M., & Whitcomb, J. H. (1998). Marital equality: What does it mean? *Journal of Family Issues, 19*, 227–244.

Rosenfeld, L. B. (1979). Self-disclosure avoidance: Why I am afraid to tell you who I am. *Communication Monographs, 46*, 63–74.

Rosenfeld, L. B. (2000). Overview of the ways privacy, secrecy, disclosure are balanced in today's society. In S. Petronio (Ed.), *Balancing secrets of private disclosure* (pp. 3–17). Mahwah, NJ: Erlbaum.

Rosenfeld, L. B., & Kendrick, W. L. (1984). Choosing to be open: An empirical investigation of subjective reasons for self-disclosing. *Western Journal of Speech Communication, 48*, 326–343.

Rosenfeld, L. B., & Welsh, S. M. (1985). Differences in self-disclosure in dual-career and single-career marriages. *Communication Monographs, 52*, 253–261.

Rosenthal, D., Gifford, S., & Moore, S. (1998). Safe sex or safe love: Competing discourses. *AIDS Care, 10*, 35–47.

Rosenthal, R., & Jacobson, L. (1968). *Pygmalion in the classroom: Teacher expectation and pupils' intellectual development*. New York: Holt, Rinehart & Winston.

Rosenzweig, J. M., & Lebow, W. C. (1992). Femme on the streets, butch in the sheets? Lesbian sex roles, dyadic adjustment, and sexual satifaction. *Journal of Homosexuality, 23*, 1–20.

Ross, M., & Sicoly, F. (1979). Egocentric biases in availability and attribution. *Journal of Personality and Social Psychology, 37*, 273–285.

Rozema, H. J. (1986). Defensive communication climate as a barrier to sex education in the home. *Family Relations, 35*, 531–537.

Rubenstein, C. M., & Shaver, P. (1982). *In search of intimacy*. New York: Delacorte Press.

Rubin, Z. (1970). Measurement of romantic love. *Journal of Personality and Social Psychology, 16*, 265–273.

Rubin, Z. (1973). *Loving and liking: An invitation to social psychology*. New York: Holt, Rinehart & Winston.

Rubin, Z. (1974). Lovers and other strangers: The development of intimacy in encounters and relationships. *American Scientist, 62*, 182–190.

Rubovits, P. C., & Maehr, M. L. (1973). Pygmalion black and white. *Journal of Personality and Social Psychology, 25*, 210–218.

Ruesch, J. (1951). Communication and human relations: An interdisciplinary approach. In J. Ruesch & G. Bateson (Eds.), *Communication: The social matrix of psychiatry* (pp. 21–49). New York: Norton.

Rusbult, C. E. (1980). Commitment and satisfaction in romantic associations: A test of the investment model. *Journal of Experimental Social Psychology, 16*, 172–186.

Rusbult, C. E. (1983). A longitudinal test of the investment model: The development (and deterioration) of satisfaction and commitment in heterosexual involvements. *Journal of Personality and Social Psychology, 45*, 101–117.

Rusbult, C. E. (1987). Responses to dissatisfaction in close relationships: The exit-voice-loyalty-neglect model. In D. Perlman & S. Duck (Eds.), *Intimacy relationships: Development, dynamics, and deterioration* (pp. 209–237). Newbury Park, CA: Sage.

Rusbult, C. E., & Buunk, B. P. (1993). Commitment processes in close relationships: An interdependence analysis. *Journal of Social and Personal Relationships, 10*, 175–204.

Rusbult, C. E., Drigotas, S. M., & Verette, J. (1994). The investment model: An interdependence analysis of commitment processes and relationship maintenance phenomena. In D. J. Canary & L. Stafford (Eds.), *Communication and relational maintenance* (pp. 115–139). San Diego, CA: Academic Press.

Rusbult, C. E., & Farrell, D. (1983). A longitudinal test of the investment model: The impact on job satisfaction, job commitment, and turnover of variations in rewards, costs, alternatives, and investments. *Journal of Applied Psychology, 68*, 429–438.

Rusbult, C. E., Johnson, D. J., & Morrow, G. D. (1986). Impact of couple patterns of problems solving on distress and nondistress in dating relationships. *Journal of Personality and Social Psychology, 50*, 744–753.

Rusbult, C. E., & Martz, J. (1995). Remaining in an abusive relationship: An investment model analysis of nonvoluntary dependence. *Personality and Social Psychology Bulletin, 21*, 558–571.

Rusbult, C. E., & Zembrodt, I. M. (1983). Responses to dissatisfaction in romantic involvements: A multidimensional scaling analysis. *Journal of Experimental Social Psychology, 19*, 274–293.

Rusbult, C. E., Zembrodt, I. M., & Gunn, L. K. (1982). Exit, voice, loyalty and neglect: Responses to dissatisfaction in romantic involvements. *Journal of Personality and Social Psychology, 43*, 1230–1242.

Russell, B. (1938). *Power: A new social analysis*. London: Allen & Unwin.

Russell, J. A. (1980). A circumplex model of affect. *Journal of Personality and Social Psychology, 39*, 1161–1178.

Russo, F. (1999, August). Keep your marriage strong at 25, 35, 45. *Redbook*, pp. 94–98.

Sabatelli, R. M. (1984). The marital comparison level index: A measure for assessing outcomes related to expectations. *Journal of Marriage and the Family, 46*, 651–662.

Sabatelli, R. M., & Cecil-Pigo, E. F. (1985). Relationship interdependence and commitment in marriage. *Journal of Marriage and the Family, 47*, 931–937.

Sabatelli, R. M., & Mazor, A. (1985). Differentiation, individuation, and identity formation: The integration of family system and individual development perspectives. *Adolescence, 20*, 619–633.

Sadalla, E. K., Kenrick, D. T., & Vershure, B. (1987). Dominance and heterosexual attraction. *Journal of Personality and Social Psychology, 52*, 730–738.

Safilios-Rothschild, C. (1970). The study of family power structure: A review 1960–1969. *Journal of Marriage and the Family, 32*, 539–552.

Safron, C. (1979). Troubles that pull couples apart: A Redbook report. *Redbook, 83*, 138–141.

Sagrestano, L. M. (1992). Power strategies in interpersonal relationships. *Psychology of Women Quarterly, 16*, 481–495.

Salovey, P., & Rodin, J. (1985, September). The heart of jealousy. *Psychology Today*, pp. 22–25, 28–29.

Salovey, P., & Rodin, J. (1986). Differentiation of social-comparison jealousy and romantic jealousy. *Journal of Personality and Social Psychology, 50*, 1100–1112.

Salovey, P., & Rodin, J. (1989). Envy and jealousy in close relationships. In C. Hendrick (Ed.), *Close relationships* (pp. 221–246). Newbury Park, CA: Sage.

Sanders, J. A. (1989, February). *The influence of gender on the uncertainty reduction strategies of disclosure, interrogation, and nonverbal immediacy.* Paper presented at the annual meeting of the Western Speech Communication Association, Spokane, WA.

Scheflen, A. E. (1965). Quasi-courtship behavior in psychotherapy. *Psychiatry, 27,* 245–257.

Scheflen, A. E. (1972). *Body language and the social order: Communication as behavior control.* Englewood Cliffs, NJ: Prentice-Hall.

Scheflen, A. E. (1974). *How behavior means.* Garden City, NY: Anchor/Doubleday.

Scherer, K. R. (1972). Judging personality from voice: A cross-cultural approach to an old issue in interpersonal perception. *Journal of Personality, 40,* 191–210.

Scherer, K. R. (1979). Acoustic noncomitants of emotional dimensions: Judging affect from synthesized tone sequences. In S. Weitz (Ed.), *Nonverbal communication: Readings with commentary* (pp. 249–253). New York: Oxford University Press.

Schlenker, B. R. (1980). *Impression management: The self-concept, social identity, and interpersonal relations.* Monterey, CA: Brooks/Cole.

Schlenker, B. R. (1984). Identities, identifications, and relationships. In V. Derlega (Ed.), *Communication, intimacy, and close relationships* (pp. 71–104). San Diego, CA: Academic Press.

Schlenker, B. R. (Ed.) (1985). *The self and social life.* New York: McGraw-Hill.

Schlenker, B. R., Britt, T. W., & Pennington, J. (1996). Impression regulation and management: Highlights of a theory of self-identification. In R. M. Sorrentino & E. T. Higgins (Eds.), *Handbook of motivation and cognition: The interpersonal context* (Vol. 3, pp. 118–142). New York: Guilford.

Schlenker, B. R., Britt, T. W., Pennington, J., Murphy, R., & Doherty, K. J. (1994). The triangle model of responsibility. *Psychological Review, 101,* 632–652.

Schlenker, B. R., & Darby, B. W. (1981). The use of apologies in social predicaments. *Social Psychology Quarterly, 44,* 271–278.

Schlenker, B. R., & Weigold, M. F. (1990). Self-consciousness and self-presentation: Being autonomous versus appearing autonomous. *Journal of Personality and Social Psychology, 59,* 820–828.

Schlenker, B. R., & Weigold, M. F. (1992). Interpersonal processes involving impression regulation and management. *Annual Review of Psychology, 43,* 133–168.

Schneider, K. T., Swan, S., & Fitzgerald, L. F. (1997). Job-related and psychological effects of sexual harassment in the workplace: Empirical evidence from two organizations. *Journal of Applied Psychology, 82,* 401–415.

Schutz, W. C. (1958). *The interpersonal underworld.* Palo Alto, CA: Science and Behavior Books.

Schwartz, J. C., & Shaver, P. (1987). Emotions and emotion knowledge in interpersonal relations. In W. H. Jones & D. Perlman (Eds.), *Advances in personal relationships* (pp. 197–241). Greenwich, CT: JAI Press.

Schwartz, P. (1994). *Peer marriage: How love between equals really works.* New York: Macmillan.

Scott, M. D., & Powers, W. G. (1978). *Interpersonal communication: A question of needs.* Boston: Houghton Mifflin.

Segrin, C. (1998). Interpersonal communication problems associated with depression and loneliness. In P. A. Andersen & L. K. Guerrero (Eds.), *Handbook of communication and emotion: Research, theory, applications, and contexts* (pp. 215–242). San Diego, CA: Academic Press.

Seltzer, J. A. (1991). Relationships between fathers and children who live apart: The father's role after separation. *Journal of Marriage and the Family, 53,* 79–101.

Sennett, R. (1970). *Families against the city. Middle class homes of industrial Chicago.* Cambridge, MA: Harvard University Press.

Shackelford, T. K., & Buss, D. M. (1997). Cues to infidelity. *Personality and Social Psychology Bulletin, 23,* 1034–1045.

Shantz, C. U. (1993). Children's conflicts: Representations and lessons learned. In R. R. Cocking & D. A. Renninger (Eds.), The development and meaning of psychological distance (pp. 185–202). Hillsdale, NJ: Erlbaum.

Sharabany, R., Gershoni, R., & Hoffman, J. E. (1981). Girlfriend, boyfriend: Age and sex differences in intimate friendship. *Developmental Psychology, 17,* 800–808.

Sharma, V., & Kaur, I. (1996). Interpersonal attraction in relation to the loss-gain hypothesis. *Journal of Social Psychology, 136,* 635–638.

Sharpsteen, D. J. (1991). The organization of jealousy knowledge: Romantic jealousy as a blended emotion. In P. Salovey (Ed.), *The psychology of jealousy and envy* (pp. 31–51). New York: Guilford.

Shaver, P. R., Furman, W., & Buhrmester, D. (1995). Aspects of a life transition: Network changes, social skills and loneliness. In S. W. Duck & D. Perlman (Eds.), *Understanding personal relationships research: An interdisciplinary approach* (pp. 193–219). London: Sage.

Shaver, P. R., Hazan, C., & Bradshaw, D. (1988). Love as attachment: The integration of three behavioral systems. In R. J. Sternberg & M. L. Barnes (Eds.), *The psychology of love* (pp. 68–99). New Haven, CT: Yale University Press.

Shaver, P. R., Morgan, H. J., & Wu, S. (1996). Is love a "basic" emotion? *Personal Relationships, 3,* 81–96.

Shaver, P. R., Schwartz, J., Kirson, D., & O'Connor, C. (1987). Emotion knowledge: Further explorations of a prototype approach. *Journal of Personality and Social Psychology, 52,* 1061–1086.

Shea, B. C., & Pearson, J. (1986). The effects of relationship type, partner intent, and gender on the selection of relationship maintenance strategies. *Communication Monographs, 53,* 352–364.

Shelov, S. P. (Ed.). (1998). *Caring for your baby and young child.* New York: Bantom Books.

Sheppard, B. M., Hartwick, J., & Warshaw, P. R. (1988). The theory of reasoned action: A meta-analysis of past research with recommendations for modification and future research. *Journal of Consumer Research, 15,* 325–343.

Sheppard, V. J., Nelson, E. S., & Andreoli-Mathie, V. (1995). Dating relationships and infidelity: Attitudes and behaviors. *Journal of Sex and Marital Therapy, 21,* 202–212.

Sherrod, D. (1989). The influence of gender on same-sex friendships. In C. Hendrick (Ed.), *Close relationships* (pp. 164–186). Newbury Park, CA: Sage.

Shotland, R. L., & Craig, J. M. (1988). Can men and women differentiate between friendly and sexually interested behavior? *Social Psychology Quarterly, 51,* 66–73.

Sias, P. M., & Cahill, D. J. (1998). From coworkers to friends: The development of peer friendships in the workplace. *Western Journal of Communication, 62,* 273–299.

Sias, P. M., Smith, G., & Avdeyera, T. (1999, November). *Developmental influences and communication in peer workplace friendships.* Paper presented at the annual meeting of the National Communication Association, Chicago, IL.

Siegert, J. R., & Stamp, G. H. (1994). "Our first big fight" as a milestone in the development of close relationships. *Communication Monographs, 61,* 345–360.

Sigall, H., & Landy, D. (1973). Radiating beauty: The effects of having a physically attractive partner on perception. *Journal of Personality and Social Psychology, 28,* 218–224.

Sillars, A. L. (1980). Attributions and communication in roommate conflicts. *Communication Monographs, 47,* 180–200.

Sillars, A. L., Coletti, S. F., Parry, D., & Rogers, M. A. (1982). Coding verbal conflicts: Nonverbal and perceptual correlates of the "avoidance-distributive-integrative" distinction. *Human Communication Research, 9,* 83–95.

Sillars, A. L., & Weisberg, J. (1987). Conflict as a social skill. In M. E. Roloff & G. R. Miller (Eds.), *Interpersonal processes: New directions in communication research* (pp. 140–171). Newbury Park, CA: Sage.

Sillars, A. L., & Wilmot, W. W. (1994). Communication strategies in conflict and mediation. In J. A. Daly & J. M. Wiemann (Eds.), *Strategic interpersonal communication* (pp. 163–190). Hillsdale, NJ: Erlbaum.

Silver, R. L., Boone, C., & Stones, M. H. (1983). Searching for meaning in misfortune: Making sense of incest. *Journal of Social Issues, 39,* 81–102.

Simpson, J. A. (1987). The dissolution of romantic relationships: Factors involved in relational stability and emotional distress. *Journal of Personality and Social Psychology, 53,* 683–692.

Simpson, J. A. (1990). Influence of attachment styles on romantic relationships. *Journal of Personality and Social Psychology, 59,* 971–980.

Simpson, J. A., & Gangestad, S. W. (1991). Individual differences in sociosexuality: Evidence for convergent and discriminant validity. *Journal of Personality and Social Psychology, 60,* 870–883.

Simpson, J. A., & Harris, B. A. (1994). Interpersonal attraction. In A. L. Weber & J. H. Harvey (Eds.), *Perspectives on close relationships* (pp. 45–66). Boston: Allyn & Bacon.

Simpson, J. A., & Rholes, W. S. (1994). Stress and secure base relationships in adulthood. In K. Bartholomew & D. Perlman (Eds.), *Attachment processes in adulthood: Advances in personal relationships* (Vol. 5, pp. 181–204). Bristol, PA: Kingsley.

Singh, D. (1993). Adaptive significance of female attractiveness: Role of the waist-to-hip ratio. *Journal of Personality and Social Psychology, 65,* 293–307.

Singh, D. (1995). Female judgment of male attractiveness and desirability for relationships: Role of the waist-to-hip ratio and financial status. *Journal of Personality and Social Psychology, 69,* 1089–1101.

Skinner, B. F. (1953). *Science and human behavior.* New York: Macmillan.

Snow, D. A., & Anderson, L. (1987). Identity work among the homeless: The verbal construction and avowal of personal identities. *American Journal of Sociology, 93,* 1336–1371.

Snyder, M., Berscheid, E., & Glock, P. (1985). Focusing on the exterior and interior. Two investigations of the initiation of personal relationships. *Journal of Personality and Social Psychology, 48,* 1427–1439.

Snyder, M., & Gangestad, S. (1986). On the nature of self-monitoring: Matters of assessment, matters of validity. *Journal of Personality and Social Psychology, 51,* 125–139.

Snyder, M., & Simpson, J. A. (1987). Orientations toward romantic relationships. In D. Perlman & S. Duck (Eds.), *Intimate relationships: Development, dynamics, and deterioration* (pp. 45–62). Newbury Park, CA: Sage.

Snyder, M., Tanke, E. D., & Berscheid, E. (1977). Social perception and interpersonal behavior: On the self-fulfilling nature of social stereotypes. *Journal of Personality and Social Psychology, 35,* 656–666.

Sorensen, R. C. (1973). *Adolescent sexuality in contemporary America.* New York: World.

Sorrentino, R. M., Holmes, J. G., Hanna, S. E., & Sharp, A. (1995). Uncertainty orientation and trust in close relationships: Individual differences in cognitive styles. *Journal of Personality and Social Psychology, 68,* 314–327.

Sorrentino, R. M., & Short, J. C. (1986). Uncertainty orientation, motivation, and cognition. In R. M. Sorrentino & E. T. Higgins (Eds.), *Handbook of motivation and cognition: Foundations of social behavior* (Vol. 1, pp. 379–403). New York: Guilford Press.

Sorrentino, R. M., Short, J. C., & Raynor, J. O. (1984). Uncertainty orientation: Implications for affective and cognitive views of achievement behavior. *Journal of Personality and Social Psychology, 46,* 189–206.

Sperling, M. B., & Borgaro, S. (1995). Attachment anxiety and reciprocity as moderators of interpersonal attraction. *Psychological Reports, 76,* 323–335.

Spiegel, D. (1992). Effects of psychosocial support on patients with metastatic breast cancer. *Journal of Psychosocial Oncology, 10,* 113–120.

Spitzberg, B. H., & Cupach, W. R. (1988). *Handbook of interpersonal communication competence.* New York: Springer-Verlag.

Spitzberg, B. H., & Cupach, W. R. (Eds.). (1998). *The dark side of close relationships.* Mahwah, NJ: Erlbaum.

Sprecher, S. (1986). The relation between emotion and equity in close relationships. *Social Psychological Bulletin, 49,* 309–321.

Sprecher, S. (1987). The effects of self-disclosure given and received on affect for an intimate partner and the stability of the relationship. *Journal of Personal and Social Relationships, 4,* 115–128.

Sprecher, S. (1989). The importance to males and females of physical attractiveness, earning potential, and expressiveness in initial attraction. *Sex Roles, 12,* 449–462.

Sprecher, S. (1998a). Insiders' perspectives on reasons for attraction to a close other. *Social Psychology Quarterly, 61,* 287–300.

Sprecher, S. (1998b). Social exchange theories and sexuality. *Journal of Sex Research, 35,* 32–43.

Sprecher, S., & Felmlee D., (1992) The influence of parents and friends on the quality and stability of romantic relationships: A three-wave longitudinal study. *Journal of Marriage and the Family, 54,* 888–900.

Sprecher, S., & Felmlee, D. (1997). The balance of power in romantic heterosexual couples over time form "his" and "her" perspectives. *Sex Roles, 37,* 361–378.

Sprecher, S., & McKinney, K. (1993). *Sexuality.* Newbury Park, CA: Sage.

Sprecher, S., McKinney, K., Walsh, R., & Anderson, C. (1988). A revision of the Reiss premarital sexual permissiveness scale. *Journal of Marriage and the Family, 50,* 821–828.

Sprecher, S., & Regan, P. C. (1996). College virgins: How men and women perceive their sexual status. *Journal of Sex Research, 33,* 3–15.

Sprecher, S., & Regan, P. C. (2000). Sexuality in a relational context. In C. Hendrick & S. S. Hendrick (Eds.), *Close relationships: A sourcebook* (pp. 217–227). Thousand Oaks, CA: Sage.

Stafford, L., & Canary, D. J. (1991). Maintenance strategies and romantic relationship type, gender and relational characteristics. *Journal of Social and Personal Relationships, 8,* 217–242.

Stafford, L., & Reske, J. R. (1990). Idealization and communication in long-distance premarital relationships. *Family Relations, 39,* 274–279.

Staines, G., & Libby, P. (1986). Men and women in role relationships. In R. Ashmore & F. Del Bocca (Eds.), *The social psychology of female-male relationships: A critical analysis of central concepts.* New York: Academic Press.

Stangor, C., & Ruble, D. H. (1989). Strength of expectancies and memory for social information: What we remember depends on how much we know. *Journal of Experimental Social Psychology, 25,* 18–35.

Stark, P. B. (1994). *It's negotiable: The how-to handbook of win/win tactics.* San Diego, CA: Pfieffer.

Steil, J. M. (2000). Contemporary marriage: Still an unequal partnership. In C. Hendrick & S. S. Hendrick (Eds.), *Close relationships: A sourcebook* (pp. 125–136). Thousand Oaks, CA: Sage.

Steil, L. K., Barker, L. L., & Watson, K. W. (1983). *Effective listening: Keys to success.* Reading, MA: Addison-Wesley.

Steinberg, L. D. (1981). Transformations in family relations at puberty. *Developmental Psychology, 17,* 833–840.

Steinberg, L. D. (1987). Impact of puberty on family relations: Effects of pubertal status and pubertal timing. *Developmental Psychology, 23,* 451–460.

Steinberg, L. D., & Silverberg, S. B. (1986). The vicissitudes of autonomy in early adolescence. *Child Development, 57,* 841–851.

Steinmetz, S. K. (1979). Disciplinary techniques and their relationship to aggressiveness, dependency, and conscience. In W. Burr, R. Hill, R. I. Nye, & I. L. Reiss (Eds.), *Contemporary theories about the family* (Vol. 1, pp. 405–438). New York: Free Press.

Stephan, C. W., & Bachman, G. F. (1999). What's sex got to do with it? Attachment, love schemas, and sexuality. *Personal Relationships, 6,* 111–123.

Sternberg, R. J. (1986). A triangular theory of love. *Psychological Review, 93,* 119–135.

Sternberg, R. J. (1987). *The triangle of love: Intimacy, passion, commitment.* New York: Basic Books.

Sternberg, R. (1988). Triangulating love. In R. J. Sternberg & M. L. Barnes (Eds.), *The psychology of love* (pp. 119–138). New Haven, CT: Yale University Press.

Stewart, J. (1973). *Bridges not walls: A book about interpersonal communication.* Reading, MA: Addison-Wesley.

Stier, D. S., & Hall, J. A. (1984). Gender differences in touch: An empirical and theoretical review. *Journal of Personality and Social Psychology, 47,* 440–459.

Stiff, J. B., Dillard, J. P., Somera, L., Kim, H., & Sleight, C. (1988). Empathy, communication, and prosocial behavior. *Communication Monographs, 55,* 198–213.

Stiles, W. B. (1987). "I have to talk to somebody": A fever model of disclosure. In V. J. Derlega & J. H. Berg (Eds.), *Self-disclosure: Theory, research, and therapy* (pp. 257–282). New York: Plenum.

Stiles, W. B., Shuster, P. L., & Harrigan, J. A. (1992). Disclosure and anxiety: A test of the fever model. *Journal of Personality and Social Psychology, 63,* 980–988.

Street, R. L., Jr., & Giles, H. (1982). Speech accommodation theory: A social cognitive approach to language and speech behavior. In M. Roloff & C. Berger (Eds.), *Social cognition and communication* (pp. 193–226). Beverly Hills, CA: Sage.

Strong, B., DeVault, C., & Sayad, B. W. (1999). *Human sexuality: Diversity in contemporary America.* Mountain View, CA: Mayfield.

Strong, S. R., Hills, H. J., Kilmartin, C. T., DeVries, H., Lanier, K., Nelson, B. N., Strickland, D., & Meyer, C. W. (1988). The dynamic relations among interpersonal behaviors: A test of complementarity and anticomplementarity. *Journal of Personality and Social Psychology, 54,* 798–810.

Struckman-Johnson, C. (1988). Forced sex on dates: It happens to men too. *Journal of Sex Research, 24,* 234–241.

Struckman-Johnson, C., & Struckman-Johnson, D. (1991). Men's and women's acceptance of sexually coercive strategies varied by initiator gender and couple intimacy. *Sex Roles, 25,* 661–676.

Struckman-Johnson, C., & Struckman-Johnson, D. (1994). Men pressured and forced into sexual experience. *Archives of Sexual Behavior, 23,* 93–114.

Student Health Services. (1998). *HIV/AIDS facts.* San Diego, CA: San Diego State University.

Sullivan, H. S. (1953). *The interpersonal theory of psychiatry.* New York: Norton.

Sunnafrank, M. (1986). Predicted outcome value during initial interactions: A reformulation of uncertainty reduction theory. *Human Communication Research, 13,* 3–33.

Sunnafrank, M. (1990). Predicted outcome value and uncertainty reduction theories: A test of competing perspectives. *Human Communication Research, 17,* 76–103.

Sunnafrank, M. (1991). Interpersonal attraction and attitude similarity: A communication-based assessment. In J. A. Anderson (Ed.), *Communication Yearbook 14* (pp. 451–483). Newbury Park, CA: Sage

Sunnafrank, M. (1992). On debunking the attitude similarity myth. *Communication Monograph, 59,* 164–179.

Swan, S. C. (1997). Explaining the job-related and psychological consequences of sexual harassment in the workplace: A contextual model. *Dissertation Abstractions International, 58*(6-B), 3371.

Swann, W. B. (1983). Self-verification: Bringing social reality into harmony with the self. In J. Suls & G. Greenwald (Eds.), *Psychological perspectives on the self* (Vol. 2, pp. 33–66). Hillsdale, NJ: Erlbaum.

Swann, W. B. (1987). Identity negotiation: Where two roads meet. *Journal of Personality and Social Psychology, 53,* 1038–1051.

Swann, W. B., De La Ronde, C., & Hixon, J. G. (1994). Authenticity and positivity strivings in marriage and courtship. *Journal of Personality and Social Psychology, 66,* 857–869.

Swann, W. B., Griffin, J. J., Predmore, S., & Gaines, B. (1987). The cognitive-affective crossfire: When self-consistency confronts self-enhancement. *Journal of Personality and Social Psychology, 52,* 881–889.

Swann, W. B., & Read, S. J. (1981). Self-verification processes: How we sustain our self-conceptions. *Journal of Experimental Social Psychology, 54,* 268–273.

Swann, W. B., Silvera, D. H., & Proske, C. U. (1995). On "knowing your partner": Dangerous illusions in the age of AIDS? *Personal Relationships, 2,* 173–186.

Tannen, D. (1990). *You just don't understand: Women and men in conversation.* New York: Morrow.

Taraban, C. B., Hendrick, S. S., & Hendrick, C. (1998). Loving and liking. In P. A. Andersen & L. K. Guerrero (Eds.), *Handbook of communication and emotion: Research, theory, applications, and contexts* (pp. 331–351). San Diego, CA: Academic Press.

Tardy, C. H. (Ed.) (1988). *A handbook for the study of human communication: Methods for observing, measuring, and assessing communication processes.* Norwood, NJ: Ablex.

Tedeschi, J. T. (Ed.). (1981). *Impression management: Theory and social psychological research.* New York: Academic Press.

Tedeschi, J. T. (1986). Private and public experiences of the self. In R. Baumeister (Ed.), *Public self and private self* (pp. 1–20). New York: Springer-Verlag.

Tesser, A., & Achee, J. (1994). Aggression, love, conformity and other social psychological catastrophes. In R. R. Vallacher & A. Nowak (Eds.), *Dynamical systems in social psychology* (pp. 95–109). San Diego, CA: Academic Press;

Thagaard, T. (1997) Gender, power, and love. *Acta Socialogica, 38,* 357–376.

"The best dating service? Try the workplace!" (1988, February 12). *New York Post,* p. 14.

Thibaut, J. W., & Kelley, J. J. (1959). *The psychology of groups.* New York: Wiley.

Thieme, A., & Rouse, C. (1991, November). *Terminating intimate relationships: An examination of the interactions among disengagement strategies, acceptance, and causal attributions.* Paper presented at the annual meeting of the Speech Communication Association, Atlanta, GA.

Thompson, A. P. (1984). Emotional and sexual components of extramarital relations. *Journal of Marriage and the Family, 46,* 35–42.

Thompson, L., & Walker, A. J. (1989). Gender in families: Women and men in marriage, work, and parenthood. *Journal of Marriage and the Family, 51,* 845–871.

Thorne, B., & Luria, Z. (1986). Sexuality and gender in children's daily worlds. *Social Problems, 33,* 176–190.

Tice, D. M., Butler, J. L., Muraven, M. B., & Stillwell, A. M. (1995). When modesty prevails: Differential favorability of self-presentation to friends and strangers. *Journal of Personality and Social Psychology, 69,* 1120–1138.

Tolhuizen, J. H. (1989). Communication strategies for intensifying dating relationships: Identification, use, and structure. *Journal of Social and Personal Relationships, 6,* 413–434.

Tolstedt, B. E., & Stokes, J. P. (1984). Self-disclosure, intimacy and the depenetration process. *Journal of Personality and Social Psychology, 46,* 84–90.

Tornblom, K. Y., & Fredholm, E. M. (1984). Attribution of friendship: The influence of the nature and comparability of resources given and received. *Social Psychology Quarterly, 47,* 50–61.

Tracy, K. (1990). The many faces of facework. In H. Giles & W. P. Robinson (Eds.), *Handbook of language and social psychology* (pp. 209–226). Chichester, UK: Wiley.

Traupmann, J., Hatfield, E., & Wexler, P. (1983). Equity and sexual satisfaction in dating couples. *British Journal of Social Psychology, 22,* 33–40.

Trivers, R. (1985). *Social evolution.* Menlo Park, CA: Benjamin/Cummings.

Trost, M. R. (1997, August). *"Let's stay friends" and other strategies for rejecting romance.* Paper presented at the annual meeting of the American Psychological Association, Toronto, Canada.

Trost, M. R., & Alberts, J. K. (1998). An evolutionary view on understanding sex effects in communicating attraction. In D. J. Canary & K. Dindia (Eds.), *Sex differences and similarities in communication* (pp. 233–255). Mahwah, NJ: Erlbaum.

Trost, M. R., & Gabrielidis, C. (1994, February). *"Hit the road, Jack": Strategies for rejecting flirtatious advances.* Paper presented at the annual meeting of the Western States Communication Association, San Jose, CA.

Trost, M. R., & Yoshimura, S. M. (1999, February). *Profiles of jealous emotions.* Paper presented at the annual meeting of the Western States Communication Association, Vancouver, BC.

Tucker, J. S., & Anders, S. L. (1998). Adult attachment style and nonverbal closeness in dating couples. *Journal of Nonverbal Behavior, 22,* 109–124.

Turner, L. H. (1990). The relationship between communication and marital uncertainty: Is "her" marriage different from "his" marriage? *Women's Studies in Communication, 13,* 57–83.

Turner, R. E., Edgley, C., & Olmstead, G. (1975). Information control in conversations: Honesty is not always the best policy. *Kansas Journal of Speech, 11,* 69–89.

Tusing, K. J., & Dillard, J. P. (1999). The sounds of dominance: Vocal precursors of perceived dominance during interpersonal influence. *Human Communication Research, 26,* 148–172.

Tutzauer, F., & Roloff, M. E. (1988). Communication processes leading to integrative agreements: Three paths to joint benefits. *Communication Research, 15,* 360–380.

Ugbah, S., & DeWine, (1986, November). *Conflict and relational development: Are the communication strategies the same?* Paper presented at the annual meeting of the Speech Communication Association, Chicago, IL.

Utech, D. A., & Hoving, K. L. (1969). Parent and peers as competing influences in the decisions of children of differing ages. *Journal of Social Psychology, 78,* 267–274.

Vangelisti, A. L. (1994). Family secrets: Forms, functions, and correlates. *Journal of Social and Personal Relationships, 11,* 113–135.

Vangelisti, A. L., & Caughlin, J. P. (1997). Revealing family secrets: The influence of topic, function, and relationships. *Journal of Social and Personal Relationships, 14,* 679–706.

Vangelisti, A. L., & Huston, T. L. (1994). Maintaining marital satisfaction and love. In D. J. Canary & L. Stafford (Eds.), *Communication and relational maintenance* (pp. 165–186). San Diego, CA: Academic Press.

Vangelisti, A. L., Knapp, M. L., & Daly, J. A. (1990). Conversational narcissism. *Communication Monographs, 57,* 251–274.

Vangelisti A. L., & Sprague, R. J. (1998) Guilt and hurt: Similarities, distinctions, and conversational strategies. In P. A. Andersen & L. K. Guerrero (Eds.) *Handbook of communication and emotion: Research, theory, applications, and contexts* (pp. 123–153). San Diego, CA: Academic Press.

Van Horn, K. R., Arnone, A., Nesbitt, K., Desilets, L., Sears, T., Giffin, M., & Brudi, R. (1997). Physical distance and interpersonal characteristics in college students' romantic relationships. *Personal Relationships, 4,* 15–24.

VanLear, C. A., Jr. (1987). The formation of social relationships: A longitudinal study of social penetration. *Human Communication Research, 13,* 299–322.

Vaughn, D. (1986). *Uncoupling: Turning points in intimate relationships.* New York: Oxford.

Verhoff, J., Young, A. M., & Coon, H. M. (1997). The early years of marriage. In S. Duck (Ed.), *Handbook of personal relationships* (pp. 431–450). New York: Wiley.

Wallace, H., & Silverman, J. (1996). Stalking and post traumatic stress syndrome. *Police Journal, 69,* 203–206.

Waller, W. W., & Hill, R. (1951). *The family: A dynamic interpretation.* New York: Dryden Press.

Walster, E., Berscheid, E., & Walster, G. W. (1973). Equity and extramarital sexuality. *Archives of Sexual Behavior, 7,* 127–141.

Walster, E., & Walster, G. W. (1978). *A new look at love.* Reading, MA: Addison-Wesley.

Walster, E., Walster, G. W., & Berscheid, E. (1978). *Equity: Theory and research.* Boston: Allyn & Bacon.

Walster, E., Walster, G. W., Piliavin, J., & Schmidt, L. (1973). "Playing hard-to-get": Understanding an elusive phenomenon. *Journal of Personality and Social Psychology, 26*, 113–121.

Walster, E., Walster, G. W., & Traupmann, J. (1978). Equity and premarital sex. *Journal of Personality, 36*, 82–92.

Ward, L. M. (1995). Talking about sex: Common themes about sexuality in prime-time television programs children and adolescents view most. *Journal of Youth and Adolescence, 5*, 595–615.

Warren, C. (1995). Parent-child communication about sex. In T. Socha & G. H. Stamp (Eds.), *Parents, children, and communication: Frontiers of theory and research* (pp. 173–201). Mahwah, NJ: Erlbaum.

Watzlawick, P., Beavin, J. H., & Jackson, D. D. (1967). *Pragmatics of human communication*. New York: Norton.

Webb, D. G. (1972). Relationship of self-acceptance and self-disclosure to empathy and marital need satisfaction. (Doctoral dissertation, United States International University). *Dissertation Abstracts International 33*, 432–43B.

Webb, L., Delaney, J. J., & Young, L. R. (1989). Age, interpersonal attraction, and social interaction: A review and assessment. *Research on Aging, 11*, 107–123.

Wegner, D. M. (1989). *White bears and other unwanted thoughts*. New York: Viking Press.

Wegner, D. M. (1992). You can't always think what you want: Problems in the suppression of unwanted thoughts. In M. Zanna (Ed.), *Advances in experimental social psychology* (Vol. 25, pp. 193–225). San Diego, CA: Academic Press.

Wegner, D. M., & Erber, R. (1992). The hyperaccessibility of suppressed thoughts. *Journal of Personality and Social Psychology, 63*, 903–912.

Wegner, D. M., Lane, J. D., & Dimitri, S. (1994). The allure of secret relationships. *Journal of Personality and Social Psychology, 66*, 287–300.

Wegner, D. M., Schneider, D. J., Carter, S. R., III, & White, T. L. (1987). Paradoxical effects of thought suppression. *Journal of Personality and Social Psychology, 53*, 5–13.

Weinbach, R. (1989). Sudden death and the secret survivors: Helping those who grieve alone. *Social Work, 34*, 57–60.

Weiner, B., Graham, S., Peter, O., & Zmuidinas, M. (1991). Public confession and forgiveness. *Journal of Personality, 59*, 281–312.

Weiner, M., & Mehrabian, A. (1968). *Language within language: Immediacy, a channel in verbal communication*. New York: Appleton-Century-Crofts.

Weis, D. L., & Slosnerick, M. (1981). Attitudes toward sexual and nonsexual extramarital involvement among a sample of college students. *Journal of Marriage and the Family, 43*, 349–358.

Werking, K. (1997). *We're just good friends: Women and men in nonromantic relationships*. New York: Guilford.

Werner, C. M., Altman, I., Brown, B. B., & Ganat, J. (1993). Celebrations in personal relationships: A transactional/dialectical perspective. In S. Duck (Ed.), *Social context and relationships* (pp. 109–138). Newbury Park, CA: Sage.

Westhoff, L. A. (1985). *Corporate romance*. New York: Times Books.

Wheeler, L., & Myiake, K. (1992). Social comparison and everyday life. *Journal of Personality and Social Psychology, 62*, 760–773.

White, C. H., & Stewart, R. A. (1990, November). *Effects of expectancy violations on uncertainty in interpersonal interactions*. Paper presented at the annual meeting of the Speech Communication Association, Chicago, IL.

White, G. L. (1981). Jealousy and partner's perceived motives for attraction to a rival. *Social Psychology Quarterly, 44*, 24–30.

White, G. L., Fishbein, S., & Rutstein, J. (1981). Passionate love: The misattribution of arousal. *Journal of Personality and Social Psychology, 41*, 56–62.

White, G. L., & Mullen, P. E. (1989). *Jealousy: Theory, research, and clinical strategies*. New York: Guilford.

Whyte, W. H. (1957). *The organization man*. Garden City, NY: Anchor/Doubleday.

Wiederman, M. W., & Allgeier, E. R. (1993). Gender differences in sexual jealousy: Adaptationist or social learning explanation? *Ethology and Sociobiology, 14*, 115–140.

Wiener, M., & Mehrabian, A. (1968). *Language within language: Immediacy, a channel in verbal communication*. New York: Appleton-Century-Crofts.

Wiggins, J. D., & Lederer, D. A. (1984). Differential antecedents of infidelity in marriage. *American Mental Health Counseling Association Journal, 6*, 152–161.

Williams, S. (1999, February). How women size you up. *Men's Health*, pp. 92–97.

Williams, S., & Andersen, P. A. (1998). Toward an expanded view of interracial romantic relationships. In V. Duncan (Ed.), *Toward achieving Malt*. Dubuque, IA: Kendall-Hunt.

Wilmot, W. W. (1994). Relationship rejuvenation. In D. J. Canary & L. Stafford (Eds.), *Communication and relational maintenance* (pp. 255–273). San Diego, CA: Academic Press.

Wilmot, W. W. (1995). *Relational communication*. New York: McGraw-Hill.

Wilmot, W. W., Carbaugh, D. A., & Baxter, L. A. (1985). Communicative strategies used to terminate romantic relationships. *Western Journal of Speech Communication, 49*, 204–216.

Wiseman, J. P. (1986). Friendship: Bonds and binds in a voluntary relationship. *Journal of Social and Personal Relationships, 3*, 191–211.

Wiseman, R. L., & Shenck-Hamlin, W. (1981). A multidimensional scaling validation of an inductively-derived set of compliance gaining strategies. *Communication Monographs, 48,* 251–270.

Witteman, H., & Fitzpatrick, M. A. (1986). Compliance-gaining in marital interaction: Power bases, processes and outcomes. *Communication Monographs, 53,* 130–143.

Wood, J. T. (1994). *Gendered lives: Communication, gender, and culture.* Belmont, CA: Wadsworth.

Wood, J. T. (Ed.). (1996). *Gendered relationships.* Mountain View, CA: Mayfield.

Wood, J. T., & Dindia, K. (1998) What's the difference? A dialogue about the differences and similarities between women and men. In D. J. Canary & K. Dindia (Eds.), *Sex differences and similarities in communication* (pp. 19–39). Mahwah, NJ: Erlbaum.

Wood, J. T., & Duck, S. (1995). Off the beaten track: New shores for relationships research. In J. T. Wood & S. Duck (Eds.), *Understudied relationships: Off the beaten track* (pp. 1–21). Thousand Oaks, CA: Sage.

Wood, J. V., & Taylor, K. L. (1991). Serving self-relevant goals through social comparison. In J. M. Suls & T. A. Wills (Eds.), *Social comparison: Contemporary theory and research* (pp. 23–49). Hillsdale, NJ: Erlbaum.

Woodall, W. G., Burgoon, J. K., & Markel, N. N. (1980). The effects of facial-head cue combinations on interpersonal evaluations. *Communication Quarterly, 28,* 47–55.

Wright, P. H. (1982). Men's friendships, women's friendships, and the alleged inferiority of the latter. *Sex Roles, 8,* 1–20.

Wright, R. A., & Contrada, R. J. (1986). Dating selectivity and interpersonal attractiveness: Toward a better understanding of the "elusive phenomenon." *Journal of Social and Personal Relationships, 3,* 131–148.

Wright, R. A., Toi, M., & Brehm, J. W. (1984). Difficulty and interpersonal attraction. *Motivation and Emotion, 8,* 327–341.

Yingling, J. (1995). The first relationship: Infant-parent communication. In T. J. Socha & G. H. Stamp (Eds.), *Parents, children, and communication: Frontiers of theory and research* (pp. 23–41). Hillsdale, NJ: Erlbaum.

Zeeman, E. C. (1977). Catastrophe theory. *Scientific American, 234,* 65–83.

Zillman, D. (1978). Attribution and misattribution of excitatory reactions. In J. H. Harvey, W. Ickes, & R. F. Kidd (Eds.), *New directions in attribution research* (Vol. 2, pp. 335–368). Hillsdale, NJ: Erlbaum.

Zillman, D. (1990). The interplay of cognition and excitation in aggravated conflict. In D. D. Cahn (Ed.), *Intimates in conflict: A communication perspective* (pp. 187–208). Hillsdale, NJ: Erlbaum.

Zimmerman S., & Applegate, J .L. (1994). Communicating social support in organizations. In B. R. Burleson, T. L. Albrecht, & I. G. Sasason (Eds.), *Communication of social support: Messages, interactions, relationships, and community.* Thousand Oaks, CA: Sage.

Zuckerman, M., DePaulo, B. M., & Rosenthal, R. (1981). Verbal and nonverbal communication of deception. In L. Berkowitz (Ed.), *Advances in experimental social psychology* (Vol. 14, pp. 1–59). New York: Academic Press.

Zunin, L. (1972). *Contact: The first four minutes.* Los Angeles: Nash.

Credits

Text and Illustrations

Chapter 1 Box 1.1 From Hara E. Marano, "PSY 101: Gottman and Gray—A Tale of Two Relationship Gurus," *Psychology Today*, November/December 1997. Reprinted with permission from Psychology Today Magazine. Copyright © 1997 Sussex Publishers, Inc.

Chapter 2 Box 2.1 Reprinted with permission from Andre Modigliani. Fig. 2.1 From *Journal of Personality and Social Psychology*, 63(4), pp. 596–612, 1992. Copyright © 1992 by the American Psychological Association. Reprinted with permission.

Chapter 3 Box 3.1 From Tardy, ed., *A Handbook for the Study of Human Communication Methods and Instruments for Observing, Measuring, and Assessing Communication Process*, Ablex, 1988. Reproduced with permission of Greenwood Publishing Group, Inc., Westport, CT.

Chapter 4 Box 4.2 From "Attributional Confidence and Uncertainty in Initial Interaction," *Human Communication Research*, Vol. 5:2, p. 149. Reprinted with permission from International Communication Association and the author. Box 4.3 From *Journal of Personality and Social Psychology*, 65, Appendix, p. 876, 1993. Copyright © 1993 by the American Psychological Association. Reprinted with permission.

Chapter 6 Box 6.1 Adapted from *Journal of Social Behavior and Personality*, 5(4), pp. 249–252. With permission from Select Press. Box 6.2 Adapted from *Journal of Social and Personal Relationships*, 9(1), p. 48. With permission from Sage Publications Ltd.

Chapter 9 Fig. 9.1 From Steven Duck, ed., *Social Context and Relationships*, p. 143. Reprinted by permission of Sage Publications, Inc.

Chapter 10 Fig. 10.1 From Steven Duck, ed., *Handbook of Personal Relationships: Theory, Research, and Interventions*. Reproduced with permission from John Wiley & Sons Limited.

Chapter 12 Fig. 12.1 From *Psychological Bulletin*, 120(3), p. 457, 1996. Copyright © 1996 by the American Psychological Association. Reprinted with permission.

Chapter 13 Fig. 13.2 From *Journal of Personality and Social Psychology*, 73(2), p. 327, 1997. Copyright © 1997 by the American Psychological Association. Reprinted with permission.

Chapter 15 Fig. 15.1 From Steven Duck, ed., *Personal Relationships 4: Dissolving Personal Relationships*, London: Academic Press, 1982, p. 16. Reprinted with permission from Academic Press Ltd.

Photos

p. 12, © Dwayne E. Newton/PhotoEdit; p. 21T, © Michael Newman/PhotoEdit; p. 21B, © Amy C. Etra/PhotoEdit; p. 37, © Tony Freeman/PhotoEdit; p. 78TL, © Reuters NewMedia, Inc./Corbis; p. 78TR, © Reuters NewMedia, Inc./Corbis; p. 78B, © AP/Wide World Photos; p. 183, © Myrleen Ferguson Cate/PhotoEdit; p. 233, © Amy C. Etra/PhotoEdit; p. 260, © Lisa Gallegos/AG Photograph; p. 284L, © Gavin Wickham, Eye Ubiquitous/Corbis; p. 284R, © Hulton-Deutsch Collection/Corbis; p. 373, Courtesy of the author

Author Index

Subject Index

Page numbers in **bold** indicate vocabulary terms. Page numbers in *italic* indicate boxes, charts, etc.